RUSSIA AND THE BALKANS
1870–1880

TSAR ALEXANDER II
ON THE DANUBE FRONT, 1877

RUSSIA AND THE BALKANS

1870 – 1880

BY

B. H. SUMNER

FELLOW OF BALLIOL COLLEGE
FORMERLY FELLOW OF ALL SOULS COLLEGE
UNIVERSITY LECTURER IN EASTERN
EUROPEAN HISTORY

ARCHON BOOKS

HAMDEN · LONDON

1962

FIRST PUBLISHED 1937
OXFORD UNIVERSITY PRESS
REPRINTED 1962 WITH PERMISSION

PRINTED IN THE UNITED STATES OF AMERICA

PREFACE

SOME years ago I was struck by the fact that very little use of Russian sources had been made by western historians in writing of the Near Eastern crisis of 1875–8. This study of Russian foreign relations has grown out of the attempt to make some of these Russian printed sources available to students. Since I began working on it important works on this subject have appeared by Professors Langer, Seton-Watson, and Harris; they have helped me very greatly, though Professor Harris's book was published too recently for me to profit from it as much as I could wish. None of these three scholars, however, aim at covering the same ground as myself or at presenting the Near Eastern question in its Russian, and in something of its Turkish and Balkan, setting. Foreign relations are not the same as the relations of foreign offices; I have therefore tried to avoid a purely diplomatic treatment and have put considerable emphasis on military factors, on forces outside the foreign office or government circles (in particular panslavism), and on the internal development of Russia and the Balkan peninsula during the generation succeeding the Crimean War.

I have not worked in the Moscow archives, and I am painfully aware that no final estimate of Russian foreign policy can be made until much more has been made known from the Russian foreign office archives than is at present the case. The utmost that I can hope is that, in the meantime, this book may be of use in setting out what is at present known from the main printed sources in Russian, supplemented by those in western languages and by a little of the material published in Serbian and Bulgarian. I have also used extensively the British foreign office papers in the Public Record Office, the Layard papers in the British Museum, and the unpublished portion of the Shuvalov papers from the archives of the former Imperial Russian embassy in London. I am extremely grateful to Professor Seton-Watson for his kindness in putting at my disposal his transcripts of the Shuvalov papers, which are of the greatest value for the months of acute crisis between Russia and England in 1878. I am also indebted to Baron A. Meyendorff for the use of transcripts and notes, relating to the years before 1876, made by him from the same embassy archives; and to

M. M. D. Stojanović for permission to utilize certain portions, based on the Belgrade and Vienna archives, of his unpublished London University doctoral thesis.

I have a number of further debts of gratitude to acknowledge. I cannot sufficiently thank the Principal of Hertford College, Dr. C. R. M. F. Cruttwell, without whose toil this book would not have emerged. Professor H. W. V. Temperley has given me much help in Chapters II and III; Professor L. M. Penson in the last three chapters; and Professor Sir Bernard Pares on a number of points. Professor L. B. Namier has saved me from numerous blunders and obscurities in the first half of the book. Mr. J. E. C. Hill has very kindly undertaken the laborious task of reading my proof-sheets. The Council of the Royal Historical Society has allowed me to republish, with some additions and corrections, a paper on panslavism which was originally published in its *Transactions* for 1935, and which now forms section 4 of my introductory chapter on the Russian background. Finally, I must express my very great thanks to the staff of the Clarendon Press for their unfailing patience and skill.

B. H. S.

BALLIOL COLLEGE, OXFORD

26 April, 1937

CONTENTS

ILLUSTRATIONS

MAPS

NOTE

ALL dates are given according to the new style, which was twelve days in advance of the old style.

ABBREVIATIONS

1. Unprinted material

British Museum Add. MSS.: British Museum, Additional MSS.: Layard Papers.

F.O.: Foreign Office papers in the Public Record Office. I have worked through for 1875–8 the series, 65, General Correspondence, Russia, and, 181, Embassy and Consular, Russia; the Simmons Papers, 358, and the Tenterden Papers, 363. I have used largely the series, 78, General Correspondence, Turkey; and for particular questions the following series of General Correspondence: 7, Austria; 27, France; 45, Italy; 64, Germany; and 195, Embassy and Consular, Turkey. In the case of documents which were published in the blue-books, references are given to *Accounts and Papers* and not to *F.O.*

Meyendorff MSS.: notes and copies made by Baron A. Meyendorff from the archives of the Imperial Russian Embassy in London. These relate to the years before 1876.

Seton-Watson MSS.: transcripts made by Professor R. W. Seton-Watson from the archives of the Imperial Russian Embassy in London. These are Shuvalov's papers, from January to May 1878: those covering 1875–7 have been published by him in the *Slavonic Review*, see below, p. 692.

Stojanović, M. D., Serbia in international politics: from the insurrection of Herzegovina (1875) to the congress of Berlin (1878). A London University thesis, which includes material from the Belgrade and Vienna foreign office archives.

2. Printed material

Particulars as to the following will be found in the Bibliographical Notes at the end of the volume, as also to those books and articles referred to in the footnotes without initials of author, date and place of publication.

A. and P.: *Accounts and Papers*, Parliamentary Proceedings. The references are to the year and number of volume, the command number, and the number of the document.

Actenstücke: *A. aus den Correspondenzen des k. u. k. gemeinsamen Ministeriums des Äusseren über orientalischen Angelegenheiten.*

Disraeli: Monypenny and Buckle, *The Life of Benjamin Disraeli*. The references are to vol. 2 of the 1929 edition.

D.D.F.: *Documents diplomatiques français . . . Ière série . . . .* The references are to vol. 2, unless otherwise stated.

G.P.: *Die Grosse Politik der europäischen Kabinette*. The references are to vol. 2, unless otherwise stated.

Hasenkampf: *Moi dnevnik 1877–78 gg.*

I.V.: *Istorichesky Vestnik.*

R.S.: *Russkaya Starina.*

Salisbury: Lady Gwendolen Cecil, *Life of Robert, Marquis of Salisbury.* The references are to vol. 2.

San Stefano: Ignatyev, *San Stefano.*

Skalon: *Moi vospominaniya, 1877–8 gg.*

S.R.: *Slavonic Review.*

Tatishchev: *Imperator Aleksandr II . . . .* The references are to vol. 2, unless otherwise stated.

Wertheimer: *Graf Julius Andrássy . . . .* The references are to vol. 2, unless otherwise stated.

I

THE RUSSIAN BACKGROUND

1. Internal Situation

THE greatest problem for the Russia of the eighteen-seventies was not the decomposition of the Ottoman empire, but the transformation of her own empire. The reforms of the sixties are rightly known as 'the great reforms', however much they were emasculated from the very start. First and foremost, the abolition of serfdom shook the whole structure of society. Taken together, the reforms plunged Russia forward into a final stage of transformation: she was becoming a country swayed by the western forces of large-scale finance, industry, and agriculture, and tied very closely to world markets and world prices. The reforms initiated the struggles between liberalism of a constitutional or democratic kind, revolutionary socialism whether of a populist, Marxian, or revisionist kind, and the Tsarist autocracy buttressed by the police-bureaucracy, the army, and the Orthodox church. These struggles came to a head in 1905 and 1917, in each case as an immediate consequence of failure in war, less than two generations after 'the great reforms', themselves the result of the collapse in the Crimean war. Between 1856 and 1904 Russia had the longest period of peace that she had ever known; if her colonial expeditions are excluded, she fought only one war, that with Turkey in 1877–8. Before embarking on it, the Tsar had been warned by his finance minister that war would jeopardize the internal achievements of his reign, and this proved to be true; for, although Russia triumphed in arms against Turkey, she did so at great cost, and she failed in diplomacy against Europe. The revulsion at home left the government almost unsupported in its struggle against revolutionary terrorism, and the assassination of Alexander II brought reaction firmly into the saddle in the person of Alexander III.

After the Crimean war Russia ceased to figure as 'the gendarme of Europe', ceased indeed to play any leading role in the affairs of Europe for twenty years. She could not fail to be important, but she was not decisive, and the great events— German and Italian unity—were accomplished with Russia in the background. The weakness of Austria in 1866 and 1867 and the simultaneous revolt in Crete might have given her the chance of moving forward again in the Balkans; so might the Franco-Prussian war. But, although in 1870 Russia did move forward in the Black Sea, she did not feel strong enough to challenge the issue of the Crimean war. Foreign affairs were still secondary, and the major issues lay at home. While Russia affected the West to a comparatively small extent, the influence of the West on Russia during these twenty years was all-important, and the borrowing from France, England, or Prussia was both direct and deliberate in the case of all the reforms, with the one exception of the abolition of serfdom.

The immense change-over was bound to be slow and extremely complex. The transformation of agriculture into a system of relations entirely based on hired labour, a money economy, and mobility of labour had not nearly been attained even by the beginning of the twentieth century. Forms of the older economy based upon labour services long persisted, and with them the corresponding psychology. Old features of the serf régime lived on, even if decaying, side by side with the new capitalistic development. That development itself inevitably had different characteristics and a different tempo according as it took place in the long-settled central and western regions or in the new lands of the south and east. The emancipation of the serfs had been prepared by the growing realization in the second quarter of the century that serfdom was incompatible with the economic requirements even of the serf-owners, the gentry. Above all, the ground was mined by the rebelliousness of the serfs themselves,[1] and Alexander II inaugurated his reign by publicly avowing that the only alternative to emancipation from above was revolution from below. When the emancipation edict was announced, in March 1861, it seemed for a moment that everything might founder beneath 'the complete and absolute distrust of the people . . . of all constituted authority. . . . Manifestos, uniforms, officials, ukases, governors, priests bearing the cross, the commands of the Tsar,—all this is a lie, an imposture, a fraud . . .'.[2] Yet, considering everything, the crisis

[1] The figures for peasant risings and disturbances are disputed, but there is no doubt of widespread nervousness among the landowners in the late fifties: the most recent figures, from official sources, are in *Istorik marksist*, 1933, no. vi, pp. 146–53, and *Krasny arkhiv*, 1936, vol. lxxv, pp. 63–82.

[2] Private letter of Samarin, from Samara, 22 Apr. 1861, extract in *Krasny arkhiv*,

was quickly overcome. The drastic use of force by the military and the police and the admirable work of the new 'arbiters of the peace', suppressed or prevented a real conflagration, and the new order began with infinite pains to take shape. However remote the terms of emancipation were from the hopes and feelings of the peasantry, the following twenty years saw no such succession of riots or risings as the preceding generation.

The terms were exceedingly complicated, but the broad results were the following. The peasantry constituted almost 50,000,000 of the 60,000,000 inhabitants of European Russia. There were about 10,000,000 male state peasants, whose position varied greatly but in most cases approximated to serfdom. Rather over 3,000,000 belonged to the imperial family and certain special categories of peasants. These two groups were dealt with separately, on much more favourable terms than the third group, the 10,000,000 male serfs of the gentry, who numbered about a quarter of a million. These were no longer to be personally bound to their owners, and were to be emancipated with land (except in certain cases), at a price. In general, they were to retain their strips in the communal fields, whether under repartitional or hereditary household tenure, and to pay for them in the form either of money rent or of redemption annuities to the state, where agreement had been reached as to the state buying out the landowners. The scales were intentionally weighted in favour of the latter process, and by 1881 nearly all the ex-serfs of the gentry were paying redemption annuities. Their allotments were diminished in size, save in the western provinces and the forest regions of the far north, and they lost very severely in the arrangements made as to pasture, meadows, and woodlands. Further, the state bought out the nobles at rates on the average much higher than the market price of land, and the redemption charges were fixed at an over-high rate. At the same time the poll-tax system, from which the gentry were exempted, continued in force (until 1886) and certain new tax dues were laid upon the peasantry. The net result was that 'the scales were weighted against the peasant; he was coming forth from the Emancipation with limited rights and little land, but abundant obligations . . .'.[1] The outstanding fact in the agrarian history

1936, vol. lxxiv, p. 17. Samarin was one of the slavophil leaders in the struggle for emancipation. His later letters show that he quickly recovered from his initial fears.
[1] G. T. Robinson, *Rural Russia under the Old Régime* (London, 1932), p. 88, a very

of the next half-century was that, although the allotment lands increased slightly and the non-allotment lands bought or rented by peasants increased steadily (from the 1880s), there was a far greater rise in the peasant population: the increase in the land they held was in no way proportionate.

This was in part due to another feature of the emancipation reforms. They aimed at preserving the bonds of the commune (*mir*) and the undivided family, as the distinctive Slav institutions upon which rested the salvation of village Russia. The commune, and to some extent the new, elected cantonal authorities, took over various obligations many of which had previously been performed by the nobles: in particular, it was the commune and the head of the family who were responsible for the poll-tax and redemption-charge payments. Thus the government made separation from the commune as cumbersome as possible, and had no intention of remoulding the peasantry along the lines of French or of American development. The communal organization meant a considerable, though from the seventies on a diminishing, amount of peasant self-government, but, with its prevailing strip-cultivation on a three-field system, it acted as the greatest impediment to better farming and modern developments. Only at the very end of the nineteenth century were there signs of a change in official circles, and it was not until 1904 and Stolypin's land legislation of 1906 that there was a reversal of policy, which now aimed at breaking up the communal system and staked the future on a rapid increase of a solid, peasant-farmer class. By then the differentiation of the peasantry into three broad classes—the rich (kulaks), middle, and poor peasantry—had proceeded far. Under Alexander II this decisive change in the agrarian situation as it developed after the abolition of serfdom was not yet pronounced, but there was already beginning to grow up a small well-off village class and a large village proletariat, landless or almost landless, subsisting as hired labourers whether in agricultural or other occupations. Conditions varied so greatly as to make generalization almost impossible; nevertheless, in the seventies the economic results of emancipation on a large part of the peasantry

careful study of agrarian conditions between 1861 and 1917. I have found this book and A. A. Kornilov, *Krestyanskaya reforma* (St. Petersburg, 1905) particularly useful in attempting to generalize about the emancipation. Lenin's *Razvitie kapitalizma v Rossii* (vol. iii of the first Russian collected ed.) is indispensable for the results of emancipation.

were judged by contemporaries to be profoundly disturbing. Arrears of payments due to the state mounted higher and higher, and it would be impossible to hold out for long against some reduction of them. On the side of the gentry matters were, relatively, no better. They had been heavily indebted before emancipation, and much of their immediate gains from being bought out of the allotment lands went towards meeting these obligations. Only a small minority of them reorganized their estates efficiently; in the seventies the rush to use the new, private land-mortgage banks showed that very many of the gentry were still in the most precarious situation; and they were already selling their land on a large scale, mainly as yet to the urban merchant or entrepreneur. By the end of the reign the fall in wheat prices was hitting them harder and harder, and Alexander III had to devote his main energies to buttressing up a resident, landowning gentry as the surest bulwark of his power.

The abolition of serfdom was the first of 'the great reforms' both in time and in importance. There followed education reform (1863), the creation of *zemstva* (1864), law reform (1864), new press regulations (1865), municipal self-government (1870), military conscription (1874). Immediate results fell depressingly short of the exaggerated hopes of the sixties. In part this was inevitable; but in part it was due to half-measures and to the determination of the bureaucracy to continue to rule with as little sharing of power as possible with new institutions and new forces. The attempted assassination of the Tsar in 1866 gave added strength to the reactionaries and the time-servers in their struggle against liberal tendencies. They captured all the most responsible posts, except three: Reutern remained in charge of finances, Gorchakov of foreign affairs, and D. A. Milyutin of the war office. The result was a deliberate policy of whittling away the reforms as they began to function. Only Milyutin's conscription measure escaped almost unscathed, and that, unlike the other reforms, had been led up to by ten years of reform in the army.

In the field of education, D. A. Tolstoi, the new minister, grappled with renewed student disturbances by stifling such independence as the 1863 university statute permitted, and inaugurated his reactionary campaign against secondary education, which was one of the main battlegrounds of the seventies. Legal reform fared likewise. The reforms of 1864 had introduced an entirely new system of courts which were originally to a very large extent divorced from the police and the departments, and in which for the first time proceedings were public and barristers and, for criminal cases, juries employed. Despite various serious defects they were hailed as, next to abolition of serfdom, the greatest of triumphs for the liberty of the individual. From 1867 a swing back began: 'temporary' ordinances were issued, which remained in force indefinitely; administrative arrests were resumed; the police jostled the new courts more and more closely; the provincial governors were armed with special overriding powers. By 1876 the wave of political offences had reached a new high-water mark. Strangely enough these trials, when eventually they took place, were in part held in public, until in April 1878 Vera Zasulich, who had shot the chief of police in St. Petersburg, was acquitted by the jury. Thereafter publicity and juries disappeared for anything of a political colouring, in exchange for administrative decisions or military tribunals.

Freedom of the press had been demanded more unanimously than anything else in the earlier years of Alexander II, but none of 'the great reforms' were more unsatisfactory from the outset than the revised press regulations issued in 1865. During the previous ten years there had been at first a violent reaction against the extreme rigours of Nicholas I's censorship during which the press blossomed forth in a strange, new air, and then doses of sharp repression, both on the right and the left, but the position had not been clarified by any new legislation. Under the 1865 regulations, designed as temporary but in fact in force for the next forty years, there was to be no preventive censorship for Russian books or translations over a certain length, or for already existent daily or periodical papers published in the two capitals. For all other publications the preventive censorship was continued. Hence the provincial press remained virtually non-existent. The actual system as applied, and with important additions introduced from 1868 onwards, placed even that portion of the press exempt from preventive censorship at the mercy of the punitive censorship. Press cases were more and more completely removed from the purview of the lawcourts. As regards the daily and periodical press, large financial guarantees were required: an administrative veto could be placed on the reporting of certain facts or the discussion of certain questions, and temporary suspension ordered in case of disobedience: three warnings, however widely separated, likewise involved temporary suspension: permanent closure of a paper could be ordered in extreme cases: street sale could be prohibited;[1] and, from 1879, advertisements. Under such conditions no cheap political press could grow up legally and the existent press in St. Petersburg and Moscow was very severely shackled in its dealings with politics.

At the same time, in despite of all these obstacles, Russia did now have a definitely political press whereas under Nicholas I she had not. In sharp contrast with the silence during the eastern crisis of 1853–6, twenty years later questions of foreign policy, and notably that of the Balkans, were publicly discussed. Foreign countries were well aware of this change. The Russian press was carefully followed abroad and complaints became frequent as to the deliberate failure of the foreign office to exercise due control. A nationalist press campaign could be, within limits, very useful to the government, as Katkov had shown in 1863 in defying the Poles and foreign intervention; and normally a much freer hand was left as regards foreign than internal affairs. The position of the foreign office was in any case difficult. Departmental jealousies and intrigues gave scope for greater freedom of expression of opinion. The foreign office could inspire, and it could threaten, but the actual censorship was, mainly, vested in the ministry of interior, and it was punitive not preventive for all the important papers.

While almost all the educated public chafed and fumed under the arbitrary uncertainty of the press censorship, liberal opinion was equally depressed by the fate of the local government reforms, inaugurated in the form of elected provincial and district councils (*zemstva*) and municipal councils. Ultimately they were to prove the most important institutional innovation of the reign, but for a full generation after their creation they were struggling even for air in which to breathe. From the first they were narrowly limited in powers and carefully weighted in composition. From the first they had to contend with the bureaucracy. They figured as means by which various sections of the gentry and the professional classes aspired to curb the police state of Tsardom by creating new fields of social and

---

[1] Most of the Russian press still depended mainly on regular subscribers, but street sale was increasing and its prohibition was a very serious financial loss.

political activity and even by securing ultimately a national representative body, and perhaps some form of constitution. There were sharp divisions of opinion as to what form any such national representation should take, and the liberals could not make common cause with any of the revolutionary groups. From 1867 Timashev, the minister of interior, and D. A. Tolstoi fought unremittingly not merely against any extension of *zemstva* activities, but even against the carrying out of those functions which had been originally allotted to them, particularly in the spheres of education and public health. The *zemstva*, if they had to exist, were to be nothing but a fifth wheel in the administrative coach; they were to be admitted on sufferance only in so far as the omnipotence of provincial governors and officialdom was not undermined.[1] The result was that the men who in the mid-sixties had enthusiastically acclaimed the *zemstva* as opening a new career of public life, in the seventies fell back, for the most part, into the prevailing pessimism of shattered illusions. When, however, after 1878 the authorities were pitted against terrorism, the opposition nests in the *zemstva* were once again prominent in their efforts to gain some share in government. The authorities were wavering: some stood for resolute struggle against any innovations; others for concessions. The outcome was Loris-Melikov's 'constitution'; cautiously selected consultative bodies, in part chosen from the *zemstva*, somewhat on the model of the procedure adopted in working out the emancipation of the serfs. Loris-Melikov himself repudiated any idea of national representation or western constitutionalism, yet his scheme might have led on towards a constitution if the pressure of revolutionary and liberal opinion had been maintained. His proposals had been accepted by Alexander II on the eve of his assassination. Alexander III turned at once to Pobedonostsev and unyielding autocracy. The revolutionaries were broken, for a time: the reformists were too alarmed and disunited to continue their struggle.

Between the liberal reformists and the revolutionary groups there had been, with rare exceptions, no links. The cleavage was largely a cleavage between two generations; as in the sixties, there was a gulf between 'Fathers and Sons'. The revolutionaries were for the most part either 'conscience-stricken nobility' or 'men of the mixed class', with the students,

---

[1] Lenin, vol. v (first ed. of Russian collected edition), p. 40.

male and female, from the universities and technical colleges as prominent as ever. They had never regarded Tsarist reforms as anything but sops of deception, and they now felt only too bitterly justified as reaction gained more and more ground. During most of the eighteen-seventies the revolutionary scene was dominated by *narodnichestvo* (populism) and the influence of Bakunin and Lavrov. Marx was not yet of consequence in Russia.[1] Bakunin stood for the destruction of state power by mass risings and its replacement by some system of federative communes; in Russia the sole power of social revolution lay with the dark, many-millioned peasantry, ripe for revolution, but unorganized and disunited. Lavrov preached the useless-ness of a political without a social revolution based on a broad mass movement; the necessity for intensive, socialistic educa-tional work among the peasantry and for direction by an orga-nized party; the primary value of individual personality in the history of progress in opposition to reliance on elemental mass waves. Both Lavrov and Bakunin, for all their differences, staked everything on the peasantry as the decisive revolutionary factor, and this was the cardinal tenet of the *narodniki* (populists). Among them two different types of revolutionary belief and psychology were mingled: belief in the miraculous effects of propaganda among the masses, and belief in a central, secret organization of a dictatorial character. The former was upper-most in the days of 'the going to the people': the latter was revivified in the terrorist campaign of the last three years of Alexander II's reign.

The 'going to the people' (1873–5) was the stirring example of inchoate, revolutionary enthusiasm which frightened the government into mass arrests and mass trials and made a stronger impression on Russian opinion than any other event in the two or three years preceding the Balkan wars. Reinforced by the recall of Russian students from abroad, the revolutionary youth sallied forth to the villages (and to a much less extent to the factories) to merge themselves in their masters and enlighten them as to their true, revolutionary and socialistic interests. The movement was hopelessly lacking in organization, and the programme preached was vague and varying: the usual essential

[1] The first volume of *Das Kapital* was allowed into Russia, and a Russian transla-tion was allowed by the censorship in 1872. Translations of Hobbes's *Leviathan*, Spinoza's works, and Lecky's *History of . . . rationalism in Europe* were prohibited.

was that the land was to belong to those who worked it and the landowners were to be expropriated; the commune (*mir*) was to be the basis for the socialist utopia. On the showing of those who 'went to the people' themselves, the movement failed almost completely; even without the roundings up by the police. Two consequences followed. In the words of one of the *narodniki*: 'We succeeded in producing that about which we did not care at all—the sympathy of the thinking layers of Russian society.'[1] The divorce between the governmental apparatus and the bulk of Russian opinion, not in itself revolutionary, was the most serious symptom of the internal crisis which convulsed Russia after the war with Turkey. The second consequence linked on directly to the internal crisis: the *narodniki* struggled to build up a new organization (*Zemlya i Volya*, Land and Liberty) and to reconstruct a programme of action (1877–9); but a split took place which led to the formation of the terrorist group known as *Narodnaya Volya* (People's Will) and to its campaign of assassination, ending with that of the Tsar in March 1881.

Meanwhile, in 1876, when the problem of Turkey again occupied the centre of the European stage, 'the going to the people' had collapsed and there was nothing positive, either from the revolutionary or the liberal side, which could act as a sufficiently powerful magnet to prevent attention being diverted abroad. The *narodniki* were disorganized, and in many cases dejected or prepared to sacrifice themselves elsewhere to a cause. The ordinary feelings of traditional patriotism could be tapped much more effectively than during the sixties (except as against the Poles) when the framing and working out of 'the great reforms' were all absorbing. War was not made with Turkey in order to distract attention from the internal front; but if there had to be war, then a victorious conclusion would be an incalculable asset to Tsardom at home: failure would mean a terrifying question-mark.

There could hardly be defeat in war against Turkey alone, for the impact of the West on Russia was transforming her technically and economically at a far more rapid rate than it was modernizing Turkey. As part and parcel of the reforms of

[1] Vl. Debagory-Mokrievich, *Vospominaniya* (St. Petersburg, 1906), p. 183, quoted in James Mavor, *An Economic History of Russia* (London, 2nd. ed., 1925), vol. ii, p. 106.

the sixties a variety of measures had been taken to develop commerce and industry along western lines.[1] Reutern, who was minister of finance from 1862 to 1878, did his utmost to assist this process. He reorganized the financial administration and provided some degree of publicity for the national budget; reformed the state bank and encouraged the foundation of private banks (previously unknown in Russia) and of new credit institutions. Company promotions were multiplied; the stock exchange ushered in a new life; almost at a bound St. Petersburg at least passed into a world of financial and commercial speculation. There were, apart from the greater mobility of labour made possible by the abolition of serfdom, three bases for this economic transition—railways, foreign investments, and low tariffs.

Prior to the Crimean war Russia had but 650 miles of railway opened. Moscow had been linked with St. Petersburg; Warsaw with the Austrian frontier and Vienna. That was virtually all. In the next twenty years the mileage was increased to 11,750, five-sixths of it opened between 1866 and 1876. It was very small in comparison with the size and needs even of European Russia, and there was as yet nothing built east of the Volga; but a big step had been made towards grappling with harvest or famine problems, towards the formation of an internal market on a national scale, and towards the expansion of industry. From the time of the congress of Paris itself the French had been foremost in the new economic penetration of Russia, and Péreire and the Crédit Mobilier were the mainstays at first of the railway projects; but their ventures ended in failure and the programme inaugurated in 1866 largely through Reutern was financed more from London than Paris. Although almost all the lines were built and operated as private companies, usually at a very high cost and with gross peculation, the state guaranteed a return and in fact stood behind them. Russian capital was quite insufficient to meet the outlay involved, and repeated flotations abroad were necessary.

[1] For the following pages I have used particularly: J. Bloch, *Les Finances de la Russie au xixe siècle* (Paris, 1899; 2 vols.); V. I. Pokrovsky, *Sbornik svedenii po istorii i statistiki vneshnei torgovli* (St. Petersburg, 1902); S. O. Gulishambarov, *Vsemirnaya torgovlya v xix v. i uchastie v nei Rossii* (St. Petersburg, 1898); Lenin, *Razvitie kapitalizma v Rossii* (vol. iii of the 1st ed. of his collected works); P. I. Lyashchenko, *Istoriya russkogo narodnogo khozyaistva* (Moscow, 1927); V. Wittchevsky, *Russlands Handels- Zoll- und Industriepolitik von Peter dem Gr. bis auf dem Gegenwart* (Berlin, 1905); M. Tugan-Baranovsky, *Geschichte der russischen Fabrik* (Berlin, 1900); B. Ischchanian, *Die ausländischen Elemente in der russischen Volkswirtschaft* (Berlin, 1913).

Even apart from railway needs, heavy foreign borrowing was necessary to restore the state finances shattered by the Crimean war and further damaged by the Polish revolt in 1863. Nicholas I, in fear of the consequences of relying on foreign credit, had attempted to borrow abroad as little as he could. Under his son the policy of as rapid a development of Russian resources as possible led to the encouragement of the investment of western capital. In twenty-five years nearly twice as much was raised in foreign loans, including railway bonds, as during the thirty years of Nicholas's reign. In 1857 approximately one-third of the total debt consisted of foreign loans; by the end of Alexander's reign about one-half. Almost all these loans paid 5 per cent., and by 1880 they absorbed about an eighth of the revenue. The strain was heavy, but unlike Turkey, which was by now immensely burdened with foreign debt, Russia never defaulted.

A low tariff was another reversal of the policy of Nicholas. From 1822 onwards Russia lived behind an immense wall of tariffs or prohibitions. In 1850 some modifications were secured, and in 1857 Bastiat and Cobden won the day. The new tariff of that year, with subsequent alterations downwards, and the tariff of 1868 opened the door liberally to the West. The railways were built almost entirely with foreign equipment entering duty free or under very low rates. American raw cotton likewise came in duty free, and a wide range of raw materials and semi-manufactured goods were specially favoured. It was not until the financial necessities of meeting the Balkan crisis in 1876 that an all-round increase in duties was made (see below, p. 231). Thereafter, with the tide flowing strongly in that direction in Germany and elsewhere, Russia in the eighties again adopted extreme protection.

Thanks to railways, foreign capital, and low tariffs, the advance was marked in almost all industries. The contribution of western technical experts and entrepreneurs was equally marked, though this was no new feature. Ludwig Knoop and Karl Scheibler, the creators of the modern textile industry of the Moscow and Lodz regions, were at the height of their activities. The former was already proverbial; 'a priest (*pop*) to every church, a Knoop to every factory'. Hubbard, Shaw, and Thornton were well-known names in the textile world. The Welshman John Hughes gave his name to the new metallurgical centre in the Donets basin (1869), though it was ten years before its phenomenal expansion began, thanks to Belgian and French enterprise. Robert Nobel paid a chance visit to Baku in 1874, and five years later the great Nobel company started to revolutionize the oil industry.[1] New industries such as machinery, steel, and beet-sugar by 1880 were expanding rapidly. Raw cotton imports rose from 4·4 million lb. (English) in 1850 to 21·7 in 1860 and 80·9 in 1876: machinery imports almost quadrupled between 1861 and 1875. The production of manufactured cotton goods and yarn doubled in value between 1860 and 1876; that of woollen goods rose sharply; so at last did that of pig-iron in the early seventies (the Ural works, still much the largest producers, were always inefficient): the production of coal increased sixfold (in weight), and by 1880 elevenfold. The total value of manufactured goods more than doubled in fifteen years (1864–79). The number of factory operatives, minute in proportion to the whole population, grew from just under half a million in 1865 to over three-quarters of a million in 1879, by which date there were approximately 250,000 miners and 175,000 railwaymen.[2]

Above all, grain prices were well maintained or were rising until the mid-seventies, and grain exports mounted until those of 1880 were worth five times those of 1860 (in weight they were three and a half times larger). Russian foreign trade was expanding continuously; the average value of exports and imports, taken together, for 1876–80 was more than three times greater than that for 1856–60, and the *per capita* increase more than twofold. Yet, whereas in almost every year of Nicholas I's

[1] The output of the Baku wells had already increased very strikingly from 1872, when the state farming-out system was abandoned in favour of substantially unrestricted private enterprise; see the figures in A. Mamedov, 'Azerbaizhanskoe neftyanoe khozyaistvo do otmeny otkupnoi sistemy (1800–72)', in *Istorik marksist*, 1936, no. iv, pp. 111–12.

[2] In addition there were a relatively large but indeterminate number of persons employed in domestic industries. The statistics for factories and industrial workers are very unsatisfactory and much disputed: they are analysed in detail by Lenin, *Razvitie kapitalizma v Rossii*, pp. 370–405, 496–502. Already (1879) a feature which was to be of the greatest importance in the twentieth century was evident: there were 390,374 workers employed in 852 factories classed as employing more than 100 persons; of these workers no less than 156,760 were concentrated in the 76 factories employing over 1,000: this concentration in large, machine-equipped factories was specially accentuated in the cotton industry, in which out of a total of 162,191 factory operatives 92,529 were so employed; ib., pp. 402–5, and Tugan-Baranovsky, *Geschichte der russischen Fabrik*, p. 431.

reign there had been a substantial excess of exports over imports, under Alexander II, with an enormous increase in imports, a favourable balance was not regularly maintained, and between 1871 and 1875, with four short harvests, there was a large deficit. Three other characteristics of Russian foreign trade between 1856 and 1881 stand out as of special interest, two of them being equally evident during the preceding quarter of a century; grain exports were still far the largest group of exports; the bulk of foreign trade, especially of exports, was still by sea; two countries, England and Germany, were dominant.

In the fifties grain (over half of it wheat) accounted for more than one-third of the total value of Russian exports: after 1865 this proportion was steadily increased until by the end of the century (1891–5) it reached 47·2 per cent. But already by 1875 the international collapse in wheat prices had begun, which, when coupled with the fall in rye and oats, was to cause catastrophic results to Russian agriculture. Wheat, the crop of the big estates, remained of primary importance in export, but the development of the German market for rye, the crop of the peasants, and oats was pronounced: for 1876–80, 29 per cent. of the value of the grain exports consisted of rye, 14·9 per cent. of oats, 38·5 per cent. of wheat.

The great bulk of foreign trade was still carried by sea, and in foreign ships, though the railways linking up with Germany and Austria-Hungary brought about a steady rise in the proportion of imports that came in over the land frontiers. Grain exports continued to be overwhelmingly sea-borne, in the case of wheat almost entirely from the Black Sea. During the reign of Nicholas the Black Sea and Sea of Azov ports had been gaining rapidly on those of the Baltic. In the reign of his son they were responsible for between 40 and 42 per cent. of sea-borne exports (1861–80); and in the following fifteen years this share rose to over 60 per cent. Since in the same period (1861–95) the proportion of sea-borne exports to total exports only fell from 77·5 to 72 per cent. and the total value of exports increased threefold, it is obvious that the economic importance of the Straits was immense. This had been keenly enough realized in the first half of the century with the initial tapping of new wheat lands in the south and the rise of Odessa, but in the second half of the century it was all the more emphasized not only by such an enormous development of the exporting latifundia, but from the end of the seventies by the beginnings of the South Russian heavy industry and of large-scale production of oil in the Caucasus.

The United Kingdom and Germany between them took at least two-thirds of Russia's exports and supplied between 54 and 68 per cent. of her imports (1861–81). The British dominance of the first half of the century had passed. The United Kingdom was still Russia's best customer, but in exports to Russia she had already yielded first place to the Zollverein, German exports jumping from an average of 15·6 per cent. of the total Russian imports for 1841–50 to 41·9 per cent. for 1872–81. The corresponding British figures were 27 and 26 per cent., with a drop to 19 per cent. in the sixties. Russian exports to Germany showed relatively an even larger increase, from an average of 8 per cent. of the total Russian exports for 1841–50 to 30 per cent. for 1872–81. Exports to the United Kingdom were well maintained until 1870; then there was a relative fall, and again, as also in exports to Germany, in the eighties (1841–50, 37 per cent.; 1851–60, 40 per cent.; 1861–70, 45·7 per cent.; 1871–80, 35·3 per cent.). The dependence of Russia on these two countries was further increased by the fact that the United Kingdom had the lion's share of the shipping and that Russian foreign trade was still mainly conducted through British and German firms.

On the other hand, neither the United Kingdom nor Germany was similarly dependent on Russia. The former after 1856 never took from Russia more than 6·7 per cent. of her total imports, and never sent her more than 3·3 per cent. of her exports.[1] The colonies, the United States, France, Germany, and ultimately Holland ranked before Russia. Turkey (including Serbia and Roumania) until the early seventies took about as much or more of British exports as Russia, though she sent very much less to England than Russia did. Nor was Russia after 1856 regularly still the largest single supplier of wheat to England. After the Civil War transatlantic competition reappeared with overwhelming effect, and during the ten years

---

[1] *A. and P.*, 1890–1, lxxvii, Trade, &c.: Statistical Tables . . . . The figures are for quinquennial periods from 1855 to 1889. In the case of exports they exclude re-exports, which were very large, but probably not on such a scale to Russia as to raise appreciably the figure of 3·3.

1876 to 1885 over half of the British wheat imports was coming from the United States.[1]

Beside the figures for Russian trade with the United Kingdom and Germany those with Austria-Hungary looked exceedingly puny. Even when they made a relatively big jump in the seventies, the percentages of the total Russian imports and exports were only 4·5 and 6·4, and the Austro-Hungarian equivalents only 3·8 and 5·5. For Austria-Hungary the Turkish dominions were very much more important than Russia. In 1874 her trade with Turkey came next after her trade with Germany, while that with Italy and Russia followed far behind. For Turkey the United Kingdom was the main provider, with well over one-third of her imports; Austria-Hungary was a poor second, but even so completely out-distanced Russia.[2] Russian industrialists on the eve of the Balkan crisis calculated that exports to Turkey represented 3·2 per cent. of total Russian exports, and imports from Turkey not more than 4·5 of total Russian imports, and it was admitted that since the Crimean war their exports of manufactured goods to Turkey had sunk almost to zero.[3] It has been said that the expansion in the productive power of Russian industry without any proportionate expansion of the internal market made it inevitable that Russian manufacturing interests should demand an energetic foreign policy to assist their capture of new markets. This view does not appear to have much relevance to the Balkans or the Levant, in which they displayed the slenderest interest, between 1856 and 1876. Their hopes lay to the East, in Persia, Central Asia, and China, where western competition might be very much less severe. Russia's Asiatic trade was a very small fraction of her total foreign trade, but something like three-quarters of her Asiatic exports was made up of manufactured goods. During the reign of Alexander II big

---

[1] Wittchewsky, *Russlands Handels-, Zoll-, und Industriepolitik* . . ., p. 344 (quoting Russian official figures). J. H. Clapham, *An Economic History of Modern Britain*, vol. ii (London, 1932), pp. 218–19, estimates that in the fifties England was dependent on foreign wheat for about 25 to 30 per cent. of her supplies, and by the end of the seventies for nearly 60 per cent. The exact dependence of England on Russian grain is very hard to estimate, particularly under Nicholas I, owing to reshipments to England of Russian grain exported, in the first place, to Mediterranean and Baltic ports.

[2] M. N. Pokrovsky, *Vneshnyaya politika* (Moscow, 1919), p. 45.

[3] A. Popov in *Avantyury russkogo tsarizma v Bolgarii*, p. 218, citing *Trudy obshchestva dlya sodyeistviya russkoi promyshlennosti i torgovlye*, 1876, vol. ix, pp. 1–13.

gains were made from China and the conquest of Central Asia was achieved (see section 3 of this chapter). It was in this direction, not in that of the Balkans, that Russian economic imperialism was showing its hand.

One illustration may be drawn from a region of particular interest in Asiatic trade which was much to the fore in the eighteen-seventies. Since 1846 Transcaucasia had been again, as from 1821 to 1831, a free transit zone for goods coming through to Persia, and the customs dues at eastern Black Sea ports had been lowered, various offsets to Russian manufactures being given at the same time. The changed policy was for long of little efficacy in repairing the damage done by the alliance between Kankrin, Nicholas I's finance minister, and Russian manufacturing interests and by the resultant closure of the free transit zone (1831–46). Armenian and British traders had organized the rival Trebizond–Erzerum–Tabriz caravan route and the smuggling business too successfully. Gradually in the sixties, owing to the final conquest of the Caucasus, to improvements in roads, and to special measures taken by Reutern, Transcaucasian trade was notably revived at the expense of the rival route through Turkey. But there followed a new attack from the side of Russian textile interests backed by Gorchakov, which were hand in glove with the new colonial expansion beyond the Caspian and aimed at the exclusion of British goods from Transcaucasia, north Persia, and Central Asia. The building of the Poti–Tiflis railway in the early seventies reinforced their arguments, and the war with Turkey gave them most of what they wanted. They failed to secure annexations which would cut the Erzerum–Tabriz trade route, but Batum, a much less unsatisfactory harbour than Poti, was at last acquired, though it was to be a free port, and at home a return was made to high protection: in 1883 the free transit zone was largely abolished and Transcaucasia substantially incorporated in the customs system of Russia proper: two years later the free-port régime at Batum was abrogated: further measures followed to assist the capture of the north Persian market.

The advance both in foreign trade and in general economic development during Alexander II's reign was great, measured in terms of Russia's past, but it was very small in comparison with that of western Europe and the United States. Russia was definitely started on the path of big-scale production based on modern communications and modern technique, but it was only a start. She was still a 'backward country'. Power, machines (especially on the land), the sharp separation between industry and agriculture, were still the exception. In the vast polygot empire the old traditions and mentality were frequently untouched, and everywhere would take long to be outgrown. The economic development both varied greatly in different parts of Russia and proceeded by fits and starts. A brief boom for a small cluster of manufacturers immediately after the Crimean war had been succeeded by many years of dislocation due to the currency crisis and above all to the emancipation of the serfs. The first effect of this had been to upset labour conditions and cause a diminution of production, notably in the Ural metal industry and the cloth mills. After 1867 the great period of railway building set in, grain prices ruled high, and industry and trade expanded as never before. In 1873 a decline set in: the international financial crisis and the general depression in the west reacted on Russia; railway construction was cut down; three successive bad harvests, famine in certain regions, reduced to almost nothing the always exiguous purchasing power of the great mass of the peasantry. It is true that some branches of industry continued to go ahead, and 1875 brought a very rare occurrence—revenue higher than expenditure, and a unique occurrence—expenditure lower than the year before: but it also brought yet another bad harvest. During that year the financial situation deteriorated in sympathy with conditions in the west, and it was highly alarming by the time that the Balkan crisis came to a head in 1876.

2. PERSONNEL

The foreign policy of Russia in Europe still depended upon her sovereign to a far greater extent than was the case in any other European country after 1870, with the exception of Turkey. Alexander II had succeeded to the throne, at the age of thirty-seven, in the middle of the Crimean war. His father had given him an education very different from his own, which had been practically confined to the parade ground, and had taken pains to initiate him into internal affairs of state. As heir-apparent none could have guessed that he would earn the name of Tsar Liberator. The emancipation of the serfs so reluctantly wrung from him and the other reforms that followed by no means meant that he regarded the basis of government in Russia as other than autocratic. He had had to yield to forces that could not be any longer blocked, and he had done so with the maximum of delay and the minimum of decisiveness. His true inclinations were better illustrated by the fourteen years of reaction beginning in 1866. Just as the catastrophe of the Crimean war brought to a head the immense internal problems of Russia which were the overriding tasks of Alexander's reign, so it left an ineffaceable mark on his outlook on foreign affairs. He could not forget the humiliation, the treachery of Vienna, the isolation save from Berlin, the imposed caution of weakness which had to be maintained during his early years as Tsar. Faced with a wholly new international situation, without experience in foreign affairs, never acquiring, as did Nicholas I and Alexander I in their different ways, a masterful interest in them, Alexander II found from the outset in Gorchakov a courtier diplomat who seemed both to mirror his own feelings and to be able to translate them into diplomatic terms as effectively as circumstances would allow. Alexander was himself a man of very mediocre character and attainments; slow and obstinate, but with little energy and little decision of will; becoming increasingly the slave of his habits and of routine. It was difficult to win his full confidence, but, once secured, difficult to undermine it. He did not possess vision or imagination, but, on the other hand, he was not to be captured readily by fantasies or far-flung aspirations; and he had a certain sober, matter-of-fact way of judging foreign affairs which, if it had been allied to wider knowledge and to real strength of character, might have saved him from the failures of his closing years.

The foreign policy of Russia was to a special degree the Tsar's policy. There was no ministry with which, in effect, he had to share control, or through which co-ordination could be obtained. Imperial councils, composed as he himself thought fit, might—or might not—be called to consider this or that particularly grave problem. His minister of foreign affairs, however influential, was *his* minister. No other member of the imperial family exercised much weight in foreign, as opposed to internal, affairs. Inevitably the Tsar's decisions were dependent upon his channels of information and his means of execution, so that the bureaucracy was usually the master. But the formulation of policy and final action of decisive importance required his sanction. Alexander did not assume that ostentatiously directing role which had been the practice of his father. Nor did he often follow his father's habit of employing his aides-de-camp general for specially important missions abroad and of thereby in a sense supplanting his own foreign office and diplomatic service. It is true that in the Caucasus, in Central Asia, and in the Far East, the war office and the governors-general and not the foreign office exercised the dominating influence and could be decisive even against the Tsar himself, but elsewhere the ministry for foreign affairs was the almost invariable channel through which he worked. The one important exception was provided by the personal links between the Romanovs and the Hohenzollerns. The relations between nephew and uncle grew closer and closer, and nothing could shake Alexander's belief in the Emperor William as the sheet anchor of his hopes.

Gorchakov was at the head of the ministry for foreign affairs throughout the reign, save for the first year during the war.[1] Twenty years older than his master, he was nearing sixty when he replaced the aged and discredited Nesselrode in 1856. He had served all his working life in the diplomatic service, but having started as a protégé of Capo d'Istria he earned the persistent hostility of Nesselrode[1] and his rise was slow. For fourteen years he remained side-tracked as minister at Stuttgart. He won favour at court through the marriage of Nicholas's favourite daughter with the Crown Prince of Württemberg, and did well as minister to the Confederation at Frankfurt, but he came to the front only in 1854, when he was charged with the thankless task of conducting the Vienna negotiations during the Crimean war. Whether justifiably or not, he succeeded in gaining the reputation of having displayed great ability and of being bitingly anti-Austrian, on good terms with the French,

[1] Aleksandr Mikhailovich Gorchakov, b. 1798, d. 1883; married; had two sons; 1817, entered the foreign office; 1821-2, attended the congresses of Laibach and Verona; 1824, at the London embassy; 1830, chargé d'affaires at Florence; 1833-8, counsellor of legation at Vienna; 1841-55, minister at Stuttgart and from 1850 at Frankfurt; 1852, attended Wellington's funeral; June 1853, death of his wife; 1854-5, special mission to Vienna; 1856, April, foreign minister; 1862, on death of Nesselrode made vice-chancellor; 1867, 25 June, on completing fifty years' service made chancellor; 1871, on day of ratification of the London Convention, 30 Mar., given the title of Highness.

[2] So he maintains in his reminiscences in R.S., vol. xl, pp. 161, 168.

and entirely hostile to the whole line of Nesselrode's policy. Thereby he seemed better fitted than any other available person to take over the foreign office on the conclusion of the war, when a new man and a new course were essential. His tone of dignified, if rather pompous, insistence on Russian rather than European interests, his calculated emphasis on his position as Russian minister for Russian foreign affairs as opposed to his predecessor's position as foreign minister for foreign affairs, his anti-Austrian tirades, his apparent favouring of liberal ideas, gave him an initial measure of popularity. This was greatly increased by his handling of the diplomatic crisis caused by the Polish rebellion of 1863, and was maintained by his ridding Russia in 1870–1 of the deeply resented provisions of the 1856 treaty which prohibited a Russian fleet in the Black Sea. His detractors said that neither in 1863 nor in 1870 did he take the lead, that Katkov forced his hand, and that he was in reality timorous and shuffling. But they did not deny that he succeeded in clothing himself for a time in the mantle of national popularity, a mantle of which he was inordinately proud. He was acclaimed by Tyutchev, the reigning patriotic poet of the day, as the direct opposite of Nesselrode, that dwarf of un-exampled cowardice, for daring to appeal to the united public spirit of Russia in her unequal struggle against Europe, for saving Russia's honour in the Balkans, and for restoring Russia's freedom in 'the sea left by testament to us'.[1]

If Gorchakov had died in 1871 his reputation would certainly stand higher than it does. His last dozen years of office go far to strip him of the laurels that might have been his due. He was already seventy-two (six years older than Disraeli) when the creation of the new German empire and the acknowledged pre-eminence of Bismarck (seventeen years his junior) ushered in a new period which was bound to be difficult for Russia and which proved more than doubly so with the development of a crisis of the first magnitude in the Balkans. Gorchakov's health was becoming more and more enfeebled; his failings more and more aggravated: by 1878 he was quite incapable of grappling with the situation. Yet he had trained up no successor. Jealousy and vanity, two of his strongest characteristics, had combined to keep around him only bureaucrats or secondary figures. On

[1] *Polnoe sobranie sochinenii F. I. Tyutcheva* (ed. 1913), particularly pp. 210, 219, 220, in poems directly addressed to Gorchakov in 1867 and 1871.

the other hand, his relations with the Tsar remained unimpaired. Twenty years of experience and service meant everything to Alexander, who disliked the effort required to make a change, had no one he trusted to put in Gorchakov's place, and was genuinely grateful to the man whom in 1871 he had rewarded with the unexampled title of Highness.

Thus Gorchakov as he will appear throughout most of this book is Gorchakov in decline. Always a clever wielder of the pen and turner of an epigram ('L'Autriche n'est pas un état, ce n'est qu'un gouvernement'; 'La Russie qui ne boude pas, mais se recueille'), he came more and more under the accusation of having 'fait des phrases au lieu d'affaires'. His delight in form and style degenerated into the production of 'spécimens de littérature avec des mots ronflants', when what his subordinates were demanding were precise instructions.[1] He had deservedly been styled 'le Narcisse de l'encrier', and he did not become less of a Narcissus. At his best he was an able technical diplomatist knowing excellently the precise importance of formulae and seeing well ahead on the diplomatic chess-board; he shone where balance, manœuvring for position, or face-saving were required: but he did not possess much constructive ability, had no driving force, and little power of decision. He was in many ways admirably adapted for the post which he held under an autocratic monarch, but as his master was himself also lacking in commanding qualities the combination of the two men was not a strong one, though it was psychologically satisfactory for each of them. Gorchakov's vanity was already a by-word even before it became of international importance in conjunction with his jealousy of Bismarck. 'Tapez-lui sur son vieux nez à grands coups d'encensoir; il n'en aura jamais assez';[2] that advice of an Austrian minister had always held good, and became sounder than ever as the little old Russian courtier's reputation dimmed before that of the Prussian giant who had once been his 'pupil' in their Frankfurt days. In the eighteen-seventies protestations that Bismarck still as ever regarded himself as Gorchakov's pupil only drew from him the sour retort: 'Oui, comme Raffael était l'élève de Perugino.'[3]

[1] Shuvalov's memoirs, quoted by Hanotaux, *Histoire de la France contemporaine*, vol. iv, p. 93.
[2] Rumbold, *Recollections of a Diplomatist*, vol. ii, p. 243.
[3] Bülow, *Denkwürdigkeiten*, vol. iv, p. 349; cf. *G.P.*, vol. i, p. 299.

GORCHAKOV, 1867
From the portrait by I. Keller

It was symptomatic of Gorchakov in his last decade that he figured as less of a Russian and more of a European. He belonged himself to an old Russian noble family, which had not come to the front before the time of Catherine II, but his upbringing in Alexander I's fashionable Tsarkoe Selo *lycée*, his social environment, and his professional connexions made of him primarily a cultivated internationalist, tied to salons and courts. If he always plumed himself on his early friendship with Pushkin, pre-eminently a Russian poet, he also liked to think of himself as something of a latinist, quoting Horace or borrowing from Suetonius to differentiate liberty from anarchy.[1] For most of thirty years he had been away from his own country, steeped in the cosmopolitan society of western diplomacy, before he appeared in the guise of a Russian defending Russia against a hostile Europe. In his old age, when social ferment again put a premium on the solidarity of states maintaining sound monarchical principles, and when a new brand of Russian nationalism was in the ascendant setting no store by those European links which had always been in some form a presupposition of his, Gorchakov reverted more and more to his earlier years and became finally the target for accusations similar to those which formerly he himself had aimed at Nesselrode. In fact the cleavage between the attitude of Nesselrode and that of Gorchakov was never so pronounced as the latter had made it appear.

Within the ministry of foreign affairs itself, still as in Nicholas's reign, the rivalry between what may be called the western and the nationalistic Russian outlooks was reflected in the two main departments, the chancellery and the Asiatic department. The considerable internal reorganization of the office which Gorchakov effected in the sixties[2] had not seriously altered the position of the chancellery as the holy of holies of Russian diplomacy, the best stepping-stone to the diplomatic service, socially superior to the other departments, working in the immediate proximity of His Highness. From it he drew, for the most part, 'le petit ministère', as his closest collaborators and adulators were styled, with their perfect French and far from perfect

---

[1] *R.S.*, vol. xl, p. 164; J. Klaczko, *Deux chanceliers* (3rd ed., 1877), pp. 5–10.

[2] The official *Ocherk istorii ministerstva inostrannykh dyel, 1802–1902* (St. Petersburg, 1902), contains useful information on the organization and personnel of the ministry and the diplomatic service.

Russian. Characteristically, the three most pertinacious and effective of these, Westmann, Jomini, and Hamburger, were men of no force, excellent civil servants, but little else; and none of the three were in the full sense Russians. Westmann he had inherited as director of the chancellery from Nesselrode, and had promoted to be assistant minister of foreign affairs in 1866; a pale, conscientious reflex of his chief, he died in May 1875 just before the outbreak of the revolt in Herzegovina. Jomini, likewise inherited from Nesselrode, came to be Gorchakov's most important factotum. He was the son of the well-known Swiss strategist and military historian who took service under Alexander I after 1812: he had spent his life in the chancellery and was soaked in the world of western diplomacy: of Russia he knew little or nothing. He was ingenious, receptive, loquacious, and incapable of holding to any opinions or line of his own: but his French style was excellent and he could turn out dispatches by the ream. Hamburger was not much more than a satellite quill-driver, who, despite an extremely unprepossessing exterior (he looked like a malformed orang-outang), succeeded in making himself almost indispensable to Gorchakov, thanks to his exceptional discretion, his command of detail, and his capacity to work at all hours. His master ultimately, in 1879, raised him to the Berne legation, where the worm turned at long last and indulged in the bitterest criticism of Gorchakov, even down to the inferiority of his cigars.[1]

In contrast, the Asiatic department contained none of Gorchakov's personal adherents and in general tended to look upon the rest of the ministry as gilded, semi-alien rivals. It was, as earlier, predominantly staffed with pure Russians, with a fair sprinkling of men of Balkan origin. Its sphere included European Turkey as well as all that lay within Asia proper, and its personnel included men who had passed through a special training in eastern languages as well as the ordinary entrants into the foreign office, though the former were somewhat looked down upon and rarely rose outside the consular service. Important questions of policy relating to the Near East were handled as well by Gorchakov and his entourage, but the detailed work and expert knowledge lay with the Asiatic department. Thus

---

[1] Feoktistov, *Za kulisami politiki i literatury, 1848–1896*, pp. 59–62; Rumbold, *Further Recollections of a Diplomatist*, pp. 190–1. Officially Hamburger was, from 1870, in charge of the establishment department.

in Balkan affairs it was of the first importance, and since it supplied most of the consular or diplomatic posts in the Near and Middle East it was in a strong position when it differed from Gorchakov. Under Nicholas I it had been in the background, but under Alexander II it acquired a new prestige and growing influence. Its connexion with slavophil or panslav circles was marked from the very beginning of the reign by the appointment as its director of Kovalevsky, a prominent nationalist, explorer, and author, and it is already typical of Gorchakov's attitude towards the Asiatic department that he was supposed to be on bad terms with Kovalevsky because the Tsar required the latter's attendance when Gorchakov made his reports on Asiatic affairs.[1] The fact that his successor for three years, 1861–4, was Ignatyev, fresh from his triumph in Pekin and already a marked man, was proof of the rising influence of the department. Ignatyev was followed as director by Stremoukhov, with whom he for long saw eye to eye and under whom the department continued to acquire an increasingly nationalist colouring. Stremoukhov himself, however, from 1872 stood for the new Austrophil policy and accordingly fell out with Ignatyev. Three years later he fell out also with Gorchakov and Jomini and retired, and his place was taken by Giers. A Protestant of Swedish extraction, Giers had served the first thirty years of his career in the Principalities, in Constantinople and Teheran, but since 1869 he had been minister at Berne and then Stockholm. Though impressed with the influence of the panslavs at home, he was no ally of theirs and was mainly intent on feeling his way through cautious balancing. Thus the crisis of 1876–8 found the Asiatic department influential but without a personality at its head and with panslavs only as subordinates: these could make a difference, but they could not give the impress which Ignatyev from Constantinople required.

Entrance into the foreign office and the diplomatic service (usually after serving a brief apprenticeship in the office) was since 1860 by examination, but the vacancies were, of course, only open to the well-off and well-connected, save in the case of a few 'orientalists'. In both, allowing for the Asiatic department as an exception, the Baltic-German and non-Russian element still, as before the Crimean war, bulked large; witness, for example, the names of Osten-Sacken, Evers, Meyendorff,

[1] M. I. Venyukov in *Golos minuvshago na chuzhoi storonye* (Paris), 1926, no. ii, p. 117.

Hillenband, Mohrenheim: but, whereas in the earlier part of Alexander II's reign the inheritance from the Nicholas-Nesselrode régime continued to dominate the major diplomatic posts, with Brunnow back in London and Budberg and Stackelberg ringing the changes on Vienna, Berlin, and Paris, the last ten years of the reign saw Orlov at Paris, Novikov at Vienna, Shuvalov at London, and at the very end Saburov in place of Oubril at Berlin. At Constantinople there was Ignatyev; but Constantinople had always been a 'Russian' preserve. These were the ambassadors with whom Gorchakov had to work during the Near Eastern crisis. Only one of them was his own man: only two of them were *diplomates de carrière*: and two of them were his bitter and influential rivals. Here again there was all too much friction, cross-countering, and hostile intrigue.

Gorchakov's own man was Oubril, whom he insisted on retaining at Berlin from the end of 1862 till the beginning of 1880, when Gorchakov himself was finished. Both his grandfather, who had migrated from Holland to Russia, and his father had been in the diplomatic service, and in it Pavel Petrovich spent all his life. He was Gorchakov's right-hand man during the Vienna negotiations in 1854–5 and the two made a firm alliance. He had been a strong Prussophil, but Prussia and the Minister-President were very different in the sixties from the new *Reich* and the Iron Chancellor in the seventies. Oubril was an ardent Catholic and he had a Polish wife. Bismarck suspected him of the worst, and at the same time despised the little man heartily: he used to maintain that he was the grandson of a French cook whose *petits pâtés* had won favour with Catherine the Great,[1] and he came to treat him accordingly. During the seventies, as Bismarck's relations with Gorchakov became worse and worse, so did his relations with the ambassador, all the more since Gorchakov refused to yield to Bismarck and move him. Nor was there anybody else in the Berlin embassy who counted. Hence, in 1876 and 1878, when it was of the utmost consequence that Russia should be well represented at the German capital she paid dearly. Hence, too, the personal links between the two emperors became all the more important if Russo-German relations were to be maintained on an amicable footing.

At Paris Orlov, the son of Nicholas's Prince Orlov, needs but

[1] Bülow, *Denkwürdigkeiten*, vol. iv, p. 315.

bare mention. A big grandee, he filled his post with adequate distinction, but given the reserved role of France throughout the Near Eastern crisis he was not called upon to play a part in it.

At Vienna Novikov (1823-1903) represented Russia continuously from 1870. If St. Petersburg were to cleave firmly to the line of agreement and compromise with Vienna initiated in 1872, he was a good man in many ways for the post, though his earlier career would not suggest it. Trained in the classics, he had begun as a learned Slavist, specializing at Moscow university in John Huss and Czech history, and in 1856 had come to the Constantinople legation filled with enthusiasm for the Slav cause. There eight years' experience, particularly of the Bulgarian extremists, produced a remarkable change, convincing him that the Bulgars were egoistic nationalists who cared nothing for Orthodoxy or Slav solidarity. Five years as minister at Athens confirmed his good opinions of the Greeks as the cultural and religious standard-bearers of Orthodoxy against the Bulgars, and his presence in Vienna meant a set-back to the panslav currents which had been previously prevailing in the Russian legation. He was only too ready to work for a rapprochement with Austria-Hungary, and he established excellent relations with Andrássy. Novikov came indeed to see everything far too much through Austrian spectacles, so that his enemies, Ignatyev at their head, had an easy task in attacking him as being completely in Andrássy's pocket, though their intrigues to get him transferred to London failed. Ineffective, at times even repellent, in personal converse, Novikov was at his best at his writing-table, supporting his views by arsenals of facts and historical or legal analyses: there was something of the learned pedant in him, and he was perhaps better suited for a chair of ecclesiastical history or international law than for an ambassador's chair. Too often he was unable to distinguish the essential from the secondary: once he had arrived at his own conclusions on some political question he could not be moved. His voluminous dispatches were apt to be so wrapped up in verbiage that St. Petersburg was more mystified than enlightened. Yet the fact remained that so long as the policy of reconciliation with Austria was preserved Novikov was a most valuable adjunct. Most of his staff had a bad reputation, particularly for their panslav intrigues, and it was currently believed that the Vienna embassy acted as the tool of the

Slavonic societies in Russia in their propaganda among the Austrian Slavs. Such charges were the reverse of true as regards Novikov himself or the military attaché, but were almost certainly justified in the case of the chaplain, the archpriest Raevsky, and of the very incautious Tatishchev, later the biographer of Alexander II, then a brilliant young second secretary, notorious at the Jockey Club and in fashionable salons. Tatishchev's career as a diplomatist was, however, cut short in the middle of the Balkan crisis under very unsavoury circumstances, gossip going to the length of saying that he had sold the embassy cipher to the Austrians![1]

In the other two embassies were the two men who were destined to be pitted against each other and Gorchakov in the final struggle of 1878. For all their differences and hostility Shuvalov and Ignatyev yet had some common background. Nearly of the same age, both were the sons of big landowning noblemen who rose high at court: both passed through the Corps of Pages, entered crack cavalry regiments, served in the Crimean war, and had a hand in the negotiation of its final peace terms. Both were rapidly advanced and secured the coveted reward of aide-de-camp general to the Tsar; Ignatyev, exceptionally young, in 1860, Shuvalov in 1866. Both fell in mid-career when barely fifty. Both were polished men of the world, commanding persons of real abilities, public figures of the calibre of ministers of state rather than of professional diplomats. But whereas Ignatyev passed from the army to diplomacy to end as minister of the interior, Shuvalov passed from the army to administration to end as ambassador.[2]

When Shuvalov took over the London embassy in the autumn of 1874 from the senile Brunnow, he was entering a new sphere

[1] Kartsov's *Za kulisami diplomatii*, pp. 6–9, contains interesting appreciations of Novikov, Tatishchev, and the Vienna embassy, though Kartsov had never himself served in Vienna or under Novikov. See also the passionate defence of Novikov by his strange protégé Ghikas, *Botschafter von Novikow über den Panslavismus und die Orientalische Frage*. For Tatishchev, see below, p. 149, note 1, and pp. 694–5.

[2] Petr Andreievich Shuvalov, b. 1827, d. 1889; m. widow of Count Orlov-Denisov; educated in Corps of Pages; 1845, joined the Life Guards; served in Crimean War, including Sebastopol; 1855, aide-de-camp to the Tsar; 1856, served under Orlov at the Paris Conference; 1857, chief police commissioner for St. Petersburg; 1860, director of department of general affairs in ministry of interior, and chief of staff of corps of gendarmes and acting chief of the Third Section; 1865, governor-general of the Baltic Provinces; 1866, aide-de-camp general, and chief of the Third Section; 1873, special mission to London; 1874–9, ambassador in London.

of action, in which neither his experience as an aide-de-camp to Prince Orlov at the Paris conference nearly twenty years before nor even his special mission to London early in 1873 to smooth down English apprehensions over the Khiva expedition can be said to have materially assisted him. Disraeli could confide with a good deal of justification: '. . . As for the charming Schou., I am perfectly convinced that, instead of being a deep and *rusé* diplomat, he does not know the A.B.C. of his business, and is perfectly sincere in his frequent asseverations to that effect.'[1] Shuvalov's appointment was in fact largely the result of the intrigues of his enemies at home, particularly, so it was said, of the Tsar's mistress Catherine Dolgoroukaya. Since 1857 he had been one of the leading figures in the police and the ministry of the interior, and a strong opponent of the emancipation of the serfs and the subsequent reforms. After Karakozov's attempt on the life of the Tsar in 1866 he was summoned to take charge of the Third Section, which meant above all the organization and control of the secret police, and for the next seven years he was one of the most powerful and feared leaders of the reaction, earning for himself the nicknames of Arakcheyev II, vice-Emperor, Peter IV. The enemy of all who professed anything resembling liberal views, Shuvalov was naturally opposed to Milyutin at the head of the ministry of war, whose army reforms he regarded as pandering to liberalism; but he was equally opposed to the slavophils and panslavs, since he had no patience with Muscovite nationalism or with any working upon 'our brother Slavs' which might embroil Russia in war; and ultimately he was also on bad terms with the Tsarevitch and with the Empress. This was the *grand seigneur*, wholly reactionary in politics, wholly delightful in personal converse, who proceeded to charm his way through London society and eventually to make himself the pivot of Anglo-Russian relations.[2]

The position which Shuvalov won for himself in London was due mainly to his very close personal relations with Derby, the foreign secretary, and to the inside information which he thereby acquired. It came to be said that his intimacy with Lady Derby was equally accountable for the leakage of cabinet secrets, which assumed such proportions in the early months of 1878 that

---

[1] *Disraeli*, p. 887: letter to Lady Bradford, 3 Nov. 1875.

[2] Eckardt, *Distinguished Persons in Russian Society*, pp. 23–35, reflects contemporary Russian opinion hostile to Shuvalov.

Disraeli formed his triumvirate, with Salisbury and Cairns against Derby, and finally severed relations with Shuvalov. Yet his ingratiating ways quickly had effect with Salisbury too: within a month of his taking over the foreign office Shuvalov had won his confidence sufficiently for the two men to negotiate in strict privacy what was substantially a peace settlement. Undoubtedly the ambassador's social gifts, even though he was slightly deaf and originally knew scarcely any English, were an invaluable asset in opening to him the big political houses: he was also on easy terms with leading members of the opposition such as Harcourt and Dilke, and kept in cautious touch with the propagandist leaders of the anti-Turkish campaign. Thus he was able to furnish St. Petersburg with an exceptionally full picture of the political situation in London, in striking contrast with the isolation and ineffectiveness of the British ambassador on the Neva.[1] Although he was accounted lazy, and gossip made much of his fondness for wine and women, and although his embassy counsellor, in malignant retrospect, had a very low opinion of him,[2] Shuvalov was a man of sufficient stature to deal on an equal footing with the leaders of British foreign policy and, for all the hostility to him, to carry weight at home. When to this is added the fact that he won the friendship and trust of Bismarck, it was almost inevitable that Gorchakov should see in him a rival only one degree less dangerous than Ignatyev.

Like Shuvalov with the mentality of a reactionary, unlike Shuvalov with the energy of a revolutionary, Ignatyev differed also from his rival in London in having some twenty years' experience of foreign affairs, and in having a definite policy.[3] Almost all that experience had been in the East. He had begun

[1] For Disraeli and cabinet leakages to Shuvalov, see *Disraeli*, pp. 1081–2, and below, pp. 321, 356; for his relations with the opposition see below, pp. 356 and 472. Shuvalov was no friend of Mme Novikov, the agent of the Moscow panslavs in England and a perfervid assistant in the Gladstonian campaign against Turkey.

[2] 'Extrait des mémoires de . . . M. Michel de Bartholomei', in *Revue d'histoire diplomatique*, vol. xlviii, pp. 100–3. Bartholomei, a professional diplomat, was at the London embassy from 1870 to 1880.

[3] Nikolai Pavlovich Ignatyev (made a count after San Stefano), b. 1832, d. 1908; educated in Corps of Pages; 1849, entered Hussar Life Guard regiment; 1851, passed War Academy; on the Guards General Staff; during Crimean War served on Berg's staff in the Baltic Provinces; 1856, military attaché in London, where he paid special attention to Chinese, Indian, and Persian problems; 1856–7, seconded to Paris as Kiselev's expert on the frontiers of Bessarabia; 1857, travel tour in Balkans and Levant; 1858, mission to Khiva and Bokhara; 1859–60, mission to

well in dealing with the Bessarabian frontier question after the congress of Paris. He was loudly acclaimed for his successful mission in 1858 to Khiva and Bokhara, though actually its practical results were almost nil. Very different were the results of his mission to China which followed in 1859 and 1860: the Amur boundary settled, Vladivostok and the Maritime Province added to the Russian empire, important commercial and consular rights gained, Russian influence at Pekin established. Ignatyev had utilized the crisis of the Taiping civil war and the Anglo-French war with China with great skill and determination. Henceforward he was a made man. If in later years his treaty of Pekin was forgotten by others, it was never forgotten by Ignatyev himself; on his gravestone he had only three words carved: Pekin San Stefano. He was immediately rewarded, though only twenty-eight, with the prize of aide-de-camp general to the Tsar and with his first official mission to Constantinople, to congratulate Sultan Abd ul-Aziz on his accession. This was a turning-point, for he returned to head the Asiatic department in the ministry of foreign affairs for the next three years where the Ottoman Empire bulked quite as largely as the Far East or Central Asia; and thereafter his career was linked for good or ill with Constantinople, the Christians in the Balkans and Asiatic Turkey, above all with the Slavs and their champions in Russia. He received the Constantinople legation in 1864 (it was not raised to an embassy till three years later) and there he remained for thirteen consecutive years. By the time that the Near Eastern crisis was renewed in changed form by the revolt in Herzegovina, Ignatyev had acquired an international reputation as the leading champion of panslavism and occupied without dispute the first position among the diplomats on the Bosphorus. That he had also acquired an international—and a Russian—reputation for being an inordinate liar, and that he was also much disliked in many quarters in Russia, more particularly among the bureaucracy, did not prevent the recognition that he was a man of the utmost address and dangerous abilities.

Pekin; 1860, made aide-de-camp general to the Tsar; 1861, special mission to Constantinople; 1861–4, director of the Asiatic department; 1864–77, minister, from 1867 ambassador, at Constantinople; 1878, January to May, the struggle for the treaty of San Stefano; 1881, March, minister for state lands; 1881, May–1882, May, minister for interior: thereafter a member of the state council but lived in retirement.

'Brilliantly aided by his seductive wife; himself combining great physical energy, unabashed self-confidence, ingratiating charm, jocular brusqueness, and unappeased talent for intrigue; supplied with a fantastic medley of agents and informers; Ignatyev, with ten years' experience of Turkey behind him and in the closest relations with Abd ul-Aziz, could feel that he was deservedly styled *le vice-Sultan*.'[1]

Apart from Ignatyev's personal influence and capacity, the Ottoman empire was studded with Russian consular officials, most of whom were his adherents and many of whom were in close touch with the Slavonic committees in Russia. In Constantinople itself he was ably supported by Nelidov, the first counsellor, Onou, the first dragoman, and Bazili and Tseretelev in junior posts;[2] and with such energetic professional backing Ignatyev stood out as the most forcible representative of a nationalistic Russian policy in the Balkans, which was in open contradiction with that of his nominal superior Gorchakov. Whereas the latter, knowing little and caring nothing for the details of the eastern question, looked at it through the spectacles of the concert of the three eastern powers and, in the ambassador's eyes, thirsted for international conferences, preferring loud-sounding phrases and diplomatic verbiage to solid practical action, Ignatyev, holding that all the powers were more or less hostile to the attainment of Russia's necessary ambitions, made it his principal aim to whittle away old obligations and avoid any new obligations *vis-à-vis* the other powers, to work for the time being for a direct understanding with Turkey, and to prepare the ground for a disruption of the Ottoman empire to be achieved solely by Russia assisted by her Slav compatriots. This policy of resolute, though as always with Ignatyev ingeniously flexible, isolation clashed ostentatiously in the eighteen-seventies with the whole basis of the *Dreikaiserbündnis*. By 1875 Ignatyev was the most powerful representative of those sections of opinion in Russia which thought primarily in terms of Slavdom and only secondarily in

---

[1] For an attempt to present Ignatyev's career at Constantinople, mainly from his memoirs, see my article 'Ignatyev at Constantinople 1864–1874', in *S.R.*, vol. xi, pp. 341–54, 556–71. His panslav views are treated later, see below, pp. 73–6.

[2] For later references to these see Index. The consul-general at Constantinople, Khitrovo, had much ability and knowledge, particularly of Macedonia, but he was supposed to intrigue against Ignatyev behind his back; Kartsov, *Za kulisami diplomatii*, p. 6.

those of Orthodoxy. While Russia as the champion of the Orthodox was pitted mainly against Turkey, Russia as the champion of the Slavs was pitted equally against the Habsburg empire, now the Dual Monarchy, a stronger power than Turkey. Gorchakov, personally disliking and increasingly jealous of Ignatyev, had embarked with enthusiasm since 1872 on the policy of rapprochement with Austria-Hungary. If Gorchakov and Andrássy were to go hand in hand together in the Balkans, where was there place for Ignatyev?

To this sketch of the Russian personnel most closely concerned with the Near Eastern crisis must be added a brief outline of the position occupied during these years by Langenau, Loftus, and Schweinitz, the representatives in St. Petersburg of Austria-Hungary, Great Britain, and Germany respectively. Baron Langenau had held his post since 1871 and was a whole-hearted supporter of a close understanding with Russia. He could not forget 1866 or forgive Bismarck. He thus represented the anti-German outlook current in certain Austrian military circles, and in proportion as Andrássy's policy of *entente* with Russia became subsidiary to reliance on Berlin rather than St. Petersburg, so did Langenau's relations with his chief become cooler and cooler. Like Loftus and Schweinitz he professed full confidence in the honourable intentions of the Tsar and Gorchakov, discounted the ebullitions of nationalism in Russia, and in general did his utmost to present Gorchakov and official Russian policy in as favourable a light as possible. Here he overshot his mark: as relations between the two countries deteriorated finally to the point almost of rupture, so Langenau's reports were less and less heeded in the Ballplatz, where he came to be regarded as impossibly russophil, very much as his opposite number in Vienna was regarded on the Neva as impossibly austrophil.[1]

The British ambassador, Lord Augustus Loftus, had likewise come to St. Petersburg in 1871, after thirty years of diplomatic experience at German courts. Like Sir Andrew Buchanan at Vienna, he earned the sharpest strictures from Disraeli: 'a mere Polonius', 'Pomposo', 'a mere Livadian parasite and afraid even of G(orchakov)'s shadow'. The British foreign office records bear out that Loftus was of no influence in St. Peters-

---

[1] Wittrock, *Gorčakov, Ignatiev och Šuvalov*, e.g. pp. 3–6, 8, contains valuable information on Langenau's attitude, based on the Vienna archives.

burg and contributed very little towards the shaping of British policy, but it should be added that, if the British government had so low an opinion of their ambassador at so critical a post, they were scarcely acting fairly towards him by leaving him there until 1879, and that one reason for the ineffectiveness of Loftus may have been his feeling that by 1877 and 1878 he had lost the confidence of his government.[1] An urbane, easy-going aristocrat, living in the ordinary rut of the St. Petersburg diplomatic world, he had the reputation of a keen sportsman rather than of a keen observer or of a hard worker. He had no real knowledge of Russia, and though on friendly enough terms with Gorchakov, and particularly with Jomini, was not in their confidence. In the main, except in regard to Central Asia, he believed in the fundamentally pacific and moderate ideas of the Russian government, until the outbreak of the war with Turkey in 1877 swept him to the very reverse of his previous views. On the other hand, he had with him as a highly effective military attaché his son-in-law Wellesley, who knew Russian, did not confine his attentions purely to St. Petersburg, and had very valuable secret channels of information, particularly in the war office as regards Central Asia. Wellesley had the confidence of Disraeli, and above all he made a very good impression on the Tsar, whose favour he succeeded in keeping even after his relations with the Russian military had been ruined in the winter of 1876–7 through the leakage of his highly derogatory views on the Russian army.

Finally there was the German ambassador, General von Schweinitz, who succeeded Prince Reuss in March 1876. He already knew St. Petersburg excellently through his most successful occupancy for six years (1863–9) of the unique and very influential post of personal military representative of the King of Prussia at the court of the Tsar of Russia.[2] He returned readily enough, for his intervening years as ambassador at Vienna had not removed his mistrust of the Austrians, and he knew himself to be *persona gratissima* with the Tsar. Schweinitz was a splendid specimen of the best type of Silesian magnate and guards officer. The soul of honour, he had the full con-

---

[1] See my article, 'Lord Augustus Loftus and the Eastern Crisis of 1875–1878', in *The Cambridge Historical Journal*, vol. iv, pp. 283–93.

[2] The post was continued after the creation of the German empire, and was held during 1875–8 by General Werder, who was, however, quite overshadowed by Schweinitz.

fidence both of his master and of the Tsar. No one better exemplified the ideal of those intimate, personal links between Potsdam and Tsarskoe Selo which for Alexander II, as much as for his father, constituted the mental and emotional reality of Russo-German relations. Schweinitz himself described his diplomacy as 'Flügel- oder Generaladjutantendiplomatik', presupposing a policy of monarch with monarch, handled through an intermediary who possessed the absolute confidence of both: 'the especial task of the military confidant of both sovereigns was to stand for the immutable laws of honour and almost sacred friendship even if *raison d'état* appeared in opposition therewith.'[1] As ambassador he continued to act in the same spirit, which was exactly what was required by both emperors. Besides his intimacy with the Tsar, he was very friendly with Gorchakov and especially so with Giers, though of Milyutin he saw little. Thus incomparably better placed than any of the other foreign representatives at the Russian capital, Schweinitz was of exceptional value to Bismarck. At the same time the general's absolute faith in the word of the Tsar, his confidence in Gorchakov, his tendency to belittle or gloss over the dangers of panslav or anti-German currents, his fundamental attitude of reliance on 'the word of a gentleman' as the centre-piece of good relations between Russia and Germany, were far from being shared by the German Chancellor. 'Generaladjutantendiplomatik' was still a necessity in the Russia of Alexander II, but Bismarck knew well enough that it was no longer sufficient in itself: the policy of neither country toward the other could remain so dependent upon dynastic and personal connexions as had been the rule in former days. Schweinitz himself was to experience all too painfully the results of the new forces operative both in his own country and in Russia before he laid down his ambassadorship sixteen years later in 1892.

3. CENTRAL ASIA

While such was the general internal situation and such the personnel in the forefront of the Russian diplomatic stage during the seventies, the international setting of the stage, the background for the eastern crisis, may perhaps best be represented by examining three leading features—Central Asia, panslavism, and the new Germany and the *Dreikaiserbündnis*, which in

---

[1] See particularly Schweinitz, *Denkwürdigkeiten*, vol. i, pp. ix–x, 201.

varying degrees had transformed the international position of Russia in 1875 as compared with that of two decades earlier.

Whereas at the time of the Crimean war the Russian threat to India appeared solely as a lateral threat to British communications through command of the Straits or of the upper Euphrates and Tigris, twenty years later it figured prominently as a direct menace. During those twenty years Russian imperialism had swallowed the greater part of Central Asia. In the late thirties Russian dominance at Teheran, the first Russian contact with Afghanistan, and Perovsky's expedition to Khiva had for a brief spell brought Central Asian and Afghan affairs to the front as an additional factor in Anglo-Russian hostility; but absorption in the second Mehemet Ali crisis resulted temporarily in at least the official drawing together of the two governments, and the complete failure of Perovsky's expedition removed for many years any widespread alarm as to Russian expansion in Central Asia. During the eastern crisis of 1853–6 the English press paid but occasional attention to Russia and India, while from the Russian side, although three plans for a diversion against the north-west frontier were put forward, they were not approved and did not receive notoriety.[1]

By 1876 the situation was startlingly different. During the first half of the nineteenth century the expansive forces of Russian Tsardom had been mainly engulfed in the Caucasus. In Asia the continued inefficacy of its policy towards the Kirghiz[2] and other nomads had resulted in Russian effective power still running little to the east or south of the great curve represented by a rough line drawn up the Ural river and east-

[1] For this section on Central Asia I have used particularly: A. Krausse, *Russia and Asia* (New York, 1899); M. N. Pokrovsky, *Diplomatiya i voiny tsarskoi Rossii v xix stoletii; Tatishchev;* F. Martens, *La Russie et l'Angleterre dans l'Asie Centrale;* M. Grulev, *Sopernichestvo Rossii i Anglii v Srednei Aziyu* (St. Petersburg, 1909); E. Schuyler, *Turkistan;* F. I. Lobysevich, *Postupatelnoe dvizhenie v Srednyuyu Aziyu v torgovom i diplomatichesko-voennom otnosheniyakh* (St. Petersburg, 1900, an historical sketch, not going farther than 1869, largely based on unpublished official sources, by the author of the semi-official history of the 1873 Khiva campaign); *A. and P.,* 1873, lxxv; 1874, lxxvi; and 1878, lxxx; Sir Henry Rawlinson, *England and Russia in the East* (London, 1875); The Duke of Argyll, *The Eastern Question,* vol. ii; F. Noyce, *England, India, and Afghanistan* (Cambridge, 1902).

[2] So the Russians called the Turkic-speaking Kazaks (nomads), clanned together into the Little Horde, the Middle Horde, and the Great Horde, who pastured and pillaged between the Ural river and Lake Balkash and the Semipalatinsk steppe. The true Kirghiz, called by the Russians Kara-Kirghiz, or Dikokamenny Kirghiz, are mainly in Semirechensk and to the south. The Soviet names of Kazakstan and Kirghizstan are accurate.

MAP I

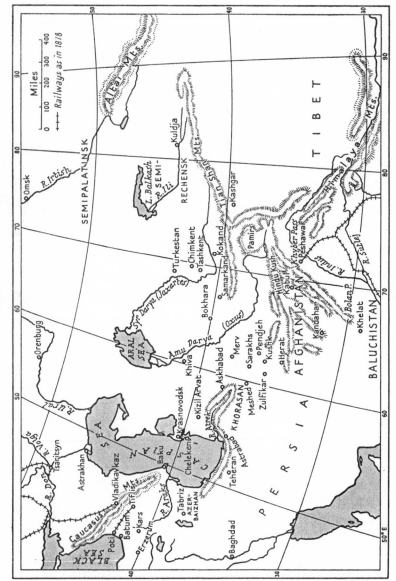

RUSSIA AND CENTRAL ASIA

wards along latitude 51° to the Altai mountains. During the second half of the century, after the subjection of the Caucasus had been substantially completed by the capture of Shamyl (1859) and the crushing of the Circassians (1864), the Russians proceeded on the one hand to extract from China by mingled force and diplomacy the Amur and Maritime provinces (1858, 1860), and on the other hand to control the steppes of Central Asia and to master, with the minimum of difficulty from man and the maximum of difficulty from nature, the settled Moslem Khanates of Bokhara, Khiva, and Kokand.

By 1864 Russia controlled the Orenburg steppe and had pushed her forts some 350 miles up the Syr Daria (Jaxartes), and, working south from Siberia, had occupied the Ili basin (Semirechensk). A gap of about 400 miles remained. In 1864 action to close that gap was begun; but distant officials in Orenburg or St. Petersburg were quite unable to control the military on the spot, who turned what had been planned as the completion of the Kirghiz steppe policy into colonial conquests of a type new to the history of Russian relations with Asia. In that year fell Chimkent and Turkestan—crumbling city of fabled renown; in 1865 Tashkent; in 1868 Samarkand— with its memories of Timur and Baber outvying even Turkestan, and, more important, controlling the water-supply of Bokhara. All were annexed except Bokhara itself, which was left as a vassal Khanate. In 1873 Khiva met the same fate as Bokhara. In 1876 the third Khanate, Kokand, was reduced, and annexed under the title of Ferghana. To the north-east the Chinese province of Kuldja (controlling the Ili gap, a key gate in the history of the steppe), having lapsed into complete chaos and being threatened by Yakub Bey from Kashgar, was occupied in 1871. Assurances were given that it would be restored to China as soon as the Pekin government could maintain order there, assurances that appeared designed merely to cloak annexation, though actually the bulk of the province was handed back ten years later. To the west a solid base was in 1869 at last established on the eastern shore of the Caspian at Krasnovodsk, whence a series of expeditions were pushed farther and farther east in the direction of Merv against the Turkoman tribes, and raised in very practical form the dangerous question as to where the Persian frontier ran in the Atrek region. Certain of the Turkoman nomads were tough fighters—almost the only such with which the Russians had to cope in their subjugation of Central Asia. Aided above all by the exceptionally difficult nature of their country, they inflicted a number of reverses upon the Russians before being broken on the wheel by Skobelev (1881). Thereby he secured Askhabad. The Merv oasis, two hundred miles farther east, was gained three years later, and at the same time Sarakhs on the Persian frontier, giving easy access to Herat and Meshed. Immediately there followed (1885) the Pendjeh affair, a hundred miles to the south-east, on the Afghan borderland. War with England was averted, but, although thereafter the Russian boundaries were not further extended except in the Pamirs, British fears continued unabated, if less vocal, as the Russians continued to develop their new colonial empire along lines which showed military considerations to be predominant.

Communications were the touchstone, and they were overwhelmingly military. In 1879 the army engineers began the construction of the Trans-Caspian railway, from near Krasnovodsk, along the northern frontier of Persia. Its commercial importance, at least for many years, would be of the slightest. It was an arm against the Turkomans, against Persia; and, as it was rapidly pushed on to the east, against Afghanistan, against India? It reached Merv in 1886, Samarkand in 1888. Branches were pushed out to Tashkent and into Ferghana. By 1883 there was direct railway communication between Baku, Tiflis, and Batum: Transcaucasia, always a reservoir of Russian troops and stores, could now dispatch them with relative quickness to Trans-Caspia and Central Asia. At the very end of the century, in 1898, another strategic line was completed, from Merv to the new fort at Kushk on the Afghan frontier, over against Herat. On the other hand, of the two great lines of economic importance, one, the Tashkent–Orenburg, was not opened until 1906; the other, the 'Turk–Sib.', scarcely left the pigeon-holes of the Tsarist bureaucracy. Thus Central Asia, whose history in the last fifty years hinges on the railway lines, was transformed by the general staff and the military on the spot. The treaty of Berlin marked no *détente* in Anglo-Russian relations in regard to Central Asia, where Russian intrigues in Afghanistan helped to bring on the second Anglo-Afghan war and where the revolution in communications was about to begin. Salisbury well summed up the situation in 1880 when he wrote: 'It is a fallacy to assume that within our lifetime any stable arrangement can be arrived at in the East. The utmost we can do is to provide halting-places where the process of change may rest awhile.'[1]

Even before this revolution in transport, the prevalent British attitude in the seventies fastened above all on the annihilation of distances intervening between Russia and India. Together with this, as the second great factor in the new element in russophobia created by Central Asia, went a firm belief in the carefully planned, far-sighted, and at the same time ruthless and faithless, character of the policy of Russia. The distances were immense and, in 1876, took substantially the same time to cover as in 1856; but by now the routes as far as Khiva, Bokhara, Tashkent, Samarkand, or Kokand were, more or less effectively, in Russian hands. The littoral of the eastern Caspian and the steppes as far as Kizil Arvat were now occupied by forts or in process of subjugation by annual 'punitive expeditions'. The Atrek and the northern rim of Khorasan, the middle Oxus, the Tian Shan, were the rough limits of the Russian empire. Boundaries in the European sense did not exist, but there did exist the contiguity of Russian power with Persian weakness and Afghan instability where twenty years before the Muscovite arms were unknown. For the first time since Alexander the Great the West was encamped on the Oxus and the Jaxartes. For the first time in human history the non-nomad West was mastering the nomad steppes of Central Asia. But to the British the more important fact was that for the first time since Dupleix or Napoleon their ascendancy in southern Asia was in danger of being challenged by another European power.

The British public from the late sixties onwards was having dinned into it the alarming prospect of losing 'the key to India' unless the Russians were forestalled by determined action. Parliament and press continuously focused attention on the problem. Opinions differed somewhat as to what was 'the key', but Merv and Herat took easy pride of place. British explorers (Baker, Napier, Macgregor, Burnaby) were dramatically active in Baluchistan, Afghanistan, north-eastern Persia, and, when they could get there, in Central Asia itself. The accounts of their travels and of the Muscovite menace were

[1] *Salisbury*, p. 377, letter to Dufferin (St. Petersburg), 4 Feb. 1880.

spread far wider than among merely political, Anglo-Indian, and technical circles. Burnaby's *Ride to Khiva*[1] was for years a best-seller, and, though he was not particularly alarmist, he gave a picture of energetic Russian officers on the Oxus confident that 'the day' would soon come and preparing for it with cheerful gusto. The most influential single English contribution to Russophobia was Sir Henry Rawlinson's *England and Russia in the East*, backed by the weight of the author's (out-of-date) Persian and Indian experience and membership of the Council of India. First published in 1875, it was in part a reprint of earlier articles, in part an analysis of the situation at that date. His views had varied considerably, and had not originally been unduly alarmist, but the final impression now was of the necessity of a forward policy in Persia and Afghanistan and of armed resistance to Russia if she pressed on too far: 'the continued advance of Russia in Central Asia is as certain as the movement of the sun in the heavens': the subjugation of the Tekke Turkomans and then the occupation of Akkal and Merv are merely a question of time: 'Russia by advancing on Merv evidently means mischief . . . Russia in possession of Herat would have a gripe on the throat of India': there lay 'the pivot of the whole Eastern question . . . *we cannot afford to expose Herat to the risk of being taken by a Russian coup-de-main*'. 'So long as she held aloof from Merv, we should hold aloof from Herat; but if she deliberately threw down the gauntlet, she must expect it to be taken up.' That meant the occupation of Kandahar as well as of Herat, whether or not Shere Ali, in whom Rawlinson now had no belief, concurred. It meant also decided action in Persia, above all 'an experimental contingent force of 10,000' Persians, 'raised, armed, fed, paid, clothed, disciplined, and commanded by British officers'—in fact an inverted harbinger of the Persian Cossack brigade.[2]

Rawlinson's views in particular were given wide currency in the Russian press since he was taken as a semi-official exponent of the policy of the government of India, which with Lytton as Viceroy from the spring of 1876 gave ample further oppor-

[1] Burnaby's *Ride to Khiva* was first published in Oct. 1876; reprinted in Nov. and Dec., seven times in 1877, twice in 1878, twice in 1881; popular edition Dec. 1881, reprinted seven times in 1882; new edition Apr. 1884, reprinted three times in 1885; illustrated edition Mar. 1895, reprinted 1900, 1907, 1913; new popular edition Apr. 1905, reprinted 1906, 1909.

[2] pp. viii, 339, 327, 344, 356–65, 132–5.

tunities for Russian counter-offensives whether on paper or in action. On the other hand, equal scope was given to the fanning of British hostility by the use that could be made of Russian chauvinist, or even moderate, publications. For even moderate military opinion insisted that 'the experience of the last years had convinced us that, after occupying any point in Central Asia, it was impossible for us to abandon it', and was careful not 'to assert that we must once for all desist from further aggressive operations'.[1] Special notice was taken[2] of the anti-British extremism of Terentyev's *Russia and England in Central Asia*, which was translated and published by the foreign department of the government of India. England was directly told by him that 'in the event of a war produced by European complications, we shall clearly be obliged in our own interests to take advantage of the proximity to India, which is afforded by our present position in Central Asia'. Treaties with Asiatic rulers were worthless: the perpetual advance of Russia in search of a secure frontier was an historical necessity which could be stayed only when 'her territories are coterminous with those of a nation which respects treaties, which is sufficiently civilized not to live on plunder and pillage, and sufficiently powerful to restrain its subjects from predatory incursions across our frontiers'. Could Afghanistan, could Persia be put in this category? Evidently the boundaries of the Russian empire were to be moved forward until they marched with those of the British empire, though even then 'we should be obliged to adopt the English system, viz., to consider sacred only those treaties, the conditions of which are disadvantageous to our opponents, and to treat as waste paper such as are injurious to our own interests'.[3]

This was in 1875. The Indian Mutiny was not twenty years behind. Here was the root of the British fears of a Russian threat to India. Actual invasion even by a small force might

[1] M. Romanovski, *Notes on the Central Asiatic Question* (Calcutta: office of superintendent of government printing, 1870), pp. 31, lxv, 8–9. His book is a defence of his actions in 1866 when he replaced Chernyaev for a brief spell in command in Turkestan, and proceeded to rout the Emir of Bokhara and to occupy additional territory. His 'moderate policy' meant only opposition to immediate conquest and annexation of the Khanates; pp. 8, 17.

[2] e.g. by the *Quarterly Review*, Apr. 1876, p. 442, which, though highly suspicious of the uncontrollable Russian military, represented on the whole a moderate conservative attitude towards Russian expansion in Central Asia.

[3] vol. i, pp. 13–16; vol. ii, pp. 45, 156, 163–4.

not prove an imminent possibility, though as to this the experts were divided. But the danger of Russian ascendancy among the Afghans, of frontier raids on the north-west frontier, of sparks being thrown into the combustible material of northern India, of some Afghan attack perhaps stiffened by Russian detachments and followed by a penetration into the plains and a widespread revolt—the danger of ignition or explosion, rather than of direct invasion by Russia, this was the core of British apprehensions, which refused to be quieted by the reflection that the opening of the Suez Canal had caused a saving of eighteen days to Bombay (twenty-four instead of forty-two), that Bombay was but five hours distant by cable, and that railway communications in India had been widely extended since the mutiny and now reached Peshawar, while the Russian termini were still not nearer than Tiflis, Vladikavkaz, or Tsaritsyn.

The Russians for their part were carefully primed with the admissions of Mayo and Rawlinson as to the disturbed state of native feeling, and were regaled with the most lurid picture of two hundred millions of oppressed and discontented people only too ready to rise and sweep out the cruel and rapacious British.[1] 'The East India Company', wrote Terentyev, meaning thereby the British rule in India, 'is nothing less than a poisonous unnatural plant, engrafted on the splendid soil of India—a parasite which saps away the life of the most fertile and wealthy country in the world. This plant can only be uprooted by forcible means, and such an attempt was made by the natives of the country in 1857, though it failed for want of sufficient skill. Sick to death, they are now waiting for a physician from the North, are hastening on his advance with eager prayers, and making him the text for discourses in their temples'. The same author again gave the lead to Russian opinion when he discounted any direct attack upon India but insisted that the true reason for the fears of England was to be found in 'the fact that even the neighbourship of Russia

[1] e.g. by Pashino, one of the very few Russians who succeeded in penetrating into India: he was in the Punjab in 1873, unavailingly pursued by the government of India. Russian ignorance of India may be instanced by the computation that between 1854 and 1881 only four Russian travellers explored India, whilst in the same period 319 explored other parts of Asia; C. Marvin, *The Russian Advance towards India* (London, 1882), pp. 191–2, citing Venyukov, a leading Russian explorer in Central Asia.

would be too much for her in view of the many secret elements of hostility which lurk throughout her Indian dominions. The proximity of a strong power would naturally weaken the authority of England, and would show clearly that after all the British colossus has only legs of clay'.[1]

Such capital made out of British alarms by Russian publicists in the seventies tended to obscure what was not seriously denied by the British, that the real reason for the conquest of Central Asia was not a desire to conquer India. By the time of the eastern crisis of 1875–8 the problem of Central Asia had come to play an important part in the bad, and finally very critical, relations between England and Russia, less, perhaps, because of its then intrinsic importance than because of the pre-existence of those bad relations. The abolition of serfdom, and the possibility of a reformed Tsardom, had had some effect on British opinion, but this had been almost obliterated by the repression of the Poles, the fervour of panslav nationalism, and the more and more marked return to reaction after 1866. Public opinion in the main returned to the old conception of the Russia of Nicholas I's day—an obscurantist autocracy ruling with the knout and the Cossacks, the enemy of freedom, the persecutor of Circassians, Poles, Jews, of all who were not Muscovites, standing in all matters of political, social, and religious organization at the opposite pole to England. And now on to this picture were smeared the virulently bright colours of deliberate massacre of Turkomans, faithless dealings with Khiva, agreements with England again and again broken, uncontrolled generals pressing on and on, menacing the outposts of India and the Indian empire itself.

To the Russian public this expansion naturally presented a very different aspect: They found it especially difficult to see wherein lay the difference, in broad outline, between their expansion in Asia and the British expansion in Asia. The British in the hundred years since Clive had moved on and on finally to the Himalayas and across the Indus, while the Russians had been pinned down to their fifty years' struggle in the Caucasus. Now in the second half of the century they were but following in the footsteps of the British during the first half. As they carefully pointed out, had not Russell admitted this comparison, recommended (like Salisbury later)

[1] Terentyev, *Russia and England in Central Asia*, vol. ii, pp. 157–8, 130.

the use of large-scale maps, and agreed that apprehensions as to a conquest of India were pure chimeras? Had not Northcote, from the India Office, explicitly informed the Viceroy that 'the conquests which Russia has made, and apparently is still making in Central Asia, appear to them [the British government] to be the natural result of the circumstances in which she finds herself placed, and to afford no ground whatever for representations indicative of suspicion or alarm on the part of this country'?[1] Twenty years earlier Nicholas I and Nesselrode had indicated to Peel the desirability of the Sutlej being the limit of British expansion to the north-west:[2] the British paid no heed, conquered the whole Indus valley, and pressed on beyond. In 1869 Clarendon proposed the Amu Darya (Oxus) as the dividing line between the two spheres of influence: what more natural than that Gorchakov should point out that Khiva was to the south of the Amu Darya, or more appropriate than that the proposal should be lost in the sands of three years' negotiations?

The clash between nomad and non-nomad in the great stretches between the Caspian and the Altai was inevitable, sooner or later, once Russia had expanded down the Volga, to and beyond the Urals. For three centuries, since Ivan the Terrible, Muscovy had struggled forward against the steppe in 'Europe', and at long last she was triumphant. But the frontiers of the steppe save on the west did not lie in 'Europe'; on the west they were the Carpathian mountains and the Pripet-Dniester forest-marshes, on the east the Altai and the Tian Shian. On the confines of the more or less settled area, from the Ural river and the long Siberian strip between tundra and steppe, the Russians had to extend control over the nearest nomad peoples; that involved action against others beyond them; and thus the Russians were led on farther and farther. The agelong conflicts on the steppe over camel- and stock-lifting, over water, over grazing grounds, took on a new appearance with the Cossack lines and the Cossack flying expeditions, ineffective though these latter usually were; for behind the Cossacks was slowly being welded a cumbrous organized power

---

[1] Russell to Lumley (St. Petersburg), 31 July 1865, in *A. and P.*, 1878, lxxx, C. 2164, App. i, no. 3 (and see no. 1); Northcote to Lawrence, 26 Dec. 1867, in *A. and P.*, 1878–9, lvi, C. 2190, no. 12.

[2] C. S. Parker, *Sir Robert Peel from his Private Papers*, vol. iii, pp. 259, 261–2.

which spelt in the long run the effective impact of a non-nomad civilization upon the nomad world. 'Russian subjects are killed, and retaliation is unavoidable.' Equally: 'Russian subjects are sold into slavery; Russians caravans are marauded; that must be stopped.' Here a different factor entered. The reasons for the subjugation of the steppe which have just been outlined, and which were repeated endlessly in varying forms by Russians,[1] merged into a justification for the subjugation of what lay within and beyond the steppe: settled oases, carefully irrigated, reputed rich; centres of ancient civilization, far-fabled, dusty-magical cities—Turkestan, Samarkand, Bokhara.

These were the magnets for the caravans: here were the slave-markets. But these Khanates were now, as political edifices, but ramshackle mud-walls, and their nominal subjects included a larger proportion of Kirghiz or Turkomans than of settled Uzbeks or Tadjiks. Their life was inextricably bound up with the nomads. Possessing but the façade of states, their sole protection lay in distance and desert: they could not serve as buffers or as boundaries. 'If we were to chastise the Khan [of Khiva], the whole fabric would fall like a pack of cards.'[2] This was equally true of Bokhara and Kokand. Yet only force would teach the Khanates the duties of states, so it was argued. Notably, only force would teach the Khans, especially of Khiva, that they must not permit kidnapped Russians (nor even Persians) to languish in slavery in the dominions they professed to rule; must not indeed permit slavery at all. Russia's civilizing mission was flourished loud in Kaufmann's treaties with Bokhara and Khiva, which required on paper the abolition of slavery. But the lengthy provisions in his treaties relating to caravans and to commerce were far from being paper concessions, slow and difficult though their practical realization proved to be. The interests of Russian direct and transit trade and of navigation and the rights of Russian merchants were carefully guarded and so widely extended that the vassal Khanates could be converted into a Russian commercial preserve but little different from the territories annexed to the empire. 'In under-

[1] e.g. particularly Gorchakov's circular dispatch of 3 Dec. 1864 in *A. and P.*, 1873, lxxv, C. 704, appendix.

[2] So Stremoukhov, the director of the Asiatic department, unburdened himself to Loftus; Loftus to Granville, disp., 19 Mar. 1872, in *A. and P.*, 1873, lxxv, C. 704, no. 81.

taking our civilizing mission in the East we had principally in
view the opening of new markets for our products, which would
not support the competition of Europe.' The same keynote was
privately expressed by Gorchakov: '. . . des intérêts commerciaux qui sont, au fond, le principal motif qui nous appelle en
Asie'.[1] Almost hand in hand with the conquering generals
went the Khludovs, Moscow textile millionaires, Pervushin with
his lead mines, Kolesnikov with his gold and coal scandals and
his Kashgar and Kokand ventures, and the big trading firms of
Pupyshev and Bykovsky. The combination of military duties
with caravan profits was only too easy, as was seen in the fla-
grant case of Glukhovsky, a highly placed general staff officer.
Lomakin, in command of Trans-Caspia, remarked with pride
on the progress of the Nobel oil concession in Cheleken, the
excellent market for oil in Central Asia, and the first convoy of
oil products about to start for Khiva. 'Latterly', he confided in
1876, 'our eastern shores of the Caspian have attracted general
attention from the capitalists and various big companies. I am
approached from all sides with applications for concessions for
fishing, salt, sulphur, oil, and ozocerite.' And he went on to
expatiate on the prospects of one specially important salt company at the head of which stood a very high court functionary.[2]

Actually the commercial and economic prospects were wildly
exaggerated; most of the early Russian ventures failed; in the
seventies there was much dispute as to the growth of trade with
Russia, disputes much aided by the lack of any accurate figures.
The local raw cotton was wretched in quality and nothing
effective was done to improve it until the introduction of American cotton in the middle eighties. By then the conquest period
was well over, there was comparative organization and stability,
and the railway had come. But the pioneer-buccaneer decades
of the sixties and seventies were the inevitable preliminaries to
the full economic conquest of Central Asia, and British commercial interests did not wait till the completion of this process
to sound the alarm. Russians, for their part, in the light of
British colonial history, found retorts enough and to spare to the

[1] Schuyler, *Turkistan*, vol. ii, p. 229, quoting from a report written in 1871 by
a highly placed officer in Turkestan; extract from letter of Gorchakov to Brunnow,
8 Mar. 1869, in *Meyendorff MSS*.

[2] Private letter of Lomakin to Bakulin (consul at Astrabad), 15 Mar. 1876, text
in V. A. Alekseyev, *Pisma N. P. Lomakina Konsulu F. A. Bakulinu (o sredne-aziatskikh
dyelakh), 1874–1878* (St. Petersburg, 1914), pp. 23–4.

accusations of aggressive commercialism. Placed in the general setting of Anglo-Russian rivalry in the Near and Middle East, this desire for commercial expansion in Central Asia, even if it cannot be accounted the determining direct explanation of the earlier stages of conquest, was an important factor in the general background against which the expeditions of the sixties took place. In the following decade, when in particular Russian textile production was increasing rapidly (it had fallen sharply at the time of the American Civil War), Central Asia and Persia beckoned with bright prospects of the elimination of British competition, though the Trans-Caspian campaigns were still (as 1878 and 1879 showed only too clearly) primarily part of the policy of strategic diversion against England. During the eighties Central Asian and Middle Eastern problems became more and more divorced from direct relation to the struggle for the Straits, and Russian commercial and industrial interests more and more in the foreground of the new colonial empire.[1]

The British, not content with their recriminations against Russian economic designs, inveighed specially against the independence of the Russian generals in Central Asia and their habit of paying no attention to the instructions, or at any rate the professions, of St. Petersburg. Tashkent had been captured contrary to instructions; annexations made without reference to the imperial government; Kuldja occupied in despite of the foreign minister; Khiva subjected in a manner irreconcilable with the assurances of the Tsar; Kokand annexed against his will. Continuously since 1865 St. Petersburg had repeated mollifying formulae; each advance was the last; the most definite instructions had positively been issued against a forward movement: yet each year marked another expedition, another advance. Clarendon had directly taxed Gorchakov at their Heidelberg meeting in 1869 with failure 'to control the ambi-

---

[1] P. I. Lyashchenko, *Istoriya russkogo narodnogo khozyaistva* (Moscow, 1927), p. 358; A. Popov, 'Ot Bosfora k Tikhomu Okeanu', in *Istorik Marksist*, 1934, no. iii, pp. 7–11; see also M. N. Pokrovsky, *Vneshnyaya Politika* (Moscow, 1919), pp. 23–4, and for his views on the economic aspects of Russian imperialism in Central Asia his *Diplomatiya i voiny tsarskoi Rossii v xix stoletii*, pp. 320–1, 328–9, 340–4, and his *Istoricheskaya nauka i borba klassov* (Moscow, 1933), vol. i, pp. 253–9. There is an interesting study in *Istorichesky Sbornik*, vol. iii (Leningrad, 1934), on the activities of certain Russian merchants and industrialists in paving the way for Russian conquests in Central Asia in the latter part of Nicholas I's reign; E. N. Kusheva, *Sredneaziatsky vopros i russkaya burzhuaziya v 40-e gody xix veka*, pp. 133–62. But she has not yet extended her studies to the sixties.

tion of military Commanders',[1] and each succeeding year had given ground for substantially similar complaints, inquiries, or warnings. Thus by the later seventies English opinion was more than ever suspicious of any protestations from the Tsar or his foreign office: they either did not have the power or they did not have the will to carry into effect any engagements. This accentuation of the distrust of Russia was to be of the greatest weight as events in the Balkans developed and shaped themselves finally into a crisis of the first magnitude.

At least in so far as Central Asia was concerned the British protests were well founded. The foreign and finance ministries were entirely unable to control the general staff, Tashkent or Tiflis. The Tsar himself was too undecided, too ill informed, and too lazy to attempt the fruitless task. All the general factors were working for continued advance, which could only have been delayed, not permanently checked. Added to these were the character of the forces operating in Asia and the struggle for power among the high officials. Russians themselves serving in the Turkestan army admitted that it was in large part 'a refuge for the scum of military society', that 'the true scourge which engenders the moral unhealthiness consists in the corps of officers', that the combination in the same hands of the military and civil administration led to enormous abuses.[2]

'A positive fever for further conquest raged amongst our troops— an ailment to cure which no method of treatment was effective, especially as the correctives applied were freely interspersed with such stimulants as honors and decorations. Not only the Russian Generals, but even the youngest Lieutenants, raved after further extension of territory, while those of the officers, who were entrusted with any sort of independent command, carried into effect their individual schemes. . . . It was indeed impossible to expect that such desires should be resisted, when by gratifying them it was possible for a Lieutenant in four years to become a General.'[3]

The effects of the struggle for power among the high officials and the departments were almost equally potent. The ministry of the interior counted for nothing. The ministry of finance

---

[1] Clarendon to Buchanan (St. Petersburg), 3 Sept. 1869, disp., extract, in *A. and P.*, 1873, lxxv, C. 704, no. 11.

[2] Schuyler, *Turkistan*, vol. ii, pp. 220–32, quoting from a report written in 1871 by a highly placed officer in Turkestan.

[3] Terentyev, *Russia and England in Central Asia*, vol. ii, p. 66, cf. also vol. i, p. 221.

waged perpetual war on the demands and maladministration of the military, but with the minimum of success. It was impossible to hide the scandals or to deny the financial unproductiveness of Russian rule in the newly won territories except by the extreme measure of presenting revenue and expenditure figures which entirely excluded the cost of the army; but Reutern's bureaucrats, though supported by a section of the press, could effect nothing substantial. Gorchakov fought a losing tactical battle without determination and probably without the full support of his own department of Asiatic affairs. The real power among the departments was the ministry of war. The real struggle was between the governors-general, almost independent satraps, each with the treasured right of personal report to the Tsar. In the early stages it was Orenburg against Omsk: then both failed to prevent the creation of the new governor-generalship of Turkestan and lost to it much of the Kirghiz steppes and Semirechensk: thereafter Orenburg and Omsk were bitter rivals of Tashkent. Here ruled Kaufmann, the governor-general of Turkestan from 1867 to 1883, the ablest of the Russian Asiatic administrators, with powerful support in the highest circles in St. Petersburg. Nominally he was subject to the ministry of war, but as he owed his position to the ministry and was, as regards Central Asia, its *alter ego*, no serious clashes occurred and the two walked hand in hand in their policy of expansion. From the outset they had wrested from the Tsar formal sanction of decisive powers: Kaufmann was entrusted with full political and diplomatic powers in dealing with the independent states of Central Asia. Thus, as in the days past with Ermolov in the Caucasus and in the days to come with Alexeyev in the Far East, the St. Petersburg foreign office was counter-checked. Gorchakov's liaison officers with Kaufmann were of no weight, and Tashkent, not St. Petersburg, spoke the final word: hence the evasions and the shifts to which Gorchakov was reduced in his efforts to pacify the British.

The one serious rival to Kaufmann was the Viceroy of the Caucasus, the Tsar's brother, the Grand Duke Michael. With the mountaineers 'pacified', the obvious outlet for the energies of the very large army of the Caucasus was Persia and particularly the eastern side of the Caspian. From Baku it was only 150 miles across to Krasnovodsk, established in 1869 as the advance base for action against Khiva, against the Turkomans, and against the disputed northern frontier of Persia. By 1874 enough progress had been made to excuse the setting up on an elaborate scale of a new Trans-Caspian military district under the control, not of Tashkent, but of Tiflis. It was typical of Russian politics that this project was rejected, owing to the protests of Gorchakov and Reutern, by the special commission formed to examine it, but immediately afterwards was sanctioned by the Tsar on the insistence of Milyutin and the Grand Duke Michael. Tiflis was now as much a thorn in the flesh to the British as Tashkent. The satellites of the two satraps eyed each other with mingled contempt and distrust, but the net result of their jealousy was that each was spurred on yet more insistently to what seemed more and more in British eyes to be carefully planned provocation.

It is true that in Russia itself there was a rising chorus of criticism against the prodigal expenditure, the high-handedness, and the corrupt administration of the military. Kaufmann's 1873 expedition to Khiva was currently reported to have been at least in part due to his desire to distract attention from powerful attacks, notably by Chernyaev, the conqueror of Tashkent, which were endangering his position with the St. Petersburg authorities. His massacre of the Yomud Turkomans, with which that expedition closed, was outspokenly condemned in Russian newspapers and the charges levelled against him were never answered. Yet it should be noted that the bulk of Russian criticism in the press was drawn from sources supplied either by rival officials or by discarded officers, and that it was directed rather to the means by which the policy of expansion was being carried out than to the general policy itself. Further, while making all allowances for a growing restiveness over the conduct of Tashkent and Tiflis, it must be remembered that criticism by Russians was one thing, by foreigners quite another. The swelling volume of British hostile criticism tended to band together Russian opinion against impertinent interference and in support of 'Russia's civilizing mission in the East'. At the very time when Kaufmann was encountering the most serious hostility from his Russian opponents, equal hostility was being shown on all sides to the Afghan boundary agreement with England. The Russian public were by then wounded, disgusted, and also undeterred by the repeated diplomatic wrangles with London and the parliamentary discussions, which were the official signs of the pressure on the British government of more and more alarmed opinion in India and at home.

By 1875 ten years of diplomatic fencing had brought but one hit by England, and that a dubious one, in the shape of the 1873 agreement as to the Oxus forming the north-eastern boundary of Afghanistan. In that same year the Khiva expedition took place, which, though not followed by official recriminations, made a deeper impress on English opinion in the years that followed than any other single event in Central Asia. Kaufmann had insisted that the expedition could no longer be deferred. Shuvalov was sent on a special mission to London immediately in advance armed with calming assurances from the Tsar in person; the sole object of the expedition was to rescue Russians enslaved, to punish brigandage, to teach the Khan a merited lesson. 'Not only was it far from the intention of the Emperor to take possession of Khiva, but positive orders had been prepared to prevent it, and directions given that the conditions imposed should be such as could not in any way lead to a prolonged occupancy of Khiva.' By June Kaufmann was in possession of the capital of the Khanate, Khiva itself. He thereupon imposed a treaty by which Khivan territory on the eastern bank of the Amu Darya (Oxus) was annexed to Russia, and the total effect of which was to reduce the Khanate to absolute dependence on Russia. There followed the massacre of Yomud Turkomans. The outburst of indignation in England was far more serious than ever before: nearly all the press indulged in what was almost a war scare.[1] It seemed impossible to reconcile the treaty with the Tsar's undertakings given through Shuvalov; equally impossible to palliate the barbarities reported to have been perpetrated against the Yomuds. The only reply that could be made was that the assurance given was meant to apply only to the town itself of Khiva, not to the whole of the Khanate.

[1] H. F. F. Chance, 'Russia and *The Times* in 1863 and 1873', in *Cambridge Historical Journal*, vol. i, pp. 96–7, 100–2. For the Tsar's undertaking conveyed through Shuvalov and quoted above, see Granville to Loftus, 8 Jan. 1873, in *A. and P.*, 1873, lxxv, C. 699, no. 3. Gorchakov later admitted: 'I am an outspoken opponent of any extension of Russia whatever; but I can do nothing against the ambition of our generals.' Stählin, 'Die Briefe L. Schneiders an . . . Waluew', in *Historische Zeitung*, vol. 155, p. 306. The massacre of the Yomud Turkomans again inflamed English opinion in 1876 owing to the version of it given by Schuyler in his book on Turkestan. Gladstone's counter-version, in the *Contemporary Review*, Nov. 1876, was concocted largely in concert with Mme Novikov and General Gorlov, the Russian military attaché in London; see W. T. Stead, *The M.P. for Russia*, vol. i, pp. 296–305.

Shuvalov himself thought the accusation of broken pledges justified. Later it was semi-officially argued that Shuvalov's declaration was only a statement of intentions or policy, not a promise or an international engagement. As the same semi-official defence expressed it: 'Ainsi les résultats de l'expédition contre le Khiva étaient impossibles à prévenir, et indépendants de la volonté du gouvernement russe.' Very well; if that were so, then according to the British it was impossible to expect that the Russian government could ever be trusted again. Khiva was not forgotten: 'it will cost Russia as much as a lost battle.'[1]

Granville, the British foreign secretary, did not, however, enter upon a controversy as to the past: the immediate future was harassing enough: Tiflis, not to be outdone by Tashkent, was pressing forward, and Afghanistan appeared to be threatened as well from the Trans-Caspian side by action against the Tekke Turkomans and Merv. Gorchakov was even more guarded than usual: he renewed his assurance long since given to Clarendon to the effect that Afghanistan lay outside Russia's sphere of action, but he refused to tie Russia's hands against the Turkomans of Merv, or to recognize any British intervention on their behalf (2 Feb. 1874).[2]

In the same month the sudden general election brought Disraeli at last to power. Derby replaced Granville, and Salisbury Argyll. But the change of government did not produce any immediate alteration in the tone or general lines of British

[1] Loftus, *Diplomatic Reminiscences, 1852–1879*, second series, vol. ii, pp. 105–6; Baddeley, *Russia in the Eighties*, p. 306; Martens, *La Russie et l'Angleterre dans l'Asie Centrale*, pp. 48–9, a defence based largely on Argyll, *The Eastern Question*, vol. ii, p. 301; *Spectator*, 4 Nov. 1876, quoted in Thompson, *Public Opinion and Lord Beaconsfield, 1875–1880*, vol. i, p. 139.

[2] Gorchakov to Brunnow, 2 Feb. 1874, in *A. and P.*, 1874, lxxvi, C. 919, no. 3. The visit of the Tsar to England in May 1874, following upon the marriage of his daughter to the Duke of Edinburgh, did, however, make St. Petersburg specially anxious that no immediate new move should be made in Central Asia. Kaufmann, busy with the fortification of his annexations at the expense of Khiva, agreed with Milyutin on 'un programme tout à fait pacifique', but there was the usual difficulty with the Grand Duke Michael; however, 'les velléités de nos troupes du Caucase ... contre les Turcomans Tekés ont été formellement repoussés'. Stremoukhov to Brunnow, 'très confidentielle', 7 Apr. 1874, extract in *Meyendorff MSS*. In fact, Lomakin's annual 'reconnaissance' in Trans-Caspia in 1874 was not on a large scale. Gorchakov, though he had just been unable to prevent the formation of the new military district of Trans-Caspia, professed more than usual optimism: 'Les ordres de l'Empereur ... ont été données en termes si péremptoires qu'aucune convoitise n'osera se permettre de les transgresser ... Donc, aucun nuage sur le terrain politique ne se trouvera lors de la visite de notre A.M. à Londres': Gorchakov to Brunnow, 'confidentielle', 6 Apr. 1874, extract in *Meyendorff MSS*.

policy towards Russia. Derby was little less placid and pacific than Granville, and was soon on the best of terms with Shuvalov, who took over the Russian embassy that autumn. Salisbury was not russophobe, was unimpressed by experts and unperturbed by the alarmists in the India Office and Simla. Disraeli had enough on hand at home and was not ready to force the pace overmuch. Lytton did not succeed Northbrook as Viceroy till two years later. Yet gradually the long interchange of communications on Afghanistan drew to a culmination which was the reflection in diplomatic terms of the hostility of the two countries.

A lengthy memorandum of Gorchakov (17 Apr. 1875) declared that the Tsar had no intention of extending his frontiers in Central Asia either on the side of Bokhara or on that of Krasnovodsk or the Atrek, and offered again to acknowledge Afghanistan as an intermediate zone provided that its independence were secured on either side from all encroachment. The proviso and past experience of the 'intentions' of the Tsar rendered this document worthless in the eyes of the departments concerned in London: in the foreign office it was interpreted as in reality meaning the abandonment by Russia of the long-discussed question of a neutral zone, and as 'an insidious attempt to get the sanction of H.M.G. for all the broken promises of Russia in regard to Central Asia'. The normal interval of six months having elapsed, the British government answered by roundly insisting on the most complete freedom of action in relation to the integrity of Afghan territory under all future contingencies (25 Oct. 1875).[1] This drew an exceptionally entangled statement from St. Petersburg closing the unpractical discussions as to an intermediate zone, and in substance amounting to the reservation by Russia of necessary freedom of action in regard to Afghanistan, while recognizing a similar freedom of action on the part of England (15 Feb. 1876). The gloves were off. A month later the conquest of Kokand was completed by its incorporation in the Russian empire. Highly suspicious communications were renewed between Tashkent and Kabul; equally suspicious intrigues were on foot with

---

[1] Minute of Bourke, under-secretary for foreign affairs, 16 May 1875, in *F.O.* 65/927. The foreign office views on Gorchakov's memorandum are in *F.O.* 65/929. Both the Russian and the British statements are printed in *A. and P.*, 1878, lxxx, C. 2164, nos. 29 and 54.

Shere Ali's nephew and rival Abdur Rahman Khan, for the past seven years an exile in Bokhara and Samarkand, now in Tashkent itself.[1] English counter-measures were pushed ahead: Lytton and the 'forward school' were now in the saddle at Simla. The second Afghan war was lowering not far ahead, and the essential cause of that war in the eyes of most Englishmen was Russia.

Thus, in the year when the Balkans exploded and Disraeli was heading England towards a firm stand against Russian designs on the Ottoman empire, the Afghan question had reached a most dangerous state and provided the maximum of additional embroilment between Russia and England. At the same time the mutual suspicions and enmity aroused by the Near Eastern crisis were further heightened by alarums and excursions in regard to Persia. In large part these were linked up with the Afghan problem. Herat, 'the key to India', had always been a centre of discord between the Afghans and the Persians, and Meshed, with the frontier post of Sarakhs and the Zulfikar Pass, was in English estimation second only in importance to Herat and Merv. Khorasan, the whole north-east of Persia, seemed threatened by the advance of the Russians in Trans-Caspia: thus also Herat, Kandahar, western Afghanistan. And only through Khorasan could the Turkoman tribes be aided in their efforts to escape subjection. Farther west, the Atrek boundary agreement between Russia and Persia appeared none too secure. The authority of the Shah in this region was extremely ineffective, and since the grazing-grounds of some of the Turkoman tribes lay on both sides of an ill-mapped and more or less nominal frontier, easy excuses for forward action were available to the Russian commanders. Such action was not of merely local importance, for the Grand Duke Michael and the Caucasus staff were pushing forward grandiose schemes for the Atrek to serve as a stepping-stone for the acquisition of the whole southern shore of the Caspian. The Central Asian question was

---

[1] *F.O.* 65/957 and 958 contain much material as to Kaufmann's negotiations with Shere Ali and fears as to Abdur Rahman Khan. The Russian foreign office at first categorically denied that an agent had been sent to Kabul by Kaufmann, though it later admitted the fact, but continued to deny that there was any intention to negotiate a treaty with Shere Ali. The annexation of Kokand was, at any rate at first, taken calmly by the British government and press, much to Shuvalov's surprise; Shuvalov to Gorchakov, 17 Mar. 1876, enclosed in Loftus to Derby, disp. .no. 158, secret, 22 Apr., in *F.O.* 65/957.

by 1875 extended, not only to Afghanistan, but to the integrity and independence of Persia. Taken in conjunction with the complete maritime control of the Caspian by the Russians, with their energetic bidding for commercial and telegraph concessions in Persia, with their activities in Azerbaizhan, with the battle over the Reuter concession and the uncertain results of the Shah's European visit two years before, such planning of direct conquests, however difficult of immediate attainment, were highly disturbing to the British government, who were kept admirably informed by their well-primed military attaché in St. Petersburg. They were scarcely to be reassured by the information that the Tsar had vetoed the designs of his brother and had given special instructions not to increase British suspicions, for ample scope was still left to the Russian generals when they were told that they 'should endeavour to avoid as much as possible any measures of aggression, and not cross our present frontiers without absolute necessity'.[1] A year later (1876) much the same account was given of the annual spring conference in St. Petersburg on Central Asian affairs; the Caucasus command were wanting another expedition against the Akkal Tekkes; the Tsar was trying to hold them back and making much of British fears for Merv.[2] Yet as usual Lomakin at Krasnovodsk sent out an expedition.

So it continued; from the Caspian to the Oxus and Kashgar British observers watched every movement of the Russians with undisguised suspicion. There were lulls, and there were pacific

[1] *F.O.* 65/927, especially: Loftus to Derby, disp. no. 134, most secret, 27 Apr. 1875, enclosing from Wellesley translation of dispatch of Milyutin to the Grand Duke Michael, 15 Apr., giving the results of the annual conference just held on Central Asian affairs: Loftus to Derby, disp. nos. 99, most secret, 29 Mar., and 123, secret, 14 Apr., with important enclosures from Wellesley, particularly text of report of Grand Duke Michael to Milyutin, 6 Mar. 1875. Loftus himself, though not in general russophobe, was thoroughly alarmist in regard to Central Asia, and urged that England should enter into no engagements which might fetter her unrestricted action: 'nor do I attach any value to the assurances which the Imperial Government may offer of their pacific and friendly relations' in regard to Persia or Central Asia; disp. no. 103, conf., 30 Mar. 1875. It is worth noting that at the beginning of 1875 Derby and Salisbury agreed that Loftus's secret dispatches (apparently those on Central Asia, particularly with Wellesley's enclosures) should not be circulated to the cabinet as a whole; minute of Tenterden (permanent under-secretary), 17 Jan., in *F.O.* 65/926. I do not know how long this practice was continued. The war office would, of course, receive Wellesley's reports.

[2] Wellesley's reports, no. 9, secret, 15 Apr. 1876, and no. 15, secret, 12 June, enclosing translations of dispatch of Grand Duke Michael to Milyutin, 14 Feb., and Milyutin's reply of 2 Mar., in *F.O.* 65/957.

speeches and articles to be quoted on either side, but the russophobia of Simla, the India Office, and certain sections of British opinion was spreading far more widely now. 'The threat to India' was popularized just when it could be allied to the acute revival of older fears of Russian Tsardom and 'the threat to the Straits'. The Russian officials and their public were almost equally on edge. Disraeli's purchase of the Suez Canal shares aroused acid comment; so did the new imperial title. Why did 6,000 English rifles suddenly make their appearance among the Turkomans? Why was the Kaulbars mission to Kashgar promptly followed by the Forsyth mission, on a far more imposing scale? What were the real terms of Forsyth's treaty with Yakub Bey, and why was he accompanied by a Turkish embassy? Not content with their wholesale bribery and arming of the Afghans as 'a living wall against Russia', the British were forcing an Afghan concentration at Herat against Merv and the Tekkes. Shere Ali was their mere tool. Lytton was bent on aggression; witness Khelat and the Bolan Pass. Neither country could trust the other. The two foreign ministers might maintain an attitude of amicable moderation and might genuinely enough smooth over difficulties, but they could not smooth them out. The clash between the rival interests at stake and the rival feelings aroused was too severe, and perhaps a clash in arms might follow soon now that the Balkan crisis was shaping so ominously.[1]

4. PANSLAVISM

Panslavism, the second new feature colouring Russian foreign relations in the eighteen-seventies, was of a very different character.[2] While the Russian conquests in Central Asia and the menace to India were clear-cut issues and while they affected directly England alone of the European powers, panslavism was the current appellation given by western Europe to a

---

[1] For the interaction of Central Asian affairs and the Near Eastern crisis in 1877 and 1878, see below, pp. 308–9 and n., 479 and n., 498, 513–14 and n.

[2] On the panslavs and the slavophils, besides some of their own writings, I have found specially useful: M. Gershenzon, *Istoricheskie Zapiski* (2nd edition; Berlin, 1923); N. L. Brodsky, *Rannie Slavyanofili* (Moscow, 1910); T. G. Masaryk, *The Spirit of Russia* (2 vols., London, 1919); A. N. Pypin, *Panslavizm v proshlom i nastoyashchem* (St. Petersburg, 1913); A. Fischel, *Der Panslavismus bis zum Weltkrieg* (Stuttgart, 1919). I am much indebted to the Council of the Royal Historical Society for permission to republish this section (with some alterations and additions), which was originally read as a paper before the Society and published in their *Transactions* for 1935.

variety of unsystematic, and partially conflicting, views which were directed against those countries which might stand in the way of Russia's fulfilment of her national mission. Here Austria-Hungary and Turkey were more deeply affected than England. Since panslavism was in general not so much an organized policy, or even a creed, but rather an attitude of mind and feeling, it was at the time correspondingly difficult to gauge its power, just as it is now to analyse its different elements. At least there is no doubt that during the eastern crisis of the late seventies panslavism bulked in the eyes of Buda-Pest and Vienna, of Constantinople and London, as the most dangerous force in Russia, and as will be seen in subsequent chapters there was much in it to give good ground for the denunciations of foreign alarmists.

One major difficulty in giving specific meaning to the term panslavism is that in proportion as it gained real influence it did so very largely by transforming itself into a very pronounced form of Great Russian nationalism. It was, in fact, during the sixties and seventies in a period of transition when the watchwords that appealed to the older generation were sounding less clearly and did not chime in harmoniously with the harsh clanging of a younger generation. In a sense panslavism was the connecting link between slavophilism and panrussianism. What had begun as the religious and intellectual strivings of small coteries of Muscovite landowners ended by being transformed into crude appeals to nationalist mass-emotions. The slavophil movement, which grew up in the two decades before the Crimean war and attracted considerable attention abroad under the description of the struggle between the slavophils and the westernizers, had neither any organization nor any clear political programme. The conditions of the later years of Nicholas I's reign made the open expression of political opinions almost impossible, but a further reason for the predominantly non-political character of early slavophilism lay in the fact that for the majority of the slavophils it was the outcome of individual struggles to express a satisfactory philosophical and theological formulation of their religious convictions and a justification of their view of the world: hence the vein of quietism or of social and political conservatism which runs through much of the writings of the slavophils—it is particularly noticeable in Ivan Kireyevsky. Yet they were by no means conservatives of the official Uvarov brand: they tended to look upon the state and the machinery of law as acting only by force and as entirely secondary in comparison with the living reality of a community morally free and morally united in the collective realization of faith. They were first and foremost steeped in Orthodoxy. At the same time they were also intellectuals belonging to the middle or upper strata of the nobility; well off and well educated; acquainted with western thought and literature; specially influenced by Schlegel and Hegel. The opposition between them and the westernizers was ultimately due less to divergence of historical or political views than to differences of temperament and divergent psychological approaches—the one religious, the other rationalistic. Nearly all of the slavophils were closely bound to the Russian land; they were not only serf-owners but born, bred, and living much of the year on their country estates. 'Like spreading oaks, these families grew in the easy soil of serfdom, their roots invisibly intertwined with the life of the people and drawing life from its waters, while their topmost branches reached up into the air of European culture.'[1] Instinctively they represented the country as against the town. Their one town was Moscow, and that was a great, sprawling clutter of gardened houses, peasant huts, and countless churches. St. Petersburg was psychologically and physically, just as it was symbolically, entirely alien to them. Thus bound to Moscow, thus linked with the land, they inevitably reacted profoundly against the catastrophic failure of the St. Petersburg bureaucracy, largely non-Russian in personnel, in the Crimean war. In the 'liberal' years that ushered in Alexander II's reign, when the press was relatively free and political activity to some extent possible, the slavophils entered the lists prominently in the struggle for reforms above all concentrated on the problem of serfdom. It was, thus, in the sphere of internal reforms that they first openly appeared upon the political scene. Though bitterly critical of the break-down of the foreign policy of Nicholas and his Baltic German diplomats, their efforts were in the first place mainly directed to saving Russia herself. Only a healthy, cleansed Russia could come forward as the saviour of Slavdom.[2]

[1] M. Gershenzon, *Istoricheskie Zapiski*, pp. 44–5, and cf. 94–5 (2nd edition, Berlin, 1923); referring to such families as the Kireyevskys, the Koshelovs, the Homyakovs, or the Samarins.

[2] A noticeable feature in the writings of the later panslavs, such as Aksakov, Danilevsky, and O. Miller, is the emphasis placed on the changed position of

The economic outlook of the slavophils was centred on the land and greatly coloured by their idealizing of the *mir* and the *artel* as spontaneous Russian forms of association. For them western liberalism and *laisser-faire* spelt civil and political freedom without economic freedom for any but the very few; spelt, in fact, the forcible keeping-down of the masses: in the end catastrophe was inevitable. Slavdom reposed neither economically nor spiritually upon individualism or the western conception of personality, but upon the principle of community and co-operation, which found expression above all in the family and in the village commune. Serfdom, having brought them to an economic impasse, was recognized to be the crying evil, and there were no more sturdy fighters for emancipation, along their own lines, than many of the slavophils. But emancipation must not usher in an era of untrammelled competition and capitalistic production, leading to the growth of a large urban proletariat. They admitted the necessity of Russian industrial development, provided that it was not unduly expanded and that factories preserved their patriarchal character and the traditional connexion of the workers with the land. They had always stood for extreme protection, and they had corresponding support from Moscow industrialists, whom they were accustomed to typify in the formula: 'the owner of the factory is the father of the family, the workers his children'. Hence the slavophils and later the panslavs, while glorifying those employed in domestic handicrafts (*kustari*) as the true source of industrial welfare for Russia, could in part at least make their peace with the new industrial developments which were already marked in the later years of Nicholas I and were to transform Russia under his son and grandson. This transformation, the pace of which was enormously increased by the reforms of Alexander II, involved the breaking-up of what the slavophils claimed as essential to Slavdom. Yet the ironical contradiction remains that the panslavs of the last forty years of the century found among their most useful allies the very cotton, iron, and steel magnates who so largely contributed to westernizing Russia. The explanation lies in part in the fact that the big industrialists

Russia *vis-à-vis* the other Slavs as a consequence of the emancipation of the serfs and the other reforms of the sixties: Russia, they claimed, could now, as she could not formerly, appeal to them in the name of liberty and a new range of cultural development.

utilized panslav diatribes against Europe and advertising of
Russia's past as a means of holding off foreign competition, particularly by a return to a high tariff; in part in the fact that
panslavism developed from its slavophil origins into autarkic
nationalism of a type closely similar to that of Katkov, who
from the end of the seventies made his *Moskovskiya Vyedemosti* the
mouthpiece of extreme protection and the big Moscow industrial interests.[1]

Prior to the Crimean war slavophil circles had in general taken
little sustained interest in the non-Russian Slavs, as to whom
they were, with a few exceptions, very poorly informed. The
linguistic and cultural revival which began among Czechs,
Serbs, and Bulgars in the first half of the century looked far
more to Russia than vice versa. Russians, when they travelled
abroad, went normally to Germany, Switzerland, or the West,
not to the Balkans or the Slav lands of the Austrian empire.
The official world looked askance at any incipient panslav
stirrings, and Nicholas I, only too thoroughly supported here
by Nesselrode and his closest confidants, frowned severely upon
any Slav movements which might infuse a further dose of
revolutionary principles, above all if they infected the Habsburg
empire. No raising of a Slav banner was possible without a
break between St. Petersburg and Vienna, and such a break
Nicholas was, to his cost, the last to think possible. Only on
the very eve of the Crimean war did he, as a last resort, sanction
an appeal to the Christians of Turkey to rise in common defence
of Orthodoxy—but not of Slavdom. It was at this point that the
first slavophil attempts to influence foreign policy were made.
These were due mainly to the activities of the energetic and
widely known Pogodin, one of the few among the friends of the
earlier slavophils to interest himself vigorously in the other Slav
peoples. Professor of history at Moscow university, Pogodin was
the leading representative of the type of academic propagandist
and philanthropist which was to be very prominent in the
panslav movement in the sixties and seventies. Though stoutly
Orthodox himself, his Slav interests and sympathies were
founded rather upon the historical achievements of the past
than upon a spiritual basis of the reuniting and redemptive

[1] G. von Schulze-Gävernitz, *Volkswirtschaftliche Studien aus Russland* (Leipzig,
1899), pp. 174–98, 208; M. Tugan-Baranovsky, *Geschichte der russischen Fabrik*
(Berlin, 1900), pp. 344–9.

powers of Orthodoxy. As for the present, he conjured up a picture of brother Slavs groaning under the yoke of the foreigner and gazing expectantly at Russia, by whose undisputed and unaided might they were to be rescued. This breezy optimism was rudely shattered by the Crimean war, but Pogodin was possessed of a buoyant perseverance, and he had the invaluable capacity of giving life to vague sympathy by organizing it to practical effect. Almost alone of the slavophil sympathizers of his generation he lived on in activity for long after the war (he did not die until 1875), and he was one of the founders, and the second president, of the Moscow Slavonic Benevolent Committee.

This committee was set up with the approval of Alexander II in 1858 with the declared aim of assisting the Southern Slavs to develop their religious, educational, and other national institutions and of bringing young Slavs to Russia to be educated. In practice it concentrated mainly upon the Bulgars, upon whom it had an important, though by no means always the desired, effect (see below, pp. 111–12). From the start it was closely connected with the church, and various ecclesiastical dignitaries both in Moscow and the provinces gave the movement influential assistance. It had the backing of the department of Asiatic affairs, and in particular the energetic support of Ignatyev. The St. Petersburg committee, founded ten years later, was largely directed by professors of the university and confined itself mainly to relations, by no means always amicable, with the Czechs. Similar committees were also set up in 1869 and 1870 in Kiev and Odessa, where the Bulgarian colony served as its nucleus. The membership of all four was very small; they did not issue propagandist literature on any scale in Russia until 1876, and they had no regular press of their own.[1] Their influence within Russia was not widespread before 1876; outside Russia, and especially in Bulgaria, they were by then of definite importance. But their greatest effect probably lay less in their actual achievements than in the exaggerated alarm which their intrigues in the Balkans and Austria-Hungary had inspired in the world of diplomacy and journalism.

The most spectacular achievement of the Moscow committee

---

[1] Aksakov founded three short-lived papers, *Dyen* in 1861 and *Moskva* and *Moskvich* in 1867 and 1868, but they fell foul of the censorship on account of internal policy, and further funds were not forthcoming until 1881.

had been the holding in 1867 of a Slavonic Ethnographic Exhibition in Moscow which was much advertised in Russia and much commented upon abroad as a thin cultural cloak for political propaganda. On the whole it was not much more than a platonic declaration of Slav sympathies, and no effect was given to the one practical proposal put forward (by the Czechs, not the Russians), namely, the organization of a permanent Slavonic institute and of biennial Slavonic cultural congresses. Its Russian organizers hailed it as for the first time arousing Russia to the Slav question and as converting what had been an abstract literary question into a living problem of actuality. Yet these same men eight years later, when the eastern question again festered into a crisis, had to confess that Russian ignorance of and apathy towards their Slav brethren were still only too widespread. By 1875 not so very much had changed since 1860, when Turgenev's *On the Eve* depicted the father of the heroine as unable to distinguish her Bulgarian revolutionary lover from 'a vagrant Montenegrin'. Yet the Slavonic committees did form a skeleton organization which might be rapidly expanded if circumstances were favourable. And they now had what they never had before, powerful supporters in the court both of the Tsar and of the Tsarevich, and powerful allies in the rising forces of anti-foreign hostility. Of their Muscovite core the most typical representative was the leader of the Moscow committee, Ivan Aksakov, a man of exceptional personality, who rose to the height of his career in the crisis of 1876 to 1878.

Ivan Aksakov—sprung from the central Russian land, bred in something of the atmosphere of his father Sergei's *A Russian Gentleman*—though born in 1823, belonged spiritually, like Dostoyevsky two years his senior, to the older slavophils born in the first decade of the century.[1] With him, as for them, the roots of Slav feeling lay in devotion to the Orthodox church. His main energies, like theirs, lay outside any professional or official service. Neither learned nor widely read, but passionately outspoken with all the conviction of an inspired fanatic, he became the prophet of the small circle of the Moscow committee, announcing in semi-apocalyptic terms the divine

---

[1] His panslav writings are collected in the first volume of his collected works, *Slavyansky vopros*; there is a valuable, though very hostile, article by A. N. Pypin, reviewing this, in *Vestnik Evropy*, Aug. 1886, pp. 763–807.

mission of Russia, the freeing of her brothers in faith and blood from a foreign religious and political yoke. This historical mission of Russia, her moral right and duty, is founded on the fact—never argued nor 'proved', merely didactically stated— of Orthodoxy as the one pure form of Christianity, the essential basis of true civilization, of which the Russian Slavs are the only true and effective repository and upholders. Over against Slav orthodoxy is set the old decaying Romano-German world of the West, with its poison of unbridled rationalism and individualism, its cancer of internecine competition, and its ruinous social and industrial struggles. As for almost all the earlier slavophils, Catholicism is the symbol for western civilization, and for Aksakov the arch-enemy. Protestantism bulks far less, appearing merely as a subsidiary form of declension from the true principles of Christianity. Thus the Catholic Slavs have been guilty of the great betrayal. The Slavs stand at the parting of the ways; either the way of the West, of Rome; or the way of the East, of Orthodox Moscow. For the Czechs and Croats there may be some hope if they return to Cyril and Methodius, to Orthodoxy: to the Poles Aksakov offers nothing but the cup of irreconcilable bitterness. The essential prerequisite for the idea of panslav fraternity is the idea of the highest spiritual unity in faith: secure the purity of the Slav ideal of faith and church, then all things will be added unto you. Hence political combinations, the political aims of Russian foreign policy, are left vague and unanalysed. All the strength of the Slavs lies in Russia; all the strength of Russia in her Slavdom. Russia cannot achieve healthy national development save through realization of her vocation as the great Slav power, through a break from the Petersburg period of her history. Just as Russia is unthinkable apart from Slavdom, since she is both spiritually and materially the leading expression of it, so also is Slavdom unthinkable apart from Russia.

These views are little else than a restatement of those of Ivan Kireyevsky and Homyakov, but the emphasis is now laid on Orthodox Slavdom rather than on Greco-Slavonic Orthodoxy, a significant transition towards the newer panslavism. And further, while earlier writers (including also Dostoyevsky) hankered after some synthesis which should save western civilization from the consequences flowing from its over-developed rationalism, Aksakov was content to summon Orthodoxy and

Slavdom to do battle with the principle of evil. Russia's messianic calling was no longer to be that of the saviour of humanity at large, but was now limited to Orthodox Slavdom alone. On the other hand, he took over from his predecessors, besides their fundamental religious outlook, their antipathy to institutional forms of constraint and regulation and their criticism of, or hostility to, Peter the Great and his semi-German successors with their tentacular bureaucratic despotism and desertion of true Russian ways of life for western importations. Thus the *mir* and later the *zemsky sobor*[1] became slogans for slavophil or panslav groups as genuine, national products of Muscovite Russia: thus the Holy Synod was repudiated as an erastian creation of Peter which had shackled the true life of the church and bent it into subservience to the state; thus the governmental machine (and notably the censorship) was attacked as an alien incubus, controlled by Baltic Germans and other non-Russians, totally unable to respond to the deep currents of national life; thus, finally, the dynasty itself was the target for accusations of being but a German brand of military autocracy without roots in the soil of Russia.

Such an attitude of mind, to some extent traditional among certain sections of the landed gentry, owing much now to the reaction against the régime of Nicholas I and something to the economic and social dislocation following on the emancipation of the serfs and other reforms, was by no means confined to Aksakov's followers. With different colourings and different trappings it was common to many among the land-owning class for whom St. Petersburg meant government by bureaucrats, loss of power, and economic displacement. Here were potent feelings, not essentially connected with panslavism, which might be utilized by it in an assault upon St. Petersburg foreign policy if that policy refused to move in consonance with the true aspirations of the Russian people as the standard-bearer of the Slav cause.

This anti-governmental element, together with the anti-

---

[1] The historical development of the *mir*, or village community, was almost completely misunderstood by the slavophils and their successors: it was, in fact, in the main a village organization for tax and police purposes imposed from above in the sixteenth and seventeenth centuries by the Russian government. The *zemsky sobor*, roughly comparable to the *États généraux*, had not met since 1682. A revival of it in some form might provide the landowners with a curb on the Tsar and the bureaucracy.

dynastic streak, in the panslavism of Moscow circles helped to make them profoundly antipathetic to Alexander II himself and to most of the functionaries of the St. Petersburg machine. Yet they were not without allies or sympathizers in the very highest circles of the court. The Empress and, later, the wife of the Tsarevich, with all the enthusiasm of converts to Orthodoxy, imbibed the traditional view of the mission of Orthodox Russia and surrounded themselves with a circle of ardent devotees of Homyakov's and Tyutchev's brand of religious, poetizing nationalism, of which the Countess Bludova's salon was the most conspicuous centre. There reigned Tyutchev's dreams of a 'great Graeco-Russian Orthodox Empire' which should gather together Slavdom with 'the Pan-Slavonic Tsar' at its head, and

> as ye gaze,
> To east and west, to south and north,
> The sun's glad tidings shall ring forth
> The summons of his conquering rays.[1]

In such an atmosphere, and with Pobedonostsev as tutor, the future Alexander III had been brought up. He was probably not deeply influenced by this mixture of pan-orthodox and panslav symbolism, but he was, while Tsarevich, generally supposed to be an adherent of panslav ideas, a supposition which could find confirmation in the undoubted fact that a number of his entourage, as well as his wife, were warm supporters of the cause. These court allies were not an initiating force, but if a crisis arose in the Balkans, if feeling rose high, they might act as a powerful influence on Russian foreign policy and as invaluable collaborators with Aksakov's following in Moscow.

Although Aksakov and his like fiercely denounced Peter the Great and so much that followed after him, they omitted from their counts the expansion of Muscovy into the Russian empire. It was Peter and the house of Holstein-Gottorp who had

---

[1] On Tyutchev's panslav ideas, see G. Florovsky, 'The historical premonitions of Tyutchev', in *S.R.*, vol. iii, pp. 337–49, and K. Pigarev, 'F. I. Tyutchev i problemi vneshnei politiki tsarskoi Rossii', in *Literaturnoe Naslyedstvo* (Moscow), 1935, vol. xix–xxi, pp. 177–256, where are printed a number of Tyutchev's letters to Gorchakov. Countess Bludova, a fanatical anti-Pole, was a close friend of Bashanov, the Empress's confessor, and of Tyutchev's two daughters, both ladies in waiting; one of them subsequently married Aksakov and was an important link between Aksakov, Pogodin, and Katkov, and court circles. Cf., for Pobedonostsev's connexion with Aksakov through the daughters of Tyutchev, 'Pobedonostsev and Alexander III', in *S.R.*, vol. vii, pp. 31–2.

annexed the Baltic provinces, Poland, the southern steppes, the Crimea, Finland, Bessarabia, the Caucasus, great tracts of Asia. This tremendous heritage was silently accepted. So far from there being any murmur of undoing any part of this work, Moscow and the panslavs were the loudest in demanding that the borderlands be fully absorbed in the great Slav mass of central Russia, the core of the old Muscovy. The Polish revolt of 1863 unleashed century-old hatreds and fears. In the years which followed, the old 'Congress Poland' was mercilessly dragooned within the framework of the administration common to Russia proper, while 'the western lands', Lithuania, White Russia, and the western Ukraine, were subjected to every measure of russianization. Contemporaneously a campaign was initiated of the same nature in the Baltic Provinces and Bessarabia; and, to show without mistaking that Russian meant Great Russian alone, the Little Russian or Ukrainian cultural revival of the time was successfully attacked by Moscow, above all by the prohibition in 1876 of the use of the Ukrainian 'dialect' for any academic or literary purposes. Symptomatically two of the men most actively associated with this denationalizing, russianizing policy were among the most prominent of the slavophil or panslav Muscovites of the day: Prince Cherkasky and Yuri Samarin, a close friend of Aksakov.

Completely different in character and attainments, they were both at one in regarding the problem of nationality within the Russian empire as requiring urgent and drastic handling. Samarin admirably summed up an increasingly widespread feeling when he ridiculed the ideal of a denationalized empire in which Russians, Poles, and Germans lived side by side but apart from each other, 'comme qui dirait la réproduction très en grande de l'hôtel Ragatz [he was writing from Brussels] où Russes, Américains et Français venaient, sans se connaître, s'asseoir à la même table d'hôte'; over against this he set a Russia in which a Russian 'would feel like a Frenchman feels in France or an Englishman in England', entirely at home.[1] For Samarin and Cherkasky the only solution possible for the great western fringes of the empire was an undeviating policy of russianization; of the success of this in the central Polish

---

[1] B. E. Nolde, *Yuri Samarin i ego vremya* (Paris, 1926), p. 186; quoting a private letter of Samarin written in 1864.

provinces with an overwhelming pure Polish population they were admittedly doubtful, but it could at least serve to stifle the nationalistic chauvinism of the upper classes until such time as the Polish peasantry had been transformed by the new legislation for which both men were largely responsible. Samarin had been one of N. A. Milyutin's right-hand men in working out the details of the abolition of serfdom in Russia and was subsequently employed in the somewhat similar task of agrarian reform in Poland. An earlier period of administration in the Baltic Provinces had likewise given him first-hand practical experience of the Letts and Estonians and their Baltic German landowners. Prince Cherkasky, a wealthy Tula landowner, had taken a prominent part in the emancipation of the serfs and also worked with Milyrtin and Samarin in Poland and distinguished himself in the campaign for reuniting the Uniats with the Orthodox church. For three years (1868-70) he was still more in the public eye at the head of the Moscow city council, until his aggressive stand against the reactionary forces in the government led to his removal. Both were noted members of the Moscow Slavonic Committee, though neither of them was deeply concerned with the Slavs outside Russia until their closing years.

Samarin and Cherkasky are significant in the panslav movement in that, unlike Aksakov or the earlier slavophils, and unlike the professorial type represented by Lamansky, Miller, or Grot, they were active in administration and politics and were well-known public figures. Cherkasky in particular represents the doer—by fits and starts—as opposed to the thinker or prophet. Samarin, endowed with an exceptional capacity for hard work, combined practical ability with deep intellectual and religious interests grounded in him by his early upbringing and his student years at Moscow university. Himself a considerable theologian as well as the author of the widely influential *The Borderlands of Russia*, the text-book of the 'russifiers' of the seventies, he may be accounted a bridge between the older style of slavophil steeped in the learning, the rites, and the mysticism of Orthodoxy, and the newer style of forceful administrator, diplomat, or soldier to whom such a religious and philosophical grounding was of little or no concern. Both men are also, above all, significant as representing the transformation of the idea of panslavism into that of pan-russianism.

To the success of their views on internal policy was largely due that continuance in western countries of the picture of Russia as the brutal oppressor of her subject peoples which remained one of the strongest springs of russophobia in England and elsewhere.

At the same time this internal aspect of developing panslavism was paralleled by the note of hectoring domination or overweening pride which was becoming more and more marked in relations with the Slavs outside the empire. It is obvious that views such as those of Aksakov sketched above would raise in an acute form the fundamental contradiction contained in the combination of panslavism and orthodoxy. A thousand years of the history of the western Slavs were virtually ignored. More than half of the Slavs living outside Russia dwelt within the bounds of the Austro-Hungarian empire; and the great majority of these were Catholic and had been for centuries deeply affected by westernizing influences. Still more formidable was the problem of the Poles, the second most numerous of the Slav races and glorying in long and great traditions of civilization binding them to Catholicism and the West. It was impossible in the long run to ignore them, and yet at this period that was the deliberate attitude of the Russian panslavs, hot with the acrid fumes of 1863. At the Slavonic Ethnographic Exhibition held in Moscow in 1867 to display to Russia and the world at large the fraternal union of Slavdom, the Poles were conspicuous by their absence. In all the round of speeches on that occasion the Poles were scarcely mentioned, save by Pogodin, who called upon them to rejoin the Slav brotherhood by humbling themselves before the Russian Tsar. At the close Rieger, the Czech leader, remonstrated in cautious terms. Promptly Cherkasky, true to his reputation, arose to pour forth minatory reproaches on any meddling with what was a purely Russian question.

It is evident that panslavism, so long as the Orthodox church remained as its basis, could only be applied in the main to the Slavs in Turkey. Only in proportion as it shed its ecclesiastical and religious elements might it be capable of appeal to the majority of the Slavs in Austria-Hungary, or to the Poles. Even then there would remain the stumbling-block of the lack of any common language. It was symptomatic that Pogodin's correspondence with Šafarik and other Czech or Croat leaders was written in German, and that the proceedings of the Prague

Slavonic congress of 1848 were likewise conducted in German. The Russians in their attempt to impose Russian as the common language for all Slavs encountered the most emphatic opposition: unedifying and fruitless wrangles with Lamansky, Hilferding, and other Russian philologists in the panslav camp were the only result.

A third stumbling-block in the path of panslavism lay in the fact that, although Russia was indisputably the only effective political and military Slav power, her claims to cultural predominance seemed thin and arrogant in the eyes of many western Slavs. Thus Homyakov's *Address from Moscow to the Serbs*, in 1860, with its tone of dictatorial superiority, had aroused much ill feeling in Serbia; Palacký and others were not behindhand in repudiating any idea of Russian hegemony; and the same antipathy to the patronizing dominance of Moscow was scarcely veiled during the celebrations of the 1867 Ethnographic Exhibition. Despite the reforms of the early sixties, Russian Tsardom ran counter to the traditions and aspirations of every other Slav people. Emancipation at the hands of the Russian Tsar might mean but an exchange of dominations. Gorchakov, always an opponent of panslav schemes, was justified in writing: 'Je ne vous dissimule pas qu'il m'est difficile de croire à une sympathie sincère des races Slaves pour la *Russie Autocratique*.'[1] However much some of the Czech leaders might blind themselves to the nature of Russian Tsardom, the trees of liberty were likely to have very queer blossoms if transported from the banks of the Neva or the Moskva. Certainly they were not recognizable along the Vistula.

These three major obstacles to the development of panslavism were abundantly apparent throughout Alexander II's reign. Towards its close they became less apparent to foreign eyes when a different form of panslavism was in the ascendant which put either no or little store on the test of purity of religion, or on the overcoming of linguistic differences, or on the civilizing mission of Russia, but stood out nakedly for the annihilation of the Habsburg and Ottoman empires through the military might of Russia. This may be said to mark the final stage of the development of panslavism into panrussianism, and this was the form in which during the eighteen-seventies panslavism was above all represented to the rest of Europe, mainly through

[1] Gorchakov to Novikov, 9 May 1872, in *Meyendorff MSS.*

the work of two men, the one forgotten, the other still remembered—Rostislav Andreievich Fadeyev and Nikolai Pavlovich Ignatyev.

Fadeyev was a military man, belonging to a country family of the nobility. He served for twenty years in the Caucasus, where he became an ardent supporter of expansion in Central Asia and a life-long henchman of Prince Baryatinsky, the conqueror of Shamyl and 'the pacifier of the Caucasus'. He was excellently fitted for the Russian type of empire-building in Central Asia, but in 1867, at the age of forty-three, inspired by Baryatinsky chafing in retirement, he joined in the attack then being engineered on D. A. Milyutin's army reforms, which he subjected to drastic criticism in a series of articles entitled *Russia's Armed Forces*.[1] As a result he was forced by Milyutin to retire from the active army, and he soon joined forces with Chernyaev, the Central Asian lion of the day who had likewise been broken by Milyutin, and with his swashbuckling friends grouped round the violent nationalist paper *Russky Mir*. From this period dates Fadeyev's championship of the Slav cause, first pronounced in strident tones in his *Opinion on the Eastern Question* (1869), which at once made his name in the Slav lands. In January 1875 he went to Egypt to reconstruct the Egyptian army at the invitation of the Khedive—an invitation which apparently was extracted by the intrigues of Ignatyev.[2] This task was undertaken as a practical means for working towards the disruption of the Ottoman empire, in the hope of being able in five or six years to utilize the Khedive's army against his suzerain in conjunction with a rising of the Balkan Slavs. Events moved too quickly; and in any case Ismail Pasha intended his army for a very different use, against the Abyssinians. Fadeyev hurriedly set out for the real scene of action and was back in Russia at the end of May 1876. The authorities succeeded in stopping him from proceeding to Serbia, but they allowed him to re-enter the active army, and he will be met with later figuring as a stormy petrel in Belgrade and Cettinje.

The views of such a man on the Slav question would naturally

---

[1] Schweinitz, *Briefwechsel*, p. 47. These articles were republished in book form and soon appeared in a German translation with an alarmist, anti-Russian preface by Julius Eckardt.

[2] Stanton (Cairo) to Derby, no. 17, very confidential, 15 Jan. 1876, in *F.O.* 181/535.

present radical differences from the ideas already analysed. Fadeyev had no interest in the past, no concern for the slavophil tradition of emphasis on the spiritual and cultural union of the Slavs, no feeling for the unique mission of the Orthodox church and the civilization based upon it, no blind belief in the virtues of the Russian peasant. He looked upon the Moscow slavophils as having finished their role and as having, since the emancipation of the serfs, no practical programme.[1] Significantly he lived, in his later years, in St. Petersburg or Odessa, not in Moscow. He had the mentality of a militant adventurer. He could be direct and briefly to the point, but was apt to be carried away by fantastic exaggeration and atrabilious judgement. Of the Slav lands he really knew very little until his unwelcome appearance in Serbia in 1877; but he imbibed much from his friend Ignatyev and from the panslav group in Odessa. Above all he had a perfectly clear idea as to two fundamentals in the Slav question—force and Austria-Hungary.

His first book, *Russia's Armed Forces*, contained little of a nontechnical character, and panslavism was only incidentally urged, and in relatively moderate terms, but it enunciated without qualification the doctrine that force is the sole final arbiter in international affairs and the inevitable prerequisite for any great nation with a mission to fulfil. That the eastern question could only be solved by war on a great scale was even more emphasized in his *Opinion on the Eastern Question*. This brief, easily read, violently provocative outburst from Fadeyev was the most influential of all the expressions of panslav views of the time. First published in 1869, it was rapidly translated into most European and all the Slav languages, and was generally taken abroad to sum up the quintessence of panslavism.

Its resounding keynote was the watchword attributed to Paskevich, 'the eastern question can be solved only in Austria, not in Turkey; the way to Constantinople lies through Vienna'. Austria-Hungary cannot without committing suicide act otherwise than in a sense diametrically opposed to Russia: free Slav states in the Balkans would be impossible for the Austrians and the Magyars with their subject Slav races. 'Austria can

---

[1] *Russkoe obshchestvo v nastoyashchem i budushchem*, in his collected works, vol. iii, pt. i, pp. 102–4. He is writing specifically of slavophilism in relation to the internal problems of Russia, but the views here expressed are, I think, typical of his attitude to slavophilism in general.

hold her part of the Slavonian mass as long as Turkey holds hers, and vice versa.'[1] Turkey is looked upon as being in complete decadence, and neither her army nor her fleet are regarded as of any consequence. Militarily Russia can always forestall her western opponents, not only in the Balkans, but on the Bosphorus: with 100,000 men to mask the Bulgarian fortresses and a striking force of another 150,000 she can be in Constantinople in six weeks. But her line of communications is fatally threatened by the strategical situation of the Austrian empire. Hence the necessity of settling with the Habsburgs and of annexing Eastern Galicia and Bukovina, with their brother Slavs 'groaning on the Russian borders'.

Russia's 'historical individuality' is now pronounced, but it is not realized, and it can only be realized by expansion as the welder of the Slavonic world. 'The whole of Europe stands up against the historical development of Russia, threatening, as it does, a still greater breaking up of present systems. . . . The historical move of Russia from the Dnieper to the Vistula was a declaration of war to Europe, which had broken into a part of the Continent which did not belong to her. Russia now stands in the midst of the enemy's lines—such a condition is only temporary: she must either drive back the enemy or abandon the position.' She 'must either extend her preeminence to the Adriatic or withdraw again beyond the Dnieper'. Save for the members of her own family, the Slavs and the Orthodox, Russia has, and can have, no reliable allies. Least of all must Prussia (which Fadeyev already regarded as virtually united Germany) be accounted such, for she will stand with Austria-Hungary for the traditional German preponderance in the Danube valley, and for continued germanization of the Slavs. 'Russia's chief enemy is by no means Western Europe, but the German race in its enormous pretensions.' Thus, foreshadowing developments of the late eighties, he went on to argue that 'all the more substantial interests of Russia and Prussia are much more antagonistic than those of *Russia and France*'.

Fadeyev was not a whit depressed by his picture of an irreconcilably hostile Europe in the struggle that was inevitably to come. He did, indeed, admit as a weakness the small amount of interest that had hitherto been shown by Russia in her Slav allies

[1] My quotations are from the second English edition, published in 1876.

and her omission to establish herself as their undisputed leader, but he readily comforted himself with the recommendation that time and propaganda would quickly rectify the mistakes of the past. In any case the immense sympathies of the Slavs for Russia could be securely counted upon as her greatest asset when the opportunity came and her armies struck victoriously against their common foes. Then seven hundred thousand Slavs (a typically exaggerated figure) would rise in arms to fight on Russia's side. The Roumanians were to be won over by the gift of Transylvania; the Greeks by the gift of Thessaly, Epirus, and the Isles, but nothing more. The political objectives of the struggle for Slav emancipation were twofold: to secure to each branch of the Slavs its independent political and social life; and to combine with Russia in some form of confederation in which Russia was to be militarily and internationally predominant. 'Each tribe requires a Sovereign of its own for its domestic affairs, and a great Slave[1] Tsar for the affairs of all collectively.' Thus foreign policy and military affairs must be in the hands of the Tsar. He added that it was very desirable that Russian grand dukes should sit upon the new Slav thrones. Russia, however, was to make no annexations, except in the case of Eastern Galicia and Bukovina, and the southern districts of Bessarabia torn from her in 1856. Constantinople was left in the vague position of a free city for the confederation. As for the Poles, they 'will have to choose between the position of a younger brother of the Russian people and that of a German province'.

Such a programme of panslavism, however reckless in what it assumed and fantastic in what it omitted, could rouse all the more alarm abroad when in the course of the eighteen-seventies the renown of the Russian ambassador at Constantinople came to be widely spread as the able, unscrupulous, tireless propagator of closely similar ideas. It was above all the influence of Ignatyev which transmuted the aspirations of the Moscow panslavs into one of the main realities of the eastern crisis of 1876–80. Something has already been said of Ignatyev, and later chapters will necessarily deal in considerable detail with his moves and counter-moves during his struggle for Russian

---

[1] Slav was frequently at this time spelt in English Slave, thus evoking a wholly different range of associations from those suggested to Russians by the word *slavyansky*; Slav, which in sound is near to *slava*, meaning glory.

ascendancy in the Balkans. Here it may be convenient to set out a summary of his own presentment of his views which will show clearly that panslavism had become but another name for an aggressive, ultra-nationalistic policy directed first and foremost against Austria-Hungary and Turkey.[1]

Ignatyev in sketching in his memoirs his general policy in the Near East laid down three aims which Russian diplomacy must follow: the revision of the 1856 treaty of Paris (including the suppression of the collective guardianship of Turkey by the powers), the command of Constantinople and the Straits, and some form of common action by the Slavs under the direction of Russia. His attitude to panslavism is predominantly political, the religious and cultural aspects being merely useful adjuncts for the attainment of Russian predominance in south-eastern Europe. Ignatyev was not a man for whom the Orthodox church meant any deep religious experience or mystical communion. His attitude during the struggle between the Greeks and the Bulgars over the Exarchate is an excellent illustration of the way in which political calculations were the determinant factor. He knew that a schism would lead to internecine struggles among the eastern churches and a general lowering of the prestige of Orthodoxy which would be not at all to Russian interests: hence his original policy appears to have been to secure a compromise which would provide some nucleus for the nascent Bulgarian nation but which would not entirely alienate the Greeks. But as the prospect of any such agreed settlement receded he was quite prepared to tip the scales more and more decisively in favour of the Bulgarian extremists. Unable to prevent the Greeks from unyielding opposition, he stood out undisguisedly as the main protagonist of those in the Russian diplomatic service who thought in terms of Slavdom rather than in those of Orthodoxy. There could be no stronger contrast than that between Ignatyev and his subordinate Leontyev, occasionally, though erroneously, classed as a slavophil. Leontyev was for some ten years in the consular service in the Balkans and Constantinople. His first-hand acquaintance with both Bulgars and Greeks served to develop his convictions as to the primacy of 'Byzantinism' (the Greek-Orthodox culture and view of the world) and caused him to recoil in

[1] The following paragraphs on Ignatyev are based mainly on my article 'Ignatyev at Constantinople, 1864–1874', in S.R., vol. xi, pp. 343–4, 569–71.

horror from the deliberate rending of the Orthodox world by the Bulgarian intelligentsia in the name of that false nationalism, linked up with the principles of 1789, which for Leontyev was the curse of Slavism.[1] For Ignatyev, on the other hand, the whole question of the exarchate was simply one as to how could be secured for the Bulgars 'un noyau national qu'on serait libre de développer ultérieurement'; and by 'on' he meant primarily Russia.

The fundamental difference between the panslavism of Ignatyev and his like and the philosophical and religious slavophilism of the older type is equally well illustrated by Ignatyev's frank repudiation of any pretence at idealism in his championship of the Slavs. Sooner or later, he held, Russia must fight Austria-Hungary for the first place in the Balkans and for the leadership of Slavdom: only for the attainment of this task should Russia make sacrifices for the Slavs under Austrian and Turkish rule and be solicitous for their freedom and growth in strength. To aim merely at emancipating the Slavs, to be satisfied with merely humanitarian success, would be foolish and reprehensible.[2] Slowly they must be united in the form of a defensive union subordinated to the direction of Russia. Against Gorchakov he insisted that the Slav standard should be borne exclusively by the Russian Tsar: better to adjourn any idea of solving the Balkan question or of liberating Bosnia and Herzegovina from the Turkish yoke than yield anything to the inevitable rivalry of Austria-Hungary. All Ignatyev's efforts were directed towards working for the time when the development of Russia's strength and favourable conditions in Europe would allow of the attainment of a purely Russian solution of the eastern question, viz. the Straits at the disposal of Russia and the creation of brother states in blood and faith linked to Russia by the firmest ties. Of first im-

[1] For Leontyev's views see his *Vostok, Rossiya i Slavyanstvo*, vol. i (Moscow, 1885), a republication with some additions of his articles on the eastern question, notably *Panslavizm i greki* (1873) and *Bizantizm i Slavyanstvo* (1875).

[2] The same attitude is apparent in Fadeyev: when urging that the new Bulgaria should be contiguous territorially with Russia and should run south as close to the sea of Marmara as possible, he writes: 'To free the Balkan Slavs and turn them into a state without establishing assured communication with them by the Danube would mean freeing them not in our own interests but in the interests of our enemies.' H. Vanag, in *Istorik marksist*, 1935, no. 10, p. 62, quoting report of Fadeyev, 1877, in *Osoboe pribavlenie k opisaniyu russko-turetskoi voiny 1877-8 gg.*, pt. vi, p. 294 (St. Petersburg, 1911).

portance was the command of Constantinople and the Straits, as necessary for the security of Russia's Black Sea coast-line as for her political and economic expansion. She must be mistress of Constantinople by one of two means, either by complete diplomatic predominance there, as was largely achieved between 1871 and 1875, or by direct conquest if the opposition of the Turks and the powers rendered the former policy impracticable. Ultimately in any case a radical solution of the eastern question would have to be found involving the disruption of the Ottoman empire in Europe and defiance of the Habsburg empire: if the other powers combined with Turkey against Russia, Constantinople and the Straits must simply be conquered, and the Greeks, Bulgars, and Armenians won over to act as obedient tools of Russian policy.

Thus with Ignatyev, as with Fadeyev, two ideas predominated; that of an independent, anti-European policy of force, and that of a Russia whose destiny was to utilize the growing nationalism of the Slav peoples so as to disrupt by her own might the Austro-Hungarian, as well as the Ottoman, empires, leaving in their stead south-eastern Europe (and for Ignatyev above all Constantinople and the Straits) under her unquestioned control.

Of this newer type of panslavism no theoretical or systematic exposition was supplied by Ignatyev or Fadeyev. This lack was met by Danilevsky's *Russia and Europe*, subsequently styled 'the Bible of panslavism'.[1] Though first published in 1869 it was not very influential in Russia or much known abroad until a later period. Ponderous and very lengthy, it was not designed for wide consumption. It did, however, introduce a new note which helped to give it some immediate vogue. Danilevsky had been trained as a student mainly in botany and the natural sciences, and throughout his career, which was that of a government inspector of fisheries and other departments of agricultural economics, he retained the closest interest in them, Darwin becoming his particular bugbear. From his botanical studies he derived the idea of the struggle for existence as the dominating factor in the relation between states; force was justified as an inevitable, natural concomitant of the

---

[1] There is no English translation of it in the British Museum. The only German translation that I know was not published until 1920, and in a very much shortened version.

development of any healthy species. *Russia and Europe*, built up with much parade of scientific argumentation, heavily loaded with scientific analogies, seemed to give to panslavism a fashionable *cachet* of science.

Danilevsky's political views, apart from their setting and presentation, are closely similar to those of Fadeyev. He, too, denies the conception of humanity or civilization as a whole, and places in the forefront that of the struggle between different cultural-historical types, based mainly on language groupings. While in general agreement with slavophils as to the opposition between the Romano-German civilization of Europe and that of the Slav peoples, he considers this opposition to be fundamental in the sense that it is insuperable. Thus he, too, repudiates anything in the nature of Dostoyevsky's striving towards a universal brotherhood to which Russia should guide, not merely her Slav brothers, but the whole suffering world. Danilevsky's nationalism is as unadulterated as is Aksakov's or Fadeyev's. Slav civilization, above all as represented by Russia, is inevitably destined for a glorious future, but this future depends upon the political emancipation of the Slavs from western Europe, and such independence can only be attained by war. Thus only can the eastern question receive its final solution. Danilevsky has no doubts as to the outcome. Russia is taken as a match even for a combined Europe, and the Slavs can have the fullest confidence in their moral superiority over a Europe diseased through centuries of violence and now through economic dissensions and the undermining threat of socialism. Victory is assured, and will bring to birth a Slav federation under the leadership of Russia, into which must enter (besides the Poles) the non-Slav Greeks, Roumanians, and Magyars, and the capital of which is to be Constantinople.

Here, again, the sketchiness of panslavism as a political programme is apparent. With too little understanding of the Slav lands and with too little facing up to the obstacles in its path, it was much more of an emotional force than a planned creed of Russian imperialism. It is significant, for instance, that on the vital question of the future of Constantinople there was no agreement among the panslavs. All were indeed agreed that Constantinople 'must be ours'; but there were wide differences as to what exactly that meant. When the crisis of 1878 was reached, the lack of any clearly thought out solution was only too evident. While Dostoyevsky feverishly preached the necessity and rightness of the annexation of Constantinople by Russia as the head and guardian of Orthodoxy,[1] and while pious Orthodox circles, and particularly the court devotees, would not be satisfied 'until they sat cross-legged upon the crescent of Santa Sofia',[2] Fadeyev and others urged some kind of internationalization in the form of a free city, and Danilevsky diatribed against such an idea as converting what should become the capital of a Slav confederation into a hotbed of anti-Russian and anti-Slav intrigues of every description.[3]

One last figure, often placed among the panslavs, must be considered. Katkov in the seventies and eighties was very well known in the West as the most influential figure in Russian journalism and was regarded as a political power of great consequence. This was true under Alexander III, but his position is apt to be misconceived, and he was the reverse of a consistent supporter of panslav ideas. Katkov had begun as a westerner, an admirer of England, and a believer in free trade. The Polish revolt and 'nihilism' turned him to the right and he eventually belonged entirely to the reactionary camp of his close friend D. A. Tolstoi, from 1866 minister for education. His famous press campaign of 1863 against the Poles and foreign intervention was followed by a campaign for the russification of the western borderlands, and he came to be the mouthpiece of Russian nationalism against cosmopolitanism and western revolutionary ideas. But Katkov was never an adherent of the slavophils, though he had many links with them, and his attitude towards panslavism veered continually. He took a brief interest in the Bulgars in 1858, but thereafter paid very little attention to Slav questions, other than Polish, until the Moscow Slavonic Ethnographic Exhibition (1867), when for a time he took up the question of Eastern Galicia. A few years later, after reflecting the current of Russian opinion favourable to France as against Prussia, he was found to be loudly welcoming the new policy of the *Dreikaiserbündnis*, ridiculing the idea of the union of all the Slavs under one sceptre, and declaring that Austria and Russia could march

---

[1] *Dnevnik pisatelya*, collected works, vol. xi, pp. 281–3; vol. xii, pp. 71–3, 78–82, 354–60.   [2] Gorchakov on the Countess Bludova, *R.S.*, vol. cxxxiii, p. 96.
[3] Danilevsky in articles published in 1877, reprinted in R. Streltsov, *Rossiya, Tsargrad i prolivi*, pp. 66–70. So, too, Leontyev in *Grazhdanin*, 1878, reprinted in his *Vostok, Rossiya i Slavyanstvo*, vol. i, pp. 249–50, 254–5: cf. 76, 239.

in agreement and even assist each other in the Balkans.[1] This did not prevent him in 1876 from heading the nationalist lists and clamouring for war to save 'our oppressed Slav brothers', and in 1878 for the seizure of Constantinople. As a result of the Berlin congress he became openly antagonistic to Bismarck and advocated a policy of the free hand, but by 1882 he had swung round and was throwing the blame for Russo-German estrangement on Gorchakov, not Bismarck, and was lauding the *Dreikaiserbund* (and the *Dreibund*) as the coping-stone of monarchical principles. This attitude was part and parcel of his adherence to extreme reaction after the assassination of Alexander II, when his friendship with the new Tsar, Pobedonostsev, and Tolstoi (now minister of interior) to a large extent justified him in regarding himself as the unofficial adviser of the autocracy. Katkov was certainly not the passionate hater of Germany and lover of France that Germans have frequently depicted him as being, but the last two years of his life (1885–7) brought another shift which largely accounts for such views. In violent disillusionment over the Bulgarian crisis, he again championed a policy of the free hand, this time combined with the closest relations with France short of a written alliance. He was unsuccessful: Alexander III preferred to conclude the reinsurance treaty; nevertheless Katkov had put the possibility of a Franco-Russian understanding on the map, and six years later Alexander concluded an alliance. Katkov's international outlook was a compound of nationalism and conservatism. The two ingredients frequently clashed, and the latter was often uppermost. Just after his death his principal paper announced that 'panslavism in Russia is not the programme of any party, but the political confession of the Russian people'.[2] That had not been Katkov's consistent view, and in so far as it could be applied to his own career it would be better to substitute for panslavism Muscovite nationalism.[3]

Such were the main strands going to make up the tangled web of panslavism. Clearly it was not the organized power or carefully devised plan which it was represented as being abroad.

---

[1] *Moskovskiya Vyedemosti*, 5 and 10 Feb. 1874, quoted in *Avantyury russkogo tsarizma v Bolgarii*, p. 210.

[2] *Moskovskiya Vyedemosti*, 1887, no. 260, quoted in Nevedensky, see next note.

[3] Nevedensky, *Katkov i ego vremya*; Sementkovsky, *M. N. Katkov, ego zhizn i literaturnaya dyeyatelnost*; Grüning, *Die russische öffentliche Meinung und ihre Stellung zu den Grossmächten, 1878–1894*, pp. 37–48.

Yet the foreign view of it, though exaggerated, was correct in emphasizing the danger which lay in it. The panslavs, divided and few in numbers though they were, represented a sounding-board of the new, restless Russian nationalism. Through their excellent connexions with the Muscovite nobility, the Orthodox church, the court, the diplomatic service, and the army, this nationalism might, if events abroad gave the requisite shock, be capable of effectually diverting or even directing the policy of the Tsar and his immediate advisers. An outbreak in the Balkans, massacres of Christians, tales of heroic resistance, could be made to arouse again among the immense mass of the illiterate population of Russia the old traditional feelings that God had made the Turks to be the oppressor of the Orthodox and the Russians to be their saviour. With the tiny minority of the educated this same appeal of the panslavs to religious sympathy for the Balkan Christians could bulk large, while they could also find support, in the case of many, in a desire to escape from aimlessness and inaction by plunging into a cause. This last element in the panslav appeal in the late seventies brings out one of the two deepest motive forces lying beneath the turgid and often bombastic externals of panslavism. In its call to self-confidence, to action, to belief in Russia as a mighty power destined to shape the history of the world and fulfil a mission of her own, it responded to a deep craving for national recognition, all the keener after the humiliation of the Crimean war was set in such sharp contrast with the achievements of Italians and Germans in moulding their national future. And as a second motive force lay the reaction, so explicit in all forms of slavophilism or panslavism, against the claim of western European civilization to set up as the one true civilization to which all other peoples are or should be adapting themselves, a reaction which still remains in different guise one of the most potent influences in Russia of to-day.

5. *THE DREIKAISERBÜNDNIS*

While the fears and hopes aroused by panslavism and by the expansion of the Russian empire in Central Asia mark essential contrasts between the setting of the Near Eastern crisis of 1875–8 and that of 1853–6, the biggest contrast lies without any doubt in the conversion of Prussia into Germany. The new great power had fundamentally changed the interplay of

European forces. Berlin had succeeded to Paris as the key capital of Europe.

This change of balance, if so great a change there had to be, was not initially unsatisfactory to Russian interests. It is true that anti-Prussian, and then anti-German, feelings were becoming increasingly expressed in influential court circles in St. Petersburg, and in some circles in Moscow; and it is true that the personal relations between Gorchakov and Bismarck had assumed a dangerous character; but the German bogy in Russia must not be antedated, and dislike of Prussians or of Baltic Germans and an alien bureaucracy must not be identified with fears of a highly industrialized, militarist colossus. Such fears had not yet taken root; though Thiers had pointed prophetically to the future when on his fruitless mission to St. Petersburg after Sedan. And the deciding voice still lay with the Tsar and not with Gorchakov or the panslavs. When he telegraphed to his uncle, on the signature of peace preliminaries in 1871, 'Je suis heureux d'avoir été en situation de vous prouver mes sympathies comme ami dévoué. Puisse l'amitié qui nous unit assurer le bonheur et la gloire des deux pays', he meant sincerely and simply what he said.

Russia had emerged from the Crimean war isolated, save for Prussia; and Prussia was not strong enough then to serve as Russia's only friend. Hence Napoleon's outstretched hand was readily grasped. But it was the hand of a friend, not of an ally. The close working with France which was the dominating feature of Russian foreign policy during the five or six years following 1856 never developed into an alliance. Morny urged it. Gorchakov would have agreed, on certain terms. Napoleon III thought a close understanding sufficient. Alexander II, Prussian by sympathy and by calculation even before the beginning of his close personal relations with the Prince Regent in 1860, was prepared to work with France, but was disinclined for anything so close as an alliance. It was essential to make the most of the divergences, or to widen the breach, between France, Austria, and England; but Napoleon was not the man, nor France the country, to inspire any confidence in the heart or mind of Alexander. French designs in the East, above all French sympathies with the Poles, were fatal stumbling-blocks, while Napoleon's only too frequent coquetting with revolutionary principles did but undermine established order as appreciated by Alexander. 1863 revealed the rift nakedly.

Russia was again isolated, save for Prussia, stout in friendship though sheering clear of alliance. Thereafter the mending of Franco-Russian relations was precariously artificial, and more than ever dependent on Franco-Prussian relations. The one possibility of French policy effacing the effects of French support of the Poles lay in whole-hearted support of Russia in the Balkans and in removing the Tsar's two 'nightmares', the articles of the treaty of Paris ceding the three southern districts of Bessarabia, and prohibiting a Russian fleet in the Black Sea. Not the least of the blunders of Napoleon and Moustier was the fact that they made no consistent effort to utilize for this end the long-drawn-out Cretan question, in which Russia finally had to accept failure. Napoleon was equally remiss in making no play with a revision of the treaty of Paris (though he had used it to secure his treaty with Russia in 1859) until war with Prussia had actually broken out. When in June 1870 the Tsar and Gorchakov met King William and Bismarck at Ems, any doubts there may have been as to the attitude of Russia in case of war with France were set at rest. A month later the war came, and with it the Russian declaration of neutrality expressly conditional on that of Austria.

The payment for this most valuable support was promptly extracted by the Russians in the shape of their repudiation of the naval clauses regarding the Black Sea imposed upon them in 1856. To the Germans such a unilateral declaration, announced at a moment (31 Oct. 1870) when its reactions might jeopardize the rapid and successful conclusion of their struggle with France, was certainly distasteful; but, even apart from their previous assurances of general support for Russian desires to be rid of such rankling interference with national defence, Bismarck in the situation as it was could only support Russia to the full. The whole eastern question, even if it led to war, was unimportant to Germany as compared with the problem of France; under no circumstances must German relations with Russia be changed for the worse. Austria in the past had already admitted to Russia the justice of a revision of the treaty of Paris to her benefit, and now, though Beust was not less active than usual in his intrigues, she was too divided internally, too uncertain of her position, and too anxious to utilize the occasion for furthering her interests in the navigation of the Danube, to take any stand against Russia.

Hence the conference demanded by England was successfully weathered by Russia. Gladstone had always opposed the
Black Sea provisions of 1856, as constituting an impossible
affront to Russian honour and interests, and it was to the form,
not the substance, of Gorchakov's action that he objected so
strongly. He duly succeeded in securing the formal recognition
that treaties could not be modified or annulled except with the
agreement of all the signatories. Gorchakov equally attained
his object: there was no withdrawal of his circular dispatch
of 31 October. Its contents were internationally sanctioned in
the treaty of London (15 March 1871); henceforward Russia
and Turkey were unimpeded in the Black Sea. But as an
offset the international regulation of the Straits, as fixed in
1841 and reconfirmed in 1856, was now altered. After almost
ludicrous confusion over the formula, it was finally laid down
that the Straits were to remain closed to warships, but that the
Sultan might open them in time of peace to warships of
'friendly and allied powers' should he judge such action
necessary for the safeguarding of the treaty of Paris. That
treaty was expressly reconfirmed, save as regards the abrogated
naval clauses and the provisions as to the Danube commissions,
which latter were changed more or less in accordance with
Austrian and British wishes. The net result was an undoubted
gain for Russia. A fortnight before the final signature of the
treaty the peace preliminaries between France and Germany
had been concluded, whereupon the Tsar and the new Emperor
had exchanged the warmest telegrams. Each had good cause to
be satisfied with the other.[1]

The seal was thus set on the close relations existent between
St. Petersburg and Berlin. There was no Polish question to
divide them; no competing or conflicting interests in the Near
East; no real divorce in views on the structure of society and
the character of constituted authority. The dynastic interests

[1] For the repudiation of the Black Sea articles and the London Conference:
Goriainow, *Le Bosphore et les Dardanelles*, pp. 144–302; Prince G. Troubetzkoï, 'Les
préliminaires de la Conférence de Londres', in *Revue d'histoire diplomatique*, vol. xxiii
(1909); Noradounghian, *Recueil d'actes internationaux de l'empire ottoman*, vol. iii,
pp. 301–37; *G.P.*, pp. 3–25; Kurt Rheindorf, *Die Schwarze-Meer (Pontus) Frage
1856–1871* (Berlin, 1925); Baron A. Meyendorff, 'Imperatritsa Evgeniya; Rossiya
posle pleneniya Napoleona III', in *Sbornik statei posvyashchennykh P. N. Milyukovu*
(Prague, 1929), pp. 497–512; A. F. Tyutcheva, *Pri dvore dvukh imperatorov* (Moscow,
1929), pp. 203–7; B. H. Sumner, 'Ignatyev at Constantinople, 1864–1874', in
S.R., vol. xi, pp. 558–62.

of the Romanovs had been dangerously .touched in 1866, but Bismarck had stepped warily with Württemberg and Hesse-Darmstadt and Oldenburg. The unexpected rapidity and completeness of Prussian success both in 1866 and in 1870 had jarred and alarmed Russian opinion, and had foiled Gorchakov's hopes of Russian participation in a remaking of the map of Europe through a general congress. But these were relatively minor considerations to set against the great and solid fact that the new power of the first rank that had now been welded by Bismarck was linked with St. Petersburg by a tradition of friendship and co-operation which, save for the years 1813–15, had never been more fruitful in results than in the decade of the sixties, and by sufficient community of interests and lack of points of friction to make the continuance of this tradition a probable factor of great consequence in the shaping of the future.

How closely Russia could work with the new Germany depended, diplomatically, on Russian relations with beaten, and republican, France, and with beaten, and reconstructed, Austria. France, staggering under the results of the war and the Commune, was somewhat in the position of Russia after the Crimean war. She needed many years of internal recovery before she could stand forth again with confidence in the role of a first-class power. For all her financial strength, her home problems, the founding of the third republic, dominated. Her external relations, for the time being, were of secondary consequence. The eastern crisis came too soon for her to do.anything but remain well in the background: its coincidence with the crisis of MacMahon's presidency and the *Seize Mai* enforced a policy of substantial abstention.

Isolated in 1870, France had fallen. Her one and obvious foreign policy was to repair her isolation. Italy, with Rome now her capital, was unlikely, and by herself too weak, to be of assistance. England was too uncertain; under Gladstone non-committal and immersed at home, under Disraeli unsteady and alarming in colonial activities. Austria, even though now Austria-Hungary, might seem a likely possibility, but in fact Andrássy and Bismarck were to be successful in rendering stillborn any union of revenge for '66 with revenge for '70. In any case Austria-Hungary would hardly move closely with France unless assured of Russia. Might the Tsar, remembering the outstretched hand of Napoleon after the Crimean war, now proffer his own? This was the bogy which haunted Bismarck, frequently in such exaggerated shapes. An understanding between Russia and France, still worse with Austria-Hungary as well, would isolate Germany and hearten her ultramontane enemies. When the Tsar declared that Europe needed a strong France, did he mean more than to emphasize the desirability of a stable régime? Did he mean that France must not be further weakened even if the rebuilding up of her strength threatened Alsace-Lorraine and called forth preventive action by Germany? Did he mean that the neutrality of Russia now no longer could be assumed?

The war-scare of 1875 was to answer these questions in a manner which caused Bismarck much perturbation, but until then Gorchakov had not gone farther than mild coquetting with France. Some playing on German fears of a revived France was an obvious course for St. Petersburg. Russia would not give Germany a free hand by guaranteeing to her Alsace-Lorraine. But Russian concern at the new preponderance of Germany did not mean that monarchical Russia would seek to offset that preponderance by any rapid and permanent alinement with a republican France that was too weak to be reliable. Gorchakov himself talked much in the vein of a balance of power which would involve a recovery of French weight, but there were other factors shaping Russian policy in the seventies towards continued understanding with Germany, either alone or in conjunction with Austria-Hungary. And Gorchakov, despite his desire for France to be a greater make-weight, was at the same time committed to the current which set for both Berlin and Vienna. Russia's immediate interests in Europe lay in the Balkans. While France could be of no avail here, Austria-Hungary, for good or ill, was of the first consequence. When the Tsar came to England in May 1874 after the marriage of his daughter with the Duke of Edinburgh, surreptitious efforts were made to induce him to visit France. They failed entirely.[1] Three months earlier the Emperor Francis Joseph had paid a state visit to St. Petersburg;

[1] Jules Hansen, *Les Coulisses de la diplomatie; quinze ans à l'étranger (1864–1879)* (Paris, 1880), pp. 277–9. The marriage, which had been difficult to arrange, did not lead to any diminution of friction between Tsarskoe Selo and Windsor; Corti, *The Downfall of Three Dynasties*, pp. 209–16 (based on the papers of the Tsar's brother-in-law, Prince Alexander of Hesse, who had helped to arrange the marriage).

eleven months earlier the Tsar Alexander had done likewise to Vienna.

This realinement of Russia and Austria, through the *entente* of the three empires, and not a rapprochement between Russia and France, was the most important feature in European international relations during the five years following Sedan. It marked a complete change in Russian foreign policy as conducted hitherto by Gorchakov, and, to a considerable degree, a return to the very policy of Nicholas I and Nesselrode which Gorchakov and the bulk of Russian opinion had jettisoned after its humiliating break-down in the Crimean war.

Austria was now Austria-Hungary, the Dual Monarchy: a painfully achieved transformation of decisive importance. 1859 and 1866 had driven the Habsburgs from their position in central Europe and the Italian peninsula, and had forced upon them the sharing of power with the Magyars. The *Ausgleich* gave to the latter both unrestricted control in Hungary itself (which included Croatia, Transylvania, and the Banat), and a joint control in common affairs which in its practical working out placed the Magyars in a specially advantageous position. The security of the new dualist system was threatened in the years immediately succeeding 1867 by the possibility that the forces in Vienna which still looked westward might combine with France in a triumphant war of revenge against Prussia, and by the possibility that the Slav peoples of the empire might compel a transformation of dualism into some form of federalism. The danger of a war was scotched, if not killed, by Bismarck's diplomacy, by Russia's antagonism, and by Moltke's overwhelming rapidity. The danger of federalism remained for fifty years the pivotal problem of the empire; but the replacement of the Hohenwart ministry in October 1871 by the Auersperg régime and, in Trans-Leithania, the manipulation of the Magyar-Croat compromise of 1868 seemed to promise, for the time being at least, a continuation of the Dual Monarchy in the form demanded by the Magyars. That meant a shift of interest to the south-east, a new emphasis on Balkan affairs, a sharper outlook on the effervescent Slav world. The change at the Ballplatz in 1871 was symbolical of the new Austria-Hungary: the departure of Beust, the Saxon, with his eyes set west and his heart envenomed against Berlin; the arrival of Andrássy, the Magyar, hanged in effigy in 1849, prime minister of Hungary, now foreign minister to his Imperial and Royal Majesty.

So, more than ever, if Russia were to be able to regain southern Bessarabia and to make headway in the Balkans, it was essential that Austria-Hungary should either be confronted with overwhelming odds, or should be squared. Ignatyev and his supporters believed in the possibility of the former alternative, but they had failed to convince the Tsar. Gorchakov, after 1870, believed the latter alternative to be the only feasible policy for the near future. On the side of Germany there were no signs of Bismarck repudiating his past policy by completing German unity at the expense of the existence of the Habsburg empire and dividing the spoils with Russia. On the contrary the immediate drawing together of Bismarck and Andrássy showed that Russo-German friendship was not to stand in the way of close relations between the Reich and the Dual Monarchy. This caused the Tsar much perturbation,[1] until he was reassured that Berlin was ready enough that this drawing together should serve as a bridge to a triple *entente*. Austria-Hungary, then, must be squared; Berlin would approve and assist, provided that the squaring did not involve any manœuvres in the direction of Paris. Such a rapprochement of St. Petersburg with Vienna would strengthen the links with Berlin, would help towards keeping England isolated, and could secure the best possible position, under the circumstances, in which to face events in the Ottoman empire.

Thus came about the official burying of the rancour towards Austria which had been so conspicuous a feature of Russian policy since the 'treachery' of the Crimean war. And it was achieved, in the high circles of St. Petersburg, with remarkable speed. The path was eased no doubt by the replacement in November 1871 of Beust, whom Gorchakov disliked and profoundly distrusted, by Andrássy, and in the same autumn by the appointment as minister at St. Petersburg of Langenau, with his Russophil predilections and his hostility towards Bismarck.[2]

---

[1] Gauld, 'The Dreikaiserbündnis and the Eastern question, 1871–6', in *English Historical Review*, vol. xl, pp. 208–9. Cf. Odo Russell's suspicions that the Russians were fearing, rightly, that Bismarck intended an Austro-German alliance which would liberate Germany 'from the protectorate' of the Tsar; Russell (Berlin) to Derby, disp., secret, 12 Sept. 1872, text in *S.R.*, vol. viii, p. 707.

[2] Wertheimer, 'Neues zur Orientpolitik des Grafen Andrássy (1876–1877)', in *Historische Blätter . . .*, no. 2, pp. 255–6.

In July 1872 a visit to the Russian capital of the Archduke William, on the initiative of Andrássy,[1] went off excellently, and the Tsar followed this up by securing in September an invitation to visit Berlin at the same time as the Emperor Francis Joseph.[2] In April of the next year, 1873, the Emperor William came to St. Petersburg. In June the Tsar visited Vienna in state. The next February (1874), the Emperor Francis Joseph returned the visit. On each occasion the foreign ministers came with their sovereigns.

From the first meeting in Berlin the Russians were delighted with the Austro-Hungarians, and in particular were loud in praise of Andrássy. The two later meetings more than confirmed Gorchakov's good impressions of him, and he fully accepted Novikov's estimate of the Hungarian as 'le rival honnête'. The 1874 meeting consummated the *entente* between St. Petersburg and Vienna. Their legations were raised to the status of embassies. Even though dislike or suspicion of Francis Joseph persisted with the Tsaritsa and the Tsar, pro-Austrian and anti-German feelings were in the ascendant on the Neva. A year before, the British ambassador had noted that the German Emperor's visit had called forth 'no enthusiasm, no popular outburst of satisfaction'. And already during the Berlin meeting Gorchakov's ever-increasing jealousy of Bismarck had been marked. The war-scare of 1875 was to sharpen this personal hostility of the two chancellors to a real danger-point.[3]

Meanwhile, though Bismarck was frustrated in his hopes that the *Dreikaiserbündnis* could achieve a definite alinement against France, it served as a shackle to the unsteadiness of which Gorchakov was suspected; while the creation of an atmosphere of co-operation between Russia and Austria was of the utmost consequence after almost twenty years of hostility. 'C'était une œuvre de paix et de réconciliation', wrote Gorchakov of the

---

[1] Loftus, *Diplomatic Reminiscences* . . ., second series, vol. ii, pp. 32–3.
[2] L. Schneider, *Aus dem Leben Kaiser Wilhelms*, vol. iii, p. 254; Loftus, op. cit., pp. 32–3; *Wertheimer*, p. 71; *G.P.*, vol. i, pp. 197–201.
[3] *Wertheimer*, pp. 75–6, 85–8, 115–20, and in *Historische Blätter* . . ., no. 2, p. 258, quoting from Langenau's unpublished memorandum on his St. Petersburg mission; Goriainow, *Le Bosphore et les Dardanelles*, p. 309; Loftus, *Diplomatic Reminiscences* . . ., second series, vol. ii, p. 69. Corti, *The Downfall of Three Dynasties*, p. 215, using the papers of the Tsaritsa's brother, Prince Alexander of Hesse, who was in St. Petersburg at the time, depicts the 1874 visit as much less successful than Wertheimer represents it to have been, and considers that the *Dreikaiserbündnis* was much more due to the Archduke Albert than to Andrássy.

Berlin meeting, 'ni écrivailleries, ni protocoles; aucun engagement positif qui modifierait notre liberté d'action; en un mot, rien pour les archives diplomatiques, mais le résultat moral est immense.'[1] There is exaggeration in this (and the current reports of a renewal of the Holy Alliance wildly overshot the mark), but it is not far from the mark if the official relations of Russia and Austria only are considered. As Gorchakov said, nothing was set down in writing at Berlin; but there the way was paved for Schönbrunn and the Russo-German military conventions which were signed in 1873. At Berlin there was only amiable converse between Gorchakov and Andrássy, as to the Poles, as to Serbia, and as to their common interest in the maintenance of Turkey; if events there were to take a different course, Turkey should be left to her fate; both professed to be agreed that no state should interfere in the relations of the Sultan with his Christian subjects; Andrássy drew the corollary that if the latter rose in arms no Russian help should be given them; Gorchakov frankly declared that any forcible Austro-Hungarian intervention would create a conflict with Russia. At the same time he reported to his master that Andrássy stigmatized the rumours then circulating as to the acquisition of Bosnia-Herzegovina as false; the least extra weight would sink the Hungarian ship.[2] Such verbal interchanges in themselves were of very slight value, but they might lead on to a nearer approximation of views, to a setting down on paper of engagements, and even perhaps to a habit of co-operation.

At Vienna, during the Tsar's visit in June 1873, a written compact between the two sovereigns, declared to be independent of any changes in their foreign offices, was achieved.[3] There was to be mutual consultation even when the interests of their countries caused divergent attitudes towards certain questions; and there was to be no separation 'sur le terrain des principes qu'elles considèrent comme seuls capables d'assurer et s'il le faut d'imposer le maintien de la paix de l'Europe

---

[1] Letter of Gorchakov to Brunnow, 11 Sept. 1872, extract in Goriainow, *Le Bosphore et les Dardanelles*, p. 307.

[2] *Wertheimer*, p. 72; copies of Gorchakov's reports to the Tsar of 9 Sept. 1872, translated text in *S.R.*, vol. viii, pp. 402–8.

[3] Text of the convention of Schönbrunn, 6 June 1873, in Pribram, *The Secret Treaties of Austria-Hungary*, vol. ii, pp. 184–6; and of the accession of the Emperor William, 22 Oct. 1873, p. 186.

contre tous les bouleversements de quelque côté qu'ils viennent' (Art. 1). In the case of aggression by a third power menacing the peace of Europe, a mutual preliminary understanding was to be reached as to a common line of conduct without seeking or contracting any new alliances (Art. 2). A Russian proposal was made to add a military convention, similar to that concluded just previously with Germany, whereby either party would assist the other with 200,000 men if attacked by a third power, but the Austrians would not go beyond agreeing that, if as a result of the preliminary understanding military action became necessary, a special military convention was to be concluded (Art. 3).[1] A two years' denunciation period was laid down (Art. 4), and Germany was to be invited to accede. This the Emperor William did when he came to Schönbrunn later in the year.

The contents of this convention, the only written basis for the *Dreikaiserbündnis*, may be styled jejune and vague, and the Russian and Austrian archives have not yet revealed any specific reference to action being taken under the convention in the following years; yet it did represent a notable step in the attempt of Russia and Austria-Hungary to draw together in close connexion with Germany. It was intended by both parties to wipe out the previous twenty years. It did not mean that acute differences might not arise between them again in the future, but it did mean that there was somewhat less chance of differences becoming acute. The autumn of 1875 was to show that Gorchakov started by regarding the revolt in Herzegovina from the standpoint of the *Dreikaiserbündnis* and in the spirit of the Schönbrunn convention. The importance of this fact was not nullified, though it certainly was minimized, by the other broad fact that Ignatyev at Constantinople and growing forces within Russia were strongly antagonistic to the new policy of the Tsar and Gorchakov towards Austria-Hungary. Andrássy himself was only too suspicious of the intrigues of Ignatyev and the panslavs, but as long as Gorchakov retained the sole confidence of his master Vienna could rest reasonably assured that at least the official policy of Russia would continue along the lines of accommodation with the Dual Monarchy. That in itself was a considerable gain as compared with the days of Buol and Beust.

[1] *Wertheimer*, pp. 89–90.

While the Tsar's visit to Vienna resulted in the convention with Austria-Hungary, the Emperor William's visit to St. Petersburg a month before, in May 1873, resulted in a military convention with Germany. Its terms provided that, if either were attacked by a European power, the other would with as little delay as possible assist with an army of 200,000 effectives (Art. 1), its cost being met by the succoured power (annex). There was a denunciation period of two years (Art. 3), and Gorchakov was careful to insert into the preamble wording to the effect that the object of the convention was to consolidate peace and mitigate the chances of war in Europe.

This somewhat strange document was the product, not of the two foreign offices (neither Bismarck nor Gorchakov signed it), but of a section of the Russian military led by the aged field-marshal Berg, one of Nicholas I's right-hand men, later notorious as viceroy of Poland (1863–6). Berg's plan was for a 'triple alliance which should impose peace in Europe and allow a reduction of standing armies'. He had advocated it the year before, but it was considered premature to broach it at the Berlin meeting of the three emperors. He renewed his project in February 1873, and now in May he was successful at least to the extent that he and Moltke exchanged signatures to the convention just summarized. But he failed to persuade the Tsar at once to agree to associating Austria-Hungary with it; according to Gorchakov both he and Bismarck disliked that idea, holding that absolute secrecy was necessary for fear of leakage to Paris and especially to London. A month later Berg was allowed to broach it when the Schönbrunn convention was negotiated, but, as already shown, he did not succeed.[1]

What precise meaning and how much significance should be attached to this convention it is impossible to estimate without more evidence than is at present available. The first of the May laws, the fall of Thiers, the German evacuation of French occupied territory, the Khiva expedition, combined in this May (1873) to create a particularly cloudy atmosphere. Bismarck apparently did not wish to commit himself to military

[1] Reuss (St. Petersburg) to the Emperor William, 16 July 1872, to Bismarck, 10 Feb. 1873, *G.P.*, vol. i, pp. 198–9, 202–3; text of two notes of Gorchakov to the Tsar, 4 May 1873, in *Russko-Germanskie otnosheniya*, pp. 22, 24; on p. 28 (and in *G.P.*, vol. i, pp. 203–4) is printed the text of the military convention, signed on 6 May, and ratified the same day.

obligations; certainly he did not intend to 'go behind the back' of Austria; privately he took the line that the validity of the convention depended on Austrian acceptance; perhaps he regarded the Schönbrunn convention as superseding it.[1] The non-definition of attack in any case left, as usual, an ample loophole. Berg himself died next year. The Russian foreign office seem to have left the convention pigeon-holed; it was not their own handiwork. And the Tsar, who was always vague about engagements, seems to have forgotten it. At any rate it played no part in the succeeding years, during which no reference appears to have been made to it.[2]

The St. Petersburg visit in all probability did little if anything to strengthen the links between Russia and Germany. Bismarck professed that Germany had no political interests in the East, and was anxious to impress on his hosts that strict instructions had been given to German consuls in the Orient not to meddle with political affairs. This was to assuage Russian complaints of various difficulties encountered, particularly with the German consul in Jerusalem. For a time the outcome was satisfactory, but it was noted in St. Petersburg that Bismarck did not do more than express in very general terms German support for Russia in the East. He spoke calmly of the religious question in Germany, and seemed more perturbed as to socialism and its ubiquitous manifestations.[3]

It was the religious and not the social problem which in the two following years was to immerse Bismarck in a struggle,

---

[1] Bismarck's marginal notes on letter of Tsar Alexander to the Emperor William, 10 June 1873, in G.P., vol. i, pp. 204–5.

[2] Reference was made to it, and to the convention with Austria, during the 1880–1 negotiations for the second *Dreikaiserbund*; see, e.g., Simpson, *The Saburov Memoirs*, p. 116, where Bismarck is represented as saying, in Jan. 1880, that the military conventions 'were to be used as a prelude to a Treaty of Alliance between the three Courts', and as throwing all the blame on Gorchakov for the failure to conclude such an alliance. Article VI of the treaty of 18 June 1881 specifically abrogated the 1873 conventions.

[3] Text of reports of Stremoukhov to Gorchakov, 30 Apr., and Gorchakov to the Tsar, 1 May 1873, reporting conversations with Bismarck, in *Russko-Germanskie otnosheniya*, pp. 12–16, 20–2. The need for combating the International had been much discussed in 1872, notably during the Berlin meeting of the three emperors, *Wertheimer*, pp. 74–5; Russell to Derby, disp., secret, 12 Sept. 1872, text in *S.R.*, vol. viii, p. 705; copy of report of Gorchakov to the Tsar, 9 Sept. 1872, translated text in ib., p. 405; Moritz Busch, *Bismarck, Some Secret Pages of his History*, vol. ii, pp. 201–4. It seems that the French were energetic in encouraging action against the International; Gabriac, *Souvenirs diplomatiques de Russie et d'Allemagne (1870–1872)*, pp. 235–52.

the international ramifications of which were ultimately of great consequence to Russia. The psychological reactions of the strain of the *Kulturkampf* on Bismarck redoubled his nervousness and suspicions of France and magnified his exaggeration of possible combinations against him, especially on the part of Gorchakov, who he came to believe was consumed by personal jealousy and was heading the Tsar away from his loyal past in the direction of a francophil future. He was the more encouraged in this estimate by the fact of the long retention at the Berlin embassy of Oubril, who was both a trusted adherent of Gorchakov, and, with his Polish wife, an aider and abettor in Bismarck's eyes of ultramontane opposition to himself. Gorchakov's own son, at the Berne legation, added to Bismarck's disgust by his pro-French extremism; while Shuvalov, to and fro from London, deliberately encouraged his aversion to Gorchakov, depicted him in the worst possible light, and worked upon the Tsar to continue his trust in Bismarck and Russo-German friendship.[1]

The war-scare of the spring of 1875 brought Gorchakov into the full limelight as the would-be maintainer of European peace. It was the role that Bismarck regarded him as playing on this occasion which stamped itself indelibly on Bismarck's mind throughout the following years. Hence Russo-German relations during the first half of 1875 are of great importance for an understanding of later developments in the Balkan crisis which grew out of the events of the second half of that year.

The winter of 1874–5 saw Bismarck engrossed in the *Kulturkampf*, and Gorchakov continuing to refuse to be drawn in Bismarck's wake by standing against Papal or Catholic interests. This attitude was in itself reasonable, and was only to be expected, since the Russian government were engaged at this very time in the liquidation of their long wrangle with the Vatican over Catholic bishops in Russian Poland. But to Bismarck the Russian attitude to the Poles caused irritable uneasiness. During the same winter there had been renewed

[1] Hajo Holborn, 'Bismarck und Schuwalow im Jahre 1875', in *Historische Zeitung*, vol. cxxx, pp. 256–77, mainly based on Reuss's reports. Shuvalov had conversations with Bismarck on 18 Mar. and 5 May 1875. As an instance of Bismarck's recriminations against Gorchakov may be cited his belief that the *Kreuz Zeitung*, then waging a violent campaign against Bismarck, was in receipt of a subvention from the Russian government and was sent free to many Russian diplomatic representatives.

signs of Russia showing friendly feelings towards France. Le Flô, the French ambassador, and Decazes, the French foreign minister, were reported as playing up more than ever to Gorchakov. Gontaut-Biron, the French ambassador in Berlin, an ultramontane and a special bugbear of Bismarck, was believed (erroneously) by Bismarck to have paid a visit to St. Petersburg. Simultaneously there were misunderstandings between St. Petersburg and Berlin over affairs in Montenegro and in Belgrade. Reuss was on leave, ill; Alvensleben, the chargé d'affaires, too junior to be of effect. Bismarck took the opportunity to send on a special mission to the Russian capital one of his most trusted lieutenants, Radowitz.

The Radowitz mission has been represented, mainly through Le Flô, as a definite attempt by Bismarck to gain a free hand in the West for the destruction of France in exchange for an alliance and a free hand for Russia in the East. There seem now no trustworthy grounds for such a view. The origin of the mission was probably Bismarck's concern at the recent trend of affairs in St. Petersburg and its object merely to clear up misunderstandings and restore a more even tenor to the course of Russo-German relations. Radowitz himself, in his subsequent memoirs, emphatically repudiated the French accusations and maintained that he was purely concerned with current difficulties between the two countries. The German foreign office archives support this contention and furnish no evidence as to far-reaching designs against France. If Bismarck secretly instructed Radowitz to sound the Russians as to such designs, the evidence of this has not been forthcoming. It is very improbable that he made proposals such as have been attributed to him, and it is not probable that he made any definite soundings.[1]

It is true, however, that the Radowitz mission, which took place in February and March 1875, was interpreted immediately, at least in French circles, as intended to bind Russia to Germany against France. A report of the French chargé d'affaires in St. Petersburg sheds clear light on French alarms during the following month and on the desperate hopes pinned on Russia. He wrote, on 25 March, that the general belief in

[1] For the Radowitz mission see especially: Radowitz, *Aufzeichnungen und Erinnerungen*, vol. i, pp. 296–314; and Hajo Holborn, *Bismarcks europäische Politik zu Beginn der siebziger Jahre und die Mission Radowitz* (Berlin, 1925).

the diplomatic corps was that Radowitz had been secretly charged by Bismarck, without the Emperor's knowledge, to inquire as to the attitude of Russia in the event of a Franco-German war and had been authorized to make offers in regard to the eastern question. He added that Radowitz had completely failed in his task and had met with immediate opposition to any idea of war.[1] This French belief, even though probably erroneous, in the real object of Radowitz and in Russian opposition to German plans against France was the most important consequence of his mission. A second consequence, of some weight, was that Radowitz returned to Berlin having found Gorchakov not at all accommodating or to his liking, and harping much on Bismarck's nervous excitability. By the time of his return, 23 March, events in the West had moved rapidly towards the war-scare in which both Radowitz and Gorchakov were to play leading parts.[2]

Bismarck with alarming energy was hitting hard at the ultramontane enemies he espied all too readily abroad. Demands on Belgium were followed up by demands on Italy, and France was warned that she might be accorded the same treatment as Belgium. Then the German military authorities, obsessed by the idea of French rearmament, poured in a stream of proofs pointing to a coalition of forces against Germany and to the certainty of French *revanche* in the near future. An embargo on the French purchase of ten thousand horses was declared; the new French army law was denounced as a deliberately provocative step towards a war of revenge. Bismarck's secret service sources (which seem to have served him very exaggeratedly at this time) informed him of exceptional financial measures taken by the French. The press campaign in both countries was producing almost unbearable tension. On 8 April appeared the famous article in the Berlin *Post* headed with the direct question: '*Ist der Krieg in Sicht?*' The possibility of a preventive war at some date before 1877, when it was calculated that the French military preparations would be completed, was now not merely discussed by the newspapers; it was

---

[1] *D.D.F.*, vol. i, pp. 387–9. Le Flô, the ambassador, was on leave during Radowitz's visit. The date of publication of this volume, 1929, is posterior to that of Radowitz's memoirs mentioned in the previous footnote.

[2] For the war-scare of 1875, see particularly W. Taffs, in *S.R.*, vol. ix (1930–1), pp. 335–49, 632–49, analysing the crisis in the light of the published material and of her researches in the London and Berlin foreign office archives.

referred to unequivocally by Moltke, guardedly by Bismarck, and, most incautiously, by Radowitz in conversation with Gontaut-Biron, who promptly sent a highly incriminating dispatch to his government. German sources deny, or do not confirm, that Radowitz ever used the argument of preventive war attributed to him. Yet on the whole it is probable that he made reference to it: at least it is certain that such language was being used by those in responsible positions. Whether Radowitz was or was not guilty of the indiscretion imputed to him, Decazes, at the Quai d'Orsay, in any case did not fail to use it to the utmost of his ability. Gontaut-Biron's dispatch, together with an urgent appeal from Decazes, was sent (29 April) to the major powers, and to Brussels, the Vatican, and The Hague. Two days later Bismarck bluntly told Belgium that she had better look to her army, for she might need it sooner than she expected. On 5 May a note was presented to Decazes protesting officially against the French army increases and the hostility of the French press. On 6 May appeared Blowitz's article in *The Times*, which was virtually a last alarm-signal of Decazes appealing for Russian help to stay Germany. It was well timed, for on 10 May the Tsar and Gorchakov were due to arrive in Berlin.

The French pressure on St. Petersburg had been assiduous from the moment of Le Flô's return from leave (11 April). The highly strung Breton did all he could both to flatter and to alarm the Tsar and Gorchakov, striving to secure at the least a moral engagement of fullest support and the taking of the strongest possible steps in Berlin. When the Gontaut-Biron dispatch reached him, it was shown *in toto* to both (4 May), as was also an accompanying confidential letter of Decazes.[1] This went so far as to refer to the Russian assurances already given as constituting an engagement 'tirer l'épée pour nous', an interpretation immediately refused by Gorchakov. The French were indeed forcing the pace, for the Tsar, though he had been rash in his encouragement of Le Flô, had not lost all discretion. 'Les intérêts de nos deux pays sont communs', he told Le Flô (15 April), 'et si, ce que je ne crois pas, vous étiez un jour menacé, vous le saurez bien vite.' Then, after a pause, he added:

---

[1] The text of this confidential letter, which is to be distinguished from Decazes's circular of the same date (29 Apr.), referred to in the text above as 'an urgent appeal', is not printed in *D.D.F.*, vol. i.

'Vous le saurez par moi.' He confirmed this verbal engagement three weeks later, but did not commit himself further. Even so Gorchakov considered that the Tsar had gone too far, and he himself was far less specific; but from the first (12 April) he assured Le Flô that all his efforts 'tiendront à contenir les impatiences de Berlin et y faire prévaloir les idées de paix et de modération'; and he continued to give the warmest avowals that he was neglecting nothing to prevent peace being troubled. The combination of the Tsar's outspoken friendliness and Gorchakov's confident sympathy left no doubt that France was assured at the least of Russia's 'concours moral'.

The effect on Germany of this definite turn towards France on the part of Russia and of the open expectation that the Russian visit to Berlin would be the occasion for direct pressure to be exercised was seconded at this juncture by the unconcerted intervention of England. Derby instructed his ambassador at Berlin (8 May) 'to use every possible means to allay the misunderstandings which had arisen between France and Germany and to support the anticipated efforts of the Tsar in the same direction'. Derby also stated his intention of asking Vienna and Rome to act likewise. On 9 May, the day before the arrival of the Tsar and Gorchakov, Lord Odo Russell officially communicated to Bülow, at the head of the German foreign office, the fears of the British government that 'peace was threatened owing to German alarm at the rapid growth of French armaments', their certainty 'that France had no aggressive designs', and their readiness 'to do all in their power to dispel misunderstandings'.[1]

Whether Bismarck had or had not been hitherto unable to bridle the alarmist extremes of the general staff and the press, he now immediately closed the crisis by alining himself with the seventy-eight-year-old emperor, who had throughout been entirely in favour of peace, and by adopting the attitude that the cause the Russians had come to plead needed no pleading. No offensive action by Germany had ever been contemplated: the alarm had been engineered by the press and magnified by misunderstandings due to the military. The Russians were at once able to give absolute assurances to the French that there was no longer anything to fear, and that the Emperor and

---

[1] Derby to Russell, 8 May, and Russell to Derby, 9 May, as paraphrased in *S.R.*, vol. ix, pp. 640–1.

Bismarck were entirely pacific. The war-scare promptly died down; not least because the tone of the press immediately and completely changed.

Yet, though the Russians had succeeded, in combination for once with the English, their success left a fatal memory of humiliation in Berlin. Nothing could have been less diplomatic than Gorchakov's cock-a-hoop bantering of Bismarck. At their first meeting, on 10 May, he had played the part of 'protector of France and mentor of Germany' in a manner which could but infuriate the over-wrought German chancellor. 'In his vanity and desire to appear as still playing an important part in affairs, this conceited octogenarian had even asked for a categorical promise that Bismarck would never go to war—a promise he had refused to give because it would imply the existence of an intention on his part he did not in any way entertain. . . .' Gorchakov for his part gaily admitted having talked of such a promise, but said that Bismarck 'had only refused it in writing, and that he had declared that his word was sufficient'.[1] As the final goad to Bismarck's resentment came Gorchakov's circular telegram: 'L'Empereur quitte Berlin parfaitement convaincu des dispositions conciliantes qui y règnent et qui assurent le maintien de la paix.' Whether or not the well-known phrase 'maintenant la paix est assurée' originally figured in it and was omitted, as Bismarck recounted three years later, owing to his own express representations, Bismarck was substantially justified in feeling that 'maintenant la paix est assurée' represented the attitude of Gorchakov, with the addition of the words 'grâce à moi'.[2]

May 1875 had brought a disquieting alinement of Russia and England requiring that France must not be further weakened. One feature alone of the crisis was satisfactory to Bismarck. Andrássy had refused to make any move; and Bismarck was aware of the English invitation to Vienna to join in pressure on Berlin. Andrássy, disturbed though he was by what he admitted to be Bismarck's nervous restlessness and lack of good sense, maintained an attitude of cautious reserve, evidently hoping that it was safe to leave it to Russia and England to put a check on German designs, if such there really were, against the peace. Thus might Austria-Hungary, the

[1] Russell to Derby, disp., secret, 11 May, as paraphrased in S.R., vol. ix, p. 642.
[2] G.P., vol. i, pp. 283, 299–300.

one power to make no move against Germany, earn full gratitude from Bismarck. He was right in his judgement. War,
which he was the last to want, faded into the future. Bismarck
for his part neither forgot nor forgave the conduct of Gorchakov.
Nor did he forget the conduct of Andrássy. If, as the latter
rightly surmised, the interests of Germany would in the last
resort decide Bismarck to opt for Austria-Hungary as against
Russia, henceforward personal feelings would help to swing
him in the same direction.

So, as the summer of 1875 began, the *Dreikaiserbündnis* was
singularly frail. Russia had openly taken a stand against
Germany on the most vital question for the latter; Russian
neutrality could no longer be securely counted upon. Austria-
Hungary by her inaction had seemed virtually to support
Germany; there was no sign of the dreaded combination
between St. Petersburg, Vienna, and Paris. That between
St. Petersburg and London, though highly unpleasant in its
unexpectedness, was unconcerted and hardly likely to survive
its immediate purpose. On the other hand Russia and Austria-
Hungary, despite their different roles in the war-scare, were
officially on good terms. That was the main achievement of
the *Dreikaiserbündnis*. Now it was to be tested. In July 1875
revolt broke out in Herzegovina.

II

THE BALKAN BACKGROUND

'THAT Turkey is weak, fanatical, and misgoverned no one can honestly deny.' So the Great Elchi wrote in extreme old age; and he went on to emphasize that Turkey could not expect a continuance of the tripartite guarantee of 1856 when reckless extravagance had brought her to financial destitution and when scarcely anything effective had been done to carry out the promised reforms; on the contrary, the provisions of the treaty of Paris combined with financial interests now gave the powers the right to impose a combined policy of tutelage, involving a strong European commission to superintend reforms and in the last resort involving even occupation, though a strictly limited one.[1] This revulsion on the part of so great a champion of friendship with Turkey bears striking witness to the two greatest changes in the international position of Turkey since the Crimean war: her loss of support through failure to carry through the *Tanzimat,* and her financial dependence on the West, itself the most far-reaching symptom of many foreign borrowings of other kinds. The *Hatti-Humayoun* of 1839 had professed to inaugurate an era of reform: little was actually done, and by the *Hatti-Humayoun* of 1856 the Sultan had undertaken to execute and extend the reforms; yet after the respite of twenty years so little appeared to have been accomplished that the moral assets of Turkey were very slender. Perhaps of even greater significance was the effect of financial dependence.[2]

This was a new feature. Since 1854 Turkey had contracted fourteen loans of various kinds with a nominal capital of about £200,000,000 sterling, requiring finally some £12,000,000 sterling a year to meet annuities, interest, and sinking fund, a sum which absorbed rather more than half the total annual

---

[1] Stratford de Redcliffe, *The Eastern Question,* a republication of his articles and letters to *The Times* between 1875 and 1878. While by then dubiously turkophil, he remained almost as anti-Russian as ever.

[2] For Turkish finances I have relied chiefly on A. du Vellay, *Essai sur l'histoire financière de la Turquie* (Paris, 1903); C. Morowitz, *Les Finances de la Turquie* (Paris, 1902); and D. C. Blaisdell, *European Financial Control in the Ottoman Empire* (New York, 1929). See also N. Iorga, *Geschichte des osmanischen Reiches . . .,* vol. v, pp. 541–4, and the references given there.

resources of the government. Three of these loans were
guaranteed on the Egyptian tribute, the remainder on the
customs and various internal taxes. There was thus an essential
difference between Turkish and Russian borrowing. Turkish
finances were becoming more and more tied to foreign banks
and foreign bondholders with guaranteed rights. In case of
default there was the probability of some measure of interference with Turkish internal affairs. Permanent financial
intervention in due course did take place in 1881 in the shape
of the Administration of the Ottoman Public Debt, and this
was the direct result of default. The internal crisis of 1875–8
in European Turkey was in part occasioned and greatly
intensified by pressure of taxation and financial penury. When
in 1874 the Ottoman Bank had to float an issue of nominally
£40,000,000 sterling at a price of 43½ (the average issue price
of previous loans had been about 60), the limit was reached.
In October 1875, three months after the outbreak of the
revolt in Herzegovina, the Turkish government, owing as was
widely believed to the influence of Ignatyev, announced that
for the next five years they could pay only half the interest due
on the foreign loans, plus a certain compensation, and by April
1876 there was a complete suspension of all interest payments,
which were not renewed until five years later.[1] Turkey could not
have faced Europe in a worse position, and the effect on the
British political world was disastrous; the change from 1853 to
1876 was drastic.

European financing of the Ottoman empire had been at first
British and French, then predominantly French. The new
banking institutions were in consequence mainly French and
British, led by the Ottoman Bank, set up in 1863, with a
Frenchman at the head and an Englishman as second in
command. Vienna began to display some activity from the
end of the sixties, mainly in connexion with Baron Hirsch's
complex railway plans. Of the crop of banks and financing
houses which appeared in Constantinople in the sixties and
seventies only one, and that small and unimportant, was
Russian. When in 1881 the Governing Body of the Ottoman
Public Debt was set up there was no Russian on it, for Ottoman
bonds were not held in Russia. Nearly 70 per cent. of these

[1] Neither the partial nor the total suspension of interest payments applied to the
1854, 1855, and 1871 loans, which were guaranteed on the Egyptian tribute.

were held in France and England; the holdings in Austria-Hungary took last place.[1]

'The borrowed sums went to meet the extravagance of the sovereign, the service of former loans, the military expense of an insurrection in Crete, and to repair the damages of the Crimean War. A bare 10 per cent. was so used as to increase the country's economic strength. The borrowing country had no budget system. Its public accounts were elementary and made no separation between the financial affairs of the state and the sovereign. No constitutional control existed over the borrowings of the sovereign or his use of the proceeds. . . . Bankers, local and foreign, matched their wits against circumstance. When one group among them would not lend another would, provided the return offered was high enough (a substantial part of the debt bore an effective interest rate of over 10 per cent).'[2]

With this foreign money a hectic beginning had been made with railway building, and by 1875 the revolution in communications had proceeded far enough to affect profoundly the finances and the economic future of Turkey. For the past fifteen years railway projects had been an unending source of financial intrigue and commercial rivalry. In the sixties the British, for the time successfully tapping the Roumanian market, built two lines from the Black Sea to the Danube, Constanza-Cernavoda and Varna–Rustchuk, but by 1870 Ignatyev's influence at the Porte was powerful enough to ruin the prosperity of the former line.[3] The Sultan's craze for railways came now to centre above all on Baron Hirsch, the cosmopolitan financier, Bavarian by origin, Viennese and Parisian by banking interests, through whom the Orient line, planned to link Constantinople with Austria-Hungary, was being built. This line was by 1877 far enough advanced to be already of great military importance for the Turks. They could rush troops by train from Constantinople and Adrianople to Philippopolis for the defence of the Balkan passes. One branch joined Adrianople to Dedeagach on the Aegean; another was thrust forward northwards to Yamboli. The main line as yet ended a little to the west of

[1] Adib Roumani, *Essai historique et technique sur la dette publique ottomane* (Paris, 1927), p. 135, gives the following percentages for the holdings of Ottoman bonds in 1884: France 39·99, England 29, Turkey 7·93, Belgium 7·20, Holland 7·59, Germany 4·7, Italy 2·62, Austria-Hungary 0·97.

[2] H. Feis, *Europe the World's Banker, 1870–1914* (Yale, 1930), pp. 313–14.

[3] Pokrovsky, *Russkaya istoriya s drevnyeshikh vremen*, vol. iv, p. 251. For railways in the Balkans see maps between pp. 240–1 and 410–11.

Philippopolis. The long gap Sofia–Nish–Belgrade remained to be filled, and to be a battleground for Austrian and Russian interests, and was not completed till 1888. An adjunct to the Orient line, the Vardar valley railway, had made more progress: by 1878 Salonica was linked with Mitrovica, the key-point of the *sanjak* of Novi Bazar. In the north of Bosnia there was one light railway from Banjaluka intended to link up with the Croatian lines. Here again Austrian commercial circles were beginning to bestir themselves with plans for a through route from Salonica via Novi Bazar and Bosnia or by effecting a junction with the Orient line at Nish, as was eventually done. It was most unsatisfactory for Vienna to see the new Turkish railways start from the sea and remain unlinked with its own system. Whereas before the Crimean war the lion's share of the external trade of European Turkey had fallen to Austria-Hungary, this (save as regards Roumania) had now passed to England. By the end of the seventies Austrian industrialists were awake to the unpleasant fact that English textile goods had a virtual monopoly of the Turkish markets, and that the needs of the Austrian army in Bosnia and Herzegovina were met more cheaply by English goods coming via the Salonica–Mitrovica railway than by Austrian goods.[1] In Asiatic Turkey the only railways as yet were from Constantinople to Broussa and two lines from Smyrna operated by British syndicates. Communications with the Caucasus frontier remained as they had been at the time of the Crimean war.

The most immediately serious feature of this railway building was the impossible strain placed upon Turkish finances. The orgy of corruption and extravagance that accompanied Baron Hirsch's numerous projects, coupled with the reactions of the international financial crisis of 1873, called forth from some of the best experts on the spot predictions of an early declaration of bankruptcy, predictions that were duly reported by Ignatyev to his government with the satisfaction of one who had con-sistently opposed the mania for Turkish railway construction and struggled against the Sultan 'en proie à une véritable fièvre de chemin de fer'.[2]

---

[1] Skazkin, *Konets avstro-russko-germanskogo soyuza*, vol. i, pp. 256–7, citing P. Dehn, *Nach dem Orient*, and *Oesterreichs Handelsinteressen im Orient* (Vienna, 1878).

[2] Skazkin, op. cit., vol. i, p. 259, quoting Ignatyev to Gorchakov, 3 May and 19 June 1873. Cf. Ignatyev's 1874 memorandum, text in *Izvestiya ministerstva inostrannykh dyel*, 1915, bk. 4, pp. 231, 234–6.

The Sultan's spendthrift passions, which reached limits excessive even for Constantinople, were in themselves an outstanding reason for Turkish bankruptcy. Abd ul-Aziz, K.G., in succeeding Abd ul-Medjd in 1861 as a young man of thirty, had succeeded also to the financial chaos left by his brother. This he drastically accentuated in the next fifteen years. Apart from personal lavishments, especially upon his palaces, enormous sums were squandered upon the navy. Although the result was the creation of an imposing fleet, British-built, with a retired British rear-admiral in control, the war with Russia was to reveal it as a costly plaything, of very little effect. Great sums likewise had been poured out on the army, but with very different results. When it came to the test, the changes introduced on the whole proved their value. The artillery in particular was well equipped and up to date. There were appalling deficiencies in the armies operating far from Constantinople, deficiencies to which the admirable, unexacting Anatolian soldiery were only too well inured, but nearer the capital they were better provided technically than ever before. Still, as of old, the army was recruited only from Moslems.

It was not only the army, the navy, railways, some economic development, international finance, that were spelling out change in the Turkey of these two decades. Much had been put on paper, something accomplished, in the way of internal reforms. These might aim at remedying the lot of the *rayas*, but they could not result in altering their fundamental position of inferiority. The continuance of Ottoman rule in Europe must still mean the superiority of the conquerors (the minority) at the expense of the conquered, a superiority rooted in the Moslem control of the army and in the working effects of Moslem law. This was the irremovable obstacle in the path both of the French idea of a fusion of races, to be achieved through the sincere application of administrative uniformity and civil and political equality, and of the somewhat similar ideas of the more extreme liberals among the 'Young Turks'. The Russian alternative of decentralized autonomy could be made to fit in much better with the historical past of the Ottoman empire, but by the third quarter of the nineteenth century it was open to fatal suspicions. As formulated by the Russians themselves it meant that 'l'on devait offrir à chacune d'entre elles [the peoples within the empire] des garanties *spéciales*, en mettant à profit les institutions religieuses et communales déjà existantes et en s'efforçant avant tout d'adapter ces dernières au principe *nationale*'.[1] Naturally this was taken to amount to a policy of dissolution, to the advantage of Russia; and in any case the Russian plan ran counter to the most essential feature of the reforms inaugurated since the Crimean war.

This feature was the attempt to transform the old, decentralized, not systematically intolerant admixture of powerful pashaliks and religious and communal autonomies, and to substitute for it a new centralization, radiating out from Constantinople by telegraph, borrowing something of the forms of the Second Empire. By 1875 the question had grown acute whether this centralizing process was to continue under the almost unlimited sway of the Sultan or whether his power was to be curbed by a constitution, by some effective ministerial control, and perhaps some species of elective assembly. The deaths of Fuad and Ali Pashas, in 1869 and 1871, had removed the two men whose complementary abilities and characters had inspired respect in western countries and had acted as a check upon the Sultan's aberrations. To what a pitch Abd ul-Aziz's mental condition was reduced may be judged from the fact that between September 1871 and February 1874 there were no less than six grand viziers, and no less than seventy-two changes in the *valis* within the space of fourteen months. Such methods, combined with his financial prodigality, were leading to disaster. 'In the old days the odium could be thrown on the Grand Vizier. Every one knew that this system was now purely personal, and criticism was thus directed straight at the Pàdishah.' The 'Young Turks' were becoming more and more urgent for revolution, and they had their man of destiny in Midhat Pasha, with his widely earned reputation for efficiency and his professed policy of greater justice to the Christians and a real share for them in local government. The deposition of a Sultan was nothing new in the annals of the Ottomans. On the other hand, a constitution was new, and Midhat had to

[1] Russian memorandum of 1867 quoted in Engelhardt, *La Turquie et le Tanzimat*, vol. i, p. 220. See also the Russian memorandum of 18 Apr. 1867, developing in detail the Russian arguments in favour of a policy of national autonomies as against one of assimilation; text in Testa, *Recueil des traités de la Porte ottomane avec les puissances étrangères*, vol. vii, pp. 446–55.

face the insuperable difficulty that 'it was not possible to have a constitution predominantly Turkish, and yet to do complete justice to Christians'.[1]

Behind the particular problem of Sultan Abd ul-Aziz, brought to a head by the revolt in Herzegovina and its repercussions, lay the deeper problem of the modernization of Turkey. 'The fish rots from the head', runs the proverb. There might be little real doubt as to the vitality of the Turks in Anatolia, but they seemed unable to save their empire in Europe by adaptations of their old system of government to meet the impact of western forces and new strivings among the peoples they ruled. The problem was of extreme complexity, involving as it did the transition of the Balkan peninsula from the Middle Ages to a new era. On the one hand, 'the European powers, which had gone through the most violent struggles and acute crises in evolving the modern state, seemed to expect the Ottoman government to effect this change on the spur of the moment, though the difficulties with which it had to contend were much greater than those faced by almost any other nation'.[2] On the other hand, the nineteenth century, by importing into the Ottoman empire western ideas of nationality, based generally upon the territorial, independent state, was causing a slow break with the hitherto almost unquestioned ideas of the continuance of the empire in some form or other, of a composite organization of partially autonomous religious communities and vassal tributary principalities. By 1875 the fermenting effects of this new nationalism were dangerously felt. Fired by the example of Italy, the Roumanians and many of the younger generation among Serbs, Bulgars, and Greeks thought and felt in terms of nationality which spelt a disruption of the old empire.[3]

In the twenty years since the treaty of Paris the control of the Ottomans over their polyglot empire had been steadily weakening in almost every quarter outside of their Anatolian bulwark of strength. Southern Arabia was the one big exception. In those regions, thanks to the opening of the Suez Canal

---

[1] Temperley, 'British policy towards parliamentary rule and constitutionalism in Turkey (1830–1914)', in *Cambridge Historical Journal*, vol. iv, pp. 169–71.

[2] Langer, *European Alliances and Alignments, 1871–1890*, p. 61.

[3] See particularly N. Iorga, 'L'origine des idées d'indépendance balcanique', in *Le Monde slave*, July 1927, pp. 73–93.

and the possibility of new naval activities, a series of campaigns had much increased Turkish authority. Elsewhere the tale was very different. The outbreak in 1860 of fighting between Christians and Moslems in Syria and the Lebanon had brought European intervention, a French occupation, and the enforced acceptance by the Turks of a special régime which greatly strengthened French predominance. In Egypt Ismail had won virtual independence of Constantinople, while at the same time subjecting himself to fatal dependence on French and British loans. In 1866 he had acquired Turkish official sanction for his contract with de Lesseps. At the outbreak of the Cretan revolt he had gained his great object, the official recognition by the Sultan of hereditary succession by primogeniture, though at the cost of the Egyptian tribute being nearly trebled. A year later, in return for his assistance in Crete, he received further important privileges and the title of Khedive, and although this was succeeded by a Turkish attempt, partly at British instigation, to deprive him of his commanding French support, the fortunes of Ismail did not suffer from the collapse of his protectors in 1870. A new *firman* in 1873, officially communicated to the powers, gave him almost complete satisfaction as regards army and navy, foreign affairs, and succession. Egypt was virtually lost to Turkey. Tribute and the possibility, continuously utilized, of playing off the powers in the Egyptian financial morass were all that substantially remained to Constantinople.

Crete, apart from Arabia, provided the one success of Abd ul-Aziz, and even there the *règlement* of 1868 had had to be concerted with the powers, and was to tie the hands of the Turks for a generation to come. Still, the revolt of 1866–8 had been quelled; the Cretan proclamation of union with Greece nullified by Hussein Avni's final repression; the powers easily kept divided by Ali Pasha's diplomacy and their own conflicting interests. The French had not seen fit seriously to use the Cretan question for a rebuilding of close relations with Russia, fatally antagonized by their support of the Polish revolt of 1863. They were to pay the cost in 1870. The Russians had failed in their support of the Cretan efforts to join Greece; and Ignatyev and others had not succeeded in their intrigues for a general rising of the Christians in conjunction with the revolt. The Greeks, despite the marriage of King George in 1867 to a Russian princess, had been ignominiously compelled to yield to an effective Turkish threat of war and to abandon assistance of their compatriots in Crete, Thessaly, and Epirus.

In Turkey itself Hellenism was being more and more seriously challenged since the Crimean war by the painful birth of a new Balkan nationality, owing much to Russian midwifery.[1] The new Bulgaria was being fashioned by four conjoined means: an intellectual and cultural rebirth, Russian assistance, the struggle for a national church, and revolutionary conspiracies. The great mass of the Bulgars, some three to four million in all, were illiterate peasants, untrained to arms and mainly without them, hard-working, by no means unprosperous, living in large compact blocks north of the Balkan range and in some areas south of it, but elsewhere interspersed with Greeks, Serbs, Turks, and other Moslems. After 1864 the settlement of Circassian colonies had still further complicated the ethnographic map and had ruinously increased banditry. In the mountains little bands of *haiduks*, half freebooters, half champions, lived a life of precarious freedom and vendetta against all whom they styled oppressors of the Bulgarian peasant. They formed the one element of peasant stock from whom could be formed daring revolutionaries (somewhat on the model of the *carbonari*), gradually to be transformed into the *comitadjis* of dubious fame.

The better-off Bulgars (the *chorbadjis*) were a small minority. This middle class had been in danger of completely succumbing to Hellenism. They had written in Greek or at best in Bulgarian with Greek script. To be cultured, to be up to date, was to copy Greek ways. The grip of the Orthodox church lay heavy on the land, and that meant the dominance of the Patriarch, the Phanar, and Athos. Church posts were almost monopolized by Greeks. Greek was the usual language of the services. The few schools were almost all monastic schools where everything

[1] For Bulgaria I have used mainly Hajek, *Bulgarien unter der Türkenherrschaft*; *Proslava na osvoboditelnata voina*, especially N. Bobchev's article 'Slavyanofilskoto dvizhenie v Rusiya i novoblgarskoto obrazovanie'; S. Radev, *Stroitelite na svremenna Blgariya*, vol. i; Prince Gregory Trubetskoy's article on the Bulgarian schism in *Revue d'histoire diplomatique*, vol. xxi; and Ignatyev's 1874 memorandum in *Izvestiya ministerstva inostrannykh dyel*, 1914 and 1915. The four volumes of Naiden Gerov's private and official correspondence are a mine of information on Russo-Bulgarian relations after the Crimean war; *Iz Arkhivata na Naiden Gerov*, and *Dokumenti na blgarskata istoriya*, vols. i and ii. Additional information and references, particularly on the struggle for the exarchate, are given in my article 'Ignatyev at Constantinople, 1864–74', in *S.R.*, vol. xi, pp. 566–71.

was Greek. Two monasteries only—one on Athos, the other the famous sanctuary of Rila—had preserved the memories of the olden days of Bulgarian greatness. Among the main mass of the Bulgars there was ample basis for material discontent, particularly against the Greek higher clergy. The taxes levied by these for their own support and that of the patriarchate and its hangers-on in Constantinople were increasingly heavy, and usually arbitrary. The winning of an independent kingdom of Greece and, thirty years later, the secularization of monastic property in Wallachia and Moldavia had very gravely damaged the financial interests of the patriarchate and its allies, and the Bulgars were additionally fleeced to make good the gaps. The net result of this and other factors was a social and economic cleavage between the great majority of the clergy and their nominal flock, which was intensified by the long and intimate connexions between the Greek hierarchy and the Turkish administration. It was inevitable that, if there were to be a Bulgarian national regeneration, it should be founded on opposition to the Greeks as largely as to the Turks.[1]

The sole initial outlets to the world at large were provided by the thriving Bulgarian colonies in Constantinople (thirty to forty thousand strong), Bucarest, and Odessa, and by connexions with Belgrade and with the Serbs in Hungary. It was from outside Bulgaria itself, above all from Odessa and Constantinople, that from the eighteen-twenties onward began the rebirth of Bulgarian nationalism, mainly with Russian assistance. Venelin, Pogodin, and other Slavophils, and the Palauzov and Toshkovich families in Odessa, aroused the first interest of Russians in Bulgaria, and started, on a very small scale, the work of educating the Bulgars. The official Russia of Nicholas I had not assisted these efforts. The Tsar and Nesselrode were deaf to any ideas of revolutionary nationalism, and took hardly any interest at all in the Bulgars. Only at the very last, in the winter of 1853–4, did Nicholas change course and contemplate the emancipation of the Bulgars: then it was too late; the scene rapidly shifted from Silistria to Sebastopol. The Bulgars looked back to two Russo-Turkish

[1] Already a generation earlier, during the 1828–9 campaign, the hostility of the Bulgars to the Greek upper clergy, as much their oppressors as the Turks, and Greek suppression of Bulgarian nationalism had been apparent to the Russians; see F. P. Fonton, *Vospominaniya* (Leipzig, 1862), vol. ii, pp. 71–3, 180, 195.

wars and two Russian occupations followed by abandonment
to the tender mercies of the Turks. However warm Moscow
might be, St. Petersburg appeared as treating the Bulgars solely
in its own interests. Russia had failed them in the hours of
victory in the past; in the Crimean war she failed them again
by revealing her feet of clay. A generation of young Bulgars
was to grow up with few romantic illusions about the fraternal
aid of Tsarist Russia.

The most complicating change in the period after 1856 was
this advent of a new generation of *émigré* nationalists imbued
with vague revolutionary socialism, usually violently hostile to
those of their own people who could be styled *chorbadjis*, the
older men of means and affairs, who wanted not to break
through old bonds, but to file them through, and who believed
in working closely with the Russians.[1] Many of the new
generation, on the contrary, looked askance at Russia, and some
came under the influence of the Polish refugees in Turkey.
The Bulgars must work out their own salvation for themselves.
Rakovsky (though himself actually of the older generation;
he was born in 1821) led the way in bitter denunciation of
Russia; and for the decade following 1856 he was the dominating influence among Bulgarian revolutionary nationalists. His
successors, as leaders of the extremist organization in Bucarest
—Lyuben Karavelov, Levsky, M. Grekov, Christo Botyov,
Stambulov—all preached a general armed revolution for a
democratic republic on an equalitarian basis. Russia to them
meant either Tsarist oppression or *narodniki* example.

In the sixties joint action with the Serbs was to the fore and
received much Russian encouragement. Plans for a Bulgar-
Jugoslav confederation were hatched in 1867, but the Russians
could not combine the divergent parties among the Bulgarian
colony in Bucarest, and in any case the success of these plans
depended on Prince Michael of Serbia, who would not finally
commit himself. Two small risings, in 1867 and 1868, brought
no Serb co-operation, only drastic reprisals by Midhat Pasha.[2]

---

[1] The attitude of the *chorbadjis* living in Bulgaria was also naturally compromis-
ing towards the Turks; for an interesting defence of such moderates see the report
drawn up for Cherkasky in Dec. 1876, by a Bulgar, T. Minkov, and printed in
Ovsyany, *Russkoe upravlenie v Bolgarii*, vol. i, pp. 259–66.

[2] The risings were in part instigated and financed by Ignatyev through Naiden
Gerov, the Bulgarian nationalist leader and Russian vice-consul at Philippopolis;
see Gerov's letter to Stremoukhov, 21 Dec. 1867, text in *Iz Arkhivata na Naiden*

Serbs and Roumanians seemed but to be playing for their own hands. On their side the Serbs regarded with increasing suspicion Ignatyev's championship of the Bulgars and the extreme claims of the exarchate; the struggle over schools was promptly inaugurated in the disputed regions of Nish and Old Serbia, and the rift between Bulgars and Serbs was already opened even before Russian policy in 1877 and 1878 so disastrously antagonized the two peoples. Meanwhile the early seventies saw the Bulgarian revolutionaries in Bucarest struggling to compose dissensions among themselves and to carry out plans of covering Bulgaria with revolutionary nuclei in preparation for a general rising. 1875 was to give them their chance, and they did their best to take it. The Turks for their part succeeded in keeping themselves well informed of these secret societies. An abortive attempt in 1872 failed miserably, and enabled them to capture and hang Levsky, the ablest of the revolutionary leaders and by then the only one widely known in Bulgaria itself. There was no one who could fill his place. Next year the Turks soon stifled an attempted terrorist campaign; but their nerves were on edge and retaliation and outrages were constant. On the other hand, Midhat's rule in the new *vilayet* of the Danube, though it had been scarred by peremptory ferocity, resulted in considerable material improvement, and, as the Russians were soon to find to their surprise, the Bulgars as a whole were relatively prosperous.[1]

The radical, democratic nationalism of the Bulgarian extremists was an entirely unwelcome result of the Russian efforts to bring to birth a new Bulgaria. Russian cultural and educational propaganda among Bulgars had been multiplied after the Crimean war thanks to the Moscow Slavonic Benevolent Committee, and it now for the first time received state assistance,

Gerov, vol. ii, p. 287: for Bulgarian plans for co-operation with Serbia and Russian relations with the Bulgars in 1867 see particularly the correspondence between Gerov and Karakonovsky, the Bulgarian doctor at the Russian embassy in Constantinople, ib., vol. i, pp. 744–58, and Gerov's reports to Ignatyev in *Dokumenti za blgarskata istoriya*, vol. i, pp. 432–41, and the valuable article of P. N. Oreshkov, 'Ruska drzhavna prepiska po nasheto osvoboditelno dvizhenie (1866–1868)', in *Spisanie na Blgarskata Akademiya na Naukitye* (Sofia, 1935), vol. lii, pp. 255–328. After much intriguing two Bulgarian delegates were allowed to come from Bucarest to St. Petersburg and Moscow at the end of 1867.

[1] F. Kanitz, *Donau-Bulgarien und der Balkan*, vol. i (Leipzig, 1875), pp. 28–32, 113–14, on the effectiveness of Midhat in his starting of the new *vilayet* system; and cf. Temperley, 'British policy towards parliamentary rule and constitutionalism in Turkey (1830–1914)', in *Cambridge Historical Journal*, vol. iv, p. 179.

as well as encouragement from various high ecclesiastics, notably Philaret, Metropolitan of Moscow. Great efforts were made to develop educational and charitable institutions in Bulgaria, with the energetic support of the Russian embassy at Constantinople and Russian consulates. Between 1856 and 1876 about five hundred Bulgars were sent to Russia to be educated at the expense of the state, the Moscow or Odessa Committees, or private individuals. Here, as in Bulgaria itself, there was very close collaboration between the Slavonic committees and the department of Asiatic affairs, the ministry of education, and the Holy Synod. Hardly any of these students received a military training, a notable difference from what happened after 1878, and a glaring deficiency when it came to armed struggle.[1] They were supposed to come to Russia to be imbued with slavophil ideas of salvation through Orthodoxy, of antagonism to western civilization, and of co-operative union of the Slav races led by Russia. To this end they were mainly sent to various theological academies in Moscow, Kiev, and Odessa; but some also attended the universities of Moscow and Odessa, and the Richelieu high school at the latter centre, where student life was anything but calculated to sow the seeds of conservative panslavism, Odessa in particular in the sixties and seventies being a hotbed of 'nihilism'. The main attractions proved to be not Homyakov or Kirievsky, but Dobrolyubov, Chernyshevsky, and Russian versions of Saint-Simon, Louis Blanc, and Proudhon. Two of the foremost of the Bulgarian revolutionary leaders, Botyov and Stambulov, had been Odessa-educated and expelled for 'nihilist' connexions; a third, Lyuben Karavelov, had returned from his Moscow studies a revolutionary socialist and a violent opponent of panslavism. Among the Constantinople leaders, Dragan Tsankov had been sent to Kiev, but his subsequent career was the reverse of Orthodox: he led the Uniate movement of 1859–61 and thereafter was one of the mainstays of the extremist russophobe wing of the fighters for the exarchate.

Not all, of course, of the Bulgars sent to Russia thus fell away.

[1] In the risings in 1876 the only person to show any military ability was one Bulgar who had served in a Russian line regiment; Hajek, *Bulgarien unter der Türkenherrschaft*, pp. 283–4. When the Russians formed a Bulgarian legion during the 1877–8 war, it was officered entirely by Russians, save for seven officers in the Russian army who were by birth Bulgars; *Proslava na osvoboditelnata voina*, p. 323.

They included a number of those who subsequently built up the Bulgarian church and filled other posts in the young Bulgarian state, among them Anthim, the first Exarch, Naiden Gerov, who was for long invaluable to the Russians as their vice-consul at Philippopolis, and Daskalov, another of their consular agents, at Varna. The Constantinople, Bucarest, and Odessa colonies continued to have an influential body of moderates who were in close touch with St. Petersburg and Ignatyev.[1] But what remains broadly true is that official Russia and panslavism had failed to be the unquestioned shapers of Bulgarian nationalism. The regenerated Bulgaria was still, by 1875, predominantly an affair of small groups, numerous now, growing, and very active (notably the school teachers), but divided among themselves; some believed in taking all they could get from Russia; others regarded her as a class despotism scheming only in her own interests; some talked vaguely of the Sultan assuming the title of Tsar of Bulgaria in some Ottoman confederation; others contented themselves with petitioning for admission of Bulgars to the army and the use of Bulgarian as an official language.[2]

The Russians had not only failed to prevent the growth of an antipathetic revolutionary movement, they had also failed to guide the struggle for a Bulgarian church along the channels they desired. The creation of the Bulgarian exarchate between 1870 and 1872 was undoubtedly an event of the first consequence for Bulgarian nationalism and a grave danger-signal of disruption for the Turkish rule in Europe; but even if as such it may be credited as a gain for Russia, the means by which it was brought about and the circumstances attending it did not represent a clear victory either for St. Petersburg or Moscow. The anti-Russian spirit which has already been emphasized among the avowed political revolutionaries found its counterpart amongst those who were concentrating on defeating Greek

---

[1] But the leaders of the Bulgarian colony in Odessa were already by the mid-sixties said to be largely out of touch with opinion in Bulgaria itself; see *Iz Arkhivata na Naiden Gerov*, vol. ii, pp. 687, 689. There is some interesting, but 'official', information on the Odessa Bulgars' committee in N. Barsov, *Tridtsatilyetie dyeyatelnosti Odesskago Bolgarskago Nastoyatelstva (s 1854–1884)* (Odessa, 1895). The committee worked in close touch with the Asiatic department and the Holy Synod and with the Constantinople embassy and the Russian consulates.

[2] As late as Jan. 1876 a petition to this effect was put forward by, or procured from, Bulgars in Sofia; text in *Dokumenti za Blgarskata istoriya*, vol. ii, pp. 141–2.

ecclesiastical and cultural dominance by the winning of an
independent church which would serve as the basis for subsequent political nationalism. And by an independent church
they meant an independent church. These Bulgarian extremists
in the struggle for the exarchate would concede nothing to the
Patriarch but the barest forms, and that only when they felt
secure of the Turkish intention to assist in keeping them bare.
They fought to the last for the widest possible territorial extension of the exarchate, and Macedonia was already something
of a powder-magazine in the struggles between Greeks and
Bulgars. They fought with almost equal tenacity against their
own moderate compatriots who were prepared for some compromise and were swayed by Russian influences and the
tortuous counsels of Ignatyev. These extremists were profuse
in their professions of contempt, of suspicion, and even of
hatred of Russian policy; and it was these men who had won
the day by 1872.

When the Greek-Bulgar church struggle was renewed in 1858,
the Russian legation had attempted a moderating influence,
without much energy and with no success. Not until the Uniate
movement, particularly in Macedonia, came to a head in
1860–1 were Russian official circles actively stirred. The Tsar
left no doubt of his alarmed interest in the securing of a satisfactory field for the development of a Bulgarian church, and
he continued throughout the long struggle to support strongly
the moderate Bulgarian claims and to debar his Holy Synod
from any action detrimental to Bulgarian interests. The policy
of the moderates aimed at securing the Patriarch's consent to
the regular appointment of Bulgarian bishops, to their representation in the Synod, to the use of Bulgarian in the churches,
to some settlement of the financial grievances, and as a maximum at setting up a Bulgarian exarchate in agreement with
the Patriarch. Such claims were very different from a breaking
away of the Bulgars from the Oecumenical Patriarch and the
defiant challenge of a national opposition church. Such an
outcome could hardly fail to result in a schism and a general
lowering of the prestige of Orthodoxy, which was bound to
be detrimental to Russia. Ignatyev represented that he had
throughout done his best 'de procurer aux bulgares, *sans
rompre avec les grecs*, un corps national en les préservant des
efforts de la propagande catholique et protestante et en les

conservant ainsi à l'orthodoxie et à notre influence'.[1] It is undoubted that this was the Russian official policy and that Ignatyev employed the most ingenious efforts to carry it through. It does, however, remain uncertain whether the belief was not well founded that he himself intended to create the nucleus for a Bulgaria even at the cost of breaking with the Greeks, if this could not be circumvented. At any rate his efforts between 1864 and 1869 to achieve a compromise brought upon him the continuous animosity of the extreme Bulgars, while at the same time he was regarded with the deepest suspicion by the Greeks.

The Turks naturally did their utmost to sow dissensions and discredit Ignatyev. Finally they came, under Ali Pasha's direction, to grant of themselves to the Bulgars far more than the Russian embassy was urging. This was the *firman* of 1870 providing for a separate 'Bulgarian Exarchate', which was to be governed by an Exarch and a Synod independent of the Patriarch, and was to include fourteen dioceses reputed to have an overwhelmingly Bulgarian population, and, in addition, any others where there was a two-thirds majority of Bulgars. This involved a territorial minimum of almost the whole of Bulgaria north of the Balkan range, and to the south of it a great part of what in 1878 became Eastern Rumelia. Among the fourteen dioceses were those of Pirot and Nish, where Serbian claims were by now to the fore, claims that were to be made good by conquest in 1878. The two-thirds provision obviously meant an intensification of the struggle between the contestants, particularly over the extension of the exarchate south-westward in Macedonia.[2] The *firman* made almost certain an entire break between the Greeks and the Bulgars, and the rupture was duly completed after three turbid years, when in 1872 the Patriarch launched a series of excommunications and the Bulgars were declared schismatic. 'Long live the schism,' shouted the Greeks in the streets of Constantinople, 'we won't be absorbed by the

[1] Italics mine: Ignatyev's 1874 memorandum, in *Izvestiya ministerstva inostrannykh dyel*, 1914, bk. 6, p. 159.

[2] The Greeks were unable to prevent the provision for a two-thirds plebiscite being applied in the dioceses of Uskub (Skoplje) and Okhrida, and Bulgarian bishops were duly installed there; but the events of 1876 resulted in their expulsion, and they were not restored until 1890; R. von Mach, *The Bulgarian Exarchate* (London, 1907), pp. 11–30, with good map of disputed dioceses in Macedonia and Thrace; A. Ischirkoff, *La Macédoine et la constitution de l'exarchat bulgare* (Lausanne, 1918), pp. 29–33; map of exarchate in Rizov, *The Bulgarians in their historical, ethnographical and political frontiers.*

Slavs. We won't let our children be bulgarized.' It seems that the *firman* of 1870 went considerably farther than Ignatyev had expected. The Bulgarian extremist leader Chomakov, an influential official in the Turkish administration, had succeeded in convincing Ali and Fuad Pashas that the best safeguard against Russian influence on the Bulgars was that the Turks themselves should promote the setting up of a Bulgarian exarchate within which healthily anti-Russian Bulgarian feelings could be developed. Ignatyev was perhaps only making the best of having been in part overreached when he claimed the *firman* as a happy culmination to five years of his efforts.[1] In any event the Bulgarian extremist press was attacking Russian influence and designs more bitterly than ever.

The exarchate came into being designedly as the political cradle of the Bulgarian people. Rightly or wrongly, Russia and above all Ignatyev were regarded by the world at large as its creators. For the Turks, if they counted on the necessity of applying the principle of *divide et impera*, the exarchate certainly served as an admirable means for antagonizing Greeks and Bulgars. For the Greeks it was a fatal blow at 'the great idea', and they laid the blame on Russia for abandoning the cause of Orthodoxy for that of Slav nationalism. It is scarcely surprising that, when, in the spring of 1878, the victorious army of Orthodox Russia was at the gates of Constantinople and its commander was within the city itself, the Oecumenical Patriarch found himself to be ill and unable to make any appearance.[2]

The emphasis that has been placed on the elements among the Bulgars which were hostile or antipathetic to Tsarist Russia may help towards a better understanding of the complex character of Bulgarian nationalism and of the clash between Russians and Bulgars in the years following 1878, yet at the same time Turkish and foreign opinion was certainly right in regarding Russia as the bulwark of the growing nationality and the Bulgars as for the most part at least initially her henchmen. For, if it came to war between Russia and Turkey, the Bulgarian nationalists would struggle actively against Turkey. Russia alone could assist them in winning freedom. Willingly or un-

---

[1] Trubetskoy in *Revue d'histoire diplomatique*, vol. xxi, pp. 396–7, citing an extract from Ignatyev to Gorchakov, 22 Mar. 1870. Ignatyev's antipathy to the Bulgarian extremists is well shown in his dispatch of 30 Jan. 1872; text in *Dokumenti za blgarskata istoriya*, vol. ii, pp. 41–6.

[2] Prince B. D. Dabizh in *R.S.*, vol. lviii, pp. 681–2.

willingly, the Bulgars would accept Russia as a means to this end, but once they had gained freedom from the Turks they would not compliantly subject themselves to any new masters. Inevitably other countries feared that the means might swallow up the end.

To the north of the Danube, in a completely different land of rich lowlands, great latifundia, and homogeneous population, the twenty years since the Crimean war again had seen profound change.[1] Roumania was Roumania in all but official title. The attempt of the congress of Paris to keep Wallachia and Moldavia separated had failed from the very start. Within three years, thanks largely to Napoleon III, Alexander Cuza, the choice of the Roumanians, was accepted as hospodar of both the principalities. Though they were to be separately administered the beginnings of joint organization were provided for, and the new name 'Principautés unies' betokened the fact that Roumanian unity was well on its way. Five years later, Cuza by his *coup d'état* of 1864 united the two, and his new constitution was accepted with only minor alterations by the powers and Turkey. There was no doubt of general Roumanian approval of Cuza's action, but he himself was not much more than a party-politician colonel. In 1866 he was forced to abdicate, and the Roumanians invited Prince Charles of Hohenzollern-Sigmaringen to take his place. His father, ex-prime minister of Prussia, agreed subject to King William's consent. King William gave it. The French failed in their efforts to bring the decision to a conference at Paris. The Russians failed in extreme proposals for compulsion to be applied to the principalities. The Roumanians were again successfully acting for themselves, and Prince Charles in October 1866 extracted, though with difficulty, the *firman* from the Porte recognizing him as hereditary prince of the United Principalities. The tribute was augmented; armed forces were not to exceed 30,000; no political treaty or convention could be concluded with a foreign power. But in fact Roumania, which had but two generations before been still the enforced granary of

---

[1] For the following section on Roumania I have used in particular T. W. Riker, *The Making of Roumania, 1856–1866* (Oxford, 1931); R. W. Seton-Watson, *A History of the Roumanians* (Cambridge, 1934); and N. Iorga, *Geschichte des rumänischen Volkes im Rahmen seiner Staatsbildungen*, vol. ii (Gotha, 1905).

Constantinople and a fertile prey to Turkish and Phanariot rapacity, was virtually detached from the Ottoman empire.

The beginning of Prince Charles's forty-eight years' reign was hazardous in the extreme, but he brought the prestige of his house, invaluable though unpopular connexions with the West, and above all his own wisdom, political ability, and efficient interest in the army. Economic development was pressed on, the French and English in the sixties leading the way in penetration, followed by the complex and much opposed German financing of the first Roumanian railways, which caused so many years of muddy strife with Strousberg and Bleichröder. These railways were planned to link up with the Austro-Hungarian system, not with the Russian. By 1875 the only Russian line in Bessarabia was the single line to Kishinev and the Pruth frontier at Ungheni, a junction with the Roumanian railways being effected only just before the war with Turkey by a hastily and ill constructed continuation to Jassy. By that date one Roumanian link was completed with Austria-Hungary, that from Bucarest to Czernowitz in Bukovina, going by Galatz and crossing the Sereth by the vital Barboshi bridge. To the west Bucarest was joined to Turnu Severin and the Iron Gate of Orsova, but no connexion had yet been made with the Hungarian railways. There was a railway south from Bucarest to Giurgevo on the Danube opposite Rustchuk. The British-built line across the Dobrudja from Constanza ended on the Turkish bank of the Danube, and the great Cernavoda bridge lay twenty years ahead in the future. This economic development was being paid for at a heavy price, mainly, as usual, by the peasantry, who, despite some efforts at improvement by Cuza, remained for another half-century at the mercy of the big landlords, of shifty politicians, and of the new middle class. There was endless intrigue among the political parties and the financial position of the country was precarious in the extreme, but none the less Roumania in her general development was more 'advanced' at this time than any of the other Balkan states. Among these she was unique in possessing a nobility, Orthodox by religion and Roumanian in feeling, though partially foreign by origin and connexions. For good or ill she had something more than the façade of the western European state system, much of it grafted from the political and administrative practices of the Second Empire upon the traditional stock of the *boyar* oligarchy. It was said that Europe during the eastern crisis of 1875–8 looked on the Balkan peoples not as *Balkanstaaten* but as *Aufstandsherde*.[1] In this sense the Roumanians were not one of the Balkan peoples; and they themselves, with their proud belief in their latinity, had no desire to be considered so.

The creation of the new Roumania since 1856 had been largely due to Napoleon III, latterly to German and Austrian help. Austria had always looked askance at the creation of a compact Danubian state which might act as a magnet for Transylvania, might serve as an example elsewhere, and might increase Russian influence in the Balkans. But Roumania came into being rather as the creation of France than of Russia; and incipient Roumanian nationalism in Transylvania, in its struggle against Buda-Pesth, looked to Vienna rather than to Bucarest, despite a number of disturbing incidents and despite the birth of what was to become the Academy of Roumanian Sciences at Bucarest. The Dual Monarchy with Andrássy conducting its foreign relations did not seek to undo what the Habsburgs had unwillingly had to accept between 1856 and 1866, and was prepared to enter into close relations with a state which offered excellent opportunities for economic penetration at the expense of Russia. The commercial treaty concluded in 1875, though it aroused Magyar opposition owing to the competition of Roumanian grain and cattle, threw open Roumania to Austrian goods to such effect that during the next seven years over half of Roumanian imports came from Austria-Hungary.[2]

Russia had been forced in 1856 to hand over to the powers as a whole the special rights which she had previously claimed in regard to the Principalities. During the period of union she could only play a secondary part. Opposed in principle to union, she was far more concerned with her *entente* with France, and was in any case too weakened in the Balkans and too much engrossed at home to do much more than derive a sardonic pleasure from voting against Turkey and especially Austria. Later she had opposed Prince Charles strongly, and had refused to recognize him for two years. Little seemed to remain of the

---

[1] Przibram, *Erinnerungen eines alten Oesterreichers*, vol. ii, p. 7.

[2] Langer, *European Alliances and Alignments*, p. 331, citing Karl Grünberg, *Die handelspolitischen Beziehungen Oesterreich-Ungarns zu den Ländern an der unteren Donau* (Leipzig, 1902), part i, and C. G. Antonescu, *Die rumänische Handelspolitik von 1875–1910* (Leipzig, 1915).

former Russian influence in the principalities. But one factor remained unchanged, the contiguity of the Roumanian stripling with the Russian colossus, with its man-power and its resources, which were bound sooner or later to affect the destiny of Roumania. And in particular there was the haunting uncertainty as to the three southern districts of Bessarabia which Alexander II had been forced to cede in 1856, and which had been handed over to Moldavia. For him it was always a question of retrocession; for the Roumanians of retaining a portion of what had been torn from them as lately as 1812. The Tsar regarded the cession extorted at Paris as an affront to his own honour and to the dignity of Russia. He regarded in the same light the stipulations as to the neutralization of the Black Sea likewise forced upon him in 1856. These stipulations he declared null and void in October 1870, and the ensuing London conference made no difference to the fact that he was rid of one-half of what he termed his nightmare. What of the other half? The outbreak of the Franco-Prussian war had aroused alarm in Bucarest lest Russia should take the opportunity of demanding the Bessarabian districts. Inquiries as to the Austrian attitude were hurriedly made in Vienna, and negotiations entered into with the Turks for possible opposition to the Russians. The results in neither case were satisfactory.[1] With the drawing together of the three empires from 1872 onwards Austro-Hungarian support of Roumania in her retention of what had belonged to the Romanovs seemed still more dubious. Roumania, for all her memories of eight Russian occupations, for all her suspicions of St. Petersburg, could not afford to alienate too sharply her overwhelming neighbour. Thus Roumanian politicians tended to be divided between those who looked to Austria-Hungary and those who regarded Russia as the safer, because ultimately the stronger, power with which to keep in close relations.

One question which was of the utmost consequence to the Roumanians and had been during the two decades prior to the Crimean war a continual source of recrimination between Russia, Austria, and England had been dealt with satisfactorily by the treaty of Paris and was not again dangerously to com-

---

[1] Iorga, *Histoire des relations russo-roumaines*, p. 330, and in *Le Monde slave*, 1928, no. 4, pp. 142–3, 145; cf. his *Correspondance diplomatique roumaine sous le roi Charles Ier* (*1866–1880*), nos. 150, 154, 156.

plicate the eastern question. The navigation of the Danube, above all of its difficult delta mouths, was in 1856 placed under a new, international system, which was at the same time guaranteed against Russian political control by the handing back to Turkey of the delta and the three southern districts of Bessarabia.[1] The Russians by this removal of their frontier from the Danube were no longer in a position to continue their policy of refusing to take adequate measures for the dredging, buoying, and lighting of the Sulina mouth, a policy which had been deliberately aimed at the detriment of the Roumanian grain trade and Austrian commerce and at the advantage of Odessa. Under the treaty of Paris a European commission, composed of the signatory powers, was set up, which in fact developed, at the expense of the more or less still-born riparian commission, into a body charged not merely with its original duties of inquiry and planning, but with the administrative and technical working of the navigation of the Danube mouths, up to Isatcha, on the basis of freedom and equality for the vessels of all nations. Set up in the first place for only two years, its life was prolonged, with much bickering, in 1866 until 1871, then until 1883, and thereafter, in fact, indefinitely. From the first the right of Turkey (and of Turkey alone, as the territorial power) to keep warships on the Danube was recognized, and this right was expressly reconfirmed by the treaty of London in 1871 occasioned by the Russian repudiation of the 1856 provisions neutralizing the Black Sea. As an offset to the Russian action the 1871 treaty also included the neutralization of the works and personnel of the commission, a provision obviously of doubtful efficacy if it came to war between Russia and Turkey, as 1877 was to prove: but the Russians did not push matters to extremes, and the Danube did not figure in the forefront as it had during the Crimean war.

The European commission had proceeded efficiently with the improvement of the Sulina mouth, and thereby had slowly revolutionized Roumanian sea-borne commerce. A marked increase in the trade through the Danube mouths was already taking place from 1846 onwards, but this developed on a far

[1] For the navigation of the Danube I have used particularly: *La Commission européenne du Danube et son œuvre de 1856 à 1931* (Paris, 1931; a voluminous, official publication of the Commission); C. I. Baicoianu, *Le Danube* (Paris, 1917; strongly anti-Austrian and anti-German); J. P. Chamberlain, *The Régime of International Rivers: Danube and Rhine* (New York, 1923).

larger scale and a far more secure basis during the sixties and seventies. Whereas in 1856 the total tonnage clearing from the Danube was 318,000, by 1875 it was 520,000, a figure which had been greatly exceeded in the peak year of 1869 (665,000 tons) and was to be completely dwarfed by the abnormal chartering of 1876 (748,000) in anticipation of war between Russia and Turkey. Greek shipping took first place until 1868, when it was displaced and soon far out-distanced by British; the Italians came third until 1872, when they collapsed and were replaced by the Austrians. Russian shipping had a diminutive share. Yet this development of Danubian trade, which meant above all increased competition of Roumanian grain exports, did not arouse so much alarm in Russia as might have been expected: grain prices were on the whole well maintained; grain exports from the Russian Black Sea ports swelled continuously. Odessa itself experienced a serious decline in commerce in the three years following 1872, but when a petition for assistance was sent in by the municipality in 1876, the question of Danubian competition, though admitted to be dangerous, received but bare mention, and all the emphasis was placed upon the need for improved rail and water communication in South Russia.[1] On the whole Russia had ceased to think of the Danube primarily in economic terms; the regaining of the territory lost in 1856 was rather a matter of 'national honour', or of linking up geographically with the Bulgars—or a matter of no interest at all. In any case it seemed improbable, when the eastern question was reopened in its fullness, that Russia would be able to set aside the twenty years' working of the European commission by reacquiring exclusive control of the Danube mouths. She did not, in fact, make any serious attempt in this direction. There were to be protracted wrangles over the navigation of the Danube in 1878 and the following years. It was not, however, the delta, but the course of the river above Galatz, and especially the Iron Gates, which were primarily in question: Austria-Hungary and Roumania were the protagonists; Russia was secondary; and the European commission itself emerged with enlarged powers.

Just as the old ties binding Bucarest to Constantinople had been snapped or weakened in the course of twenty years, so it

[1] *Mémoire sur la recherche des mesures propres à développer le commerce d'Odessa*, p. 35.

was with the ties binding Belgrade. Serbia, like the Principalities, had in 1856 been given a species of guarantee by the signatory powers. The Turks might have to deal no longer with a sole Russian protector, but with European intervention. This was likely in most cases only to reveal disunity of views and to be ineffective in practice, but from the Turkish point of view the substitution of joint European, for Russian, patronage still further complicated an already tangled situation and, for all the apparent success of the Turks in playing off the powers against each other, essentially weakened their hold on the Balkans. Serbia, like the Principalities, secured the Sultan's recognition of a new, hereditary dynasty, though unlike her neighbour the dynasty was not a foreign house, but the returned Obrenović family. Serbia likewise, though less thoroughly, began under Prince Michael to take the first steps in the evolution towards a modern European state.[1]

Miloš Obrenović, after twenty years of exile, ended as he began, Prince of Serbia, and 1859 saw the expulsion of the Karageorgević for forty-four years. Miloš was seventy-eight; tough, despotic, wily, he had done much for his countrymen, but he belonged to the past, to the Serbia of clan-chiefs and a people patriarchically organized as fighting irregulars, with few institutions that were not the cat's-paw of violence and fraud. It was fortunate for Serbia that he died in 1860. With all his abilities he was not the man for the new times. His son Michael, well educated and with some knowledge of non-Balkan countries, combined much of his father's diplomatic skill with a realization that was all his own of Serbia's need for efficient internal organization. His brief reign of eight years laid the basis of a modern Serbia. The tragedy was that what must have in any case been a laborious and chequered process was rendered doubly erratic by the early death of the one man who might have supplied continuity of guidance. Worse still, when Michael was obscurely assassinated in June 1868, his successor, Milan, was only fourteen. The inevitable regency had two special defects. It gave small cliques of politicians a taste for more or less arbitrary power in the working of the semi-

---

[1] In the following pages on Serbia, the Jugoslavs, and Montenegro, I am particularly indebted to H. W. V. Temperley, *History of Serbia* (London, 1917); R. W. Seton-Watson, *The Southern Slav Question* (London, 1917); and E. Haumant, *La Formation de la Yougoslavie* (Paris, 1930).

western constitutionalism which had been partially introduced by Michael and was, on paper, carried much farther in the constitution of 1869. Secondly, Milan's upbringing and the circumstances of his accession and of his minority imbued him with fear for his own position and life and with habits of double-dealing and spendthrift selfishness. The West meant for Milan mainly the music-halls and coffee-houses of Vienna or Paris. The depravity of his private character was not compensated by outstanding gifts in public affairs. He had considerable political abilities, but they were from the first distorted in the unhealthy atmosphere of Belgrade. He had little real know-ledge of the Serbian peasantry, who constituted nine-tenths of his people. He tended to look at everything merely from the angle of Belgrade, an attitude which was the more natural in that it was to a great extent shared by the ablest, and most dangerous, of his ministers, Ristić.

Thus, when the crisis of the late seventies came, Serbia had a prince without strong personality, and therefore without commanding influence, and politicians divided among them-selves, ambitious too frequently in their own interests alone, no longer trained as first and last peasant leaders, not yet schooled by habit in new standards. The beginnings of a regular army had been made by Michael, and had been continued with very fair efficiency. Something had been done in the way of com-mercial and banking legislation. But in twenty years there had not been much economic change. A free, land-owing peasantry was the basis of the state. Their economic links with the outer world were predominantly confined to Austria-Hungary. No railways had yet been built: the proposals to link up with the Hungarian system had been rejected, and the Orient railway, though planned to join Constantinople with Buda-Pesth, had a long and difficult gap between Philippopolis and the northern bank of the Danube in the Banat. Serbia was consequently, in contrast with the Principalities, unsaddled with the problems of foreign financial control of railway and other new develop-ments. But she was a poor and small country (with a population of not more than 1,500,000), and any real development of the army on a modern basis and any use of the army in a war would require at once money from abroad.

Prince Michael had pursued a cautious and successful foreign policy. In 1862, after the Turkish commander in the fortress of Belgrade had lost his head and bombarded the town for four and half hours, he had rid Serbia of all Moslems in the country other than the Turkish garrisons and had secured the dismantling by the Turks of two of their fortresses. Five years later he rid his country entirely of the Turkish garrisons in Belgrade and the three other fortresses they occupied. Gorchakov in 1862 had supported Michael's claims, and in 1867 the Russians were pinning their hopes on Serbia as the centre of their influence in the Balkans. But by the end of that year St. Petersburg was changing course, and anti-Russian Serbs found sharp complaint with Russian policy when in 1868, on the election of Milan, the Sultan finally acknowledged the Obrenović claim to hereditary succession to the principality. Prince Michael's assassination removed the last possibility of carrying into effect the plan of a Balkan alliance, which was to include Roumania, Greece, and Montenegro, and to utilize risings in Bulgaria, Bosnia-Herzegovina, and Old Serbia for the final overthrow of Turkish rule in Europe. This grandiose foreshadowing of the Balkan League of 1912 was similarly assisted by the Russians; above all by Ignatyev, who, from the Austro-Prussian war until the death of Michael, was doing his utmost to bring Serbia and Greece together and to combine the Cretan revolt with a general assault of the Christians upon the Turks. Treaties were concluded by Serbia with Greece, Roumania, and Montenegro, but in November 1867 the removal from office of Garašanin, the Serbian minister for foreign affairs, a strong russophil and well-known protagonist of a 'Greater Serbia', seems to show that Prince Michael was not prepared to commit himself to very risky action until circumstances were more favourable. It is doubtful what exactly was his conception of a 'Greater Serbia', but it apparently included, besides the acquisition of Bosnia and Herzegovina, some form of union with the Bulgars. Although these plans did not materialize, they had an effect in intensifying Slav efforts in the Balkans to rid themselves of the Turk and in stimulating the growth of Jugoslav ideas, and there was ample, if conflicting, encouragement from Russian agencies for the Balkan Christians to believe that Russia, in the last resort at least, would not fail them.[1]

[1] For this paragraph see the references in my article, 'Ignatyev at Constantinople, 1864–74', in S.R., vol. xi, pp. 349–53; A. Popov, 'Nastuplenie tsarskoi Rossii

Prince Michael, at least until his closing months, when the international situation had been completely changed by the *Ausgleich*, had worked well with Russia. His assassination ushered in the troubled times of the regency, with Blaznavac and Ristić at its head. The former was regarded by the Russians as a tool of Austria-Hungary, and the new constitution conferring some legislative power on a national assembly elected on an extremely wide franchise was strongly disapproved of by St. Petersburg. Russian favours were immediately withdrawn from Belgrade and showered upon Cettinje. During 1870 the worst suspicions were aroused by Austrian soundings of Ristić for some treaty for the partition of Bosnia and Herzegovina. A year later came a turning-point: on Ignatyev's suggestion Blaznavac took Prince Milan for a visit to the Tsar in the Crimea, and was won over by his reception. The regency proceeded to follow Russian advice and to draw away from Vienna. The young prince came of age in 1872, but retained Ristić in office and with him Russian predilections to balance Austrian pressure, though the autocratic ways of Shishkin, for many years the Russian consul-general in Belgrade, continued to cause resentment. There were difficulties that same year over the election of the Orthodox Metropolitan of Karlovči (Karlowitz), thanks, so it was alleged, to the intrigues of the *Omladina* and the Moscow panslavs.[1] The Serbs also showed particular opposition to Austro-Hungarian railway schemes, and the visit of Prince Milan to Vienna in 1873 did nothing in itself to mend matters.[2] Andrássy suspected Ristić of bad faith, while added grievances had been given by schemes for a marriage with a Russian princess and by the celebration of Milan's majority in an aggressively nationalistic manner; not only were representatives from Russia and Montenegro invited: similar invitations were

---

na Balkanakh', in *Avantyury russkogo tzarizma v Bolgarii*, pp. 197–205; and T. W. Riker, 'Michael of Serbia and the Turkish occupation', in *S.R.*, vol. xii, pp. 133–54 and 409–20, for the events and negotiations of 1862.

[1] Mollinary, *46 Jahre im österreich-ungarischen Heere*, vol. ii, pp. 248–52; Giacometti, *Russia's work in Turkey*, p. 35, a very suspect source; see below, pp. 130, n. 4, 244, and 681.

[2] He was received with sovereign honours, much to the anger of the Sultan, to whom further offence was caused by the fact that Milan did not visit him until after having paid court to Vienna: the visit to Constantinople, in the spring of 1874, was not auspicious in its outcome; F. Kanitz, *Das Königreich Serbien und das Serbenvolk* (Leipzig, 1914), vol. iii, p. 233; E. Engelhardt, 'La confédération balcanique', in *Revue d'histoire diplomatique*, vol. vi, p. 43.

extended to the Serbs of the Banat, the Croats, the Dalmatians, the Slovenes, and the Czechs.[1] In the autumn of 1873, however, Andrássy's immediate fears of Serbian nationalism were quieted by the replacement of Ristić by Marinović, and for the ensuing eighteen months internal party struggles in the principality made impossible any striking activities in foreign policy.[2]

At the root of the Austrian and Magyar distrust of Serbia lay the problem of the Jugoslavs. The word itself had received, as it were, official baptism in the Croatian diet in 1861. The very fact that the Jugoslav movement was only being brought to birth in these years rendered it obscure and liable to be attributed over-readily to Russian panslav agencies. 'Les différentes familles Iugo-Slaves ont de vagues aspirations communes', wrote the Balkan expert Engelhardt, 'mais des rivalités intérieures et étrangères tendent incessamment à les séparer, laissant planer sur leur sort futur le doute qui voile encore l'avenir de la Monarchie des Habsbourgs.'[3] There could be no doubt as to the sharp divisions between Catholic Croat and Orthodox Serb. The Serbs had looked askance at Gaj's Illyrianism in the second quarter of the century—the romantic dream of an Illyria strangely likened to a lyre, the 'triangle between Scutari, Varna, and Villach'—and in the third quarter they were even more suspicious of the Jugoslav cultural propaganda of the great Bishop Strossmayer. Behind his preaching of a new future of freedom in which Catholic and Orthodox would find reconciliation they felt the menace of Croat predominance and the shadow of Uniatism; and their fears that Habsburg and Croat might combine to prevent them uniting with their kinsmen in Bosnia proved all too justified when in 1878 a Croat general carried through the Austrian occupation and Croats filled most of the posts in the new administration.

[1] Text of Gorchakov's report to the Tsar on his conversation with Andrássy in Berlin, 9 Sept. 1872, in S.R., vol. viii, pp. 402–3; Iorga, Correspondance diplomatique roumaine sous le roi Charles Ier (1866–1880), no. 222.

[2] For the early years of Prince Milan see the article by Vaso Trivanovitch in The Journal of Modern History, vol. iii, pp. 414–26, and particularly Slobodan Jovanović, Vlada Milana Obrenovića, vol. i, pp. 110–26, 167–9, 207–11, 246 n.; Seton-Watson, 'Les relations diplomatiques austro-serbes entre 1868 et 1874', in Le Monde slave, Feb., May, and Aug. 1926, based on Kállay's reports; J. A. Reiswitz, Belgrad–Berlin, Berlin–Belgrad (Munich, 1936), chaps. v, vi, vii, based on the very anti-Russian reports of Rosen, the German consul in Belgrade.

[3] Engelhardt (French consul at Belgrade), 4 Feb. 1872, in D.D.F., vol. i, pp. 127–30; an excellent analysis of the Jugoslavs in Austria-Hungary at that date.

For their part the bulk of the Croats were struggling hard to make the best of matters with Buda-Pesth. In 1868 they had to accept a very unsatisfactory but not impossible compromise with the Magyars. After five fractious years their autonomous régime was altered slightly in their favour, and they were given as *Ban* a Croat of peasant stock who did well and appeased the moderates with important administrative and educational reforms (including one which hit hard the Orthodox schools and correspondingly antagonized the Serbs of Slavonia). On the other hand, the Croat extremists, Starčević's Party of National Right, so far from seeking alliance with Belgrade, preached a virulent 'pan-croatism' and poured the bitterest scorn upon the Serbs of the principality, inferior offspring of effete Byzantine culture, bowed for centuries beneath the Ottoman yoke.

If Belgrade had no cause to smile on Zagreb, it equally had no intention of abdicating in favour of Zagreb. The principality had grown markedly in prestige and confidence under Michael, and the links were being multiplied with the Serbian Orthodox in Bosnia, where they vastly outnumbered the Catholics. The Magyar Kállay, consul-general at Belgrade during the regency, was right enough in emphasizing again and again the prime importance of Bosnia in Serbian eyes, and he had no doubts that the Serbs were counting on some form of union with it. Some Magyar opinion even dallied with the idea of Serbian extension into Bosnia as a counterweight to the Croats; but Vienna, equally perplexed and undecided, was drifting towards the military view of annexation as a strategical, perhaps political, necessity.

While Zagreb dreamt now of a resuscitation of the Triune Kingdom (Croatia–Slavonia–Dalmatia), now of a great Jugoslavia under Croat dominance, while Belgrade dreamt of a smaller, predominantly Orthodox Jugoslavia, across the Danube the Serbs of the *Voivodina* (brief creation of 1849, reincorporated in Hungary in 1860) were confusedly voicing a third idea, that of a great Slav confederation, to include even the Bulgars. It was among these Serbs, who had a comparatively developed commercial middle class, that had taken place during the last two generations the cultural rebirth of Serbian nationalism. Karlovči (Karlowitz), the residence since 1690 of the fugitive Metropolitan of Ipek, and Novi Sad close by, with its Serbian college, printing-presses, and newspapers,

had been the centres of Serbian national culture, and their
connexions with the principality were still close. During the
early years of Prince Milan the position of 'uncrowned king of
the Serbs' was currently allowed to Miletić, by birth a Serb
from the military frontiers, by upbringing and career identified
with the Banat. His *Zastava* (*Standard*) was reputed to have a
wider influence than any other Serbian paper, and his views,
though frequently changing and difficult to pin down, acted
as a dangerous stimulant to the younger Serbian patriots. Yet
Miletić illustrates once again both the divisions among the
Jugoslavs and their dubious relation to Russia. He was at
daggers drawn with the regency. His past had been in the
romantic, Kollár panslav tradition, far more influenced by
L'Histoire des Girondins than by Homyakov or Russian slavophils.
His anti-clericalism caused a series of quarrels with the leaders
among the Serbian clergy, which widened the gulf between him
and the Slavonic societies in Russia. When in 1876, despite
his parliamentary immunity, he was imprisoned by the Magyar
authorities, the charges put in the forefront were not any connexions with Russia, but his efforts to raise a corps of volunteers
for Serbia, his championship of the *Omladina*, and his public
toasting of Prince Milan as 'King of the Serbs'.

The *Omladina*, the most important of the Serbian secret
societies, was perhaps the most harassing source of Magyar and
Austrian fears. Founded in 1866 with Miletić as one of its
chief leaders, it was a semi-secret society mainly recruited from
the new type of radical student youth from both sides of the
Danube, tapping some of the money of the wealthier Serbs of
the *Voivodina*. The very fact that its aims and influence were
doubtful rendered it doubly obnoxious. In Serbia itself Prince
Michael had in the end broken with it, and the regency yielded
further to Austro-Hungarian pressure, though Ristić was
suspected of being hand in glove with it. It was frequently
supposed to be a tool of Russian panslavism. This it certainly
was not: but money was welcome from any source, and Russian
panslavs were often enough in the dark as to the real use made
of the help which from time to time they gave. The Serbian
Orthodox clergy, rather than the *Omladina*, were the main
beneficiaries of the Slavonic societies, and official St. Petersburg
frowned anxiously on conspiratorial organizations of revolutionary youth. Nor was it Russia that supplied the main

literary and cultural influences on which youthful Serbian nationalism was fed: German romanticism, then French and Italian influences, bulked much larger; and young Serbs had an awkward predilection for sympathizing with the Poles as another oppressed people.[1] At the same time the multiplicity of Russian consulates and the general reputation of their officials throughout the Jugoslav lands fostered a growing belief in the ubiquitous, golden power of Muscovite panslavism (which was greatly exaggerated) and in the duality of Russian policy (which was largely true).

Besides the consulate-general at Belgrade there were Russian consulates or vice-consulates at Widdin, Orsova, Sarajevo, Mostar, Ragusa (for Cettinje), Scutari, Fiume, and Trieste; farther afield, at Prizrend, Janina, Monastir, and Salonika. There was little Russian commerce in these parts, few Russian subjects to require help: what, then, did the numerous Russian officials have to do except to act as liaison officers for the panslavs? If Shishkin at Belgrade reported on the *Omladina* as a purely revolutionary body, it was depicted in the Constantinople embassy as a national, patriotic body, untainted with the colours of revolution.[2] If Petkovich at Ragusa had been listless and ineffective, Ionin, his successor, was the reverse and established the closest relations with Cettinje and the border chieftains. His brother had been still more notorious at Mostar and elsewhere; so notorious, indeed, that he had to be removed to Syria. At Widdin Baikov had been for years consul; dubbed by Kállay 'véritable type de l'agent russe fanatique, rusé et intrigant', sticking at nothing, violently anti-Austrian.[3] The Rauch-Reichherzer accusations of 1871 against the Croat National Party, charging it with being financed by Russian panslavs and with plotting rebellion in concert with Belgrade, were clumsy forgeries:[4] Russian connexions with the Croats

---

[1] H. Wendel, *Aus dem südslawischen Risorgimento* (Gotha, 1921), pp. 83–96.

[2] Kartsov, *Za kulisami diplomatii*, p. 12.

[3] Quoted from a report of Kállay (Belgrade) to Beust, Sept. 1868, by Seton-Watson in *Le Monde slave*, May 1926, pp. 187–8. For the two Ionins, see below, pp. 138 n. and 170, n. 3.

[4] As perhaps were also the later accusations (Giacometti, *Les Responsabilités*) published by the Turks in the shape of alleged panslav documents, dated 1872 and 1873, and incriminating in particular Ignatyev, Novikov, and the Slavonic societies in Russia. In them the Russian consulates at Sarajevo and Mostar figure prominently. The English translator perhaps inadvertently remarked that the documents revealed 'the real feebleness of the hold of the Panslavonic idea'.

were of the slenderest. But behind the accusations lay two substantial, if vague, truths: that among the Jugoslavs, and especially in Novi Sad, Belgrade, and Cettinje, there were little groups of men intent on making the most of any trouble among the Slavs of the Dual Monarchy and the Ottoman empire; and that the belief was gaining ground that if a real fire broke out money, munitions, perhaps even an army itself would be forthcoming from the great Slav Tsar. Among an illiterate peasantry and small knots of excitable intelligentsia with no political education and little or no knowledge of other countries the myth of Russian confraternity and Russian might could work as an additional virus; spasmodic, uncertain, but inciting.

The *Omladina* itself in 1871 had elected as its president a Montenegrin, a symptom of its estrangement from official Belgrade, and in the years immediately preceding 1875 it was Montenegro, not Serbia or even the Banat, which was the main centre of the leaders of revolutionary nationalism. In no case, however, would the Black Mountain have been on easy terms with the Serbian regency or the Serbian prince. Prince Nicholas was too much of a personality not to inspire comparisons very invidious to Prince Milan; too able a leader not to arouse hopes that it was through him rather than through Milan that Serbian ambitions might be realized.[1] In Serbia itself there was scheming for the deposition of Milan in favour of Nicholas. The Belgrade government looked upon Cettinje with a jealous and fearful eye. Serbia had not been accustomed to regard Montenegro as a serious political factor, but now the events of twenty-five years and the capacity of Nicholas had changed the situation.

Prince Nicholas at the age of nineteen had succeeded his uncle in 1861 in circumstances almost as difficult as those in which, as exiled king, he was to leave the defunct independent Montenegro fifty-eight years later. His predecessor Danilo had abolished the two- to three-hundred-year-old combination of prince and bishop in one person as the head of Montenegro, and had begun to curb brigandage and the blood-feud, and to bring his country 'up to date'. This policy was pursued with

---

[1] Thus, for instance, the official Montenegrin newspaper, on 8 June 1875, had to deny emphatically that Prince Nicholas might be called to the Serbian throne and would accept; Schulthess, *Europäischer Geschichtskalendar*, 1875, p. 482.

wise caution. It was a necessary policy, if the Montenegrins were not to remain merely a small band of freebooter fighters. If they so remained they would play no important part in the transformation of the Jugoslav peoples which was slowly taking place. From the middle of the century onwards Danilo and then Nicholas were involved in three tasks simultaneously: that of introducing changes in the customs and laws of their very unruly subjects, that of extending Montenegrin connexions in the surrounding lands, particularly in Herzegovina, and that of combating the Turk. In any case they could not prevent the traditional support of fellow Christians across the borders, a support which in certain cases was an economic necessity. But it was extremely difficult, and at times impossible, to control such support in such a way as to avoid a mere repetition of frontier raids and brigandage and the chances of very severe Turkish counter-measures. The Montenegrins had combated the Turks for centuries, and almost the only result had been the proud boast of Montenegrins that the Black Mountain itself had never been conquered. They were justly proud, but unless they changed their methods, would they ever succeed in building up a larger Montenegro or in playing a big role in the Balkans? It was the object of Danilo and of Nicholas to defeat the Turk by a policy of combination: combination with the diplomacy of the powers and with the efforts of the Jugoslav peoples living in Serbia or still under direct Turkish rule.

This dual combination was exceedingly difficult to effect, and the Turks did not propose to make it any easier. They were becoming more and more convinced that Montenegro and Serbia were having a fatally disruptive effect on their rule in Europe. The outbreak of a revolt in Herzegovina in 1857, prepared and supported by the Montenegrins, gave the Turks every excuse to strike hard at the Black Mountain: but they met, instead of victory, resounding defeat at Grahovo. They also met Napoleon III. Danilo had turned to France, and French diplomacy at Constantinople and Scutari had worked to prevent the Turkish invasion and to extend the boundaries of the principality. Unable to hold back the Turks, Napoleon was not unable to insist that the Turks should accept, for a time, the verdict of Grahovo. They yielded in 1859 and allowed European commissioners to delimit somewhat enlarged Montenegrin frontiers.[1] But two years later, after Danilo had been murdered, the young prince Nicholas found himself immediately faced with another rising throughout Herzegovina. Nicholas himself was directed by his father, the formidable Mirko, the victor of Grahovo, 'the boa-constrictor'.[2] It was impossible to restrain his rather nominal subjects. It also proved impossible to make headway against Omer Pasha and an army of 50,000. He was forced to accept a humiliating but not over-drastic peace, which provided for Turkish blockhouses on the route from Scutari through Montenegro to Herzegovina. Nicholas, though he had made the worst possible beginning with defeat in battle, quickly proved his abilities. In 1863, thanks to the pressure of France and Russia, he gained the abandonment by the Porte of the matter of the blockhouses.[3] Three years later he was on the point of gaining, through negotiation at Constantinople, the long-coveted access of Montenegro to the sea. At the last moment he failed, through British and French obstruction. Henceforward Russia displaced France at Cettinje.

For the ten years following the treaty of Paris Russian influence had been in the background, even in Montenegro, specially accustomed to look to St. Petersburg. Danilo saw in victorious France and Napoleon's reputation as supporter of struggling nationalities the surest aid. Out of favour with St. Petersburg, he looked more and more to the French embassy on the Bosphorus and to Paris, whither he paid a not too successful visit in 1857. Gorchakov, anxious as he was for the closest relations with Napoleon, was yet jealous of French predominance in what had traditionally been a Russian preserve. Although the French and Russian naval flags flew side by side off Dulcigno in 1859, Danilo found more to hope for from Napoleon than Alexander. Aksakov, visiting Montenegro in 1860, was horrified to hear French rather than Russian talked around the prince, Paris rather than St. Petersburg the chief

[1] Zablotsky-Desyatovsky, *Zhizn Grafa P. D. Kiseleva* (St. Petersburg, 1882), vol. iii, pp. 62–3; Thouvenel, *Trois années de la question d'Orient* (Paris, 1873), pp. 243–5, 263–5.

[2] Temperley, 'The Yugo-Slav movement in British eyes 1860–71', in *Šišićev Zbornik* (Zagreb, 1929). Mirko died in 1867, in the cholera epidemic which swept Montenegro in that year.

[3] Noradounghian, *Recueil d'actes internationaux de l'empire ottoman*, vol. iii, pp. 202–4; Bamberg, *Geschichte der orientalischen Angelegenheit im Zeitraume des Pariser und des Berliner Friedens*, pp. 372–3.

topic of conversation; horrified to see full-length portraits of Napoleon and Eugénie, but none of Alexander.[1]

As the sixties wore on French support became hesitant and ambiguous, but it was again to Paris (where he had made his studies as a youth) that Nicholas paid his first foreign visit, in 1866. He returned with hopes of territorial extensions dangled before him, and he entered into encouraging negotiations with the Porte. But he found the expected French support lacking. The British obstructed any Turkish allowance of Montenegrin access to the sea: that would be tantamount to sanctioning a Russian port in the Adriatic. The only pronounced backing that the Montenegrin envoy did receive was from Ignatyev, prodigal with persuasiveness that 'it was Codlin, not Short'. The Cretan question showed that France was far from prepared to play the liberator of the East. Ignatyev's star was rising. Ionin, the new Russian consul-general at Ragusa and Cettinje, devoted himself to the Montenegrins. At the end of 1868 Nicholas paid his visit to St. Petersburg, and the old close relations were re-established: three of his daughters were in due course dispatched there for their education. The collapse of 1870 removed France entirely from the scene. Three years later, when the Tsar came to Vienna, Prince Nicholas hurried to welcome him there, bearing a blunt appeal for assistance from twenty-two of the leaders in Herzegovina conspiring for revolt. By the time that revolt broke out in 1875 Montenegro had resumed her place in the eyes of Russian nationalists as the representative of 'four centuries of protest of *all* the Slav peoples against the Moslem tyranny in Christian Europe: ... powerless as a state; unconquerable as an armed camp, as a community of warriors.'[2]

Herzegovina and Bosnia, the most distant of the European provinces of the Ottoman empire, still formed the great blunt wedge thrust in between Dalmatia and Croatia-Slavonia.[3] The inhabitants, save a few Jews and Gypsies, were Slav by

[1] Ch. Roux in *Revue historique*, 1912, vol. cix, pp. 275–8; Pokrovsky, *Vnyeshyaya politika*, pp. 36–7; Goriainow in *Revue de Paris*, 1 Jan. 1912, p. 26; Aksakov, *Slavyansky vopros*, pp. 72, 75.

[2] *Tatishchev*, vol. i, pp. 418–20, vol. ii, p. 67; Ignatyev's memorandum of 1874 in *Izvestiya ministerstva inostrannykh dyel*, 1914, bk. 3, pp. 116–17; *Spomenica o hertsegovačkom ustanka* . . ., pp. 91–4; Aksakov, *Slavyansky vopros*, pp. 55–6.

[3] For Bosnia and Herzegovina I have mainly relied on Sosnosky, *Die Balkanpolitik Österreich-Ungarns seit 1866*; Temperley, *History of Serbia*; A. J. Evans's historical survey in the second edition of his *Through Bosnia and Herzegovina on foot* . . .; and consular reports from Sarajevo and Mostar in *A. and P.*, 1876, lxxxiv, C. 1475

origin and Serbian by language, but there were four centuries of cleavage between the dominating, armed, Moslem minority and the Christians, for the most part unarmed, dependent serfs or *métayer* peasants, in fact though not in law attached to the soil. Out of a total population of perhaps 1,200,000, approximately 60 per cent. were Christians, divided acrimoniously between Orthodox and Catholic in the rough proportion of 42 to 18. Here ruled the conservative fanaticism of the Bosniak Moslem landowners with their fierce semi-feudal retainers. Earlier they had held despotic sway practically uncontrolled from Constantinople. Then Sultan Mahmud II had attempted to bring them to book, at the same time as he suppressed the Janissaries.[1] Some twenty-five years of struggle culminated in the rebellion of 1850, when Omer Pasha (himself a renegade Croat) overcame the Bosniak *begs* and finally forced them to accept a whittling down of their powers and the supervision of Ottoman, or non-Bosniak, officials. The *rayas* gained little by this introduction of new officials. Though they were less fanatical and cruel than the Slav Moslem nobles, their rapacious tax-farming, their labour and horse requisitions, their parody of justice and brutal police resulted in chronic misgovernment. The only mitigation might be a strong governor-general. This Bosnia had for a time in the person of Osman Pasha, but after his recall early in 1869 there were repeated changes and no strong hand. Nor had the economic and social power of the Moslem landlords been seriously shaken. Bosnia and much of Herzegovina still remained in a condition of semi-feudal serfdom. A paralysing paradox lay in the fact that the attempts of Constantinople to apply the *Tanzimat* in these distant provinces could not proceed far without an absolute break with the native Moslem aristocracy, the very class with which in the last resort Turkish interests had to be identified.

Along the Austrian frontier the heroic traditions of permanent struggle against the Moslem oppressor had never been lost, but in the bulk of the country until the mid-years of the century the fundamental problems of Bosnia, economic, social, and religious, were not deeply affected by feelings of Slav

and C. 1531, 1877, xcii, C. 1739. Yriarte, *La Bosnia e l'Erzegovina*, pp. 130–52, and Spalaïkovich, *La Bosnie et l'Herzégovine*, pp. 8–23, are also useful on the agrarian, taxation, and administrative systems.

[1] See particularly H. W. V. Tempèrley, *England and the Near East: the Crimea* (London, 1936), pp. 199–218, for Bosnia and Herzegovina, 1820–50.

kinship or by foreign influences. After 1848 there was a change, but agrarian discontent, taxation, and judicial abuses still provided the real fuel for fires. Outside instigation only fanned the flames. In Herzegovina there was a difference. Conditions here were at the same time worse and more hopeful than in Bosnia: worse in that most of the land, save the Narenta valley, is barren limestone mountain country, and economic pressure was bound to be more severe, even apart from oppression, than in Bosnia, most of which is well watered, well wooded, and fertile: more hopeful in that the southern districts of Herzegovina were almost solidly Orthodox and joined on to the unsubduable fastnesses of Montenegro. 1857 and 1858 had seen the Orthodox bands out in full force on the mountains, with the Montenegrins aiding. Three years later the most dangerous of the risings occurred under Luka Vukalović, and a bloody struggle followed between the Turks and Montenegrins. The peace of 1863 lasted till 1875, but it was an ominous interlude. The peace had imposed upon the *rayas* in Herzegovina a land settlement which they felt to be crushing, but it had also recognized the six most southerly districts as almost completely autonomous; they were to govern themselves with their own headmen and militia, and the headmen in fact were more under Prince Nicholas than the Sultan. There was thus a permanent nucleus of some 10,000 more or less armed mountaineers, in close connexion with Cettinje and Cattaro, capable of being used to lead a general insurrection in Herzegovina. In so far as they were held to Turkey at all, they were held by the garrisons of a few Turkish forts and by money grants from the Turkish government. It was a North-West Frontier region on a miniature scale.[1] It could well be said that 'any one who wished to raise the eastern question need only spend 300,000 francs in Herzegovina'.[2]

[1] How difficult the suppression of a rising could be in those bitter Karst lands is shown by the failure of the Austrians to suppress the Bocchesi amid their tremendous cliffs to the north of Cattaro, in Krivošije. Their revolt (1869) required 13,000 troops and took twelve months to put down, and even then they kept their arms, received an amnesty, and were excused compulsory service: see Sosnosky, op. cit., vol. i, pp. 71–92. Sosnosky, without citing his evidence, considers that panslavism and the activities of Ionin, the Russian consul at Ragusa, contributed to the rising; so too Kállay, the Magyar consul-general in Belgrade, quoted by Seton-Watson in *Le Monde slave*, May 1926, p. 194. Rosen, the German consul-general, though he was very anti-panslav, did not agree; J. A. Reiswitz, *Belgrad–Berlin, Berlin–Belgrad* (Munich, 1936), p. 176.

[2] Attributed by Blowitz to Andrássy, *Memoirs of Prince Hohenlohe*, vol. ii, p. 159.

Miles

0	20	40	60

▬▬▬ Boundaries in 1875.   +++ Railways in 1875.

*In 1875 Bosnia and Herzegovina formed
the vilajet of Sarajevo.*

*Herzegovina, with NoviBazar, had been made a separate
ejalet in 1831, but was reunited to Bosnia in 1856.*

The six semi-autonomous nakhie in Herzegovina are underlined

AND ADJACENT LANDS

III

HERZEGOVINA AND THE ANDRÁSSY NOTE

IN the summer of 1875, as usual, the diplomats wanted their holidays. Gorchakov was making a prolonged stay in Switzerland, where his son was the Russian minister. Nelidov, the counsellor at the Constantinople embassy, was likewise enjoying leave, in Germany, but it was terminated rather brusquely by his ambassador. Ignatyev wanted to go on leave himself, also to Germany, where his father was taking a cure. As he was on the point of starting early in July news reached Constantinople of some outbreak in Herzegovina: it would only be one of the usual boundary incidents; so he handed the matter over to Nelidov and departed. A month later he hurried back to Constantinople. It was not an incident: it was a revolt; matters were serious.[1]

It is significant that the first Austrian red book on the eastern crisis of 1875-8 begins not with July 1875 but with June 1873, when twenty-four merchants alleging persecution by Turkish officials fled for refuge from Banjaluka into Austrian territory. Typically enough, the negotiations that ensued dragged on for nine months before the incident was officially considered to be closed. Andrássy was cautious and moderate in this dispute; but immediately afterwards a long wrangle began over a gift of bells to the Catholic church at Durazzo, and in this he was not at all accommodating. How often, if at all, were the bells to be rung? Andrássy insisted that they should be rung on the Emperor's birthday, and the Turks in the end had to agree to Sundays and feast days as well.[2] Then in October 1874 there was the Podgorica affair; the murder by a Montenegrin of a Turk who had violated a Montenegrin girl. Feelings

---

[1] Nelidov, 'Souvenirs d'avant et d'après la guerre de 1877-8', in *Revue des deux mondes*, 15 May 1915, vol. xxvii, pp. 302-3; Ignatyev's memoirs in *I.V.*, vol. cxxxv, pp. 443-4. Zichy, the Austro-Hungarian minister at Constantinople, was also on leave and did not return until 16 Aug.

[2] *Actenstücke*, i, nos. 1-52. There is a good summary of this in Sosnosky, *Die Balkanpolitik Österreich-Ungarns seit 1866*, vol. i, pp. 119-25. Cf. *A. and P.*, 1877, xcii, C. 1739, nos. 44 and 74, incl., for Turkish accusations against the Austrian consular officials. Those at Sarajevo, Banjaluka, and Scutari were all three Slavs, and Andrássy seems to have suspected that the two former may have encouraged, even if they did not inspire, the complaints: he removed the vice-consul at Banjaluka from his post.

were running dangerously high in Montenegro. Ionin, ardent supporter of Prince Nicholas and his mountaineers, painted the situation in strong colours and foretold most serious clashes between Moslems and Christians. Ignatyev, who at this time disapproved of Ionin's policy, and was at enmity with Stremoukhov and the Asiatic department, criticized Ionin's reports as greatly exaggerated, and as highly dangerous in that Ionin contended that Austria-Hungary had radically changed her policy towards Russia and Montenegro and could now be counted upon to oppose Turkish intentions of destroying Montenegro and reducing Serbia to chaos. In Ignatyev's eyes Ionin was recommending a policy which would only result in the abandonment to Austria-Hungary of all the Slavs in the north-western Balkans.[1]

At the least Ionin was incontestably right in insisting that Jugoslav affairs were of immediate consequence in the eyes of Vienna. By March 1875 it had been decided that the Emperor Francis Joseph should make an official tour in Dalmatia. 'That will mean a blaze', was the comment of Mollinary, the Croat general commanding at Agram, when he was informed of this decision. It represented the victory of the military group which aimed at the annexation of Bosnia; in particular of General Beck, the chief of the military chancellery, and of General Rodić, the governor of Dalmatia, an Orthodox Dalmatian. Andrássy was unable, perhaps unwilling, to prevent the tour. He told Schweinitz, then German ambassador at Vienna: 'The Dalmatian trip is a Cis-Leithan affair with which I have nothing to do.' Accordingly the Emperor, after a meeting with King Victor Emmanuel in Venice, left on 7 April for Pola and Zara and spent a month travelling all through Dalmatia. There was the utmost excitement on both sides of the frontier. The Catholics in Herzegovina, headed by the Franciscans, sent in a number of addresses to the Emperor.

---

[1] Ignatyev's memoirs in *I.V.*, vol. cxxxv, pp. 72–4. For the Austrian account of the Podgorica affair and ensuing negotiations see *Actenstücke*, i, nos. 53–98. It is not clear from Ignatyev's very biased references exactly what Ionin recommended as his policy. Derby to Loftus, disp., no. 26, 29 Jan. 1875, in *F.O.* 65/905, repeating a telegram of 28 Jan. from Elliot, described Ignatyev's anger at Ionin's interference with the Turk-Montenegrin negotiations over the Podgorica affair. Aleksandr Semenovich Ionin was a Balkan expert in the consular service. He had been consul at Yanina before being moved to Ragusa, where he was accredited as diplomatic agent to Cettinje. Since his consulate was at Ragusa, he was technically under Novikov, not Ignatyev.

Rumour buzzed; there were reports of renewed oppression of Catholics by the Turks on the ground of their plotting in favour of the Habsburgs; Christians began to flee across the border. Dervish Pasha, the *vali* of Sarajevo, was ordered by his government to pay an official visit to Francis Joseph. He did so, at Ragusa on 28 April. Dervish Pasha had been made *vali* a year before; he was well known as an iron-fisted extremist who openly threatened the Montenegrins with the sword. His visit was stiff and coldly formal. Four days later the Emperor was at Cattaro, and received a very different visitor. Prince Nicholas, with Peter Vukotić, his cloest adviser, came down the winding mountain track from Cettinje, eager to renew his cordial protestations of Montenegrin belief in the might and benevolence of the Habsburgs which he had expressed two years before when visiting Vienna. It appeared that the Montenegrins were ready to form a right covering wing for the Austrians.[1]

Neither Rodić, nor Ionin, nor the Franciscans in Mostar and Sarajevo had long to wait for the aftermath of this inciting tour of the Emperor. At the end of June Nevesinje, a storm-centre near Mostar, was the scene of an outbreak between Orthodox and Moslems, due to a combination of the iniquities of the tax-farmers, the faithlessness of the Turks, and the plottings of secret societies among some returned fugitives. At the same time a Moslem caravan from Mostar was plundered by Christians and seven Moslems were killed, and other outrages were committed by armed Christian bands in southern Herzegovina as reprisal for the alleged murder of a Franciscan for having acclaimed Francis Joseph on the Dalmatian border. Uprisings began in the Catholic district of Popovopolje, and hostile report accused Rodić of fomenting them.[2] The Moslems retaliated

---

[1] Mollinary, *46 Jahre im österreich-ungarischen Heere*, vol. ii, pp. 281–4; Plener, *Erinnerungen*, vol. ii, p. 91; Sosnosky, *Die Balkanpolitik Österreich-Ungarns seit 1866*, vol. i, pp. 138–9; Schweinitz, *Denkwürdigkeiten*, vol. i, p. 309; Wertheimer, pp. 258–9, maintains that Andrássy was unable to prevent the Dalmatian tour, though he succeeded in his resolute opposition to the annexation which its promoters aimed at achieving. Koetschet, *Aus Bosniens letzter Türkenzeit*, pp. 1–4; Fournier, *Wie wir zu Bosnien kamen*, p. 14; Glaise-Horstenau, *Franz-Josephs Weggefährte: das Leben des Generalstabchefs Beck*, pp. 179–83 (does not confirm Beck's actual responsibility for the tour); Taylor (Ragusa) to Derby, dis., pol., no. 5, 15 May, in *F.O.* 7/860. The Emperor, in conversation with the King of Italy, seems to have referred to the possibility of an eventual Austrian taking over of Bosnia, in which case Italy might hope for something in the way of compensation though not in the direction of Trieste; Chiala, *Pagine della storia contemporanea*, vol. i, p. 266.

[2] Holmes to Derby, in *A. and P.*, 1876, lxxxiv, C. 1475, nos. 1, 2, and 6; Koetschet,

with indiscriminate pillage and murder of Christians, and the
Turks failed deplorably to prevent the revolt becoming general
in Herzegovina and spreading slowly northwards into Bosnia.
There at the head of one of the rebel bands figured Peter
Karageorgević, fighting in a struggle very different from the
last war he had served in, the Franco-Prussian; not so different,
in aim, from his next war, when as King Peter of Serbia he was
to inaugurate the world-struggle in 1914. As the leader of an
insurgent band he soon acquired an almost legendary fame,
which rendered him, the head of the rival Serbian dynasty, of
yet greater danger to Prince Milan, and which was to be one
of the main factors driving Milan to yield to the popular clamour
for war against Turkey.[1]

In the initial stages of the revolt the Catholics in Herzegovina
were prominent and there was some combination between
them and the Orthodox. Within six weeks the revolt was in
the hands of men who regarded fighting the Turks 'as a pastime,
or as a superior kind of field sport', the men of the *nevabnakhie*,
the 'mutiny districts' in the southern corner of Herzegovina
abutting on the Bocche di Cattaro and Montenegro, where the
frontier had always been but nominal. The strategical situation
for the revolt, perhaps purposely chosen, could hardly have
been bettered. The rebels close to the Dalmatian and Montenegrin frontiers found easy access there for refuge, for arms,
for money, for their families. Sutorina, their strong point on
the sea, over against the Bocche di Cattaro, was never closed
to them by the Austrians, as it had been in the 1861 rebellion.[2]

It is uncertain to what extent the outbreak of the revolt was
deliberately planned by the Slav committees in Dalmatia and
Montenegro, but it is clear that the very effective sympathy of

---

Aus Bosniens letzter Türkenzeit, p. 7; Čubrilović, *Bosanski ustanak 1875–1878*, pp.
41–2, 49–53; Mollinary, *46 Jahre im österreich-ungarischen Heere*, vol. ii, p. 284;
Wesselitsky-Bojidarovich, *Dix mois de ma vie, 1875–6*, p. 230. These versions of the
beginnings of the revolt differ as to the details, but not incompatibly, except that
Holmes, the consul at Sarajevo, regarded the outbreaks as due merely to fomenta-
tion from outside. For the fugitives from Nevesinje and their return, see also
Actenstücke, i, nos. 99–105.

[1] A point very strongly emphasized by Seton-Watson, *The Role of Bosnia in International Politics*, p. 14; cf. Jovanović, *Vlada Milana Obrenovića*, vol. i, pp. 284, 293.

[2] From Herzegovina the sea could only be reached through the two enclaves of
Klek and Sutorina. Klek, above Ragusa and just south of the mouth of the Narenta
up which a route led to Mostar, served, by Austrian permission, as the only Turkish
point of communication from the sea with Herzegovina. Much to the disgust of the
Turks, the Austrians closed Klek to them in the summer of 1876, see below, p. 173.

the Dalmatian Slavs, once the rebellion was under way, was of the first importance. The outbreak almost certainly was not due directly to Russian intrigues. Russian influence through committees and secret agents was at first of secondary account. Ionin was described by the biased but well-informed *Times* correspondent at Ragusa as not much in favour with the insurgents until about the New Year of 1876. There was an implacable feud between him and certain of the rebel leaders, of whom one of the foremost, Lyubibratić, whose connexions were mainly with Serbian secret societies, was most impolitically anti-Russian and anti-Montenegrin.[1] Another English observer, though possessed of no previous local knowledge, rightly, ridiculed the idea that the insurgents took up arms as 'the champions of Pan-Slavism or the "Cosmopolitan Revolution"... this insurrection was in its origin Agrarian rather than Political'.[2] Once the raiding, burning, and killing had begun, once the border bands were out, what was in essence a rising against agrarian conditions, grinding taxation, and brutality became a weapon in the hands of Austrian, Russian, and Serbian Slav societies, of Montenegrin captains, and of the *pandours* of the border districts. The Turks by their initial incompetence and cruelty gave the opportunity for these outside elements to exert their influence.

Prince Nicholas was from the outset unable and unwilling to prevent direct help being given to comrades in arms just across the fictitious border. But he knew that the Russian government were not prepared for decisive backing, and that Vienna must be cautiously handled. Hence he was careful at least to appear to be doing what he could to limit Montenegrin assistance and to avoid a break with the Turkish government. But from the New Year onwards, more and more encouraged unofficially by Russian agents, and spurred on by fear of Serbian action, he pushed forward his plans for directing the rebellion to his own ends. It is noticeable that Holmes, the British consul at Sarajevo, who never failed to paint the Montenegrins in the worst light and to ascribe the strength of

[1] For the evidence as to Ionin and Russian influence, see Appendix I. Holmes had not thought that his Russian colleague at Sarajevo, Kudryashchev, who had been there since 1868, was active or dangerous, and had described Bosnia as not being under Russian influence, and Russian agents there as having been for some time extremely quiet; Holmes to Elliot, no. 3, 12 Jan. 1874, in *F.O.* 195/1031.

[2] Evans, *Through Bosnia and Herzegovina on foot*, pp. 334–6. So, too, Yriarte, *La Bosnia e l'Erzegovina*, pp. 128–9, putting the main emphasis on tax-exactions.

the revolt to outside support, admitted that in its early stages
Nicholas was not fostering it, and at first laid the blame on the
Austrian Slavs, without particular mention of Russian intrigues.[1]

Very soon after the beginning of the revolt in Herzegovina,
there was a general rising and *sauve qui peut* (it was a mixture
of both) on the part of the Christians. The rapidity of this
flaring-up and the Turkish excesses and lack of control quickly
brought the powers on to the scene. St. Petersburg, fearing
that if the Turks failed to score a prompt success the Montenegrins would certainly intervene, was anxious to concert
through Novikov at Vienna steps amounting to unofficial mediation at Constantinople by Russia, Austria, and Germany; acting
on identical instructions the three ambassadors might put
collective pressure on the Porte to take adequate measures for
pacification under the moral guarantee of the three powers.
Out of this proposal Andrássy elaborated, with the agreement
of Novikov and Schweinitz, the German ambassador, instructions to the three ambassadors at Constantinople to communicate to the Porte, though not in identic terms, their good
offices for an accommodation with the rebels which was to be
reached mainly through a consular commission on the spot.
The Porte was formally approached to this effect on 18 August.
But the field by now had been widened. Decazes, at the Quai
d'Orsay, was anxious that matters should not be left entirely to
the three eastern powers; and the Russians, without any consultation with Vienna, promptly invited French participation
(14 August), and followed up this step by similar invitations
to London and Rome. The latter accepted readily, the former
hesitantly, and the upshot of the *démarches* in Constantinople
was that the Porte agreed to a consular commission composed
of representatives of the six, not the three, powers. The centre of
action, however, still lay in Vienna.[2]

This at least was satisfactory to Andrássy, though he would
have preferred that the Turks in the first place should have

---

[1] See Holmes's reports in *F.O.* 78/2402: so, too, Taylor's reports from Ragusa,
in *F.O.* 7/860. Later Holmes castigated Ionin and Prince Nicholas with the
utmost severity; see Appendix I. For Nicholas's attitude see the discussion in
Čubrilović, *Bosanski ustanak 1875–1878*, pp. 57–60, who suggests that he had, from
August onwards, to commit himself more deeply than I have allowed; and *Spomenica o hertsegovačkom ustanka*, pp. 32–3.

[2] *Actenstücke I*, especially Andrássy to Seiller (Berlin), disp., 7 Aug., no. 114, and
to Zichy (Constantinople), disp., 7 Aug., no. 113; and see the French official documents, especially Bourgoing (Constantinople) to Decazes, 25 Aug., republished

been left to deal with the revolt by themselves, while he himself pursued a policy of temporizing neutrality. He opposed successfully the efforts of Rodić, the governor of Dalmatia, to secure rapid intervention: only if the Turks failed to maintain themselves and reforms proved quite impossible would Austria-Hungary be required to take their place; the essential was to prevent any increase of Serbian or Montenegrin power and to avoid European complications. He was thoroughly suspicious of the Russians and believed that Gorchakov aimed at manœuvring him into the position of jointly extracting from Constantinople a new autonomous régime for Bosnia and Herzegovina similar to that of the Principalities. Such a project was 'downright nonsense', and must be forestalled: meanwhile the consular commission, if he kept control of it, might do no harm.[1]

It is not surprising that the commission proved to be little better than a farce. In the first place its rather hazy function was at one and the same time to keep a close watch on Server Pasha, the Turkish commissary sent to Bosnia and Herzegovina,[2] and to explain to the rebels that they had nothing to hope from the powers except diplomatic pressure upon the Porte to consider favourably a petition which the rebels should send to Constantinople—waiting quietly, and not rebelliously, in the meantime. This was impossible conduct to expect of a half-terrified, half-exultant population. The rebels would not look at any terms that were not under the express guarantee of the powers. In the second place the rebels, encouraged by secret instructions from Cettinje to make a bold front, had good reason for disbelief in the official actions of the consuls. The commission was composed of six consular representatives. The French and Italian members in secret strongly supported Serbian aspirations. Vasić, lately Austrian consul-general at Sarajevo, though now at Scutari, was believed to be neutral.

from the French Yellow Book in *Staatsarchiv*, vol. xxxii, nos. 5972–76. There is a full account in Harris, *A Diplomatic History of the Balkan Crisis* . . ., pp. 72–89.

[1] *Wertheimer*, pp. 254–64. According to Stojanović, *Servia and International Relations* (MS.), citing from the Vienna archives Andrássy's instructions of 12 Aug. to Rodić, the latter was to abstain from doing anything which might compel Austria-Hungary to intervene, but his neutrality should not be absolute and his task was to retain the sympathies of the Christians and to make them understand that the final decision of their fate lay with Vienna.

[2] Server Pasha was later minister for foreign affairs. Ignatyev, who considered him a mild and easily guided man, gave himself the credit for the appointment; *I.V.*, vol. cxxxv, p. 444.

The Russian member was Yastrebov, who had served at Scutari and Prizrend and was now consul-general at Salonika, and was known as an open supporter of the Slavs. So was the German member Lichtenberg. Only Holmes, the British consul at Sarajevo, favoured the Turks. To cap the ineffectiveness of the consuls, they had with ironical gravity been instructed to avoid the appearance of united action.[1]

In the third place, the commission, being Andrássy's creation, was energetically opposed by Ignatyev. He had cut short his leave, and was back in his embassy on 13 August, intent on concentrating policy in his own hands. He quickly re-established his ascendancy over his Austrian and German colleagues and expanded to Elliot, not without some effect, on Andrássy's designs for imposing on the Turks measures concocted in Vienna by the three eastern powers alone. There was an immediate bout between Ignatyev and Novikov in which the former succeeded in supplanting Ionin, from Ragusa, who was originally intended as the Russian representative on the consular commission, by one of his own men, Yastrebov. Ignatyev emphasized to the Tsar, then in the Crimea, the danger of instituting in Bosnia-Herzegovina any régime such as that elaborated for Crete or the Lebanon, and the necessity of the initiative for the required reforms coming from Constantinople. With this end in view he endeavoured to checkmate Andrássy by proposing, without success, that the consular commission should be made dependent on the Constantinople embassies, and should draw up a scheme of reforms in consultation with Server Pasha, the Turkish commissioner; and by playing for time by confusing the issues in Constantinople.[2]

---

[1] *Spomenica o hertsegovačkom ustanka*, pp. 36–7, from the Cettinje archives; Čubrilović, *Bosanski ustanak 1875–1878*, pp. 92–3, citing letters of Božo Petrović and Peter Vukotić to the rebel leaders; Koetschet, *Aus Bosniens letzter Türkenzeit*, p. 10.

[2] Derby to Loftus, disp., conf., no. 270, 6 Oct., enclosing copy of Elliot to Derby, disp., very conf., no. 565, 17 Sept., in *F.O.* 181/528; Buchanan to Derby, disp., very conf., no. 327, 5 Oct.; Elliot to Derby, disp., conf., no. 580, 24 Sept.; disp., nos. 596 and 597, conf., 26 Sept.; nos. 627 and 649, most conf., extenders of tels., 3 and 8 Oct.; copies in *F.O.* 181/529. There is disagreement as to the details of Ignatyev's proposals between the version sent to London by Elliot and that sent to St. Petersburg; Doria to Derby, disp., no. 297, 28 Sept., in *F.O.* 65/911; Elliot to Derby, nos. 693 and 714, 22 and 28 Oct., copies in *F.O.* 181/529. Harris, *A Diplomatic History of the Balkan Crisis* . . . , pp. 94–5, 133–43, usingt he Vienna archives, throws new light on Ignatyev's moves and counter-moves, but further evidence is needed to elucidate them. Ignatyev's memoirs, *I.V.*, vol. cxxxv, pp. 443–53, dwell mainly on his capture of Zichy and Werther and his efforts to pre-

The consular commission, labouring under such severe handicaps, proved entirely ineffective. By the beginning of October it ceased to function except as a centre of information, while Vienna proceeded to press forward negotiations with St. Petersburg which by the end of the year were to bear fruit as the Andrássy note. This was not achieved, however, without strenuous endeavours on the part of Ignatyev to counteract the Russian *entente* with Austria-Hungary by making Constantinople and not Vienna or St. Petersburg the key centre. His main object was to use his personal influence with the Sultan, with the grand vizier, and with the Christians in Constantinople for the introduction by the Turks themselves of reforms in Bosnia and Herzegovina, and also throughout the European portion of their empire. This would checkmate Austrian designs, would secure an independent Russian policy, and would assure to him an all-powerful position at Constantinople.

Ignatyev, with justice, considered his influence there to be at its highest. He was in close personal relations with the Sultan, notably through the Sultana Validé and Abram Effendi, Ismail's representative in Constantinople.[1] Late in August 1875 he succeeded in restoring his old ally Mahmud Nedim as Grand Vizier, who was prepared to work for reforms under Russian influence and to avoid drastic measures against the rebels and their supporters, Montenegro and Serbia. His opponents, headed by Hussein Avni Pasha, the fiery old bitter-ender, and Midhat Pasha, were strongly hostile to Russian or foreign intervention, were equally strongly in favour of the most stringent suppression of the insurrection, and were contemplating a military occupation of Serbia, as instigator of the rising, and as being less open to European intervention and more easy to subdue than the fastnesses of the Black Mountain. But early in October Hussein Avni was replaced as war minister by Riza Pasha, a milder man, and Ignatyev attributed to himself the credit of preventing the launching upon Serbia of an army of some 50,000 to 60,000 men.[2] Midhat Pasha, however, the leader of the 'young Turks' and a bitter opponent of

vent any precipitate action by Serbia or Montenegro which would facilitate Austrian intervention.

[1] Bamberg, *Geschichte der orientalischen Angelegenheit im Zeitraume des Pariser und des Berliner Friedens*, p. 444; Kartsov, *Za kulisami diplomatii*, p. 31.

[2] Letter of Ignatyev to Kartsov, 17 Mar. 1876, extract in Kartsov, *Za kulisami diplomatii*, p. 21; Ignatyev's memoirs in *I.V.*, vol. cxxxv, p. 806.

Ignatyev, remained as minister of justice. In mid-November the latter gained another success; the foreign minister was changed: Safvet Pasha, closely bound up with Midhat and a year later to be his collaborator in constitutional experiment, handed over foreign affairs to Reshid Pasha, coming from Vienna. He was supposed to be pro-British, but Ignatyev believed he had him in his hands. A month earlier the announcement had been made of the partial suspension of the Turkish foreign debt payments, a measure widely attributed to the influence of Ignatyev. At the end of November Disraeli startled Europe by his purchase of the Khedive's Suez Canal shares, to which the Russian foreign office reacted in silence and the Russian press in less hostile terms than might have been expected.[1]

Such was the situation during the autumn when Ignatyev was making his bid against Andrássy. According to his own subsequent account he succeeded at Constantinople, and failed at Livadia. On Ignatyev's advice the Sultan issued on 2 October an *irade* granting tax reductions and promising fiscal and administrative reforms. Abd ul-Aziz declared his readiness to carry out the Tsar's wishes in regard to these, and to submit to the Tsar's decision the question of the frontier districts in Herzegovina, subject to two conditions: that the negotiations with the Tsar should be of a strictly personal and confidential character, to be carried on through Ignatyev and not through the Porte, and that the Tsar, as in the case of Nicholas I and Sultan Mahmud, should give his word that he would not take part in any measures to bring pressure upon Turkey. Ignatyev's version of these negotiations cannot be fully trusted, but it seems that at any rate the Sultan was secretly prepared to take into the closest consideration Russian advice, and it is clear that under no circumstances would he tolerate effective official intervention by the powers. He desired Ignatyev to report personally to the Tsar at Livadia in the Crimea. Thither accordingly he went on 19 October.[2]

The Russian foreign office was still without its head, since Gorchakov did not return to Russia until the beginning of December. In his absence Jomini was in charge. The Tsar

---

[1] For press and other opinions on the purchase of the Suez Canal shares see Lee, *Great Britain and the Cyprus Convention policy of 1878*, pp. 14–22, and Wirthwein, *Britain and the Balkan Crisis 1875–1878*, pp. 29–32.

[2] Ignatyev's memoirs in *I.V.*, vol. cxxxv, pp. 453–6. The French text of the *irade* of 2 Oct. is in *Staatsarchiv*, vol. xxix, no. 5567.

was back at St. Petersburg by August, and later went down for his usual autumn visit to Livadia, the Russian equivalent of Balmoral. Jomini was probably anxious not to antagonize Ignatyev, but the Tsar's consent was not likely to be forthcoming for any new departure in foreign policy in the absence of Gorchakov. Hence Russian official policy from July to October had on the whole gone hand in hand with Austrian. At the same time the eyes of the foreign office remained conveniently closed to the activities of Ionin, the Montenegrins, and the secret societies. Both the Tsar and Jomini believed that events might lead to a speedy reopening of the whole eastern question; in that event their main concern was that there should be no repetition of the isolation from Austria which had been so disastrous during the Crimean war. The Tsar telegraphed to the Emperor William, on 11 October: 'Le malade l'est encore plus qu'on ne le croyait; il agonise, mais je ne veux pas de son cadavre, nous ne saurions qu'en faire. . . . Il faut donc prolonger l'agonie.'[1]

Jomini for his part was prolific in warnings. At the beginning of August, after speaking of the common efforts of the three eastern powers to agree upon joint action, 'morale jusqu'à présent', to be primarily under Austrian direction, he added: 'Quoi qu'il arrive, ce qui se passe est un avertissement que *la question d'Orient* peut éclater comme une bombe d'un moment à l'autre et qu'il faut prévoir.' He likened Turkey to an infant with a severe illness, in which it was impossible to foretell what phase it might take at any moment.[2] For the benefit of Vienna he painted a horrifying picture of the possibility of Serbia going to war followed by Montenegro, and risings in Albania, Epirus, and Thessaly (Bulgaria apparently he forgot); Egypt might even make a bid for Syria; Europe would be unable to conjure away the eastern question; 'il faudrait prévoir le cas où elle se présenterait, et alors il ne suffirait plus des moyens qu'on a employés jusqu'ici.'[3] Jomini was a great and calculatingly incautious talker. A month later in September he expounded to the Greek representative the fatal consequences of isolated action by the Turkish Christians and encouraged Greek action

---

[1] Gontaut-Biron to Decazes, tel., 12 Oct., extract in *D.D.F.*, p. 10, note.
[2] Le Flô to Decazes, tel., 5 Aug., in *D.D.F.*, p. 2; Doria to Derby, disp., most conf., no. 239, 4 Aug., in *F.O.* 65/910.
[3] Langenau to Andrássy, disp., 19 Aug., in *Actenstücke*, i, no. 127; Jomini read to Langenau a dispatch he was about to send to Novikov.

to raise revolt in Crete. In October he was airing his views to the French chargé d'affaires, insisting on the necessity of being prepared in advance for grave events in the spring, and going on to speak of Russia's moral obligation to the Serbs and their neighbours. 'Nous avons pris l'engagement de veiller nous-mêmes au sort des chrétiens.' Then he sketchily referred to a future for the Christian provinces, after the withdrawal of the Turks, in the form of some kind of federal union with Constantinople as an oriental Frankfurt. About the same time he threw out suggestions to the Austrian embassy as to collective intervention by the powers, first through a conference, then if necessary in the shape of military occupation by Russia and Austria, similar to that undertaken in 1860 by France in Syria.[1] Such feelers were not at all to Andrássy's liking; he did not approve the idea of a conference; he would not look at the idea of joint occupation.[2] Jomini could not have been surprised. He had already received very different proposals from Andrássy (16 October). But at this juncture Ignatyev arrived at Livadia.

He urged the Tsar strongly to accept the Sultan's offers: he foretold that refusal would mean the collapse of Russian influence and the triumph of hostile intrigues at Constantinople, and war in the near future between Russia and Turkey. The Tsar declined to be led along the path of a separate and secret understanding with the Turks; the only possibility which he would allow was that of persuading Vienna and Berlin to wait and see whether the proposed reforms would amount to anything. Ignatyev, though he failed in his major task, did thus at least gain time, and Novikov in Vienna was instructed to defer Andrássy's proposals for fuller consideration. In reply to Ignatyev's forecast that Andrássy's policy would alienate Turkey from Russia and would lead to the break-up of the Ottoman empire, the Tsar remarked that he regarded this break-up as

[1] Report of Greek representative at St. Petersburg to Athens, 20 Sept., quoted in Driault and Lhéritier, *Histoire diplomatique de la Grèce de 1821 à nos jours*, vol. iii, p. 383; Hanotaux, *Histoire de la France contemporaine*, vol. iv, pp. 69–70, quoting apparently a dispatch of Laboulaye recording the conversation which took place on 21 Oct. It is not in *D.D.F.*, vol. ii. Stojanović, *Serbia and International Relations* ... (MS.), citing Mayr (St. Petersburg) to Andrássy, 27 Oct., in Vienna archives. Jomini was likewise sounding Loftus as to the precedent of Syria in 1860 providing the only means of dealing with Bosnia and Herzegovina; Loftus to Derby, disp., no. 338, conf., 10 Nov., in *F.O.* 65/912.
[2] Harris, *A Diplomatic History of the Balkan Crisis* ..., p. 152, citing from the Vienna archives Andrássy to Mayr (St. Petersburg), 4 and 18 Nov.

unavoidable and that he therefore set more store than ever on agreement with Austria-Hungary and Germany, agreement in which he would like the other powers to join.[1]

The net result of Ignatyev's efforts with the Tsar was failure: the Tsar would not cut loose from Austria-Hungary. A semi-official announcement in the *Pravitelstvenny Vestnik* on 16 November followed a similar announcement of 10 November in the *Wiener Zeitung* in emphasizing the collaboration of the three eastern powers in Constantinople.[2] Yet Ignatyev still hoped to prevent Andrássy from presenting some form of joint demands on the Porte. He had returned to his embassy by 4 November and continued to urge his policy on the Tsar, addressing his reports by special permission direct to him at Livadia, while on the other hand he was confabulating with Mahmud Nedim a detailed plan of reforms, developing those granted in the *irade* of 2 October. The upshot of this was the *firman* of 12 December which contained comprehensive reforms for the whole empire, and marked a momentary success over Andrássy.[3]

Ignatyev hoped thereby to avoid a general rising of the Christians and to make the Turkish rule more or less bearable for the time being. If the winter months could not be successfully utilized, it would become impossible to hold back Montenegro and Serbia in the spring. He held that Andrássy's reform proposals would be hotly resisted by the Turks and would, in fact, act as an incitement to risings elsewhere in Turkey.

[1] Ignatyev's memoirs, in *I.V.*, vol. cxxxv, pp. 456–60. For Andrássy's proposals see below, p. 151. Novikov, the Russian ambassador at Vienna, was evidently much perturbed by Ignatyev's visit to Livadia, though the evidence is very unsatisfactory as to his action. Ignatyev in his memoirs, *I.V.*, vol. cxxxv, p. 459, maintains that Novikov was so alarmed at his visit to the Tsar that he sent Tatishchev from the Vienna embassy to the Crimea, while Ignatyev was there, armed with arguments in favour of the Austrian proposals, and that Tatishchev was then sent to Gorchakov at Vevey to keep him firm for Andrássy's policy. *Tatishchev* himself, pp. 297–8, gives a different, and incompatible, version.

[2] The texts of these two communiqués are given in *Staatsarchiv*, vol. xxx, nos. 5572 and 5571. See also ib., no. 5570, and *Tatishchev*, pp. 296–7, for the text of the semi-official Russian communiqué of 29 Oct., in reply to the Turkish promise of reforms of 2 Oct.: this was on the whole more in consonance with Ignatyev's views, though it caused him considerable difficulty on his return to Constantinople.

[3] This and the two following paragraphs, except where otherwise stated, are based on Ignatyev's memoirs, in *I.V.*, vol. cxxxv, pp. 461, 805–36, and mainly on two lengthy reports which are given in full, 22 Nov. to the Tsar, and 6 Dec. to Gorchakov. He closed the former report by the avowal, typical of his chameleon-like methods, that the situation in the Ottoman empire was so complicated that his views might have to be changed very rapidly. The French text of the *firman* of 12 Dec. is in *Staatsarchiv*, vol. xxx, no. 5575.

But the essential point was that the reform proposals introduced by the Turks themselves would in fact be controlled by the Russians. Ignatyev would be able to capitalize one of Abd ul-Aziz's leading characteristics, personal vanity. Refusal of the Sultan's offer would probably result in flinging him into the arms of Hussein Avni and Midhat. He made no pretence of ascribing to the two pronouncements of reforms the importance of a political guarantee for the rebirth of Turkey: on the contrary, he professed to be acutely conscious of the impossibility not only of the salvation of the Ottoman empire by this means, but even of its continued existence for much longer. What he did maintain, and this was the inner spring of the whole of his policy, was that his proposals were the only means of preventing the eastern question coming to a head at a time which was not favourable to Russia. Why allow Austria-Hungary to eat up a leaf of the Turkish artichoke without any compensation for Russia? 'Dans un pareil cas je préfère préserver l'artichaut tout entier de l'effleurement prématuré.'[1] In fact he considered a second Franco-German war as inevitable: that would be, again, Russia's opportunity in the Balkans.

The second part of the programme which Ignatyev was engaged in formulating with the Sultan and the grand vizier related to Herzegovina. Bosnia he represented as still relatively quiet, save for the north-western part, but in Herzegovina the revolt was genuinely national and could not be settled by merely administrative reforms. He proposed that the southern part of Herzegovina, up to Stolac and Nevesinje, should be virtually united to Montenegro, and that Prince Nicholas should recognize the suzerainty of the Sultan over these districts and pay annual tribute for them. (Montenegro itself neither recognized the suzerainty of the Sultan nor paid any tribute.) Serbia would require some compensation for these concessions to Montenegro, and should receive Little Zvornik, the fortress on the Drina. He told St. Petersburg that it would be difficult to extract these concessions from the Turks, but that it would be possible. What he did not tell St. Petersburg was that he had already sounded the Sultan and the foreign office and felt assured of their agreement: he feared that if he revealed this to Gorchakov he would let it out to Andrássy. An an alternative

---

[1] Ignatyev to Jomini, lettre personnelle, 31 Nov., text in *Revue d'histoire moderne,* Sept.–Oct. 1935, p. 385.

to this, he suggested the formation of further semi-autonomous *nakhie* in southern Herzegovina, similar to the six *nakhie* specially privileged after the 1861 revolt; but he doubted whether Prince Nicholas could be brought to agree to this.

Early in December he secured direct negotiations between the Porte and Prince Nicholas, through Constant Effendi, a Christian official acting as special commissary in the rebel districts in Herzegovina, who was instructed to offer certain territorial advantages, including Spizza, to Montenegro.[1] How far the Porte was serious in desiring an accommodation with Montenegro may be doubted. Prince Nicholas, at any rate, who was now working hard to remove his differences with the Serbs, put forward conditions which were absolutely refused by the Turks, and by the end of January 1876 these negotiations had collapsed.[2] By then the seal had been set on Ignatyev's failure by the Andrássy note. Gorchakov had made no detailed reply to Ignatyev's proposals: he had merely stated his desire to continue to go hand in hand with Andrássy, and instructed Ignatyev to abstain from taking the initiative.[3]

Meanwhile Vienna had been successfully pressing St. Petersburg into the announcement of agreed measures. Andrássy had expounded his programme at great length on 16 October: after diagnosing the origin of the revolt as due to 'l'exploitation des souffrances des raias par les comités révolutionnaires', he stated that the object to be aimed at must now be not merely to prevent the revolt spreading, but to provide remedies for the misgovernment of Bosnia and Herzegovina; any possibility of the two provinces being made autonomous on the model of Serbia or the Principalities was repudiated in the strongest possible terms; there remained only remedies in the shape of moral and material reforms, notably absolute religious liberty

[1] Ignatyev's memoirs, in *I.V.*, vol. cxxxv, pp. 461–2.
[2] Koetschet, who was in Cettinje in Jan. 1876 and took a hand in the negotiations, gives as Prince Nicholas's conditions for co-operation in the pacification of Herzegovina: the renunciation by the Sultan of his claims to suzerainty, the cession of Spizza, the free navigation of the Boyana under the Montenegrin flag, and a small territorial cession on the right bank of the Morača: *Aus Bosniens letzter Türkenzeit*, pp. 31–5, 41. Both Holmes and Elliot favoured the cession to Montenegro of certain frontier districts and Spizza, possibly in return for recognition of Turkish suzerainty, *A. and P.*, 1876, lxxxiv, C. 1531, nos. 37, 38; cf. nos. 82 and 83 for Andrássy's opposition.
[3] Ignatyev's memoirs, in *I.V.*, vol. cxxxvi, p. 50. His disgust at the effect of Gorchakov's return to St. Petersburg is well reflected in two letters of his to Jomini, 13 and 20 Dec., extracts in *Revue d'histoire moderne*, Sept.–Oct. 1935, pp. 386–7.

for the Christians, abolition of the tax-farming system, and abolition of the remnants of the semi-feudal system. These proposals had in the first instance been unfavourably regarded by Jomini, owing to the influence of Ignatyev.[1] But on 16 November a revised version of them was dispatched to the Neva.[2] A fortnight later the return of the Tsar to the capital (4 December), preceded the day before by that of Gorchakov, made final decisions possible, though disputes over the *firman* of 12 December delayed the conclusion of the negotiations for a month.

Gorchakov had halted for a few days in Berlin on his way home and had assured the Germans that he would not allow minor dissonances to impair relations with Vienna and that he would continue to take his stand on the *Dreikaiserbündnis*. Bismarck had already laid down the guiding line of his policy throughout the ensuing three years: he would agree to any decisions and measures concerted by Russia and Austria together, but so long as they were not in agreement he would not take any steps either in the one direction or the other.[3] For the time being, at any rate, his position was not to be rendered difficult. Gorchakov refused to be won over by Ignatyev's arguments, and sent Andrássy the warmest assurances. If he seemed to be favouring some form of consular surveillance for Bosnia and Herzegovina, he was not prepared to press this on Vienna. Thence, on Christmas Eve, an amended draft came, which four days later was accepted by Gorchakov and on 30 December was circulated to the powers.[4]

The Andrássy note comprised various reforms in the government of Bosnia and Herzegovina, including the institution by the Turkish government of a mixed commission of Christians and Moslems to see to the carrying out of the reforms, and the communication by the Sultan to the powers of his firm intention to put all the proposed reforms fully into practice. Disraeli, piqued by the fact that these proposals had been put forward

---

[1] Harris, *A Diplomatic History of the Balkan Crisis* . . ., pp. 148-50, citing from the Vienna archives, Mayr (St. Petersburg) to Andrássy, conf. letter, 21 Oct., Hamburger (Livadia) to Novikov, 24 Oct., Jomini to Novikov, 31 Oct. The text of Andrássy's proposals to St. Petersburg of 16 Oct. is in *Actenstücke*, i, no. 183.

[2] Harris, op. cit., pp. 152-3. Andrássy included an outspoken complaint as to the impossibility of trusting Ignatyev.

[3] Bülow to Alvensleben (St. Petersburg), 8 Dec., in *G.P.*, vol. i, pp. 207-8.

[4] Extract from Gorchakov (from Berlin) to Novikov, 30 Nov., quoted in Harris, op. cit., p. 154; Loftus to Derby, disp., nos. 345, 16 Nov., 369, most conf., 396, conf., and 397, 8, 21, and 22 Dec.; tel., 30 Dec.; in *F.O.* 65/912.

without consultation with England, was inclined to refuse participation, but since the Porte itself asked the British to agree to them they could not be 'more Turkish than the Sultan', and after some delay they consented.[1] On 13 February the Porte accepted the note, with certain reservations regarding taxation, and on 22 February offered the insurgents an amnesty and an armistice. In reality the Turks foresaw that the note would be a dead letter and were preparing for drastic action against the twin fountain-heads of trouble, Montenegro and Serbia. Ignatyev was right in saying that the Andrássy note destroyed his position in Constantinople; it also ruined both Mahmud Nedim and the Sultan himself, unable to stand up against the wave of Turkish fanaticism, revolutionary spirit, and military pride, which in a few months was to submerge him.

The Tsar and Gorchakov had insisted on working with the Austrians, but how far they really believed in the efficacy of the note is doubtful.[2] Gorchakov had never taken any detailed interest in eastern affairs; he knew little of Balkan conditions, and almost nothing of Balkan geography. He thought purely in terms of the great powers and refused to examine the consequences that would follow if the Andrássy note failed to achieve anything: 'alors comme alors' was all that he would say.[3] When asked what was the Russian programme in the probable event of Milan being forced to flout the powers and give in to the rising war-movement in Serbia, he made vague gestures but no intelligible reply.[4] Probably Gorchakov was content to let events run their course and meanwhile to pave

---

[1] *Disraeli*, pp. 890–1; extract from Shuvalov to Gorchakov, disp., 13 Jan., in *S.R.*, vol. iii, p. 658. The text of the Andrássy note is in, e.g., *British and Foreign State Papers*, vol. lxvi, pp. 921–31. Elliot's and Buchanan's reports, copies in *F.O.* 181/535, show Ignatyev as urging the Turks not to accept the note. For the exact terms of the Turkish acceptance see *Staatsarchiv*, vol. xxx, no. 5587. For a full account of the negotiations between the powers and with the Turks in regard to the presentation and acceptance of the note, see Harris, op. cit., pp. 170–230.

[2] Goriainow, *Le Bosphore et les Dardanelles*, p. 315, citing letter to Oubril, 12 Jan.

[3] Jomini's letters to Ignatyev in Dec. 1875, quoted in brief extracts in Ignatyev's memoirs in *I.V.*, vol. cxxxvi, pp. 50–1. Jomini himself professed to Ignatyev to have little or no hope in the success of the Andrássy note; the outlook was very dark; Russia was faced with a catastrophe which would probably lead to war; the only thing to do was 'faire la meilleure mine devant le mauvais jeu'. Yet a month later he was arguing hotly against Nelidov's views as to the inefficacy of the Andrássy note; Nelidov's memoirs in *Revue des deux mondes*, 15 May 1915, vol. xxvii, p. 310.

[4] Kartsov, *Za kulisami diplomatii*, p. 19. Kartsov, the consul-general in Belgrade, was in St. Petersburg at the end of Dec. 1875; he described the Andrássy note as an impotent palliative.

the way for a far-reaching understanding with Austria. In December and January two important visitors came to St. Petersburg: the Archduke Albert, the leader of the Austrian military party, and Prince Alexander of Hesse, the Tsaritsa's brother, on a confidential mission from the Emperor Francis Joseph. Through the latter the Tsar seems to have assured the Emperor that he would not undertake any action of a panslav character. Slowly the ground was being prepared for the Reichstadt agreement of July.[1] Gorchakov continued to retain the confidence of his master, and Ignatyev's efforts in his absence to capture the Tsar had failed. It is questionable in any case whether the situation in European Turkey had not become too explosive to allow of Ignatyev's temporizing policy. Nelidov, his own second in command at Constantinople, thought that this was so and urged that only two solutions were possible: either to leave the Turks to stamp out the revolt; or openly to support it and put the strongest pressure on the Porte, even going to the length of war and setting up an autonomous principality of Bosnia and Herzegovina. This solution could not be criticized for not being anti-Austrian; but Ignatyev had doubted the wisdom of such direct encouragement of the Christians in arms, since he thought that they might be left in the lurch by the foreign office in St. Petersburg. Hence without abandoning them he had adopted the middle line of trying to win over the Sultan and the Tsar to reforms under the sole protection of Russia. The Andrássy note destroyed this possibility. Henceforward Ignatyev began to change course in favour of an immediate panslav programme, and the Balkan Christians found more and more encouragement in extreme action from his embassy on the Bosphorus.[2]

---

[1] Kartsov, *Za kulisami diplomatii*, p. 13. Corti, *The Downfall of Three Dynasties*, pp. 219–20, mentions Prince Alexander's visit, but says nothing of politics. Bismarck expressed deep suspicion of the Archduke Albert's visit; Russell to Derby, disp., 2 Jan. 1876, text in *The Journal of Modern History*, vol. iii, pp. 433–6, p. 449.

[2] Nelidov's memoirs in *Revue des deux mondes*, 15 May 1915, vol. xxvii, pp. 305–10, where he also summarizes a memorandum of his, which Gorchakov refused to read but which met with approval from the Tsarevich: the Straits were to be occupied on the first excuse; Constantinople was to be a free city under Russian protection; in place of Turkey in Europe there were to be independent Christian states; Serbia and Montenegro greatly enlarged; Greece with Epirus, Thessaly, and the islands; Bulgaria, and Macedonia (Ignatyev, on the other hand, would not hear of a separate Macedonia); Syria was to go to France, Egypt to England; what Austria's share was to be is not stated. This panslav programme was drawn up in the autumn of 1875. Nelidov was in St. Petersburg in Jan. 1876, urging that the hour for reforms had passed and that force was the only remedy.

IV

THE BERLIN MEMORANDUM AND THE REICHSTADT AGREEMENT

THE early months of 1876 were in the main marked by a confused lull in the storm. The rebels in Herzegovina and Bosnia were being quite unsuccessfully enticed to accept the Andrássy proposals, while the Turks, the Montenegrins, and the Serbs were pushing on preparations for war.

The Turks had signally failed in their military measures to suppress the revolt. They had lost heavily in men, particularly during the bitter winter. They were at their wits' end for money. They had likewise failed entirely to provide any kind of security with which to lure back the refugees. Divided responsibilities, frequent changes in appointments, paper reforms officially promised and then not acted upon ruined any chances of the main mass of the Christians believing in the capacity or wish of the Osmanli officials to protect them either from the Moslem *begs* and their retainers or from the Christian rebel chieftains. In Bosnia no general rising had broken out, but there were continual raids and outbreaks along the Save frontier and in the north-west, and the country was becoming more and more of a powder-barrel. In eight months the only practical concession that the Turks had allowed was the ringing of the bell of an Orthodox church in Sarajevo: 'it is true it is a very small one and the sound produced resembles rather the striking of a clock than the ringing of a bell, but now that a beginning has been made the Turks will get accustomed to the sound, and probably make no opposition if eventually a larger and more sonorous bell be used.'[1]

The vital point was clear. Would the insurgents lay down their arms and accept the promised reforms? It did not seem likely. They began the year by issuing a manifesto in which they appealed especially to Russia on behalf of their struggle 'for complete independence, or death'.[2] They refused to accept

---

[1] Freeman (Sarajevo) to Elliot, 7 Apr., in *A. and P.*, 1876, lxxxiv, C. 1531, no. 137, incl..

[2] Dated 26 Feb.: an English translation of its text is given in Stillman, *Herzegovina and the Late Uprising*, pp. 170–3. He maintains that this manifesto forestalling the attempts to induce the rebels to accept the Andrássy proposals was issued despite the official efforts of Ionin and Monteverde (another Russian agent) to

the amnesty and armistice offered by the Turks, or to discard their belief that Austria and Russia would shortly intervene on their behalf by force. Help from Montenegro and Serbia was steadily increasing. Two Russian 'relief' organizations were spending more and more money on them. Ragusa was filled with Russian agents, including Col. Bobrikov from the war office, and Col. Monteverde, the panslav correspondent of *Russky Mir*, later to figure on Chernyaev's staff in Serbia. Among the Austrian Slavs feelings were unrestrained even in the highest quarters. Rodić, who had been instructed on 21 February to negotiate with the rebels, was rightly or wrongly suspected of desiring his mission to fail so that the way might be left open for annexation. Jovanović, his brother-in-law, in command of the troops in southern Dalmatia, made no effort to conceal his sympathies with the rebels and his desire for annexation. In addition, Gorchakov now had on the spot an unofficial mediator of the most dubious character in the person of Wesselitsky Bojidarovich.

The result was that Andrássy's efforts to induce the insurgents to accept his proposals met with no success.[1] When Prince Nicholas brought about a final meeting at Sutorina on 6 and 7 April between Rodić and some of the rebel leaders, their demands (concocted in advance under Montenegrin influence) were pitched very high. They demanded one-third of the land for the Christians, remission of taxes for three years, evacuation of Turkish troops except for garrisons in six towns in which there were to be stationed permanent Austrian and Russian agents, a series of immediate safeguards and relief measures which were to be under the control of a European commission, and the application of administrative reforms to the whole of Herzegovina and Bosnia; they also refused to lay down their arms until the Moslems were disarmed and the promised reforms accomplished.[2] These were clearly impossible demands for the Turks, and hostilities were resumed by Mukhtar Pasha,

prevent it, and that the subsequent toning down of the rebels' demands was due to moderating Russian influence.

[1] For the details see Harris, *A Diplomatic History of the Balkan Crisis* . . ., pp. 242–53, using the Vienna archives.

[2] Čubrilović, *Bosanski ustanak 1875–1878*, pp. 117–19, 122–5, using the Vienna archives and Serbian printed sources; *Actenstücke*, i, especially nos. 249, 281, 287–9. For the text of the rebels' demands see *A. and P.*, 1876, lxxxiv, C. 1531, no. 144 incl., and Wesselitsky Bojidarovich, *Dix mois de ma vie, 1875–6*, pp. 162–6, also giving the names of the signatories, five of whom were priests; and see pp. 153–4,

whose appointment early in the year to command all the troops in Bosnia and Herzegovina had been a victory for the Turkish war party anxious to overwhelm the *rayas* by force of arms.[1]

The resistance of the insurgents, even before the putting forward of the Sutorina points, had been widely attributed to Russian influence. The British government, in particular, complained that Prince Nicholas was actively supporting the revolt and that Russian representatives in the Balkans were openly encouraging it with funds from Russia.[2] Gorchakov and Giers, now assistant minister for foreign affairs, protested amiably against such disbelief in their loyal collaboration in helping to keep the peace and in putting pressure on Cettinje and Belgrade to refrain from support of the insurrection. These protestations, however officially correct, did not square very well with what Monson, the first secretary at the British embassy at Vienna, could see at Ragusa, whither he was sent in March to report at first hand. Henceforward London was kept well primed with information, drawn from the spot and not retailed through Constantinople, as to Ionin and other Russian agents; and Monson came to have no doubts that 'had it not been for the money spent by Russian and by Dalmatian Panslavist Committees upon certain influential Chiefs, the insurrection would long since have collapsed'.[3]

To Ionin and Monteverde had now been added a third Russian emissary, Wesselitsky Bojidarovich.[4] His own account, written in extreme old age when the unity of the Jugoslavs under Serbia had been achieved, attributes a strictly pacific role to his mediatory activities with the Herzegovinan leaders, and a purely charitable aim in his distribution of funds to the refugees. But the fact that, himself of Herzegovinan origin, he

stating that two of the most important chiefs had been instructed by Prince Nicholas not to attend the final meeting.

[1] Koetschet, *Aus Bosniens letzter Türkenzeit*, p. 24.

[2] White (Belgrade) to Derby, 5 Feb. 1876; Derby to Loftus and Buchanan, 16 Feb.; Derby to Loftus, 23 Feb.; Loftus to Derby, 29 Feb.; in *A. and P.*, 1876, lxxxiv, C. 1531, nos. 2, 3, 17, 28, and 29. Rodić reported on 13 January that Nicholas had abandoned any pretence at maintaining a closed frontier; Harris, *A Diplomatic History of the Balkan Crisis . . .*, p. 266.

[3] Monson to Derby, 14 June, in *A. and P.*, 1876, lxxxiv, C. 1531, no. 479. He had reported of Ionin that he 'will be exceedingly disappointed if Baron Rodich's mission produces any pacificatory results'; disp., no. 16, 6 Apr., in *F.O.* 7/882. For Taylor, the ineffective British consul at Ragusa, see p. 580: he left in March 1876.

[4] The following paragraph is based on Wesselitsky's memoirs, *Dix mois de ma vie, 1875–6*.

had been in the Russian diplomatic service and all too closely
embroiled in the plans for a Balkan alliance and rising in 1867
and 1868 did not make his appearance on the Dalmatian coast
in October 1875 likely to have a calming effect. This was additionally the case in that he was in close touch with the Metropolitan Michael at Belgrade, and above all in that he began
by taking up his quarters with Ionin at Ragusa. He came as
the self-appointed secretary of a propaganda body largely of
his own creation, *Le comité international de secours pour les femmes
et les enfants de Bosnie-Herzégovine*. He succeeded in gaining the
Metropolitan Michael as its official president, and (a stroke
upon which he particularly prided himself) Bishop Strossmayer
as vice-president. Orthodox Serb and Catholic Croat nationalism were thus ostensibly united. In January 1876 he went as
the unofficial agent of the Herzegovinans to St. Petersburg,
where he was received by the Tsar and Gorchakov, by the
Tsarevich and his wife, and semi-triumphantly by Countess
Bludova, Aksakov, and other panslavs. The effect of his visit
was to stimulate very considerably Russian interest in the two
provinces in rebellion and to increase largely the supply of
money for the refugees. This was the essential prerequisite
for the continuance of the revolt: the rebels, secure in the
knowledge that their families (and they themselves during
temporary periods of crossing the frontier) were being looked
after and confident that a large portion of the relief funds would
find its way into their pockets or armouries, could afford to take
the high line of their Sutorina demands.

In Russia until the middle of the winter not very much
interest had been aroused by the events in Bosnia and Herzegovina, even though the Red Cross had early started a campaign for the refugees and had received ten thousand roubles
from the Tsar. Most of the press had supported the general
policy of the government, had not given much space to the
insurrection, and relied mainly on news from the Austrian
papers. The insurgents were generally described as such; only
later did they become transformed into brothers and Christian
martyrs. But by the end of the year the activities of the Slavonic
Benevolent Committees in St. Petersburg and Moscow had
effected a change. Much use had been made of two impassioned
appeals from the Serbian and Montenegrin Metropolitans, and
it was claimed that over 300,000 roubles had been collected

by the committees and other bodies. The Moscow municipality voted twenty thousand roubles for the victims of the insurrection in Herzegovina, a highly improper proceeding. According to the law a municipality could only vote money for charitable purposes within its own limits. A circular to provincial governors was officially published by the minister of interior, Timashev, who had no sympathies with 'the Slav cause', reminding them of the legal regulations. This caused an ominous outburst of dissatisfaction, and Timashev was overridden by the Tsar, who authorized the Slavonic Benevolent Committees to organize subscriptions throughout the empire for the victims of the insurrection, on condition that the funds should be dispensed only to the suffering refugees and not to the insurgents—a condition that did not in the least hamper the activities of the committees. The censorship did little but alter 'for the Slavs of the Balkan peninsula' to 'for the wounded and sick'. There was much genuine sympathy and self-sacrifice tapped by the panslavs, but, after all, 'in order to tend the wounded one must first procure them to tend. That will cost us half our money; the other half we will scrupulously employ in healing them.'[1]

Wesselitsky returned to Ragusa entrusted, so he stated, by Gorchakov with the mission of inducing the Herzegovinans to accept the decisions of the powers, but he himself made no secret of aiming at an *administration provinciale particulière*.[2] He

[1] Attributed to Vasilchikov (? Vasilevich), in charge of panslav medical relief at Cettinje, in 'Panslavists and the Slav Committees', in *Macmillan's Magazine*, vol. xxxvii, p. 69. For the rest of the paragraph: Loftus, *Diplomatic Reminiscences, 1862–1879*, second series, vol. ii, pp. 137–8; Meshchersky, *Moi Vospominaniya*, vol. ii, p. 281; and particularly G. K. Gradovsky's article (9 Jan. 1876) on relief work in Russia, printed in the panslav propaganda volume *Bratskaya pomoch postradavshim semeistvam Bosnii i Hertsegoviny*, pp. 482–93, giving details as to the sums collected and the text of the Metropolitan of Serbia's appeal. Considerably smaller figures are given in a contemporary propaganda pamphlet *Hertsegovinskoe vozstanie i vostochny vopros*, p. 84. The total number of refugees from the two provinces during the period 1875–8 was estimated at between 200,000 and 250,000, of whom there were believed to be some 80,000 in Montenegro; Evans, *Illyrian Letters*, pp. 4, 218; Mollinary, *46 Jahre im österreich-ungarischen Heere*, vol. ii, pp. 291–2; Sosnosky, *Die Balkanpolitik Österreich-Ungarns seit 1866*, vol. i, pp. 178, 182; Monson (Ragusa) to Derby, 19 Nov. 1876, in *A. and P.*, 1877, xc, C. 1640, no. 1075.

[2] He states that Andrássy entirely approved of his mission, and warned him of Rodić's intrigues to obtain for himself a similar mission of pacification which would allow him in reality to arrange for annexation, *Dix mois de ma vie, 1875–6*, pp. 135–40. It is in the last degree improbable that Andrássy took Wesselitsky into his confidence, but the latter's account is typical both of himself and of rumours current as to Rodić, Andrássy professed officially to find Wesselitsky's views very

went by way of Vienna, where he had two interviews with Andrássy, and was back at Ragusa by March. There he proceeded to quarrel with Ionin, who in his absence had switched all the funds from Russia over to his own pet Cettinje committee. He next entered on confused negotiations with the rebel leaders and Prince Nicholas with the aim of cutting the ground from under Rodić, and played a conspicuously tortuous part at the Sutorina meeting. Thwarted by his enemies in Cettinje and the Ballplatz, he left the rebel scene of action; made a smuggled journey to Constantinople at Ignatyev's request; claimed to have been secretly offered the governor-generalship of Bosnia and Herzegovina; accompanied Novikov to Berlin in May; and in the summer, appropriately enough, postured for a time as a volunteer in the Montenegrin army.

This type of peacemaker did not exactly allay suspicions as to the sincerity of the professed desire of Russia to work in conjunction with the other powers. Further, while Austria-Hungary stigmatized the Sutorina demands of the rebels as inadmissible, Gorchakov began by maintaining that they might serve as a basis for agreement and be fitted into the Andrássy scheme of reforms, since they did not aim at separation from Turkey. He even went farther and broached ideas of the grant of autonomy to the two provinces and of a rectification of frontiers for Montenegro (11 April).[1] This step appeared the more serious in that Russian opinion was beginning to be dangerously aroused and hostility towards Austria-Hungary was becoming more and more marked among army officers, young and old alike. In particular Rodić's activities were being given the worst interpretation in Russia, and *Russky Mir* went so far as to accuse him of having urged the rebels to place no

moderate and reasonable; to Langenau, disp., 17 Mar., in *Actenstücke*, i, no. 266. See also the appendix on Wesselitsky in Harris, *A Diplomatic History of the Balkan Crisis* . . . . Wesselitsky, according to what he told Monson, was opposed to the designs of Ionin and Prince Nicholas for an extension of Montenegro at the expense of Herzegovina, probably with an eye to the chance of his securing as big a position as possible for himself; Monson (Ragusa) to Derby, disp., conf., no. 11, 30 Mar., disp., no. 48, 4 June, in *F.O.* 7/882. For violent personal accusations against Wesselitsky see Ghikas, *Botschafter von Novikow über den Panslavismus und die orientalische Frage*, pp. 35–8, and Meshchersky, *Moi Vospominaniya*, vol. ii, p. 281. For a favourable opinion of him see the obituary notice in *S.R.*, vol. ix, 1931, pp. 732–5.

[1] Harris, *A Diplomatic History of the Balkan Crisis* . . ., pp. 256–7, citing from the Vienna archives Andrássy to Langenau, tel., 8 Apr., to Zichy, tel., 9 April.; Čubrilović, *Bosanski ustanak 1875–1878*, p. 159, citing from the Vienna archives Langenau to Andrássy, disp., 11 Apr.: so too Harris, op. cit., p. 261, and cf. p. 259.

reliance on Russian promises, since Russia was incapable of carrying them out; had she not once before been defeated in war by their Turkish oppressors?[1]

In the latter part of April the possibility that Russia might play a lone hand seemed to be increased when news reached St. Petersburg that the Turks intended to attack Montenegro. 'C'est un soufflet qu'on me donne', the Tsar minuted on Ignatyev's telegram reporting this. The Tsaritsa wrote of 'Turkey's latest infamy in wishing to attack Montenegro'. Ignatyev was instructed to inform the Porte that such a step would lead to the dissolution of the Ottoman empire by bringing about risings elsewhere, and on 22 April Gorchakov formally asked in the name of the Tsar that the powers should support Ignatyev's representations. Novikov was to tell Andrássy that no further pressure on Serbia was to be expected from Russia if Montenegro were attacked. As Giers remarked to Schweinitz: 'Nous n'avons pas de programme si ce n'est pas la paix, mais nous ne pouvons pas laisser écraser la Serbie.' The Turks protested that they had no intention of attacking Montenegro: it was Prince Nicholas who was allowing his men to attack them. The British accepted this statement as an excuse for declining any combined pressure on the Porte, and joined the Turks in countering with a request to Gorchakov that *he* should use his influence to restrain Prince Nicholas. Gorchakov sharply refused: the Turks had carried out none of their promises, and had, whatever they might say, massed troops on the frontiers of Montenegro. The rift between Russia and England was widening.[2]

The seriousness of the situation led the Tsar to propose that Gorchakov, Bismarck, and Andrássy should take the opportunity of his own forthcoming visit to Berlin to meet together and devise joint measures. This was not an easy task. Loftus, though ill informed as to Russian intentions, did express much of the truth when he wrote home: 'I could perceive though

---

[1] Wittrock, *Gorčakov, Ignatiev och Šuvalov*, p. 5, citing private letter of Langenau to Andrássy, 12 Apr.; pp. 8–9, citing Langenau to Andrássy, 7 June, reporting opinions of Klepsch, the military attaché. See also Harris, op. cit., pp. 254–5.

[2] Harris, op. cit., pp. 266–76; Loftus, *Diplomatic Reminiscences*, second series, vol. ii, pp. 156–9; Tsaritsa to her brother, Prince Alexander of Hesse, letter, 21 Apr., extract in Corti, *The Downfall of Three Dynasties*, p. 221; Schweinitz, *Denkwürdigkeiten*, vol. i, pp. 320–5; Loftus to Derby, disp., 22, 26, and 30 Apr., Derby to Loftus, disp., 27 and 28 Apr., and Elliot to Derby, 30 Apr., in *A. and P.*, 1876, lxxxiv, C. 1531, nos. 163, 187, 249, 169, 177, and 267.

there is a cordial wish—and moreover a decided intention to act and co-operate with Austria in these Eastern complications, there is no harmony of views in regard to the mode or basis on which such an arrangement can be come to.'[1] Andrássy had been putting increasingly threatening pressure on Serbia to stop her military preparations and had not been supported in the least adequately by Russia, whose consul-general in Belgrade caused perpetual recriminations. At the same time he was refusing to consider any enlargement of Montenegro. The Russians suspected him of working for the incorporation of Bosnia and Herzegovina, while they themselves professed to be working merely for the restoration of order under the sovereignty of the Sultan. It was now, however, becoming clear that these professions of the Russian government must be interpreted as in fact involving vital changes for the Jugoslav lands. The Russian attitude towards the demands of the rebels at the Sutorina conference showed that far-reaching proposals were likely to come from Gorchakov at the Berlin meeting. What exactly these proposals would be remained unknown, but Vienna cannot have been encouraged to learn from Constantinople that Ignatyev had put forward to Gorchakov as the policy to be pursued at Berlin the two alternatives: either the creation of Herzegovina as an autonomous province under Prince Nicholas; or independence and territorial extension for Montenegro, including annexation of the immediately adjoining districts of Herzegovina, wide privileges for the rest of Bosnia and Herzegovina, cession of Little Zvornik to Serbia, and introduction of general reforms throughout Turkey.[2]

How far Ignatyev's ideas had been adopted or what precise line the Russians would take were still uncertain when, on 11 May, the Tsar and Gorchakov arrived in Berlin, accompanied by Jomini, Novikov from Vienna, and, a few days later, Ionin from Ragusa. Andrássy, on Bismarck's request, had come a day earlier, fresh from his successful renewal of the *Ausgleich*. At the same time arrived the perturbing news of a serious outburst at Salonika in which the German and French consuls had been killed. Inevitable orders to warships and

---

[1] Loftus to Derby, no. 171, 26 Apr., in *F.O.* 65/936; tel. and extender, no. 194, 9 May, in *F.O.* 65/937.
[2] Čubrilović, *Bosanski ustanak 1875–1878*, p. 161, citing from the Vienna archives, letter of Zichy to Andrássy, 5 May.

stiff diplomatic measures followed. Constantinople was in the throes of approaching revolution. Bulgaria was about to explode. Was a complete break-down of Turkish control in the provinces at hand?

In this perplexed atmosphere in Berlin Gorchakov expounded to Andrássy a programme based on an elaborate memorandum which rehearsed the course of the revolt in a sense highly favourable to the insurgents and demanded of the Porte suspension of hostilities and direct negotiations with the rebels on the basis of their Sutorina demands. The essential was the inclusion, as a final measure, of 'une intervention directe et une occupation'.

'Jusqu' à présent la Porte envisage l'entente des Cabinets comme purement *négative*. Elle ne croit pas à la possibilité d'une entente active. . . . Il semble donc inaispensable qu'en se concertant sur les meilleurs moyens d'apaiser la crise présente, d'en prévenir le retour périodique, les Puissances s'entendent également sur le principe d'une coercition éventuelle, afin d'affirmer aux yeux des Turcs leur ferme résolution de ne point laisser la paix générale à la merci de leur incurie ou de leur fanatisme.'[1]

Worse still, from an Austrian point of view, Gorchakov also renewed the proposal which he had already suggested to Vienna at the end of March for the establishment of autonomous states under the suzerainty of the Sultan on the model of Roumania and Serbia. Any such solution as regards Bosnia and Herzegovina was, of course, assured of extreme opposition from Andrássy. After a hard struggle in private colloquy he obtained the abandonment for the moment of the broader Russian plans. Two months later he had to face them again, at Reichstadt. For the moment Gorchakov seemed 'as soft as butter', and Andrássy even claimed to have extracted his verbal agreement to a possible Austrian annexation of Turkish Croatia.[2]

Finally, agreement was reached on a document which but for its 'tail' was the handiwork of Andrássy: the 'tail' was

[1] Text of original proposal made by Gorchakov, in Harris, *A Diplomatic History of the Balkan Crisis . . .* , pp. 447–50.

[2] Andrássy to Francis Joseph, tels., 12 May, extracts in Harris, op. cit., pp. 295–7; Wittrock, *Gorčakov, Ignatiev och Šuvalov*, p. 8, citing Langenau to Andrássy, 25 Mar. (cf. above, p. 160); Odo Russell to Derby, disp., very conf. and secret, no. 234, 26 May, and disp., very conf., no. 257, 5 June, in *F.O.* 64/852, adds some points. Wertheimer's account, pp. 296–9, is very unsatisfactory.

claimed to be the handiwork of Gorchakov, couched in the language of Jomini.[1] This was the Berlin memorandum. It was communicated on 13 May to the British, French, and Italian ambassadors, in one of Gorchakov's most polished orations, while Bismarck scribbled in contemptuous disgust 'Pompon, pompo, pomp, po!' It was stillborn, except for the 'tail'. For, if the proposed reform measures failed, then (and here entered the Russians) the three powers announced that it would be necessary 'd'ajouter à leur action diplomatique la sanction d'une entente, en vue des mesures efficaces qui paraîtraient réclamées dans l'intérêt de la paix générale, pour arrêter le mal et en empêcher le développement'.

The preceding portion of the Berlin memorandum is of interest primarily in so far as it represents an advance from the Andrássy note towards the proposals of the end of year at the Constantinople Conference. The best means of preventing any repetition elsewhere of the deplorable events at Salonika and of a general revolt of the Christians was stated to be energetic collective action by the powers to compel the Porte to perform the obligations accepted by it in the face of Europe. A two months' armistice was proposed, during which the powers were to use their utmost influence to keep all parties quiet. Direct negotiations between the Turks and the insurgents on the basis of the demands of the latter were to be opened. Five points were then named which included the retention of arms by both Christians and Moslems, a mixed commission of Christians and Moslems for certain questions, and a measure of control to be exercised by the foreign consuls in the carrying out of the terms.

What had been decided upon by the three powers was to be carried out by the six powers. Was this second, reinforced version of the Andrássy note likely to be accepted by Disraeli, suspicious and angry at being excluded from the deliberations of the three emperors? The chances of acceptance were all the slenderer when it was fired at London during a week-end. The 13th was a Saturday, and Gorchakov had told Lord Odo Russell that he and Andrássy were remaining in Berlin till the Monday and that they hoped they would receive an answer

---

[1] Schweinitz, *Denkwürdigkeiten*, vol. i, pp. 329–30, quoting a conversation with Gorchakov. The French text of the Berlin Memorandum is in *A. and P.*, 1876, lxxxiv, C. 1531, no. 248, incl. 2.

from London before they left.[1] That might be all very well for
the French, who had not yet borrowed the week-end habit and
did at once accept on the Sunday,[2] but it was adding insult to
injury to the English. Gorchakov had a reasonable excuse, if,
as is possibly the case, Lord Odo Russell had indeed blundered
into 'offering his personal opinion, that our Government would
accept the Russian note—an unheard of step!'[3] In fact the
British cabinet decided, but not until 16 May, not to accept the
Berlin memorandum. Disraeli feared 'being drawn, step by
step, into participating in a scheme, which must end very soon in
the disintegration of Turkey', and he suspected that 'des mesures
efficaces' would mean measures efficacious only in breaking up
the Ottoman empire. The British attitude remained entirely
negative, for Northcote's proposal of a constructive counter-
proposition was not agreeable to Disraeli. The British refusal was
therefore peculiarly bleak and destructively argumentative.[4]

This was the most important result of the Berlin memorandum. It irritated the Emperor William,[5] and it made the worst
impression upon the Tsar, who from now on became more and
more firmly entrenched in the belief that nothing but hostility
to Russia could be expected from Disraeli and his government.
The ordering of the British fleet to Besika Bay on 13 May was
ugly confirmation, which was not mitigated by the diplomatic
assurance a month later that the admiral in command had
been explicitly instructed 'to be careful to avoid any occasion
of contravening' the treaties regulating the Straits.[6] There were

[1] Schweinitz, Denkwürdigkeiten, vol. i, p. 330.
[2] D.D.F., p. 60. The Italians also accepted on the 14th.
[3] Disraeli, p. 900, letter to Derby, 29 May.
[4] Disraeli, pp. 895–900; Andrew Lang, Life, Letters and Diaries of Sir Stafford
Northcote, vol. ii, p. 101. What Northcote's alternative proposal was is not revealed
by Lang. Disraeli had been informed from Vienna that Andrássy had explained
the request for an immediate answer by saying that Russell in Berlin had expressed
his personal opinion that the memorandum would be accepted by his government;
Russell to Derby, disp., conf., no. 445, 2 June, in F.O. 64/852. Gontaut-Biron's
dispatch to Decazes of 13 May supports Andrássy's view; Staatsarchiv, vol. xxxii,
no. 5979. Russell's own reports at the time show him as merely receiving the
memorandum ad referendum, but as urging his government to accept it. For
Disraeli's bitterness at what he regarded as the ultimatum from Berlin, cf. Shuvalov
to Gorchakov, letter, 19 May, text in S.R., vol. iii, pp. 664–7. The British press
approved the rejection of the memorandum, and the Liberal leaders made no
criticisms; Wirthwein, Britain and the Balkan Crisis, 1875–1878, pp. 45–7.
[5] Text of letter of the German Emperor to the German Empress, 3 June, in
The Letters of Queen Victoria, 1862–1878, vol. ii, pp. 459–60.
[6] Loftus to Derby, tel., 19 June, in F.O. 65/938.

good grounds for the British criticism of the Berlin memorandum and natural reasons for British distrust of the way in which it had been drawn up and presented, but angry isolation at this moment merely left the field open to the three eastern powers and the Christians in the Balkans.

That the consequences of the manner in which he had rejected the Berlin memorandum might be awkward was perhaps recognized by Disraeli. Queen Victoria gave but regretful approval and strongly urged the great importance of acting with the powers through a conference, if England were not to be isolated and run the risk of drifting into another Crimean war. Disraeli himself by the end of May was talking to Derby of a conference being 'the only practical solution in the long run'.[1] He had hopes of being able to take the lead in this direction with the backing of Bismarck, but he was also soon indulging in very secret overtures to Shuvalov for a direct understanding with Russia.[2]

Opening out in 'after-dinner talk' on 10 June, Disraeli, according to Shuvalov's reports, inveighed against the Berlin memorandum on the special ground that it was the work of Andrássy, in whom he had lost all confidence.

'Si la Russie veut écarter le Mémorandum et proposer une solution à elle, nous examinerons et montrerons bonne volonté, mais que cela vienne directement de la Russie: nous refuserons tout ce qui viendra par Decazes et Andrássy . . . il me semble que si la Russie nous disait en ce moment ce qu'elle veut, nous pourrions encore nous arranger avec elle.'

Then, after a warning as to Afghanistan and as to the pernicious influence of Ignatyev, he proceeded to give very incautious expression to 'what we want'. This amounted to a 'hands off' policy, leaving it to the Christians and the Turks to fight it out. Shuvalov and Gorchakov were intrigued rather than impressed by this appearance of brusque reversal of Disraeli's attitude towards Russia. The former considered that no definite formulation of a policy could be expected from England and

---

[1] *Letters of Queen Victoria, 1862–1878*, vol. ii, pp. 453–6; *Disraeli*, p. 902.

[2] The following account of the Anglo-Russian negotiations is based on the telegrams and reports from and to Shuvalov and Gorchakov, between 10 June and 2 July, printed textually or in extracts in *S.R.*, vol. iii, pp. 669–82. *Disraeli* has nothing upon them except one cryptic reference (p. 904) and an account of his conversation with Shuvalov of 23 June (pp. 906–7). The British foreign office papers are not of much more than formal interest. Gorchakov communicated Disraeli's overtures to Andrássy; Harris, *A Diplomatic History of the Balkan Crisis* . . . , p. 360.

that, if she were to be brought back into the concert of the powers, Russia should initiate proposals. Gorchakov, who was at Ems with the Tsar, was evidently somewhat nervous lest Shuvalov should go too far. 'Nous ne saurions nous faire d'illusion', he wrote to him privately on 14 June, 'sur les ouvertures des ministres anglais. Outre une revanche d'amour propre, elles sont évidemment inspirées par le désir de rompre notre entente avec l'Autriche et la France. . . . L'entente des 3 Cours Impériales reste la base immuable de la politique de Notre Auguste Maître.' The chancellor thought, however, that it might not be impossible to reconcile this principle of his policy with an exchange of ideas with London, and he instructed Shuvalov, while strictly avoiding 'l'initiative de propositions formelles', to coax the British cabinet 'à faire un pas de plus dans le sens d'une autonomie tributaire des provinces insurgés', and in the sense of a port and other territorial acquisitions for Montenegro and Little Zvornik for Serbia.

Thereupon followed a fortnight of conversations with Disraeli and Derby, in an atmosphere poisoned by the increasingly alarming news that was coming through from Constantinople and the Balkans. The British seemed prepared to admit an extension of territory for Montenegro, though not a port, but they shied at the Russian conception of 'autonomie vassale et tributaire' according to the precedents of Roumania and Serbia, despite Shuvalov's endeavours to explain this away as only administrative, and not a military or political autonomy. Nor could the two ministers be persuaded that the imminent risk of conflict in the Balkans demanded urgent action. The utmost that could be hoped was that the British government would adhere to non-intervention, as advocated by themselves. At the beginning of July the expected explosion occurred. By then the British military and naval preparations, though not regarded by Shuvalov with much seriousness, suggested that non-intervention might not be long continued. There had been enough of talk with London. The fruitless interlude of feelers and counterfeelers between London and Ems was closed by an exchange of letters between the Tsar and the Queen. The frigidity of the latter's reply was thought to betray the hand of Disraeli and had the effect of confirming the Tsar yet more strongly in his adhesion to Vienna and Berlin. The Queen's letter bore the date of 9 July. One day previously the

Reichstadt agreement had been concluded. Disraeli's efforts, if seriously meant, had entirely failed to secure a reorientation of Russian policy.[1]

In the meantime events in the Ottoman empire had far out-paced diplomatic talks in London and elsewhere. Whatever the merits or demerits of the Berlin memorandum, chaos and fanaticism rendered it a dead letter in Constantinople. It was to have been presented to the Porte on 30 May. During the preceding night the Sultan was deposed. Thereafter France drew aside, much to Gorchakov's distaste, and no common procedure in regard to the new situation could be concerted.[2] Throughout the spring Constantinople had seen growing excite-ment among both Moslems and Christians. Khitrovo, the Russian consul-general, and Zelenoy, the Russian military attaché, made no secret of their ardent hopes: no more did the Roumanian and Serbian agents in the capital of their suzerain. The Turks were massing troops for combat with Montenegro and Serbia. They were not going to send out of the country what little money they had; so in April they declared the com-plete suspension of the interest payments on their foreign loans. Rising feeling in Constantinople and mass demonstrations of the *softas* forced the retirement on 11 May of the Grand Vizier, Mahmud Nedim, and of the Sheykh ul-Islam. Their places were taken by Mehemet Rushdi and a *mollah* who was likely to sign the *fetva* required for deposing a sultan. Hussein Avni again became war minister; Midhat minister without port-folio (19 May). Anti-Russian feeling was boiling and the Russian embassy ostentatiously guarded. The military extremists were almost in the saddle. One final touch was needed. Plans, of which Midhat was the heart and soul, were pushed on for the deposition of the Sultan and for radical changes in the system of government. Ignatyev, aware of an imminent *coup d'état*, advised forcible action by the Sultan. The plot was hurried forward in fear of his arresting the leaders or taking refuge in the Russian embassy, and on the night of 29 May Abd ul-Aziz was forced to abdicate. Six days later he was found in his bedroom dead, perhaps murdered.

[1] Texts of these letters of 4 and 9 July, and Gorchakov to Shuvalov, 24 July, recording the Tsar's mortification, in *S.R.*, vol. iii, pp. 682–3.

[2] Dreux, *Dernières années de l'ambassade en Allemagne de M. de Gontaut-Biron*, pp. 208–47. He was with the Tsar and Gorchakov at Ems from 1 to 18 June And see Harris, *A Diplomatic History of the Balkan Crisis* . . . , pp. 336–46.

In his place the eldest son of Abdul-Medjid was proclaimed Sultan as Murad V, and he was immediately made to announce the preparation of a comprehensive reform scheme. Murad was a mild and amiably progressive person, with a pretty taste in poetry and music, a passion for building, and an addiction to drink. Unfortunately the events of his succession were too much for him, and he promptly went out of his mind—or was declared to have done so. On 16 June further tragedy was enacted. A young Circassian officer with a grudge against Hussein Avni forced his way into a meeting of the ministers and shot him; additionally he shot Reshid and some attendants: then he was overpowered by guards and killed. With Hussein Avni was lost both the most powerful and strong-willed of the Turkish military leaders and the most redoubtable opponent of reforms. Midhat, as President of the Council, was now the most influential single personage. Safvet Pasha, his close ally, returned to the foreign office. Mehemet Rushdi, indecisive as regards reforms, remained Grand Vizier. Abd ul-Kerim, a hardened soldier, but far advanced in years, was made Seraskier and commander-in-chief in Rumelia and Bulgaria.[1]

The revolution was taken as constituting a fatal blow to Ignatyev's influence and a corresponding gain to Elliot's. Ignatyev himself summed up the situation in June as hopeless. 'There is complete anarchy here; a debauch of fanaticism in the provinces. There is no possibility of any diplomatic action until a serious government is formed and the Sultan becomes master in his own house. At the moment he is a prisoner in the hands of an oligarchy of pashas.' He added, in reference to the British instigation of Midhat's constitutional reform schemes: 'I remarked the other day to Elliot before the whole diplomatic corps "qu'un steeple chase entre nous sous ce rapport

[1] For this and the preceding paragraph: Bamberg, *Geschichte der orientalischen Angelegenheit im Zeitraume des Pariser und des Berliner Friedens*, pp. 452–63; [Cherbuliez], 'L'Angleterre et la Russie en Orient', in *Revue d'histoire diplomatique*, vol. x, pp. 70–85 (accusing Butler-Johnston of financing the arming of the *softas* and Elliot of backing the conspirators); Wertheimer, p. 303; Nelidov's memoirs in *Revue des deux mondes*, 15 May 1915, vol. xxvii, pp. 311, 328, 322; Elliot, *Some Revolutions and other Diplomatic Experiences*, pp. 230–4, 236–42 (arguing strongly that Abd ul-Aziz committed suicide), 243–5; Gallenga, *Two years of the Eastern Question*, vol. ii, pp. 48–114. The text of the Turkish reform proposals announced on 1 June is given in Noradounghian, *Recueil d'actes internationaux de l'empire ottoman*, vol. iii, pp. 395–6. Midhat was subsequently put on trial by Abd ul-Hamid under the accusation of having planned the murder of Abd ul-Aziz; see his defence in Ali Haydar Midhat Bey, *The Life of Midhat Pasha*, pp. 196–233, and Pears, *Life of Abdul Hamid*, pp. 53–6.

est impossible et que je lui abandonne volontairement le prix".'[1]

This month of intrigue and blood in Constantinople had been accompanied by revolt in Bulgaria, in which the Turks saw the decisive hand of Russia and the beginning of the end of their empire in Europe. An abortive rising had already occurred in September 1875.[2] The effect of the success of the rebels in Herzegovina was now becoming decisive, and on the western borders of Bulgaria Serbian and Russian agents were more and more active. The Turkish government, in desperate financial straits, were squeezing out arrears of taxes. A general revolt was planned to break out in May by the Bulgarian revolutionary group in Giorgiuvo and Bucarest. They had the active support of the agent of the St. Petersburg Slavonic Bene-volent Committee, Ionin, who had always been even more of a stirrer of troubled waters than his brother at Ragusa.[3] Divided among themselves and with no military capacities, the Bulgarian revolutionary committee were working frenziedly on

[1] Letter of Ignatyev to Kartsov, 29 June, extract in *Za kulisami diplomatii*, p. 32.

[2] Hajek, *Bulgarien unter der Türkenherrschaft*, pp. 252–4; Naiden Gerov's reports to Ignatyev in *Dokumenti na blgarskata istoriya*, vol. ii, pp. 121–6. There is a very frank account of this rising and that of 1876 by a participant, Zachary Stoyanov, in his *Pages from the autobiography of a Bulgarian insurgent*.

[3] I. S. Ivanov's memoirs in *R.S.*, vol. lxii, p. 137; *Proslava na osvoboditelnata voina 1877–8 g.*, p. 224. Vladimir Semenovich Ionin (1838–86), the brother of the consul at Ragusa, is worth notice as one of the best examples of the Russian emissaries of panslavism so loudly denounced in the West. He had been one of the most energetic of the 'panslav consuls' under the Asiatic department. After seven years' service in Mostar, Belgrade, and Ragusa his impetuous extremism made further employment in the Balkans impossible, and he was removed in 1867 to Beirut and later to Damascus. He was pensioned off in 1872 and withdrew to the customs department until the autumn of 1875, when he left that service and went south to his Slavonic revolutionary haunts. At Bucarest he was one of the main leaders of the Bulgarian revolutionaries, and was in close touch with Chernyaev in the summer of 1876, planning raids into Bulgaria and later organizing Bulgarian volunteers. After the Russian declaration of war Ionin returned to Serbia and Bosnia, where in the course of 1877 he plunged into a feud with Despotović, the principal Bosnian rebel leader, and set himself up as the head of a provisional national Bosnian government. At the critical moment he fell out of the window of an upper chamber and broke his leg; whereupon his government also broke down. He lived on in St. Petersburg until his death in 1886, doing what he could to help refugees and others from Bosnia and Herzegovina. Letters of Ionin, 15 May and 28 Oct. 1877, to Prince Vasil-chikov, the president of the St. Petersburg Slavonic committee, text in *Trudy Instituta Slavyanovedeniya*, vol. ii, pp. 220–5; Freeman (Sarajevo) to Derby, 16 Nov. 1877, in *A. and P.*, 1878, lxxxi, C. 1905, no. 563; Loftus to Derby, disp., no. 549, 10 Oct. 1877, in *F.O.* 65/969, enclosing translation of an article on Ionin by the Bosnian correspondent of *Russky Mir*; Čubrilović, *Bosanski ustanak 1875–1878*, pp. 401–5; *Russky biografichesky slovar*.

very insecure bases. A fortnight earlier than had been intended the revolt broke out in two villages to the north of Philippopolis. Manifestoes were distributed summoning all Bulgars to arms; the hour of deliverance had struck; skeleton revolutionary committees were multiplied stirring up the dour, slow-moving Bulgarian peasantry to fling off the Turkish yoke. The Turks, with Moslem fanaticism running higher and higher, were rendered desperate at the prospect of the spread of revolt so near the capital and at the severance of one of their main routes to the north-west, the historic Adrianople–Philippopolis–Nish road. They allowed free rein to their Circassians and Bazi-Bazouks, and the blood-bath of the Bulgarian atrocities followed.[1]

Bulgaria was added to Bosnia and Herzegovina. The effect of the atrocities on Europe was profound, and it was evident that the Turks, sooner or later, would have to accept the intro-

[1] For a violently anti-Russian view of the Bulgarian rising, belittling the subsequent massacres and laying the utmost blame on panslav committees and the Russian vice-consulate at Philippopolis (where both the vice-consul, Naiden Gerov, and the dragoman were from one of the first villages to rise), see article in the *Levant Herald*, 21 July, in *A. and P.*, 1876, lxxxiv, C. 1558, no. 24, incl. For a good account of the rising see Hajek, *Bulgarien unter der Türkenherrschaft*, pp. 259–93, mainly based on Bulgarian sources; to which should be added Naiden Gerov's reports in *Dokumenti na blgarskata istoriya*, vol. ii, pp. 144, 147, 152–91.

The *Daily News* from 23 June onwards, and the *New York Times*, published the most lurid accounts of what happened through Edwin Pears. This was followed by the investigations of McGahan, correspondent of the *Daily News*, and Schuyler, the American consul-general, backed by Dr. George Washburn, of Robert College, and by Ignatyev; see MacGahan, *The Turkish atrocities in Bulgaria*. Schuyler was furnished with a Bulgarian graduate of Robert College as an interpreter; Washburn, *Fifty years in Constantinople* . . . , pp. 109–10. The first accounts were in part exaggerated, but the investigation conducted by Baring from the British embassy, who knew Greek and some Turkish but no Bulgarian, reported 59 villages destroyed and 12,000 victims killed. Schuyler's report put the number killed at about 15,000. Ignatyev had sent up to Philippopolis in mid-June one of his favourite secretaries, Tseretelev, as vice-consul, who was most active in organizing relief work, exposing the barbarous conduct of the Turks, and shepherding Baring; his reports to Ignatyev are in *Dokumenti na blgarskata istoriya*, vol. ii, pp. 191–224. Disraeli was very badly served by Elliot and the foreign office, and, as he had shown at the time of the Indian Mutiny, was always inclined to disbelieve newspaper atrocities. Whatever the precise figures there can be no doubt that appalling atrocities did take place. See particularly Temperley, *The Bulgarian and other Atrocities, 1875–8, in the Light of Historical Criticism*, pp. 10–37. The Turks later tried to throw the blame for the excesses of the Bazi-Bazouks on Ignatyev, stating that the Grand Vizier under the influence of Ignatyev refused to send the regular troops, applied for by the Turkish authorities, who would have prevented the necessity of using irregulars; *A. and P.*, 1877, xc, C. 1640, no. 334; so, too, in Ali Hayder Midhat Bey, *The Life of Midhat Pasha*, p. 75, and *Memoirs of Ismail Kemal Bey*, p. 123. The latter, who was a member of the Turkish official commission of inquiry into the massacres, admitted 6,000 killed (p. 129).

duction of 'reforms' in Bulgaria from the hand of the foreigner. A third complication, of decisive importance, immediately followed. Prince Nicholas had already in May given warning that his position would become impossible if he were expected to hold in his forces much longer.[1] The grisly events in Bulgaria precipitated in June the conclusion of the long negotiations for a treaty between him and Milan. Belgrade believed that war would be the signal for a general rising of the Christians in Turkey, and that the Ottoman government were too weak for effective resistance. The tribute due from the Serbs at the beginning of the month was not paid, whereupon the Turks demanded Serbian disarmament. To this Milan replied, on 22 June, with an ultimatum couched in intentionally impossible terms, which included a demand to be recognized as viceroy of Bosnia under the suzerainty of the Sultan, and on 2 July the two princes began hostilities. The Bosnian insurgents proclaimed Milan, the Herzegovinan Nicholas, as their sovereigns. The fate of the Turkish rule in Europe rested with Abd ul-Kerim (old and very fat) at the head of some 150,000 troops.

Serbia and Montenegro were added to Bulgaria, Bosnia, and Herzegovina: Europe was again face to face with the eastern question almost at its fullest extent. It was no longer a question of two Turkish provinces in revolt, but of more than half of the Turkish dominions in Europe in flames. How was the conflagration to be dealt with? What should follow it?

For Russia it was essential to square Austria. Already in Berlin the Tsar was anxious to arrange a meeting with the Habsburg emperor. During June the way for it was prepared by a visit of the Archduke Albert and the warm-hearted support of the Emperor William.[2] The old Emperor clung firmly to his reliance on Alexander's word. By the beginning of July he was exceedingly perturbed by direct reports from Münster in London of very strained relations between England and Russia and of British naval and military preparations. While urging Bismarck (in vain) to initiate pressure on London in a sense friendly to Russia, he was all the more anxious that Russian difficulties with Austria should be smoothed away by a personal meeting

---

[1] Memorandum of Prince Nicholas, 8 May, to the Emperor Francis Joseph, communicated by Božo Petrović at Berlin, 15 May, in *Actenstücke*, i, no. 341.

[2] *Wertheimer*, p. 320, and his article in *Historische Blätter*, no. 2, p. 264; Harris, *A Diplomatic History of the Balkan Crisis* . . . , pp. 432–3, using the Vienna archives.

between the two emperors.[1] Within a week of the Serb-Montenegrin declaration of war, Alexander on his way back home broke his journey at Reichstadt to see Francis Joseph. With the Tsar came Gorchakov, with the Emperor was Andrássy, and the result was the Reichstadt agreement of 8 July.

In the train, alone with Andrássy in a *coupé*, Gorchakov produced a memorandum which he started to read. Andrássy stopped him and asked point blank: 'Do you want Constantinople?' 'Oh, no!' Gorchakov replied, taken aback. 'God be praised, for otherwise we should have had a war.' Andrássy followed this up: 'Do you want Bessarabia?' 'Certainly; we have been robbed of it.' Andrássy pressed his hand.[2] Their further exchange of views was recorded in writing, but by each separately, and though their several impressions of what was agreed upon for the most part tallied there was one important divergence which was to cause the greatest difficulty during the negotiations of the following winter.[3]

They began by agreeing that they would observe the principle of non-intervention for the present, reserving the right of coming to a subsequent understanding should circumstances require it. Non-intervention was thus not to be an absolutely fixed principle. Gorchakov had already proposed non-intervention on 26 June and had failed to secure Andrássy's adhesion.[4] How could Austria-Hungary remain passive if the Serbs and Montenegrins were victorious? On the other hand Gorchakov, as he noted privately, did not wish to bind his hands in certain eventualities, such as a complete collapse of the Serbs, improbable as that was accounted at the beginning of July. Klek and Cattaro were to be closed to both Moslems and Christians, but Andrássy's version makes the closure conditional.[5] In no case would assistance be given to

---

[1] Wittrock, *Gorčakov, Ignatiev och Šuvalov*, pp. 12–21, 79–91, printing the texts of Münster's direct reports to the Emperor of 25 June and 3 July, of the Emperor to Bismarck, 3 July, of Münster to Bismarck, 11 July, and of Bismarck to the Emperor, 15 July; Bismarck, *Gesammelte Werke*, vol. viii, p. 178. Münster in his first report emphasized the sharp drop in Russian stocks and the refusal of the Rothschilds and other financiers to handle any Russian loan.   [2] *Wertheimer*, p. 326.

[3] For the texts of the Reichstadt agreement see Appendix II.

[4] Harris, *A Diplomatic History of the Balkan Crisis* . . . , pp. 428–30, citing the Vienna archives.

[5] Gorchakov had been pressing at least since April for the closure of Klek; Schweinitz, *Denkwürdigkeiten*, vol. i, p. 325. The British had been particularly disturbed in June at reports of large consignments of arms being allowed by the

the Turks. Gorchakov records that Andrássy added Cattaro, the closure of which had been asked for by the British, in order to give a more impartial appearance, but had intimated that it would be impossible to prevent assistance being given to the Christians owing to the keen sympathy of the Dalmatians. If the Turks won the war, Austria would concert measures with Russia to stop them if they committed excesses against the Christians. The two powers would require the *status quo ante bellum* for Serbia; but Serbia was not to be recognized as an independent state, though Montenegro might be. (The Russian version is silent as to their independence.) As regards Bosnia and Herzegovina the two powers would insist that the Sultan should apply reforms based on the Andrássy note or the Berlin memorandum, or at least on the Cretan regulations of 1868.[1] Andrássy excluded any territorial alterations whatsoever.

If the Turks lost the war, Russia and Austria, according to Gorchakov, would act in accord to regulate the consequences of the war. They would not favour the setting-up of a large Slav state ('un grand état slave'), a proviso which is specifically mentioned only in the Russian text. Then comes the serious divergence between the two versions of the agreement. Andrássy understood that Serbia was not to be allowed to acquire anything in Bosnia which should threaten Dalmatia and Croátia, but might be allowed acquisitions on the Drina and in Novi Bazar in the direction of Old Serbia and of the Lim, while Montenegro might be enlarged by the adjacent portion of Herzegovina, Spizza, and in the direction of the Lim, the *sanjak* of Novi Bazar being thus divided between Serbia and Montenegro, whose frontiers would be contiguous: but in that case Austria would annex the rest of Bosnia and Herzegovina. Gorchakov understood that Serbia was to be given 'quelques parties de la vieille Serbie et de la Bosnie', that Montenegro was to be given Herzegovina and a port on the Adriatic, and that in that case Austria would have the right of annexing Turkish Croatia 'et quelques parties de la Bosnie contiguës à ses frontières, d'après un tracé à convenir'. Gorchakov noted against this Austrian compensation that the Vienna cabinet considered it a

Austrians to come into Montenegro through Cattaro; *A. and P.*, 1876, lxxxiv, C. 1531, e.g. no. 487.

[1] The Cretan *règlement* of 1868, as Gorchakov pointed out in his pro memoria (see below, p. 588), had been suggested by England; Derby to Loftus, 14 June, in *A. and P.*, 1876, lxxxiv, C. 1531, no. 427.

vital condition without which she could not admit an aggrandizement of Serbia and Montenegro. It appears, therefore, that Andrássy thought that he had gained Gorchakov's agreement to the annexation by Austria of almost the whole of Bosnia and Herzegovina, in the event of certain gains by Serbia and Montenegro, while Gorchakov thought that he had agreed only to the annexation by Austria of north-western Bosnia and some other frontier districts of Bosnia, the whole of Herzegovina going to Montenegro. What is most curious is that Andrássy seems at this time to have been prepared to sacrifice Novi Bazar to Serbia and Montenegro. Gorchakov was abysmally ignorant of geography, and it can well be supposed that he was in fact very confused as to what was the exact outcome of their conversations as to frontiers in Bosnia and Herzegovina, additionally since annexation only, and not occupation, was recorded. Subsequently he maintained that Herzegovina had not been assigned to Austria at Reichstadt.[1] This appears to be directly contrary to the Austrian evidence, although it is claimed that Andrássy made an admission to Novikov to the effect that the non-mention of Herzegovina was due to a mere slip of the pen.[2] Andrássy also promised to send Gorchakov a detailed sketch of the proposed frontier rectifications, which Gorchakov complained Andrássy did not do.[3] It is at least possible that it was not entirely a case of Gorchakov being muddled, but that Andrássy himself was confusedly ambiguous, being undecided as

[1] Gorchakov to Novikov, projet de lettre particulière, encl., 5 Dec. 1876, text in *S.R.*, vol. iv, p. 442. See also Gorchakov's correction in Loftus's account of his interview with the Tsar on 2 Nov., below, p. 225, note 1.

[2] Goriainow, *Le Bosphore et les Dardanelles*, p. 329, citing, but not quoting, a dispatch of Novikov to Gorchakov of 15 Nov. 1876. It is possible that either Goryainov misconstrued the dispatch, or Novikov what Andrássy said to him. A further possibility may be that Novikov in writing down to Andrássy's dictation the original of the Austrian version (see App. II) omitted 'et Herzégovine' after 'l'Autriche s'annexera le reste de la Bosnie', while the omitted words were added to the copy made from this original and kept by Andrássy. It is worth noticing, however, that, when Andrássy on 13 Sept. verbally informed the German ambassador at Vienna of the full provisions of Reichstadt, he was reported as speaking only of Bosnia, no mention being made of Herzegovina: Stolberg to Bismarck, 13 Sept., *G.P.*, p. 46.

[3] Gorchakov to Novikov, as in note 1. Harris, *A Diplomatic History of the Balkan Crisis* . . . , pp. 437–8, prints an extract from Andrássy to Novikov, 19 Dec., in which Andrássy admitted that in Berlin in May he had spoken only of Turkish Croatia, but insisted that at Reichstadt he had expressly designated both Bosnia and Herzegovina to the Tsar on the map. 'Cette carte étant à petite échelle, je promis au prince, sur sa demande, de lui désigner exactement les limites du territoire en question sur une carte plus détaillée.'

to how much of Bosnia or Herzegovina it was desirable for Austria to bite off; and there may be some truth in the statement that the Archduke Albert and the annexationists convinced Francis Joseph after the Reichstadt meeting that the whole of Bosnia, and not merely Turkish Croatia, must be united to Austria-Hungary.[1]

By the Reichstadt agreement the Russian *quid pro quo* for Austrian gains was to be the retrocession of the portion of Bessarabia ceded by Russia in 1856. The Russian frontier would thus again reach the Danube. It was also understood that Austria would give Russia a free hand in the annexation of Batum, if she so desired, and as regards acquisitions in Asiatic Turkey equivalent to the territorial gains of Austria-Hungary.

Finally, if the result of Christian victories was to bring about the complete collapse ('l'entier écroulement') of the Ottoman empire in Europe, Constantinople might be made a free city ('ville libre'); Thessaly and Epirus (according to the Austrian version, Thessaly and Crete) might be annexed to Greece; Rumelia and Bulgaria (according to the Austrian version, Albania as well) might form independent principalities 'dans leurs circonscriptions naturelles' (according to the Austrian version, autonomous states).

The whole of this understanding, according to Andrássy's version, was to be kept secret, in particular from the Serbs and Montenegrins, a proviso which did not prevent the Russians informing Belgrade that even in the case of defeat Serbia would lose no territory. Of the Austrian diplomats only Károlyi at Berlin and Langenau in St. Petersburg were informed of the details: of the Russians only Novikov.[2]

On the whole Gorchakov might well feel that he had been highly successful at Reichstadt. He had initiated the lines of agreement with Austria, and, though Austria was to drive a hard bargain, when Russia finally went to war with Turkey in April 1877 she was in a stronger diplomatic position than she had ever been before in the nineteenth century at a time of crisis with Turkey.

---

[1] Goriainow, *Le Bosphore et les Dardanelles*, p. 319, without citing any authority.

[2] *Wertheimer*, p. 350, citing Kállay (Belgrade) to Andrássy, 1 Aug., and p. 324. Gorchakov also revealed in an outburst to the Serbian envoy in St. Petersburg that Andrássy at Reichstadt had vetoed any large Serbian or Slavonic state and that Serbia would not gain Bosnia; Jovanović, *Vlada Milana Obrenovića*, vol. i, p. 329, quoting extract from Protić (St. Petersburg) to Ristić, 22 July. For Bismarck's subsequent knowledge of the Reichstadt agreement, see below, p. 204. Ignatyev was not informed of it in detail, see below, p. 405, n.

V

SERBIA AND THE PANSLAVS

'CE Piémont a besoin d'une France: où est-elle?' Serbia did not doubt. 'Servia will not move', wrote Disraeli, 'unless she is confident that Russia will step in, in case of Servia being wasted.' She had good grounds for this belief, in part through the ambiguities of the official policy of the Russian government, above all through the channels of unofficial and semi-official nationalism in Russia. By May 1876 Chernyaev's arrival to head the Serbian forces in the field pointed to direct Russian encouragement, and was, in fact, the harbinger of the first outburst on a big scale of Muscovite panslavism in the cause of a Greater Serbia. The eastern question was thus most dangerously accentuated from the summer of 1876, not only by the new problems of Bulgaria and the Serb-Montenegrin attempt to disrupt the Ottoman empire by open war, but as well by this wave of nationalism in the one great Slav protector state which was to sweep the Tsar on to the reefs of national dignity and war.

Reichstadt was as necessary for Austria as for Russia. She could not delay close probing of Russian policy, now that she had failed to prevent the Serbs drawing the sword, even though (and partly just because) she considered that the Russian foreign office had played a double game in its lukewarm co-operation in putting a curb on Belgrade. There is little doubt that the outbreak of the Serbian war would not have occurred if the Serbian government had really believed the protestations of the foreign office at St. Petersburg to be sincere and effective, and if the Balkan Christians had not come to believe that the true policy of Russia was guided by Ignatyev and the panslavs. In this sense Disraeli had some justification for asserting: 'Servia declared war upon Turkey. That is to say the Secret Societies of Europe declared war upon Turkey.' But the real reason for Russian influence in the Balkans was given in the statement in the *Fortnightly Review*: 'The best, nay the only means of anticipating the triumph of Panslavism is to emancipate the southern Slavs.' The essential fact was concisely put by the English liberal leader, Forster, after a visit to Constantinople in September 1876: 'Without doubt for many years the Russian aim has been to replace the Turks by Christians, whereas our aim has been to keep the Turk where he is. Therefore the Christians have naturally looked to the Russians, as the Turks have to us.'[1]

Shortly after the outbreak of revolt in Herzegovina, Prince Milan had paid a hurried visit to Vienna. On his return, early in August 1875, he found Ristić triumphant at the general election with a majority in the Skupština heading for war.[2] Milan's first action throws a lurid light on what was possible in diplomatic relations between Belgrade, St. Petersburg, and Vienna. He telegraphed to the Russian government informing them that a rising in Bosnia was planned for 18 August, and asking point blank whether, if Serbia went to war with Turkey, she could count on Russian protection from Austria-Hungary. Both the information and the request were immediately communicated by St. Petersburg to Vienna, together with a suggestion that the *Dreikaiserbündnis* should intervene at Belgrade to maintain peace. Andrássy preferred that the Tsar alone should reply to Prince Milan, and that Austria-Hungary, acting separately, should support his reply. The Tsar acted accordingly: Milan was told that he could not count on Russian help and he would have to shoulder all the consequences of any war with Turkey.[3]

Thereupon Prince Milan proceeded to do what he could to depict himself as standing against the revolutionary and belligerent demands of his ministers. At the beginning of October the Ristić ministry was replaced by one less suspect. Austria-Hungary, supported by France and England, was putting the strongest pressure on Serbia to prevent her provoking a rupture with Turkey, and Russia was officially collaborating. It was,

[1] *Disraeli*, p. 908, and his Aylesbury speech, 20 Sept. 1876; *Fortnightly Review*, Aug. 1876, quoted in Thompson, *Public Opinion and Lord Beaconsfield, 1875–1880*, vol. i, p. 363; T. Wemyss Reid, *Life of . . . W. E. Forster*, vol. ii, p. 140.

[2] Jovanović, 'Serbia in the early seventies', in *S.R.*, vol. iv, pp. 390–1; Ristić, *Diplomatska istorija Srbije*, vol. i, pp. 41–4; Wrede (Belgrade) to Andrássy, disp., 19 Aug., in *Actenstücke*, i, no. 124.

[3] Čubrilović, *Bosanski ustanak 1875–1878*, pp. 190–1, 70–1, 62, citing from the Vienna archives Langenau to Andrássy, 16 Aug., Andrássy to Langenau, 17 Aug., and Hoffmann (St. Petersburg) to Andrássy, 20 Aug. Čubrilović also paraphrases a report of 17 Aug. from Andrássy to the Emperor Francis Joseph, which shows him as disbelieving in a Serbian victory in the event of war with Turkey, but as much concerned over the spread of Jugoslav revolutionary ideas and determined to take energetic action, even perhaps in the shape of an occupation of Belgrade, to safeguard Austrian interests. Harris, *A Diplomatic History of the Balkan Crisis . . .*, pp. 114–16, adds some points, including the fact that Andrássy communicated (19 August) to the Turks Milan's threatened declaration of war.

indeed, Jomini who initiated the idea of a 'démarche commina-
toire', which took final shape on 6 October in a declaration by
the powers that if Serbia did not refrain from aggressive
measures against the Porte the guarantor powers would not take
any measures to prevent a Turkish occupation.[1] But the position
of Kartsov, the Russian consul-general at Belgrade, was a highly
dubious one.[2] The Serbian military preparations, castigated
by Novikov at Vienna as offensive, were being encouraged by
Ignatyev from Constantinople in so far as they could be made to
appear defensive, and caused Kartsov the greatest difficulty,
since he was repeatedly being asked as to the attitude of St.
Petersburg towards them. In October took place Prince Milan's
marriage with the daughter of a Bessarabian landowner, Keshko.
Princess Natalia, as she became, had ambition, much capacity
for political intrigue, and great beauty. She was to cause years of
trouble to Milan and to her adopted country, but at the moment
Milan was delighted with his luxurious acquisition, and all the
more so since the Orthodox marriage-rite requires the bride's
father to be sustained by a proxy and the Tsar himself filled this
position, *in absentia*. After the marriage Kartsov went to St.
Petersburg, in December, to give a very dark picture of rising
war feeling in Serbia and to try to extract from Gorchakov
definite instructions. In this he failed, but on his return to
Belgrade he did succeed in extracting from Giers the very
equivocal statement that the Tsar and Gorchakov approved of

---

[1] *Actenstücke*, i, especially nos. 144, 151, 154, 159, 176.

[2] Andrei Nikolaievich Kartsov (b. 1835, d. 1907) had only taken over the
consulate-general in May 1875, apparently much to the satisfaction of Ignatyev,
who considered that his predecessor, N. P. Shishkin, had held the post far too long
and had antagonized the Serbs by his autocratic ways. Kartsov had been in the
Asiatic department, secretary at Belgrade 1858–9, and consul first at Jerusalem
and then at Corfu. He appears to have been a man of little personality or ambition,
who had few illusions about the panslavs, but did not dare to offend them. He
certainly failed to perform what Saburov described as his task: 'vous auriez dû vous
encanailler avec les Serbes comme Ionine s'est encanaillé avec les Monténégrins.'
He was represented by Novikov as an aider and abettor of the panslav movement,
while, on the other hand, Serbian politicians and Russian volunteers criticized his
lukewarmness and evasive ambiguities. His nephew, who put together his papers,
represents him as throughout strongly antipathetic to the whole Serbian venture.
He was certainly so by Sept. 1876, but seems to have been playing a double game
prior to the declaration of war by the Serbs. He himself declared that his relations with Milan were ruined by the return to power of Ristić in May 1876 and
the arrival of Chernyaev; to the Tsar, 26 May, copy in *F.O.* 65/953. Kartsov was
removed from Belgrade in the summer of 1877 (see below, p. 327) and was
subsequently consul-general in Buda-Pesth, Naples, and Paris (1880–1903).

his instilling into the Serbs that Russia was united with Austria-Hungary in working for peace, but that the Serbs should be ready in case these peace efforts should be fruitless. Yet even if Kartsov attempted to balance judiciously between official Russian and unofficial panslav policies, there seems no doubt that the Serbs believed that he spoke his true mind when he encouraged them to go to war secure in rapid support from Russia.[1]

Naturally the Serbs pressed on their preparations. Money was their most severe difficulty. They failed to obtain a loan from German, French, and English houses, and then turned to the Dutch.[2] Meeting again with no success they were forced to raise an internal loan of about £500,000 sterling. Russian financial aid on any scale was not yet forthcoming; the Russian money-market was not technically organized for loan operations, and money found its way from Russia, not yet in any large sums, only through the relief funds for refugees. Arms and munitions were bought abroad, notably in Germany.[3] Rebellion in Bosnia was being energetically fomented and feeling in Belgrade grew increasingly warlike, partly in jealous suspicion of Prince Nicholas. During the earlier months of the Herzegovina rebellion Serbian negotiations with the Montenegrins had failed to make any definite progress.[4] Mutual suspicions were strong and the internal situation in Serbia too uncertain. But at the

---

[1] Kartsov, Za kulisami diplomatii, pp. 18–19, 21–2, quoting extract from private letter of Giers to Kartsov, 24 Jan. 1876; Jovanović, Vlada Milana Obrenovića, vol. i, pp. 293, 295–6.

[2] Letter of the Metropolitan of Belgrade to N. N. Durnovo, 2 Mar. 1876, text in I.V., vol. lxxv, pp. 533–4. This and a second letter of 20 Mar. show the Metropolitan as eager for war against Turkey, if possible in conjunction with the other Balkan Christians, and as complaining strongly of the restraining efforts of the foreign diplomats. The financial difficulties remained paramount; e.g. letter of Prince Milan to Chernyaev, 17 June, text in Russky Arkhiv, 1914, no. 1, p. 38. The Tsar vetoed an attempted loan in Moscow; Harris, A Diplomatic History of the Balkan Crisis ..., p. 398, citing Károlyi to Andrássy, 3 June. Later, in August, the Serbs did succeed in raising a 6 per cent. loan nominally of about £500,000 in Moscow; Jovanović, Vlada Milana Obrenovića, vol. i, p. 313; Loftus to Derby, disp., nos. 365 and 394, 16 Aug. and 2 Sept., in F.O. 65/939; White (Belgrade) to Derby, disp., no. 107, political, 17 Aug., in F.O. 78/2487.

[3] Sturdza (Belgrade) reported to Bucarest on 7 July 1876 that ten batteries of artillery and 120,000 rifles had arrived from Germany; text in Iorga, Correspondance diplomatique roumaine sous le roi Charles Ier (1866–1880), no. 295.

[4] For the Hristić mission to Cettinje in Oct. 1875 see Engelhardt, 'La Confédération balcanique', in Revue d'histoire diplomatique, vol. vi, pp. 47–8; Čubrilović, Bosanski ustanak 1875–1878, pp. 196–8, and Stojanović, Serbia and International Relations ... (MS.), both citing from the Belgrade archives report of Hristić, 6 Dec. 1875; Jovanović, Vlada Milana Obrenovića, vol. i, pp. 282–3.

beginning of 1876 Milan, with the knowledge of the Russians, renewed, and extended, his efforts for combined action, sending General Alimpić to Cettinje and Garašanin to Athens. The latter failed to achieve anything more substantial than underground relations with a Greek 'war committee' at Salonika which was busy stirring up insurrection in the Greek regions of Turkey.[1]

Alimpić fared rather better. Early in March 1876 he brought Nicholas a draft of a treaty of alliance and a military convention for concerted action in case of war, containing an article by which the two princes bound themselves to support the rebellion. This, as Milan admitted, was flying in the face of official Russian advice. Nicholas does not seem to have worried overmuch as to this, but he would not trust anything but very specific commitments from Belgrade; he was under strong Austrian, as well as Russian, pressure; and he did not want to commit himself until the outcome of the Sutorina conference could be gauged. In the end, while accepting the Serbian proposals in general, he refused to sign anything before the prospect of war was certain. Novikov, in Vienna, was particularly suspicious of Nicholas, and inveighed angrily against the whole proceeding. Gorchakov was careful officially to rebuke the prince in very stiff terms. Ignatyev, though largely responsible for the negotiations being opened, likewise disapproved of the draft convention, but for very different reasons. He did, it is true, consider that its terms were unsatisfactory and might compromise Russia, but he was mainly perturbed at the clumsy rashness which the Serbs had shown in their negotiations, and at Novikov's knowledge of them, for he would be certain to pass on information to Andrássy and had instigated the Greeks, through Saburov, the Russian minister at Athens, to refuse to consider the Serbian overtures.[2]

---

[1] Stojanović, *Serbia and International Relations* . . . (MS.), citing from the Belgrade archives report of Garašanin on his mission to Greece, Mar. 1876. The Greek government were at this time anxious to follow the advice of the powers and continue their policy of watchful passivity, hoping in return to gain compensations against the Slavs. Fearful of the creation of a Greater Serbia, they informed the Serbs that they were not prepared to take part in the projected war. Later, after the first defeats in August, Ristić approached the Greeks again without success. One important reason for Greek caution was that their military preparations were far from complete. Lascaris, *La Politique extérieure de la Grèce avant et après le Congrès de Berlin*, pp. 25–7, 36–7, 49; Kanitz, *Das Königreich Serbien und das Serbenvolk*, vol. iii, p. 239; Driault et Lhéritier, *Histoire diplomatique de la Grèce de 1821 à nos jours*, vol. iii, pp. 388–91, 396; Ristić, *Diplomatska istorija Srbije*, vol. i, pp. 184–99, 306–31 (bitterly anti-Greek).

[2] Stojanović, op. cit., citing from the Belgrade archives report of Ranko Alimpić,

Ignatyev was justified in his fears. As a result of these danger-ous pourparlers there came 'la bombe Wrede'. The Austro-Hungarian consul-general at Belgrade, in an official audience on 16 March and in the name of the Emperor, declared to Milan that Austria-Hungary and Russia demanded the cessa-tion of his military preparations and equivocal attitude: they were firmly resolved to carry through their policy of pacifica-tion: if Serbia did not give a clear reply and act on it, she would be faced by a 'sommation unanime' from the powers. Milan at once applied to Kartsov to know whether Wrede was em-powered thus to speak for Russia. Gorchakov, using as an excuse for inaction the breaking off of the Serbian-Montenegrin negotiations, delayed a week before definitely instructing Kar-tsov to support Andrássy's threats, and even then the Russian declaration at Belgrade was little more than a categorical denial of rumours as to disaccord between Russia and Austria-Hungary and as to Russian approval of Serbian armaments. The Serbs eventually (25 March) gave Wrede an official declaration that they had no intention of attacking Turkey or hindering the task of pacification, but Kartsov's tardy and shuffling reply could but confirm them in the belief that Russia was very far from standing shoulder to shoulder with Austria-Hungary. This belief was still further fortified by the outspoken energy displayed by St. Petersburg in the second half of April, when, as already re-counted, the reports of the Turkish intention to attack Monte-negro and Serbia appeared alarmingly well founded.[1]

By then Prince Milan was faced with a situation in Belgrade which might have caused the loss of his throne or his life had he decided to stand out against the war party, who at the beginning of May signalized their ascendancy by the formation of a new government with Ristić in charge of foreign affairs. Already a month before the Serbian representative in Bucarest, Catardzhi, the uncle of Princess Natalia, had spoken to Prince Charles of

17 Apr.; Čubrilović, *Bosanski ustanak 1875–1878*, pp. 198–200, citing the same and telegram of Alimpić to Belgrade, 17 Mar.; Andrássy to Langenau, 4 Mar., to Wrede, 6 Mar., in *Actenstücke*, i, nos. 244 and 245; Novikov to Ionin, tel., 30 Jan.; to Gorchakov, tel., 14 Feb.; Gorchakov to Novikov (for Ionin), tel., 13 March; copies in *F.O.* 65/953; Kartsov, *Za kulisami diplomatii*, pp. 22–5, extracts from letters of Ignatyev to Kartsov, 17 Mar. and 14 Apr.; White (Belgrade) to Elliot, disp., no. 99, 6 Dec. 1875, in *F.O.* 78/2399, and nos. 18 and 53, 25 Feb. and 10 May 1876, in *F.O.* 78/2486 (on Ignatyev's influence).

[1] *Actenstücke*, i, especially nos. 257, 258, 260, 262, 270, 271, 279, 282, 283; Kartsov, op. cit., pp. 25–6; White to Derby, 20 Mar., in *A and P.*, 1876, lxxxiv, C. 1531, no. 88.

war having been decided upon and had asked for his participation. Prince Charles had been wisely reserved and had warned Milan against rashly endangering his country and against counting on Roumania as anything but strictly neutral. Milan expostulated in reply that the only choice before him was war or revolution.[1]

May brought Bulgaria into the field, revolution in Constantinople, and Chernyaev to Belgrade. Surely he must be the advance guard of the Russians. Surely the Autocrat of all the Russias would have stopped his coming if he did not approve of it. In fact he did not at all approve of this stormy petrel. At the time when Chernyaev was smuggled into Serbia the Tsar was at Ems, whither he and Gorchakov had proceeded direct from the Berlin meeting, and they did not return to Russia until 10 July. To Ems Kartsov was summoned early in June. He found Alexander bent upon peace, and incensed against Chernyaev. Kartsov was categorically instructed not to allow Serbia to go to war. But the Tsar, despite his titles, was not an autocrat. Moscow and Belgrade were more decisive than Ems. As Kartsov left to return to his post Gorchakov remarked: 'All the same, don't forget that though the Tsar is against war, the Heir Apparent stands at the head of the movement.' Hardly had Kartsov arrived back in Belgrade, after assuring Vienna on his way as to the pacific views of the Russian government, than he received a letter from Giers, in charge at St. Petersburg in Gorchakov's absence, breathing the spirit of court panslav circles and reminding him pertinently that he was to take into account the state of opinion in Russia.[2] Kartsov duly delivered the Tsar's admonition against war (7 June), but within twenty-

---

[1] *Aus dem Leben König Karls* . . ., vol. iii, pp. 15, 21–2, under date 6 Apr., and text of letter of Prince Charles to his father, 26 Apr. A further effort was made by the Serbs immediately after their declaration of war to enlist the support of Roumania, likewise without success; ib., p. 47.

[2] Kartsov, *Za kulisami diplomatii*, pp. 30–1. His personal relations with Milan were by now extremely cold; Kartsov to the Tsar, 26 May, copy in *F.O.* 65/953. Giers seems to have regarded the failure of the Berlin memorandum as making it impossible to hold back the Serbs. Immediately after the Constantinople revolution of 30 May he said to the Greek minister at St. Petersburg: 'Rien ne pourra retarder les Serbes d'une action belliqueuse, si la Turquie répond négativement aux propositions contenues dans le mémorandum des puissances.' Lascaris, *La Politique extérieure de la Grèce avant et après le Congrès de Berlin*, p. 30. Cf. Giers's advice to the Greek minister in June, op. cit., p. 27: 'Nous ne conseillons à personne de faire la guerre, mais l'amitié et la préparation sont toujours une bonne chose.'

four hours he also delivered thinly disguised inquiries from Ignatyev stimulating war feeling. There was no actual disavowal of Chernyaev; Kartsov was speaking with two voices. The Serbs interpreted his unofficial encouragement as meaning that they could rely on the panslavs' forcing the Russian government to come to their help, if need be, within two or three months of the outbreak of war.[1]

It was not delayed. Their military preparations were being pushed forward so as to be ready for the opening of July.[2] By the middle of June the long-deferred treaty with Nicholas was signed and it only remained to take the final steps for war.[3] The Montenegrins were relatively well armed and provisioned, buoyant and eager for war, friendly enough to the Serbs (despite some intrigues against Milan), and confident of Russian assistance. A few Garibaldians added a halo of successful revolution.[4] Chernyaev at the head of the Serbian army seemed to give a similar halo of intrepid victories.

Mikhail Grigorovich Chernyaev, born in 1828, had sprung into prominence in Russia in 1864–6 as a result of his dashing successes in Central Asia culminating in the capture of Tashkent. This last exploit had been carried out contrary to orders and earned him the lasting hostility of Milyutin. He was recalled and sent off on leave. He had already become fired with enthusiasm for the cause of the Slav peoples through Aksakov's paper *Dyen*, and the Cretan revolt and rumours of Michael of Serbia being likely to lead a Balkan war of Slav emancipation led him to offer his services to the prince, 'l'enthousiasme étant l'unique modèle de ma démarche', as he characteristically and

[1] Wrede to Andrássy, tel. and disp., extract, 8 June, in *Actenstücke*, i, nos. 434, 440 (for the *démarche* of 7 June); Jovanović, *Vlada Milana Obrenovića*, vol. i, pp. 318–19.
[2] Wrede to Andrássy, disp. extract, 25 May, tel., 21 June, in *Actenstücke*, i, nos. 367 and 479.
[3] Shchatokin (Ragusa) to Novikov, tels., 28 and 31 May, copies in *F.O.* 65/953; letter of Milan to Chernyaev, 17 June, text in *Russky Arkhiv*, 1914, no. 1, pp. 36–8. The negotiations with Montenegro had been renewed upon Ristić's return to power at the beginning of May; Ristić, *Diplomatska istorija Srbije*, vol. i, pp. 85–6, 88–9. They were by no means satisfactory from a Serbian point of view, since no adequate combined action was secured; Jovanović, *Vlada Milana Obrenovića*, vol. i, pp. 303–4.
[4] Memoirs of Marko Petrović Dragović, in *R.S.*, vol. xxxviii, pp. 363–82. Monson reported to Derby from Ragusa, 14 June, that Ragusa was again filled with Russian agents and that Prince Nicholas was hastening on his military preparations and purchasing rifles from the Austrian war department; no. 56, in *F.O.* 7/882. Last-minute attempts by the Turks to separate the Montenegrins from the Serbs, by the lure of territorial concessions to the former, failed to have any effect; Harris, *A Diplomatic History of the Balkan Crisis* . . . , pp. 402–6.

quite truthfully expressed himself.[1] Chernyaev was an adventurous knight-errant, a fighting leader without political or diplomatic understanding or ability. This offer became known to Milyutin and the Tsar: there was a violent scene between the former and Chernyaev; and the conqueror of Tashkent was thereupon placed upon the retired list. After much heated intriguing he succeeded in procuring his reinstatement in the active army, and served in Poland until 1875, but he then left the service and took over the editorship of the extreme nationalist paper *Russky Mir*. Thus when he appeared in Serbia he was no longer actually in the Russian army.

In the autumn of 1875 Chernyaev had been planning to equip 500 volunteers and take them to Serbia, but the Moscow Slavonic Committee could not find the money.[2] In February 1876 he came to the Moscow head-quarters of the panslavs and again offered his services to the Serbs in the forthcoming war. Ristić was decidedly cool, and said that he would prefer General Fadeyev, who was much better known in Serbia through his military and panslav writings and was expected by the Serbs to be coming. Chernyaev was exceedingly annoyed and was inclined to give up his idea, but, since Fadeyev was not yet back from reorganizing the Khedive's army in Egypt (see above, p. 70), both Milan and Ristić finally agreed to his coming. There was no difficulty in securing the visa necessary for every Russian proposing to go abroad, for in this case the necessary local authority was the governor-general of Moscow, Prince Dolgorukov, who was favourably enough inclined. On 19 April Chernyaev left Moscow in great secrecy for Belgrade, getting into touch on his way with Bulgarian patriot revolutionaries in Kishinev and Bucarest. He arrived in Serbia in May and took command of the main Serbian army destined to operate up the Morava and towards Sofia. In the middle of the month the *Novoe Vremya*, already backing such a venture, came out with an article announcing the news and declaring: 'All Russians who understand the importance of the task with which Russia and Europe have now to deal wish him every success.'[3]

[1] Letter of Chernyaev to Prince Michael, 7 March 1867, text in *Russky Arkhiv*, 1914, no. 1, p. 34.
[2] Aksakov, *Slavyansky vopros*, p. 220.
[3] N. N. Durnovo's memoirs, in *I.V.*, vol. lxxv, pp. 532–5; I. S. Ivanov's memoirs, in *R.S.*, vol. lxii, p. 136. Durnovo was, by appointment of the Moscow Slavonic Benevolent Committee and the Metropolitan Michael of Belgrade, bursar of a

With the outbreak of the Serbian war the panslav excitement in St. Petersburg and Moscow, which had been notably intensified in May and June during the absence of the Tsar and the exit from the capital of most of the official world, swelled to its crescendo of July to November. Wildly optimistic news appeared in the press, grossly exaggerating Serbian numbers and successes.[1] At the Constantinople embassy, Zelenoy, the military attaché, was ultra-Serbian and equally optimistic: Nelidov was busy sending to Belgrade all the military information as to the Turks which he could collect: Ignatyev was hoping for the best and stirring up the Slavonic committees in Russia.[2] In Herzegovina, Yastrebov, the Russian member of the defunct consular commission of the previous autumn, still remained at Mostar and was plying Ionin with news as to the Turkish movements for transmission to Cettinje.[3] The Bulgarian atrocities, made known through the energy of Ignatyev and the western press,[4] added blazing fuel to the fire of the panslavs and stirred them to an appeal which well illustrates the character of their propaganda.

'Monstrous cruelties; the wildest Saturnalia of the most hideous passions; the destruction of young girls by fire after their outrage and dishonour; the massacre by tens of thousands of harmless inhabitants; the devastation of a whole region by fire and sword—in a word every description of torment and disaster is now being

Serbian hostel in Moscow which had been opened in 1874. The arrangements for Chernyaev's going to Serbia were made through him and the Metropolitan. It is noteworthy that, apart from Milan, Ristić appears in their correspondence as the deciding person, though he had not yet officially returned to power. *Novoe Vremya*, 19 May; précis of the article in Loftus to Derby, 24 May, in *A. and P.*, 1876, lxxxiv, C. 1531, no. 319; *Dnevnik A. S. Suvorina*, p. 81 (Suvorin was the editor). The semi-official *Agence Russe* weakly countered this by declaring, on 25 May, that Chernyaev was in Belgrade solely as a journalist; *A. and P.*, loc. cit., no. 329.

[1] Some idea of these can be obtained from Loftus, *Diplomatic Reminiscences, 1862–1879*, second series, vol. ii, pp. 172–3, and *A. and P.*, 1876, lxxxiv, C. 1531, no. 492. *Russky Mir*, Chernyaev's paper, naturally led the way.

[2] Nelidov's memoirs in *Revue des deux mondes*, 15 May 1915, vol. xxvii, pp. 334–5; Kartsov, *Za kulisami diplomatii*, pp. 33–4; Jovanović, *Vlada Milana Obrenovića*, vol. i, p. 305 (emphasizing Ignatyev's exaggerations of Turkish weakness).

[3] Freeman (Mostar) to Holmes (Sarajevo), disp., no. 15, 4 Aug., copy in *F.O.* 78/2489; cf. Monson (Ragusa) to Derby, disp., no. 130, conf., 22 Aug., in *F.O.* 7/883.

[4] Besides using to the utmost the reports of Tseretelev from Philippopolis (see p. 171, note 1), Ignatyev assiduously fed the Russian press, in particular Katkov: he appointed Burmov, one of the leading Bulgars in Constantinople, as special press attaché at the embassy; St. Danev, 'Za stogodishninata ot rozhdenieto na graf Ignatyev', in *Slavyanski glas*, 1932, nos. 1–2, pp. 7–8.

inflicted on the unarmed Bulgarian population by a fanatically enraged Asiatic horde, which has planted itself on the ruins of an ancient and a great Orthodox Empire and of other Orthodox Slavonian States. This horde, this monstrous iniquity and monstrous falsehood, which in former days was curbed by Russian Sovereigns but which through envy to Russia and hatred to the Slavonian race has now again been exalted by the united efforts of the whole of Western Europe and introduced, be-powdered and be-rouged, into the family of Christian nations;—this Turkey again meditates, in the face of Europe, to trample under foot the Bulgarian race and to destroy within her own limits the last bulwark of Slavonian nationality—Servia and Montenegro.

'The cup of patience, even Slavonian patience, has at last overflowed. The spark ignited by Herzegovinian despair has burst into a broad flame. Bulgaria, Servia and Montenegro have seized their arms and rushed into the fray; the last terrible bloody struggle between Slavism and Islam has commenced. For Slavonians this contest is one of life and death; they have determined to attain independence or perish. They have neither sufficient arms nor money. . . .

'While the English Government is encouraging Turkey with both moral and material aid, and Austria-Hungary shielding Turkey as with an iron wall along the whole of her extended frontier with the view of preventing the supply of bread and arms to the struggling Slavs, the other Western, European Powers remain neutral spectators of the unequal, mortal conflict. . . . Why have the Bulgarians and Servians suffered so terribly and so long? Solely because they are Slavonians of the Orthodox Faith; and because they are brethren in faith and race with the Russians. This is the sin for which they are being punished, and they have no protectors in the whole world *save Russia alone*. But is this not sufficient?

'Leaving the solution of this question, as regards its political aspects, to higher powers, the Moscow Slavonic Committee appeals to the public conscience of Russia and implores aid for the victims of the insurrection slaughtered for the sin of Orthodoxy, for the sin of uniformity of religion and race with ourselves. . . .'[1]

In such excitement of national feelings the panslavs found a ready ally in the Orthodox church, the most effective organization for propaganda in the empire. On 13 July the Metropolitan

---

[1] Loftus to Derby, disp., no. 322, 17 July, enclosing translation of the appeal, in *F.O.* 65/938. In the autumn translations of Gladstone's pamphlet *The Bulgarian Atrocities and the Eastern Question* were given the widest distribution possible. 10,000 copies, a very large edition for the Russia of that time, were issued of the first translation, at a cheap rate.

of Moscow held a special service for the success of Serbian and Montenegrin arms—a manifestation which was not, however, followed by his colleague at St. Petersburg[1]—and an appeal issued by the Metropolitan of Belgrade was distributed broadcast by the clergy. Already before July church collections had been claimed as being the largest source of income for the relief funds of the Slavonic Benevolent Committees.[2] Now these were vastly swelled. Khludov (who had already been financing Chernyaev) and other Moscow millionaires began to open their pockets.[3] The Red Cross under the very active patronage of the Empress began organizing medical work on a large scale in Serbia. In St. Petersburg society ladies collected money in the tramcars and steamboats, and by house-to-house visiting. The spectacle of the aged Countess Protasova, the Empress's mistress of the robes, and of the equally highly placed Countess Adlerberg publicly collecting money in the streets of the capital left no doubts that one section, at least, of the court was doing its utmost to further 'the Slav cause'.[4] The backing given by the Tsarevich and his wife was equally notorious.[5]

On the outbreak of war in July a new feature was added to the movement in the shape of the volunteers. Hitherto money and propaganda had been the means of action: now, while these were feverishly increased, men were sent to seal by their blood the sacred cause of the fraternal union of the Slav peoples. Aksakov and his adherents in Moscow worked at the highest pressure, adding to their activities a recruiting office publicly

---

[1] As Y. P. Polonsky, the poet, bitterly complained in his diary, the Metropolitan Isidore of St. Petersburg refused to hold a memorial service for the Slavs who had been killed, and in August censured a St. Petersburg priest for holding one for those fallen in Serbia; *Na chuzhoi storonye*, 1924, vol. iv, pp. 88, 97.

[2] For emphasis on the assistance of the church and the amount of small contributions, particularly from church collections in the towns and villages, see Aksakov, *Slavyansky vopros*, pp. 216, 220, 228; Miller, *Slavyanstvo i Evropa*, pp. 203, 413–14, 331; Gradovsky in *Bratskaya pomoch postradavshim semeistvam Bosnii i Hertsegoviny*, pp. 482, 485–9.

[3] Pokrovsky, *Russkaya istoriya s drevnyeshikh vremen*, vol. iv, p. 253.

[4] Schweinitz, *Denkwürdigkeiten*, vol. i, pp. 340–1.

[5] Chernyaev maintained touch with the Tsarevich through V. V. Zinoviev, his marshal of court; Pokrovsky, *Diplomatiya i voiny tsarskoi Rossii v xix stoletii*, p. 259; Kartsov, *Za kulisami diplomatii*, p. 30. One of the Tsarevich's confidants, Count Vorontsov-Dashkov, a general-adjutant and the chief of staff of the Guards corps, was an energetic supporter of the panslavs and encouraged Guards officers to volunteer to Serbia; Schweinitz, *Denkwürdigkeiten*, vol. i, p. 341; Wittrock, *Gorčakov, Ignatiev och Šuvalov*, p. 32, citing private letter of Langenau to Andrássy, 16 Aug.; Ovsyany, *Blizhny vostok i slavyanstvo*, p. 108.

opened without interference by the government. The streets of Moscow were gay with the badges of the Slav tricolour, blue, white, and red; the great camp on the outskirts of Moscow was pestered by agents of the Slavonic committee trying to recruit officers for Serbia; visas were easily arranged, for Prince Dolgorukov, the governor-general of Moscow, undertook to issue them to all who presented the blank certificates issued under the signature of the Slavonic committee stating that the holders were going to enter the Serbian army.[1] The railway administration was as accommodating as could be, and in numerous cases granted free tickets and free transmission of baggage and stores.[2] The departure of the volunteer trains provided admirable copy for panegyrics in the press; and for Tolstoi the closing scene (originally censored) of Vronsky's tragedy. Officers who volunteered for service in Serbia had indeed to resign their commissions, but they were promised reinstatement. Only after the irresponsible declaration of Serbian independence by Chernyaev did the Tsar finally prohibit any volunteering of those in the active army.[3] Until then the authorities had seemed powerless or unwilling to intervene effectually, perhaps regarding the movement 'comme une soupape de sûreté sans laquelle une explosion eût été malaisée à prévenir'.[4]

It was not the actual number of these volunteers that was significant, but the fact that some of them were officers in the regular army and highly placed in society, the fact that the court appeared to head the movement, and above all the fact of such a vehement campaign in the press and in various forms of meetings. Those who sallied off amid the cheering and the strains of *Bozhe Tsarya Khrani* to Belgrade and the Morava valley were probably not more than 5,000 in all.[5] They included

---

[1] Aksakov, *Slavyansky vopros*, pp. 223–4; Tcharykow, *Glimpses of high politics*, p. 91: Porokhovshchikov's memoirs, in *I.V.*, vol. lxvii, pp. 542–3. For both capitals, see also the hostile, but confirming, extracts from Vasilchikov's letters; he had just been made president of the St. Petersburg Committee, but was not a member of the directing 'special commission'; Golubev, *Kn. A. I. Vasilchikov*, pp. 113–17.

[2] I. S. Ivanov's memoirs, in *R.S.*, vol. lxii, p. 143. He is speaking of his experience at Kishinev, where he was organizing the passage of the volunteers.

[3] Von Rosenbach's memoirs, in *R.S.*, vol. clxv, pp. 73–4. He was in command of the Pavlovsk life-guard regiment. A Baltic German, he had no sympathy with 'the Slav cause', and his sense of discipline was outraged by the volunteer movement.

[4] Leroy Beaulieu, 'Les réformes de la Turquie: la politique russe et le panslavisme', in *Revue des deux mondes*, Dec. 1876, p. 513.

[5] Pokrovsky in *Diplomatiya i voiny tsarskoi Rossii v xix stoletii*, p. 260, allows 6,000 as

men of very diverse political views, fired with high idealism and deep patriotism.[1] But such were in a minority. Taken as a whole they impressed an ardent Russian nationalist eyewitness as a rabble of undesirables; and a more restrained judge strongly criticized the panslavs for concentrating on quantity rather than quality.[2] Very few of the volunteers seem to have been from the peasantry. There was a detachment of 120 Don Cossacks specially fitted out by the St. Petersburg Slavonic Committee. There were a certain number from the rank and file of the army. Of the officers, some eight hundred in all, many belonged to the best society in St. Petersburg and Moscow and went in search of military glory, to fight and not to dabble in politics; others were retired military men who wanted adventure or a chance of making some money. Far too many were 'scum' who filled the coffee-houses of Belgrade, ran up debts, and insulted the Serbs in their drunken orgies.[3] Most of the volunteers who actually reached the front fought bravely, as the Serbs, especially their peasant soldiers, admitted. At the final disaster of Djunis, when the Serbs were demoralized and without fight, the Russian volunteers almost alone displayed bravery and steadiness.[4]

At the head of them, and in command of the main Serbian

a maximum. Aksakov stated that there were about 4,000, of whom 1,176 were directly supported by the Moscow Slavonic Benevolent Committee; *Slavyansky vopros*, pp. 227, 233. I. S. Ivanov gives the number of volunteers as about 5,000, of whom some 1,500 were Bulgars; *R.S.*, vol. lxii, p. 143. Ristić, *Diplomatska istorija Srbije*, vol. i, p. 154, gives the number actually serving with the Serbian army as not more than 3,000, of whom 600 were officers. Jovanović, *Vlada Milana Obrenovića*, vol. i, p. 347, cites an official Serbian estimate as giving 718 officers and 2,000 rank and file, figures which are very close to those of Chernyaev himself, but refer only to the number of volunteers actually at the front: cf. Chernyaev's letter in the *Daily News*, 24 Feb. 1877, giving 646 officers and 1,806 other ranks in the Morava and Timok army, quoted in Thompson, *Public Opinion and Lord Beaconsfield 1875–1880*, vol. ii, p. 53.

[1] Among them were Stepniak (Kravchinsky), later well known as a terrorist and revolutionary, and Rodichev, later well known as a liberal *zemstvo* leader and *kadet*.

[2] Prince V. P. Meshchersky, at that time the inflammatory, anti-Austrian proprietor of *Grazhdanin*, who paid a flying visit to Serbia during the late summer filled with enthusiasm for the cause of the Slav peoples, and returned entirely disabused; see his *Moi Vospominaniya*, vol. ii, pp. 286–302, and *Pravda o Serbii* (published early in 1877), which give an exceedingly caustic view both of the volunteers and of the Serbs. Heisman, *Serbsko-turetskaya voina 1876 g.*, pp. 76–80, 83, 151–3. Heisman was serving at the front.

[3] Extracts from letters of Russian volunteers, in *Trudy Instituta Slavyanovedeniya*, vol. ii, pp. 211–13; Kartsov, *Za kulisami diplomatii*, p. 41. He was one of the volunteers, and the nephew of the Belgrade consul-general.

[4] Parensov's letters, in *R.S.*, vol. cxxiv, p. 634; *Aus dem Leben König Karls . . . ,*

army, Chernyaev played a most unfortunate role. He was not the man for supreme command of an army. His enemies described him as a mere politician, sitting at Deligrad surrounded by a swollen staff and busy with manifestoes, culminating in that proclaiming Milan king of an independent Serbia. Yet he was personally brave and uncorrupt, and the old soldiers among the Russians described him afterwards as an excellent commander and liked by the troops and the peasantry. He was surrounded with intrigues. His second chief of staff, Komarov, a henchman journalist-soldier, who had founded the *Russky Mir*, quarrelled hopelessly with the Serbs from the beginning. Another Russian general, Novoselov, arrived to add to the recriminations and rivalries. Chernyaev himself, when the defeats began, fell out completely with the government, and especially with Colonel Nikolić, the minister of war. There was bitter criticism of Chernyaev's generalship and he was roundly accused of having as his true objective Bulgaria, the Serbs complaining that they were treated as nothing but 'd'instruments entre les mains des comités panslavistes pour tenter de créer une Bulgarie comme dépendance russe'.[1]

After the complete collapse of the Serbs and the armistice, he

vol. iii, p. 68; reports of Sturdza (Belgrade) to Bucarest, 8 Sept. and 29 Oct., in Iorga, *Correspondance diplomatique roumaine sous le roi Charles Ier (1866–1880)*, nos. 372, 389. Sturdza reported that the general opinion in the army and among the upper classes was beginning to turn against the Russians by the beginning of September, but not that of the priests, who received a good deal of money from Russian monasteries, nor that of the peasants, 'qui voient les officiers russes se faire tuer bravement à leur tête sur tous les champs de bataille'. And again: 'C'est encore l'élément russe de l'armée qui paye le plus largement de son sang.' So, too, Humphry Sandwith, the English doctor with the Serbs, in *The British Quarterly Review*, vol. lxv, p. 217; and Salusbury, *Two months with Tchernaieff in Servia*, p. 131; he thought the Serbian infantry (but not the artillery) usually displayed great cowardice, and was indiscriminate in praise of the Russian volunteers, pp. 67, 132, 223; Heisman, *Serbsko-turetskaya voina 1876 g.*, pp. 94, 117, 128–9, admits the poor morale of the Serbian army. Monson (Ragusa) to Derby, 17 Sept., in *A. and P.*, 1877, xc, C. 1640, no. 381, describes Russian officers' disgust at Serbian cowardice and treatment of Russian volunteers. Ashmead-Bartlett spoke of anti-Russian feeling among the Serbs as being intense by October, *A. and P.*, 1877, xc, C. 1640, no. 797; for consul-general White's more moderate opinion, ib., no. 1085. The English press carried stories of Russian officers shot in the back by the Serbian rank and file; *Quarterly Review*, Oct. 1876, vol. 142, pp. 571–3.

[1] Kartsov, *Za kulisami diplomatii*, pp. 41–3; Kartsov to Gorchakov, disp., no. 67, 6 Oct., copy in *F.O.* 65/953 (Kartsov was very hostile to Chernyaev); Ovsyany, *Blizhny vostok i slavyanstvo*, pp. 109–11; *Skalon*, vol. i, p. 18, and Naglovsky's diary in *R.S.*, vol. cxii, pp. 252, 254–5, recording impressions received later at the Grand Duke Nicholas's head-quarters at Kishinev; letters of Prince Milan to Chernyaev of 30 Aug., 4 and 24 Oct., texts in *Russky Arkhiv*, 1914, no. 1, pp. 44, 58;

left Belgrade in a steam of mutual accusations, went to the Grand Duke Nicholas Nicholaevich at Kishinev to describe conditions in Serbia, and then, typically enough, paid a flying visit to Prague, where he was fêted so vociferously that the government hastily removed him across the frontier.[1] When war came between Russia and Turkey, he and his other boon companions were allowed to re-enter the army, but Alexander II relegated them to the general staff in the Caucasus. Later on under Alexander III the wind blew from a different quarter, and Chernyaev was to return, for a brief period, to the scene of his early triumphs in Turkestan as governor-general.

The Russian volunteers to Serbia certainly did not achieve anything of what had been hoped. Serbian antagonism was created above all by the fact that they were looked upon as the advance guard of Russian regulars and of official intervention. None came. It was later admitted even in panslav circles that the mass of the Serbian peasantry cared nothing for the war or the cause of Slavdom and that the divisions between Russians and Serbs, and Bulgars and Serbs, were deplorably evident.[2] The politicians and intelligentsia in Belgrade, trained in the west, found little or nothing ·in common with their eastern 'Slav brothers'. In general they either disliked or could not understand them, and the Russians, in far too many cases, gave

no. 2, pp. 185–6; Meshchersky, *Pravda o Serbii*, pp. 155, 178–92 (on Chernyaev and Nikolić); Iorga, op. cit., no. 372 (on suspicions as to Bulgaria): but Grujić, at the time in command of the artillery under Chernyaev and later minister of war, maintains that the Serbian plan of campaign had been decided on before Chernyaev's arrival, and that the concentration on the Morava valley and the secondary attention paid to the Bosnia and Novi-Bazar fronts were sound strategically, and were not due to political pressure (he makes no mention of the Austrians); abbreviated Russian translation of his *Srpsko-turski rat 1876-1877* in Ovsyany, *Blizhny vostok i slavyanstvo*, pp. 162–3. I. S. Ivanov in his memoirs describes his attempt in the summer of 1876 to organize Bulgarian *comitadjis* in Serbia and the hostile obstruction he encountered from the Serbian government, especially Colonel Nikolić the minister for war; *R.S.*, vol. lxii, pp. 137–42. For the Bulgars serving in Serbia it became 'more a war with the Serbs than with the Turks'.

[1] B. A. Evreinov, 'Voina za osvobozhdenie balkanskikh slavyan . . . i cheshskoe obshchestvo', in *Trudy V^{go} syezda russkikh akademicheskikh organizatsii za granitsei*, vol. i, pp. 356–7. Perhaps it was as well that the Austrians so speedily removed Chernyaev: a Czech journalist in a last-minute interview was disgusted to find that he knew absolutely nothing of John Huss! He also paid a brief visit in December to London, where he was befriended by Mme Novikov; W. T. Stead, *The M.P. for Russia*, vol. i, p. 309. Her brother was the first of the Russian volunteers to be killed at the front in Serbia.

[2] Miller, *Slavyanstvo i Evropa*, pp. 338–9, 357–8, in an address to the St. Petersburg Slavonic Committee, 26 Feb. 1877, published at the time in *Nedelya*.

themselves a bad name both by behaving as if they were in a
conquered country and by quarrelling and intriguing violently
amongst themselves. Novoselov fought against Chernyaev,
Kartsov against Chernyaev, Tokarev, the Russian Red Cross
agent, against almost all the Russian medical and sanitary units;
the Russian press correspondents fell out equally heatedly.[1]
After the break-down of the Serbs and the armistice enforced
by the Tsar at the beginning of November, the volunteers began
to stream back to Russia and something of the truth appeared.
The whole Serbian venture of the panslavs was chastised and
ridiculed; for a time during mid-winter they were reduced to
the defensive. When they revived their nationalist appeals, with
success, in March 1877 the Serbs were left on one side. It was
now the Bulgars who were to be rescued from tyranny and to be
assigned the role of mainstay of Russia's mission in the Balkans.

The strength of the reaction even in the panslav camp is
strikingly revealed in a letter of Aksakov at the end of the year to
his agent in Belgrade, in which the keynote is the necessity for as
complete and rapid a liquidation of the whole affair as possible:
popular movements, however strong, cannot be a normal
method of action: 'romanticism is not commissariat, as I wrote to
Chernyaev. . . . All that has happened in Russia this summer is
an unheard-of phenomenon in the history of any country: public
opinion conducted a war apart from the government and without any state organization in a foreign state. The phenomenon
is prodigious, but also in the highest degree monstrous, scanda-
lously abnormal; a matter of state interest can be dealt with
only by the state.' Having failed in their design to push the
government into rapid action, the Slavonic committees could
only cut their losses and turn elsewhere: 'the whole evil of
the Serbian war lay in this, that it was begun as if it were for
the emancipation of the southern Slavs, and not simply for the
casting off of Turkish suzerainty and the acquisition of Old
Serbia and Bosnia; in a word it was begun with a lie and a
catchword'. Now all activity must be concentrated on Bulgaria:
'it is much more important for us and for the future of Slavdom
than Serbia'.[2] This avowal, written at the opening of the

[1] Meshchersky, *Pravda o Serbii*, pp. 197–204, 370, 374, 323–40.
[2] Letter of Aksakov to the representative of the Slavonic Committees in Belgrade, 16 Dec. 1876, text in *Russky Arkhiv*, 1897, vol. ii, pp. 257–61. Cf. the similar
views which Pr. Vasilchikov, his opponent, had been vainly pressing on the St. Petersburg Committee, of which he was nominally president; Golubev, op. cit., pp. 118–20.

Constantinople conference, shows only too clearly how the fiasco of Chernyaev and the volunteers encouraged the idea of a big Bulgaria at the expense of Serbian aspirations.

But, while making full allowance for the failure of the pan-slavs' venture in Serbia, the prolonged outburst of nationalist feelings and the unexpected energy of panslav organizing were features new to Russian life and of far-reaching significance. It is true that this manifestation of what was claimed to be public opinion was in the main stimulated and canalized by a very small minority, in Moscow and St. Petersburg; and it may be said that their propaganda and the amount of money collected were rudimentary and not very impressive in comparison with western countries. Yet down to November 1876 the Slavonic committees had raised over 1,500,000 roubles, and another million and a half had been collected by other bodies, without counting large gifts in kind.[1] And the fact remains that for Russia the campaign was on a scale never before attempted, even in 1863, and was largely conducted by means never pre-viously allowed. As has been pointed out, the public collection of money throughout Russia by non-official bodies had pre-viously been prohibited. Now the government had had to yield to mere voluntary associations, the Slavonic committees. The power exercised by these committees was largely due to the support they received from the Empress and the Tsarevich and from high functionaries in Moscow, so that the resistance of the government was undermined by the panslav capture of a part of the official world itself. Similarly, their strength in the con-sular and diplomatic services, above all through Ignatyev, made it clear to the outside world as well as to Russians themselves that there were two voices in Russian foreign policy and that the unofficial was making itself heard with effect.

[1] 1,500,000 roubles would have represented rather under £250,000 at the then rate of exchange, if the money had had to be expended in England, but, of course, this was not so and its value was probably far higher. Interesting details as to the amounts raised and the items of expenditure are given in the article on the Slavonic Benevolent Society in Brockhaus and Elfron, *Entsiklopedisky slovar* (for the St. Petersburg committee, from its official figures), and in Aksakov's speech of 5 Nov. 1876, in his *Slavyansky vopros*, pp. 227–35 (for the Moscow committee). Down to 20 Oct. 1876, the St. Petersburg committee had collected 811,000 roubles, of which 425,000 had been distributed, mainly to the Serbian government, Ionin, and other agents: subsequently the Montenegrins received the lion's share. The Moscow committee had collected 742,000 roubles (152,000 down to July, and 590,000 in the three following months) and had expended 583,000 roubles, mainly on the volunteers, though 136,000 had been sent to Ragusa (Ionin).

Foreign opinion, already for some years past introduced to the bogy of panslavism, now tended to see in the ebullition of messianic nationalism, which sent the volunteers as an advance guard to Serbia, the ultimate dictator of Gorchakov's chancellery and of the Tsar's inner councils. By the autumn of 1876 even the best-informed foreign offices of Europe were in doubt whether the Tsar could hold out against the bellicose demands of the nationalist press, headed by the redoubtable Katkov, and of court panslav circles, fired by Aksakov. An autocracy is not all-powerful: some vents must be provided; while discussion of internal affairs in the press was rigorously curtailed, some latitude must be permitted elsewhere; hence, it seemed, the lack of control over the foreign columns of the newspapers. Had not the authorities allowed feelings to be aroused which they could not now master? Was not the Tsar in danger of being carried away by the panslavs claiming to express the true voice of Holy Russia? As is to be seen in the following chapter he did in fact yield to them enough to influence vitally the subsequent development of the eastern crisis. 'Un gouvernement absolu est, moins que tout autre, en mesure de s'opposer à un pareil courant des sentiments nationaux', a semi-official apologist wrote in retrospect; and he added: 'ce mouvement instinctif eut une importance capitale. Il engagea l'honneur de la Russie.'[1]

[1] 'La guerre russo-turque', in *Nouvelle Revue*, 1880, vol. vi, pp. 726–7, perhaps written by Jomini. For an interesting account of Gorchakov's fears of panslavism, as expressed by him to Schneider in May 1876, see Stählin, 'Die Briefe L. Schneiders an . . . Waluew', in *Historische Zeitung*, vol. 155, pp. 306–7.

VI

LIVADIA

THE nationalist outburst in Russia and the war were the deciding factors during the summer and early autumn of 1876 which impelled the Tsar and Gorchakov to an interventionist policy in Turkey culminating, for the moment, in the ultimatum of 30 October, the Moscow speech of 11 November, and partial mobilization. This new lead from Russia was combined with far-reaching soundings of Berlin and Vienna, and a step forward was made from the Reichstadt agreement towards the secret conventions of 1877.

The Tsar and Gorchakov did not arrive back in Russia until 10 July. Their return did not cause any toning down of nationalist propaganda. Katkov, in part alliance with the Moscow merchant Old Believers and the cotton millionaire Tretyakov, appealed vociferously for funds for the Serbs and Bulgars; heroized Chernyaev; demanded, when defeats could not be wholly denied, that the powers impose an armistice to save the Serbs.[1] Led by him, the press in July and August became more and not less violent, and was noticeably anti-British until somewhat checked by the foreign office in September; but in October even the moderate papers joined in a renewed chorus of belligerent nationalism now specially directed against Austria-Hungary.[2] The Slavonic committees, as described in the last chapter, were at the height of their energy. It was not until the beginning of September that some steps were taken to curtail their activities, and even these steps were soon reversed.[3] In part the Tsar may have been badly informed by his chief of the Third Section as to the character, aims, and influence of these committees.[4] In part he may have been unwilling to make any

---

[1] Nevedenski, *Katkov i ego vremya*, pp. 364–7, quoting from *Moskovskiya Vyedemosti*, July to October.

[2] Berchem, German chargé d'affaires in St. Petersburg, 15 Aug. and 3 Sept., cited in *Wertheimer*, p. 340; Loftus to Derby, 25 Sept., in *A. and P.*, 1877, xc, C. 1640, no. 460; Loftus's dispatches for October in *F.O.* 65/941; Austrian chargé d'affaires to Andrássy, 30 Sept. and 12 Oct., cited in Wittrock, *Gorčakov, Ignatiev och Šuvalov*, pp. 34–5.

[3] Porokhovshchikov's memoirs, in *I.V.*, vol. lxvii, pp. 544–6, 552.

[4] Schweinitz, *Denkwürdigkeiten*, vol. ii, p. 91, recording bitter criticisms, four years later, by Shuvalov, of Mezentsov's incompetence. Shuvalov had been

difficulties with the Empress at the head of the Red Cross, in view of his relations with Catherine Dolgoroukaya which were at this time still more or less veiled.[1] At least it is clear that for long he much disliked the agitation of the panslavs, and never sympathized with their methods or leaders even when he yielded, in September and October 1876, to their influence. He returned to Russia anxious to keep the peace; in August he declared his determination not to go to war: but this was to his very pacific finance minister; in addressing his officers at the end of the August manœuvres another note was, discreetly, sounded: 'L'honneur du pays m'est cher; jusqu'ici j'ai pu maintenir la paix, et je désire la conserver: mais si l'honneur du pays serait atteint je saurais la défendre, et alors je compte sur vous.' To outside observers of the court and military circles the panslav movement appeared so strong that it was impossible for the Tsar to resist it.[2]

For Gorchakov patriotic effervescence in Russia was in one sense far from unwelcome. It could be used to strengthen his hand abroad, provided that it did not go beyond controllable limits. He steadily maintained that it was a spontaneous manifestation of Russian public opinion which must be allowed reasonable scope and due weight, and that it would not sweep the government into isolated and extreme action, if the powers accepted his own moderate interpretation of Russian interests. In June this had meant common action by the powers to gain for Bosnia and Herzegovina the status of autonomous vassal principalities and for Montenegro and Serbia some acquisition of territory, including a port on the Adriatic for the former. Derby was prepared to envisage this only if the Turks failed to subdue Bosnia and Herzegovina, and made it harshly clear to Shuvalov that England did not regard the insurrection as

Mezentsov's predecessor as chief of the Third Section and is a biased witness, but there is no doubt as to Mezentsov's general ineffectiveness.

[1] Schweinitz, *Denkwürdigkeiten*, vol. i, p. 340.

[2] Reutern's journal, under date 24 Oct. 1876, in *R.S.*, vol. cxliii, p. 39; Loftus to Derby, 25 Aug., *A. and P.*, 1877, xc, C. 1640, no. 146; Wittrock, *Gorčakov, Ignatiev och Šuvalov*, p. 32, citing private letter of Langenau to Andrássy, 13 Aug., in which he describes the impressions of Prince Windischgrätz and an Austrian military mission who were visiting St. Petersburg. Bechtolsheim, the military attaché, regarded the situation far more calmly. Loftus's reports at the end of July and during August, in *F.O.* 65/939, show him as regarding the wave of panslavism as of a religious and not a political character (he did not analyse the difference), but as being very dubious as to Gorchakov's assurances that the Tsar had sufficient power not to be carried away by it.

having been caused by Turkish oppression. Andrássy was, as always, entirely opposed to such a solution of the Bosnian question, though he now recognized the necessity for something to be given to Montenegro.[1]

Early next month at Reichstadt he secured the abandonment of Gorchakov's idea of autonomy, but by then the war had just broken out and took first place. To the surprise of the Russians the Serbs failed completely. By 24 August Milan was asking the guaranteeing powers for their good offices in obtaining a prompt cessation of hostilities and the re-establishment of peace.[2] Nicholas followed suit. On 1 September the Turks heavily defeated Chernyaev and captured Deligrad. The Morava valley was gravely threatened and Serbia seemed about to be overrun. Thus auspiciously was the reign of Abd ul-Hamid II inaugurated. The day before his brother Murad had been deposed, as being permanently out of his mind. Midhat remained in power in Constantinople, but from the very first he failed to bind down the new Sultan and to secure the key appointments in the palace. He only with great difficulty secured the promulgation of a further dose of governmental reforms, but he neither desired nor was able, had he desired, to jeopardize in any way the exceedingly favourable military situation.[3]

Gorchakov had already suggested to Andrássy an armistice for two or three months and a European conference to arrange peace terms.[4] This proposal in the first instance may not have been meant very seriously, but as the Serbian military operations began to go from bad to worse, both a conference and

---

[1] *Tatishchev*, pp. 310–15; *Wertheimer*, pp. 313–14; Andrássy to Károlyi and Beust, disp., 27 June, in *Actenstücke*, i, nos. 496 and 497.

[2] This step appears to have been due to Chernyaev and a section of the Serbian government rather than to Milan, who wrote to Chernyaev, 30 Aug., urging the necessity of continuing the struggle: his *démarche* to the powers amounted to nothing: he could easily wriggle out of it: some one should be sent to Russia to work on the Slavonic committees so as to counteract the bad effect of having asked for an armistice. The text of this letter is printed in *Russky Arkhiv*, 1914, no. 1, pp. 42–4. By 15 Sept. Milan was fully convinced of the necessity for an armistice; ib., p. 44. One main difficulty was that Milan's and Chernyaev's opinions as to the desirability and length of an armistice were constantly changing according to their estimate of the military situation; Jovanović, *Vlada Milana Obrenovića*, vol. i, e.g. pp. 326, 336.

[3] Ali Haydar Midhat Bey, *Life of Midhat Pasha*, p. 104. The text of the *Hatti Sherif* of 10 Sept. is printed in Noradounghian, *Recueil d'actes internationaux de l'empire ottoman*, vol. iii, pp. 397–9.

[4] *Tatishchev*, pp. 320–1.

especially an armistice became more and more desired by St. Petersburg. Early in August Gorchakov was pressing Bismarck, through Schweinitz, to take the lead in the calling of a conference of the six powers. He was at the same time complaining that Bismarck kept his door shut against Oubril while he gave every opportunity to Lord Odo Russell to see him. Bismarck retorted that Oubril's complaints were quite unfounded, and that he would not take any initiative for a conference: no direct German interests were at stake in the Balkans: the divergent views of Russia, Austria-Hungary, and England would merely be intensified: the conference would fail, with everybody blaming Germany for lack of support.[1] Andrássy was hardly more accommodating; he objected to an armistice of more than a month, and his consent to a conference was dependent on a general programme being previously concerted by the three eastern powers: that programme did not go farther than the *status quo ante bellum* for Serbia, frontier rectifications for Montenegro, and reforms in Bosnia and Herzegovina according to the Andrássy note and the Berlin memorandum. He added tardily somewhat similar reforms for Bulgaria.[2]

This, however, bore no relation to what the triumphant Turks demanded. They refused to agree to any armistice of more than ten days without peace preliminaries being signed, and their terms, as stated on 12 September, were so severe that even the British thought them impossible.[3] All that the Turks would do was to order their troops on 15 September to suspend hostilities until 25 September, provided that the Serbs did likewise, which they did.[4] This was the utmost that British pressure

[1] *G.P.*, p. 32, note, referring to Schweinitz to Bismarck, 6 and 7 Aug.; Bismarck to Bülow, 14 Aug., in *G.P.*, pp. 31–4; Wittrock, *Gorčakov, Ignatiev och Šuvalov*, pp. 92–3, citing Schweinitz to Bismarck, 8 Aug. Schweinitz was instructed on 18 Aug. to refuse Gorchakov's suggestion of a conference.

[2] Langenau to Andrássy, tel., 29 Aug.; communication from Gorchakov transmitted by Novikov, 2 Sept.; aide-mémoire handed by Andrássy to Novikov, 6 Sept.; in *Actenstücke*, i, nos. 628, 652, 660; Čubrilović, *Bosanski ustanak 1875–1878*, pp. 232–3, citing Andrássy to Langenau, 12 Sept., and his telegram of 17 Sept. in *Actenstücke*, i, no. 696 (for Bulgaria). Whether Andrássy put any real faith in his programme is dubious.

[3] The terms included, for Serbia, reduction of the army to not more than 10,000 men and 2 batteries, abolition of the militia, occupation by the Turks of four fortresses, war indemnity or increase of tribute, a construction and exploitation by the Turks of a railway from Belgrade to Nish, and solemn recognition of the Sultan by Milan in Constantinople; for Montenegro, *status quo ante bellum*; Ristić, *Diplomatska istorija Srbije* . . ., vol. i, pp. 201–2.

[4] Elliot to Derby, 14 and 16 Sept.; White (Belgrade) to Derby, 17 Sept., in

on the Porte could achieve. The situation was further embroiled by Chernyaev's stampeding the army into proclaiming Milan king (16 September), a step which he hoped would make any peace impossible. Both the prince and the Tsar (who had not been consulted in advance) roundly disapproved of this gesture, which inevitably inspired grave misgivings among the powers.[1] Derby for once was stirred to activity, for he regarded peace as urgently necessary; the campaign against the Bulgarian atrocities was at its height, and he considered that it would be practically impossible for the government to interfere even if Russia declared war on Turkey.[2] His new proposals for a conference and peace failed at Constantinople, but he was partially successful at Vienna and at St. Petersburg: both entered into negotiations with London which it would be difficult to snap abruptly.[3]

The main divergences between the powers arose over the length of the armistice to be demanded and (as usual) over the question as to whether compulsion should be put upon the Turks. In regard to the former there was a complete *volte-face*, owing to the rapidly shifting estimates as to the military advantages to be gained by each side from a long or a short armistice, and owing to bitter divisions of opinion among the Serbs. At

A. and P., 1877, xc, C. 1640, nos. 226, 254, 259. The Turks later agreed to prolong the suspension of hostilities till 2 Oct., but this was not observed by the Serbs; Elliot to Derby, 24 Sept., ib., no. 374.

[1] Jovanović, *Vlada Milana Obrenovića*, vol. i, pp. 340–1. Milan had written to Chernyaev, 15 Sept., absolutely refusing his consent to this step: the proclamation of independence would alienate all the powers, and he doubted whether the Tsar would, or could, back him up; text of letter in *Russky Arkhiv*, 1914, no. 1, pp. 44–6. The Russian government in fact at once admonished Belgrade severely; Ristić, op. cit., pp. 138–40. The Tsar wrote on the telegram announcing Chernyaev's action, 'C'est une farce qu'on nous joue'; Loftus to Derby, disp., no. 446, 26 Sept., in *F.O.* 65/940.

[2] Derby to Elliot, tel., 29 Aug., omitted in the earlier blue-book and published separately, in *A. and P.*, 1877, xci, C. 1660. The fullest account of the campaign aroused by the Bulgarian atrocities in parliament, press, and public meetings in England, June to September, is in Thompson, *Public Opinion and Lord Beaconsfield 1875–1880*, vol. i, pp. 310–440; see also Seton-Watson, *Disraeli, Gladstone and the Eastern Question*, pp. 54–85, and Wirthwein, *Britain and the Balkan Crisis, 1875–1878*, pp. 65–101.

[3] The British proposals as finally formulated on 21 Sept., in *A. and P.*, 1877, xc, C. 1640, no. 324, were the same as those repeated by Derby in his circular of 4 Nov., which was the basis for the Constantinople conference, see below, p. 232. Derby's first proposals in September, which had owed much to Gorchakov, had included 'autonomy' for Bosnia and Herzegovina; this alarmed Andrássy, and Derby then qualified it by 'local and administrative autonomy'; Lange, *Die Orientpolitik Österreich-Ungarns vom Ausgleich bis zum Berliner Kongress*, pp. 13–14; Andrássy to Beust, tel., 8 Oct., in *Actenstücke*, i, no. 762.

first Russia and Serbia had stood for an armistice of six months, so as to give time for reorganizing the Serbian army, procuring Russian aid, and bringing pressure to bear on Constantinople. The Turks would only agree to one month or six weeks. But on 3 October Gorchakov proposed that the powers should impose an armistice of six weeks, for now the Serbs did not wish to leave the Turks for so long in occupation of much of Serbia, and Chernyaev believed that the Turks would collapse in a winter campaign. The Turks in their turn changed ground and would accept an armistice only if it were for six months, i.e. until the end of March. The Russians, and the Serbs perhaps rather unwillingly following suit, would not budge from a four to six weeks' armistice, though on 14 October Gorchakov allowed of a prolongation if necessary for the continuance of negotiations. This seemed to provide a possible bridge, and during the last ten days of October Ignatyev at Constantinople was busily trying to effect an agreement. Then when he believed himself on the point of scoring a success came the Russian ultimatum of 30 October. The Austrians had supported a six months' armistice. So had the British at first, though the cabinet on 4 October were ready to support any armistice of not less than one month. Bismarck had been careful not to commit himself and had veered with Russia.[1]

Behind this 'gâchis diplomatique' of the armistice negotiations were taking place far more important soundings by the Russians of Berlin, Vienna, and London leading towards decisive action against Turkey, whether in combination or in isolation. The real key to those months of September and October lay in the growing feeling of the Tsar and his entourage that drastic action must be taken and compulsion used. The main links in the chain were the Manteuffel mission and the Werder telegram, the Sumarokov-Elston mission and the negotiations with Austria-Hungary, the imperial councils in mid-October at Livadia, Russian mobilization, the ultimatum to Turkey of 30 October, and the Tsar's Moscow speech of 11 November.

On 29 August the Tsar, with Gorchakov and the Tsarevich,

---

[1] *Actenstücke*, i, especially nos. 745, 785, 790; *Wertheimer*, pp. 348–9: *Tatishchev*, pp. 325–6: Gorchakov to Shuvalov, tels., 13, 14, and 17 Oct., text in *S.R.*, vol. iv, pp. 192–3; *A. and P.*, 1877, xc, C. 1640, nos. 505, 506, 585, 611, 621, 630, 634, 661, 746; Ristić, *Diplomatska istorija Srbije*, vol. i, pp. 142–8.

left St. Petersburg for a week's visit to Warsaw, for manœuvres. These provided the opportunity for Bismarck to arrange an invitation to Manteuffel, though his Emperor at first objected to the choice of so highly placed a personage.[1] Bismarck was uneasy as to the effect of his refusal to take the initiative in bringing about a conference. He feared that the Tsar might be worked upon by Gorchakov to take far-reaching decisions. His unwonted accompanying of the Tsar to manœuvres seemed to portend important discussions, and Bismarck, not yet informed fully of the Reichstadt agreement, suspected (wrongly) that the Archduke Albert might put in a sudden appearance at Warsaw. General Field-Marshal Freiherr von Manteuffel, aide-de-camp to the Kaiser and already on excellent terms with the Tsar, was exactly the type of military diplomat who could tighten up those close personal links of the Tsar with his uncle which were always of such consequence. If anything Manteuffel was too well suited to his task, for his presence at this moment could not but recall vividly to the Tsar his mission to him ten years before, after Königgrätz, and the letter of the Emperor William which he now brought expressly evoked these sentiments. 'Le souvenir de Votre attitude pour moi et pour mon pays depuis 1864 jusqu'en 1870/1 guidera ma politique vis-à-vis de la Russie, quoi qu'il arrive. Voilà le résumé de ce que Manteuffel Vous dira en mon nom.'

What exactly Manteuffel did say during his five days in Warsaw (2–7 September) is by no means clear. He certainly did not fail to give assurances, in accordance with Bismarck's instructions, that Germany would in no case resort to any hostile manœuvres, diplomatic or otherwise, against Russia. But in addition he appears to have come to Warsaw with verbal instructions from Bismarck to sound the Tsar, with great caution, as to a Russo-German alliance by which, in return for a Russian guarantee of Alsace-Lorraine, Germany would support Russia 'through thick and thin'. In what form Manteuffel touched upon this very delicate question is not known. The silence on the Russian side as to any such offer in return for a guarantee

[1] Telegrams to and from Bülow, who was with the Emperor, texts in Wittrock, *Gorčakov, Ignatiev och Šuvalov*, pp. 95–6. The Manteuffel mission is known only from the German side: Manteuffel to Bülow, tel., 4 Sept., cited by Wittrock, op. cit., p. 27; instruction of Bismarck, 30 Aug.; letter of Emperor William to the Tsar, 2 Sept.; Manteuffel to the Emperor, disp., from Warsaw, 6 Sept.; letter of the Tsar to the Emperor William, from Warsaw, 7 Sept.; in *G.P.*, pp. 34–45.

of Alsace-Lorraine, coupled with the later denial by the Tsar of any knowledge of it on his part, suggests that, if it were broached by Manteuffel, it was not understood by the Tsar. At any rate it seems evident that the Tsar was encouraged by Manteuffel to put great emphasis upon the phrase 'quoiqu'il arrive' in the Emperor's letter, and to hope that Germany would in the last resort act towards Austria-Hungary as Russia had acted in 1870.[1]

Neither the Tsar nor Gorchakov gave Manteuffel the impression that they either wanted war or despaired of a peaceful solution, but the possibility of isolated and forceful action was beginning to come into the foreground. Gorchakov explained that Slav sympathies in Russia, especially for the Bulgars, had reached such a pitch that a war against Turkey would be accepted unanimously as a national, religious crusade: the government were strong enough not to be overpowered by public feeling and were aiming at a peaceful solution; a war, whatever its results, would put back internal reforms in Russia for years and would ruin her finances: there would be war only if the honour of Russia demanded it. As Manteuffel remarked, national honour is 'a far-reaching idea'. The Tsar's reply to the Emperor William was still more significant.

'Moins que personne je puis être indifférent à ce qui se passe en Orient. Malgré tout mon désir de maintenir l'accord des Puissances, sur lequel repose la paix, je puis être obligé de prendre une position particulière et séparée. En ce cas le puissant concours de l'Allemagne pourrait m'aider à satisfaire ma dignité et le sentiment national Russe, sans que la paix soit troublée. — J'aime à compter sur Vous comme Vous pouvez toujours compter sur moi. . . .'

[1] This is also the view of Schweinitz, who is very critical of the Manteuffel mission; *Briefwechsel*, 115–16 (from his diary); *Denkwürdigkeiten*, vol. i, p. 348. On the thorny question of the 'through thick and thin' offer, see Schüssler, 'Bismarcks Bündnisangebot an Russland "durch dick und dünn" im Herbst 1876', in *Historische Zeitschrift*, vol. cxlvii, pp. 106–14. There is no evidence concerning the sounding of the Tsar as to a possible alliance either in the German foreign office documents or in Manteuffel's papers: hence the assumption that Bismarck's instructions, as later to Schweinitz, were verbal. The evidence consists of two categorical statements that Manteuffel at Warsaw broached the subject but found the ground unfavourable; letter of Herbert Bismarck to his brother, 24 Aug. 1879, and Bismarck's instructions to Schweinitz, 6 Feb. 1880. In view of the dates of this evidence and of the complete change in German relations with Russia at that time, it is safer to await further evidence on the Manteuffel mission before reaching any definite conclusions. See also p. 223, note 1, for the similar alliance offer made through Schweinitz.

Bismarck pertinently minuted on this: the question is what is to be the 'position particulière', and what is to be the 'concours' expected of Germany? It seems clear from what subsequently happened that the Tsar thought that this letter, coupled with his verbal explanations to Manteuffel, constituted a discreet request to the Emperor for assistance, if necessary, against Austria-Hungary similar to that afforded Germany by Russia in 1870, and that there would be an answer. The Germans, either because Manteuffel did not understand what the Tsar expected, or because they wished to avoid any answer to so awkward a question, interpreted the Tsar as referring only to the possibility of war against Turkey. For Bismarck, a few days after Manteuffel's return, was in possession of the details of the Reichstadt agreement: on 13 September, despite the conditions of absolute secrecy, Andrássy informed the German ambassador at Vienna of its provisions.[1]

The Russians followed up the Manteuffel mission by pressing at Berlin to clear up the question as to what Germany's attitude would be if the honour of Russia imposed on her isolated action, and to discover what alternative Bismarck might propose to the conference suggested by them. Bismarck was unduly furious at this approach of Gorchakov through the despised Oubril, and he proceeded to vent his spleen upon the ambassador for his method of sounding the Germans.[2] The answer to the first question was immediately and simply assumed by the Emperor to be benevolent neutrality: the official answer, given through the St. Petersburg embassy on 22 September, was that this question had already been disposed of in the letters exchanged between the Kaiser and the Tsar.[3] This was far from satisfying Alexander and Gorchakov, who in the bellicose atmosphere of Livadia were attempting to shape some decisive policy and felt that they could not do so until certain of the attitude both of Berlin and of Vienna. The estrangement since August between Andrássy and Gorchakov must be overcome, and what could

---

[1] Stolberg to Bismarck, 13 Sept., in *G.P.*, pp. 45–7.

[2] A minor, but not unimportant, blundering of Manteuffel at Warsaw is emphasized by Schweinitz, *Denkwürdigkeiten*, vol. i, pp. 348–9. Manteuffel told the Tsar that the Kaiser was quite satisfied with Oubril. On the other hand, he explained clearly to Gorchakov that Oubril must be replaced, e.g. by Shuvalov, if really confidential relations with Bismarck were to be established. This increased the difficulty of removing Oubril from Berlin, since it reinforced Gorchakov's determination not to sacrifice Oubril merely to Bismarck's ill temper.

[3] *G.P.*, pp. 47–52; Schweinitz, *Denkwürdigkeiten*, vol. i, p. 349.

be expected from Vienna must be definitely known: the consequences of Reichstadt must now be broached. This was the object of the Sumarokov-Elston mission to Vienna.

It is essential in trying to understand this overture and all the Russian steps during September and October to remember that throughout this period the one centre of official Russian action had been removed to the imperial autumn residence at Livadia. On the Crimean Riviera, amid palaces and orangeries, between the sea and the mountains, in enchanting climate and enchanting scenery, fifty miles from the nearest railway, all that counted politically in Russia were gathered. The Tsar had arrived there on 9 September, direct from Warsaw. He did not leave till 7 November, *en route* for Moscow. With him were the Empress, and court officials, and ladies-in-waiting; two of these latter prominent leaders of ultra-orthodox or panslav circles in St. Petersburg;[1] the inevitable Adlerberg, minister of court, never pronounced, urbanely balancing towards nationalist feeling; the chaplain in residence, in close touch with the Moscow Slavonic committee.[2] Ignatyev was there; Milyutin, the war minister, and General Obruchev, one of his closest and most influential collaborators; Gorchakov, with Jomini and Hamburger. Early in October the Tsarevich was hurriedly summoned. By mid-October Reutern, the finance minister, and the Grand Duke Nicholas Nicholaevich, the Tsar's brother, had arrived. Giers and the ambassadors were in St. Petersburg, which was nothing but a post office. Of the foreigners only Werder, the Prussian military plenipotentiary, was at Yalta. Living in a remote corner of the empire, in a feminine

[1] Countess Alexandra Tolstaya and Mme Maltseva; Schweinitz, *Briefwechsel*, p. 124. Countess Bludova, an ardent panslav, was also there.
[2] The archpriest John Rozhdestvensky. When the Moscow panslavs were nervous at the end of September that Ignatyev was about to be sent back to Constantinople, it was to the archpriest that a telegram was sent to get him to stop Ignatyev going; Porokhovshchikov's memoirs, in *I.V.*, vol. lxvii, pp. 546–7. Porokhovshchikov himself paid a flying visit to the Crimea, 1–4 Oct., as an unofficial envoy of the Moscow Slavonic committee to intercede (successfully) with the Tsar against measures taken to check the activities of the committee. He found Ignatyev and Adlerberg helpful, Milyutin not prepared to decide anything without reference to the Tsar, Gorchakov evasive and, when finally cornered, hostile and inconclusive. His account of his visit is in *I.V.*, vol. lxvii, pp. 547–52. The panslavs, and Porokhovshchikov in particular, were denounced by Pobedonostsev, who was alarmed at the lack of leadership by the government and the prolonged stay in the Crimea; letters (from St. Petersburg) to the Tsarevich, 15, 24, and 30 Oct., text in *Pisma Pobedonostseva k Aleksandru III*, vol. i, pp. 48–57.

atmosphere of exalted nationalism, with all news from the West arriving late and that from the Balkans arriving early, the Tsar yielded to the prevailing pressure and advanced a long step towards war.

Gorchakov likewise was becoming highly militant in mood. Personal vanity and the desire to close his long career by a dramatic success in the eastern question were generally attributed to him as dominating motives. But to him, a life-long diplomatist, dramatic success spelt a European conference at which he carried off all the honours; war was no necessary ingredient of his triumph. It might, however, become a necessary means towards it. It was impossible to continue with exchanges of notes *ad infinitum*. Russian concern with the Balkan Christians, so stridently voiced in these months, could not be ignored; the military failure of Serbia, culminating late in October in complete collapse, necessitated urgent action. The powers must agree on a programme; and agree to enforce it on Turkey. Agreement on a programme seemed dubious, agreement on compulsion, as always the heart of the difficulty and now the central object of Russia, more than dubious. If the powers would not agree, Russia must act alone with Austria-Hungary, with Germany friendly in the background. The league of the three emperors must be given reality. If Austria-Hungary would not agree, could Russia move forward alone, rapidly and decisively? Perhaps; if Germany would answer for Vienna in the last resort. And England? She had no army; and Turkey was far away; besides, Gladstone was thundering for the Bulgarians, and the old solid pro-Turkish England no longer existed; the cabinet were divided, and might not last much longer; war on behalf of Turkey was scarcely possible; 1854 was twenty years and more outlived. Vienna and Berlin were the essentials for Russia. Berlin was only partially satisfactory. Benevolent neutrality and the memories of 1866 and 1870 were not 'the great things' for which Gorchakov hoped, and the Tsar as September closed was almost daily pressing Werder for an answer to his question to Manteuffel; was he justified in hoping that if it should come to war with Austria-Hungary the Emperor would act as the Tsar had acted in 1870?

On 25 September Werder put this question to the Berlin foreign office in an allusive *en clair* telegram from Livadia, which was not understood. On 1 October he telegraphed it in cipher in all its naked directness. It certainly was a drastic move of the Tsar, but it was typical of his outlook on the conduct of foreign relations as in essentials based upon the personal word of honour of uncle and nephew, upon the confidential family ties between the Winter Palace and Potsdam to which he was accustomed for fifty years. It was through Werder, military representative of King William to Tsar Alexander, the post itself the embodiment of those close monarchical ties, that six years before in the fateful summer of 1870 Alexander had promised to march 300,000 men to the Austrian frontier if Austria armed against Prussia. And now the same Werder, in the same post, was at Livadia, and Alexander had just received through Manteuffel his uncle's reminders of 1870. Pressed by Gorchakov and Milyutin that the attitude of Germany must be made quite clear, the Tsar took for him the obvious step of using the Werder line to the full.[1]

But Werder telegraphed not to the Emperor but to the foreign office. Bismarck, furious at Werder's clumsy meddling in politics, taken by surprise at this brusque stab in the back of the Austrian partner, faced with the most awkward of questions which it was extremely difficult to wriggle out of answering, hard put to it to restrain the old Kaiser's loyal directness, took three weeks in successfully insisting that the answer, if answer there must be, should be transferred to Schweinitz and should be merely verbal. He had believed that Austro-Russian relations were on a better footing and that Reichstadt supplied a satisfactory basis for the subsequent handling of eastern affairs.[2]

A few days before Werder's bombshell, the approach to Vienna had been made. General Sumarokov-Elston, one of the Tsar's general-adjutants, was sent with a letter, dated 23 September, from the Tsar to the Emperor Francis Joseph. It was delivered on 27 September.[3] He brought at the same time a

---

[1] Schweinitz defends on these lines the Tsar's pressure on Werder; *Denkwürdigkeiten*, vol. i, p. 350.

[2] Werder's two telegrams are in *G.P.*, pp. 52–3; the resultant German deliberations, pp. 54–79. See also below, pp. 221–2. Werder telegraphed again on 8 Oct. that the Tsar declared that in the event of continued opposition by Turkey and of the break-down of the conference he was determined on war and asked for German assistance in keeping it localized: ib., p. 77, note. For Bismarck's own later version see his *Reflections and Reminiscences*, vol. ii, pp. 228–31.

[3] Goriainow, *Le Bosphore et les Dardanelles*, p. 322. The text is printed in *S.R.*, vol. iv, pp. 187–9. *Wertheimer*, pp. 341–2, gives a summary of it, using the original, and one extract from Gorchakov's letter to Andrássy, also dated 23 Sept. The

letter from Gorchakov to Andrássy, which spoke of no longer
leaving events to take their course and of cementing Austro-
Russian friendship with a sanction. What this meant was indicated more clearly in the Tsar's letter. The object of this was to
convince Francis Joseph that, since united action by Europe
was impossible, the moment had now come for Austria-Hungary
and Russia to take concerted and drastic action to stop further
complications of the Balkan crisis and further massacres of
Christians. The situation in Turkey was painted in the darkest
colours. '. . . Il n'y a plus de Gouvernement sérieux en Turquie.
Les hommes au pouvoir sont débordés par les masses fanatisées,
habituées au meurtre et au pillage. Elles sont incapables
d'accepter des transactions modérées. Il n'y a que la force qui
puisse les dompter.' Later, an echo of Reichstadt was added:
'Je comprends Ta répugnance pour la formation d'un grand
Etat Serbe. Je repousse comme Toi cette combinaison.' But
besides suggestions of an indefinite character which were obviously meant to involve negotiations in pursuance of the Reichstadt agreement, the letter also proposed the contemporaneous
occupation of Bosnia by Austria-Hungary and of Bulgaria by
Russia, and the dispatch of the fleets of the great powers to
Constantinople to enforce the will of Europe upon the Turkish
government under the guise of protecting the Christians there.

Andrássy (as also Novikov, who had had no warning of
Sumarokov-Elston's mission) was additionally annoyed by Gorchakov's simultaneous communication of this proposal to the
other cabinets, in the belief that Andrássy himself would do
so in any case.[1] The British would have nothing to do with it.
Disraeli delightedly 'sent Schouvaloff off with a flea in his ear',
and countered by minatorily demanding an armistice of the
Turks.[2] But Andrássy was in a far more difficult position. On
far from easy terms with England, with his own militarists
anxious to enter Bosnia, he could not afford to leave Russia to
march alone or to rebuff her by anything which closed the door

proposals as to occupation and a fleet demonstration were probably due to Ignatyev;
see paraphrase of his report to Gorchakov, early in September, in his memoirs,
I.V., vol. cxxxvi, pp. 58–9.
    [1] Gorchakov to Shuvalov, tel., 26 Sept., text in *S.R.*, vol. iv, p. 190.
    [2] *Disraeli*, pp. 951–2. *Salisbury*, p. 88, records that on 4 Oct. the cabinet agreed
to occupy Constantinople if Russia occupied Bulgaria, Cairns being very much for
action, Derby disagreeing. Disraeli had been made Earl of Beaconsfield in the
previous August, but I shall continue to call him by the name by which he lives.

to further conversations. He characterized the proposals as absurd, but they were absurd only because he did not believe that Turkey was falling to pieces of herself, and did not propose to assist Russia in bringing about the collapse of the Ottoman empire in Europe. In fact Gorchakov's bait of Bosnia was shrewd, and Andrássy seems to have found considerable difficulty in persuading his Emperor to refuse it.[1] On the other hand, the suggested Russian occupation of Bulgaria caused Andrássy to expostulate strongly with Sumarokov-Elston, on the grounds that Reichstadt only envisaged an Asiatic advance on the part of Russia.[2] The Vienna press contained much on the mission, and in accordance with unofficial inspiration emphasized strongly the refusal to co-operate with Russia, but actually the refusal was not so absolute as made out.[3]

Sumarokov-Elston left for Russia with Francis Joseph's answer on 3 October.[4] It contained a refusal of any occupation, with lengthy emphasis on the impossibility of Austria-Hungary accepting political autonomy for Bosnia and Herzegovina, on the disastrous consequences that would probably result from a temporary occupation, and on the impossibility of a permanent occupation, whether of Bosnia, Herzegovina, or of Bulgaria. A fleet demonstration at Constantinople was accepted, provided that the other powers took part. Francis Joseph urged insistence on an armistice and the fullest support of the British peace proposals. If the Turks refused to yield to such combined pressure, the impossibility of a continuation of the Ottoman empire would be clear to the world. Turkish resistance would probably be accompanied by new massacres. Then would be the moment for the intervention of Austria-Hungary and Russia; and only then would the Reichstadt hypotheses become actual. While thus removing action à deux into the realm of future possibilities and while urging common European action, the Emperor gave the assurance that if Russian troops marched into Turkey he would not put any obstacles in the way, though

[1] Przibram, *Erinnerungen eines alten Österreichers*, vol. ii, p. 11.
[2] Goriainow, *Le Bosphore et les Dardanelles*, p. 323.
[3] Plener, *Erinnerungen*, vol. ii, pp. 97–8.
[4] Letter of Francis Joseph to Alexander II, 3 Oct., summarized in *Wertheimer*, pp. 343–6. Schweinitz, *Denkwürdigkeiten*, vol. i, pp. 352–3, adds some points, notably that if Russia were compelled to declare war on Turkey the occupation of Bosnia with a view to annexing the northern portion of it might be possible. Berlin was informed by the Tsar through Werder of this and the Tsar's previous letter; cf. also *G.P.*, p. 77, note.

he added the warning that partial mobilization would have to take place to guard the interests of the monarchy and the bases of the Reichstadt conversations. There was a quick response from Livadia (10 October).[1] The Tsar insisted on the necessity of a definite programme which would guarantee a real autonomy or self-government in the Balkan lands; he did not believe that the Turks would cease their opposition to solid reforms; he was resolved in that case to withdraw his representative from Constantinople and to demand freedom of action for Russia, which would mean in the final resort the realization of the Reichstadt provisions. He therefore offered to enter into negotiations in strictest secrecy for the conclusion of a detailed treaty. Vienna from this understood the Tsar to be preparing for an Austro-Russian war with Turkey in the coming spring, and in reply (23 October) made it clear that Austria-Hungary would not do anything to hasten the dissolution of Turkey, but at the same time agreed to negotiate a secret treaty, through Novikov.[2] The Tsar seemed assured of no hostile steps by Austria-Hungary; possibly of co-ordinate, if not joint, action, at a price. The negotiations, difficult though they might prove, ought successfully to forearm Russia against any repetition of the paralysing Austrian conduct during the Crimean war.

But the Russians did not know that prior to the Austrian reply of 23 October Andrássy had certain knowledge of their request through Werder as to the attitude of Germany in case of an Austro-Russian war. Immediately after Sumarokov-Elston's departure from Vienna Andrássy had sent a special agent, Münch, to Bismarck to sound him on the basis of the letters of 23 September and 3 October, and Bismarck had told him of the Werder telegram.[3] The suspicions and alarms of

---

[1] Letter of Alexander II to Francis Joseph, 10 Oct., summarized in *Wertheimer*, p. 349.

[2] Letter of Francis Joseph to Alexander II, 23 Oct., summarized in *Wertheimer*, p. 350.

[3] For the Münch mission see Wertheimer, 'Neues zur Orientpolitik des Grafen Andrássy (1876–1877)', in *Historische Blätter*, no. 2, pp. 269–73. It is not mentioned in his life of Andrássy. Bismarck apparently was not alarmed at the prospect of a Russian occupation of Bulgaria, since he did not believe they would annex it. He welcomed an Austrian occupation of Bosnia-Herzegovina if the Russians entered Bulgaria. Münch put up a kite for a German promise of assistance in case of any threat from Italy. (Cf. *Wertheimer*, p. 354, for Austrian nervousness at this moment as to Italian designs on the Trentino.) Bismarck was very unaccommodat-

Vienna were naturally intensified. The Russians would have a very severe and a very delicate task ahead of them.

Meanwhile, in mid-October, while in Moscow and St. Petersburg the press reached its culminating point of virulence and while military preparations were already being hurried on, at Livadia—after the dispatch of Alexander's letter of 10 October, before the receipt of Francis Joseph's answer of 23 October—decisive consultations took place between the Tsar and his ministers. Should Russia take immediate and drastic action, and if so, how, and with what ultimate aims? Could she take immediate and isolated action? Should autonomy for the Balkan peoples continue to be the basis of Russia's policy? Or should she aim at fundamental changes in the political structure of Turkey, involving its immediate collapse and the putting into effect of the Reichstadt outlines? What should be the instructions for Ignatyev on returning to Constantinople?

Ignatyev had returned to Russia on leave on 25 July. He had immediately expressed his views as to the military position of the Turks being favourable to rapid Russian military action, whereas if Turkey were given a few months she would be vastly stronger both in men and munitions.[1] From the beginning of September he was in the Crimea, where he employed all his skill, and much ink, to bring home the necessity of coercive measures. He was inexhaustible in combinations, but throughout his schemes ran two guiding threads, the need of force or the threat of force, and enmity towards Austria-Hungary.[2]

Ignatyev's minimum programme, based on the hypothesis that Russia could not take decisive action on her own and that an immediate armistice should be imposed, was to the following effect. The only solution of the Herzegovina rebellion was to give the whole, or the greater part, of the southern portion of Herzegovina to Prince Nicholas, for which districts, as Ignatyev had suggested in the previous year, he should recognize the

---

ing, arguing that this would be merely anti-Russian, since Austria-Hungary would not need German assistance unless at war with Russia as well as with Italy. He seems to have regarded Münch's overture rather in the same light as the Werder telegram, and he refused to be drawn by it.

[1] Ignatyev's memoirs, in *I.V.*, vol. cxxxvi, p. 57.

[2] The following analysis of Ignatyev's proposals is based solely on his own account, as given in three reports for Gorchakov, which he gives in great detail in his memoirs, *I.V.*, vol. cxxxvi, pp. 59–81. They are not dated precisely by him. Ignatyev had not yet been initiated into the details of the Reichstadt agreement, see below, p. 405, n.

suzerainty of the Porte and pay tribute. In addition, Turkey should cede Spizza, the whole right bank of the Morača, and certain other districts to Montenegro, and recognize her full sovereignty. For Serbia nothing less than the *status quo ante bellum* could be accepted, together with two small frontier rectifications. If it were impossible to obtain full autonomy for Bosnia, the northern part of Herzegovina, and Novi Bazar, they should be guaranteed 'Cretan autonomy' with important additions. Similar guarantees should be demanded for Bulgaria, since it would probably be impossible to achieve the better alternative, i.e. the creation of an autonomous, vassal state on the 1856 model of the Principalities. Here, as elsewhere, a European commission would have to supervise the putting into force of the new reforms, disputed matters being settled by the ambassadors at Constantinople. The extent of this Bulgaria was to be approximately the same as that of the Bulgaria and Eastern Roumelia ultimately set up by the Berlin congress, except that it was to include Nish and the Adrianople region. It did not include the Macedonian regions or the Aegean littoral, and thus was far smaller than the divided Bulgaria suggested by the Constantinople conference, or than the big Bulgaria of San Stefano. Ignatyev proposed that this programme should first be approved in Berlin and London, and that only then should Vienna be approached, by a special mission (thus side-tracking Novikov) which should make clear that non-acceptance would mean the end of any concerted attempt with Austria-Hungary to settle the eastern question. He admitted that the proposals as to Montenegro and Serbia would arouse Vienna, and that compensation would probably be demanded; the utmost that Russia could permit would be the cession of Turkish Croatia. But if it were possible to count on the genuine and open co-operation of England it would be better to avoid, as far as possible, any promise of cessions to Austria-Hungary. He closed by allowing that there would be great difficulties in imposing this joint policy on the Turks and that the threat of immediate war-like demonstrations might be necessary.

Gorchakov found Ignatyev's idea of a moderate policy far too dangerous, and he was anxious to remove his rival by sending him back to his post to present his credentials to the new Sultan. Ignatyev, however, succeeded in staving off his departure. He was emphasizing more and more strongly that the Turks must not be given all the winter for their preparations, and that it was urgent to strike quickly while the Serbs and Montenegrins were still in the field. Ignatyev's anti-Austrian bias and his harping on rapid and if necessary isolated action by Russia perhaps worked on the Tsar to secure the Werder telegram, and certainly contributed powerfully to the general feeling at Livadia and Yalta that some kind of energetic action was necessary. Yet, according to his own retrospective version, he failed to win the field for bold measures in September or October which according to him would have forced the Turks, insufficiently prepared, to yield without any war and would have paved the way for a revival of Russian influence in the Balkans, unhampered by suicidal commitments to Austria-Hungary.

By the beginning of October Gladstone's campaign in England on behalf of the Bulgarians was making itself felt on the shores of the Crimea, and supplied Ignatyev with a new combination. He wrote of Gladstone's programme as involving in essentials the removal of Turkish troops and officials from Bulgaria and probably a European commission and a temporary military occupation, and as being approved by the great bulk of the British press and public opinion. Gladstone might even again become prime minister. Let the Russians weave the Gladstone programme into a declaration of their own policy, to be presented as an ultimatum. They would have to be prepared to support it by force; but Disraeli would probably be unable to form an alliance against such proposals, and might even support the Russian ultimatum. Russia, at least, would have to fight a Turkey without allies. The Tsar did not share this optimism: he minuted coldly on the unlikelihood of any support from the Disraeli government. Gorchakov and Jomini were equally critical, particularly of the idea that the British would allow force to be used without coming to some agreement with Vienna. After all, they had just refused to consider the Russian suggestions for joint naval and military measures of compulsion.

Ignatyev's relations with Gorchakov were worse than ever. Now he was to return to Constantinople. But his departure was preceded by three days of imperial councils, and the results of these were the definite discussion of war, and the decision in principle to mobilize.[1] To Ignatyev this was but a half-measure,

---

[1] For the evidence as to these imperial councils and as to mobilization see Appendix III.

since immediate mobilization was not sanctioned and there was no withdrawal from the offer of negotiations with Austria-Hungary. Still, he had succeeded in pushing the Tsar and chancellor towards energetic action. Mid-October saw the Russians committing themselves to the effective threat of force: measures for war were begun: they were difficult to stop. If the threat were not sufficient for the Turks, what then but war?

Gorchakov was insisting that an answer to the Tsar's letter of 10 October to Francis Joseph must be awaited, and he apparently believed that Vienna would prefer radical political changes in the Turkish empire in Europe to reforms for the Christians within the limits of broad administrative autonomy. If the Austrians agreed to conclude a detailed treaty, Gorchakov was prepared for radical political changes. If they refused to bind themselves and to reveal their intentions, nothing would remain except to pursue the pacification of the East alone. He allowed that there were greater advantages in taking military action against the Turks at once, within a month, than in deferring matters until the spring, but he promptly qualified this by asking how such immediate action could be taken without a rupture with Europe, how the negotiations for an armistice, for peace conditions, and for a conference could be broken off. Ignatyev was therefore to be sent back to Constantinople to press forward armistice and peace negotiations on a moderate basis. But at the same time partial mobilization was to take place early in November. Gorchakov considered this the best means of frightening the powers into support of a moderate Russian programme. This seemed the last possibility of a peaceful outcome. Should it fail and Russia have to undertake war, she could choose the favourable moment and move quickly. If, however, no armistice was achieved and hostilities continued in the Balkans, if the diplomatic efforts of the powers were thus shown to be useless, Russia could then refuse further negotiations and deliver an ultimatum, which would bring either a satisfactory peace or immediate hostilities, or 'an expectant position' if Russia agreed with Austria-Hungary to wait until the spring. All this Gorchakov made conditional: no final decision was to be taken until the receipt of replies from Vienna and Berlin.[1]

---

[1] Memorandum of 13 Oct., drawn up by Jomini and Gorchakov, and read to the council on 15 Oct., and additional conclusion to this memorandum added by

These ideas were accepted at the imperial council of 15 October and served in the stead of written instructions for Ignatyev, together with an additional memorandum which set out in very general terms what was to be meant by the moderate Russian peace programme.[1] It was less far-reaching than Ignatyev's suggestions a month before, except in the one point of the abolition of slavery (*genel*) which was included for consideration by the proposed conference, but it was so vague, especially as to boundaries, that it left ample scope for elastic interpretation. Serbia was to receive the *status quo ante bellum*, possibly with slight frontier rectifications, and—a significant sign of the hardening of official Russian opinion against the 'independent' Serbs— was in principle to pay a war indemnity, in accordance with her capacity to pay. The least that Montenegro was to gain was the annexation of those regions necessary for the increase of her food-supply and for access to the sea, a usefully ambiguous formula. Bosnia and Herzegovina should be governed on an autonomous basis by local elected officials, with Turkish regular troops confined to certain garrisons and no employment of irregulars, and with a Turkish governor-general appointed by the Sultan with the previous approval of the powers. The difficulties as to mixed areas were to be dealt with in detail by the conference. Similar provisions were to be applied to Bulgaria, with the necessary local changes. It was not stated of what Bulgaria was to consist. The idea of a European commission in Bosnia, Herzegovina, and Bulgaria was abandoned. Finally the conference was to examine the question of prohibiting the settling of Circassians in European Turkey and the employment of Bazi-Bazouks. Armed with these instructions, and with the Tsar's order to enter into negotiations with the other ambassadors on the British bases approved by Russia, Ignatyev left for Constantinople on 16 October, where he arrived on the 19th.

He left also with partial mobilization decided on in principle,

---

Gorchakov, 15 Oct.; text in Russian in Ignatyev's memoirs in *I.V.*, vol. cxxxvi, pp. 432–40. Goriainow, *Le Bosphore et les Dardanelles*, p. 325, gives brief extracts from what appears to be the same memorandum, although he dates it 30 Oct. Possibly this is a misprint for 30 Sept., i.e. 12 Oct., new style.

[1] The text of this additional memorandum, in a Russian translation, is in Ignatyev's memoirs, *I.V.*, vol. cxxxvi, pp. 440–3. It was drawn up by Ignatyev and Jomini on the basis of the decisions of the council of 15 Oct. and confirmed by Gorchakov.

and perhaps already for 13 November. The military were holding that if war had to come the sooner it came the better. Since
the beginning of October the military departments in St. Petersburg had been working at full pressure in preparation for the
mobilization of the southern military circles. Milyutin, however, who had been Alexander's war minister for the last fifteen
years, had not been either by temperament or by policy anxious
to believe that war had to come. A man of great reserve, stoical
determination, and massive industry, he had never sympathized
with panslavs and had been for years opposed, publicly and
privately, by many of this type who strongly criticized his army
reforms and disliked him personally. His position now seems to
have been by no means secure, and this may account for his
apparently succumbing to the militant atmosphere of Livadia,
even though technical considerations inclined him against war.[1]
Even more unsympathetic to a nationalistic crusade was the most
widely known of Russian military men, Totleben, the famous
defender of Sevastopol, who put in a brief appearance at this
moment at Livadia. Totleben was head of the engineers and
was still high in reputation, but he carried no social or political
weight and was suspect for his open disapproval of the volunteer
movement to Serbia and for his view that war should be avoided
and that money would be better spent in completing the reorganization of the army and building up the Black Sea fleet.
He had been summoned by the Tsar early in the month and
appeared at Livadia on 9 October, when he was appointed to
direct the Black Sea coast defences, a task which he carried on
with the utmost energy, until recalled to St. Petersburg a couple
of months later. He was to remain angrily side-tracked until
the Plevna failures overrode the bias against the Courlander
from the counting-house.[2]

In the Crimea in mid-October it was not, however, Totleben
who carried the greatest weight with Milyutin but Obruchev;
an academic strategist, and a political general; distrusted by, or
at odds with, the regular soldiers; never forgiven by the Grand

---

[1] Schweinitz maintains that Milyutin was against war, e.g. *Denkwürdigkeiten*,
vol. i, p. 342; cf. to the same effect *K. P. Pobedonostsev i ego korrespondenty*, vol. i, pt. 2,
p. 1016, text of letter of the Tsarevich to Pobedonostsev, from Livadia, 4 Nov. 1876.
For the technical condition of the Russian army see below, p. 304. Milyutin had
not built strategical railways with a view to war with Turkey: the only line leading
towards the Danube had not been due to his initiative and was still uncompleted.

[2] Shilder, *Graf E. E. Totleben*, vol. ii, pp. 727–30, 734–5.

Duke Nicholas Nicholaevich for his 'liberal' attitude during the Polish revolt of 1863 and his refusal to fight in a fratricidal war. He was no friend to Austria-Hungary, and believing it impossible to avoid conflict with England thought that it was better to meet her at Constantinople than on the shores of the Black Sea. He was ready enough with a plan of campaign for a war to wrest Bulgaria from Turkish rule. Rapidity of action and no sieges were his essentials for achieving decisive results. And by decisive results he meant that it might be necessary to press home to Constantinople itself. He calculated on being there in three to four months; on reaching Adrianople in seventy to eighty days. To accomplish this he allowed for the equivalent of four corps, and reckoned on the active assistance of the Roumanians and on the main Turkish army being locked up against the Serbians and Montenegrins. Transcaucasia was to be an entirely secondary field of operations—a view diametrically opposed to that of Ignatyev, who always harboured far-flung schemes for Asia Minor as the main Russian front.[1]

The whole plan was almost naïvely optimistic, for it assumed that there would be very little effective Turkish opposition, and put a premium on immediate action, but yet admitted that it would take a fortnight to mobilize and seven to ten days to concentrate on the frontier, and that the Russian military railway time-tables were applicable only up to 20 November, after which nothing could be guaranteed owing to snow and frost. It thus involved immediate mobilization and an almost immediate break with Turkey, and the other powers. As has been seen, Gorchakov was inclining to some such break, but was not carried away so far as to snap the new links with Austria.

Obruchev's general plan was approved by the Tsar on 15 October, but Constantinople was to be occupied only as an extreme measure to achieve the aim of the war, which was to be not the disintegration of the Ottoman empire but the freeing of Bulgaria. No date was definitely fixed for the mobilization of

---

[1] Text of Obruchev's memorandum of 13 Oct., in *Hasenkampf*, appendix 1. His later memorandum of 19 Feb. 1877, ib., appendix 2, makes clear important additional points in his October plan. Obruchev had made a study of Bulgaria and the Balkan passes on the spot in 1871. Two general staff officers had done likewise in 1875. St. Petersburg was also supplied with detailed plans of the environs of Constantinople. *Nouvelle Revue*, 1880, vol. iv, p. 476. For the visit of a Roumanian mission to Livadia at this same time, in the second week of October, see below, pp. 294–5.

the four corps, though 13 November seems to have been accepted. The final decision as to war was to depend on the outcome of diplomatic negotiations. The command in the Balkans was to be given to the Grand Duke Nicholas Nicholaevich, despite the fact that he was at loggerheads with both Milyutin and Obruchev.[1] The Grand Duke immediately expostulated on the insufficiency of four corps, an expostulation which he reiterated in the coming months, and to which the reply was made that the danger from the side of Austria-Hungary made it impossible to spare more troops.[2]

It is easy to understand Ignatyev's severe condemnation of these half-measures; they were arrived at in response to the pressure for immediate action; but they provided neither for immediate nor for efficient action. On the other hand, they made eventual war extremely probable, and gave the Turks time for hurrying on preparations and for finishing with the Serbs. The final key to the situation was the refusal of Gorchakov to abandon his offer of negotiations with Austria-Hungary for a treaty or to withdraw his approval of the British peace basis which had likewise been approved by Austria-Hungary. Though decidedly bellicose, he was determined that Russia if she went to war with Turkey should do so placed in a diplomatic position which was as advantageous as could be. In this he was to succeed.

Of all those at Livadia only Reutern, the finance minister, appears to have made a direct effort for peace. He was a trusted but not a close counsellor of Alexander; cautious and meticulous; at the opposite pole to the panslavs; accustomed to a hard routine of office work and a narrow circle of friends mainly from his own Baltic Provinces. The general financial and

---

[1] *Tatishchev*, p. 328, summarizing the results of the imperial council held on 15 Oct. See Appendix III for the evidence as to this imperial council and as to mobilization.

[2] *Nouvelle Revue*, 1880, vol. iv, p. 480: the Grand Duke, if he had to have only four corps, then pressed for immediate hostilities, while the Turks would be still occupied with Serbia and Montenegro. The Grand Duke later spoke of its having been first proposed to give him command of the army against Austria: there were to be five armies, one in Poland, one against Austria, one for the Danube, one in the Caucasus, and one under the Tsarevich round St. Petersburg: *Skalon*, vol. ii, p. 20, under date 8 Dec. 1877. It is worth noticing that according to Ovsyany, *Russkoe upravlenie v Bolgarii*, vol. i, pp. 25–6, the question of the formation of a Bulgarian legion was decided while the Tsar was at Livadia. Though it was, in the first place, recruited from Bulgars in Russia, the decision is a further indication of the extreme likelihood of war.

economic situation had been increasingly serious. There was a severe fall in Russian funds, particularly in London, where in this very week of 13–20 October Russian five per cents. (1873) dropped fifteen points. Throughout the year international financial speculators, in particular certain German banking circles, were hammering hard at Russian state credit. The drain of gold, which rose from five million roubles in January to seventeen in June, jumped to sixty million in October. On the St. Petersburg stock exchange there was a panic. The exchange successfully kept up by the government in September to 81·465 could no longer be pegged, and in October fell to 78·735, to drop to 75·071 on the announcement of mobilization.[1]

Reutern, beset by this financial crisis, arrived in the Crimea on 13 October, where he was, as would be expected of him, appalled by the dominance of militant nationalism.[2] 'L'Empereur s'est mis à la tête du mouvement national' was the triumphant *mot d'ordre* of the court ladies. Gorchakov struck him as particularly bellicose; Milyutin as much preoccupied with the difficulties of a winter campaign; Adlerberg as very saneminded, but reserved; Ignatyev as talking endlessly, not always to the same effect, but apparently inclined to war. The Tsar was determined on military measures of some description and refused to pay heed to Reutern's exposition of financial and economic difficulties.[3] The net effect of his report was that war was impossible without sacrificing the results of the previous twenty years of reforms; that it would mean ruin for the economic future of Russia and a crisis incomparably more severe than any previous one; and that there were no resources for carrying on a war. The Tsar was furious, put the worst con-

---

[1] Bloch, *Les Finances de la Russie au XIXᵉ siècle*, vol. ii, pp. 233–4; *The Economist*, 21 and 28 Oct. 1876, pp. 1221, 1257, and 22 June 1878, p. 731; Propper, *Was nicht in die Zeitung kam*, pp. 38–42, 44–6. The Constantinople conference raised the exchange to 75·7. During the war it sank to 63. The exchange in question is that of the credit rouble in relation to the gold rouble.

[2] Reutern's journal, under date 24 Oct., St. Petersburg, in *R.S.*, vol. cxliii, pp. 39–41, on which the following paragraph is based, and to which his later entry in Sept. 1877, ib., p. 48, adds a few points. He left St. Petersburg for a holiday on 16 Sept. On 25 Sept. he received a telegram informing him of the Sumarokov-Elston mission and that if the Austrian reply were not satisfactory up to 200,000 men would be mobilized. He thereupon returned to the capital, and was asked to go down to Livadia on 6 Oct.

[3] Reutern's memorandum laid before the Tsar on 15 Oct. is printed in a German translation in Reutern–Nolcken, *Die finanzielle Sanierung Russlands . . . durch . . . Reutern*, pp. 221–30.

struction on Reutern's remarks, and insisted that there were resources if people knew how or wished to use them. Besides the Tsar only the Tsarevich had read his report, and there was no discussion of it at the council meetings. Reutern did not expect to secure at once any direct backing against the Tsar, but he had some hopes that it might be possible 'mettre de l'eau dans son vin'. He left deeply resenting as a personal affront the Tsar's refusal to listen to him, and cogitating resignation.

As October drew to a close and the Russians were anxiously waiting for replies from Vienna and Berlin, the Serbs completely broke down. While Kartsov's reports to the foreign office had been mordantly portraying the situation in Serbia—the egoism and timidity of Milan, the greed of the metropolitan Michael, the corrupt duplicity of Ristić, the lies of the press, the refusal of the Serbs to fight, the systematic efforts of the Slavonic committees to get the better of Russian official policy[1]—these same committees had been redoubling their efforts in Russia and above all in the Crimea, culminating in the Countess Bludova's appeal to Gorchakov on 27 October. At the same moment came the disaster of Djunis, after which the Serbian army ceased to exist as a fighting force and the Turks pressed forward down the Morava valley towards Belgrade. Even Chernyaev abandoned hope and on the 29th declared that nothing remained but to appeal to the Tsar for an immediate armistice. Milan telegraphed frantically, through Kartsov, that Belgrade was lost if an armistice were not at once imposed; Gorchakov was determined on some decisive action to save the Serbs; and on 30 October the Tsar ordered Ignatyev to demand from the Turks that they should agree within forty-eight hours to an armistice for six or eight weeks and that they should take immediate steps to cease hostilities, on pain of a severance of diplomatic relations.[2]

Ignatyev was none too well pleased at this ultimatum, partly no doubt, as he tried to urge on Gorchakov, because it did not include anything concerning Bosnia, Herzegovina, and Bulgaria. In addition he flattered himself that he was on the point

---

[1] Kartsov, *Za kulisami diplomatii*, pp. 43–4.

[2] Ristić, *Diplomatska istorija Srbije*, vol. i, pp. 150–1; 'Knyaz A. M. Gorchakov v ego razskazakh iz proshlago', in *R.S.*, 1883, vol. xl, pp. 178–9. The text of the ultimatum as presented by Ignatyev in the evening of 31 Oct., together with that of the Turkish acceptance on 1 Nov., is printed in *A. and P.*, 1877, xc, C. 1640, no. 989, incl.

of succeeding in his own negotiations with the Porte for an armistice. He delayed delivering the ultimatum until late on 31 October, while he was consulting the other ambassadors and pressing Gorchakov to cancel it. But it had already been given for publication to the official government journal, where it had appeared on the morning of 31 October; Reuter telegrams had reported it in the London evening papers, and Shuvalov had privately confirmed it at the same time to Derby. It was accepted unconditionally by the Porte next day.[1]

The news of the Turkish acceptance did not reach Livadia until 2 November. By then both Vienna and Berlin had been heard from. Francis Joseph's letter of 23 October had arrived by 29 October, and Gorchakov learned that Austria-Hungary would not join Russia in a war and apparently wished to delay matters until the spring, but agreed to negotiate a secret treaty. Thereupon Gorchakov, convinced that the Turks were dreading immediate action by Russia, again put up to the Tsar the much debated question: would it be better to strike at once, or to wait until some arrangement had been reached with Austria-Hungary, which would assure Russia of benevolent neutrality and prevent Austria-Hungary from doing more than annex Bosnia-Herzegovina?[2] The ultimatum to Constantinople shows that the Tsar confined himself to the question of the armistice, and recoiled from immediate war: what he threatened was the rupture of diplomatic relations.

In the evening of 31 October, at the very moment when Ignatyev finally presented the ultimatum to the Porte, the eagerly awaited Schweinitz arrived at Yalta, bringing what there was of the German answer to the Werder telegram of a month before. There had been long cogitation and much argument by the Germans.[3] Finally Schweinitz, after a complicated fortnight between Berlin, Varzin, and Baden, set out for Russia

[1] Ignatyev's account is in his memoirs, in *I.V.*, vol. cxxxvi, pp. 448–50. He claims to have reached already a final agreement with the Porte as to the exact text of an armistice. This is not quite borne out by Elliot's evidence, which does, however, show that Ignatyev was much more accommodating than those at Livadia: see *A. and P.*, 1877, xc, C. 1640, nos. 980–2 and 1001; and *D.D.F.*, p. 106, and *Actenstücke*, i, nos. 823 and 825.

[2] Extracts from memorandum by Gorchakov of 29 Oct., quoted in Goriainow, *Les Bosphore et les Dardanelles*, pp. 326–7.

[3] See above, page 207. For Schweinitz at Livadia see his *Denkwürdigkeiten*, vol. i, pp. 359–64, and *Briefwechsel*, p. 120; and his two reports of 1 and 2 Nov. from Yalta in *G.P.*, pp. 80–4.

with Bismarck's very guarded reply. In the event of an Austro-Russian war Germany could not bind herself to a course of action which should have no regard to the circumstances of the war, the attitude of other powers, and the consideration that it was not in Germany's interest that either Russia or Austria-Hungary should be essentially weakened. That was the core of the ambassador's instructions. He was, of course, to emphasize that Germany would observe the same friendly relations as in the past, but he was to give no binding assurances and put nothing in writing. To add to the difficulty of his task, Bismarck, perhaps repeating approaches made through Manteuffel at the time of his Warsaw mission, had given him secret verbal instructions to sound the Russians as to the possibility of a guarantee of Alsace-Lorraine in return for full German support of Russia in the East.

Schweinitz was forthwith invited to Livadia (1 November); struggled through a gloomy and trying lunch at the imperial table; and then, closeted with the Tsar, fulfilled his far from easy instructions. Thence he proceeded to a long, lively, and unfriendly conversation with Gorchakov.

'We expected great things from you, and you bring nothing that we have not already for long known. . . . I want more, I will write to Prince Bismarck what I want: he should speak out, he should declare to the world that Russia has a right as mandatory of Europe to make an end of intolerable conditions. . . . We do not ask of you any material aid, but do you know what I said to the Tsar in 1870 after I had returned from Switzerland and he had declared that he would at once put in the field 300,000 men if Austria attacked you? I said to him: Sire, you ought to have concluded a treaty binding Prussia to similar action. . . .'

And so forth; to and fro between Gorchakov and Schweinitz.

'Redensarten' was Bismarck's comment on the report of this conversation; but it was more than this, for the Russian initial dissatisfaction was not soon dissipated, and Schweinitz's cautious, quickly dropped, broaching of a possible guarantee for Alsace-Lorraine had failed to draw anything but the cynical rejoinder: 'That would be of little use to you: in our day treaties are of very slight value.' On which Bismarck minuted 'sic'. Three years later he was to make one of his counts against Gorchakov this refusal of what he called his offer of an alliance, and then apparently for the first time the offer came to the knowledge of the Tsar. Schweinitz, a Silesian, thought more of the central Polish provinces than of Alsace-Lorraine, and did not personally favour the idea of a treaty as adumbrated by Bismarck. He carried out the chancellor's instructions, but he seems to have been quite ready to take Gorchakov's gibe at the worth of treaties as a rejection, and therefore to have never approached the Tsar himself on the subject. Nor did Gorchakov. Did he understand it as a serious offer? It is not clear that Schweinitz made this evident. It is clear that he dropped the matter at the very first opportunity.[1]

Both the Tsar and his foreign minister made immediate replies, in letters dated 2 November, but written before the news of the acceptance of the ultimatum to Turkey. The Tsar declared that it was impossible for him to continue sterile negotiations: '. . . puisque l'Europe ne veut pas accomplir ce qu'elle reconnaît juste, humain et nécessaire, je suis décidé à le faire seul.' But 'seul' did not mean a break with Austria: on the contrary Alexander wrote confidently, though not at all clearly, of agreement with Francis Joseph, of Werder supplying details of this entente and the projected treaty, and of his own determination to do his utmost to maintain intact the 'entente à trois'. He appealed to Germany for friendly support, exactly in what was not clear to Bismarck. 'J'ai le droit d'attendre qu'on me laisse agir, si l'on ne veut pas coopérer avec moi.' Here was the keynote of Russian policy in the coming months. Gorchakov, in much the same strain, appealed, as he had forewarned Schweinitz, for 'une adhésion morale publiquement et nettement exprimée', and announced measures of coercion to be the sole means of action on behalf of the Balkan Christians.[2]

---

[1] On the controversial question of a German offer of a free hand to Russia in the East in return for a guarantee of Alsace-Lorraine, see page 203, note 1; and Frahm's discussion in his 'Bismarck vor der Option zwischen Russland und Österreich', in *Historische Zeitschrift*, vol. cxlix, pp. 522–43. Schweinitz gives important information and explanations in *Denkwürdigkeiten*, vol. i, pp. 355–6, 361–2; vol. ii, pp. 86–90, 224; *Briefwechsel*, p. 141. For Bismarck's position see *G.P.*, p. 80, note, and vol. iii, p. 28. In *Russko-Germanskie otnosheniya* (Moscow, 1922), p. 72, Saburov reports a conversation with Bismarck on 26 July 1879: 'Si Vous nous aviez garanti la possession de cette province [Alsace-Lorraine], j'étais prêt à Vous suivre "durch dick und dünn" et à engager toutes les forces de l'Allemagne au service de Vos intérêts en Orient.' Against this Alexander II minuted: 'Je ne me souviens pas, qu'il nous en ait jamais fait la proposition.' Bismarck went on: 'Mes ouvertures à ce sujet sont restées sans réponse, ou plutôt on a fait la sourde oreille.'

[2] With the Tsar's 'je suis décidé à le faire seul' compare Gorchakov's instructions to Novikov of the same date, 2 Nov., below, p. 277. The texts of the letters of the

It seemed clear that the Russians meant to come to an agreement with the Austrians, and to use force alone if the conference would not agree to joint compulsion. The former policy might be satisfactory enough to Bismarck, but he went to the extremes of suspiciousness as to Gorchakov's real intentions, attributing to him the idea of a deep-laid policy of winning over the Tsar to an anti-German grouping of Russia, Austria, and France by putting to Germany exorbitant demands which she could not accept and then pointing out to the Tsar that he could not reckon upon her. He was morbidly distrustful of Russian attempts to separate Berlin and Vienna, and he contrasted sharply what he termed the business-like negotiations of the Russians in Vienna and London with their high-handed ambiguities in Berlin.[1]

Bismarck was certainly beside the mark in his reference to London. Anglo-Russian relations were going from bad to worse. The Queen boiled over at 'the rash and intemperate act' of presenting the Sultan with an ultimatum, and Disraeli was further encouraged in his endeavours to take a firm line.[2] The Tsar on his side was complaining sharply of English distrust of his intentions, and was suspecting Disraeli of being about to send the fleet to occupy the Straits and Constantinople.[3] Hoping to penetrate the obscurity in which Russian designs were wrapt, Derby somewhat tardily (16 October) had instructed Loftus to arrange a visit to the Crimea. Loftus did not manage to arrive there until 27 October, when he was politely kept by Gorchakov in ignorance of all that was afoot, and had to wait five days before his first audience with the Tsar in the afternoon of 2 November, when the news had come of the all but certain acceptance of the ultimatum. His audience had first been

Tsar to the Emperor William and of Gorchakov to Bismarck, both of 2 Nov., are in *G.P.*, pp. 85–7. The Tsar added as a postscript that the Porte had just accepted his demands—a further proof that the Turks only yielded to threats: 'Puissent les autres s'en convaincre quand il s'agira des Conférences de paix, qui j'espère ne tarderont pas à s'ouvrir à Constantinople.'

[1] For Bismarck's extravagant analysis of Gorchakov's aims see Bismarck to Bülow, 10 Nov., in *G.P.*, pp. 93–6. The replies of the Emperor William and Bismarck of 14 Nov. contained nothing more than generalities; text in *G.P.*, pp. 96–8. Bismarck was careful to emphasize to Oubril his difficulties in overcoming the pro-English influence of the Empress, Crown Prince, and Crown Princess; Oubril to Gorchakov, 24 Nov., cited in Goriainow, *Le Bosphore et les Dardanelles*, pp. 337–8.

[2] *The Letters of Queen Victoria 1862–1878*, vol. ii, p. 493; *Disraeli*, pp. 958–60.

[3] Schweinitz, *Denkwürdigkeiten*, vol. i, pp. 361, 363; and his report to Bülow of 2 Nov., in *G.P.*, p. 83.

arranged for 1 November, but was deferred at the last moment
since it was discovered to be the anniversary of the death of the
late Empress: Schweinitz had just arrived. No anniversaries
interfered with *his* immediate reception.

When the Tsar finally did see Loftus, he stated clearly that,
if at the coming conference the Porte defied Europe by paralysing negotiations and reforms, Russia was not prepared to put
up with a continuation of rebuffs and would be compelled to
take isolated action if the other powers would not act with
resolution. He said emphatically that he wanted no conquests
and had not the smallest wish to be possessed of Constantinople;
and he gave his word of honour that he had no intention of
acquiring it. If circumstances obliged him to occupy a portion
of Bulgaria, such occupation would last only until peace was
guaranteed and the Christians safeguarded. He ridiculed
English fears of Russian designs on Constantinople and of a
future invasion of India which he described as completely
unrealizable. He finally summed up thus: the immediate convocation of a conference on the basis proposed by England to
agree upon such reforms in Bosnia, Herzegovina, and Bulgaria
as would give the Christians autonomy; and the demanding of
adequate guarantees for the full carrying out of these reforms.[1]

There is no reason to doubt the genuineness of this attempt of
Alexander to disabuse the English of their lack of faith in him,
and Gorchakov a day later expressed privately to Shuvalov the
advantages to Russia of the keys of the Black Sea being left in
the feeble hands of the Turks.[2] The assurances of the Tsar,

[1] For Loftus at Livadia see his telegrams and dispatches in *A. and P.*, 1877, xc,
C. 1640, nos. 669, 793, 824, 835, 950–5. *F.O.* 65/941 adds nothing material: nor
do Loftus's *Diplomatic Reminiscences, 1862–1879*, second series, vol. ii, pp. 176–92.
He telegraphed a very brief version of his audience of 2 Nov. on that afternoon
which was received that night. The full version of it, no. 952, was sent as a dispatch
and did not reach London until 14 Nov. It was dated 2 Nov., but does not seem
to have been actually sent off until the 4th, after it had been read over by Gorchakov and accepted as a correct summary, save in one particular which was
corrected. Loftus, by request, left a copy of the dispatch with the Tsar. It was
published in the *London Gazette* on 21 Nov. Its original wording had made the
Tsar, in referring to the Sumarokov-Elston mission, speak of 'the occupation of
Bosnia and Herzegovina by Austria'. Gorchakov pointed out that the proposal
had referred to Bosnia only, adding that the object of excluding Herzegovina was
'in case of occupation by the Austrian and Russian troops to place a neutral zone
between the two armies'. Loftus accordingly omitted Herzegovina.

[2] Lettre particulière of Gorchakov to Shuvalov, 3 Nov., published in the semi-
official *Journal de St. Pétersbourg* on 21 Nov., and printed in *A. and P.*, 1877, xc, C.
1640, no. 1065, incl.

however, did not cover a temporary occupation of Constantinople; they were unpleasantly indefinite as to Bulgaria; and they were coupled with the virtual certainty that Russia in the near future would insist that Turkey be coerced. Disraeli's first impression of the brief telegraphic report of this conversation was that it represented merely a 'sentimental ebullition' on the part of the Tsar. The full report did not reach London until 14 November, at the same time as the announcement of Russian mobilization, which of course intensified English fears. The one positive result of the Loftus interview was that the way was clear for a formal proposal for a conference. This was accordingly made in Derby's circular of 4 November, and Loftus remained at Yalta until the 8th busied with the details of its terms, as will be explained in the next chapter.

Yet the prospects for a successful outcome of the conference did not appear bright, especially since Gorchakov was emphasizing the need of some form of occupation to bring the Turks to their senses. When Disraeli had to speak at the Guildhall dinner of 9 November he closed what was otherwise an unalarming review of the eastern crisis with a peroration which inevitably concentrated all attention.

'Peace is especially an English policy. . . . She covets no cities and no provinces. . . . But although the policy of England is peace, there is no country so well prepared for war as our own. If she enters into conflict in a righteous cause—and I will not believe that England will go to war except for a righteous cause—her resources, I feel, are inexhaustible. She is not a country that, when she enters into a campaign, has to ask herself whether she can support a second or a third campaign. She enters into a campaign which she will not terminate till right is done.'[1]

Two days later there came from Moscow what appeared to be a direct answer to this speech. It had been arranged that the Tsar should stop at Moscow on his way north to the official capital, and should address the Muscovite nobility and civic authorities. His speech was drafted in the train on the way up, before Disraeli had uttered his warning, which was probably not known in full in Moscow in advance of the delivery of the Tsar's speech.[2] Moscow gave the Tsar the inevitable, trium-

[1] *Disraeli*, p. 964.
[2] Schweinitz, *Denkwürdigkeiten*, vol. i, p. 366. Although very well informed, he was not then with the Tsar, having left Livadia on 6 Nov. direct for St. Petersburg, and he does not allow for the draft being altered after receipt of a telegram from

phant welcome. On 11 November, amid intense enthusiasm, he spoke thus:

'I thank you, gentlemen, for the sentiments which you desire to express to me regarding the present political situation. That is now clearer, and I am therefore prepared to accept your address with pleasure. You know already that Turkey has complied with my demand for the immediate conclusion of an armistice to put an end to useless carnage in Serbia and Montenegro. The Montenegrins have shown themselves, as always, true heroes in this unequal struggle. Unfortunately it is impossible to say the same of the Serbs, despite the presence in their ranks of our volunteers, many of whom have paid with their blood for the cause of Slavdom. I know that all Russia joins with me in taking the deepest interest in the sufferings of our brothers by faith and by origin; but for me the true interests of Russia are dearer than everything, and I would do my utmost to spare precious Russian blood being shed. That is why I have striven and am continuing to strive to achieve by peaceful means a real improvement in the life of all the Christian inhabitants of the Balkan peninsula. Deliberations between the representatives of the six great powers are shortly to be begun at Constantinople for the determination of conditions of peace. I much desire that we shall reach a general agreement. If this is not attained and if I see that we are not gaining such guarantees as would assure the execution of our just demands upon the Porte, then I firmly intend to act independently and I am convinced that in such an eventuality all Russia will respond to my appeal, when I count it necessary and the honour of Russia requires it. I am convinced likewise that Moscow, as always, will set the example. May God help us to fulfil our sacred mission.'

It was so exceptional for the Tsar to speak in public on a burning issue that his words created even more effect than was strictly their due. He had linked together Orthodoxy and the Slav cause, and he had appealed to Russia's sacred mission. Away in St. Petersburg Timashev, responsible as minister of

Shuvalov on Disraeli's speech. I cannot trace when this telegram was received or exactly what it reported. There seems, however, no doubt that the Tsar had decided to make a speech at Moscow before leaving Livadia. He left on the 7th, arrived in Moscow on the 9th, and reached St. Petersburg on the 13th. The Tsar told Werder, the Prussian military plenipotentiary, on 20 Nov. that he had had no knowledge of the Guildhall speech before his own Moscow address; Loftus to Derby, disp., no. 553, 20 Nov., in *F.O.* 65/942. I have translated the text of the Tsar's speech from the original Russian as printed in *Tatishchev*, pp. 335–6. The official French version of it as published in the St. Petersburg press on 12 Nov. is printed in *A. and P.*, 1877, xc, C. 1640, no. 930, sent and received 12 Nov.

the interior for the official publication of the speech, could not believe the correctness of the text as telegraphed from Moscow and wired to Adlerberg for confirmation: but it was correct, including 'our sacred mission'. The panslavs were to do their utmost to prevent these words from being forgotten. Katkov greeted the speech with triumph, and urged on immediate, isolated, armed action against Turkey. Aksakov, despite the references to the Serbs, was in transports: commenting later in hyperbolical terms on the address he hailed Alexander as the glorious successor of Ivan the Great, Peter the Great, and Catherine the Great, assigning to him exactly the role which Alexander himself had so emphatically repudiated to Loftus.[1]

Two days after the Moscow speech, on 13 November, the Tsar gave the final order for the mobilization of six army corps and the corresponding reserves, and it was officially published on the following day.[2]

---

[1] Meshchersky, *Moi Vospominaniya*, vol. ii, pp. 308–11 (he was in Moscow); Nevedensky, *Katkov i ego vremya*, pp. 367–8, quoting from *Moskovskiya Vyedemosti*; Aksakov, *Slavyansky vopros*, p. 238, speech of 18 Mar. 1877 to the Moscow Slavonic committee.

[2] The mobilization of 'une partie de l'armée' was announced to Europe, with the necessary explanations, in a circular of Gorchakov of 13 Nov., published officially next day in St. Petersburg; text in *A. and P.*, 1877, xc, C. 1640, no. 1011. There were to be three armies in the south, the Danube operations army, the coast army (Odessa–Crimea), and the Caucasus operations army, the official total for these three being 332,634. Only four corps and some extras (about 190,000 all arms) were allotted to the Grand Duke Nicholas in command of the Danube army. Sarauw, *Der russisch-türkische Krieg 1877–8*, pp. 24–5; Springer, *Der russisch-türkische Krieg 1877–8*, vol. i, pp. 30–1; Tatishchev, p. 337.

VII

THE CONSTANTINOPLE CONFERENCE

THE fortnight which crowded together the ultimatum to Turkey, the Moscow speech, and the partial mobilization marked the culmination of the patriotic movement. Shortly after the return of the Tsar to St. Petersburg a cooler period set in, and the year ended with pessimistic forebodings and pacific possibilities much in the air. The cautious routine of the bureaucrats and the international connexions of society in the capital were again to the fore. Mobilization proceeded worm-like to the south, working on the whole with fair success, considering that it was the first of its kind; but there was for a time almost complete dislocation on the southern lines, and the Grand Duke Nicholas was continuously complaining of shortage or mismanagement in all departments. Nevertheless, by the beginning of 1877 he was at his head-quarters at Kishinev, himself seriously ill, but with some 190,000 men tolerably prepared for action.[1]

The immediate effect of the Tsar's Moscow speech had been to encourage a warlike tone: an occupation of Bulgaria was essential; war with Turkey was spoken of as inevitable; the terms of peace must be dictated at Constantinople. There were enthusiastic scenes at a review of the Guards on 15 November, when the Tsar addressed the officers in appropriately stirring terms. Patriotic addresses to the Tsar flowed in; some of doubtful spontaneity, including as they did one from Warsaw and another from the Orenburg Moslems. The fitting out of privateers in the event of war with England was actively canvassed. The newspapers were filled with anti-British outbursts, harping on a favourite theme: 'The secret and real policy of England in the East consists in obtaining payment at all hazards of the money which she forced on Turkey at Jewish rates of interest or in procuring guarantees for such payment, and secondly in keeping the Mussulman markets always open for the absorption

---

[1] For the working of the mobilization: *Opisanie russko-turetskoi voiny 1877–78 gg.* ..., vol. i, pp. 325–30; *Vestnik Evropy,* Jan. 1877, pp. 400–3; Wellesley, no. 52, conf., 19 Dec., in *F.O.* 65/942, and no. 3, very conf., 14 Jan. 1877, in *F.O.* 65/963 (painting the failure of the mobilization plans in over-dark colours). For the complaints of G.H.Q.: *Skalon,* vol. i, e.g. pp. 9–11, 15.

of English manufactures.' England, in the role of Shylock relying 'on the written instrument when he demanded the blood
of a Christian', could be brought to her senses by a blow at the
Suez Canal and threats to Gibraltar from Spain and to her
insecure Indian empire from her oppressed native subjects.[1]

But from the beginning of December official inspiration
moderated the press, and by the time of the opening of the Constantinople conference the enthusiasm for war was reported to
have almost entirely subsided.[2] Military circles in St. Petersburg came to be filled with gossip on the unpreparedness of
the army and the necessity of avoiding war. After the cold
douche of the Tsar's contemptuous references to the Serbs at
Moscow, Chernyaev became the butt for bitter attacks and
the Serbian scandals were widely advertised, much to the fury
of Aksakov.[3]

On the side of finance the outlook was as dark as ever. Efforts
to raise a loan in Amsterdam met with rebuffs.[4] The 100,000,000
5 per cent. internal loan which was publicly offered on 19 November, 'for the purpose of securing peace in the future', failed
severely: neither Moscow nor the provinces subscribed to any
extent. Reutern, when he saw the Tsar on 24 November,
painted another very gloomy picture of the difficulty of meeting
foreign obligations and of the bad effects of inevitable issues
of paper money; for the next month he continued to do his

[1] Wellesley, no. 37, 17 Nov.; Loftus to Derby, disp., no. 540, 17 Nov., enclosing
articles of 12 and 14 Nov. from *Birzheviya Vyedemosti* (not usually an extremist paper),
and *Russky Mir* (extreme nationalist); disp., nos. 571 and 577, 4 and 6 Dec. (on
privateering); in *F.O.* 65/942.

[2] Loftus to Derby, disp., nos. 586 and 600, 6 and 19 Dec., in *F.O.* 65/942.

[3] Schweinitz, *Denkwürdigkeiten*, vol. i, pp. 366–7. Schweinitz's impressions must
be taken cautiously; he always looked for signs of a peace disposition. His Austrian
colleague likewise emphasized the lack of sabre-rattling by the end of November,
and was supported as to this by Klepsch, the military attaché; Langenau to
Andrássy, 27 Nov., Klepsch to Andrássy, 22 Nov., cited in Wittrock, *Gorčakov, Ignatiev och Suvalov*, p. 36. Prince Meshchersky, *Moi Vospominaniya*, vol. ii, pp. 313–17,
just returned from Serbia via Moscow, gives a striking picture of the changed tone
of St. Petersburg as compared with the summer. The great majority of the military
in St. Petersburg belonged to the Guards and other regiments which had not been
mobilized. Aksakov, *Slavyansky vopros*, pp. 235, 241–2, 246–8. For examples of
press attacks on Chernyaev: articles in *Birzheviya Vyedemosti*, 2 and 4 Nov., enclosed
in Doria to Derby, disp., no. 12, in *F.O.* 65/941; précis of letter in *Golos* (liberal),
19 Nov., from its Belgrade correspondent, in *A. and P.*, 1877, xc, C. 1640, no. 1066
incl. According to Loftus, disp., no. 525, 6 Nov., from Yalta, in *F.O.* 65/941,
the Tsar refused to receive Chernyaev when he arrived back in Russia from
Serbia.

[4] Loftus to Derby, disp., no. 557, 21 Nov., in *F.O.* 65/942.

utmost to take advantage of the Tsar's pacific mood, and finally presented him with a new memorandum expatiating on the financial impossibility of war. Finance was not one of the Tsar's strong points: he would never believe that his mighty empire was unable to engage in war, should war prove necessary, merely because of monetary conditions, and the memorandum did not make a convincing impression upon him.[1]

One very important step had been taken already on 10 November with a view to ensuring that Russia's external obligations would be duly met. Announcement was made that from 1 January 1877 customs duties were to be paid in gold. This was tantamount to raising them at one stroke by about 33 per cent., and was the first important alteration of the tariff since 1868. Thus, while the close of the Crimean war ushered in a period of comparatively low tariffs in Russia, her next Balkan war heralded the return to fiercely protective duties. The more immediate effect of this step was regarded as satisfactory in that there was no default on her foreign loans, and in general Russian finances staggered through the war somewhat better than Reutern had prognosticated, thanks to a good harvest and heavy exports in 1877 and to the later internal loans being well taken up. But he was, of course, right in maintaining that war would mean a gigantic increase of paper money, and an immense burden for the future.[2]

Although, as the year drew to its close, the symptoms of war fever had declined, yet two dangerous facts remained: a part of the army had been mobilized and would be ready for action by the spring; and secondly, the Tsar and Gorchakov were firmly maintaining that real reforms must be introduced in Turkey with adequate guarantees for their being carried out. After the last eighteen months in the Balkans, Russia might be able to

---

[1] For the failure of the internal loan: Bloch, *Les Finances de la Russie au XIXe siècle*, vol. ii, p. 249; Reutern–Nolcken, *Die finanzielle Sanierung Russlands . . . durch . . . Reutern*, pp. 221–2; *Vestnik Evropy*, Jan. 1877, pp. 403–5. For official details as to the issue of the loan: *A. and P.*, 1877, xc, C. 1640, no. 1063 incl. Reutern's journal, 24 Nov. and 22 Dec., in *R.S.*, vol. cxliii, pp. 41–2, records his two interviews with the Tsar. The text of his memorandum, presented to the Tsar on 29 Dec., is in Reutern–Nolcken, op. cit., pp. 134–40.

[2] Bloch, op. cit., vol. ii, pp. 253–5, and 237–60 for Russian finances, 1876–9, during which period only one foreign loan was raised, in 1877 in Amsterdam under very unfavourable terms and with great secrecy. It is generally stated that the payment of the customs in gold had the effect of raising the tariff approximately by 33 per cent., but the rise is put at only 10 per cent. in Reutern–Nolcken, p. 215. 468,000,000 roubles in paper money were issued in two years.

present a good case for asking whether, if the powers agreed as to the reforms to be introduced in Turkey, they could well do nothing to impose them, or whether they could take action against Russia if she finally took this responsibility upon herself. No doubt issues might be raised going far beyond mere reforms for the Christian subjects of the Sultan, and it would be essential for Russia to safeguard herself by some agreement with Austria-Hungary. She would also have to make some arrangement with the Principalities if her army on the Pruth were to be moved forward. Hence Russian diplomacy during the six months from November 1876 was aiming at reaching an agreement with the powers as to real reforms in Turkey, at implementing such agreement by the necessary action, and if agreement proved impossible at so manœuvring that isolated Russian intervention would involve the minimum of difficulties. This triple task was carried through in the Constantinople conference, the London protocol, and the conventions with Austria-Hungary and Roumania.

It has been mentioned in the previous chapter that Derby had issued his formal proposal for a conference at Constantinople while Loftus was in the Crimea (4 November). The Russians and British had already agreed that the six powers should come to a preliminary understanding amongst themselves at Constantinople before the conference was formally opened with the Turks present.[1] The Derby circular of 4 November proposed that each power should be represented by two representatives, thus providing, as Disraeli calculated, that the conference should not simply be a reunion of the ambassadors on the spot under Ignatyev's dictation.[2] The bases for the deliberations were the same as those put forward by Derby on 21 September. The independence and territorial integrity of the Ottoman empire were to be reaffirmed and the powers to declare that they would not obtain any exclusive territorial advantages, influence, or concessions. For Serbia and Montenegro there was to be the *status quo* 'en termes généraux', a formula to be pressed hard by the Turks at the conference. A protocol was to be signed by the Porte and the powers granting to Bosnia and Herzegovina local, or administrative, autonomy, carefully

[1] Derby to Loftus, 30 Oct., informing him of Shuvalov's communication from the Tsar to that effect, in *A. and P.*, 1877, xc, C. 1640, no. 799.

[2] *Disraeli*, p. 961. Salisbury on 3 Nov. had agreed to go out; *Salisbury*, p. 90.

phrased to meet Andrássy's objections, and making clear that there would be no question of a tributary state. There were to be guarantees of a similar kind for Bulgaria. The reforms outlined in the Andrássy note and already accepted by the Porte were to be included in the administrative reforms for Bosnia and Herzegovina and to be applied to Bulgaria in so far as they might be applicable.[1]

These bases for the conference were eventually accepted by all parties, but not without some difficulty with the Russians. The Tsar agreed on 6 November to Derby's proposals except as regards 'the territorial integrity of the Ottoman Empire'. That, as Gorchakov pointed out to Loftus, might exclude the possibility of any occupation: some form of occupation would be necessary as a guarantee for the execution of the reforms, and he suggested that it might be European in character, as in the case of Syria in 1860, and might be entrusted to Russia and Austria acting in the name of Europe. This avowal added to the alarm in London and greatly perturbed Shuvalov, who pressed Gorchakov hard to give way. He was successful: on 10 November he was able to inform Derby in writing that Gorchakov accepted the English programme 'tel quel'.[2]

It was obvious, however, that the question of occupation would certainly arise at the conference in some form or another, and British distrust was further accentuated by the official publication in the *Journal de St. Pétersbourg* for 21 November of a lengthy justification of Russian policy, which began by emphasizing that the independence and integrity of Turkey must be subordinated to the necessary guarantees. Since Turkey had been the first to infringe the stipulations of the 1856 treaty as regards the Christians, Europe had the right and duty to dictate to her the conditions which alone could provide for European agreement to maintain the political *status quo* created by that treaty; and, since Turkey was incapable of fulfilling these conditions, Europe had the right and duty to substitute herself for Turkey in so far as was necessary for assuring the fulfilment of these conditions. Gorchakov was careful to emphasize his

[1] The text of the Derby circular of 4 Nov. is in *A. and P.*, 1877, xc, C. 1640, no. 873.
[2] Loftus to Derby, tel., 6 Nov., and disp., 6 Nov., rec. 21 Nov.; Derby to Loftus, 7 and 10 Nov.; in *A. and P.*, 1877, xc, C. 1640, nos. 891, 1028, 896, and 917. The occupation of Syria in 1860 was solely by the French, though with the approval of the great powers.

desire for concerted action, but isolated measures were hinted at as a possibility.[1] Accompanying this was the publication in the same paper of a letter of 3 November of Gorchakov to Shuvalov, which after explicitly disclaiming any ideas of territorial annexation went on to state that feeling in Russia was too strong to limit itself to academic expressions of sympathy. 'Cela impose à l'Empereur des devoirs auxquels Sa Majesté ne saurait se soustraire.' Then, with a deft turn: 'Mais ses devoirs sont partagés par toute l'Europe civilisée.' And the letter closed on the note of the eastern question being not solely of Russian but also of European concern.[2]

While these long-range interchanges were proceeding, at Constantinople the Turks, who had only accepted the conference with extreme reluctance on 18 November, were anxiously preparing every means of obstruction, and Ignatyev was energetically scheming for a large Bulgaria and a Russian occupation.[3] He had prepared a maximum and a minimum draft. Gorchakov, while authorizing him in the first place to put forward the former, emphasized that the latter was quite sufficient to assure a satisfactory degree of autonomy to the Bulgars, and he thought that there was a fair chance of these minimum proposals being accepted by the other powers: in that case 'ce serait un grand résultat qui nous épargnerait la campagne militaire chanceuse et politiquement et matériellement, et onéreuse surtout par son influence sur notre position financière'. If, in the preliminary conference, to be held apart from the Turks, neither of the Russian proposals were accepted, Ignatyev was to continue to participate and to take *ad referendum* any other proposal which included serious guarantees. Ignatyev reacted to these instructions by asking: Was he to insist on a Russian occupation of Bulgaria or not? Was the armistice to be prolonged or not? In case of the failure of the conference, would the military authorities prefer the rupture to come in December, in January, or in the spring? The differences between the

[1] Gorchakov to Shuvalov, 19 Nov., communicated to Derby, 27 Nov., published 21 Nov.; in *A. and P.*, 1877, xc, C. 1640, no. 1053.

[2] Loftus to Derby, 21 Nov., enclosing text of letter as published that day; in *A. and P.*, 1877, xc, C. 1640, no. 1065.

[3] Ignatyev's memoirs contain little but generalities on the preparation for and course of the Constantinople conference. He states that he was originally opposed to it, *I.V.*, vol. cxxxvi, p. 452; but once it was decided upon he worked his hardest to capture it.

two men are again clearly revealed by Gorchakov's evasive answer.

'Si minimum, qui ne contient pas notre occupation militaire, est accepté, tout est dit. Sinon et un autre projet avec garanties est proposé, ne le rejetez pas, prenez *ad referendum*. Nous pèserons ici la valeur des garanties. Vous direz dans Conférences préalables que, convaincus que l'Europe veut avec nous une œuvre réelle, devons insister sur garanties et si d'autres ne sont offertes, il nous serait difficile de nous soustraire au devoir d'une occupation militaire temporaire. Une fois la discussion ouverte, soutenez une marche accélérée. On ne saurait dès le début demander prorogation que désirons éviter. L'Empereur veut que notre rôle dans les Conférences porte le caractère d'une entière franchise et loyauté, sans arrière-pensée quelconque. Nous n'avons rien à cacher. Sa Majesté préfère avant tout solution pacifique et se féliciterait hautement si démonstration militaire ne nous est pas imposée par notre dignité. Pénétrez-vous de ces principes.'[1]

Little as Ignatyev can have welcomed his chief's conciliatory generalities, they did, at least, leave him with ample scope for a display of his great abilities, and moreover he was not to be impeded by the presence at the conference of a second Russian representative. He and his brilliant wife made a formidable pair, with ten years' experience of Levantine intrigue and a motley army of agents and informers; Ignatyev, 'much more like a Sarmatian grandee than a Russian general', with his high tenor voice, his mocking smile, his unabashed sleights of hand, his jocose bullying of the Turks; the Countess Ignatyev, with her face a combination of a ballerina's grace and strength, an adept second in political capacity, having Zichy in her pocket and Corti in her toils. Chaudordy, coming out from Paris, fell equally before this ingratiating couple. Calice, coming from Bucarest and Vienna, did not: a diplomat by profession and an expert in the Balkans, with judgement and with an excellent knowledge of English, he was a wise choice on the part of Andrássy to balance the incompetence of the internuncio, Zichy, who had no better claims to his post than that he was a rich Magyar

---

[1] Gorchakov to Ignatyev, tels., 24 and 27 Nov.; Ignatyev to Gorchakov, tel., 26 Nov.; texts in *S.R.*, vol. iv, pp. 450–1. Later (23 Dec.) Gorchakov mentioned to Ignatyev 13 Apr. (1 Apr. according to the Russian calendar) as the date to which the armistice should be prolonged; loc. cit., p. 455. Mid-April was the time favoured by the military for starting operations, and the negotiations with the Austrians would be completed by then.

nobleman in favour at court, and had served as imperial commissioner with the Russian army in Hungary in 1849. The Germans had at first only their ambassador, Werther, who was on good terms with Ignatyev but was of no weight. Later they were reinforced by Busch, an ex-dragoman and an ex-consul-general at St. Petersburg, a dangerous man, with knowledge.[1]

The English were fatally divided. Elliot, more than ever at daggers drawn with Ignatyev, was pushed by his anger at the attitude of Salisbury into the extremes of pro-Turk support. Salisbury had little use for Elliot's consular advisers, Calvert from Philippopolis, Blunt from Salonika, and Holmes from Sarajevo, and depended mainly on his protégé, White, from Belgrade. White, a man of great gifts, later to receive the Constantinople embassy from Salisbury himself, was as yet new to the Balkans. Despite his knowledge of Russia and panslavism, his previous service in Warsaw and Danzig did not seem to qualify him as an expert counsellor on Bulgaria, and his views on Elliot's entourage were highly unfavourable. The available members of the embassy staff he described as of very little ability and as 'chiefly distinguished by their Russophobia which they bring prominently forward in and out of season': the dragomans were 'all Levantines of a very bad type and suspected of being corrupt'.[2] It was widely believed that Elliot spoke the true voice of Disraeli and that Salisbury did not really represent his government, and the Turks in particular were encouraged to pin their faith to Elliot and to British support of them.[3] They were further incited to take this course by the presence of

[1] For the personal impressions made by Ignatyev and his wife: Przibram, *Erinnerungen eines alten Österreichers*, vol. ii, pp. 37–9; du Chastel, *Les Événements d'Orient et le Congrès de Berlin*, p. 11; Nelidov's memoirs in *Revue des deux mondes*, 1915, vol. xxviii, pp. 256–7; *Salisbury*, pp. 107–11. Przibram, who was sent to Constantinople in temporary disgrace from the Ballplatz press bureau, gives a very lively, unpretentious record of his impressions of Constantinople at the close of the conference. He recounts that Ignatyev, besides profiting from Zichy's numerous indiscretions to him, had in his pay one of the Austrian chancellery clerks, finally discovered in the act of passing correspondence to the Russians.

[2] Salisbury to Derby, tel., 13 Dec., in *F.O.* 78/2677; private letter of White to Sir R. Morier, 16 Jan. 1877, text in Edwards, *Sir William White*, p. 116. White, consul-general at Belgrade since the beginning of 1875, was attached to Salisbury's mission for the conference. Baring, the first secretary, was absent at the time.

[3] *Salisbury*, pp. 112, 117–20, 123; Hohenlohe's dispatch of 6 Jan. retailing French news of the conference, in *G.P.*, p. 121; Busch's diary, in *Deutsche Rundschau*, vol. cxli, p. 21. Elliot's disgust with Salisbury's policy and treatment of him is vented in his account of the conference in *Some revolutions and other diplomatic experiences*, pp. 276–92.

Butler-Johnstone, the rabidly turkophil M.P. for Canterbury, posing as the secret emissary of the prime minister.[1] Salisbury throughout had the greatest difficulty with Elliot and finally wired home that Elliot was refusing to leave if the conference broke down, and asked that he should be recalled. That this was not done was perhaps partly due to the same course having just been suggested by Ignatyev.[2]

Salisbury was the most eagerly awaited new-comer, for he was unknown personally and was the only member of a government among the foreign representatives. It was his first essay in diplomatic negotiations. He was still secretary of state for India, not yet for foreign affairs. He looked, as one observer remarked, 'like a rabbi or one of the thirteen minor prophets'.[3] One must put out of mind that he was later to be numbered among the major. He had travelled out, on the suggestion of the Prince of Wales and contrary to the advice of the foreign office,[4] by Paris, Berlin, Vienna, and Rome. These visits gave him the general impression that there was a consensus of opinion that the Ottoman empire could not be upheld for any length of time, and possibly not at all.[5] This nearly corresponded with his own tentative views on leaving England, which could be summed up as 'the Turk's teeth must be drawn even if he be allowed to live'. The India office had failed to impress on him the bogy of Russia, certainly at least as regards Turkey: the North-West frontier not the Straits was the key to India. He had been in private favouring an understanding with Russia, deploring the Crimean war and heartily wishing the Turks were out of Europe, though the difficulties seemed to him insuperable. Thus he reached Constantinople, on 5 December, with a strong bias against the Turks, believing that it would be Turkish, and not Russian, obstinacy that would be the main obstacle.[6]

---

[1] Ignatyev to Shuvalov, tel., 23 Dec., text in *S.R.*, vol. iv, p. 454; Salisbury to Derby, letter, 21 Dec., extract in *Salisbury*, p. 111 (Butler-Johnstone's name is left blank); *Wertheimer*, p. 380. See also Seton-Watson, *Disraeli, Gladstone and the Eastern Question*, pp. 129–30, and the references there cited.

[2] *Salisbury*, pp. 119–20; Seton-Watson, op. cit., pp. 131–2.

[3] Przibram, *Erinnerungen eines alten Österreichers*, vol. ii, p. 36.

[4] *Salisbury*, p. 94.

[5] *Salisbury*, pp. 96–9, 103, 107. For the German versions, which tally with Salisbury's, of his visit to Berlin, see *G.P.*, pp. 105–11, and Radowitz, *Aufzeichnungen und Erinnerungen . . .*, vol. i, pp. 363–4.

[6] *Salisbury*, pp. 84–7, 93, 102.

Contact with the Turks soon sharpened Salisbury's prepossessions against them. He described their objections as 'simply childish . . . like a street-sweeper complaining that he has been splashed'. A month of the conference drew the following private avowal from him: 'I think the Conference has done good. It has, I hope, made it impossible that we should spend any more English blood in sustaining the Turkish Empire. . . . Every day I am more convinced of the deplorable folly of the Crimean War.'[1] He did not hide his feelings of disgust, notably with Midhat.[2] The impression he made was congealed into the remark attributed to him: 'Nous serions enchantés de nous débarrasser d'un allié aussi gênant que la Turquie.'[3]

It was easy enough in these circumstances for Ignatyev to keep Salisbury separated from Elliot. Salisbury, personally amused and interested by the vivacious Menteur Pasha, was puzzled by his attitude and realized quite well that he was a queer customer, but Ignatyev's telegrams during the conference show him as loud in Salisbury's praise and thinking that they were on terms of mutual confidence.[4] 'Another bad thing here', wrote one of the British military agents, 'has been Sir H. E. was Philo-Turk. Lord S. Anti-Turk. Lady S. violent Anti-Turk. Miss E. violent Philo-Turk. The two embassies were like oil and water, the old embassy considered that they were professionals, the new embassy amateurs who were bumptious. The old embassy said what ignoramuses, the new embassy said what duffers—Ignatieff said it took me 4 minutes to set the two embassies by the ears.'[5]

The attitude of Salisbury much perturbed Disraeli. In the prime minister's view the powers were acting merely as mediators; a refusal on the part of the Porte to accept their recom-

[1] *Salisbury*, pp. 111, 122-3.
[2] Busch's diary, under date 12 Jan., in *Deutsche Rundschau*, vol. cxli, p. 22; Werther to Bülow, 14 Jan., in *G.P.*, pp. 123-5.   [3] *Aus dem Leben König Karls . . .*, vol. iii, p. 82.
[4] *Salisbury*, pp. 109-10. Telegrams from Ignatyev to Gorchakov and Shuvalov during the preliminary conference and the conference itself are printed in *S.R.*, vol. iv, pp. 453-62. As an illustration of Ignatyev's relations with Salisbury may be given the story which the former was fond of retailing in after years as to how he convinced Salisbury that Christian children were secretly put up for sale in Constantinople by himself buying a young Bulgar girl and presenting her to Salisbury and his wife; note by the editor of Ignatyev's memoirs, in *I.V.*, vol. cxxxvi, pp. 54-5; cf. Stead, *The Truth about Russia*, p. 279.
[5] Private letter of Lt.-Col. Home to General Sir Lintorn Simmons, Constantinople, 16 Jan. 1877, in Simmons papers, *F.O.* 358/1. Home had recently been sent out to report on means of defending Constantinople and the Straits against the Russians. There are important military memoranda of his in the Simmons papers.

mendations would not be an offence to the dignity of Europe: still less could there be any question of discussing in the conference the possibility of coercion. Thus Salisbury's original instructions, dated 20 November, included an explicit statement to that effect. But a week later (27 November) very secret additional instructions were dispatched to him which did *not* entirely rule out coercion. In two contingencies which might lead to the proposal of coercive measures after the close of the conference the government reserved complete freedom of action: first, if the Porte refused to agree to any scheme of reforms and guarantees accepted by all the other powers; secondly, if the Porte eventually failed to carry out promises made by it at the conference. In either of these two contingencies the government would not pledge themselves to reject or oppose the employment of foreign troops.

This represented a radical change. What Disraeli had in mind in agreeing to these altered instructions may perhaps be gauged from his letter to Salisbury of 1 December. In this he recommended in case of necessity as a last card that the British should not say that they were unequivocally opposed to a temporary occupation, but that such a step must only be taken at the instance and with the full consent of the Sultan; then the Porte should be induced to consent to an occupation by England, not by Russia and Austria. But during December Salisbury's reports from Constantinople so highly alarmed the prime minister that he was determined to tie him down as closely as possible, and he accordingly persuaded the cabinet on 22 December to revert to his own original policy and to instruct Salisbury that England would not participate in any coercive measures against the Porte and that if Turkey declined the proposals of the conference he and Elliot were to leave Constantinople, but without breaking off diplomatic relations.[1]

On the following day (23 December) the full conference was opened. The preceding ten days had been occupied with the preliminary conference of the representatives of the powers among themselves. It was held at the Russian embassy with

[1] For this and the preceding paragraph: *Disraeli*, pp. 967, 977–81; Salisbury's instructions, dated 20 Nov. and 22 Dec., in *A. and P.*, 1877, xci, C. 1641, nos. 1 and 78. The secret instructions of 27 Nov., Derby to Salisbury, no. 16, most conf., are in *F.O.* 78/2674, marked in Derby's handwriting as approved by the cabinet on 23 Nov., and also marked as sent to the Queen 23 Nov., as returned by her 25 Nov., as not to be printed, and as not to be circulated to any embassies.

Ignatyev in the chair. Bulgaria occupied his chief attention, and he succeeded in winning acceptance for the essentials of his scheme, with three important changes.[1]

In the first place, his proposed Bulgaria was to consist of what was later set up by the treaty of Berlin as Bulgaria and Eastern Rumelia, and in addition the Dobrudja, the *sanjak* of Nish, and a great part of Macedonia, stretching right across the Vardar to the west of Skoplje and Monastir. The population was computed to be just short of four millions, and was believed to be overwhelmingly Bulgar. It was substantially the same as the San Stefano Bulgaria, except that instead of Nish and the Dobrudja the latter included the Lule Borgas district and southern Macedonia with the Aegean sea-coast from the Mesta to Salonika.

Salisbury took the lead in opposing this large Bulgaria, since the Austrians told him that it was entirely unacceptable to them, while he himself thought that it would be fatal to the independence of the Sultan. After two days Ignatyev yielded, and on Salisbury's suggestion the new Bulgaria was to be cut into two portions longitudinally, thus forming an eastern and a western Bulgaria. This longitudinal, as opposed to a latitudinal, division came as a complete surprise to the British foreign office. It was justified by Salisbury on the grounds that, whereas the big Bulgaria with some system of self-government would have been in the hands of the Slav majority, his proposal would result in the creation of an eastern Bulgaria in the hands of Turks and Greeks which would include the Black Sea coast, the Balkan passes, the approaches to Constantinople, and the greater part of the lower Danube.[2]

[1] Ignatyev had three drafts for Bulgaria: two are in *A. and P.*, 1877, xci, C. 1641, nos. 50 and 56, incls.: the third is printed in the text of the minutes of the *réunions préliminaires*, ib., nos. 112 and 135, incls. The two first drafts were the work of Tseretelev and Schuyler, who had worked together in investigating the Bulgarian atrocities, and according to Russian embassy gossip were to be on the proposed international commission for Bulgaria; letter of Karakonovsky, the embassy doctor, a Bulgar, to Naiden Gerov, 1 Jan. 1877, in *Iz Arkhivata na Naiden Gerov*, vol. i, p. 776. The first draft had been drawn up in closest collaboration with leading Bulgars, notably Burmov; St. Danev, 'Za stogodishninata ot rozhdenieto na graf Ignatyev', in *Slavyanski glas*, 1932, nos. 1–2, pp. 11–12. The final decisions of the preliminary conference as presented to the Turks are printed in Noradounghian, *Recueil d'actes internationaux de l'empire ottoman*, vol. iii, pp. 409–22.

[2] Salisbury to Derby, tel., 13 Dec., in *F.O.* 78/2677; Derby to Salisbury, draft, no. 30, most conf., 11 Dec., in *F.O.* 78/2674; Salisbury to Derby, 4 Jan. 1877, in *A. and P.*, 1877, xci, C. 1641, no. 167.

BULGARIA ACCORDING TO THE CONSTANTINO

RUSSIA

To Czernowitz

BESSARABIA

Ungheni

Jassy · Kishinev

NSYLVANIA

R. Pruth

(Built during the war)

Odessa

Galatz

Reni · Kilia

Barboshi Bridge

Ismail · I. of Serpents

Sulina

Dobrudja

St. George's Mouth

LITTLE

es

VALLACHIA

Ploeshti

O

U

M

A

N

I

A

Bucarest

BLACK

Giurgevo

Cernavoda

Zimnitsa

Rasova

Constanza

at R. Danube

Silistria

D

Rustchuk

Mangalia

a

Rahova

Razgrad

Bazardzhik

dchik

Nicopolis

Sistova

Plevna

R. Lom

Shumla

SEA

R. Isker

Lovcha

Varna

Tirnovo

Balkan Mts. Shipka Pass

Burgas

Kazanlik

olkhtiman

Jamboli

Sizepoli

R. Maritsa

Philippopolis

Despoto D.

Rhodope

Rodosto

Adrianople

Midia

Constantinople

Mts.

Lule Burgas

Bosphorus

R. Mesta

Seres

Rodosto

Sea of

Ismid

ka

G. of Rendina

Dedeagach

Marmara

Brusa

Mt. Athos

Gallipoli

Dardanelles

Besika Bay

rias

GEAN

SEA

Mytilene

Miles

0   50   100

+++ Railways as in 1878

NFERENCE AND THE TREATY OF SAN STEFANO

On the other hand, Ignatyev might console himself with the thought that if two such Principalities could be set up it would not be long before steps for their union could be engineered. In addition, he had gained the very important admission that the frontiers of his projected Bulgaria were substantially justified on grounds of nationality. There does not seem to have been strong opposition raised in the preliminary conference, except by Elliot, to Ignatyev's views as to what constituted the regions primarily inhabited by Bulgars. The struggle for the exarchate, it is true, had already created the beginnings of the Macedonian problem, but its infinite complexity was not yet generally appreciated, and the most striking feature of the maps available for the conference was that they were, broadly speaking, in agreement with each other and with Ignatyev in giving a very wide westward extension to the Bulgars.[1]

In the second place, Ignatyev's draft for Bulgaria confined the Turkish regular troops to fortresses and the principal towns. This was modified to allow of their employment in either province in case of war or on demand of the governors-general.

Thirdly, there was the crucial question of occupation. Ignatyev had demanded a temporary foreign occupation, by a Russian force if no other were available. This, after prolonged discussion, was altered to the provision of a special gendarmerie, 2,000 to 4,000 strong, initially to be composed of Belgians (though they were not actually named), which was to carry out the decisions of the international commission appointed for one year by the powers to see that their detailed administrative, police, and judicial reforms were put into operation. These reforms, as drafted by Ignatyev and accepted by the other representatives without vital alterations save that they were duplicated in consequence of the division of Bulgaria, included a provincial elected assembly with important powers, a militia

[1] See the ethnographical maps in Rizoff, *The Bulgarians in their Historical, Ethnographical and Political Frontiers*, particularly those by Guillaume Lejean (1861), Kiepert (1876), G. M. Mackenzie and A. P. Irby (1867), M. F. Mirkovich (Bulgaria according to the map prepared for the Moscow Slavonic congress, 1867), and Elisée Reclus (1876). It was believed in Vienna that the Kiepert map, which was the one regularly used, was untrustworthy in that it had been prepared to Russian order and at Russian cost; Elliot to Derby, disp., conf., no. 232, 21 Mar. 1878, in *F.O.* 7/729. With this should be compared Teplov's statement in his *Materialy dlya statistiki Bolgarii, Thrakii i Makedonii*, pp. xxx–xxxi, that the first Kiepert ethnographical map aroused violent protests from panslav quarters as being too favourable to the Greeks, and that the second edition was altered in favour of the Bulgars.

and gendarmerie composed proportionately of Christians and Moslems, and a governor-general, to be appointed for five years by the Porte with the agreement of the powers.

On the whole, this *projet de règlement organique*, and above all the appointment of the governors-general and of the international commission, which in separate draft instructions was given extended functions, represented a marked success for Ignatyev. He had indeed been compelled to yield in respect of a foreign occupation and to accept the French compromise of a Belgian gendarmerie, but he had succeeded in killing tentative suggestions from London that the gendarmerie proposal might be made more palatable to the Turks by the withdrawal of the Russian forces from the frontier,[1] and he comforted himself with the calculation that the gendarmerie was a means of bringing about a Russian occupation of Bulgaria, for he reckoned on the Moslems getting out of hand and the Belgians being unable to maintain order; then would be the occasion for Russian troops to march in.[2]

While Ignatyev battled his hardest for his infant Bulgaria, it is not so clear that he exerted such efforts on the other problems before the preliminary conference. Serbia needed none; there was no question save of the *status quo ante bellum*, except for the possible gain of Little Zvornik, the fortress on the Drina in dispute since 1833. This the powers agreed to recommend, implicitly, for inclusion within the boundaries of Serbia. For Montenegro Ignatyev hoped especially to gain the fortresses of Spuž and Žablyak together with the whole right bank of the Morača and the coastal strip with Spizza, Antivari, and Dulcigno, and three border districts at least of Herzegovina (Banyani, Piva, Drobniak). The Austrians and Italians would not hear of Montenegrin seaports,[3] and substituted the completely anodyne

---

[1] Salisbury to Derby, disp., most conf., no. 43, 21 Dec., in *F.O.* 78/2675, and tel., 21 Dec., in *F.O.* 78/2677.

[2] Ignatyev's memoirs, in *R.S.*, vol. clxi, pp. 33–4. The proposal for a Belgian gendarmerie was strongly opposed by the Belgian chargé d'affaires, du Chastel; *Les Événements d'Orient et le Congrès de Berlin*, p. 13.

[3] Salisbury to Derby, tel., 11 Dec., in *F.O.* 78/2677. According to Monson (Ragusa) to Derby, 10 Nov., Prince Nicholas specially demanded the cession of Nikšić, the plain on the right bank of the Morača, and Spizza: Monson urged British support for a Montenegrin port and ridiculed the idea that it would become a Russian base; *A. and P.*, 1877, xc, C. 1640, nos. 1045 and 1021. Holmes, the consul at Sarajevo, also had advised the cession to Montenegro of Spizza, as well as of the districts of Piva, Drobniak, Banyani, and Zubči. Salisbury's instructions

formula of free navigation of the Boyana, but it was agreed to demand most of Ignatyev's other territorial requirements.

In regard to Bosnia and Herzegovina he had to walk with special wariness in view of Austria-Hungary. The minutes of the preliminary conference only record him as putting forward five points, without detailed elaboration, but amongst them figured an international commission with wide powers. It was accepted, and, as in Bulgaria, it was to be aided by a special European gendarmerie: so, too, there were to be a governor-general similarly appointed, a gendarmerie in part Christian, and a number of new administrative reforms.

Nine meetings of the guaranteeing powers (11 to 22 December) had brought them, in Chaudordy's euphemistic phraseology, to the point of agreement as to 'l'ensemble des mesures que nous croyons de nature à assurer le succès de l'œuvre qui doit être commune'. It now remained to open the conference proper and with these agreed measures to face the real masters of the situation.

The Turks, as usual, counted for much more than is generally allowed, and of their attitude there was no doubt whatever. It was one of furious opposition to European interference of any kind and to the conference in particular. Their hostility had been aggravated by the Russian ultimatum and the preliminary conversations to the pitch of a most dangerous war feeling, full advantage of which was taken by Midhat Pasha. The conference was due to open on 23 December. Just before this Midhat succeeded in being made grand vizier and entered on a brief eight weeks of semi-dictatorship. His first act was to greet the opening session of the conference with the booming of guns announcing the proclamation of a new constitution, more or less on the model of the Liberal Empire, with an elected assembly, some equality of rights for Moslems and Christians, a ministry to control the Sultan, and a whole series of reforms aiming at centralized efficiency and the fusion of the diverse peoples of the empire. It was received in Constantinople with wild enthusiasm as an unanswerable blow to the conference. Bands of *softas* paraded the streets shouting for war. Although there were still fears of a massacre of Christians, the relations between them and the Moslems were better than usual. Both

of 20 Nov. included a paragraph agreeing to the general desirability of some such changes. For the Montenegrin frontiers, see map between pp. 136 and 137.

combined in forming the new national guard. The Greeks and Armenians were filled with hatred for Russia and at least professed to welcome the constitution as the opening of a new era. They felt themselves ignored by the conference and were opposed to it tooth and nail, the Greeks egging on the Turks to resist the big Bulgaria, the Armenians regarding themselves as insulted because, while 'an outrage on an Armenian is thought nothing of in Europe, if a Bulgarian is trod on all Europe is up at the bidding of Russia'. Before the conference closed the Turkish propaganda service was ready with a damning booklet on panslav intrigues, *Les Responsabilités de la guerre*, consisting of alleged secret correspondence between Novikov, Ignatyev, Russian consuls in the Balkans, and panslav head-quarters in Russia. The revelations were, of course, denounced by the Russians as clumsy fabrications, but they had the desired effect of adding potently to Turkish anger at Russian complicity in the risings of the *rayas*, and they were carefully devised to enlist the maximum of Greek alarm by apparently circumstantial evidence as to Russian designs on the Mount Athos monasteries. To encourage the Turks still further there arrived in January a delegation of Hungarian students, ostentatiously supported by Zichy's son, and armed with a sword of honour for presentation to Abd ul-Kerim as conqueror of the Serbs. They were effusively entertained and afforded the Turks the pleasantry of inviting the Russian ambassador to an official reception for them. With feeling in the capital running thus fever-high Abd ul-Hamid, but four months Sultan, could not with impunity have bowed, had he even so desired, to foreign intervention.[1]

In the conference itself the Turks could not be moved from their initial refusal to entertain the proposals of the powers. They were represented by two strongly contrasted types, Safvet

[1] For Turkish hostility and the attitude of the Christians: de Moüy, *Souvenirs et causeries d'un diplomate*, pp. 44–5, 51 (de Moüy was first counsellor at the French embassy and a secretary of the conference); *Aus dem Leben König Karls . . .*, vol. iii, pp. 76, 90; memoranda of 17 and 25 Dec. presented to Salisbury by Greek representatives in Pera and the Greek minister, in *F.O.* 78/2687; private letter of Lt.-Col. Home to General Sir Lintorn Simmons, 16 Jan. 1877, in Simmons papers, *F.O.* 358/1 (for the Armenians); Busch's diary in *Deutsche Rundschau*, vol. cxli, p. 22. For the drafting and contents of the constitution, which did not go so far as Midhat himself desired, see Engelhardt, *La Turquie et le Tanzimat*, vol. ii, pp. 161–71; the text of the constitution is in *A. and P.*, 1877, xci, C. 1641, no. 118 incl. For Giacometti, *Les Responsabilités de la guerre*, see p. 681. For the visit of the Magyar students: Przibram, *Erinnerungen eines alten Österreichers*, vol. ii, p. 49; Ignatyev's memoirs, in *R.S.*, vol. clxi, p. 30; *Aus dem Leben König Karls . . .*, vol. iii, pp. 97–8.

and Edhem Pashas. The former was the foreign minister: an old man, he made a pitiful impression with his wretched French and his feeble attempts to appear conciliatory. Edhem Pasha, ex-minister at Berlin, violent and imperious, was belligerently anti-Russian, indignant with Germany, contemptuous of Italy, and undeceived by Austria. Firmly convinced of the active friendship of England, he would not hear of European intervention in Turkish affairs. He reflected excellently the dominating influences outside the conference itself.[1]

It at once became apparent that the agreement reached among the powers themselves was gravely imperilled. Ignatyev attempted to secure from the powers the signature of an act binding them to sustain their proposals to the Porte. This was to remain a cardinal element in his policy for the next three months. The representatives of the powers had as a result of their preliminary conference come to an agreement as to the reforms which they considered necessary in Turkey. These reforms, although by no means as far-reaching as the Russians desired, did represent, as has been seen, an advance in the right direction from the point of view of St. Petersburg. If the powers could be pinned down to them the Russian position would be greatly strengthened. From the first, however, Ignatyev encountered the utmost opposition from London and Vienna to his scheme, strongly pressed at the New Year, for the signature of an identic note or protocol embodying the results of the preliminary conference.[2]

He was compelled to abandon his efforts for the time being, and was reduced to struggling to save as much as possible of the original demands. Even the whittling down of these was wasted labour. De Moüy, the French secretary of the conference, well

---

[1] Przibram, *Erinnerungen eines alten Österreichers*, vol. ii, pp. 41–2; de Moüy, *Souvenirs et causeries d'un diplomate*, pp. 49–50.

[2] Salisbury to Derby, tel., 28 Dec., with minutes from Tenterden and Derby objecting to Ignatyev's proposal, in *F.O.* 78/2677; tels., 30 Dec. and 9 Jan., in *A. and P.*, 1877, xci, C. 1641, nos. 116, 149: cf. also nos. 123, 147. During the conference Odian Effendi, an Armenian high official at the Porte and an agent of Midhat, arrived in London on a special mission to explain the impossibility of the acceptance of the proposals of the preliminary conference and to 'puff' the new constitution; Ignatyev to Shuvalov, tel., 2 Jan., text in *S.R.*, vol. iv, p. 457; and the Disraeli MSS., Hughenden, cited by Temperley in *The Cambridge Historical Journal*, vol. iv, p. 176. Hohenlohe later reported to his government (4 Feb.) that Odian felt assured from Derby that the English would do nothing if the Turks caused the conference to fail and had reported this to Constantinople just before the final refusal of the Turks; *G.P.*, pp. 133–4.

expressed the situation: 'comme les navigateurs en détresse, on jetait la cargaison à la mer: c'était le vaisseau même dont la Porte voulait le naufrage.' The Turks played the waiting game of entrenching themselves behind the bases set out in the Derby circular of 4 November, their new constitution, and the Andrássy note. They did this with exasperating success. After three weeks they found themselves confronted on 15 January with greatly reduced demands in respect of Bosnia, Herzegovina, and Bulgaria, expressed in brief general terms. Above all, the European gendarmerie had disappeared: the previous agreement of the powers to the appointment of the governors-general was to be required only for the first five years: the international commissions appointed by the powers still remained under the designation of commissions of control, but their special instructions (a vital point) were to be drawn up subsequently. This was the last word of the powers. Each of the plenipotentiaries announced that in case of refusal he was instructed to leave Constantinople, but not to break off diplomatic relations. There was no word of further threats, of any form of combined coercion. The Turks made an offer of negotiating further if the two points as to the appointment of the governors-general and the international commissions were dropped. The offer was refused, whereupon a grand council of two hundred and thirty-seven Moslem and Christian dignitaries unanimously declared the two points to be unacceptable, and the conference terminated two days later, on 20 January. The dramatic effectiveness of the prearranged collective departure of the plenipotentiaries was ruined by an inconvenient storm which deterred all but Salisbury by the prospective pangs of seasickness.[1]

The conference had failed, yet it had not failed in a manner

---

[1] Protocols of the conference, in Noradounghian, *Recueil d'actes internationaux de l'empire ottoman*, vol. iii, pp. 400–94; de Moüy, *Souvenirs et causeries d'un diplomate*, p. 53; *Salisbury*, p. 125. The Turks tried hard to secure the attendance at the special council of the Greek Patriarch and the Bulgarian Exarch, but they, and the Armenian Patriarch, absented themselves on grounds of ill health: their representatives, however, came and voted for resistance; Busch's diary in *Deutsche Rundschau*, vol. cxli, p. 25; Salisbury to Derby, 18 Jan., in *A. and P.*, 1877, xci, C. 1641, no. 226; *Memoirs of Ismail Kemal Bey*, p. 141. There is a copy of a long, racy report by Ignatyev on the Turkish grand council in *F.O.* 78/2688. Abd ul-Hamid took up the attitude that he himself saw no fatal objection to the final terms of the powers but that he could not manage his ministers and feared dethronement; Salisbury to Derby, disp., nos. 117 and 128, secret, 15 Jan., in *F.O.* 78/2676.

which made it impossible for Ignatyev to profess satisfaction. After all, he had secured the agreement of the powers to two sets of reform proposals, and though the second represented a much mitigated version of the first it did include provisions for autonomy in Bulgaria and for international commissions of control, two far-reaching novelties. It might be possible for Russia to prevent the powers from backing away from these final demands of 15 January and to put the question, so far not squarely faced, as to whether they were prepared to see them remain a dead letter. No doubt, if Russia without attempting further joint action abruptly presented the Porte with a new ultimatum, it might be difficult for the powers to switch round into immediate support of the Turks, but Ignatyev did not at this moment favour drastic solitary action. Despite the hopes he had of Salisbury's influence on his return home, he was apprehensive of a British seizure of the Dardanelles (which had been in fact urged by one of the British officers on the spot): military action by Russia would not be possible till the spring, though by then the Turks would be in great strength: nothing was to be hoped for from the Serbs, who were completely exhausted.[1]

Serbia indeed provided the one immediate practical outcome of the conference, at which it had been decided (28 December) to prolong the armistice until 1 March. The Serbs were in a distracted plight, heightened by the undisciplined remnants of the Russian volunteers. Getting wind of the Austro-Russian conventions then under negotiation, they feared that they were being sacrificed to an understanding between the two empires, and might even suffer an Austrian occupation. They could not extract any definite answer from St. Petersburg as to what was expected of them in the event of a Russo-Turkish war. Russian disgust with the Serbian collapse and the politicians of Belgrade forced a ministerial crisis, which was much complicated by the intrigues of Kartsov against Ristić, who had to abandon a projected mission to St. Petersburg. In his stead Marinović, his

---

[1] Ignatyev's memoirs, in *I.V.*, vol. cxxxvi, pp. 453–7, in part paraphrasing a dispatch to Gorchakov; Salisbury to Derby, disp., conf., no. 131, 18 Jan., in *F.O.* 78/2676, enclosing a memorandum from Lt.-Col. Home advocating occupation and retention of Gallipoli and a *tête du pont* on the Asiatic side. Ignatyev's account of his policy on the break-up of the Constantinople conference is particularly unsatisfactory. He appears to have wavered between extracting the utmost possible from the powers and inducing the Turks to come to a direct agreement with Russia, thus escaping the clutches of Andrássy, and to have ended by recommending both courses simultaneously.

ablest opponent, who had always stood against the war, was sent in mid-November as a special envoy, in company with Kartsov. He painted a picture of the Serbs having been dragged into war by the *Omladina* and having no real sympathy with either Bosniaks or Bulgars. There was no appeal to the Tsar to draw the sword for the Slav cause. On the contrary, according to the accusations of his enemies, Marinović openly opposed the Russian militarists and fell foul of the authorities. Prince Milan likewise emphatically declared that the Serbs were strongly against a continuation of the war, and that only direct action by Russia would bring them into the field; yet he had also expressed a desire for two Russian divisions to be sent to Serbia. The Grand Duke Nicholas ruled out this suggestion emphatically. Instead there arrived in Belgrade early in January 1877 a letter from the Tsar, stating that in the event of war he expected energetic co-operation from Serbia; followed by a commission under General Nikitin with one million roubles for the reorganization of the Serbian army. The Serbs quite genuinely did not want war; they quite genuinely did want the million roubles. They found a ready tool in Nikitin, but the money could not be expended without the sanction of Kartsov and Richter, an official of the Russian ministry of finance, who set their faces rigidly against waste and embezzlement. A month of wrangles and intrigue followed. In mid-February the Nikitin mission was withdrawn—and 850,000 of the precious million: whereupon the Serbs promptly concluded peace with the Turks, on the basis of the *status quo ante bellum.*[1]

The attitude of the Russian government towards Serbia inevitably was double-faced. Since they were themselves uncertain whether or when there would be war with Turkey, they desired on the one hand that Serbian strength should be reconstituted as a useful auxiliary if it came to fighting, and on the

[1] For Ristić and the Marinović mission: résumé of incl. in lettre particulière of Gorchakov to Novikov, 5 Dec., in *S.R.*, vol. iv, pp. 442–3; Ristić, *Diplomatska istorija Srbije*, vol. ii, pp. 2–19; Schweinitz, *Denkwürdigkeiten*, vol. i, pp. 367–8, 378; White (Belgrade) to Derby, disp., no. 207, 20 Nov., in *F.O.* 78/2487; Loftus to Derby, disp., no. 583, 6 Dec., in *F.O.* 65/942. For the general situation in Belgrade, the withdrawal of the volunteers, and the Nikitin mission: Kartsov, *Za kulisami diplomatii*, pp. 46–51; Ristić, op. cit., vol. ii, pp. 15–16, 19–21; *Wertheimer*, pp. 387, 401–2; letters to and from Aksakov, text in *Russky Arkhiv*, 1897, vol. ii, pp. 257–81; Naglovsky's diary, under date 9 Jan., Kishinev, in *R.S.*, vol. cxii, p. 259 (Grand Duke Nicholas opposing withdrawal of Nikitin). There is a good summary in Jovanović, *Vlada Milana Obrenovića*, vol. i, pp. 354–5, 360–4.

other hand that nothing should be done by Serbia to bring about an explosion. Hence they did not put difficulties in the way of Serbian negotiations for a peace with the Turks.[1] These had been opened by Midhat in the latter part of January and were concluded on 28 February, the day before the lapse of the armistice, which the Turks had refused to extend. The Serbs, on the basis of the Constantinople conference, attempted to secure recognition of their claims to Little Zvornik, but counter-demands from the Turks for guarantees for the future and the non-extension of the armistice forced the Serbs, unsupported by any of the powers, to give way. The peace terms accordingly provided simply for the restoration of the *status quo ante bellum*. Ristić maintained that the only alternative was a life-and-death struggle under the most precarious circumstances; plumed himself on securing a bilateral peace protocol instead of a mere *firman*; and recalled that Custozza and Novara had cost Carlo Alberto a far greater price. Privately he believed that Russia would not go to war and that diplomacy would find a peaceful exit from the difficulties of the international situation.[2]

The Russian relations with Belgrade during the winter gravely alarmed the Austrians, already stiff and exacting in their prolonged negotiations with St. Petersburg. At the Constantinople conference they proved very unsatisfactory. They had early expressed nervousness lest England might too readily make concessions to Russia in respect of autonomy in the Turkish provinces,[3] and they had let London and Paris know early in November that they would allow very little rope to their representatives at the conference: all the more important questions arising were to be taken *ad referendum*.[4] Ignatyev complained bitterly of Calice's opposition and perpetual reference to Vienna.

---

[1] Ristić, op. cit., vol. i, pp. 233, 236, 241.

[2] Text of private letter of Ristić to Hristić, at Constantinople, 30 Mar., in *Pisma Jovana Ristića Filipu Hristiću . . .*, p. 243. The text of the protocol concluding peace is in Martens, *Nouveau recueil général de traités . . .*, second series, vol. iii, pp. 171–2: additional documents concerning the peace are printed (in Serbian) in Ristić, *Diplomatska istorija Srbije*, vol. i, pp. 281–8: see also his account of the negotiations, pp. 231–90, and the Austrian account in *Actenstücke*, i, especially nos. 955, 978, and 979.

[3] Buchanan to Derby, disp., no. 780, most conf. and secret, 5 Nov., 1876, in *F.O.* 7/874.

[4] Derby to Buchanan, 7 Nov., 1876, in *A. and P.*, 1877, xc, C. 1640, no. 898; cf. *D.D.F.*, p. 109.

Andrássy boasted of 'privately propping up' the Turks, and appears to have agreed only with extreme reluctance to the Bosnian proposals of Ignatyev and Salisbury, and to have sanctioned Austrian participation in the final demands on the Porte only in the certain expectation of their being refused.[1]

The Russians were not only finding the Austrians unaccommodating; an ugly squall blew up unexpectedly from Berlin. Bismarck had made a satisfactory speech in the Reichstag on 5 December, and a little later, interrogated by Oubril, he urged prompt, in any case sudden, military action and expatiated on the friendly aims of his policy. This was pleasant hearing, but why had Gorchakov to complain continuously of Werther at Constantinople following tamely in Calice's footsteps and taking the Russian proposals *ad referendum*? The answer, which was that Werther in each case had only waited until the Russians and Austrians were in agreement, was not satisfactory either to Gorchakov or to the Tsar. There was a most painful interview between the latter and Schweinitz (16 January), who left the imperial presence with the word 'Adieu' ringing in his ears and a consequent exaggeration of the seriousness of the situation. Bismarck, poorly served by Werther, wished to avoid appearing to support either Russia or Austria-Hungary separately at the conference. He was uncertain as to what the Russians precisely were aiming at, and complained of being kept in the dark by them. As the conference wore on news of the intimacy of Ignatyev with Chaudordy (news retailed to Berlin by Andrássy amongst others) aroused the chancellor to one of his repeated scares of a Russo-French understanding. Decazes, the foreign minister, was held in Berlin to be deliberately aiming at it. A press campaign broke out in the three countries, with the usual accompanying recriminations between the foreign offices and

[1] Derby to Salisbury, tel., 11 Jan., in *F.O.* 78/2674; Ignatyev's memoirs, in *I.V.*, vol. cxxxvi, pp. 458–9; *Wertheimer*, p. 381, vol. iii, p. 2, both of which references are to explanations made subsequently, and not at the time, by Andrássy. Cf. Ignatyev's account, during his Vienna visit in Mar. 1878, of Andrássy declaring to him that he attributed no importance to the big, divided Bulgaria of the Constantinople conference, since he had disapproved of the decisions of the conference and had only allowed them to be accepted because he was quite convinced that they would lead to no practical results while the Turks remained masters of the situation; *I.V.*, vol. cxliii, p. 362. Whatever the later representations of Andrássy, it seems as if Ignatyev had, with Salisbury's aid, succeeded in placing him in the awkward predicament of being the only one to oppose the final demands of the powers, a risk which he decided not to take.

rumours of troop movements. Moltke revised his military plans to meet the case of a Franco-Russian war against Germany, though he professed to regard such a combination as improbable and had just previously been considering the possibility of a Franco-Austrian war against Germany, if Russia should be absorbed in the Balkans. What added to the tension was that Decazes believed that Bismarck wanted the conference to fail and war to follow,[1] and that he had approached London, late in January, with suggestions for an alliance against France and Russia. This was a good deal more than the truth, which was that conversations had been opened with Vienna and London which might lead to an alliance with the former and an assurance of goodwill from the latter. These German overtures to England in fear of a Russo-French *rapprochement* duly came to the ears of Shuvalov, who, of course, reported on them to his government.[2]

In St. Petersburg the New Year had opened in a fog of uncertainty, which was only thickened, not created, by the difficulties with Berlin. The single point of agreement was that the conference would now fail. Reutern, as has been seen, was urging the impossibility of war. Milyutin was wavering between arguments for immediate war and arguments showing it to be impossible on technical grounds. Jomini wrote of general chaos, impatient suspicions of Vienna, and gloomy oscillations between fears of a repetition of 1854 and heart-searchings that brusque action had not been taken the previous summer. Giers, the

---

[1] Cf. Salisbury's information from Constantinople that Werther's sudden change of attitude to one of energetic pressure on the Turks meant that Bismarck wished no concessions to be made to the Turks and war to follow; tels. to Derby, 7, 8, and 11 Jan., in *F.O.* 78/2678.

[2] *Tatishchev*, pp. 349–53, quoting extracts from Oubril's reports to Gorchakov of 29 Dec. and 4 and 14 Jan.; Bülow to Schweinitz, 18 Dec., and Bismarck's private letter to Schweinitz, 24 Jan., in *G.P.*, pp. 119–20, 125–31; Schweinitz, *Denkwürdigkeiten*, vol. i, pp. 370, 378–86, and (on the overtures to England and Austria) *Briefwechsel*, pp. 125–6; *Wertheimer*, p. 381; Moltke, *Die deutschen Aufmarschpläne 1871–1890*, pp. 62–7, memoranda of Jan. and 3 Feb. 1877; *D.D.F.*, pp. 134–5, 140, 144; Shuvalov to Gorchakov, lettres très confidentielles, 30 Jan. and 20 Feb., texts in *S.R.*, vol. iv, pp. 738, 746. There is nothing in *D.D.F.* on Decazes aiming at an understanding with Russia or on Chaudordy's conduct at Constantinople, except a passage in Decazes's supplementary instructions to him and Bourgoing that they would do well discreetly to let Russia know that France was quite ready that she should take back Bessarabia, provided that it were not likely to be opposed by Germany; pp. 118–20. On Bismarck's previous approach to England in Jan. 1876, see the article by Harris in *Journal of Modern History*, vol. iii, pp. 441–56, and Langer, *European Alliances and Alignments*, pp. 76–81.

coolest head in the foreign office, thought that the force of circumstances would bring war with Turkey, though Gorchakov disagreed and seemed to him, as also to Loftus, extremely anxious to avoid a war. So was the Tsar; but his hopes of peace were becoming weak. The country at large, to judge from the majority of the New Year reports of the secret police, was but little concerned with the question of war or peace. Revolutionary societies and student riots bulked far larger than foreign affairs. On 18 December a demonstration before the Kazan cathedral in St. Petersburg had been forcibly broken up, and opinion was further antagonized by the severity of the sentences passed next month on those arrested. Everywhere there was open talk of the disorganization and the internal difficulties, luridly written up in the English press. With an exaggeration not quite amounting to travesty a foreign diplomat in St. Petersburg could write:

'Nothing is left of the war fever, which appeared in Moscow. They only await a more or less favourable excuse for withdrawal. They cry from the official housetops their complete military powerlessness, their administrative chaos, their financial disorder. What is most comical of all, the Chancellor does not worry in the least about the Turks or Bulgars or reforms for the Christians. All his attention is concentrated on the successful rise of General Ignatyev, whom he wishes at any price to keep reined in.'[1]

The most ominous-coloured streak in the Russian kaleidoscope was the appointment at the end of November of a civil governor for the occupied area of Bulgaria. Actually, of course, there was no occupied area of Bulgaria—as yet. The holder of the post, Prince Cherkasky, was equally unassuring. A well-known public figure, he had played an important part, as has been mentioned earlier, in Poland after 1863 and in the Baltic provinces as one of the main advocates of a denationalizing policy. Energetic and dictatorial, he was now acclaimed, now attacked, as among the most forceful representatives of Musco-

[1] Extracts from Jomini's letters to Ignatyev, Dec., from letter of Giers to Ignatyev, 17 Jan., from letter of an unnamed secretary of one of the embassies; all in *I.V.*, vol. cxxxvi, pp. 461–5, 468, 833. Ignatyev is concerned to paint a picture as full as possible of confusion and incompetence. Loftus to Derby, disp., no. 610, 28 Dec., and conf., no. 14, 11 Jan., in *F.O.* 65/942 and 963; Schweinitz, *Denkwürdigkeiten*, vol. i, pp. 375–7 (overemphasizing peace signs), 431 (on secret police reports); Shuvalov to Gorchakov, lettre particulière, 17 Jan., text in *S.R.*, vol. iv, p. 737 (on English press).

vite nationalism. Thanks to Milyutin, he was received back into the favour of the Tsar, during his visit to Moscow, and was appointed head of the Red Cross and civil administrator in Bulgaria, under the Grand Duke Nicholas. Cherkasky's domineering ambition immediately brought him into enduring conflict both with the Grand Duke and his staff and with the foreign office: if he had had his way, he would have established himself as a semi-independent satrap controlling not merely civilian affairs but the formation of a Bulgarian military force and diplomatic relations. Without any concealment of his duties he set about recruiting a staff, in close touch with Aksakov and other panslavs, and collecting information about Bulgaria, of which hitherto he knew nothing. In this latter task he was much assisted by the arrival in St. Petersburg of a Bulgarian delegation.[1]

The delegation consisted of two persons, Marko Balabanov and Dragan Tsankov. The former, a Paris-trained lawyer, was a leading adherent of the russophil moderate nationalists, but Tsankov had at one time been intimately concerned with the Bulgarian Uniate movement and on bad terms with Ignatyev. After a good deal of intriguing among the Bulgarian colony in Constantinople, Ignatyev and the Exarch Anthim, with cautious approval, deputed them in August 1876 to visit the main European capitals and plead the cause of the Bulgars. They were furnished with a memorandum drawn up by the invaluable Naiden Gerov. This, presented in the name of the Bulgarian people to the great powers of Europe, demanded full autonomy with a national government, guaranteed by the powers. It judiciously preserved complete silence as to the territorial extent of Bulgaria and as to all details. The delegates proceeded to present their case before the foreign ministers and

---

[1] For Cherkasky, see Ovsyany, *Russkoe upravlenie v Bolgarii*, vol. i, pp. 2–25, 151–64. For the Bulgarian delegation, see Bobchev's article 'Blgarskite delegati pri chuzhdite dvorove i pri Tsarya-Osvoboditel', in *Proslava na osvoboditelnata voina 1877–1878 g.*, pp. 263–86, mainly based on Balabanov's own account, *Stranitsa ot politicheskoto ni vzrazhdane* (Sofia, 1904), a book which I have been unable to obtain; Muromtseva's article on the Exarch Anthim in *Russky Vestnik*, vol. clii, pp. 339–40. Balabanov and Tsankov were not at all to the taste of the Bulgarian extremists in Bucarest; letter of V. S. Ionin to Prince Vasilchikov, 14 Dec., extract in *Trudy Instituta Slavyanovedeniya*, vol. ii, p. 202. Avril, *Négociations relatives au traité de Berlin*, pp. 129–33, gives the French text of the memorandum, dated 26 Aug. 1876, which the two delegates brought with them. This is also printed in the English pamphlet *Bulgaria* issued by them in London in Oct. 1876.

to make propaganda in the western capitals. In mid-December they delightedly left the chilly atmosphere of the Ballplatz for a welcome on the Neva, the reverse of wintry. They saw the Tsarevich, who questioned them as to whether the Bulgars could assist in case of war. They saw Cherkasky, who picked their brains on the situation in Bulgaria. They visited Moscow, where Aksakov organized an effusive reception. At the foreign office Gorchakov was mainly concerned as to whether there was any Bulgar fit to rule an autonomous Bulgaria: the delegates said they wanted a foreigner. The culminating point was their audience with the Tsar, on 23 December. Alexander told them clearly that, though he wished for peace, he would not be satisfied with empty promises from the Turks: 'If the other powers content themselves with mere words we shall call God to our help and move forward and fulfil our duty: tell this to those who sent you.'

This was almost exactly what was to happen in the course of the next four months.

VIII

THE LONDON PROTOCOL

THE Constantinople conference had collapsed with the Turkish refusal of demands for reforms in Bosnia, Herzegovina, and Bulgaria which had been agreed upon at one stage by all the powers as a necessary minimum. What did the powers now propose to do? This, like many apparently simple questions, was an exceedingly difficult one to answer; and the powers found it so when they received Gorchakov's circular of 31 January inquiring what measures should be taken in concert to answer the Turkish flouting of Europe and to guarantee the carrying out of the rejected agreement. The circular was couched in terms of joint action, but there was a significant reference to the other powers 'avec lesquels nous nous sommes efforcés jusqu'à présent et désirons autant qu'il sera possible continuer de marcher en commun'.[1]

Gorchakov felt the Turkish refusal to be a box on the ears and he considered that the other powers should feel it similarly, but he did not see his way to any very rapid action. Only the military convention had as yet been settled with Austria, and the outstanding questions were protracting the negotiations with Vienna uneasily. Something might be hoped from the effect of Salisbury's return to England with his hostile impressions of the Turks; and at Rome on his way home he had expressed himself very flatteringly on Russian policy. Something also might come out of the English parliamentary debates. Both were to prove a disappointment to the chancellor, but meanwhile it was in any case best to await replies to his circular, 'dans notre attitude d'expectative armée'.[2]

This was additionally so in view of new developments on the Bosphorus. Midhat had become insufferable to Abd ul-Hamid. Regarding the new constitution partly with the pride of its maker, partly as a means for his own power, he was dictating

---

[1] The text is in *A. and P.*, 1877, xci, C. 1713, no. 1. Derby's general attitude was well expressed in writing to Odo Russell, 24 Jan.: 'If you are asked what steps England is going to take next, your true answer should be "none". We shall wait, say little, and pledge ourselves to nothing.' Newton, *Lord Lyons*, vol. ii, p. 107.

[2] Text of dispatch of Russian minister in Rome, 4 Feb., in Ignatyev's memoirs, *R.S.*, vol. clxi, pp. 31–3; Gorchakov to Shuvalov, 31 Jan. and 12 Feb., text in *S.R.*, vol. iv, pp. 738–9, 742.

boldly on all subjects to the other ministers, and to the Sultan himself. He reckoned without Abd ul-Hamid, even as a young man unrestrained by anything but fear for himself. On 5 February Midhat was kidnapped, placed on the imperial yacht, and deported to Brindisi.[1] His place was filled by Edhem Pasha as grand vizier. This did not augur well, but the appointment was accompanied by an imperial *hatt* announcing a grandiose scheme of reforms in part based on those recommended by the Constantinople conference. Hopes were entertained that these reforms were really going to be translated into practice. The British made play with them to suggest giving the Turks the benefit of the doubt by granting a year's grace, and Disraeli opened out to Shuvalov in most friendly confidences, which suggested the possibility of a radical change of attitude. The Russians expostulated that they could not keep their army mobilized for such a length of time, and that they could not demobilize without guarantees. But the Turks also were mobilized by now: could not Turkish demobilization be secured as a guarantee? The Russians (rightly) suspected the reforms of Edhem Pasha as being due to British influence, but apparently they were somewhat impressed by them as providing a bare chance of a peaceful solution of the crisis, provided that some form of guarantee satisfying to Russia's dignity could be given.[2]

Contemporaneously with Edhem's reforms in February and March, obscure intrigues were being woven by Ignatyev's agents and Nelidov, in charge of the Russian embassy, for the dispatch by the Turks of a special mission to treat directly with the Russians. Gorchakov, however, refused to move in this

---

[1] De Moüy, *Souvenirs et causeries d'un diplomate*, pp. 56–61; Busch's diary, under date 8 Feb., in *Deutsche Rundschau*, vol. cxli, p. 25. Midhat was restored later to some favour as Vali of Smyrna, but was again disgraced, to die in the Hedjaz, probably murdered by the Sultan's orders.

[2] Text of the *Hatti-Sherif* of 6 Feb., in *A. and P.*, 1877, xci, C. 1738, no. 121, incl.; Loftus to Derby, disp., conf., no. 76, 20 Feb., recording a conversation with Gorchakov on the previous day, in *F.O.* 65/963; Shuvalov to Gorchakov, letter, 21 Feb., text in *S.R.*, vol. iv, pp. 747–9; Busch's diary, under dates 20 and 28 Feb., in *Deutsche Rundschau*, vol. cxli, p. 27 (on the English and the reforms); Schweinitz, *Denkwürdigkeiten*, vol. i, pp. 399–401, recording conversations with Gorchakov and the Tsar, 26 and 27 Feb., cf. *D.D.F.*, pp. 146–7. According to Derby to Loftus, nos. 32, 33, and 45, 9, 12, and 19 Feb., in *F.O.* 65/960, Shuvalov had suggested to him pressing the Turks to adopt on their own initiative the reforms of the Constantinople conference, and Derby did so: on 19 Feb. Shuvalov informed Derby that Gorchakov was favourably inclined to Edhem's reforms provided that they were really put into practice.

direction, and the Sultan either would not or could not yield to the advice of those Turks who feared the worst if it came to war. Ignatyev himself, too, was soon deeply involved on another line.[1]

He had returned from Constantinople by way of Athens and Vienna. His Greek visit was the occasion for manifestations by the Greek irredentist groups and for confused dealings with the political parties. Ignatyev was regarded with unconcealed alarm as the champion of Slav ascendancy in the Balkans, and himself was doubly suspicious of the Athens government owing to rumours of an Austro-Greek political and military agreement in the event of war between Russia and Turkey. His efforts to distract Greek politicians from Macedonia and Thrace by encouraging them to concentrate on Epirus, Thessaly, and Crete were frustrated by Greek reliance on British influence; and he left giving the advice to Saburov, the Russian minister, and Gorchakov that it was essential somehow to compromise the Greeks in the eyes of the British, since they had in their hands the means to exploit the Greeks to the extreme prejudice of Russian interests.[2] Forty-eight hours in Vienna convinced him that no sincere agreement could be reached with Austria-Hungary unless Andrássy were supplanted, preferably by Count Alfred Potocki or, better still, by Mollinary, the Croat general commanding at Agram.[3] Early in February he reached St. Petersburg.

Ignatyev sharply criticized the circular of 31 January. It was the work of his rival, and it had been carefully issued without waiting for his advice. It was obnoxious to him less from its actual content, which he derided as vague phrase-making, than from its imposing on Russia a costly and indefinite period of waiting. He was at one grave disadvantage: the air was full of rumours of the Austro-Russian conventions, but he could not penetrate into the secrets of these carefully shielded negotiations. Nor could he make any impression on Milyutin with a repeti-

---

[1] Ignatyev's memoirs, in *I.V.*, vol. cxxxvi, pp. 460–1, 838–40, 853–4; vol. cxxxvii, pp. 55–7; Nelidov's memoirs in *Revue des deux mondes*, 15 July 1915, vol. xxviii, p. 261. It was schemed to send Ahmed Vefik, the president of the new elected chamber: he had been minister at Teheran and Paris, and was a learned orientalist, in which capacity he had in 1876 attended a congress in Russia, where he had links with Jomini: he was reputed to be an independent man, though taxed with being anglophil, and to be very alarmed at the prospect of war.

[2] Ignatyev's memoirs, in *R.S.*, vol. clxi, pp. 34–45.

[3] Ignatyev's memoirs, in *R.S.*, vol. clxi, pp. 45–6. There is nothing specific in *Wertheimer* on Ignatyev's passage through Vienna.

tion of his favourite theme of the importance of the Asiatic front as Russia's main field of operations.[1]

Ignatyev was not able to gain his principal object, to occupy the centre of the scene, until a series of imperial consultations at the end of February, when he found an ally, perhaps unexpectedly, in the war minister. Both the Tsar and the foreign office in mid-February had given the impression of being in a pacific mood. 'The current here is strong for Peace,' thought Loftus, 'and I doubt very much whether under any circumstances the Emperor would plunge into a single-handed contest with Turkey . . . Gorchakov is in a ditch. He wants us to pull him out—and if we do not, he will try to pull us into it. Our interest is to pull him out.'[2] However that might be, the current was soon altered when a few days later Milyutin presented the Tsar with a memorandum which made a deep impression and led on to the imperial councils of 22, 24, and 27 February.

The Milyutin memorandum, which was circulated to the ministers, was a most curious document, for it consisted of three parts, and the third part was in flat contradiction with the second. It began with a statement of the forces available. It continued by emphasizing that both the internal and the external situation required the avoidance of war. It ended in a completely different tone by insisting on the impossibility of remaining inactive. Either alone or in conjunction with the powers Russia should demand the effective carrying out of the Constantinople conference reforms: if European diplomacy or Turkish delays threatened indefinite prolongation, then an ultimatum should be presented, to be followed in case of rejection by war. 'Reasons—', the pacific Valuev remarked on this conclusion, 'general phrases—Russia, the Tsar's Moscow speech, our traditional eastern policy etc.'[3] But Alexander reacted very differently. 'I am certainly with Milyutin', was his greeting to Reutern when he came to make his report on 23 February, 'there are moments in the life of states, as of individuals, when it is necessary to forget everything save the defence of honour.'

---

[1] Ignatyev's memoirs, in *I.V.*, vol. cxxxvi, pp. 827-8, 835-8.

[2] Loftus to Tenterden, private letter, 14 Feb., in *F.O.* 363/2.

[3] *Hasenkampf*, appendix 2, prints a five-page memorandum drawn up by Obruchev for Milyutin and dated 19 Feb. I have taken this as being at least substantially the same as the Milyutin memorandum handed to the Tsar, although the evidence is not conclusive; Reutern's journal, under date 25 Feb., in *R.S.*, vol. cxliii, p. 43; Valuev's diary, under date 23 Feb., *Dnevnik*, pp. 5-6.

Though the Tsar was calmer next day, Reutern could carry no weight with his financial arguments or with his pleadings that feeling in Russia had cooled down and that war would not be simply against Turkey but against a coalition.[1]

At the imperial council on the 22nd Milyutin had again urged strongly the necessity of energetic and prompt action, while Gorchakov had created general amazement (if Ignatyev can be believed) by first supporting Milyutin's line and then suggesting that, since neither the entente with Germany and Austria-Hungary nor the Constantinople conference had brought any practical result, and since the question was not purely Russian but European, a still better policy would be for Russia to announce her withdrawal from further collective negotiations and to demobilize her army, leaving herself full freedom of action for the future—'full freedom of inaction', as Ignatyev naturally styled it.[2]

The peace party, Reutern, Valuev, and Timashev, did their best, all three standing unconditionally against war, but they were of no effect. On the 24th there was another imperial council. It opened with a 'prise de bec': Gorchakov at Ignatyev; the Tsar ordered his chancellor to behave himself.[3] Then Ignatyev produced a lengthy analysis of the whole situation, interlarded with stinging references to the mistakes of the foreign office. He repeated with emphasis that the most favourable moment for military action, i.e. the previous summer or autumn, had passed and that war would now be a most serious affair, with a completely different aim from before. It would be impossible to keep to a limited programme, for events in the Balkans would move too fast and would lead to the complete collapse of Turkish rule in Europe. Once war was decided on, every effort should be made to hasten this collapse by stirring up 'our native allies'. His final conclusion was in essentials very close to the advice of Milyutin. Let the negotiations over

---

[1] Reutern's journal, under date 25 Feb., in *R.S.*, vol. cxliii, pp. 43–4; text of Reutern's memorandum for the Tsar, 23 Feb., in Reutern–Nolcken, *Die finanzielle Sanierung Russlands . . . durch . . . Reutern*, pp. 141–6.

[2] Ignatyev's memoirs, in *I.V.*, vol. cxxxvi, pp. 840–1, paraphrasing the memorandum read by Gorchakov, and stating it to have been drawn up for him by Jomini.

[3] Valuev's diary, under dates 23 and 24 Feb., *Dnevnik*, pp. 6–7; Reutern's journal, under date 25 Feb., in *R.S.*, vol. cxliii, p. 44; both were present at the council of 24 Feb. Cf. Polovtsov's diary, under date 22 May, recording Timashev's general attitude to the war, in *Krasny arkhiv*, vol. xxxiii, p. 171.

the replies to the circular of 31 January be speeded up by sending a special envoy to Berlin and London. If the answers to the
circular prove favourable, sign immediately a protocol with the
powers which would tie down the Porte to binding responsibilities and would give Europe the right of supervision and
intervention. With the signature of such a protocol Russia
could demobilize, though keeping an observation force ready
in Bessarabia and Transcaucasia. The Turks must demobilize
their reserves and reduce their striking force. If the negotiations
for the protocol fail, make agreements at once with Germany
and Austria-Hungary for decisive action. Only after the complete break-down of all diplomatic negotiations should an
ultimatum be presented to the Porte (about the beginning of
April) in agreement with the central powers; the ultimatum to
be followed, in case of rejection by immediate advance, in case
of acceptance by demobilization (about the end of April).[1]

The suggestion of a special mission and of a protocol was
accepted, and at the third imperial council (27 February) it
was decided to send Ignatyev to the chief capitals, Gorchakov
failing in his opposition to the choice of his rival, Ignatyev failing (as he doubtless intended) in his professions of extreme
reluctance to go.[2] Ignatyev had not only to face entire lack of
support from his foreign office; he had as well to count upon the
opposition of Shuvalov in his key post at London. Shuvalov at
once telegraphed emphasizing the very bad effect Ignatyev
would create in London, and he induced Salisbury to ask
Ignatyev to defer his visit. In view of this, the Tsar at the last
moment (1 March) instructed him not to proceed to England
without special telegraphic permission from St. Petersburg.
Clearly he would have to see to it that this permission was
extracted: his mission would be a fiasco if it omitted London.[3]

Ignatyev left on 2 March, nominally to consult an oculist in
Paris. As instructions he took with him, so he declares in his
memoirs, only a draft protocol. The draft was drawn up in the
foreign office, but was evidently, at least in the main, Ignatyev's

[1] Text of Ignatyev's memorandum, in *I.V.*, vol. cxxxvi, pp. 841–57.
[2] Valuev's diary, under date 1 Mar., *Dnevnik*, p. 7 (he was present at the council
of 27 Feb.); letter of Gorchakov to Shuvalov, 1 Mar., extract in *S.R.*, vol. iv, p. 753;
Ignatyev's memoirs, in *I.V.*, vol. cxxxvi, p. 858.
[3] Shuvalov to Gorchakov, tels., 27 Feb. and 1 Mar.; Salisbury to Ignatyev, tel.,
1 Mar.; texts in *S.R.*, vol. iv, pp. 750, 753; Ignatyev's memoirs, in *R.S.*, vol. clviii,
p. 5.

own handiwork. He had himself, immediately after the refusal of the Turks to accept the demands of the powers at the Constantinople conference, asked the ambassadors to sign a declaration binding them to support these demands,[1] and the essential feature of the draft protocol was its close linking up with the conference. The Porte was called upon to make peace with Serbia and Montenegro on the terms laid down at the conference, to demobilize, and to put into operation without delay the reforms enumerated in the protocols of the conference and in the *Hatti-Sherif* of 6 February. The powers were to announce their right of surveillance over the carrying out of these reforms. If their hopes were yet again deceived, they reserved their right to consider in common the action necessary to secure the well-being of the Christians and the interests of the general peace. The language throughout was emphatic and minatory (even though the close bound the powers only to further discussion and less definitely to action), and there was the definite formulation of the requirement to demobilize.[2]

Did the Russians genuinely desire the acceptance of the protocol? Or did they desire to fight? There was no one answer. Ignatyev under the circumstances wanted *his* protocol to succeed, but not any other.[3] The foreign office, just because it was *his* protocol, were apathetic or hostile to it; Gorchakov's adherents a little later expressed unmeasured delight at what they termed the fiasco of Ignatyev's mission.[4] The military wanted a quick decision one way or the other, and on the whole preferably for war. Reutern and his associates wanted peace at any price, but they counted for little. The Tsar was swayed this way and that. Some of those at court spoke of him as filled with suspicion of his advisers and very averse to war, and even of the Tsaritsa as now backing away from the policy of force, but after the middle of March hopes of a peaceful outcome dwindled. The Tsar still spoke of peace, but he would not

---

[1] Ignatyev's memoirs, in *I.V.*, vol. cxxxvi, pp. 859–60, without giving any details as to the document: cf. above, p. 245.

[2] See Appendix IV for this text of the draft protocol and the text as finally signed in London on 31 Mar.

[3] Loftus to Derby, disp., no. 100, 6 Mar., in *F.O.* 65/964, thought that Ignatyev would do his best to succeed, and obtain thereby his great ambition, the London embassy. His dispatches show that he thought that the mission was genuinely meant for peace, though not at any price.

[4] Langenau to Andrássy, 6 Apr., reporting Jomini's remarks, cited in Wittrock, *Gorčakov, Ignatiev och Šuvalov*, p. 46.

withdraw his troops without having gained some tangible result; he could not indefinitely keep them mobilized and inactive, and the English requirement of Russian demobilization aroused him to the most dangerous insistence on his honour.[1] A new wave of panslav agitation was now at its height. Aksakov in the middle of March poured forth the vials of his wrath on St. Petersburg in a speech in Moscow, of which the published text, though confiscated by the authorities, was widely circulated in secret. Harking back to the Tsar's Moscow speech of November he clamoured for the fulfilment by arms of 'our sacred mission'.[2] The one effectively determined worker for peace was Shuvalov, and as such he stoutly fought Ignatyev's protocol, for it could never be accepted by England without severe emendation, and in Shuvalov's eyes it was the first essential not to antagonize England further. With no alternative, save war, in the field it was clearly the best policy to outrival Ignatyev by substituting for his protocol one which would be compatible with British views, and Shuvalov in conjunction with his foreign office proceeded to act accordingly.

Ignatyev was in Berlin by 4 March, whence he wrote glowingly of the friendly welcome of the Emperor, Bismarck, and others. Bismarck had never met him before, and found him less excitable and more serious than he had expected, but not less loquacious and involved.[3] He approved orally the general lines of the protocol, provided that all the other powers consented— a nullifying proviso since he did not imagine that the English would consent and warned Ignatyev that he must expect much opposition from them. He assured him in general terms of German friendly neutrality in the event of a Russo-Turkish war and of his desire to keep the *Dreikaiserbündnis* intact, and he empowered Schweinitz to give specific assurances to this effect should the necessity arise.[4] Finally, he gave great delight to the

---

[1] Wellesley, no. 16, 14 Mar., in *F.O.* 65/964, reports at length the views of one of the Tsar's senior aides-de-camp (name not given), which laid stress on the change towards peace at the beginning of March. Cf. Polovtsov's diary, in *Krasny arkhiv*, vol. xxxiii, p. 171.

[2] Aksakov, *Slavyansky vopros*, pp. 236–51, text of speech of 18 Mar. to the Moscow Slavonic committee; Schweinitz, *Denkwürdigkeiten*, vol. i, pp. 412–13.

[3] Radowitz, *Aufzeichnungen und Erinnerungen*, vol. i, p. 365; Bismarck, *Gesammelte Werke*, vol. viii, pp. 194–5. Radowitz, who knew Ignatyev well, piloted him about Berlin.

[4] Bismarck to the Emperor, 4 Mar., reporting his conversation of that day; Bülow to Schweinitz, 8 Mar.; in *G.P.*, pp. 134–8.

Russian envoy by a bitter personal attack on Gorchakov for his conduct in 1875. Ignatyev on his side was careful to deny any connivance at intrigues with France and to declare himself a determined supporter of alliance with Germany. He reported that Bismarck had emphasized the loss to the prestige of Russia if she backed away from war, and had remarked that Bleichröder could easily arrange a large loan. On the whole so far so good.[1]

Paris, however, was far from satisfactory. Ignatyev arrived there on 8 March to find Shuvalov before him, on a flying visit from London, and to encounter much suspicion from the French government, and from the circles of Thiers and Jules Simon to whom he also laid siege. Decazes laid stress on difficulties with England and put forward a counter-draft of the protocol which was far too anodyne for Ignatyev. One essential point was gained in Paris in the shape of the reluctant acquiescence of Salisbury to act as Ignatyev's host if he came to England. Armed with this he obtained the required telegraphic permission from the Tsar to cross the Channel.[2]

On 16 March he reached London, and was at once embroiled in an unequal struggle with Shuvalov on his own ground. Apart from long-standing personal rivalry, Ignatyev was now incensed against the London ambassador for his efforts to prevent his visit, for his having already started negotiations on the protocol with Derby, and for what Ignatyev regarded as his commitments respecting demobilization by Russia. This last point he found on arrival to be the crux of the negotiations.

It had been raised on 11 March, when Shuvalov communicated to Derby a draft of the protocol, and a pro memoria, which included a clear warning that the Tsar desired 'la paix, mais non pas une paix à tout prix'. Derby had asked whether he could count on Russian demobilization if England signed the protocol and Turkey demobilized. Shuvalov had answered evasively, whereupon Derby made it quite clear that the British signature could be obtained only at that price, and Shuvalov urged St. Petersburg for authority to give the required assurance. Gorchakov replied on the 12th: if Derby accepts the protocol as communicated by Ignatyev to Bismarck and if

---

[1] Ignatyev's memoirs, in *R.S.*, vol. clvii, p. 515, and 502–13, for his account of his Berlin visit, including a long extract of his dispatch to Gorchakov of 13 Mar.

[2] Ib., vol. clviii, pp. 15–16, 242, 443–6; Shuvalov's memoirs, in *Krasny arkhiv*, vol. lix, pp. 85–6; *Salisbury*, pp. 132–3.

Turkey puts her army on a peace footing, you and Ignatyev are empowered to communicate secretly to the cabinet that we are prepared to demobilize; but the Porte must take the initiative and immediately proceed to demobilization; otherwise we shall consider only our own interests and the opportunity of a peaceful solution will be let slip. Gorchakov followed this up by telegraphing on the same day, by order of the Tsar, that the Tsar did not consent to any promise of demobilization being included in the protocol itself; an idea which Shuvalov promptly protested he had never entertained.[1]

The gap, however, between St. Petersburg and London was still very wide, for Gorchakov, probably merely for bargaining's sake, had linked the possibility of Russian demobilization with acceptance by England of Ignatyev's draft protocol, and it was evident that the British cabinet would never accept so harsh a document. The draft upon which Shuvalov had entered into conversations represented a slight toning down of Ignatyev's provocative phraseology, and he and Derby were soon busy with further whittling away, particularly by virtually omitting reference to the Constantinople conference. Negotiating with Derby was never a light-footed affair (Shuvalov compared it to dancing on a carpet to a piano), and Derby, besides requiring some formal pledge of Russian intention to demobilize, posed two further conditions: that the protocol must be accepted by the other powers, and that it should not be signed by the Turks.[2]

Such was the situation when Ignatyev attempted to interpose in London. He was fatally handicapped by the utmost secrecy on the part of Shuvalov, by bad relations with Derby (to whom he took an immediate dislike) and Tenterden (with whom he had a heated discussion at Hatfield), and not least by his general reputation in English eyes. His efforts to preserve his own draft protocol proved quite unavailing, and he made no impression on the foreign office as regards the question of demobilization. He explained in vain that Russia could not promise demobilization while the Montenegrin question was still unsettled, while

[1] Text of telegrams of Shuvalov to Gorchakov, 11, 12, and 13 Mar., and Gorchakov's replies of 12 Mar., in *S.R.*, vol. iv, p. 754, and *R.S.*, vol. clviii, pp. 11, 243–5. For the draft and pro memoria communicated by Shuvalov to Derby on 11 Mar., see Appendix IV.

[2] Derby to Loftus, 13 Mar., in *A. and P.*, 1877, xci, C. 1738, no. 280; no. 71, 16 Mar., in *F.O.* 65/960; Gathorne-Hardy, *Gathorne-Hardy, First Earl of Cranbrook*, vol. ii, p. 17.

the Turks were not convinced of the necessity of yielding, while the Christians were not assured of improvements in their conditions, while something was not achieved to satisfy public opinion in Russia. In the end he suggested to Derby that no reference to Turkish demobilization should be made in the protocol, the question being left to direct discussions between Russia and Turkey. Derby did not take this idea as seriously meant and persisted in requiring that some agreement as to Russian demobilization must precede the signature of the protocol. Faced by this insistence Ignatyev abandoned his attempts to negotiate and departed on 22 March for Vienna, leaving the field to Shuvalov.[1]

He started homeward under no illusions now as to the political strength of the Tories or the influence of Gladstone's views. He was much struck by the almost universally anti-Russian and anti-Slav standpoint of London society, and in particular of the foreign office and the army, but long conversations with Disraeli and Salisbury confirmed him in the belief that the idea of the imminent collapse of the Ottoman empire was making headway and that the English had in mind guarantees for the safety of their communications with India in the shape of one of the Aegean islands, Cyprus, or Mytilene. Gorlov, the military attaché, told him that English plans for seizing the Dardanelles were all ready, in case of necessity. He thought on the whole that, if Russia avoided making serious mistakes, the state of opinion in England would make it impossible for any government to give Turkey material support against Russia, although in the event of a Russo-Turkish war some gage would certainly be demanded by England.[2]

Breaking his journey for twenty-four hours in Paris, Ignatyev discoursed to Lyons on the inadequacy of Shuvalov and on the

---

[1] Ignatyev's memoirs, in *R.S.*, vol. clviii, pp. 447–8, 452–5, 458; Rumbold, *Further recollections of a diplomatist*, pp. 78–9; Derby to Loftus, 21 and 23 Mar., in *A. and P.*, 1877, xci, C. 1738, nos. 338 and 366.

[2] Ignatyev's memoirs, in *R.S.*, vol. clix, pp. 5–13, in part quoting from his dispatches. *Disraeli*, pp. 999–1000, gives nothing on the Ignatyev mission beyond the extreme awkwardness of the Hatfield invitation (and the diamonds at dinner): so too Marquis of Zetland, *Letters of Disraeli to Lady Bradford and Lady Chesterfield*, vol. ii, pp. 108–10. *Salisbury*, pp. 130–5, shows that he was urging the cabinet to accept the Russian proposals and was adumbrating a policy of some kind of partition of Turkey, a policy of which the cabinet would not hear. Forster, a guest at Hatfield, records a long but uninforming conversation with Ignatyev; see his life by T. Wemyss Reid, vol. ii, pp. 166–71.

impossibility of a public undertaking to disarm, though, as Lyons reported to Derby, he 'was willing to whisper in your ear . . . the most positive assurance that the Army would be demobilized . . .'. Such whispers made as little impression on the British ambassador as they did on the foreign secretary.[1] If Ignatyev hoped for any assistance from Vienna, where he arrived on 25 March, he was promptly undeceived. Andrássy, who a week before had signed the second secret convention with Russia, unknown to Ignatyev, seemed to him to support the British view as to Russian demobilization, considering it as the natural, immediate consequence of the signature of the protocol, and proposing an entirely distasteful formula. A suggestion of Austrian mediation between St. Petersburg and London was likewise unacceptable to Ignatyev, though Andrássy appears to have put this forward in the genuine belief that St. Petersburg was seeking a bridge by which to withdraw. In Vienna the news that Ignatyev collected all pointed to both the Turks and the Montenegrins standing to their guns.[2] He heard more talk of war from Bismarck on his return through Berlin on 29 March. 'If I were a Russian subject . . . I should say: we will be moderate in our demands, but we will fight, if we cannot attain by peaceful methods results satisfactory to our national feeling.'[3] It is no wonder that Ignatyev travelled home with little thought of a protocol in his mind and much hope of the best solution being speedy war. He was all the more convinced of this when he found that within twenty-four hours of his arrival in St. Petersburg (evening, 30 March) Shuvalov's protocol had been signed in London. Yet again his foreign office had carefully forestalled him.

The protocol as signed on 31 March by the six powers was a very different document from Ignatyev's draft, and was not in

[1] Lyons to Derby, disp., very conf., no. 229, 23 Mar., in *F.O.* 27/2236.

[2] Ignatyev's memoirs, in *R.S.*, vol. clix, pp. 195–202 and 402, including text of his dispatch to Gorchakov of 28 Mar.; Andrássy to Károlyi, 27 Mar., cited in *Wertheimer*, p. 403 (for St. Petersburg anxious for a bridge: Andrássy had received from the counsellor of the embassy a letter dated 18 Mar. describing the spread of nihilism in Russia in the darkest colours), and p. 399 (for Andrássy's impression of Ignatyev wanting war).

[3] Ignatyev's memoirs, in *R.S.*, vol. clix, pp. 402–4, including text of a dispatch to Gorchakov. I do not know of any German version of this conversation. Oubril in dispatches to Gorchakov of 18 Mar. and 1 Apr., extracts quoted in *Tatishchev*, p. 367, reported Bismarck as urging Russia not to demobilize, to act for herself, and not to be deterred by financial difficulties; Bleichröder would see to the raising of a hundred-million-rouble loan in Germany: cf. above, p. 263.

fact regarded with any favour by St. Petersburg. The tone of aggressive insistence had given place to one of polite exhortation. Above all there was complete omission of the requirement to carry out the reforms agreed upon as necessary by the powers at the Constantinople conference, and these included, it will be remembered, the appointment by the powers of international commissions of control and of the governors-general. The Porte was invited to place its army on a peace footing, with the exception of such troops as were indispensable for the maintenance of internal order. The exception clearly offered a large loophole. The Porte was further invited to put into effect as rapidly as possible the necessary reforms. What constituted necessary reforms was not stated, a general reference only being made to the *Hatti-Sherif* of 6 February.[1] The Porte finally was warned that if the condition of the Christians were not adequately ameliorated the powers reserved the right of deliberating in common as to what they might do. This terrible threat concluded the protocol itself, but with it went a declaration of Derby to the effect that the British government would not in the future consider themselves bound by their adhesion to the protocol if it failed to attain its object, 'namely, reciprocal disarmament on the part of Russia and Turkey, and peace between them'. Russian demobilization was not mentioned in the text of the protocol, but on Shuvalov's initiative a formula had been devised to which both Derby and Gorchakov could agree.[2] A special declaration was made by Shuvalov that, if Turkey showed herself ready to place her troops on a peace footing and to undertake the task of reform seriously, she should send a special envoy to St. Petersburg to treat of disarmament to which the Tsar on his side would also consent: if there were a recurrence of massacres of the Christians, that would necessarily put

---

[1] Ignatyev in his memoirs strongly attacked the protocol for its failure to pin the Turks to precise reforms. Yet a minute of Derby, dated 17 Mar., in *F.O.* 65/987, shows that on that day Ignatyev himself suggested the omission of an enumeration of the reforms which figured in the draft protocol at that date. Presumably he did so because the reforms in question were Edhem's, and not those of the Constantinople conference, and he preferred to replace the list by a sentence which included specific reference to the conference.

[2] Derby to Loftus, 23, 24, 27, and 29 Mar., in *A. and P.*, 1877, xci, C. 1738, nos. 366, 369, 405, 407. Shuvalov apparently proposed his declaration on his own initiative, and it was also he who proposed the idea of Derby's declaration; Derby to Loftus, disp., no. 98, 27 Mar., in *F.O.* 65/960. For the text of the protocol and declarations see Appendix IV.

a stop to Russian demobilization measures. One further condition was ultimately inserted in this declaration, a condition which figured as its opening words: 'If peace with Montenegro is concluded.'

The two main stumbling-blocks in the whole question of Russian demobilization had been the dignity of Russia and the obstinacy of Montenegro.[1] The Black Mountain has always produced trouble disproportionate to its size, and it did not fail to do so in March 1877. Whereas Serbia, worn out and defeated, had yielded and made peace, Montenegro, successful in arms and confident of the future, had not. Prince Nicholas was encouraged by the fact that the Roman Catholic Mirdites in the mountains of north Albania had been goaded by Turkish stupidity into a serious rising (ascribed by the Turks to money doled out by the Russian consul Yastrebov); he turned a deaf ear to warnings from Andrássy to make peace, and preferred to believe that Gorchakov's silence during March meant that Russian policy intended him to stand firm and was most truly represented by the much needed grain consignments which were being shipped through the Slavonic committees in Russia.[2]

The armistice indeed had been prolonged, first until 21 March, then until 13 April, and Nicholas yielded so far as to abandon his original requirement of Vienna as the seat of peace negotiations and to send two delegates to Constantinople, where they arrived on 2 March. But no real progress could be made in the negotiations: they were broken off on 12 March, renewed again on the 24th, and then after a few fruitless days remained suspended, though the delegates were persuaded to remain at hand in Constantinople. At first they pitched their territorial demands impossibly high, and in no case would they make anything tantamount to an admission of Turkish suzerainty. Nicholas finally whittled down his essential demands to Nikšić and the Duga pass, the right bank of the Morača, and Spizza, and even on these, under strong Austrian pressure, he professed

---

[1] Giers wrote significantly to Kartsov in Belgrade, on 16 Mar.: 'we seem to be approaching a peaceful exit from the present crisis: Ignatyev's mission will probably be successful, but the difficulties encountered over the Turk-Montenegrin negotiations may ruin matters.' Kartsov, *Za kulisami diplomatii*, p. 54. For the importance of Montenegro in the negotiations for the Austro-Russian secret conventions, which were not concluded until 18 Mar., see below, pp. 280, 284.

[2] *A. and P.*, 1877, xci, C. 1738, nos. 22, incl., 98, 99; xcii, C. 1806, no. 31; *Actenstücke*, i, nos. 1002, 1007, 1030.

at the close of March to be ready to compromise. But he did so only because of a report from Vienna that Ignatyev himself and the Russians had deserted him on Nikšić: as soon as Ignatyev denied this, the Prince was ready enough to insist upon its acquisition as a point of honour, and to pin his faith to the Russians' not demobilizing before peace was concluded between Montenegro and Turkey.[1]

On the Russian side, Nelidov at Constantinople does not seem himself to have encouraged the more extreme claims of the Montenegrins; but the Turks were hearing from their ambassador on the Neva that Gorchakov was insistent on their yielding to Nicholas, and it was true that the chancellor was in fact becoming more and more restive, maintaining that it was impossible for Russia to abandon Montenegro with the Turks treating her like a vassal.[2] In the London negotiations Gorchakov had initially stood for no signature of the protocol until peace between Turkey and Montenegro had been signed, and had secured Derby's concurrence; but by 27 March Gorchakov had modified his position to this extent, that the protocol itself only urged freedom of navigation on the Boyana and a rectification of Montenegrin frontiers without specifying the cessions agreed on by the powers at the Constantinople conference, while it was the separate Russian declaration that made Russian demobilization dependent on the conclusion of peace between Turkey and Montenegro.[3]

It was this requirement, together with the clause relative to the recurrence of any massacres such as those which had taken place in Bulgaria, which above all exasperated the Turks and

---

[1] *Actenstücke*, i, especially nos. 959, 968, 972, 987, 999, 1001–4, 1008–9, 1017, 1020, 1022, 1041, 1053; Monson (Cettinje) to Derby, nos. 71, 76, 78, 82, 85, and 95, 29 and 31 Mar., 2, 3, and 11 Apr., in *F.O.* 7/912. Busch's diary, under dates 4, 15, and 17 Mar., in *Deutsche Rundschau*, vol. cxli, pp. 27–8, gives a good idea of the extreme claims of the Montenegrins, which according to him at one time included even Ipek as a *sine qua non*. Busch saw the Montenegrin delegates in company with Nelidov. For the Montenegrin frontiers see map between pp. 136 and 137.

[2] Nelidov's memoirs, in *Revue des deux mondes*, 15 July 1915, vol. xxviii, pp. 265, 269. Loftus's dispatches in *F.O.* 65/964 report a marked change for the worse in the Russian press from 15 Mar. onwards, and Gorchakov as making more and more of a stumbling-block out of Montenegro. This insistence on Montenegrin claims was perhaps heightened by the presence in St. Petersburg of Ionin, the Russian diplomatic agent at Cettinje, who had been summoned back at the end of November 1876, and did not return to his post until the outbreak of war in Apr. 1877.

[3] Derby to Loftus, 24, 27, and 28 Mar., in *A. and P.*, 1877, xci, C. 1738, nos. 369, 405, 409.

played into the hands of Mukhtar Pasha and the extremists. At the same time they professed to the British chargé d'affaires that they suspected the Russian insistence on their sending an envoy to St. Petersburg as being designed to lead on to negotiations to force an alliance and the conclusion of another treaty of Unkiar Skelessi, and that they also suspected that an offensive alliance between Russia and Persia had lately been arranged.[1] While they stigmatized the protocol itself as an entirely unwarranted humiliation, they regarded the appended Russian declaration as an insulting device for encouraging the Montenegrins and Christian disorders and ensuring that Russian demobilization should not take place. By the Russians equal emphasis was placed on the declaration. Gorchakov explained to Loftus that if the Porte replied verbally or evasively the result would be immediate war; but it was not acceptance of the protocol that he emphasized, but acceptance of the conditions in Shuvalov's declaration.[2]

A copy of the protocol and of the two declarations was officially left with the Porte on 6 April. The representatives of all the powers urged acceptance. As the British cabinet in the same sitting as that in which they had approved the protocol had also approved the announcement of Layard, already a well-known friend of Turkey and opponent of Russia, as ambassador at Constantinople, the Turks felt all the less reason to doubt that they could rely on English support in the last resort, while the Russians were correspondingly confirmed in their belief in British duplicity. A Turkish circular of 9 April announced the rejection of the protocol and Shuvalov's declaration. On the 10th negotiations with Montenegro were broken off by a final refusal of any extension of territory, the armistice ceasing three days later. On the 12th the Turkish circular was handed to Gorchakov.

There could be no doubt of the result, and the diplomatic fumblings in other quarters to avert a final rupture were wasted labour. The campaigning season was at hand: the press was thoroughly bellicose. Already in the first week of April almost all the foreign diplomats in touch with the Tsar were convinced

[1] Jocelyn (Constantinople) to Derby, tel., secret and conf., 7 Apr., copy in *F.O.* 181/553.

[2] Loftus to Derby, 6 Apr., recounting interview with Gorchakov that day, in *A. and P.*, 1877, xci, C. 1738, no. 518.

that war was unavoidable. Alexandf   the
English, disliked the protocol, and   the
Tsaritsa and the general atmosph   usy
explaining to all and sundry ho   v.[1]
Cherkasky was now in the   cly
appearing as imperial civil a   co-
vite nationalist circles were delig   le
forebodings of those dismal days' of iv   s
diplomatic twaddle' of the protocol. The Sla   s
were again in the forefront, and were about to   al
legal recognition.[2] Gorchakov was working on drai   r
manifesto. On 13 April this was finally approved: it w   e
issued on the 24th, and the Pruth was to be crossed on th   ie
day.[3] The Tsar on the 19th travelled south to his army ..ith
Milyutin and Ignatyev, and there, from the Grand Duke
Nicholas's head-quarters at Kishinev, issued his manifesto of
war on the appointed day.

Just after his departure from St. Petersburg unexpected news
came that Germany was sending back an ambassador to Constantinople: Prince Reuss, formerly ambassador to Russia.
Austria followed suit with Zichy. Most of the Russian press
favoured this step, believing that Reuss, a great nobleman with
imperial connexions, would be a counterweight to Layard; but
Gorchakov boiled over: 'Je le regrette profondément', he exclaimed to Schweinitz, 'et l'Empereur le regrettera aussi; vous

[1] Letter of the counsellor of the Austrian embassy to Andrássy, 5 Apr., cited in
Wertheimer, pp. 407–8.

[2] Valuev's diary, under date 6 Apr., recording a ministerial council on that day
attended by Cherkasky, *Dnevnik*, p. 9; extracts from letters of Mme Novikov, then
in Moscow, in W. T. Stead, *The M.P. for Russia*, pp. 338–9, 344; Aksakov, *Slavyansky
vopros*, pp. 258–61.

[3] The final text of the war manifesto was drawn up by Valuev, Adlerberg, and
Urusov on the basis of four drafts by Gorchakov; Valuev's diary, under date
14 Apr., *Dnevnik*, p. 10. This may explain why the emphasis of the manifesto was
on Russia's readiness to sacrifice her blood for the oppressed Orthodox in Turkey,
while no reference was made to community of Slav interests; Russian text in
Zhigarev, *Vostochny vopros*, vol. ii, pp. 166–7; French in Avril, *Négociations relatives
au traité de Berlin . . .*, p. 187; English in *A. and P.*, 1877, xcii, C. 1806, no. 156, incl.
Similarly the keynote of the Tsar's speech in Moscow (which had just promised a
gift of a million roubles) on his way back from the front was not the Slav cause, but
the old refrain of 'divine blessing on our glorious armies, setting out to fight for the
faith, the Tsar, and the fatherland': text in Meshchersky, *Moi Vospominaniya*, vol. ii,
pp. 333–4. Andrássy had telegraphed on 16 Apr. to urge that the manifesto should
not lay stress on common Slav interests; Goriainow, *Le Bosphore et les Dardanelles*,
p. 344: this ruffled Gorchakov, but does not seem to have influenced the wording
of the manifesto already decided upon three days before Andrássy's telegram.

vous mettez sur une ligne avec l'Angleterre; vous faites une position magnifique à la Turquie.' To his emperor he reported: 'plus que jamais j'arrive à la conviction que Votre Majesté ne doit compter que sur Dieu et son épée.' 'Personne n'est plus persuadé que moi' was the answer of Alexander in the midst of his troops.[1]

[1] Schweinitz, *Denkwürdigkeiten*, vol. i, pp. 416–20; Schweinitz to Bülow, 22 Apr., in *G.P.*, p. 150 note; Gorchakov's report of 22 Apr., quoted in Goriainow, *Le Bosphore et les Dardanelles* ;p. 344.

IX

THE CONVENTIONS WITH AUSTRIA-HUNGARY

THE most serious problem confronting Russia was the internal situation of the country. War accentuated its seriousness. The finances, even if Reutern's gloomy forebodings were belied, were certain to be put to the severest strain, and one bad harvest could throw the whole economic life of the country out of gear, with quite incalculable repercussions. It was only by lucky chance that the two famine years which were due did not occur until the direct strain of war was over, until 1879 and 1880. Reverses or a long-drawn-out struggle might bring a wave of revolutionary outbreaks leading to a collapse of the home front and recourse to drastic suppression, perhaps combined at one and the same time with efforts to prop up the social structure by a new series of reforms complementary to those which had followed the Crimean war in the early years of the Tsar Liberator. Many of the revolutionaries welcomed the war as the prelude to an inevitable exposure of the incompetence of the government and the military and of the hollowness of panslav nationalism, an exposure which would result in a general breakdown with revolution following in its wake. Those who were not revolutionaries feared that such hopes might be only too well justified, above all if the war dragged on or Russia found herself again facing a hostile European coalition. None could forget the spectre of 1854. Least of all could the Tsar and Gorchakov.

Their words of nettled impatience with which the previous chapter closed did less than justice to the saner judgement that had on the whole characterized their course of action during the six months preceding April 1877. Though Russia was alone in drawing the sword and did not do so as the mandatory of Europe, her isolated action was taken under circumstances far different from those of 1853 and never more favourable to herself. For eighteen months she had talked internationally: three times all the powers had agreed together as to the reforms necessary in Turkey: twice the Turks had refused them; once the Turks had accepted them—and been unable to put them into practice: were they really likely to carry out even the reforms which they themselves were advertising?

England it is true was both very suspect and very suspicious; public opinion was easily stirred by Central Asia and the menace to India; Queen Victoria was as russophobe as twenty years before; Disraeli almost as dangerous as Palmerston; Layard prepared to follow in Elliot's footsteps according to the example of Stratford de Redcliffe. But the old attitude of unquestioning support of Turkey had been seriously undermined. Not only in high places were there grave doubts as to the continuance of the Ottoman empire in its existing form; there was a large and vocal section of opinion which genuinely believed that Turkish oppression of Christians culminating in the Bulgarian atrocities was a blot on the face of Europe which must be removed. The diversity of view so dramatically represented by the clash between Disraeli and Gladstone gave reasonable hope that British armed support of the Turks, however much they intrigued for it and believed in it in the last resort, would not be forthcoming *if* Russia played her cards with the moderation which her foreign office professed.

But the key for Russian foreign policy lay in Vienna rather than in London. There Gorchakov had made his diplomatic name twenty-two years earlier, struggling to prevent the malevolent neutrality of Austria being converted into actual hostilities. Thence Alexander had received the ultimatum which had brought the Crimean war to its humiliating close. Never had the strategical advantages of the Habsburg empire been more glaringly displayed, when the Russians were forced to evacuate the Principalities at its behest and one-third of their forces were immobilized by its threat of attack. Whatever happened St. Petersburg must never allow that situation to be repeated. Mutual suspicions and conflicting interests made it impossible for Russia to go forward against Turkey in agreement with England. Therefore, if she were to move, some understanding with what was now the Dual Monarchy was all the more necessary, however much against the grain. Mutual suspicions no doubt were plentiful here too, but conflicting interests possibly less dominating. There was no question of rivalry in Asia. Rivalry in the Balkans there must be, but it might not be a cause of fatal dissension if the panslavs did not have their way. This was an essential condition.

The panslavs were a growing force, but they were still few in number, though they occupied influential positions; above all

Ignatyev. For them, and him in particular, Gorchakov had the greatest dislike. They talked an alien language (Russian in fact) and thought in terms which paid no regard to the mysteries of the European equilibrium and of nicely calculated diplomacy, on his mastery of which the ageing chancellor plumed himself so jealously. The Tsar until the autumn of 1876 looked upon the panslavs with lazy disfavour, when he looked at all. Thereafter he might waver dangerously, but, until the triumphant successes of his armies in the winter of 1877–8, he never wavered so far as to forget his belief in the necessity of securing himself against his brother emperor on the Danube, and he never wholly discarded the old banner of Orthodoxy for the new banner of Slavdom which would mean conflicting interests with Austria-Hungary of the gravest character.

Thus the official wielders of Russian policy had advanced from the renewal of friendly relations with Vienna in 1872 and 1873, through the joint action of the Andrássy note and the Berlin memorandum in 1876, to the Reichstadt agreement of July. As has been already explained, that agreement was an attempt to sketch what should happen, and what should not happen, as a result of the war which had just broken out between Turkey and Serbia and Montenegro; in the event of the Turks winning, in the event of the Turks losing, and in the event of a complete collapse of the Ottoman empire. As has also been seen, the Tsar was later prevailed upon to change his ideas as to what should happen if the Turks won, which by September they unexpectedly were on the point of doing, and he made approaches to Francis Joseph which resulted in the offer and acceptance of negotiations for a secret treaty to supplement the Reichstadt understanding in the more and more probable event of Russia acting on the claim she was now putting forward to freedom of action in the Balkans.[1]

At the beginning of November 1876 these negotiations were started, in strictest secrecy, between Gorchakov, Langenau, Novikov, and Andrássy, and dragged on throughout the winter in an atmosphere heavily charged with mutual distrust.[2] While

---

[1] For the letters exchanged between Alexander and Francis Joseph in September and October, see above, pp. 207–10.

[2] The following summary of the negotiations is based, except where otherwise stated, on *Wertheimer*, pp. 384–95, Wertheimer, 'Neues zur Orientpolitik des Grafen Andrássy (1876–1877)', in *Historische Blätter*, no. 3, 1921–2, pp. 448–63, and Goriainow, *Le Bosphore et les Dardanelles*, pp. 327–36, using respectively the

the extent of the demands of the Austro-Hungarians and their attitude to the Constantinople conference served to intensify the irritability and uncertainties of Gorchakov, on Andrássy's side the more and more pronounced hostility of the Magyars to Russia, his well-founded fears as to Ignatyev, and not least his knowledge, of which St. Petersburg was unaware, of the substance of the Werder telegram (see above, p. 210) combined to ensure the greatest caution and the most stubborn bargaining. Andrássy told his ambassador, on leave in November, that he was prepared to go to extreme limits to maintain agreement with Russia and that he would never follow the Buol policy of 1854; but there was an ominous symptom for the future in his remark 'my bark is not worse than my bite', which was not at all to the taste of Langenau, who still maintained his belief in the loyalty of the Tsar and his hatred of Bismarck. Only the extremely austrophil Novikov introduced into the discussions a spirit of unreserved collaboration.[1]

The situation as understood by Gorchakov and the course to be followed are fully set out in his instructions to Novikov of 2 November, dispatched from the Crimea in the excited mood of the ultimatum to Turkey and steps towards mobilization.[2] Francis Joseph's letter of 23 October shows that he admits common action only if the Ottoman empire collapses of itself, but also that he considers such dissolution as not far distant, and further that if the Tsar finds himself compelled to take immediate action Francis Joseph will consent to action in appearance independent, but in reality concerted. Russia cannot, Gorchakov continues,

'attendre impassible l'issue du procès de dissolution qui ne s'accomplirait probablement qu'au milieu de convulsions plus effroyables encore que celles qui ont révolté la conscience publique. L'Empereur

Austrian and the Russian archives; and on Wittrock, *Gorčakov, Ignatiev och Šuvalov*, pp. 49–54, 100–13, using the Austrian and German archives. For documents concerning the negotiations and for the texts of the conventions see Appendix II.

[1] Wertheimer, in *Historische Blätter*, no. 2, p. 269, using unpublished memorandum of Langenau. Ghikas, *Botschafter von Novikow über den Panslavismus und die orientalische Frage*, pp. 48–9, relates, without giving any dates, that Novikov clinched his arguments as to the necessity of an understanding with Austria-Hungary by reporting that Andrássy was negotiating an agreement with Turkey whereby, in case of a war of conquest by Russia, Austria and Turkey would jointly oppose her in arms. I do not know of any confirmation of this very unsatisfactory evidence.

[2] Text in *S.R.*, vol. iv, pp. 438–40, from a copy, apparently made for Andrássy's use, in the Vienna archives.

est décidé à en finir. Sa Majesté n'a plus de confiance dans la diplomatie européenne, que nous avons loyalement travaillé depuis un an à réunir dans un but d'humanité et de paix. Notre Auguste Majesté est résolu à agir seule et sans retard.'

Novikov is to work for precise engagements as to combined though independent action which would put into practice the complete solidarity of the two powers in regard to their common end. If Gorchakov really believed that agreement between him and Andrássy as to their common end was of a positive character, he was to be disabused, for Andrássy made it quite clear in the following months, not only that Austrian action would at best be only concomitant and parallel, not conjoint and combined, but also that, since Austria-Hungary desired to postpone any intervention until the continuance of Turkish rule was admitted on all sides to be impossible and since Russia was not prepared thus to wait, they could not be said to have a common positive aim but only the negative one of at all costs avoiding any collision between the two monarchies. It remained true, however, that this negative community of aim was of great importance to Russia.

Novikov's instructions further directed him to secure an engagement to maintain completely benevolent neutrality in the face of isolated action by Russia and to paralyse any attempts at intervention or collective mediation by other cabinets; an engagement which was duly accepted by Andrássy, together with an undertaking to renounce any obligations under the secret treaty of 15 April 1856 with England and France. Vienna also was to allow the use of the Lemberg–Czernowitz railway for hospital trains,[1] to allow the placing of orders for military supplies in Austria-Hungary, and to make the necessary arrangements for transport of material (but not of troops). 'Dans le cas où le Cabinet de Vienne jugerait nécessaire d'entrer en Bosnie, le moment et le mode d'y procéder dépendront de son appréciation.' But any action in Bosnia should not be given the appearance of hostility to Russia. It was indispensable that Vienna should engage not to extend her military influence to

---

[1] This represents a modification of a suggestion of Obruchev in his memorandum of 13 Oct. 1876 (see p. 217), that Austrian friendliness should be tested by asking for the use of the Lemberg–Jassy railway for the transport of war material and troops. The Warsaw–Cracow line, and certain others in Russian Poland were normal gauge: thus this Russian rolling-stock could run through direct to Roumania via Galicia.

Roumania, Serbia, Herzegovina,[1] or Montenegro, which must constitute a zone between the Austro-Hungarian and Russian armies; and Vienna was also to engage not to put any difficulties in the way of Russian military operations nor of those of the Christian provinces joining Russia against the Turks. The question of the Danube was recognized as very delicate, since Russian operations would have to involve the breaking of the international regulations: Austria-Hungary was to prevent this becoming a first-class dispute; Russia would be ready to bind herself to respect the principle of the neutrality of the Danube and to re-establish it in fact as soon as war necessities allowed.[2] The consequences of the war should be regulated by a separate engagement on the lines of Reichstadt.

Thus the negotiations were initially to be concentrated on a military convention which should guarantee Austro-Hungarian neutrality and diplomatic assistance and should delimit military spheres of action. What should follow the war was to be left for a second political convention. Gorchakov failed, however, to bind Andrássy during the war before he was assured as to Russian intentions as to the results of the war. The negotiations for the two conventions were intertwined, and Andrássy's signature of the military convention on 15 January 1877 was specifically dependent on the conclusion of the political convention to follow. Two further months of wrangling (a draft of Andrássy, alterations by Gorchakov, and a second draft of Andrássy) were necessary before the political convention was signed on 18 March, and it was then antedated to 15 January in order to show that the two conventions were to be regarded as one whole.

This long delay seems to be attributable partly to Russian procrastination and ill humour with Vienna, partly to Austrian suspicions of St. Petersburg. Already early in December Gorchakov was complaining to Novikov of Andrássy's lack of goodwill. 'Il semble perdre de vue les nuances qui séparent la neutralité bienveillante non seulement de la neutralité absolue, mais même de l'hostilité voilée sous l'apparence de la neutralité' (4 December). Six weeks later (19 January), very

---

[1] In the copy of Novikov's instructions in the Vienna archives Herzegovina is put in pencilled brackets and queried.

[2] At this point there is an Austrian note: 'Nous devrions déclarer que la Russie doit sortir de la Bulgarie.' In the conventions as finally agreed upon there was no mention of Russian evacuation of Bulgaria, although any possibility of annexation was excluded.

sore over the concessions he had been compelled to make in the military convention just signed and further disabused with Austrian conduct at the Constantinople conference, he was writing: 'Ce n'est pas d'hier que je suis arrivé à la conviction que nous ne devons compter que sur nous-mêmes, tout en conservant l'apparence de croire aux protestations qu'on nous prodigue. C'est le cas en parti à Berlin, mais surtout à Vienne.'

On that same day (19 January) Andrássy sent Gorchakov a draft for the political convention which was by no means satisfactory. No reply came from St. Petersburg till 7 February. It was now Vienna's turn for delay; and Andrássy did not dispatch counter-proposals until 28 February. By the time of their arrival the Ignatyev mission had been decided upon, and Gorchakov received them with contemptuous coolness, declaring, if Andrássy is to be believed, that the negotiations were not now of urgent importance. This would indeed have been, in Andrássy's words, 'a brainless policy', if seriously acted upon, but thanks apparently to the insistence of the Tsar instructions were sent to Novikov on 12 March to complete the negotiations, which were successfully concluded a week later.[1]

Probably Andrássy was genuinely relieved at this result. He had not only been disturbed by the sudden European tour of his adversary Ignatyev—a tour in which Vienna was the last of the capitals to be visited (25 March); he had also been alarmed in February by reports which reached him that the military convention had become known in London through Shuvalov. This would be particularly awkward since Andrássy had carefully kept Beust in ignorance of the negotiations. In addition, Andrássy believed that deliberate efforts were being made in London to discredit him in the eyes of St. Petersburg. An English blue-book had just been published in which Salisbury represented Andrássy as urging the British to combat at the Constantinople conference any Russian proposal for an occupation of Bulgaria. This led to a lengthy protestation to St. Petersburg from Andrássy denying any double dealing and the accusation of being an opponent of Russia which had been levelled at him by Buchanan, the British ambassador in Vienna

[1] Stolberg to the German foreign office, tel., 10 Mar. 1877, cited by Wittrock, *Gorčakov, Ignatiev och Šuvalov*, p. 53. Stolberg was reporting Gorchakov's remarks as retailed by Andrássy who had them from Langenau. Gauld, 'The Dreikaiserbündnis and the Eastern Question, 1877-8', in *English Historical Review*, vol. xlii, p. 561.

(Andrássy to Langenau, 22 February). In fact it appears that Andrássy was unnecessarily perturbed. It is doubtful whether Shuvalov really knew anything circumstantial of the negotiations with Vienna, and what exactly he said to Derby or to others as to the convention. In any case he would seem to have been acting by himself, and Gorchakov accepted Andrássy's explanations of the revelations in the English blue-book without demur. Yet, even though Andrássy's fears may have been exaggerated, they help to explain the delay in the conclusion of the political convention and to illuminate the difficulties of the negotiations.[1]

Once these had been seriously entered upon, it soon became evident that Gorchakov's limitation of Austrian occupation and military influence to Bosnia alone was totally unacceptable to Andrássy. This was the double point which nearly wrecked the negotiations in December. Gorchakov probably by a genuine, but inexcusable, mistake had left Reichstadt in the summer under the impression that Andrássy had agreed only to annex a portion of Bosnia and that Herzegovina should go to Montenegro, but he now found that Andrássy maintained on the contrary that what had been agreed upon was that all Bosnia and almost all Herzegovina were to go to Austria-Hungary (see pp. 174–6). He claimed these two provinces as the exclusive domain of Austrian influence and consequently the privilege of himself laying down what frontiers on that side should be granted to Serbia and Montenegro: as to Serbia he was very severe, though as to Montenegro he promised to give some satisfaction in the bordering districts of Herzegovina, without specifying details: extensions of territory for the two principalities on the side of Old Serbia and Albania were to be arranged between him and the Russians.[2]

To Novikov Bosnia was a matter of no importance: he could see nothing against some hundred thousands of Bosniaks, most of them Catholics and Mussulmans, being joined to Austria, which would treat them far better than Turkey.[3] Herzegovina

---

[1] Wittrock, *Gorčakov, Ignatiev och Šuvalov*, pp. 40–3, 101–5, deals at some length with Shuvalov's conduct in London and the English blue-book and its effect on Andrássy, and gives amongst other documents the text of his dispatch of 22 Feb., 1877, to Langenau.

[2] Novikov to Gorchakov, 5 Dec., extract in *S.R.*, vol. iv, p. 443. (In Goriainow, *Le Bosphore et les Dardanelles*, p. 331, dated 6 Dec.)

[3] Extract from letter of Novikov to Gorchakov, 2 Oct., quoted in Goriainow,

also was of small concern, and he tried to argue that its occupation by the Austrians would really be an advantage to Russia, since it would draw them into war with Turkey and thus lighten Russia's task. For him the essential was to avoid making Andrássy's position more difficult than it already was, and to avoid stimulating further the increasing russophobia of the press. But to his superior in St. Petersburg this large extension of Austrian claims, as he viewed it, was extremely distasteful, especially since the Austrians were also manœuvring to secure Russian recognition of their right to occupation as the price merely of benevolent neutrality, and not of combined intervention as Gorchakov had originally understood: while Russia bore the weight of a war, Austria would quietly sweep up her pickings. In addition, an Austrian occupation of both Bosnia and Herzegovina, whatever it might be in form, could hardly fail in reality to be permanent. Andrássy emphasized that, while it was possible for the Russians to evacuate Bulgaria after a temporary occupation had provided for the satisfactory setting up of a new order, conditions in Bosnia and Herzegovina were such that a semi-independent position was impossible and absorption sooner or later in Serbia or Montenegro was the only alternative to continued Austrian occupation. Gorchakov had to yield, and the military convention accordingly gave Austria the right to choose the moment and the mode of occupation of both Bosnia and Herzegovina, while the subsequent political convention expressly used the word annexation. All that Gorchakov could secure in return was that the occupation was not to be made to appear as the counterpart of a Russian occupation of Bulgaria or as an act of hostility towards Russia.

He had not only been forced to yield on Herzegovina; he also failed to preserve Russian freedom of action in Serbia. This had been the main object of his original idea of confining Austrian military influence to Bosnia. But Andrássy was insistent. Making the utmost of parliamentary considerations and of Magyar feeling, he demanded as an essential point in the

---

Le Bosphore et les Dardanelles, pp. 323–4. This was in the end substantially also the real view of St. Petersburg. When in Mar. 1877 two envoys from the Bosnian rebels surreptitiously appeared there, they were cold-shouldered as being agents of Ristić, and even by panslav sympathizers were bluntly told that Russia did not mean to have a new Crimean war and that Bosnia would go to Austria; Čubrilović, *Bosanski ustanak 1875–1878*, pp. 280–1, citing from the Belgrade archives the report of the envoys.

military convention (to the especial disgust of the Tsar) that
there should be a neutral zone between the Austro-Hungarian
and Russian spheres of action consisting of Serbia, Montenegro,
and Novi Bazar. Vienna was at this moment particularly
suspicious as to Russian designs in Serbia and the discussions
which preceded the Nikitin mission (see pp. 248–9). Andrássy
explained openly to Gorchakov his fears as to panslavism: if
Russia planned to combine the Slavs of Turkey and to transform
a Russo-Turkish war into a Slav revolutionary movement the
reactions on the Dual Monarchy would be fatal, and Germans
and Magyars would combine to insist on energetic action being
taken in advance by the government (aide-mémoire of 26 December). Novikov from the first had been convinced of the
impossibility of obtaining consent to any entry of Russian troops
into Serbia: the very idea alarmed him mightily. The Austrians,
he said, would have no objection to the Russians' crossing the
Pruth and the Danube, always provided that they did not
march through Serbia, or, he added, advance across the Balkans
to Adrianople.[1]

Gorchakov had no better success in his attempt to smuggle
through permission for the Russians to combat the Turks in
Serbia if after the armistice they continued to advance in Serbia
or to occupy it. He was compelled to drop this suggestion in
view of Andrássy's refusing to alter his view that any entry of
Russian troops into Serbia would be in furtherance of political
aims rather than of military operations. The military convention as signed prohibited any crossing of Russian troops into
Serbia, Novi Bazar, and Montenegro. The same prohibition
was applied to the Austrians, whose military action was also not
to extend to Roumania. As regards operations outside the
boundaries of Serbia and Montenegro the Austrians agreed not
to oppose any combined action of Serb or Montenegrin troops
with the Russians. Although Gorchakov was furious at not
being able to obtain his immediate aims in respect of Serbia, he

[1] Letters of Col. Parensov to Levitsky, deputy chief of staff to the Grand Duke
Nicholas, 27 Dec. and 6 Jan., text in *R.S.*, vol. cxxiv, pp. 605–9, 613. Parensov
was in Vienna for a few days at Christmastime to find out for G.H.Q. the intentions
of Austria, particularly in the event of Russian troops crossing into Serbia. He
knew nothing of the details of the negotiations for a convention. He described
Novikov, and Feldmann, the military attaché, as being for peace at any price, and
in Andrássy's pocket. Novikov, while assuring him that Andrássy had not the
slightest objection to the Russians entering Roumania, warned him strongly
against Roumanian intrigues.

had secured substantial advantages: the provision in respect of Roumania was vital to Russia: and the Serbian situation as it had been in December and January was radically changed by the peace of 28 February 1877 after which the Turks evacuated what they were occupying of Serbia; if subsequently the Serbs were to fight again they would start from their frontier, and co-operation with the Russians, according to the convention, would have to be allowed by the Austrians, provided that the Serbs were not driven back into their own territory.

Shortly before Christmas General Obruchev, from the Russian war office, had arrived in Vienna to assist (and doubtless to stiffen) Novikov, and on 27 December St. Petersburg approved the signature of the military convention, though subject to its own interpretation of certain verbal assurances said to have been given by Vienna. By this convention, agreement, on terms very satisfactory to the Russians, was reached on the two technical clauses in the military convention which dealt with hospital trains and provisioning arrangements and on the clause respecting the navigation of the Danube; but the chief matter which seems to have been raised by Obruchev was of far wider importance and linked on with the political convention to follow. He brought with him a map marking the changes in the western Balkans proposed by Russia, and intended to serve as an annex to the political convention, and also a memorandum describing these new frontiers. A copy of this map was left with Andrássy, who proceeded to raise much discussion as to the extension of Montenegro, but apparently made no remarks on what was intended on the map to represent the boundaries of the new Bulgaria. These boundaries were almost the same as those of the big, divided Bulgaria of the Constantinople conference. Fifteen months later Ignatyev in defending his treaty of San Stefano before Andrássy was to make the most of the Obruchev map. Montenegro was to be enlarged, not on the side of Herzegovina, but to the coast and to the east and north-east, including Ipek and a portion of Novi Bazar where her frontier would join the new Serbian frontier along the Lim.[1]

[1] For the Obruchev visit and map: *San Stefano*, pp. 340, 266; Ignatyev's memoirs, in *I.V.*, vol. cxliii, pp. 365–7; and Stolberg's dispatch to Bismarck, 1 Apr. 1878, in *G.P.*, pp. 253–4, where Obruchev is not actually mentioned by name. Parensov (see previous note) mentions that Obruchev had returned to St. Petersburg just before his arrival in Vienna on 23 Dec. Ignatyev was writing long subsequently with the express purpose of justifying his big Bulgaria, and at the time of the Obruchev

Novi Bazar had not caused difficulties at the Reichstadt meeting in the summer, when Andrássy accepted a division of it between Serbia and Montenegro, but here again the Russians were now to find his attitude stiffened. Gorchakov insisted that, if Austria-Hungary took in over a million new subjects in Bosnia and Herzegovina, it was impossible not to allow Montenegro to have the port of Antivari and a rich slice of Novi Bazar, the rest of it and old Serbia going to Serbia (aide-mémoire confidentielle for Novikov, presented to Andrássy 28 February). Andrássy at Reichstadt had appeared willing to grant Montenegro Spizza (which was a worse anchorage than Antivari), but he was now, both in Vienna and in the Constantinople conference, stubbornly opposing any Montenegrin access to the sea. On Novi Bazar he was arguing as to the necessity of Austria-Hungary's being assured of her commercial outlet through it to the Vardar valley (a harbinger of the Sarajevo–Mitrovitsa railway argument so strongly developed in 1878), and Gorchakov could not secure more than a compromise by which the question of Novi Bazar (save that it should not be annexed by Austria-Hungary) was to be settled by subsequent agreement. In respect of the other Montenegrin frontiers the political convention was still more unsatisfactory, for it contained no specific reference to any enlargement of the principality, nor indeed to that of Serbia.

On the other hand, an implication of territorial gains for the two principalities was evident in the very important third article of the political convention. This expressly reaffirmed the understanding reached at Reichstadt: 'un grand état compact slave ou autre est exclu': Bulgaria, Albania, and the rest of Rumelia might be constituted as independent states: Thessaly, Crete, and (added by Gorchakov) part of Epirus might be annexed to Greece: Constantinople, with a surrounding district to be subsequently determined, might become a free city. But in reaffirming Reichstadt the convention signed on 18 March did not exactly repeat Reichstadt. The provisions of Article III just described were stated to be envisaged as the result of territorial changes or of a dissolution of Turkey, just as the preamble (drafted by Andrássy) to the whole convention described it as 'destinée à régler d'avance les remaniements territoriaux que la

visit he was in Constantinople and was being carefully kept in ignorance of the negotiations. Obviously his evidence is very suspect, but Andrássy's admissions to Stolberg confirm the possession by Andrássy of some such map. See below, p. 451.

guerre ou la dissolution de l'Empire Ottoman pourrait avoir pour résultat'. The Reichstadt agreement, on the other hand, made the sentence as to not setting up any large Slav state (the words 'ou autre' did not appear in it) refer to the eventuality of a defeat of the Turks by the Serbs, while it mentioned Constantinople and Bulgaria, &c., a few lines lower, under the different hypothesis of Christian victories bringing about the complete collapse of the Ottoman empire.

This difference between the Reichstadt agreement and the political convention has a twofold importance, in relation to Bulgaria, and in relation to the question as to when the convention was to come into force. A strange confusion over Bulgaria seems to have prevailed during the negotiations for the conventions. The Russians began by understanding the prohibition at Reichstadt of a large Slav state as applying only (or at least primarily) to an aggrandizement of Serbia or Montenegro, and the Austrians knew this. Alexander in his letter to Francis Joseph of 23 September repudiated the idea of a large *Serbian* state (see p. 208). The ambiguities on the Russian side were also apparent in a later statement (5 December) of Gorchakov specially written for communication to the Emperor and his foreign minister.[1] After writing of the misunderstandings as regards Herzegovina, he turned to the other Turkish provinces: '*nous resterons fidèles à l'idée de ne pas y favoriser l'établissement d'un grand état compact slave ou autre.* Les différentes provinces s'y organiseraient sous l'influence de leurs mœurs et de leurs traditions, c'est à dire pratiquement.' Well and good: but there immediately followed: 'Pour ce qui regarde l'organisation qui serait donnée à la Bulgarie, M. le Comte Andrássy n'objecte pas à ce qu'elle soit aussi large que possible. Ses préoccupations se portent sur l'Herzégovine et la Bosnie, vu leur voisinage avec l'Autriche-Hongrie. Nous nous proposons d'y être aussi modérés que ce sera nécessaire pour leur assurer une existence améliorée et garantie.' Now, although the expression 'the organization to be given to Bulgaria' seems to relate primarily to the securing for a new Bulgaria of as large a measure of autonomy as possible, it can hardly have failed to be clear that the Russians linked closely together the question of autonomy and that of frontiers, for in the preliminary conference at Constantinople

[1] Text of enclosure to Gorchakov's projet de lettre particulière to Novikov of 5 Dec., in *S.R.*, vol. 4, pp. 441–2. The italics are Gorchakov's.

they were urging a large Bulgaria with a large degree of autonomy, and at the same time the Obruchev map brought to Vienna appears to have repeated this large Bulgaria. The Austro-Hungarian representatives in Constantinople were behind Salisbury in dividing the large Bulgaria longitudinally, but in the negotiations between Vienna and St. Petersburg for the conventions there seems to be a veil of silence over Bulgaria.

As a result of a Russo-Turkish war it was practically assumed that Serbia and Montenegro would become independent states: Russia agreed to undertake that they should not be so enlarged as to constitute a large Slav *state* and to hand over Bosnia and Herzegovina to Austria as the price of her benevolent neutrality. That was clear to both sides. But in the case of Bulgaria a Russo-Turkish war might lead either to the erection of a principality with a large measure of autonomy or to the creation of an independent *state* in the event of a dissolution of Turkey in Europe. The Russians appeared to be taking the line that in the former case a large, but not independent, Bulgaria was permissible: an autonomous principality would not be a large Slav *state*. But would there not be strong opposition to this line, since such an autonomous principality was undoubtedly most likely to form the nucleus for a subsequently independent *state*? Was it entirely clear from the political convention that any form of a large Bulgaria was ruled out? Until further evidence is available the best provisional conclusion is that during the winter of 1876–7 confusions, whether deliberate or not, and whether fully realized or not, between the two parties over Bulgaria were not cleared up.[1]

The second question raised by a comparison of the Reichstadt agreement with the convention of 18 March is that as to when

[1] There is no mention in Wertheimer, Goriainow, or Wittrock of the extent of Bulgaria being discussed during the negotiations, but their treatment of the negotiations is not sufficiently complete to allow of their silence being used in support of Ignatyev's subsequent statement that Andrássy raised no questions as to the boundaries of Bulgaria in connexion with the Obruchev map. Fournier, *Wie wir zu Bosnien kamen*, p. 44, mentions an Austrian map with a line drawn on it by Novikov showing that he recognized the Timok–Vardar line as the division between Austrian and Russian spheres of influence. Throughout it should be remembered that, whereas the names Serbia and Montenegro represented quite definite areas, the names Bulgaria and Rumelia did not. Since the reign of Mahmud II the old Turkish names of Boulgaristan (Bulgaria) and Roumili had been abandoned with the break-up of the *eyalets* bearing those names into *vilayets*.

the convention should be considered to be applicable. Its object, as has already been quoted from the preamble, was to provide in advance for 'les remaniements territoriaux que la guerre ou la dissolution de l'Empire Ottoman pourrait avoir pour résultat'. Gorchakov had struck out the words 'la guerre ou' in Andrássy's first draft with the object of restricting Russian consent to an occupation of Bosnia and Herzegovina, but he had been obliged ultimately to leave them in the final text. Unlike the Reichstadt agreement, the articles of the political convention did not draw any distinction between changes resulting from a war which did bring about the dissolution of Turkey and changes resulting from a war which did not. Gorchakov, at least in December 1876, argued that the Ottoman domination in Europe would not disappear as the immediate, direct consequence of a war: it would be undermined by an internal process of dissolution, and only on that supposition must the 'arrangements éventuels' of Reichstadt be discussed.[1] He had wished to conclude a military convention guaranteeing Austrian neutrality and to defer to some indefinite date the signature of a political convention, this to be effective only in the event of the dissolution of the Ottoman empire; while Andrássy had been successful in tying together the two conventions and was maintaining that the latter must hold good whatever the results of the war. As the preamble shows he again had his way, but not before this divergence of view, combined with their differences over Montenegro, had brought matters to a complete standstill. Andrássy had thus made doubly certain of freedom of action as regards Bosnia and Herzegovina; whatever happened either occupation or annexation was recognized. He had also secured that in any event no important territorial changes in the Balkans could be made by Russia without reference to Austria-Hungary. Further, Article I of the political convention expressly limited Russian annexations in Europe to the portion of Bessarabia ceded in 1856, Austrian annexations being similarly limited to Bosnia and Herzegovina; and Article II provided for mutual diplomatic support if the territorial changes resulting from a war or from the dissolution of Turkey gave rise to collective deliberations of the great powers—an article due to Gorchakov, who

---

[1] Text of enclosure (for communication to Francis Joseph and Andrássy) to Gorchakov's projet de lettre particulière to Novikov of 5 Dec., in S.R., vol. iv, p. 441.

did not foresee how great a service it was to be to the Austrians a year later. What still remained obscure and was never settled, was: what does the dissolution of Turkey mean? In Andrássy's language, the dissolution of a state is like baldness: when does baldness begin? when is it completed? A state does not collapse in a day; is its dissolution to be reckoned from the first attack upon its integrity? or from its final and complete disintegration? Andrássy feared that the Russians meant the former: he himself meant the latter. On the other hand, the Russians throughout seem to have attributed to the Austrians the desire for dissolution in the latter sense. The result was yet another series of misunderstandings to embitter mutual relations.

Finally, nothing was said as to Russian acquisitions in Asia. At Reichstadt it had been understood by both sides that Russia might annex Batum and some further territory, and by Austria that such annexations were to be in the nature of an equivalent for what was to be annexed by Austria herself. Gorchakov was anxious during the negotiations for the political convention to keep a free hand in Transcaucasia as being outside the sphere of any Austrian interests, and, in despite of warnings from Novikov against arousing suspicions that Russia intended to acquire in Anatolia more than what Austria acquired in Bosnia and Herzegovina, he removed from the draft of the convention any reference to Asiatic gains.

The conventions were to be kept secret, except from Bismarck who was informed by both parties; of the text of the military convention at the end of December 1876, of that of the political convention at the beginning of May 1877.[1] Andrássy not only never revealed their contents to the British, but when pressed by them continued to deny stoutly their very existence. Their contents were not known until 1903, and the texts were not published until 1919.

In the preceding pages much emphasis has been laid on the strained relations between St. Petersburg and Vienna engen-

---

[1] *G.P.*, note on pp. 91–2, where it is also stated that Germany exercised no influence on the course of the negotiations. On pp. 111–14 is printed the text of the draft military convention as communicated by Károlyi to Bismarck on 30 Dec. 1876: it is word for word the same as the text finally signed on 15 Jan. Andrássy, though he immediately supplied Berlin with information as to the second convention, did not communicate its final text until after some pressure: apparently he was nervous lest its terms became known to London; Wittrock, *Gorčakov, Ignatiev och Šuvalov*, p. 54. For Ignatyev's knowledge of the conventions, see below, p. 405, n.

dered in the process of negotiating the two conventions. This should not, however, obscure the essential fact: by them Russia when she opened her campaign in April 1877 was secured on the side of Austria-Hungary. Events were to shatter the basis of agreement, but they had not yet occurred.

X

THE CONVENTIONS WITH ROUMANIA

IN a war with Turkey in Europe it was a necessity for Russia to assure herself against the danger of an Austrian threat to her long line of communications through Bessarabia and Roumania. This she had done. But it was also necessary to make some arrangement with the country which barred her access to the Danube and what lay beyond. Roumania, nominally a portion of the Ottoman empire, actually an almost independent state, must be squared. Negotiations to this end had been proceeding dilatorily since November 1876. After the agreement with Austria-Hungary had been reached on the eve of war, they were concluded by the signature of two conventions on 16 April 1877.

It was clear from a military point of view that, since the crossing of the Danube by the Delta alone was impracticable and since therefore the main Russian forces would have to move through Roumania to points on the river between Silistria and Widdin, elaborate preparatory measures must be made for their transport and provisioning, as well as for the prevention of any Turkish crossing of the river, particularly at Kalafat opposite Widdin, and of any attempts to blow up the Barboshi bridge over the Sereth, which was the keystone of the Roumanian railway system. This, with the exception of the short stretch finished on the outbreak of war from Jassy to the Bessarabian frontier, was of normal gauge, and, since hardly any Russian wagons were fitted with telescopic axles, Roumanian rolling-stock would be required. There was thus more than enough staff work to be done by the Grand Duke Nicholas's headquarters, quite apart from the thorny political questions as to the international status and the attitude of Roumania if it came to war between Russia and Turkey. During the winter of 1876–7 the Principalities were filled with Russian military agents, and the Grand Duke was pressing for the immediate conclusion of detailed arrangements which would secure the passage of his troops: if the Roumanian army would collaborate in the campaign, so much the better.[1]

[1] His two principal agents, General Bobrikov and Colonel Parensov, were able and effective officers. For their memoirs see below, pp. 676 and 689. Bobrikov had been

The natural desire of the military for clear-cut engagements was not, however, shared by the foreign office in St. Petersburg. Gorchakov's general attitude towards the Roumanians was one of dilatory disdain. The legal status of Roumania provided ground both for much argument and for caution. Technically, if the Russians crossed the frontier, they would be entering Turkish territory. The districts of Bessarabia ceded by Russia in 1856 had been ceded not to Moldavia, still less to the United Principalities which at that date did not exist, but to Turkey. Subsequent agreements had transferred these districts (but not the Delta) from the direct rule of the Ottoman government to the vassal principality of Moldavia, after 1864 merged with Wallachia in the United Principalities. The Tsar was determined that no long drawn-out legal interpretations should obstruct what he regarded as the clearing of his honour. The whole of Bessarabia must again be his. Exactly how this retrocession was to be effected Gorchakov did not greatly trouble to think out in advance. If it came to force, force would decide, as against both the Turks and the Roumanians. Provided that he was secured against any Austrian hostile action, he knew that Roumania must in the last resort yield to the overwhelming strength of Russia, and he was averse from condescending to enter into confidential discussions with Bucarest or in any way to ease the task of those Roumanian politicians who were inclined to accept in advance the inevitable and to bargain for compensations to the south of the Danube. He was prepared, at first, only to allow the military situation which would arise in the event of war to be in part regularized by the signature by the military authorities of a technical convention, bereft of political implications.

This graceless policy of calculating drift was to be to some extent circumvented by Prince Charles, and by Ignatyev. In Bucarest the Russian diplomatic agent, Baron Stuart, was not the man to take a lead or to carry much weight in St. Petersburg. He had only been transferred there from the Asiatic department in July 1876, succeeding Zinoviev, whose rising star had gained him the Teheran legation. Stuart had the reputation among the

for long well acquainted with the Balkans, particularly northern Bulgaria: he had spent the previous winter in Dalmatia and Montenegro: he had made himself *persona grata* with influential Roumanians at their manœuvres in 1874, and he now established very close relations with Brătianu, the prime minister, and was on good terms with Prince Charles. For the places mentioned, see map between pp. 240 and 241.

Russian general staff officers of being a discreet, hard-working administrator: he had no belief in the Serbian venture, was pessimistic as to the outcome of the crisis at hand, and was no admirer of the Slavonic committees.[1] In this last respect he was very different from the other Russian consul-general, Jacobson at Jassy, who, with a Roumanian wife, was the centre of Russian intrigues and acted as an avowed forwarding agent for the Moscow panslavs.[2]

The outbreak of the Serbian war placed the Roumanians awkwardly between two fires. The passage of Russian volunteers, arms, ammunition, and medical supplies caused endless recriminations, culminating in an affair over an 'excursion train' crammed with 300 volunteers. The Serbs belaboured the Roumanians with accusations of acting as gendarmes for the Turks. The Russian foreign office, egged on by the Empress, persistently complained of Roumanian interference with the transit of Russian ambulance material and munitions.[3] The Turks for their part protested that Roumanian neutrality was a farce, and that no real efforts were made to prevent the plotting by Bulgarian revolutionaries of raids across the Danube. The Bulgarian émigrés, backed by the agents of the Slavonic Benevolent Committees, were redoubling their activities. In mist or darkness small groups were constantly slipping across the Danube to rouse their unfortunate homeland. Rumour even credited the Russian panslavs with a projected dash for Varna and the gift of it to Prince Charles.[4]

In fact the Roumanian neutrality was highly benevolent to

---

[1] Parensov to Levitsky, letter, 6 Jan. 1877, text in *R.S.*, vol. cxxiv, pp. 613–14; Bobrikov's memoirs, in *R.S.*, vol. cli, pp. 340–1; *Skalon*, vol. i, p. 19.

[2] Mansfield (Bucarest), no. 12, 24 Sept. 1876, in *F.O.* 78/2484; Parensov's letter, 6 Jan., ib., p. 615. Stuart had under him a first secretary whom he did not trust, but his second secretary, Zolotarev, was a tireless worker who had five years of experience of Bucarest and spoke Roumanian and Bulgarian fluently; Parensov to Levitsky, letter, 7 Jan., ib., p. 620.

[3] Mansfield (Bucarest) to Derby, nos. 4, 9, and 10, 8, 20, and 21 Sept., in *F.O.* 78/2484; reports from the Roumanian diplomatic agents in Belgrade and St. Petersburg in Iorga, *Correspondance diplomatique roumaine sous le roi Charles Ier*, nos. 314, 361, 365, 366, 385.

[4] St. John (Bucarest) to Derby, no. 97, conf., 14 Aug., in *F.O.* 78/2484. For the official Turkish protests to Bucarest against non-observance of neutrality, see the documents in Sturdza, *Charles Ier, Roi de Roumanie*, vol. ii, pp. 143 ff. *Trudy Instituta Slavyanovedeniya*, vol. ii, pp. 200–1 and 205–6, gives extracts from letters of V. S. Ionin (see above, p. 170, note 3) showing his activity in organizing the Bulgars in Bucarest and his complaints of Roumanian obstruction: the St. Petersburg Slavonic Committee, of which Ionin was the agent, protested direct to Brătianu.

the Serbs. The prince himself, though refusing commitments, in private warmly supported the Serbs and did not need Russian advice that he had better close his official eyes to much that was going on.[1] He was credited by the British diplomatic agent with desiring an ambitious forward policy, and it is probably true that, being a far-sighted and consequential man, he was working so as to place Roumania at the opportune moment side by side with Russia, to win on the field of battle independence and some offset to the inevitable loss of the Bessarabian districts. But Prince Charles never let his ambitions outrun probable chances of success. The time for action would not arise until Russia was committed to war. Meanwhile, throughout 1876 he was doing his best to bring his army up to strength and a reasonable pitch of efficiency, and here as in other matters he was finding the chambers exceedingly difficult to manage.

The five years of Conservative monopoly of power had ended in May 1876, and the ensuing elections in June resulted in the usual Roumanian manner in an overwhelming victory for the government party, this time the Liberals. The new minister of foreign affairs, Kogălniceanu, a man of 1848 and one of the most prominent of the liberal nationalists, was prompt to seize the opportunity of the Serbian declaration of war to adopt a line of aggressive hostility to the Turks. On 7 July he put forward to Constantinople far-reaching demands which included recognition of the name Roumania, the admission of the Roumanian representative to the diplomatic corps, various questions affecting the rights of Roumanian citizens, and the handing over of the Delta.[2] A month later he followed up this step by broadly hinting that public opinion might make the continuance of Roumanian neutrality impossible. Thereupon public opinion as manipulated by his political rivals in Bucarest declared that Kogălniceanu had entirely misinterpreted it. A ministerial crisis occurring at the same time resulted in Prince Charles being forced to accept Brătianu at the head of a reconstructed Liberal ministry, which, besides being extremely distasteful to him on grounds of internal policy, was originally tilted against Russia and in favour of a policy of neutrality and of reliance upon Austria and England. The Brătianu ministry

---

[1] *Aus dem Leben König Karls* . . ., vol. iii, pp. 40, 67.
[2] The text of this note to the Porte is in *Documente Oficiale, Ministeriul Afacerilor Straine* (Oct. 1876), pp. 76–88.

remained in office until April 1877, though not without various changes among the ministers and acute divergences of opinion. The consequent political instability and wavering tortuousness of policy go far to explain Russo-Roumanian relations during these months. Brătianu himself, starting with radical ideas borrowed from the Paris of the Second Republic, was little inclined towards Tsardom; but in the course of a few months he swung round towards a policy of some understanding with Russia. Ionescu, the successor of Kogălniceanu at the foreign office, made no such decisive turn and remained on the whole true to vague, anglophil ideas of resistance to Russian pressure and insistence on neutrality. In this attitude he had strong support from other members of the ministry, but not apparently from the minister of war. Prince Charles had succeeded in keeping this office in the same hands as before, those of Slaniceanu, and though there were very various opinions as to his abilities and intentions it does not seem that he obstructed either the prince's views or Russian military preparations.

At the end of September 1876 news of the Sumarokov-Elston mission to Vienna bred alarming rumours. Had there been an agreement at Reichstadt for some partition of Roumania? Was there now going to be a Russian occupation of Bulgaria, which would involve also something approaching an occupation of Roumania? Was the die about to be cast and Russia determined on coercion of the Turks? It seemed that no concessions could be extracted from the Porte; must not some effort be made to broach closer relations with the Tsar? Seizing this opportunity, Prince Charles, on 3 October, secured the dispatch of a mission to Livadia, composed of Brătianu, Slaniceanu, and two court officials. Significantly it did not include the foreign minister. It left on the 8th and was back by the 16th.

Considerable obscurity surrounds this mission to Livadia, which arrived just when the Russians were engrossed in trying to formulate their own policy.[1] At the least, however, it is clear

---

[1] For the Livadia mission: *Aus dem Leben König Karls* . . ., vol. iii, pp. 60, 62–3, under dates 3 and 16 Oct. (including interview with Brătianu on his return), 66–7 (text of letter of 22 Oct. to his father); Brătianu, *Le Problème des frontières russo-roumaines pendant la guerre de 1877–8 et au congrès de Berlin*, pp. 45–7 (recording later reminiscences of the prime minister); Adamov, 'Le problème bessarabien et les relations russo-roumaines', in *Le Monde slave*, 1928, no. 1, pp. 98–9 (quoting extract from Gorchakov's annual report, for 1876), 101 (quoting extract from dispatch of Stuart to Gorchakov, 14 Mar. 1877). Three reports of Lt.-Col. Mansfield, the British diplomatic agent in Bucarest, are of interest, and include information given by

that the Roumanians returned much impressed by the strength of Russian war feeling; that they realized that the Russians were resolved in the event of war to use Roumania as the basis of their operations, and would demand the conclusion of a military convention; and that they were met with a mixture of threats and equivocations in regard to political issues. Even if the question of Bessarabia was not directly discussed, a point which is not clear, Brătianu must have understood at least from Gorchakov's general tone that its retrocession would be required. It had been common knowledge for years that the Tsar set the greatest store on wiping out the humiliation of 1856, and it is quite certain that he was later told by Gorchakov that at Livadia Brătianu had been informed in sufficiently obvious diplomatic language that Roumania, as a result of an eventual war, would have to lose Bessarabia, though she would gain in exchange equivalent compensation elsewhere as well as independence. In any case Gorchakov's attitude at Livadia made it apparent that any attempts officially to settle these political issues in advance by a treaty would be met by very strong opposition from him. Brătianu and Slaniceanu returned with the belief that a policy of some understanding with Russia should if possible be undertaken. This, broadly speaking, meant that Brătianu was won over to Prince Charles's general outlook, though it did not mean that such a shifty and precariously placed politician would, or could, run a straight course. The anti-Russian element in the cabinet required very delicate handling.

Hence, during the month of November, Brătianu entered into negotiations at one and the same time with both the Russians and the Turks. Whether satisfactory concessions were seriously expected from the Turks is problematical. Certainly Brătianu's choice of an intermediary—Sir Henry Lakeman—could not inspire initial confidence. Lakeman, on the testimony of the British representatives both in Bucarest and in Constantinople, was an utterly unreliable, extremely egotistical adventurer of no particular ability or importance, except that he was related by marriage to Slaniceanu, the minister for war. Lakeman spun

Ionescu and D. Sturdza, but neither had been at Livadia; nos. 19, 23, conf., and 46, conf., 7 and 19 Oct. and 12 Dec., in *F.O.* 78/2484. Mansfield was a cool and resourceful man, but he had only arrived in Aug. 1876, and never penetrated behind the scenes.

enormous stories of Brătianu being prepared to put the Roumanian army, with himself in command, at the disposal of the
Porte in joint resistance to the Russians, and of the Porte being
prepared to negotiate an agreement to that effect, acknowledging in return the title of Roumania. Brătianu for his part denied
that Lakeman, who had gone from Bucarest to Constantinople
about the middle of November, had any official mission, and
maintained that he had only told him that the Roumanian
government would examine favourably the idea of an occupation of Bulgaria by a Roumanian police force if the Porte and
the powers so desired, a suggestion which was in fact raised a
month later in the preliminary discussions of the Constantinople
conference. It is unlikely that the Turks took Lakeman any too
seriously, but at the close of November they did officially send
Ali Bey, the President of the Danube Commission, to sound
Bucarest, and he appears to have offered 50,000 Turks to support the Roumanians if they would take sides against Russia.
He effected nothing, and early in December left to obtain instructions in Constantinople. Close on his heels came the prime
minister's brother, Dimitrie Brătianu, on a special mission to
pursue the negotiations and to present to the powers at the
Constantinople conference Roumanian claims to the Delta and
to a guarantee of neutrality and territorial integrity. He also
effected nothing. Any chance there may ever have been of
some Roumanian understanding with Turkey was ruined by
the proclamation of the new Turkish constitution, in which
was included reference to Roumania as one of the 'privileged
provinces' and as an integral part of the Ottoman empire.
This raised a storm of protest in Roumania and led to bitter
exchanges with Constantinople, thereby easing the path towards
an understanding with Russia.[1]

At the very time when Ali Bey was in Bucarest negotiations
had been simultaneously opened with the Russians. The initiative for these appears to have come from Ignatyev and from the
Grand Duke's staff at Kishinev. While Ignatyev was in the

[1] For Sir Henry Lakeman's and Ali Bey's negotiations; Mansfield to Derby,
nos. 36, 38, 40, and 41, conf., 24 and 27 Nov., 6 and 8 Dec., in *F.O.* 78/2484; Elliot
to Derby, nos. 1280 and 1290, conf., 1300 and 1301, 16, 17, and 22 Nov., in *F.O.*
78/2467. The text of the Roumanian memorandum presented to the Constantinople conference is in *A. and P.*, 1877, xci, C. 1641, no. 172, incl. A Roumanian
green book, *Ministeriul Afacerilor Straine; Documente Oficiale, 1878*, was later published
giving the official version of Roumanian efforts at the conference.

Crimea in October, it had been arranged that Nelidov, his counsellor of embassy, should fill the post of chief of the diplomatic chancellery of the Grand Duke Nicholas. Both Ignatyev and the Grand Duke were anxious to force Gorchakov's hand and to arrive at a settlement with the Roumanians. In consequence the former, hoping to achieve a *fait accompli* before the Constantinople conference, accredited Nelidov to negotiate and sign a military convention with Brătianu,[1] and in the middle of November Nelidov left Constantinople for Bucarest via Kishinev. On the way Nelidov received instructions from St. Petersburg to decline absolutely any political conversations and to concern himself solely with a military convention, and he was given the technical services of Colonel Prince Michael Cantacuzene, a transport expert on the Russian general staff and a member of one of the best-known Phanariot-Roumanian families.[2]

By 28 November Nelidov was in Bucarest, in strict incognito, entering upon negotiations with Brătianu alone, with elaborate precautions to preserve secrecy. It quickly became evident that Brătianu and Prince Charles would not accept Nelidov's proposal for a purely technical convention to be signed by himself and Brătianu and to be ratified by the Grand Duke Nicholas and Prince Charles: should events render an agreement necessary it must take the form of a treaty and be regarded as a political affair.[3] Difficulties were raised as to Nelidov's full powers, and the crucial question as to Bessarabia appears to have been discussed at some length between Nelidov and the prime minister. Despite the instructions from St. Petersburg, a formula was concerted, which, according to Nelidov's very much later account, without explicitly tying the hands of the Russians, could satisfy Roumanian anxieties as to territorial integrity and safeguard the position of Prince Charles and Brătianu. But the urgent representations of the Grand Duke Nicholas and Ignatyev for the prompt signature of a convention[4] were of no avail against the refusal, from different motives,

---

[1] Letter of Ignatyev to Brătianu, 17 Nov., extract in Sturdza, *Charles Ier, Roi de Roumanie*, vol. ii, p. lx.

[2] For the Nelidov mission, except as otherwise stated; Nelidov's memoirs, in *Revue des deux mondes*, 15 July 1915, vol. xxviii, pp. 244–54. These were written long subsequently from memory, and can only be used with great caution. Ignatyev's memoirs do not deal with the negotiations. They remained entirely unknown to Mansfield, the British diplomatic agent in Bucarest.

[3] *Aus dem Leben König Karls* . . ., vol. iii, pp. 77–8, under dates 28 and 29 Nov.

[4] Parensov to Levitsky, letter of 10 Jan. 1877, text in *R.S.*, vol. cxxiv, p. 622.

of Prince Charles and of Gorchakov to enter into binding commitments.

Although the main points of the military convention had been provisionally agreed upon as early as 5 December in Bucarest, Prince Charles was determined not to move too rapidly and to secure sufficiently explicit political assurances. Roumanian finances were a source of great difficulty, and the divisions among the ministry were being sharply accentuated. He therefore parried Baron Stuart's pressure for signature of the military convention by replying that the results of the Constantinople conference must be awaited. He was supported in his caution by Bismarck's advice, which he sought late in December and which was to the effect that a clash between Russia and Austria was not probable, that a treaty regulating the passage of Russian troops was preferable to the alternative of being compelled to give the Russian army *carte blanche*, but that there was no necessity for precipitate action. Hence, although in mid-January the prince considered that Turkish extremism over the constitution provided a favourable opportunity for signature, he yielded to Brătianu's arguments that more time must be given for the preparation of public opinion and allowed him to offer to sign the military convention only if certain military requirements were promptly met, including a credit of two million francs for the purchase of rifles in Paris.[1]

In St. Petersburg there was equal disinclination to hasten matters. Reutern was objecting to the stipulations in the draft convention respecting payment for provisions. Gorchakov had not yet completed his secret conventions with Austria-Hungary and seems to have deliberately left the Bucarest negotiations in the air and Stuart without instructions. He was all the less inclined to yield to Roumanian exigencies as to some form of political treaty in that he was aware of the Roumanian approaches not only to Turkey but also to Austria and England. Public announcement had been made in October of the dispatch of Ion Ghica to Vienna and London and Rosetti to Paris, for the conclusion of commercial conventions. Both were important politicians and the former was well known to be very biased

---

[1] *Aus dem Leben König Karls . . .*, vol. iii, pp. 78–81, 85–6, 91, under various dates in Dec. and 16 Jan. 1877; Parensov to Levitsky, letter, 16 Jan., text in *R.S.*, vol. cxxiv, p. 628 (for Brătianu's conditional offer to sign the military convention).

against Russia. It is therefore not surprising to find Gorchakov retailing reports (which were in fact tolerably correct) to the effect that Ghica's real object was to obtain money and munitions from England and to secure the support of the powers if Roumania resisted a Russian occupation.[1] There was actually still more to arouse Gorchakov in the relations with Austria-Hungary of the anti-Russian party in Roumania, who were hoping to prevent any agreement with Russia, to withdraw the army to Little Wallachia on the Hungarian border, and to adopt an attitude of defiant expectation in concert with the Austrians. Such a policy had even been recommended by Andrássy, according to the Roumanian diplomatic agent in Vienna; but Prince Charles, who was on a friendly footing with the former, did not hesitate to inform him uncompromisingly that his own views were diametrically opposed to any such course.[2]

Events other than Roumanian were to decide the issue. When Gorchakov had concluded his negotiations with Vienna, when the London protocol failed to achieve any result, when war was certain and a Russian entry into Roumania a matter of weeks or even days, action finally became necessary. The inevitable political crisis in Bucarest resulted, amid wild excitement and ultra-alarmist rumours, in the victory of the russophils and the return to the foreign office of Kogălniceanu. He and Stuart immediately signed, on 16 April, two conventions, the one technical and military, in substance handing over the Roumanian railways to the Russians, the other of a political character. By this second convention, which represented a signal withdrawal by Gorchakov from his original attitude, the passage of Russian troops through Roumania throughout the war was guaranteed in return for payment in gold (a final concession extracted from St. Petersburg at the last moment[3]) and for an undertaking by the Tsar 'à maintenir et à faire respecter les droits politiques de l'État roumain, tels qu'ils résultent des lois intérieures et traités existants, aussi qu'à maintenir et à défendre l'intégrité actuelle de la Roumanie'. Such was the formula

---

[1] Ignatyev's memoirs, citing a report to him from Gorchakov at the end of Oct., in *I.V.*, vol. cxxxvi, pp. 445-6; Gorchakov to Shuvalov, tel., 2 Dec., text in *S.R.*, vol. iv, p. 443.

[2] *Aus dem Leben König Karls . . .*, vol. iii, p. 81, under date 18 Dec., summarizing a report from Bălăceanu in Vienna; p. 92, text of letter to his father, 20 Jan. 1877.

[3] Ib., vol. iii, p. 116, under dates 10 and 13 Apr. 1877.

designed to safeguard Roumanian claims to Bessarabia and destined a year later to provide the bitterest controversy.[1]

At least it served the immediate purpose of assisting greatly to secure approval of the conventions by the Chamber and the Senate on 28 and 29 April; by which time the Russians were already across the Pruth, and the Grand Duke Nicholas was pressing for the active co-operation of the Roumanian army. As to this the conventions said nothing. Prince Charles was actively engaged in conversations with the Grand Duke to this end, and Brătianu was in agreement with him as to the impossibility of a merely passive attitude; but Kogălniceanu thought otherwise.[2] He appealed to the threatening attitude of Vienna and the dangers of a prompt Austrian intervention.[3] In fact he shared with most Roumanian politicians fears as to the prince utilizing war to set up some form of dictatorship. He had an additional argument for inaction in that no move could be made without a loan of five million francs, the need for which was urgently impressed on Iancu Ghica, who was sent as special envoy to Kishinev and St. Petersburg for ratification of the conventions. Ratifications were exchanged on 7 May, but the money was not easily forthcoming. Gorchakov referred Ghica to Reutern, who was very reserved. One million had already just been advanced through Baron Stuart, and Ghica could not obtain more than a loan of three millions in gold.[4] By then, the middle of May, Roumania was at war with her suzerain, the Turks having declared war on the 8th, the Roumanians follow-

---

[1] I know of no evidence on the final course of the negotiations or on Gorchakov's change of attitude in admitting political commitments. The texts of both conventions, in the original French, are printed in Sturdza, *Charles Ier, Roi de Roumanie*, vol. ii, pp. 550–8. The text of the political convention is also printed, in the original French, in Avril, *Négociations relatives au traité de Berlin* . . ., pp. 219–20.

[2] *Skalon*, vol. i, pp. 76–7 (the first personal meeting between the Grand Duke and Prince Charles, without any of his ministers, was on 14 May); *Aus dem Leben König Karls* . . ., vol. iii, pp. 141–4.

[3] Ghica to Kogălniceanu, 20 Apr. (from Kishinev), Kogălniceanu to Ghica, 22 Apr., texts in *Corespondenţa Generalului Iancu Ghica*, pp. 29, 33.

[4] Iancu Ghica, op. cit., pp. 36, 39, 54–9, 69–70 (Ghica's reports from Kishinev and St. Petersburg). Iancu Ghica is to be carefully distinguished from Ion Ghica. He was a russophil nobleman, who promptly established excellent relations with the Grand Duke Nicholas and was on very good terms with Giers, whom he had known well when Giers was diplomatic agent at Bucarest. Sent on 16 Apr. to effect ratification of the conventions, he was appointed Roumanian representative in St. Petersburg and then at the Grand Duke's and the Imperial Head-quarters. He was detained at Kishinev seeing the Grand Duke and the Tsar, and did not reach St. Petersburg until 6 May.

ing suit five days later. There was now no stopping the movement towards a complete repudiation of any links with the
Ottoman empire, and on 21 May independence was formally
proclaimed. The fate of the new state, unrecognized by any of
the powers, rested with the Russian army pouring into the
country towards the Danube, with the Grand Duke Nicholas,
the Tsar, and Gorchakov, who in the last resort would decide
the still unresolved question as to whether the new Roumania
was to seal her independence on the field of battle fighting side
by side with the Russian soldiery.

XI

PLEVNA

THE war opened with attention concentrated on the line of the Danube and the Grand Duke Nicholas's army of operations, with a total strength of nearly 190,000 men, a combatant strength of 144,000, and about 500 guns. As immediate reserve to this were available 73,000 troops and 210 guns in the Kiev district, and a further 80,000 in partially trained reserve battalions. For the defence of the Black Sea coast a force of 72,000 men and 216 guns was allotted. On the Transcaucasian frontier, where the Grand Duke Michael was in command, a striking force of 58,000 was ready, with another 60,000 of the active army mobilized. These numbers might look impressive on paper, but the essential fact was that when war was declared there were under 150,000 combatant troops for immediate action against the Turks in Europe. The Grand Duke Nicholas had not ceased to urge his insufficiency of men and material, but he was not able to secure adequate satisfaction until mid-April, when a supplementary mobilization of nine divisions and various reserve formations was ordered.[1]

Rapidity of action was the keynote of the Russian plans: to secure the line of the Danube, cross the river, drive the Turks out of northern Bulgaria, force the Balkan passes, and then sweep down for 'the full, irrevocable decision of the eastern question, the unconditional destruction of Turkish rule in the Balkan peninsula'.[2] This was the dream, though not the officially sanctioned aim, of the Russian military. Its realization required speed and decisive force. Slow-moving reinforcements thrown in piecemeal would not avail. Yet, in fact, after a few months the Russians were thrown back upon the defensive while they awaited anxiously the arrival of reinforcements which should have been made available from the outset.

By the spring of 1877 the Turks had had six months in which to push forward their counter-measures. To meet the Russian

---

[1] *Opisanie o russko-turetskoi voiny 1877–78 gg. na balkanskom poluostrove*, vol. i, pp. 254, 258; *Voenny Sbornik*, vol. cxxv, pt. 2, pp. 142, 144; *Skalon*, vol. i, pp. 52–3 (giving G.H.Q.'s figures for striking strength in mid-Apr.), 252.

[2] Memorandum of Obruchev, printed in *Hasenkampf*, appendix 4: it is on p. 462 given as dated 4 Apr. 1877: in *Skalon*, vol. i, p. 251, it is dated 13 Apr.

invasion across the Danube they had succeeded in mustering approximately equal numbers, though they were much scattered, were far less heavily gunned, and were fatally lacking in unity in command. The best estimates of the Turkish strength in Bulgaria varied between 160,000 and 180,000 men. In the western Balkans there were approximately another 100,000; in and around Constantinople perhaps 20,000; on the Caucasus frontier between 70,000 and 100,000. The reserve man-power was uncertain, but in any case far less than that of the Russians.[1] On the other hand, the Turks had the control of the Black Sea. The Russians had not pushed forward any effective building programme since 1870, whereas the Sultan had poured out money on his warships. The Russians could only operate by land, and the Danube was threatened by the Turkish monitors and gunboats. Actually, however, the Turks signally failed to utilize their sea-power. Throughout the war the most glaring weakness was their staff work, which was fantastically accentuated by intrigue and indecision in Constantinople and by personal animosities between the commanders. Another defect lay in the system (not followed by the Russians) by which the almost untrained reserves were formed into separate battalions of little worth, while the excellent formations composed of the regulars and the time-expired men were allowed to dwindle away without any incorporation in them of the new cadres.[2] Yet in technical equipment the Turks, at least in Europe, were superior to their foe. Most of their first-line infantry were armed with the new Peabody-Martini rifle, the remainder with Schneiders; and they were fully supplied with ammunition. Their field-guns were of the latest Krupp patterns, and were on the whole well served. Their pack-trains were well equipped with entrenching tools, and their soldiers were admirable diggers.

On the Russian side, the infantry had, initially, no entrenching tools, and they were still trained in their old bayonet tradition,

---

[1] The strength of the Turkish forces is impossible to determine accurately, but both the estimates of the Grand Duke's G.H.Q. and Turkish official sources agree closely as to the troops available on the outbreak of war in Bulgaria and Constantinople, but much less closely as regards the rest of Turkey in Europe; *Opisanie . . .*, vol. i, pp. 44–5 (giving both sets of figures), Skalon, vol. i, pp. 42–3 (giving another estimate of the Grand Duke's staff). See also Springer, *Der russisch-türkische Krieg 1877–78 in Europa*, p. 35, *La Guerre d'Orient en 1877–8*, pp. 59, 61 (differing widely except for the Danube army), Sarauw, *Der russisch-türkische Krieg 1877–8*, p. 22 (giving much lower estimates).

[2] Baker Pasha, *War in Bulgaria*, vol. ii, pp. 24–5, 326–33.

deliberately avoiding, in contrast with the Turks, long-distance fire. Only the Guards, and some of the troops in the Caucasus, had been rearmed with the excellent Berdan rifle; old-fashioned Krynks were still used by the rest of the infantry. Both the cavalry and artillery were armed with a variety of models, with the maximum resultant confusion in munitionment. The field-artillery was the weakest arm and was in the main composed of out-of-date models. The Russian army was still undergoing reorganization consequent upon the adoption of conscription in 1874: strengths existed, to an unusual degree, often only on paper. Its two greatest weaknesses were officially described as the absence of a reserve of officers and the extremely insufficient reserve of trained rank and file. After mobilization the officers were found to be 17,000 under strength, while in the case of the rank and file reserves there was eventually a shortage computed at no less than 550,000.[1] During the course of the campaign two other failures in organization, in the medical and in the supply services, attained such scandalous proportions that they aroused most dangerously opinion at home in Russia, which after the failures before Plevna became violently critical of the whole conduct of the war.

Neither the Grand Duke Nicholas nor the Grand Duke Michael had any real qualifications as commanders-in-chief. The latter in particular, who had been viceroy of the Caucasus since 1862, laid himself open from the first to the most damaging charges of the kind usually, and with justice, directed against Russian grand dukes. Only the abilities of the two Armenian generals, Tergukassov and Loris Melikov, and later of Obruchev, finally transformed the Caucasus theatre of war from a chaos of mismanagement into one of the most illustrious examples of the fighting qualities of the Russian soldiery. The Grand Duke Nicholas had held a series of high military posts and had some technical knowledge, but it was admittedly as the Tsar's eldest brother that he took command of the European front. He fell out continuously with the ministries of war and foreign affairs, and personally disliked both their chiefs. Being without any

[1] For the Turkish armament: *Opisanie* . . ., vol. i, pp. 33–5, 39–40; Sarauw, op. cit., pp. 20–1; Pokrovsky, *Diplomatiya i voiny v tsarskoi Rossii v xix stoletii*, p. 270. For the Russian armament, etc.: Pokrovsky, op. cit., pp. 267–9; Nikolsky, 'Osvoboditelnaya voina', in *Proslava na osvoboditelnata voina 1877–1878*, pp. 311–12; *Opisanie* . . ., vol. i, pp. 70, 81, 84, 245; Greene, *The Russian Army and its Campaigns in Turkey in 1877–1878*, pp. 52–73.

subtlety or width of mind he had an acute distaste for diplomatic considerations and could appreciate only straightforward and unambiguous decisions. He did, however, possess a certain simplicity and directness of manner which were of some value, and his good relations with Prince Charles of Roumania were undoubtedly an asset. Unfitted though he was for such command, the Grand Duke had no intention of being a mere figurehead. He had vehemently refused to have as chief of staff Milyutin's choice, Obruchev (who, whatever his faults, had at least vigour and independence), and had selected Nepokoichitsky, a routine-bound Crimean veteran, far too old for his post. The deputy chief of staff was Levitsky, formerly a professor at the War Academy, hard-working and tenacious, but with a remarkable gift for making himself unpopular. Both were of Polish origin, a fact which led to much savage comment when the fortune of war ceased to smile.

During the greater part of the war operations in Europe were seriously hampered by the presence in the field of the Tsar and a number of other grand dukes for whom suitable employment had to be found. The Tsarevich in particular had to be given the command first of a corps, then of an army, and although he acquitted himself well on what became the very critical left flank it was impossible that the fact that he was the heir apparent should not operate as a disturbing factor. Yet another royal complication was added in August when Prince Charles took the field at the head of his troops. The military disadvantages arising from the existence of two head-quarters, the grand-ducal and the imperial, were obvious. However much the Tsar might protest that he left the entire command to his brother, it was inevitable that as more and more critical situations arose they could not be met by the Grand Duke without consultation with the Tsar and his staff, and as this included Milyutin, whose views were usually sharply divergent from those of the Grand Duke's G.H.Q., such consultation almost invariably meant prolonged recriminations.

The consequences of this virtual duplication of military head-quarters were paralleled by the friction arising from the fact that the diplomatic campaign was handled in no less than four different quarters. From 2 June until 22 December the Tsar was continuously absent from St. Petersburg, at his head-quarters on the Danube, absorbed in his army. With him, besides Milyutin, was Ignatyev, all the more dangerous in that he was complaining loudly of having no adequate duties assigned to him.[1] Gorchakov had been opposed to the Tsar's isolating himself in the far south in the dangerous atmosphere of the military, but had made the best of a very awkward decision by securing leave to accompany him.[2] He was not, however, actually with the Tsar at his head-quarters: at no age was Gorchakov the man for a bivouac, even on an imperial scale. He remained in the rear, with Jomini, in Bucarest, where his enemies declared that he was entirely shelved and spent his whole time in senile courtships. A third wheel in foreign affairs was supplied by the Grand Duke's diplomatic chancellery, at the head of which was Nelidov. At first busied primarily with relations with the Roumanians and the Serbs, it was throughout hostile to Gorchakov and was later to be a deciding element. Also under the Grand Duke, and in certain respects influencing foreign relations, was Prince Cherkasky, the civil commissioner for those parts of Bulgaria which came under Russian occupation. Finally, as the fourth wheel, thirteen hundred miles away from the real centre of events there was the foreign office in St. Petersburg, reduced for all important questions to the role of a glorified post office. The task of Giers, who had been left in charge, was not exactly facilitated by the contradictory orders which he on occasion received from the Tsar through Ignatyev without the knowledge of Gorchakov.[3] All the diplomatic representatives remained in the capital. Imperial head-quarters included Werder and Bechtolsheim, the Prussian and Austrian military representatives, and (belatedly, after a serious incident) Wellesley, the British military attaché. Gaillard, his French colleague, had been with the Grand Duke since the beginning of the year.

The shortcomings of the Russian army and its leadership which have just been stressed did not at the first tell heavily. Against them must be set, on the one hand, the fighting quali-

---

[1] Ignatyev's memoirs, in *I.V.*, vol. cxxxvii, pp. 71–2. After accompanying the Tsar to Kishinev for the review and the declaration of war, Ignatyev, according to his own account, was side-tracked and retired to his family in Kiev until 20 May, when he was ordered to join the Tsar as one of his general-adjutants. He arrived at Ploeshti on 4 June. It appears that he was not in St. Petersburg during Shuvalov's visit there, 16 May–4 June.

[2] Schweinitz, *Denkwürdigkeiten*, vol. i, p. 422.

[3] Valuev, *Dnevnik*, p. 16, under date 30 Aug. 1877.

ties of the Russian soldiery together with the personal prowess
or skill of a few of the higher command, and on the other hand
the failure of the enemy, with one famous exception, either to
collaborate in a concerted plan of campaign or so to organize
and inspire their men as to make fully effective the almost
equally redoubtable qualities of the Turkish soldiery. During
the first three months of the war the Turkish forces in Europe
were so badly handled that the Russians scored a series of
successes which appeared to show the correctness of the opinion
generally held outside Russia as well as within that the war
would be brief and decisive. The Russians began by immediately securing against the Turkish river flotilla the Barboshi
railway bridge over the Sereth, and in Asia by occupying
Bayazid (30 April) and capturing Ardahan (17 May). This
hasty advance on the Caucasus front was followed by a number
of set-backs and retreat, but all eyes were riveted on the Danube,
which, after a successful feint by the Delta, was crossed in
strength in the closing days of June. While the main forces
pressed forward rapidly in northern Bulgaria, a flying column,
of not more than 16,000 sabres and bayonets, sent under Gurko
to seize the main Balkan passes, secured the Shipka (19 July),
almost cut the Orient railway, and for a few days caused a
panic in Constantinople itself. Then the tide turned. The
weakness of Gurko's detachment was quickly discovered: Suleiman Pasha, rapidly transporting far superior numbers by sea
from the Montenegrin theatre of war, drove it back beyond the
Balkans: only the Shipka pass itself remained precariously in
Russian hands. At the same time the hero of the war appeared
at the little, unknown town of Plevna. On 20 July Osman
Pasha bloodily repulsed a rashly executed Russian attack.
When, ten days later, he repeated his performance on a far more
serious scale the Russians suddenly found that they had overshot their strength: they were reduced to a desperate defensive
struggle against Suleiman's army from the Maritsa and Mehemet
Ali's based on Shumla, while they directed the main weight of
their forces without success against Plevna. Thus, down to the
last week of July, the Russians appeared to be carrying all before
them: then with a dramatic reversal of fortune the war took on
a wholly different colouring.

So, on the diplomatic stage, three months of increasingly
menacing tension gave way to a period of pause and balance

until the outcome of Plevna could be determined. The tension as would be expected was most severe between Russia and England. Andrássy was watchful and nervous, particularly as to Serbia, but he would not take anything approaching hostile action unless the Russians gave him conclusive proof that they were not going to abide by the secret conventions. He professed to trust in the Tsar's word, and he was not at all forthcoming in the dilatory negotiations which he carried on with the British during May, June, and July. Only for a moment at the end of July does he appear to have been on the point of considering a break with Russia. Internal politics in the Dual Monarchy as usual rendered difficult a clear-cut policy: the Czechs welcomed the Russian war for Slav liberation; in Zagreb there were pro-Russian demonstrations; in return the russophobia of the Magyars was becoming more and more outspoken. In Russia anti-Austrian, mainly anti-Magyar, opinion was vocal, but the invectives of the press and society were chiefly showered upon England.[1]

At the beginning of the war, as was to be expected, the general tone was one of chauvinism and over-confidence. The Moscow merchants now at last came forward with their moneybags, and the first internal loan was a striking success. 'The Muscovite dream of possessing Constantinople' seemed about to come true. But for England there would have been no war; Turkey would not have dared to flout Russia had she not felt confident of English assistance. Articles pointing at India as the Achilles' heel of England and boasting of countering English designs on the Straits by a forward move from Central Asia were typical of the stock-in-trade of the Russian press. Loftus was not alone in emphasizing the bitterness of anti-English feeling in the capital: 'Ils ne parlent de l'Angleterre que l'écume à la bouche' was Shuvalov's impression when he arrived in the middle of May.[2] A telling symptom of the unbalanced nerves which accompany the beginning of every war was the paean of enthusiasm with which was greeted a successful

---

[1] Plener, *Erinnerungen*, vol. ii, pp. 103–4; Glaise-Horstenau, *Franz Josephs Weggefährte: Das Leben des Generalstabchefs Grafen Beck*, p. 189; de Vogüé to Decazes, 10 May 1877, in *D.D.F.*, pp. 168–9. For Andrássy's attitude and the Anglo-Austrian negotiations see below, pp. 319–22. For Austrian fears in Apr. and May as to a Turkish occupation of Kladova, on the Danube, in Serbia, and thus precipitating Russo-Serbian counter-measures, see *Actenstücke*, ii, nos. 7, 8, 13, 14, 21, 22, 26, 29.

[2] Schweinitz, *Denkwürdigkeiten*, vol. i, p. 425.

action in May against the Turkish monitors on the Danube: no successes had been expected at sea, where the Turks were vastly superior, and the most extravagant hopes now ran riot: the crowning delight was the fact that the Turkish navy was a British creation and was commanded by an Englishman, Hobart Pasha. Not only at sea were there Englishmen aiding the infidel: General Sir Arnold Kemball, freed from delimiting the Serbian armistice line, was now with the Turkish army in Armenia, and Russians did not forget the part played by Fenwick Williams twenty years before in the defence of Kars. In Bulgaria Baker Pasha, previously engaged in forming a gendarmerie, and already suspect for his 'hunting expedition' on the Atrek, was infusing energy and confidence into the Turkish resistance. Russians believed that British officers were being allowed to serve in the Turkish army (Baker did hold a command from November 1877 onwards), and they were also aware that for months past the defences of Constantinople and the Straits were being studied by experts sent out from England. To cap these examples of direct British aid to the enemy they were fed on press revelations inveighing against Wellesley, the military attaché, and finally accusing him of being a spy.[1]

All these minor incidents, to which was added from July onwards intense indignation against English accusations of Russian atrocities, assisted to work up to fever-heat the inevitable anglophobia, which both reacted on and was itself intensified by the attitude adopted by the British government in the opening months of the war. Ten days before its declaration Derby had seen fit to issue a blue-book exposing the Russian persecution of the Uniates. From May onwards there was a renewal of alarmist telegrams from Simla as to Russian plans for an advance on Merv, and the India office succeeded in obtaining an official warning to St. Petersburg that such action would be met by a corresponding advance by the British.[2] It

---

[1] Wellesley, *With the Russians in Peace and War*, pp. 169–75. His reports had dwelt heavily on the unpreparedness of the Russian army and bear out his general hostility; see further, below, pp. 316–17.

[2] *F.O.* 65/990, particularly Sir Louis Mallet (India office) to Derby, 6 June, and Derby to Loftus, disp., no. 244, 13 June (the draft was initialled by Disraeli as well as by Derby). The official reply of Giers was in the usual terms, that Lomakin was engaged solely on a punitive expedition and that there were no designs on Merv; *F.O.* 65/1028. By October, Lomakin had returned to Krasnovodsk. *F.O.* 65/991 shows the continuance during the summer of British alarms over the Atrek frontier and the Kizil Arvat expedition and Russian counter-accusations of British assistance

is symptomatic of the relations between the two countries that on the very day of the declaration of war Derby paid serious attention to rumours of a possible blockade of Egypt by the Russian Mediterranean fleet and at once proceeded to warn Shuvalov emphatically of the danger of any such action; notwithstanding the fact that the foreign office had information that the little squadron which made up this fleet had received orders months before to repair to North American waters and had already arrived there.[1] The choice of such waters was explained by the dispatch to the United States of a Russian admiral to purchase and equip vessels of the *Alabama* type to act as commerce-destroyers in the event of war with England.[2]

Such news did not improve the atmosphere in London. The ministry had agreed upon a note dated 6 May which represented a compromise between the two wings in the cabinet and hedged about British neutrality in an unpleasantly conditional form. It was described publicly by Disraeli as 'the charter of our policy', 'the diapason of our diplomacy', but in reality (as Shuvalov correctly informed his government) he was already aiming at a much more decisive policy. Together with Cairns and Gathorne-Hardy, he held exaggerated fears as to rapid Russian successes and as to Gallipoli falling into Russian hands. He was opening negotiations with Vienna and offering to transport Austrian troops to Gallipoli and Constantinople in case of necessity; but he did not expect satisfactory results in that quarter, and preferred the idea of an invitation from the Porte to occupy the Dardanelles and send the fleet to Constantinople.[3]

to an envoy from the Sultan of Turkey to the Amir of Afghanistan. The Russians were additionally restive owing to the British occupation of the Khanate of Khelat. Salisbury, the secretary of state for India, continued to be unimpressed by Lytton's alarms and to be opposed to his forward policy; see especially his dispatch to Lytton, no. 68, secret, 18 Oct., in *F.O.* 65/992 (cordially approved by Derby).

[1] Derby to Loftus, disp., no. 150, conf., 24 Apr., in *F.O.* 65/961.

[2] Loftus to Derby, disp., nos. 286 and 286A, secret, 29 May, confirming and extending telegram of same date, in *F.O.* 65/966. According to Butkovsky, 'Tainstvennaya ekspeditsiya v Ameriku v 1878 g.', in *I.V.*, vol. xi, pp. 602–3, the Russian Mediterranean squadron consisted of five old ships, only one of which was armoured: Admiral Butakov, in command of it, had received orders in mid-Nov. 1876 to sail to the United States, and then in the spring of 1877 to return to Russia: in the latter half of 1876 plans were being refurbished for eventual cruiser action against English commerce, more or less on the lines worked out in 1863, when war with England seemed likely and when there was likewise a Russian squadron in American waters: see also below, pp. 472–3.

[3] *The Letters of Queen Victoria, 1862–1878*, vol. ii, pp. 529–33; *Disraeli*, pp. 1005–7,

The note of 6 May informed the Russian government that the interests of England would be affected in case of any military action threatening the Suez Canal, Egypt, the Persian Gulf, and Constantinople and the Straits, and that in such a case it might be impossible to continue a policy of abstention and neutrality.[1] This communication was handed to Shuvalov, who was about to go to St. Petersburg, whither the Tsar returned from his visit to his army on 7 May. Shuvalov was doubtless convinced that his presence at home was badly needed to counteract extremist influence and to bring home to the Tsar and Gorchakov the urgency of placating England. When he saw Derby just before leaving (11 May), he was evidently nervous that in his absence the army might be put on a war footing or the fleet sent to the Dardanelles, and he begged that no steps of a decisive character might be taken, to which Derby replied that any such action was in the highest degree improbable.[2] But, as he was to be absent for at least three weeks and Loftus as usual was more or less side-tracked, it was evident that there would be a very awkward period of delay before he brought back the Russian answer.

Shuvalov on his way saw the Emperor William and Bismarck, showed the English note to the latter, and professed to be very well satisfied with his attitude. On 16 May he reached St. Petersburg, and plunged into a fortnight's struggle for what Bismarck termed 'la petite paix'. Gorchakov, who does not seem to have wanted an unrestricted war with the military in the saddle and catastrophic results for Turkey, inclined on the whole to his side, but the current was flowing powerfully against half-measures and 'la petite paix'. Shuvalov urged unceasingly the danger of a British entry into the war and strongly pressed that the Russians should not cross the Balkans. His great hope was that peace could be attained rapidly after a few victories, a peace which would involve only autonomy for Bulgaria, a territorial extension for Montenegro, and the retrocession of Bessarabia. His great fear was that the war would drag on until it would become impossible to keep it localized. Presumably

---

1011–15; *Salisbury*, pp. 140–1 (the offer to Austria was never conveyed by Derby). As early as 18 Apr. Shuvalov reported that the government were studying the possibility of an occupation of the Dardanelles and Crete; tel., secret, 18 Apr., text in *S.R.*, vol. v, p. 416.

[1] *A. and P.*, 1877 (ii), lxxxix, C. 1770, no. 1.

[2] Derby to Loftus, disp., no. 182, conf., 11 May, in *F.O.* 65/961.

he was supported by Novikov, who arrived from Vienna on 27 May, but he was unable to tie the hands of the military tightly in advance or to obtain sufficient assurances as to Constantinople.[1]

He arrived back in London on 7 June bringing Gorchakov's reply, dated 30 May, to the British note of 6 May and confidential instructions as to the Russian war aims, the substance of which were to be communicated in a separate memorandum.[2] On the following day he gave Derby the two documents. The note was fully satisfactory in respect of the Suez Canal, Egypt, the Persian Gulf, and any threat to India, but with reference to Constantinople it stated only that, without prejudging the course and issue of the war, Russia recognized that the fate of the Turkish capital constituted a question of common interest which could only be decided by a general understanding: if the question as to whom it should belong to should arise, it could not belong to any of the great powers: as regards the Straits, that question should be decided at the conclusion of peace by common agreement ('entente générale'). Finally, Russia would not extend the war beyond the limits constituting the object of the war as announced by the Tsar—an obscure and elastic undertaking. Thus Gorchakov had carefully refrained from touching on the possibility of a temporary occupation of Constantinople. He had, in fact, in his instructions to Shuvalov expressly warned him against giving any engagements as to 'une approche éventuelle ou même une occupation temporaire de Constantinople'. In confidential explanation to Derby (8 June) Shuvalov accordingly interpreted the Russian assurances as relating only to 'une prise de possession ou une occupation permanente', and added that the Russians could not tie their hands in advance as to military operations. A temporary occupation of Constantinople

---

[1] Loftus to Derby, disp., no. 275, conf., 27 May, extending tel. of same date (for Novikov, and the visit to Bismarck), in *F.O.* 65/966; *Tatishchev*, p. 384; Goriainow, *Le Bosphore et les Dardanelles*, pp. 345–6, quoting a memorandum by Shuvalov of 22 May; Schweinitz, *Denkwürdigkeiten*, vol. i, pp. 425–7. Loftus saw Shuvalov four times while he was in St. Petersburg, but his reports indicate that Shuvalov told him almost nothing as to the discussions proceeding among the Russians: see also below, p. 314.

[2] Text of reply and of the memorandum in *A. and P.*, 1878, lxxxi, C. 1952, no. 1; text of the confidential instructions, also dated 30 May, in *S.R.*, vol. v, pp. 422–7. Shuvalov did not leave St. Petersburg until 4 June. The Tsar and Gorchakov left for the seat of war on 2 June. If 30 May represents the date when these final decisions were taken, it is not clear why Shuvalov did not hasten his return to London.

and the Straits remained as an alarming possibility. Who could say what temporary might mean?

The memorandum on the Russian peace terms raised different but equally grave issues. In communicating it Shuvalov made two conditions as to a discussion of the 'question of the possible conditions of peace, supposing the Porte to be willing to come to terms before the Russian forces have crossed the Balkans': his proposals were not to be made public without his sanction; and, if the British government declined to enter on an exchange of ideas, the terms proposed should not be communicated to the Porte. Derby accepted both conditions.[1]

The terms, which were also communicated to Austria-Hungary and Germany, comprised the following points: Bulgaria north of the Balkans was to form an autonomous, vassal principality under the guarantee of Europe, with self-government and a national militia: Turkish troops and officials were to be evacuated from it, and the fortresses were to be razed: Bulgaria south of the Balkans and the other Christian districts of Turkey were to receive full guarantees of a just administration: Serbia and Montenegro were to receive territorial enlargement to be defined with the common consent of the powers: Bosnia and Herzegovina were to receive fully satisfactory institutions, in the settlement of which Austria-Hungary was to have a preponderating voice: Serbia was to remain a vassal state: the independence of Roumania could be regulated only by general agreement: Russia was to acquire Batum and adjacent territory and the Bessarabian districts ceded in 1856 (but not the Delta): Roumania was to be compensated either by the recognition of independence or by part of the Dobrudja: if Austria-Hungary demanded compensation, Russia would not oppose her seeking it in Bosnia and part of Herzegovina. Turkey could secure these conditions provided that she accepted them before the Russians crossed the Balkans. If she refused them, Russia would carry on operations until Turkey was compelled to accept a peace, the conditions of which might be different. The Tsar desired to know whether, within the limits indicated, he could count on the neutrality of England, a neutrality which would exclude any occupation of Constantinople and the Straits by England.

[1] Derby to Loftus, disp., 8 June, in *A. and P.*, 1878, lxxxi, C. 1952, no. 2.

Herein lay the real object of the conversations: to assure the neutrality of England. Even Shuvalov did not believe that the Turks would accept these peace terms until they had been taught a sound lesson, though he did have hopes that they might learn their lesson before a crossing of the Balkans. When Derby emphasized that even if the British government were to assent to the terms proposed it did not follow that the Porte would follow suit, Shuvalov explained that the object of his government was not that the British should press for acceptance at Constantinople, but rather that the neutrality of England should be ensured 'by the evidence thus afforded of the moderation of their intended demands'.[1]

The statement of war aims did not result in softening the effect of the Russian refusal to undertake not to occupy Constantinople and the Straits in any circumstances. Reports had been arriving from Loftus in St. Petersburg which fitted in admirably with the worst constructions put on the Russian statements, and which represented Gorchakov's object as being to lure England by delay into a passive attitude until it was too late to prevent the occupation of Constantinople by Russian troops.[2] Loftus was convinced that the Russian government would demand from Turkey at the conclusion of peace free navigation of the Dardanelles by Russian warships, and that their ultimate aim was 'the subjection of Turkey to Russian domination and the reduction of the Ottoman Empire to a Russian province'. The occupation, if not the acquisition, of Constantinople would be soon effected, unless timely measures of defence were taken. England should act firmly, and if necessary alone: upon the Russians crossing the Danube she should take immediate measures for the occupation of Constantinople and the Dardanelles for defensive purposes, as being 'the surest means of coming to an understanding with Russia in regard to the future of Turkey . . . as a measure for ensuring peace and not for making war—for enabling England to have a commanding voice in the settlement of the Oriental Question'. Such

---

[1] Derby to Loftus, disp., 11 June, in *A. and P.*, loc. cit., no. 3, printed as an extract: the copy in *F.O.* 65/961 shows that nothing material was omitted.

[2] Loftus to Derby, disp., nos. 253, conf., 21 May, confirming telegram of same date, 266, most conf., and 267, secret, 23 May, received 28 May; in *F.O.* 65/966. In his disp., no. 330, very conf., 20 June, in *F.O.* 65/967, Loftus repeated these views at length. All these reports are marked as having been seen by the Queen and Disraeli.

pleas for a resolute policy could not have been read by Disraeli without the admission that for once 'the Livadian parasite' judged the situation in the same light as himself. The urgency was great: the danger-point was the crossing of the Danube, not of the Balkans.

Any lingering chance of success for Shuvalov was now removed by the capture of the Tsar by the military. Alexander had left St. Petersburg on 2 June, two days before Shuvalov's departure for London, accompanied by the Tsarevich, Gorchakov, Jomini, and Milyutin. On the 6th he arrived at the Grand Duke Nicholas's head-quarters at Ploeshti in Roumania. Ignatyev was already there, urging on the need for a rapid campaign to be pushed even to Gallipoli and Constantinople; ruling out of court any ideas of a promise not to cross the Balkans or of the subordination of military operations to diplomatic pressure from the powers.[1] The army leaders scarcely needed such incitement: at the very outset of the campaign they obviously would not be inclined to accept the imposition of any limits to their operations, and were incensed against Shuvalov and his policy of 'la petite paix'. Gorchakov in fact had omitted, presumably deliberately, to send the Grand Duke a copy of his note and instructions of 30 May. When he arrived at Ploeshti a heated struggle at once began. On the same day, 6 June, a special council was held (not attended for some reason by the Grand Duke himself) at which it was decided to withhold the delivery in London of the note and the memorandum containing the obnoxious peace conditions. But—so the version of Skalon, one of the Grand Duke's trusted subordinates, continues —Gorchakov secretly refused to move: he did not send the cancelling telegram. Four days later Skalon discovered this and reported matters to the Grand Duke. A violent scene followed between the commander-in-chief and the chancellor; and the belated telegram was dispatched (11 June). It was three days too late. On 8 June Shuvalov had made his communication to Derby. 'Horrible fellow! Horrible fellow! Pigwash! Pigwash!' was the Grand Duke's unburdening on Gorchakov in particular and diplomatists in general. The temperature at head-quarters was at the same time heightened by an inflammatory signed article by Prince Meshchersky in his paper *Grazhdanin* trouncing the Russian diplomats for taking their orders from London and

[1] Ignatyev's memoirs, in *I.V.*, vol. cxxxvii, pp. 64, 66, 68–9.

Vienna. The Tsar's comment upon it, 'quite right, though very malicious', promptly went the round of the staff.[1]

Thus encouraged, the Grand Duke refused to accept Gorchakov's *fait accompli*. The conditions must be modified: it was impossible to circumscribe the military sphere of action: the provision for an autonomous Bulgaria confined to the north of the Balkans was an absurdity; it would leave under Turkish rule precisely those Bulgars who had suffered most atrociously. The Tsar yielded. 'Mature examination' caused him to require that Bulgaria, both north and south of the Balkans, should form one vassal autonomous principality. The ambassadors in London, Vienna, and Berlin were to inform the respective governments of this change in the Tsar's conditions. Shuvalov did so on 14 June.[2] The change was tantamount to a withdrawal of the previous conditional engagement not to cross the Balkans. The Turks would never accept so enlarged a Bulgaria until reduced to the last extremity. Layard was confident that they would not agree even to the unmodified terms and that it would be dangerous to suggest them to the Porte.[3] The English russophobes were incontestably supported by this new proof of Russian prevarication. The Austrians in alarm turned a somewhat closer ear to the offers of London and warned the Russians that they would require explanations as to the creation of so large a Slav state.[4] Shuvalov and his foreign office were definitely defeated. As will be seen later, Gorchakov was able at this time to hold back the extremists only as regards the participation of Roumania and Serbia in the war.

In London the effect of the alteration in the Russian conditions was aggravated by a personal incident, insulting to the honour of England and correspondingly provoking Queen Victoria. Certain reports of her military attaché, Colonel Wellesley, owing to some leakage in London, had early in the year become known to the Russians. As they were couched in

---

[1] The above account is based solely on the diary of Skalon, vol. i, pp. 112–23, 134. I know of no source with which it can be checked, except to some extent the version given in *Nouvelle Revue*, 1880, vol. iv, pp. 500–1, which also represents the standpoint of G.H.Q., and which is erroneous in dating, and imprecise.

[2] The text is printed in *A. and P.*, 1878, lxxxi, C. 1952, no. 6.

[3] Layard to Derby, disp., no. 612, most conf., 13 June, received 22 June, extending telegram of same date; copy in *F.O.* 181/555. Derby had not telegraphed to Layard the Russian proposals until 12 June.

[4] Andrássy to Beust, tel., translation handed to Derby, 14 July, text in *S.R.*, vol. x, p. 457.

very unfavourable terms, Wellesley fell under a cloud, and by the Grand Duke's head-quarters was regarded as an arch-enemy of Russia. His name was ostentatiously omitted from the list of invitations to accompany the Tsar to Kishinev for the review on the declaration of war. This slight was angrily resented by the British government, but was for the moment smoothed over by Shuvalov and Adlerberg in St. Petersburg, who secured an invitation from the Tsar to Wellesley (30 May) to join the army of operations in the same capacity as his French colleague, Gaillard. Wellesley accordingly went to the Grand Duke's head-quarters. He arrived on 12 June, at the very moment when the Grand Duke was so incensed against English efforts to checkmate his plans. He was received with an 'arrogant and overbearing' outburst in which the Grand Duke told him that he would be treated virtually as a spy. He refused to take up his position and wrote home for instructions. The cabinet protested stiffly through Shuvalov (20 June), whereupon Gorchakov intervened and arranged that Wellesley should be attached to the imperial, not the grand ducal, head-quarters (27 June). Wellesley was quickly again on very frank terms with the Tsar personally, but the whole affair ruined his position with the Russian military and additionally embittered Anglo-Russian relations.[1]

By this last week of June they were acute enough in any case. On the night of 26/27 June the main crossing of the Danube was easily effected at Zimnitsa, and strong Russian forces advanced successfully in the face of weak resistance. July opened with a complete Russian victory seemingly near at hand. Immediately, while the Tsar was expressing his nervousness at relations with England being 'of the most delicate nature', and was complaining that his word of honour as a gentleman should be sufficient to appease 'the aggressive ideas' of Disraeli, the British government, despite much divergence of views, began active counter-measures. On 30 June the fleet was ordered to Besika Bay, outside the Dardanelles, a reply to the Russian passage of the Danube which created a sensational impression at head-

[1] Wellesley's reports, nos. 27 and 37, 25 Apr. and 1 June, from St. Petersburg, in *F.O.* 65/965 and 966; nos. 1 and 2, 12 June (rec. 20 June) and 27 June, from Bucarest, in *F.O.* 65/985; draft to Shuvalov, 20 June, initialled by Derby and marked as approved by Disraeli, Gathorne-Hardy, and the cabinet, in *F.O.* 65/986. For the opinion of Wellesley at the Grand Duke's head-quarters: *Skalon*, vol. i, pp. 123–4; *Hasenkampf*, pp. 35–6.

quarters.[1] In the middle of July, with the news of Gurko forcing the Shipka pass, the pace was forced. Queen Victoria poured forth italics on the necessity of preventing even a temporary occupation of Constantinople. On the 17th Disraeli pushed Derby into officially warning Shuvalov that in the event of a Russian occupation of Constantinople the government would be free to adopt any measures they might think fit. Shuvalov was unable to give any reassurances and had to admit that the Russians would not hear of any idea of mediation.[2]

Meanwhile Wellesley was reporting on the growing intoxication of the military party, and Layard's telegrams were becoming more and more alarmist, culminating in one of 27 July which described Constantinople as panic-stricken, the Russians as being likely to advance to Adrianople and Gallipoli, and the seizure of the Dardanelles as urgently necessary.[3] It appears even, though this was not known to the ambassador, that the Sultan had dispatched his specially trusted minister of marine, Reouf Pasha, to meet the Russians empowered, if it was impossible to stop them at Adrianople, to ask for an armistice.[4] The British cabinet on 21 July had been induced by the prime minister to decide that it would be necessary to declare war if the Russians should occupy Constantinople without arranging for immediate retirement, and on the 28th they informed Layard that they would be ready on the invitation of the Sultan to send the fleet up to Constantinople at once, and instructed him to tell the Sultan that he might rely on their friendly offices to obtain as favourable a peace as possible. Shuvalov was simultaneously warned that the fleet might be ordered to the

---

[1] Wellesley to Derby, no. 4, most conf., 3 July, reporting an interview with the Tsar on that day, and no. 5, most conf., 11 July, in *F.O.* 65/985.

[2] *Letters of Queen Victoria, 1862–1878*, vol. ii, pp. 547–9; secret and confidential memorandum of Derby to Shuvalov, 17 July, in *F.O.* 65/986 (drawn up by Derby in moderate language, and only slightly altered by the cabinet); Derby to Loftus, disp., no. 291, very conf., 21 July (reporting an interview on that day with Shuvalov), in *F.O.* 65/962, and text of tel. of Shuvalov to Gorchakov, 19 July, in *S.R.*, vol. v, p. 432.

[3] Layard to Derby, tel., 27 July, rec. same day, in *F.O.* 78/2598. For Wellesley's reports, see Appendix V.

[4] So Reouf told Ignatyev, in March 1878; Ignatyev's memoirs, in *I.V.*, vol. cxxxvii, p. 67. There is a similar account, derived from Ignatyev, in Parensov's memoirs, *Iz proshlago*, pt. 3, p. 456. Reouf had been sent up to take command on the Rumelian front, until the arrival of Suleiman from Montenegro. For the crisis in Constantinople and the Turkish changes in command, see Raschdau, *Ein sinkendes Reich*, pp. 50–4, 57–8.

Golden Horn.[1] Andrássy was almost as anxious as Disraeli: for the moment he swayed from his attitude of balancing caution and was believed to be harbouring ideas of revenge for Világos, of dictating to the Russians by armed force, of cutting Russian communications in Roumania.[2]

But 1877 was not 1878. The apprehensions of July were almost ludicrously falsified by the events of August. Already a little cloud had arisen in western Bulgaria. On 20 July Osman Pasha had won his first Plevna victory. It made at first no impression abroad, for all eyes were concentrated on Gurko and the Balkan passes. But his second victory, on 30 July, at once transformed the situation by deflecting the main Russian strength to Plevna. The Turks, discovering that Gurko's crossing of the Balkans was a mere raid, rallied, drove him back, and advanced on all sides with energy and success. The Russians were now on the defensive, while they concentrated a decisive blow on Plevna. They met instead their third, and severest, defeat at the hands of Osman on 11 and 12 September; and the whole situation of their armies south of the Danube became precarious in the extreme. Thus August and September removed effectively for the time being the fears of imminent catastrophe for the Turks with which July had closed. A relief of the international tension was the inevitable result.

In London, the transformation of the military situation effectually strengthened the negative resistance of Derby, Carnarvon, and others in the cabinet to Disraeli's forceful policy. Until December restored the critical conditions of July, the prime minister was unable to secure decisive steps to anticipate a repetition of Russian victories. In Vienna, any idea of the adoption of a vigorous line of action was abandoned, and no further progress was made with the negotiations which had been proceeding with London during the previous three months.

[1] *Disraeli*, p. 1026 (for cabinet decision of 21 July); Derby to Layard, tels., nos. 384 and 385, 28 July, drafts in *F.O.* 78/2561 marked 'settled in Cabinet'; confidential memorandum of Derby to Shuvalov, 28 July, in *F.O.* 65/986.

[2] Glaise-Horstenau, *Franz Josephs Weggefährte: Das Leben des Generalstabchefs Grafen Beck*, pp. 193–4. According to Beck, the chief of the Emperor's military chancellery, he had some difficulty in arguing Andrássy out of his bellicose ideas. There is no confirmation of this aggressive mood of Andrássy in *Wertheimer*, who speaks only of Tisza's apprehensions and of an eventual mobilization of two divisions, primarily against Serbia; vol. iii, pp. 44–6. Plener, *Erinnerungen*, vol. ii, p. 106, writes of a joint council of ministers on 31 July which approved military preparations against Serbia as a demonstration against Russia.

Passing reference has already been made to these negotiations, which must now be considered more fully, since they were known to the Russians and were a factor of some consequence in the diplomatic history of the summer of 1877.[1]

Disraeli in his ardent desire to confront the Russians with a bold stroke desired to secure concerted action with Austria-Hungary: if the Balkans were crossed, material guarantees for a satisfactory peace must be ensured by joint English and Austrian action by sea and land respectively. Derby accordingly on 19 May broached the idea of such an understanding, and a full, but leisurely, exchange of views took place during the next two months. Prospects of success were much diminished by the fact that Andrássy was regarded with much suspicion in London and that the two ambassadors concerned, Beust in London and Buchanan in Vienna, were not trusted by either party. Beust, it is important to note, knew nothing of the secret of Reichstadt or the Austro-Russian conventions, and indeed was expressly authorized by Andrássy to remove English suspicions by stating that, though certain assurances had been given, no secret understanding or engagement existed between Austria-Hungary and Russia (16 July). Buchanan was regarded as 'a hopeless case' by Disraeli, who sent to Vienna two unofficial agents, Lord Denbigh and Butler-Johnstone, to put the desired pressure upon Andrássy.

It was at once made clear by Andrássy that he was not prepared to intervene in the war unless it was absolutely certain that Russia was about to override vital Austrian interests, 'which we are determined to defend against all eventualities of the war' (29 May). He had as yet no cause to believe that Russia would not act in accordance with the secret conventions, and held firm to the central basis of his policy: 'mettre à l'abri nos intérêts sans nous exposer à la nécessité de devoir les sauvegarder les armes à la main.' He regarded England as in the last resort primarily responsible for the war, and he suspected her overtures as being designed to put him into the position of pulling English chestnuts out of the fire. On the other hand, it

[1] For the following three paragraphs: Lee, 'The Anglo-Austrian understanding of 1877', in S.R., vol. x, pp. 189–200, 449–65 (printing texts of the relative documents in the Public Record Office); Wertheimer, vol. iii, pp. 26–41 (largely based on the same material in Vienna); reports from Shuvalov in S.R., vol. v, pp. 427–34. See also the account in Seton-Watson, Disraeli, Gladstone, and the Eastern Question, pp. 198–203.

was possible that Russian victories might force the hand of the Tsar, and good relations with England would then be of decisive importance. Hence Andrássy was prepared for a confidential exchange of views provided that it led to no commitments. He kept steadily to this proviso. He refused to consider a Russian crossing of the Balkans as ground for any action against Russia. He refused to bind himself in regard to a purely temporary occupation of Constantinople, or in regard to the necessity of maintaining unchanged the existing regulations as to the Straits, though he fully admitted that any modifications should only be made by common agreement among the guaranteeing powers. He refused to admit an extension of Bulgaria to the south of the Balkans as a *casus belli*, laying the main emphasis here on the necessity of preventing a Russian occupation or protectorate of Bulgaria. Finally, he refused to do more than agree to a strictly secret declaration, setting out what consequences of the war would be regarded by each as inadmissible: only if events did in fact belie the assurances given by Russia, 'nous serions prêts à aviser, au moment donné, en commun avec le Gouvernement de la Reine, aux mesures ultérieures pour la sauvegarde matérielle et pour la défense de ceux de nos intérêts réciproques qui seraient menacés d'une atteinte' (26 July). With this very anodyne declaration the British government had to be content, and on 14 August replied with a similar statement. Thereupon, with the military situation transformed by Plevna, the negotiations ceased.

Meanwhile Shuvalov, as usual excellently informed, had been keeping Gorchakov accurately primed with the tenor, and even with much of the details, of the conversations. It was thus revealed to the Russians that Andrássy had admitted some doubts as to how far the Tsar might be able to keep his engagements, and that he had expressed no alarm at a Russian crossing of the Balkans, on the ground that the Russian military position would thereafter become increasingly difficult and that a naval demonstration by England and a military demonstration by Austria-Hungary could easily render the position untenable. On the other hand, Shuvalov does not appear to have learnt of Andrássy's important qualifications as to Bulgaria or Constantinople and the Straits. He did, however, obtain correct information of the seven points enumerated by Andrássy on 29 May as being those which Austria-Hungary could not tolerate, which figured again substantially unchanged in his final statement of 26 July. They were: the exclusive protectorate of the Balkan Christians by any one power; the definitive settlement of the results of the war without the concurrence of the guaranteeing powers; any territorial acquisitions by Russia on the right bank of the Danube; the incorporation of Roumania by Russia or a Russian protectorate over her; the establishment of a Russian or Austrian *secundogenitur* in the Balkan countries; the possession ('la prise de possession') of Constantinople by Russia; the establishment of a great Slav state to the detriment of the non-Slavs in the Balkans. It was natural that the Russians should be deeply concerned at these conversations, although Shuvalov's reports were by no means alarmist. Andrássy was careful to represent himself to the Tsar as standing out against the insidious wiles of the English, and he had revealed to them nothing as to the future of Bosnia and Herzegovina. The Tsar, in his turn, anxiously reassured the Ballplatz that he had no intention of arriving at a definitive settlement alone; that there would be no lasting occupation of Bulgaria; that no democratic régime would be introduced there; in short, that there would be no departure from the Reichstadt programme (26 July). Here for the time being matters rested. There could be no question of any such departure (save possibly in connexion with Serbia) until the defiance of Osman Pasha had been overborne.

During the critical month of July, Alexander had not been content merely to reaffirm his engagements with Vienna. He attempted also to stave off English hostility by a direct approach to London, which furnished Disraeli with the opportunity of retorting with a special warning to the Tsar himself. In the midst of the Russian advance, when head-quarters were elated at the easy capture of the Shipka pass, Ignatyev with his ingratiating duplicity had been attempting to secure the confidence of Wellesley, and he persuaded the Tsar to offer through Wellesley to entertain 'suitable' propositions of peace if made by the Sultan, though military operations would not be suspended. A telegram to this effect was dispatched by Wellesley on 20 July. It was delayed and did not reach London until 27 July, at which moment, the darkest of the whole month, it naturally made no impression.[1] But it was shortly followed by

[1] Wellesley to Derby, tel., 20 July, rec. 27 July, in *A. and P.*, 1878, lxxxi, C. 1929, no. 1.

Wellesley in person on a special mission from the Tsar. In strict secrecy from Gorchakov and Shuvalov, Wellesley was directed to repeat the Tsar's assurances as to the object of the war being 'solely the amelioration of the condition of the Christian population of Turkey', and as to the conditions of peace being still those communicated by Shuvalov in the previous month, so long as England maintained her neutrality; 'if, however, England abandons that position, matters will have entered a new phase'. The Tsar suggested that British influence should be brought to bear upon the Porte to offer suitable proposals for peace; but mediation in favour of Turkey could not be entertained. Although the Tsar committed himself to the general undertaking that 'Europe will be invited to a Conference for the final settlement of the conditions of peace', he added a new stipulation in the shape of the necessity for a temporary occupation of Bulgaria, and in regard to Constantinople he did not go farther than stating that he would not occupy it 'for the sake of military honor, but only if such a step is rendered necessary by the march of events'.[1]

Wellesley's final interview with Alexander took place on 29 July, the day before the second Plevna, and he did not reach London until 7 August, by which date the immediate occasion of his mission had been dissipated by the Russian reverses. The cabinet approved on 14 August an evasive but not unfriendly reply restating 'strict, though conditional, neutrality', which was brought to the Tsar by Wellesley, who arrived back at the imperial head-quarters on 29 August. But he brought also a very secret message from Disraeli, to which Queen Victoria alone was privy. Wellesley had represented to them that despite the recent Turkish successes the Russians were bound to win in the end, and he had agreed with the Queen that the best chance of preventing too great a weakening of the Turks and of obtaining peace was a strictly confidential warning to the Tsar himself as to '*what* we could *not* stand, viz. their going to Constantinople'. It was then arranged between the three that Wellesley was to tell the Tsar that, should 'the war be prolonged and a second campaign undertaken, the neutrality of England

[1] For this and the following paragraph: *Disraeli*, pp. 1045–7 and 1082 (informing Salisbury in December of the secret warning to the Tsar); *The Letters of Queen Victoria, 1862–1878*, vol. ii, pp. 560–7, text of cabinet memorandum of 14 Aug. in *A. and P.*, 1878, lxxxi, C. 1929, no. 4; text of Wellesley's reports in Appendix V; and his *With the Russians in peace and war*, pp. 200–1.

could not be maintained and she would take her part as a belligerent'. Such a forewarning was very unpleasant hearing. In the meantime, however, the campaign of 1877 was more than enough to occupy Alexander, and there were no immediate reactions to Wellesley's return to head-quarters. Forebodings of 1878 were swamped by the crisis on the Danube caused by the complete defeat of the third attempt to capture Plevna on 11 and 12 September.

The three Plevnas—the first an oversight, the second an error, the third a crime[1]—, besides their effects which have just been described upon relations with England and Austria-Hungary, inevitably also produced deep reactions in the Balkans and not least in Russia herself.

In the Balkans, first and foremost the pressing need of the Grand Duke Nicholas for reinforcements brought the Roumanians actively into the war in August. As was explained in the last chapter, May had seen the Grand Duke and Prince Charles anxious to arrange for the co-operation of the Roumanian army, in all 50,000 strong; but the politicians in Bucarest were divided and hesitant, and Gorchakov in St. Petersburg was most unwilling to compromise the international situation by the armed support of Roumania. In his view the military assistance of Roumania should be confined to defence of her actual territory, and for three months he was successful in combating the wider plans of the Grand Duke's head-quarters and of Ignatyev, in which task he was much assisted by the financial disputes that arose between the two countries. Iancu Ghica, the special envoy from Bucarest, found St. Petersburg in May reminiscent of another capital which he knew well. 'Que Pétersbourg', he wrote to his wife, 'ressemble à Constantinople! Même insouciance pour temps perdu, même enchevêtrement d'attributions dans les ministères, même centralisation, même indécision sur toutes choses, mêmes tâtonnements, même laisser-aller et en foi de compte, même incurie! C'est exaspérant.' Ghica was officially told by Gorchakov (21 May) that the Tsar did not desire the co-operation of Roumania, and that if she nevertheless decided on crossing the Danube she must do so at her own expense. A week later this was expanded in a note

[1] Botkin, *Pisma iz Bolgarii*, p. 213.

which Nelidov was compelled to address to the Roumanian government: Russia had no need of the assistance of the Roumanian army; all the arguments against its participation in hostilities were renewed; if it did so its plan of campaign must not obstruct the Russians; therefore it must either make no move, or act under the Grand Duke Nicholas.[1]

Gorchakov, on arrival in Bucarest in June, continued to hold firm against Prince Charles and the Grand Duke. The Roumanian troops remained guarding the left bank of the Danube even after the Russian crossing, though Prince Charles did all he could to prepare to follow suit.[2] The Roumanians were divided as to what to do, and with a large foreign army sprawling through the country and high-handed Russian officers issuing orders and counter-orders unending friction was inevitable. The main question at issue, Bessarabia, was not squarely faced. Brătianu and the few others who appear to have recognized that the loss of Bessarabia was a foregone conclusion believed that they could not defend its cession without being swept from power, and admittedly did nothing to prepare their country in advance.[3] The prince himself did not endorse his subjects' sentiments on the question, and was primarily concerned that the compensation should be fully adequate. If the Roumanians did not take an active share in the war, would there be any compensation? at any rate would it not be far less than if they did? The Russians still refused to discuss the question of Bessarabia with the Brătianu ministry, which for their part either did not dare or were unwilling to find out exactly what was intended. Gorchakov, indeed, in private converse with the prince made no concealment that Russia must have the Kilia (northern) mouth of the Danube, and Kogălniceanu, the foreign minister, returned from Vienna, which he visited at the very beginning of August, fully convinced at last that Roumania had been sacrificed at Reichstadt and that Austria would do nothing to save Bessarabia, though she would not object to the

---

[1] Letter of Iancu Ghica to his wife, 16 May, and tel., to Kogălniceanu, 21 May, in *Corespondenţa Generalului Iancu Ghica*, pp. 60, 75; *Hasenkampf*, p. 24, under date 23 May; text of note of Nelidov in *Aus dem Leben König Karls . . .*, vol. iii, pp. 167–9, under date 29 May.

[2] *Aus dem Leben König Karls . . .*, vol. iii, pp. 178–9 (recording interview with Gorchakov on 14 June), p. 194.

[3] Cf. the later admission of Brătianu during the congress of Berlin, in Bobrikov's memoirs, in *R.S.*, vol. cli, p. 338.

compensation being as large as possible in the Dobrudja.[1] But there still was no effectual broaching of the problem. Nelidov privately believed that the Roumanians did not want to annex the Dobrudja (as distinct from the Delta), since it was in population entirely Bulgarian or Turkish, and that they were casting eyes on the triangle formed by the Danube, the Lom, and the Serbian frontier, which contained a few Roumanians and in particular the important fortress of Widdin. From a Russian standpoint this would have important advantages: Russia had already declared that she had no intention of annexing the Delta; it would have to be given to Roumania, for the gift of it to Bulgaria would arouse the powers too seriously since the Russian and Bulgarian frontiers would in that case be contiguous; but if Roumania were compensated for Bessarabia by the Delta and the Widdin district and Bulgaria received the Dobrudja, then the two frontiers would be brought as close to each other as was practicable.[2]

The calculations of Russians and Roumanians alike depended on defeat of the Turks. They were rudely upset by Osman Pasha. On the day after his second victory Prince Charles was asked by the Grand Duke for immediate assistance against Plevna. Urgent action was imperative. Delay might not merely imperil disastrously future relations with Russia; the war itself might be fought out on the northern side of the Danube. On the part of the prince there was no hesitation; his ministers tried to negotiate and to extract another treaty from the Russians; he himself wanted to insist only on certain personal and military conditions. But once they were met, his carefully nursed army took the field. The prince was to be in command of all the troops, Russian and Roumanian alike, investing Plevna, under the Grand Duke Nicholas as commander-in-chief and with a Russian general as his chief of staff. By the end of August 35,000 Roumanians were across the Danube facing Plevna. They were an invaluable reinforcement and were to acquit themselves well in a furious baptism of fire. In recompense for their aid, so pressingly sought, in recompense

---

[1] *Aus dem Leben König Karls* . . . , vol. iii, pp. 178, 195, 218; *Corespondenţa Generalului Iancu Ghica*, p. 177; Brătianu, *Le Problème des frontières russo-roumaines* . . . , pp. 19–20.

[2] Letter of Nelidov to Ignatyev, 27 May, text in *I.V.*, vol. cxxxvii, pp. 65–6; memorandum of Jomini, 17 June, summarized in *Hasenkampf*, p. 38. See also below, pp. 402, 410, for Bulgaria and the Dobrudja.

for their blood, so gallantly shed, would not Prince Charles have the strongest claims when the final outcome of the war was reached? But the precise nature of the recompense was left unspecified by any new engagement.[1]

The results of Plevna on Russian relations with the Serbs were important, though not decisive. Here again there were serious divergences between Gorchakov and general head-quarters. The essential fact was that only Gorchakov and Novikov, in Vienna, knew the precise stipulations in the secret conventions with Austria-Hungary which prohibited any entry of Russian troops into Serbia, though not co-operation between Serbs and Russians outside Serbia. The Grand Duke Nicholas and his diplomatic adviser, Nelidov, while they were aware in general that the attitude of Vienna required cautious handling of affairs at Belgrade, knew only that some agreement with Austria-Hungary had been reached. The former in particular was so distrustful of St. Petersburg diplomacy that he tended to regard policy towards Serbia solely as a military question which should be decided by his head-quarters. This attitude found support from Ignatyev, who urged the Grand Duke to take independent action and present the foreign office with *faits accomplis*. General head-quarters considered that action on the part of the Serbs could only be useful if taken in fullest co-opera-tion with the Russian armies, which virtually meant a Russian-directed campaign after the crossing of the Danube. At the same time, however, they realized that the situation in Serbia was difficult and that another war was, at any rate from a technical point of view, very risky.[2]

The internal condition of Serbia was indeed so unstable that she could only wait upon events and waver between Vienna and St. Petersburg. Relations with the latter were additionally prejudiced by the entanglements of Kartsov, the Russian consul-general, in internal intrigues, which were perhaps in part deliberately due to Prince Milan's desire to compromise him effectually and thus secure his recall, in which aim he was successful in the course of the summer.[3] Once hostilities had

---

[1] For the organization and condition of the Roumanian army and its entry into the war see Rosetti, 'Roumania's share in the war of 1877', in *S.R.*, vol. viii, pp. 551–9.

[2] Correspondence between Nelidov and Ignatyev, May, in *I.V.*, vol. cxxxvii, pp. 60–5; Bobrikov's memoirs, in *R.S.*, vol. clii, p. 252.

[3] Kartsov, *Za kulisami diplomatii*, pp. 52–3; *Skalon*, vol. ii, p. 23.

begun, Serbia could not under all circumstances passively await
the outcome, especially since the Montenegrins, their armistice
denounced, had again taken the field. She could not, even if
she had wished, immediately follow suit; her army was still
entirely disorganized, and she had no money. Vienna was
pressing her to suspend arming; Buda Pesth was talking of an
occupation of Belgrade if she moved.[1] St. Petersburg, as usual,
spoke with two voices.

In the middle of April there arrived in the Serbian capital
the notorious austrophobe panslav, General Fadeyev—on a
'travel tour' to Zagreb! While the Russian foreign office denied
any knowledge of how he had slipped out of Russia and while
the Serbian professed to turn a deaf ear, rumours buzzed in
Belgrade of his preparing pontoons for a Russian crossing of the
Danube into Serbia, of his numerous interviews with Prince
Milan and the government, of his plotting with the leaders of
the foreign legion. Fadeyev was probably acting merely as a
self-appointed agent without the connivance either of the Grand
Duke Nicholas or of the foreign office, but he inevitably aroused
Serbian suspicions or hopes, as in 1876, that the final arbiter of
Russian policy was Muscovite panslavism.[2]

The official spokesmen of that policy declared that the Serbs
must take no definite action until the Russians had crossed the
Danube, when they would be informed further as to Russian
wishes, and that they must avoid any provocation, but at the
same time should take defensive measures on their own account.[3]
Yet simultaneously the Tsar was said to have told Catardzhi,
the Serbian representative at Kishinev, that Serbia would sign
her death-warrant if she remained inactive throughout the war,
and the Grand Duke dispatched Prince Imeretinsky, one of the
most prominent and most capable of his staff officers, to Bel-

[1] D.D.F., vol. ii, pp. 169, 184.

[2] Letter of Giers to Kartsov, 6 May, extract in Za kulisami diplomatii, p. 54; St.
John (Belgrade) to Derby, 16 Apr., in A. and P., 1877, xcii, C. 1806, no. 126, and
disp., no. 48, 21 Apr., copy in F.O. 181/553; Wrede (Belgrade) to Andrássy, disp.,
1 May, in Actenstücke, ii, no. 26. Fadeyev was in Belgrade again in Aug., offering
his services to the Serbian army and meeting with emphatic refusal; text of letter of
Ristić to Hristić, 28 Aug., in Pisma Iovana Ristića Filipu Hristiću, p. 251; cf. Hasenkampf,
p. 95; Skalon, vol. i, p. 276.

[3] Georgewitsch, Die serbische Frage, pp. 50–1, citing the Tsar to Prince Milan,
1 May, and Gorchakov to Kartsov, 8 May; Nelidov to Ignatyev, letter, 9 May,
text in I.V., vol. cxxxvii, p. 60; Aus dem Leben König Karls ... , vol. iii, p. 156, under
date 15 May.

grade to discuss the financial assistance which the Serbs claimed had already been pledged by Ignatyev.[1] In an attempt to clear up the situation and to obtain money Prince Milan decided on a personal visit to the Russian head-quarters, in company with Ristić.

They arrived at Ploeshti, where the imperial and grand ducal head-quarters then were, on 16 June, and left for Serbia on the 22nd. Gorchakov had attempted to prevent the visit, and it proved obviously embarrassing.[2] The Serbs failed in their principal object, a subsidy; and they were no more successful in extracting a clear statement of Russian policy. The military had little faith in the possibility of any rapid, effectual assistance from the Serbian army and were not prepared to fling good money into Prince Milan's coffers without effective guarantees that it would be suitably expended and that the eventual Serbian campaign should be controlled by them. They were greatly handicapped by not having any reliable agent in Serbia, so that their information as to the situation there was very defective.

Consequently, although the military did their usual best to counteract Gorchakov, they had no specific alternative proposals with which to confront the fluctuating Tsar. Gorchakov insisted to Prince Milan and Ristić that Serbia must confine herself to defence, and did not reveal to them that the agreement with Vienna allowed of offensive Serbian co-operation with the Russians. He argued that a Serbian offensive following this visit and the Russian crossing of the Danube would arouse so violent a feeling in Austria-Hungary as to render Andrássy's position impossible. For the present Prince Milan was told to hold his hand: at a later date Serbian co-operation might be useful, or even necessary; if it became so, he would receive special instructions, after Gorchakov had communicated with Vienna. This aroused the ire of the Grand Duke, who expostulated at length, but without substantial success. No agreement was reached on the essential question of a subsidy, and the Tsar plainly told Prince Milan that money would be given only after he had begun hostilities so that no accusations of inciting Serbia might be made by Vienna. Thus to a considerable extent Gorchakov had prevailed.[3]

---

[1] Text of letter of Nelidov to Ignatyev, 9 May, in *I.V.*, vol. cxxxvii, p. 60.

[2] *Aus dem Leben König Karls* . . . , vol. iii, pp. 180, 183; *Skalon*, vol. i, pp. 126–7.

[3] Summary of memorandum of 17 June by Jomini for Gorchakov, in *Hasenkampf*, pp. 37–8; *Skalon*, vol. i, pp. 130, 132–3, 288; Bobrikov's memoirs, in *R.S.*, vol. clii, p. 252.

On the other hand, some personal remarks of the Tsar led the Serbs to believe that, once the Danube had been crossed, they could go to war if they wished and need not in that case fear an attack from Austria-Hungary. On the whole they received the impression that the Tsar, the Grand Duke, and Ignatyev desired their entry into the war, after the Danube had been crossed.[1] They returned home with no very clear line of action emerging from the divergent counsels of the Russians. Vienna was given mollifying versions of the effect of the visit, but feeling was running dangerously high in the Serbian parliament,[2] and the government had already avowed openly that if the war were to lead to wider results than the mere carrying out of the programme of the Constantinople conference they would be unable to remain as spectators without compensation: thus the neutrality of Serbia could only be regarded as precarious.[3] In any case, a Russian subsidy for the purchase of equipment and munitions remained the essential prerequisite for action.

The Plevna defeats decided this issue. A diversion by the Serbs might now prove invaluable. Already after the first Plevna a million roubles were to be promptly forthcoming. But the promise was accompanied by the demand of the Tsar, backed by Ignatyev, that Serbia should enter the war within twelve days; if she did not, she would be ruined and her national future compromised for ever.[4] Any such immediate action was quite out of the question, and the demand, if it were not meant merely as a threatening spur to military preparations, only showed how nervous the Tsar was and how grossly he misjudged conditions in Serbia. But there was some appreciation of these at the Grand Duke's head-quarters, where long discussions took place as to whether Serbia was not too ill prepared to do anything but provide yet another victory for the Turks.[5] Again the absence of any effective Russian representative in Belgrade was acutely felt. To remedy this, Prince Tseretelev was sent late in August on a brief mission, with the first half of the million roubles. Tseretelev was a bad choice, since he was a champion

[1] Ristić, *Diplomatska istorija Srbije* . . ., vol. ii, pp. 38–43.

[2] Seton-Watson, *Disraeli, Gladstone, and the Eastern Question*, p. 230, citing the Vienna archives.

[3] Wrede to Andrássy, disp., extract, 21 May, in *Actenstücke*, ii, no. 43.

[4] Ristić, op. cit., vol. ii, pp. 60–3, quoting reports from Catardzhi, the Serbian representative at Russian head-quarters.

[5] *Skalon*, vol. i, p. 213; *Hasenkampf*, p. 95.

of the big Bulgaria, and he bitterly antagonized the much divided Ristić government. He returned with the gloomiest verdict on the Serbs: the one bright spot, according to his reports, was the peasantry, who were eager to fight.[1]

Tseretelev was followed early in September by Bobrikov, an efficient general-staff officer who was sympathetic to the Serbs and remained with them until the following May as the Grand Duke Nicholas's official representative. He was to see whether the Serbs could not rapidly come into action and divert Turkish troops from the relief of Plevna, but at the same time he was to avoid any commitments in case of a Serbian disaster. His written instructions, a masterpiece of hedging ambiguity, show clearly enough how urgently the Russians desired that something, if only the concentration of troops on the frontier, should be done by the Serbs to draw off Turkish reinforcements. Bobrikov found, however, that conditions in Serbia made any immediate action still impossible. All that was feasible was the gradual concentration during the next three months of troops on the frontier. To the pressure of the Grand Duke the Serbian government replied with requests for more money, which were in part met, and for satisfactory assurances of financial assistance during the war, which were not at first forthcoming. They did not comply with the final demand of the Russians that their army should cross the frontier within ten days until Plevna was on the point of falling and the Russian star again was bright-shining. Plevna had put a premium both on Serbian assistance and on Serbian delay. What was for Roumania a danger to her own soil, to be met by joining the Russians in arms, was for Serbia an additional warning that she must enter the war only when success was certain.[2]

For Greece—the third of the Balkan states whose reactions to Plevna must be traced—the Russian reverses were equally important. The outbreak of the war, while it accentuated Greek fears of Ignatyev and the panslavs, at the same time gravely complicated Greek calculations. The war, at first, seemed almost certain to result in sweeping territorial changes in the

[1] White to Derby, 27 Aug., in *A. and P.*, 1878, lxxxi, C. 1905, no. 310; Ristić, *Diplomatska istorija Srbije*, vol. ii, pp. 64–6 (dating Tseretelev's mission a month too early); *Hasenkampf*, pp. 118, 471 (recording later Serbian accusations against Tseretelev); Bobrikov's memoirs, in *R.S.*, vol. clii, p. 505.

[2] Bobrikov's memoirs, in *R.S.*, vol. clii, pp. 252–5, 506, 509, 514–15; Ristić, op. cit., vol. ii, pp. 67–73; Jovanović, *Vlada Milana Obrenovića*, vol. i, pp. 385–7

Balkans: in that case Greece must not go empty-handed, and
she had better keep in close relations with a victorious Russia,
despite the latter's espousal of extreme Bulgarian claims. Active
participation in hostilities, or perhaps only active support of
insurrections among the Greeks still under direct Turkish rule,
might give a solid backing to Greek claims. On the other hand,
Greece had no navy and no money; Turkey had the one,
England had both. The conservative government in England
could be counted upon to support Turkey up to a point, but up
to what point was uncertain. They were sure to oppose to
the utmost panslav designs in the Balkan peninsula and thus
might lend some support to Greek irredentist demands. If a
liberal government displaced Disraeli's, they were likely to
favour Greece strongly against the Turks, if not against the
Bulgars. The Greeks were roughly divided between two parties:
the one in power, under Deligeorges, the democrat leader,
believed that more was to be gained by working closely with
England; the other under Coumoundouros believed that an
active policy of intervention in concert with Russia would be
more profitable. The King aimed at maintaining neutrality,
while pushing on military preparations so as to be ready if
necessary for action.

Russian policy as usual was hesitant. Saburov, at the Russian
legation, was exerting all his energies in fomenting rebellions in
Epirus and Thessaly and in attempting to secure the entry of
Greece into the war. His foreign office confined itself to approval of the former policy, but refused to give the undertakings
required if Greece were to be persuaded to effect a diversion
against the Turks by a declaration of war. These undertakings
were naturally some form of guarantee that Greece would
acquire an extension of territory. Soundings made by Coumoundouros in the winter of 1876–7 failed to produce anything
but oracular and nebulous answers. At the same time English
opposition successfully quashed attempts to float a loan. Later
on, in April, in the heat of the final break with Turkey, Gorchakov so far unburdened himself as to telegraph to Saburov:
'Toute diversion en faveur de nos troupes serait actuellement
désirable. Préférerions arriver à démembrement définitif de
Turquie. Armes seront déposées à Corfou pour Epire et Thessalie. Conseillez prudence envers Garibaldiens.' But in a second
telegram on the same day (17 April) he went back upon this

avowal of the object of the war about to be declared: 'Prendre engagements formels avec Grèce serait prématuré; c'est à elle à choisir d'abord le rôle qu'elle veut remplir lors de notre rupture très prochaine avec Porte pour amélioration du sort des chrétiens. Nous ne nous opposons pas à annexion.'[1]

In the following three months the Russians, flushed with success, felt no need for Greek co-operation, while on the other hand the Greeks became increasingly nervous of the consequences of a final decision reached without their participation. In June Tricoupis, the minister for foreign affairs, met with a rebuff from Derby when he tried to secure his backing for Greek territorial claims: Derby's reply spoke only of administrative reforms in the Greek provinces of Turkey. This disillusionment, together with suspicions that the British intended to seize Crete, contributed towards a turn in favour of Russia, and in June and July conversations were carried on with Saburov in Athens and Giers in St. Petersburg with a view to an alliance. But Saburov was unable to give satisfactory engagements to Tricoupis, who was making unacceptable claims to part of Macedonia: Giers was not in a position to speak with authority, and put off the Greek minister in St. Petersburg with evasive encouragement: while, in the third place, protracted negotiations for the loan of Russian warships from the Baltic proved fruitless, and there was no getting round the difficulty of the lack of a Greek fleet.[2]

From the end of July the situation was reversed, with the Russians now anxious for Greek aid and the Greeks correspondingly cautious in committing themselves. The first defeat before Plevna (20 July) resulted in general head-quarters opening communications with Athens for the unloosing of insurrections in Turkey, and then in general head-quarters directly appealing to Saburov for an immediate diversion by the Greeks. Saburov was only too ready to urge the Greek government to move, and Gorchakov was prepared to authorize him to conclude an alliance. Tricoupis, wearied of Giers's indefiniteness, insisted on obtaining from Gorchakov himself clear assurances

[1] Driault and Lhéritier, *Histoire diplomatique de la Grèce de 1821 à nos jours*, vol. iii, pp. 403–4, 410–11, citing telegrams to and from Saburov; and p. 415, text of Gorchakov to Saburov, tels., 17 Apr.

[2] Driault and Lhéritier, op. cit., pp. 416, 421–2, using the Greek foreign office archives and Saburov's reports; Lascaris, *La Politique extérieure de la Grèce avant et après le congrès de Berlin*, pp. 63, 85–7, using the Greek foreign office archives.

that the legitimate claims of Hellenism would be met by the eventual peace. Gorchakov, however, would not, in August, go farther than a formal repetition of previous informal Russian protestations that, in the event of territorial changes in Turkey in Europe, Russia would not oppose a Greek annexation of Epirus and Thessaly. But after the third Plevna (12 September) he did offer actual Russian support for such acquisitions, if the Greeks took action. The negotiations for an alliance which the Russians now pushed forward failed to achieve any success. The Greek army was not ready for taking the field immediately, which was the prime requisite in Russian eyes, and the Russian defeats had greatly increased the force of all the arguments weighing with the Greeks against intervention. Hence Plevna resulted in King George and his government swinging back from St. Petersburg to London and Vienna. By the end of September they stated that they intended to remain at peace, though the British failed to secure any formal engagements to this effect.[1]

While such were the effects of the three Plevna reverses on Russian relations with Roumania, Serbia, and Greece, their effects on Russia herself were immediate and far-reaching. From the mood of exaggerated confidence a plunge was made into the extremes of pessimism and hostile criticism. The seriousness of the situation at the front was apparent from the decision to call up the first ban of the militia and to mobilize the Guard corps and four other divisions and move them across the Danube. Not even in the Crimean war had the Guards gone to the front. During August the wildest rumours of a complete *débâcle* and the capture of the Grand Duke by the Turks were afloat in St. Petersburg. A free vent was given to the hitherto pent-up mutterings against 'the Grand Dukes' war'. There was a chorus of panslav attacks upon the army leadership—delivered into the hands of Poles and Germans. Aksakov expounded apocalyptically that the reason for failure lay in Russia's having been untrue to her own national spirit, and called for an *union sacrée* of the Orthodox against the Moslem, and against the West, more particularly England and that 'monstrous political compound of German-Jewish culture and Magyar-Bazi-Bazouk

[1] Driault and Lhéritier, op. cit., pp. 423, 433-5, citing telegrams to and from Saburov; Lascaris, op. cit., pp. 87-8, using the Greek foreign office archives; Avril, *Négociations relatives au traité de Berlin* . . ., pp. 241-7.

savagery which goes by the name of Austria-Hungary'.[1] The reaction against the panslavs themselves for having dragged the
Tsar into war was equally strong. The trickle of news from the
Danube had swelled into a stream of revelations as the weeks
went by and more and more wounded found their way back to
Russia. Intense indignation especially was aroused by the complete break-down of the medical service and by the scandalous
inefficiency of the commissariat department, which had been
handed over to the speculations of Günzberg and Polyakov,
an unsavoury pair of contractor-financiers.[2]

At the front, the disastrous third attempt to storm Plevna
was almost followed by a retirement behind the Danube. The
Grand Duke Nicholas despaired of any other course; but
Levitsky, his deputy chief of staff, supported by Milyutin, energetically combated retreat, and urged the blockade or siege of
Plevna. To this the Tsar agreed. More troops were mobilized,
and the all-important decision was taken to summon Totleben
to the front. He had been left behind fretting in inaction in St.
Petersburg. Now, with all his prestige as the engineer hero of
Sevastopol, he in effect took command against Plevna; pronounced decisively for blockade as against a retreat, a siege, or
an attempt at storm; and for the next two months stubbornly
refused to be swayed from his starving out of Osman.[3]

So during the late summer days, the autumn fogs, and the
first frosts of winter, while Radetsky clung on to the Balkans,
imperturbably playing cards, laconically reporting 'All quiet
on the Shipka front'; while the Tsarevich battled against the
efforts of Mehemet Ali and Suleiman to roll up the Russian left
wing; Osman Pasha, against his better judgement pinned to
Plevna, watched starvation edging nearer, waited for the
thudding of relieving guns, and Russia watched the casualty

---

[1] Speech of 8 Oct. to the Moscow Slavonic Benevolent Society, text in Aksakov,
Slavyansky vopros, pp. 266–80. According to Eckardt, *Russia before and after the war*,
p. 320, Aksakov had also been publicly urging the convocation of a species of
national assembly to supervise the conduct of the government.

[2] Pobedonostsev's letters to the Tsarevich during Sept., Oct., and Nov. give a
good picture of the nervousness and depression of St. Petersburg and of the violence
of the attacks, even from very conservative official circles, upon the Grand Dukes
(especially Nicholas Nicholaevich and Michael Nicholaevich), Levitsky, Cherkasky,
and the medical and supply services; texts in *Pisma Pobedonostseva k Aleksandru III*,
vol. i, pp. 69–101.

[3] *Tatishchev*, pp. 402–4, using the records of the war councils of 13 and 27 Sept.,
at the latter of which Totleben was present.

lists mounting, waited for victory—or a break-down on the home front.

During that autumn of tense gloom, when the Guards were hissed as they marched through Odessa, when the rouble touched its lowest point, when even the Russian press had to admit that scarcely one-third of the new external loan was taken up, when risings in Daghestan seemed likely to set fire to the Caucasus, on all sides the prophecy was heard that whatever the issue of the struggle beyond the Danube the real crisis would be at home. In Kiev, Odessa, and other southern towns revolutionary circles were multiplying their activities, which culminated in an outbreak in September and a serious peasant rising ('the Chigirinskoe affair'). In St. Petersburg the trial of the 193 before the Senate, the largest and most famous of the crop of state trials of the *narodniki*, which began on 30 October and dragged on until the end of January, inflamed the public most dangerously. Liberal opinion lived in hopes that the rottenness of the whole system was such that a change for the better must come: the government itself would be forced, if only through financial necessity, to make concessions leading to some form of constitution, some limitation of autocracy through an elected assembly: how could the Tsar stand forth as the giver of freedom to the Bulgars and not give with it a constitution? how could he then refuse to resume his role of the Tsar Liberator in Russia itself? Calculating politicians thought that the immense strain of the war would necessitate sops to the people; it was time to be getting ready drafts for a constitution. A strong reactionary, and opponent of the panslavs, such as Trepov, the chief of police in St. Petersburg, took it for granted that the finish of the war would bring loud demands for a constitution, 'and', he added bitterly, 'the Tsar will grant it too'. The Chief of the Third Section was even more pessimistic: if another campaign were necessary in 1878, it would be accompanied by revolution at home.[1]

[1] Letter of Pobedonostsev to the Tsarevich, 22 Oct. (inveighing against the decision to start the trial of the 193), text in *Pisma Pobedonostseva k Aleksandru III*, vol. i, pp. 84–7, cf. p. 47; letter of A. I. Livanov (a St. Petersburg liberal student, on trial with the 193) to his mother, 19 Dec., text in *Krasny arkhiv*, vol. v, pp. 141–2; Polovtsov's diary, under date 28 Sept. (recording conversation with Valuev), in *Krasny arkhiv*, vol. xxxiii, p. 175; private letter of Langenau to Andrássy, 10 Oct. (recording conversation with Trepov), cited in Wittrock, *Gorčakov, Ignatiev och Šuvalov*, p. 64; Bechtolsheim to Andrássy, 16 Aug. (recording Mezentsov's views), quoted in *Wertheimer*, vol. iii, p. 9. Away in London, Marx wrote jubilantly: 'This

The fact that for some the silver lining of defeat was hope of a new era at home, whilst for others defeat was even welcome as the harbinger of revolution, showed that once more the strain of war had laid bare the sapping of the foundations of Romanov bureaucratic absolutism. Either the Tsar Liberator would have to move forward again, impelled by the conflicting forces of the nihilists and social revolutionaries, of the *zemstva* liberals, and of the conservative constitutionalists among the panslavs, or he would have to rely on nakedly reactionary militarism. But for the time being the Tsar himself could only be immersed in the fate of his armies. Tied to the Danube, he could not leave until military honour had been re-established.

By now this was the immediate object of the war. All ideas of the freeing of the Bulgars had perforce for the time being faded into the background. In any case, first-hand acquaintance with the Bulgars had cured the Russian troops of any enthusiasm for shedding their blood to emancipate Bulgaria. The Russians had been fed with stories as to their Orthodox brothers, harried or massacred by the Turks, awaiting with despairing eagerness the day when they would greet triumphally the victorious legions of the Tsar and rise like one man to free their country. In sober fact they found themselves in a foreign land among a close-fisted peasantry who, in most cases, seemed to show little spontaneous joy at their 'liberation'. The most striking impression made upon the Russians was that, whereas they had expected to find but the remnants of a persecuted, miserable people, the Bulgars on the whole seemed to be materially far better off than the average Russian peasant. Since the Russians were only in northern Bulgaria, they saw

crisis is a *new turning point* in European history. . . . The gallant Turks have hastened the explosion by years with the thrashing they have inflicted, not only upon the Russian army and finances, but in a highly personal and individual manner on the *dynasty commanding* the army. . . . The upheaval will begin *secundum artem* with some playing at constitutionalism and then there will be a fine row. . . . All sections of Russian society are in complete disintegration economically, morally, and intellectually. This time the revolution will begin in the East, hitherto the unbroken bulwark and reserve army of counter-revolution.' His chief anxiety was lest the Poles should try to rise before there was a conflagration in St. Petersburg and Moscow, and thus cause the intervention of Bismarck and the rallying of Russian chauvinists to the Tsar. Letter to Sorge, 27 Sept. 1877, text in *Karl Marx and Friedrich Engels: Correspondence, 1846–1895* (London, 1934), pp. 348–9. The correspondence between Marx and Engels in the *Gesamtausgabe*, dritte Abteilung, Bd. 4 (Berlin, 1931), is mainly of interest for Engels's military criticisms. There are no letters between 25 Aug. 1877 and 17 Sept. 1878.

few traces of the much-bruited massacres. When finally they swept forward victoriously, it was the Turks not the Bulgars who were the corpses and the starving fugitives. Nor did the Bulgars flock in arms to join their liberators. At the beginning a Bulgarian legion had been formed, mainly of émigrés, with Russian officers, which grew to a strength of 7,000. Detachments of it fought, and massacred, fiercely in Gurko's July raid and on the Shipka, but the Russian authorities treated it so badly that recruiting soon dwindled away to nothing.

It is easy to understand the unhappy position of the Bulgars, placed as usual now in the frying-pan now in the fire. Bitter experience in the past had taught some of them the value of Russian words. The loud-sounding proclamation of the Tsar to the Bulgars in June, with its hopes held out of the widest possible extension of Bulgaria, with its promises of some measure of local self-government in the occupied areas, with its assurance of the fraternal beneficence of the Russian army, sounded hollow when Gurko, living on the country, first swept forward and then abandoned the Bulgarian villages to the tender mercy of the Turks; when Cherkasky, as civil administrator, soon quarrelled with the few Bulgars he had deigned to appoint and enforced an alien military régime; hollower still when in the autumn the Russians were struggling even to maintain themselves on the right bank of the Danube. Few occupying armies commend themselves to the occupied: none when the period of occupation is likely to prove fluctuating. If the Russians disliked the Bulgars, the Bulgars equally disliked the Russians. Yet, when all allowances have been made on the dark side, the Bulgars knew that in the last resort only through the Russians could their freedom be won; Alexander was to them the Tsar Liberator: and there were bonds of a kind between the two peoples which in the years to come were never wholly effaced either by the twists and turns of politicians and diplomatists or by the overbearingness of governing generals.[1]

[1] For the Russian attitude to the Bulgars: Botkin, *Pisma iz Bolgarii*, pp. 90, 98, 353–4; Vereshchagin, *Na voine*, pp. 75, 121–7, 131; *Hasenkampf*, pp. 54–5. Cf. the similar views of foreigners: Sayn-Wittgenstein, *Souvenirs et Correspondance*, vol. ii, pp. 503–4; Liegnitz, *Aus drei Kriegen*, pp. 135, 230, 248, 274; Wellesley to Derby, nos. 22 and 27, 29 Oct. and 24 Nov., in *F.O.* 65/985; Vice-Consul Sankey (Constanza), in *A. and P.*, 1878, lxxxi, C. 2089, no. 33, incl.; Forbes, *Czar and Sultan*, pp. 332–5, 389; Wentworth Huyshe, *The Liberation of Bulgaria*, pp. 145–9. For the Bulgarian volunteer legion: Ivanov's memoirs, in *R.S.*, vol. lxii, pp. 144–8, 157–8;

Meanwhile, Plevna held the key to the hopes and fears alike of Bulgars, of Russians, and of Turks. Far away on the other front the great eastern stronghold of the Ottomans fell for the third time in fifty years before Russian audacity and courage: on 16 November Kars was taken by assault. For all this heartening news, it was plain enough that the real issue lay by the Danube. It could not be delayed much longer. The Turkish commanders in the field and at Constantinople, virulently at odds and constantly changing, had squandered their opportunities: Suleiman sacrificed his finest battalions in frontal assaults on the Shipka pass, and refused to combine with Mehemet Ali in a massed offensive on the Russian left flank; Mehemet Ali would only attack indeterminately on the Lom; Constantinople ordered Osman to hold on to Plevna, and devised no concentration to keep open his communications with Sofia. The investment was made complete: the scales were tipping in Totleben's favour. Finally, one last effort of Osman to hew a way out; and then, on 10 December, surrender. The Tsar handed him back his sword.

Just as the defeats before Plevna with unimagined suddenness changed the whole course of the war for four months, so now its capture with equally dramatic rapidity ushered in the final stage of the war, which, within another four months, was to lead the Russians to the gates of Constantinople, to the brink of armed rupture with Great Britain and Austria-Hungary, and at the last to the long conference-table in Berlin.

Proslava na osvoboditelnata voina 1877–1878 g., p. 323. The text of the Tsar's proclamation to the Bulgars, which was the work of Cherkasky, is printed, in a French translation, in *A. and P.*, 1878, lxxxi, C. 1905, no. 31, incl. For Cherkasky's administration: Ovsyany's defence in his *Russkoe upravlenie v Bolgarii*, vol. i; Anuchin's defence in *Vestnik Evropy*, 1893, vol. v, and *R.S.*, vol. lix; Ivanov's attack in *R.S.*, vols. lxii and lxvi; Dabizh's attack in *R.S.*, vol. lvii: see also *Iz Arkhivata na Naiden Gerov*, vol. i, pp. 160–1, 166, 719–23 (letter from a Bulgarian patriot inveighing against the graft and inefficiency of his compatriots), vol. ii, pp. 834, 925–8; and two disillusioned letters of the conservative, Odessa Bulgarian leader N. Kh. Palauzov to Aksakov, in N. Barsov, *Tridtsatilyetie dyeyatelnosti Odesskago Bolgarskago Nastoyatelstva (s 1854–1884 g.)*, pp. 58–68. See also the very frank defence of the Bulgars against Russian accusations by Nemirovich-Danchenko in his *God voiny*, vol. ii, pp. 247–64, 335–7.

XII

ADRIANOPLE

THE fall of Plevna produced everywhere the impression that the war was virtually over and that the Turks would promptly sue for peace. But at the Russian head-quarters opinions were sharply divided as to what exactly should be the next step. The Grand Duke and his chief of staff, backed by the impetuous Gurko and partially supported by Obruchev (recently back from the Caucasian front), urged an immediate crossing of the Balkans and an advance to Sofia and the Maritsa valley. Most of the military experts regarded such a campaign as too risky and advised its deferment till the spring. The Grand Duke, however, won the day with the Tsar, and on 12 December the decision was taken which within six weeks was to result in the Cossack advance guards being almost within sight of Constantinople itself.[1]

At the same time discussions were taking place as to what should now be the Russian terms of peace. That they would no longer be the same as those stated in June to the English was taken for granted. As November drew to a close, the Grand Duke's diplomatic chancellery had been busy drafting the preliminary terms. Nelidov brought his proposals to the Tsar's head-quarters at Poradim, then to Gorchakov at Bucarest. On 9 December they were approved by the Tsar, with only two alterations of substance. Three days earlier, Ignatyev, who had been on nominal sick-leave in semi-disgrace since October, had arrived back at Poradim, urging that no binding obligations towards the powers should be entered into; acting as usual as a powerful stimulant to extremist action.[2]

The bases of peace drawn up by Nelidov included the following main points:[3]

1. Bulgaria, within the limits of Bulgarian nationality and in no case smaller than those agreed upon at the Constanti-

---

[1] *Tatishchev*, p. 413; *Skalon*, vol. ii, pp. 31, 40, 114; Wellesley, *With the Russians in Peace and War*, p. 270; for Gurko see especially Puzyrevsky, 'Vospominaniya o voiny 1877–8 gg', in *Voenny Sbornik*, vol. cxxvi, pt. 1, pp. 230–70.

[2] *Hasenkampf*, under date 25 Nov., pp. 181–2; Nelidov's memoirs in *I.V.*, vol. xci, p. 67; Ignatyev's memoirs in *I.V.*, vol. cxxxvii, p. 74.

[3] *Tatishchev*, pp. 425–6, citing Milyutin's diary for 9 Dec.

nople conference, was to form one autonomous principality, paying tribute, but with a national militia and with
exclusion of Turkish troops.

2. There was to be a Russian occupation of Bulgaria for two
   years.

3. Serbia and Montenegro were to be recognized as independent states and to receive territorial acquisitions: likewise
   Roumania, which was to obtain the Dobrudja.

4. Bosnia and Herzegovina were to have an autonomous
   administration with adequate guarantees in which Austria-
   Hungary should have a special position.

5. Similar reforms were to be introduced into the other Christian provinces of Turkey.

6. Turkey was to pay a war indemnity.

7. Turkey was to cede to Russia the southern districts of
   Bessarabia, and in Asia Kars, Bayazid, Ardahan, and
   Batum.

8. There was to be a revision of the provisions as to the
   Straits, by which the warships of all other powers should
   be prohibited from passing through them, while the warships of Black Sea powers might pass one at a time.

Two alterations, each of them greatly widening the scope of
possible Russian combinations, were made in these terms at the
instance of Ignatyev. Instead of a statement of the Russian (and
Roumanian) acquisitions, the Porte was to undertake to compensate Russia for the sacrifices entailed by the war in money or
territorial cessions. Secondly, point eight was altered so that the
Sultan was to enter into an agreement with the Tsar whereby
the rights and interests of Russia as regards the Straits were
protected. At the end of December three further changes were
made: point two was omitted: the expression 'frontier rectifications' instead of 'territorial acquisitions' was used in regard to
Serbia: and the reference to Austria-Hungary in point four was
omitted.[1] Otherwise, these bases of peace drawn up at the time
of the fall of Plevna were the same as those presented to the
Turks two months later after the fall of Adrianople. The bewil-
dering successes of the Russians in January did not cause any
stiffening of the terms. But, as Gorchakov expressed it, they

[1] Ignatyev's memoirs, in *I.V.*, vol. cxxxvii, pp. 76–7; Goriainow, *Le Bosphore et
les Dardanelles*, pp. 355–6.

had been carefully framed so as to be 'assez vagues, mais assez élastiques pour contenir toutes nos conditions ultérieures'; and they took the slenderest account of obligations towards Austria-Hungary.

Gorchakov, side-tracked in Bucarest, does not seem to have raised any special opposition to these bases of peace, which had been concerted with the minimum of participation on his part; but the treatment of the question of the Straits can hardly have met with his approval, as he showed by his efforts during the ensuing three months to secure the abandonment of point eight. Gorchakov recognized the necessity of some kind of agreement being reached among the powers as regards questions arising out of the war which were of general interest, but the initial difficulty was the decision as to what were such questions, and he had a hard task to extract from the Tsar unqualified agreement that the problem of the Straits was so reserved. 'Le principe posé par nous,' Gorchakov wrote at the end of the month, 'd'une délibération et d'une sanction collective pour les questions touchant aux intérêts généraux, reste intact. Il nous serait impossible de préciser, dès à présent, la nature de ces questions ni le mode de leur discussion.' As will be recounted shortly, it was another three weeks before Gorchakov could begin to win back any of the ground gained by Nelidov and Ignatyev at Poradim and could bind Russia to an abandonment of any separate arrangement in regard to the Straits.[1]

At the beginning of December it was not the terms of peace themselves but the method of negotiation which caused the main difficulties, and here Ignatyev did not, for the time being, secure a victory. In the first place, he, and Obruchev, urged without success the necessity of not being lured into armistice negotiations until the Dardanelles and the Bosphorus had been reached. The imperial council held on 12 December merely decided that an armistice should not be granted until the bases of peace were accepted.[2] In the second place, Ignatyev pro-

[1] Gorchakov to Shuvalov, letter, very secret, 31 Dec., text in *S.R.*, vol. vi, p. 432. The Tsar appears to have believed that the question of the Straits could be settled between Russia and Turkey without affecting the principle, which he accepted, of the powers agreeing together as to the stipulations affecting general interests; Gorchakov to Shuvalov, letter, very secret, 2 Dec., in which he includes the text of the Tsar's ideas as to peace: these were very similar to those of Nelidov, with whom he had just been conferring; text in *S.R.*, vol. vi, pp. 427–8.

[2] Ignatyev's memoirs, in *I.V.*, vol. cxxxvii, p. 75; *Tatishchev*, p. 426, citing Milyutin's diary for 12 Dec. (for Obruchev); Nelidov's memoirs, in *I.V.*, vol. xci,

posed that he himself should be in control of the negotiation of preliminary peace conditions and that for this end, after the armistice and bases of peace had been accepted, he should be sent to Constantinople; and he linked up this proposal with the idea of meeting the danger of European intervention in the peace negotiations by a renewal of the Constantinople confer- ence, in which, with the victorious Russian armies at his back, he would be a virtual dictator. The Tsar, however, refused to commit himself, taking refuge in the argument that Gor- chakov, who would not be able to travel to Constantinople, could not thus be displaced. Ignatyev then suggested Odessa or Sevastopol as the meeting-place, whereby he would still gain one of his primary objects—the removal of negotiations from the influence of the Grand Duke's head-quarters, of which he was extremely distrustful. But the only definite decision reached (12 Dec.) was that it should be the Grand Duke who should conclude the negotiation of the armistice and of the bases of peace, the terms of which in their final form together with full powers would be sent later from St. Petersburg.[1]

Now at last the Tsar was free to make a homecoming to his capital in triumph. On the 22nd he was back on the Neva; to be greeted with inevitable jubilations, but also with the rever- berations of the trial of the 193, and with mutterings of a European storm. Much to Ignatyev's indignation, the proposed bases of peace had been at once communicated to the two emperors, and also to Shuvalov in London, where the atmo- sphere was so stormy that he did not dare divulge them.[2]

The news of the fall of Plevna had brought the struggle in the British cabinet to a head. Disraeli during the autumn had been unavailingly prodding Derby towards mediation or even eventual intervention. Now he was induced at least to repeat, though in very polite terms, the warning given in May that in

p. 68. Milyutin's diary dates this council 12 Dec.; Ignatyev the 13th; Nelidov gives no date.

[1] Ignatyev's memoirs, in *I.V.*, vol. cxxxvii, pp. 78–81; Nelidov's memoirs, in *I.V.*, vol. xci, p. 68.

[2] Ignatyev's subsequent statements, *San Stefano*, pp. 90, 307, 322, that the terms were communicated to Vienna before his return to the Danube at the beginning of December, are incorrect. See below, p. 428, for the Tsar's communication to Vienna of 9 Dec. Shuvalov had been sent a copy of the proposed terms on 2 Dec., though the terms decided on 9 Dec. were not sent to him until 21 Dec.; Goriainow, *Le Bosphore et les Dardanelles*, p. 358; Shuvalov to Gorchakov, 27 Dec., text in *S.R.*, vol. vi, p. 430.

the event of any occupation, however temporary, of Constantinople or the Dardanelles the government would be forced to
take 'whatever course may appear to them necessary for the
protection of British interests' (memorandum of Derby to
Shuvalov, 13 Dec.). After further tussles in the cabinet, it
was decided on the 18th that Parliament should be summoned
for 17 January to vote supplementary estimates, and that an
offer of mediation should be made. Disraeli immediately
encouraged the Turkish ambassador to believe that effective
British aid was forthcoming,[1] but Derby's ingrained dislike for
anything that savoured of prompt action caused further delay

The Turks, even before the capitulation of Plevna, had been
sounding the great powers, and immediately after its fall they
appealed to them for joint mediation. When this move failed,
mainly owing to the German Emperor, the English attempted
to persuade the Austrians to join with them in mediation. It
was not until 24 December, after Andrássy had refused to compromise himself, that Derby officially offered to Constantinople
the good offices of England alone. This was eagerly accepted
by the Turkish government, and on 27 December Derby telegraphed to St. Petersburg to inquire whether the Tsar would
entertain overtures of peace. The answer was that the Porte
must apply to the Grand Dukes Nicholas and Michael who
would state the conditions for an armistice (Loftus to Derby,
29 Dec., received same day). This was followed by the communication to Derby on 2 January of the reply to his warning
of 13 December as to Constantinople and the Dardanelles.
Gorchakov, though he was much exercised as to the likelihood
of the British fleet seizing the Dardanelles and appearing before
Constantinople, merely repeated his statement of June that the
fate of Constantinople must be decided in agreement with
Europe, that it could not belong to any of the great powers, but
that the Tsar was unable to limit the freedom of action of his
troops (Gorchakov to Shuvalov, 28 Dec.). Thus the under-

---

[1] According to Layard the Sultan told him that Disraeli 'had himself suggested
to Musurus Pasha an appeal from the Porte to the British government for their
mediation, hinting that they would be prepared to offer mediation, even if left
alone by the other powers and that if Russia [refused] the offer and persisted in
continuing the war England would then proceed to take other measures to bring
it to an end. . . . The Sultan was greatly delighted with Lord Beaconsfield's language
and at once counted upon armed support from England at no very distant period.'
Layard memoirs, *British Museum, Add. MSS.* 38935, ff. 307–8.

taking not to occupy temporarily Constantinople or the Dardanelles was again not given, and the issue of events was left in the hands of the military. A belated endeavour of Derby to obviate this by suggesting direct discussions as to the armistice between the Russian and Turkish governments was stonily repulsed (Derby to Loftus, 4 Jan.; Loftus to Derby, 5 Jan.). It was not realized in London until as late as 11 January that the Grand Duke's instructions had not yet reached him, nor that the conclusion of an armistice was made dependent upon the acceptance of preliminary terms of peace. Both facts added greatly to the fears that Russia was bent on prolonging hostilities until the complete collapse of the Ottoman empire might be realized.[1]

The instructions to the Grand Duke had been dispatched on 2 January by courier, and did not reach him until the 14th. Whether the telegraph was purposely not used so as to delay the conclusion of an armistice is not certain, but it is impossible not to suspect strongly this motive, though admittedly the instructions were of exceptional length. St. Petersburg would have preferred to await the Austrian views on the bases of peace before sending them off to G.H.Q. in their final form, but by the end of December further delay was felt to be impossible. It was therefore decided to forestall probable Austrian objections by confining the peace conditions to general terms without specification in detail of territorial changes or Russian acquisitions. These bases of peace were the same as those described at the beginning of this chapter. Their acceptance was to be the condition of granting an armistice to the Turks. The armistice was to insist unconditionally on the evacuation of those of the Danube fortresses which they still occupied and of Erzerum, but no mention was made of the evacuation of Shumla, Varna, or Batum. The two commanders-in-chief were to demand the occupation of the strategical points which they considered most important. The Turkish signature was to be followed by the dispatch of plenipotentiaries to Odessa or Sevastopol (Ignatyev had for the moment won his point here) for the further negotiation of the preliminary peace.[2]

---

[1] For this and the previous paragraph: *Disraeli*, pp. 1054–6, 1067, 1070, 1082; *Salisbury*, pp. 161–72; *A. and P.*, 1878, lxxxi, C. 1906 and 1923. The drafts for Derby's telegram of 27 Dec., in *F.O.* 65/962, show that it had been under discussion by the cabinet since 19 Dec.

[2] *Tatishchev*, pp. 427–8, 430, citing imperial rescript of 29 Dec. and letter of

For the next month the military situation in the Balkans dominated the diplomatic struggle with kaleidoscopic breathlessness. On the right wing Gurko, battling as much against the elements as the enemy, forced the western passes of the Balkans and on 4 January occupied Sofia, at the same time making connexion with the Serbs, who had finally gone to war again when the fall of Plevna seemed to spell its speedy termination. While Gurko swung eastwards for the Ikhtiman pass and the Maritsa valley in pursuit of Suleiman Pasha, Skobelev and Radetsky forced the central Balkan passes after heavy fighting: on 9 January the Shipka was turned and 36,000 Turks capitulated. Skobelev swept forward to Kazanlik and the main railway line. Away to his right on 15-17 January Gurko smashed to pieces Suleiman's forces and entered Philippopolis. The Turkish army, half taken prisoner, half streaming away in headlong panic through the Rhodope to the Aegean, had ceased to exist as a fighting force. On the 20th the Russian cavalry entered Adrianople without resistance. By the 29th they had taken Lule Burgas and Chorlu and were three short days' march from Constantinople. In less than a month the Russians had forced the snow-drifted, ice-bound Balkans, destroyed two Turkish armies, and advanced some three hundred miles almost to the gates of Constantinople. There, on the 31st, they stopped—outside the gates. On that day the armistice was signed.

It had taken three weeks and two days for the Turks to extract an armistice from the Grand Duke. This delay was not under the circumstances so unreasonable as the enemies of Russia at the time represented. When the Russians found that the Turkish resistance was completely broken, they inevitably desired to press forward as far as possible before any suspension of hostilities, but they faltered in their tactics of deferring the conclusion of the armistice, and in the earlier stages at least the Turkish government were themselves considerably to blame, for they would not face squarely the imminence of a complete break-down. Already in the middle of December Suleiman Pasha, just transferred from the Varna to the Balkan front, had expatiated on the hopelessness of the position, and had person-

Milyutin to the Grand Dukes Nicholas and Michael of 1 Jan. The Grand Duke Nicholas evidently did not believe that it was impossible for the instructions to be sent by wire, see below, p. 348, note 1.

ally urged the Sultan to make immediate peace with the Tsar
without attempting European intervention: any help from
England would take at least a month to materialize; by then
the Russians would have pushed on, and the Greeks would have
entered the war. This advice to come to a direct understanding
with Russia was strongly supported by the German ambassador,
Prince Reuss, in Layard's eyes 'more Russian than Ignatyev
himself and scarcely less mischievous', but neither Abd ul-Hamid
nor his closest advisers would be convinced, and preferred to
believe in Layard's private encouragement and the reports of
Musurus from London that English preparations were being
pushed forward in extreme secrecy and that Disraeli would
soon secure a declaration of war. Suleiman was ordered to hold
up the Russians for a month, while Turkish diplomacy did its
utmost to procure the collective mediation of the powers or the
mediation of England alone.[1]

The Turks, finding that Vienna and Berlin would not look at
any form of collective mediation,[2] pinned their hopes the more
to prompt English assistance, hopes that were additionally
encouraged by the activities of Colonel Home and other British
officers in and around Constantinople. Even when Gorchakov
stated (29 Dec.) that an armistice could only be had from the
Grand Duke Nicholas, and when Suleiman renewed (2 Jan.)
his appeals for peace and declared that the formation of the
reserve army round Adrianople would take three months,[3]
the Porte still clung to the skirts of the London foreign office.
At last, on 8 January, when Sofia had fallen and the Shipka was
trembling in the balance, Reouf Pasha, now Seraskier, telegraphed to the Grand Duke stating that the new commander-
in-chief, Mehemet Ali, had just been given full powers by the
Porte to conclude an armistice. The immediate reply was that
negotiations could only be conducted with the Grand Duke

[1] Faust Lurion, *Campagnes de Suleyman Pascha*, pp. 408–9. Suleiman paid a flying
visit to Constantinople between 15 and 20 Dec.: his evidence is extremely biased:
he was suspected of treachery and subsequently court-martialled. Layard to
Derby, disp., no. 1476, conf., 13 Dec., and no. 69, secret, 16 Jan. (repeating strictures on Reuss), copies in *F.O.* 181/564; private letter of Layard to Lytton, 2 Jan.,
copy in Layard Papers, *British Museum, Add. MSS.* 39131, f. 5 (for Reuss); Layard
memoirs, in *British Museum, Add. MSS.* 38936, ff. 15–16, 22–5.

[2] Russell (Berlin) to Derby, disp., no. 482 and 495, secret, 26 and 29 Dec.; tel.,
3 Jan., reporting Bismarck and Andrássy as being agreed in trying to compel the
Turks to appeal direct to the Tsar; copies in *F.O.* 181/564.

[3] Faust Lurion, op. cit., pp. 460–1.

himself, and that no armistice could be obtained without the
acceptance at the same time of preliminary bases of peace.[1]

For this the Turks, divided and distracted among themselves,
were not prepared. Edhem Pasha, the Grand Vizier, had
intended that the armistice should contain no political conditions, and the powers to treat which had been dispatched had
been so drafted.[2] If it was necessary to accept a linking up of
armistice conditions with preliminary bases of peace, the negotiations could not be left to the Turkish military but would
require the dispatch of plenipotentiaries from Constantinople,
thus involving further delay. Hence, even apart from the chaos
in both armies, nothing resulted from the original Turkish
proposal to entrust the armistice to their commander in the
field, although the Grand Duke Nicholas had immediately
ordered Gurko, on the evening of the 9th, to tell Mehemet Ali
to come to G.H.Q., but not to stop energetic military action
until the receipt of further orders.[3]

At this moment Nicholas Nicholaevich took a step which
most seriously aggravated an already complicated situation.
At 10 p.m. on 9 January, after he had replied to Reouf and had
so informed the Tsar, the news arrived that the Shipka pass
had been captured. Next morning he moved forward from
Lovcha, and for the next three days his head-quarters were
plunging through the mountains, halting only for the night,
until on the evening of the 12th they reached Kazanlik, well on
the south side of the main Balkan range. The commander-in-
chief of the Russian armies in Europe had thus placed himself
almost literally at the head of his troops, a position certainly not
conducive to the maintenance of effective communications. It
was obvious, as Nelidov had urged in vain,[4] that by thus pushing forward he would cut himself off from any certainty of rapid
communication with the outside world. To a large extent the
fate of Turkey both now and during the next two months rested
in the hands of the signal service. At Lovcha the Grand Duke

---

[1] Reouf to the Grand Duke, 8 Jan., rec. 4.30 p.m., 9 Jan.; Grand Duke, from
Lovcha, to Reouf, 9 Jan.; texts in *Hasenkampf*, p. 286, and *Skalon*, vol. ii, p. 108.
The Grand Duke informed the Tsar that evening and urgently asked that his
instructions should be telegraphed.

[2] Faust Lurion, *Campagnes de Suleyman Pascha*, pp. 510–12, text of instructions
sent on 9 Jan. by Edhem Pasha, for the Porte; confirmed by Layard's résumé of
them, tel., no. 27, 10 Jan., copy in *F.O.* 181/564.

[3] *Hasenkampf*, pp. 286–7.

[4] Nelidov's memoirs, in *I.V.*, vol. xci, pp. 68–9.

had been linked to St. Petersburg by a field telegraph to the
Danube, where there was a break, and then by a land line via
Bucarest and Kishinev. When he moved forward he was dependent in part on a very hastily laid line joining up with Lovcha,
and mainly on relays of orderlies. The new line, crossing a
4,000-ft. pass and exposed to all the severities of mid-winter in
the Balkans, was subject to repeated breaks, which were not
made less frequent by the fact that telegraph-poles are good for
firewood and telegraph-wire good for almost anything. Under
any circumstances there would be the maximum of difficulty
in keeping the lines working, and there were in fact appalling
delays which on at least four occasions were of very serious
consequence.

Even greater difficulties confronted the Turks in communicating with the Grand Duke, for they were not in direct touch
and had to rely on the circuitous route via Trieste and Bucarest.
But the continued delays were at first as much due to the confusion reigning in Constantinople. The Turks had hopes that
something might be achieved by a personal appeal from Queen
Victoria to the Tsar, and even from the Sultan himself. Both
efforts were as fruitless as a simultaneous attempt to induce the
Grand Duke to reveal the bases of peace in advance.[1] At the
same time the Sultan was engaged in re-forming his government.
Edhem Pasha, though honest and conscientious, was unable to
cope with the crisis or to combat palace intrigues against him,
and was momentarily replaced as Grand Vizier by Hamdi
Pasha, a mere nullity (11 Jan.). After the fall of Plevna the
war office had been entrusted to Reouf Pasha, an arch-enemy
of Suleiman, and the admiralty to Said Pasha, both 'honest,
intelligent, and active' men according to Layard, and the latter
'in daily—I had almost said hourly—communication' with the
British ambassador. Said's influence was further increased by
his appointment as marshal of the palace. These changes for
the moment merely had the effect of adding to the confusion,
and, despite Layard's trust in Said, they were not to the immediate advantage of England. The Turks, misled by their hopes
and their ambassador in London, now felt that they had been
deceived and abandoned.[2]

---

[1] The Grand Duke to Reouf, tel., 12 Jan., *Hasenkampf*, p. 318.

[2] Layard's memoirs, *British Museum, Add. MSS.* 38936, ff. 33, 3, 34; Raschdau, *Ein sinkendes Reich*, pp. 121–4, 135 (also describing the dispatch of the plenipotentiaries).

On 13 January the final decision was taken to treat directly with the Grand Duke Nicholas, and Server and Namyk Pashas were appointed as plenipotentiaries. Server had considerable European experience and thanks to his marriage was one of the leading politicians under Abd ul-Aziz: he had been Reis Effendi since the preceding August and had the general reputation of being russophil. Namyk, now an octogenarian, the fierce old relic of the days of Mahmoud and Abd ul-Medjid, hating the foreigner and refusing to speak French, had been cajoled out of his long retirement to face the Russians once more in conference as he had done half a century before at Akkerman: but in the eyes of the English he appeared as particularly hostile to them, and was believed to have advised that Turkey ought to accept almost any conditions from Russia and to enter into a close alliance with her.[1] The two plenipotentiaries did not leave Constantinople until the 15th. It was two days before their train reached the Russian outposts, where it was promptly commandeered; another three before they drove wearily into Kazanlik, on the evening of the 19th.[2]

By then the Grand Duke was in receipt of his instructions and full powers to treat—and of much else, little to his liking, from St. Petersburg. His brother, elated at the news of success after success, was urging him to press on to the utmost without hastening the communication of the peace terms, yet was wavering before the prospect of a break with the western powers.[3] At long last, in the middle of January, the Austrian reply to the Tsar's letter of 9 December enclosing the bases of peace had arrived. Andrássy directly accused the Russians of breaking the terms of the secret convention and declared that he would recognize as valid only such peace terms as were consonant with Austrian interests, and in the case of those

---

This Said Pasha is to be distinguished from the Sultan's secretary of the same name. For another very favourable impression of Reouf, see Baker Pasha, *War in Bulgaria*, vol. i, pp. 6–7, 322–4.

[1] Private letter of Layard to Derby, 16 Jan., copy in Layard Papers, *British Museum, Add. MSS.* 39131, f. 15. For Server, see below, p. 365.

[2] *Hasenkampf*, pp. 335–6, 338; *Skalon*, vol. ii, pp. 144, 153; Dukmasov, *Vospominaniya o russko-turetskoi voine gg. i M. D. Skobeleve*, pp. 272, 278, 280; Nelidov's memoirs, in *I.V.*, vol. xci, pp. 69–72. Vereshchagin, who was an eyewitness, gives a vivid description of the meeting of the Turkish plenipotentiaries with Skobelev at Hermanli; *Na Voine*, pp. 238–40.

[3] Tsar to the Grand Duke, tels., 10 and 15 Jan., rec. 11 and 16 Jan., text in *Hasenkampf*, pp. 308, 323.

touching the general interests of Europe only such conditions as might be confirmed by all the signatories of the 1856 treaty. On 15 January a formal declaration to the same effect from the British government arrived. The effect of this double warning was that the Russian government decided that direct negotiations for peace should immediately follow the conclusion of the armistice, and that the great powers should be informed that this peace would be only preliminary and that all questions affecting general European interests would be decided only in agreement with them.[1] The Tsar wrote accordingly to the two emperors (16 Jan.), and Gorchakov followed with a circular to the same effect on 25 January.

Far more serious in its immediate consequence was the English belief that the armistice was being purposely delayed so as to allow of a maximum Russian advance. On the 12th Loftus was instructed to ask Gorchakov to give an assurance that no Russian force would be sent to the Gallipoli peninsula. The answer, which was not given until the 15th, represented a substantial setback for Ignatyev: there was no intention of directing military operations upon Gallipoli if the Turks did not concentrate regular troops there, it being understood that England would not occupy it with her troops. Derby immediately replied (16 Jan.) that 'Her Majesty's Government contemplate no occupation of that position under present circumstances'. Neither answer was satisfactory to either party. What did regular troops mean? And why should the Turks have to leave Gallipoli virtually undefended? How long would present circumstances last? And was Derby really speaking with the voice of the cabinet? The reassembling of Parliament on the 17th was marked not by the strength of Gladstonian opinion from which St. Petersburg hoped so much, but by a speech from the throne which scarcely veiled the hurrying on of preparations.

As the stream of confused telegrams recording these far-away moves and counter-moves filtered into G.H.Q., the Grand Duke became more and more perplexed and out of patience with his old enemies the diplomatists. Nervous and wearied, he was

---

[1] *Tatishchev*, p. 431, citing Milyutin's diary for 16 Jan. on imperial council held that or the previous day. Schweinitz, *Denkwürdigkeiten*, vol. ii, p. 4, 16 Jan., shows that Novikov was in St. Petersburg *en mission* from Vienna: his influence, such as it was, must certainly have been to placate Austria to the utmost. The diplomatic communications referred to in this and the following paragraphs are printed in *A. and P.*, 1878, C. 1923.

the prey of moods varying between elation at each new success and desire to press to a final conclusion on the one hand, and on the other hand lassitude, doubt as to the wisdom of a total destruction of the Ottoman empire, and desire to get finished as quickly as possible and return home with a prompt peace. On 19 January, in the morning, some hours before the Turkish plenipotentiaries reached his head-quarters, he received a decisive telegram from Gorchakov informing him of the Tsar's desire that he should delay the communication to the Turks of the bases of peace by asking first for their proposals and referring them to St. Petersburg, thus giving time for some agreement with the Austrians to be reached: in any case, operations were not to be stopped.[1]

This telegram threw the commander-in-chief off such balance as he still possessed. In his first access of anger he so far lost control of his senses as to order the telegraph lines connecting him with St. Petersburg to be cut.[2] After having declared to Constantinople that Turkish plenipotentiaries must be sent to receive the terms from him, how could he be expected to fob them off with such diplomatists' by-play and ask them for *their* terms? Military men at least had a sense of honour. Clearly Gorchakov and Ignatyev were intensely jealous at not taking part in the peacemaking and wanted to hold everything up till one or other could play the chief role. Diplomatists were past understanding. Here were the Turkish delegates about to arrive, and St. Petersburg had upset everything. But he would *not* be upset by Gorchakov. After all, it was not the Tsar's command; only his desire. And he could repay the foreign office in its own coin: he could point out (which he duly did next day) that any artificial prolongation of negotiations while the headlong Russian advance continued would only make the worst impression on the other powers: he could point out that if he pressed right on to Constantinople he would then have to occupy Gallipoli, exactly what St. Petersburg had warned him not to

[1] Gorchakov to the Grand Duke, 17 Jan.; text in *Hasenkampf*, p. 339; *Skalon*, vol. ii, p. 148.

[2] This incredible action is vouched for only by his adjutant, Skalon, who heard him give the verbal order; vol. ii, pp. 148–9. That it was actually carried out is still more difficult to believe, although Skalon definitely states (vol. ii, pp. 150–2) that two telegrams reporting the latest successes of Gurko and Skobelev although dated 9 p.m. 19 Jan. were not actually sent off till 21 Jan. He does not, however, make any reference to the Grand Duke's telegrams dated 20 Jan. not being dispatched on that day. Hasenkampf has no indication of the lines being cut.

do: for the Grand Duke, just as the English, looked upon an occupation of the Dardanelles as a necessary safeguard if he went to Constantinople.[1]

So next morning, on 20 January, when his first meeting took place with Server and Namyk, he played the blunt soldier; handed them the armistice terms and bases of peace; said they could not be altered; and gave the Turks twenty-four hours for their consideration.[2]

That very evening the situation was entirely transformed. With dramatic tardiness, about 8 p.m. Nicholas Nicholaevich learnt that the key fortress of Adrianople (in command of Namyk's son) was defenceless. It had taken twenty-four hours for Strukov's telegram from the farthest advanced cavalry to reach Kazanlik. The impression produced in head-quarters was sensational. Skobelev and Radetsky were forthwith ordered to race forward to the city. Was this the knell of the Turkish rule in Europe? Would the Turkish panic spread to Constantinople? Would the Christians rise and the British fleet steam up to occupy it before the Russians could arrive? The Grand Duke swayed nerve-strained between his hopes and fears, scarcely knowing which were which. Next day (21 Jan.) the Turkish plenipotentiaries, despite the news of Adrianople, declared that the big Bulgaria and the reforms demanded for the other Christians meant the end of Turkey in Europe, that their instructions would not permit them to sign, and that they must consult their government. When the Grand Duke was faced with this refusal to sign, all the motives, all the influences working for a final sweep to Santa Sofia, to the Chanak narrows, gathered strength. For a few days, for the first and only time, Nicholas Nicholaevich was ready to act hand in hand with Ignatyev far away in St. Petersburg. 'My conviction is that the time has come when it is necessary to go to the end, to the heart of Turkey' (letter to the Tsar, 23 Jan., rec. 2 Feb.). The Turks were told that the advance would continue, that they could

[1] The Grand Duke to Gorchakov, tel., 20 Jan., sent after the first meeting with the Turks that morning; text in *Hasenkampf*, p. 342, and *Skalon*, vol. ii, p. 158. For the Grand Duke's attitude towards Gorchakov's telegram of 17 Jan., ib., pp. 339 and 148–9.

[2] This and the following four paragraphs are based on *Skalon*, vol. ii, pp. 156–69, 174, 183–5, and *Hasenkampf*, pp. 342–55, 360–1, 372, 376, 381, 386, where are given the texts of all the telegrams and letters mentioned; and on Nelidov's memoirs, in *I.V.*, vol. xci, pp. 73–8.

communicate with Constantinople, but that the original terms no longer held good, at least until further instructions were received from St. Petersburg. At the same time the Grand Duke decided to move forward his head-quarters and dispatched to St. Petersburg the first of three vital telegrams (evening, 21 Jan.).

He asked whether, if the Turkish government accepted the bases of peace, he should conclude the armistice or whether he should await new instructions. Then he raised the decisive question of an advance to Constantinople itself, which might now easily occur in view of the Turkish panic. What should he do: (i) if the British fleet came to the Bosphorus; (ii) if the British landed in Constantinople; (iii) if there were disorders in Constantinople and appeals from the Christians to come to their help; (iv) as regards Gallipoli, whether the British fleet was or was not there?

Later that evening (21 Jan.) the news arrived, as usual very delayed, of Gurko's final rout of Suleiman's army and his capture of 97 guns; next morning (22 Jan.) that of Strukov's entry into Adrianople. In a vein of glowing optimism the Grand Duke sent the second and third vital telegrams (22 Jan.): the complete panic of the Turks and their non-acceptance of the bases of peace make it impossible to call a halt and necessary to go on to Constantinople, which may be reached even by the end of the month, and to occupy Gallipoli; no armistice will be concluded until an answer is received, and meanwhile 'with God's help I shall advance'. The answer took a week. No reply to these three telegrams reached him until 2 o'clock on the afternoon of the 29th.

During this final week the Russian advance-guards wearily pressed forward along the railway line to Constantinople, while Gurko's forces were brought up to Adrianople, an observation force was pushed down to Dedeagach and Enos, and a strong screen thrust out towards the Bulair lines. The troops were admittedly worn out, lacking in every kind of equipment, particularly boots and ammunition, and unsupported by artillery; but G.H.Q. maintained that their morale was excellent, their health good, their provisioning sufficient thanks to the capture of Turkish supply depots, and that every effort should be made to press on while the Turks were in a state of panic. The Grand Duke, though increasingly anxious at the absence of any reply to his three urgent telegrams, continued on the whole in his mood of unstable exultation. On the 24th he was once more on the move, and on the 26th made a triumphant entry into Adrianople (marred only by the dubious behaviour of the Greek metropolitan). There he fixed his head-quarters; but he was soon talking of moving forward yet again, to some point on the sea of Marmara, and was busy with plans for the transport of a division from Sevastopol to effect a *coup de main* on the Asiatic shore of the Bosphorus and for meeting the eventuality of a war with England.

This now seemed more and more probable. The final struggle in the British cabinet and the taking of decisive measures might be precipitated at any moment. The occasion was provided by reports from Constantinople that the Russian bases of peace included a settlement of the question of the Straits by Russia and Turkey alone, which was the exact opposite of what Shuvalov had privately assured Derby.[1] Thereupon, on 23 January, the fleet was ordered to pass the Dardanelles and go to Constantinople. Carnarvon at once resigned: Derby did likewise; and then came back. For 'like a bombshell' on the 24th there arrived further news from Layard: the Sultan had just accepted the Russian conditions, and these provided for a European, not a Russo-Turkish, settlement of the Straits. Immediately countermanding orders were sent to Admiral Hornby, who had already entered the Dardanelles but then withdrew. Next day (25 Jan.) the cabinet received the peace conditions in greater detail from Layard: it was found that the question of the Straits *was* reserved for bilateral treatment. Hornby's orders could not yet again be countermanded. 'How we gnashed our teeth!' wrote Northcote. So did Layard in Constantinople: 'we are taunted with cowardice and are a public laughing stock. The Russians are now completely masters of the situation.' Thus, with pardonable exaggeration, he exploded to Hornby, for whom he had with great difficulty succeeded in extracting a *firman* from the Porte.[2]

---

[1] Derby to Loftus, disp., no. 49, secret, 21 Jan. (Shuvalov privately telling Derby that day that there was no mention in the bases of peace either of the Dardanelles or of the Bosphorus), in *F.O.* 181/564.

[2] Egerton, *Admiral Sir Geoffrey Phipps Hornby*, pp. 229–32 (including text of the Admiralty telegram to pass the Dardanelles and the countermanding order: the fleet was at Vourla Bay near Smyrna, not at Besika Bay; hence the countermanding order reached it in time); Andrew Lang, *Life, Letters and Diaries of Sir Stafford*

During these critical days Shuvalov had been making desperate efforts to avert an explosion before the cessation of hostilities,
and to secure the retention of his friend Derby at the foreign
office. He was in daily contact with him and other ministers,
and was even in communication with leaders of the opposition.[1]
On 24 January he was at last given the text of the bases of peace
and empowered to communicate them in full to Derby, which
he did next day.[2] Moreover, on the 26th he was able to give an
official assurance, which he repeated on the 28th and 29th, that
the passage of warships through the Straits was a question of
European concern with which Russia did not intend to deal
separately.[3] Thus Gorchakov had taken a decisive step in his
battle with Ignatyev over the Straits, a step taken just after the
latter had left St. Petersburg for the Balkans. As has been seen,
while the bases of peace provided for a bilateral agreement
whereby the rights and interests of Russia in respect of the
Straits were to be protected, the Tsar had assured the German
and the Austrian Emperors, on 16 January, that these bases
were only preliminary terms and that questions of general concern would only be decided in agreement with the powers. On
the 25th Gorchakov gave the same commitment to England,
in the form of a circular to all the powers. Now on the 26th the
Straits were formally declared to be included among such
questions of general concern. Ignatyev was thus assured of a
doubly stiff struggle if he were to effect his aim of actually concluding the bilateral agreement which he had originally succeeded in inserting in the bases of peace.

But Ignatyev was not the man to abandon any struggle until

Northcote, pp. 111–12; private letter of Layard to Hornby, 25 Jan., copy in Layard
Papers, *British Museum, Add. MSS.* 39131, f. 22.

[1] Private letters of Shuvalov to Gorchakov, 24, 25, and 27 Jan., and (for communication with the opposition) tel., 26 Jan., and disp., 28 Jan., texts in *Seton-
Watson MSS.* Seton-Watson, *Disraeli, Gladstone and the Eastern Question*, pp. 254–60,
shows from the Granville and Harcourt papers that Shuvalov was pouring out
mystifying confidences to Harcourt three weeks earlier.

[2] Shuvalov to Gorchakov, tels., 22, 23, and 24 Jan., texts in *Seton-Watson MSS.*;
A. and P., 1878, lxxxi, C. 1923, no. 38.

[3] Goriainow, *Le Bosphore et les Dardanelles*, p. 360; Derby to Loftus, 28 and 29
Jan., in *A. and P.*, 1878, lxxxi, C. 1923, no. 43, and C. 1925, no. 12. Gorchakov
had telegraphed to this effect to Shuvalov, 20 and 22 Jan., but apparently without
permitting him to inform Derby officially until the 26th, although Shuvalov had
privately assured him on the evening of the 23rd that all questions concerning the
Straits were reserved; confidential letter to Gorchakov, 24 Jan., text in *Seton-Watson
MSS.*

all means had been exhausted. At the very time when the British cabinet so nearly sent the fleet to Constantinople, the advisers of the Tsar were also in the throes of a crisis. Between 21 and 24 January the Tsar was in almost continual conclave with Gorchakov, Milyutin, and Ignatyev, in the midst of which arrived the Grand Duke's telegrams of the 21st and 22nd. The reply to these was naturally of decisive consequence. Ignatyev redoubled his efforts, urging that orders be sent for the occupation of the heights commanding Constantinople and the Bosphorus and insisting that the Bulair lines be also seized: such energetic action would be the best means of staving off a conflict with England, for it would show her the uselessness of a struggle. Among the inner ring round the Tsar Ignatyev received influential support for his extreme measures only from the Grand Duke Constantine, the head of the admiralty, who gaily proposed the immediate occupation of Constantinople, a proclamation announcing the cessation of Turkish rule over the Christians, and the summoning of a conference at Constantinople. On the other side, Milyutin and Gorchakov pointed out the dangerous complications which a final collapse of the Ottoman empire would cause, and succeeded in dissuading the Tsar from sanctioning an immediate rupture of the armistice negotiations and from giving unconditional approval to the advance on Constantinople. Ignatyev could not secure more than that the Turkish delegates should be presented with a stiff ultimatum. He likewise failed to win his way in regard to the negotiations that were to follow the armistice. The earlier idea of conducting these at Odessa and Sevastopol having been dropped in view of the changed military situation, Ignatyev renewed his proposal that he should be sent direct to Constantinople with a staff of his own picking, and now added the suggestion that he should there arrange for Russian troops to enter the city on the request of the Christian population. This was not accepted. It was decided that he should be placed in charge of the negotiations for the preliminary peace (a decision that was bound to give him great scope), but he was to carry them on with Nelidov at G.H.Q. and was accordingly to leave immediately for Adrianople.[1]

[1] Milyutin's diary for 21 Jan., recording an imperial council of that date, cited in *Tatishchev*, p. 435 (for the Grand Duke Constantine, Milyutin, and Gorchakov); Ignatyev's memoirs, in *I.V.*, vol. cxxxvii, pp. 87–91, and *San Stefano*, pp. 10–11,

This and the other conclusions of the Tsar's deliberations, constituting the answer to the Grand Duke's telegrams of 21 and 22 January, were dispatched on the morning of the 24th, before the news had reached St. Petersburg of the ordering of the British fleet to Constantinople.[1] The fact that the arrival of this news coincided with that of the countermanding order operated to leave the instructions to the Grand Duke unchanged, although there were still fears of an immediate rupture with England. The Tsar had abandoned his earlier desire to spin out the armistice negotiations and now recognized the importance of hastening their conclusion so as to avoid the accusation of desiring to get as near Constantinople as possible.[2]

In the instructions of 24 January the Grand Duke Nicholas was again directed not to call a halt until the armistice and bases of peace were signed. He was to give the Turkish plenipotentiaries an ultimatum stating that, if within three days of their telegraphing to Constantinople for instructions they did not receive full powers to sign, the Russians would no longer consider themselves bound by the conditions they had offered, and the issue would have to be decided under the walls of Constantinople.[1] Thus the reply to the first of the Grand Duke's questions was that the original terms were to hold good until the expiration of the time-limit. To his other four questions the replies were: (i) if the British fleet comes to the Bosphorus, get into touch with the authorities to arrange for the joint preservation of order in Constantinople; (ii) if the British land in Constantinople, avoid any clash with them and keep your troops under the walls of Constantinople; (iii) if asked by the Chris-

20–1. Ignatyev maintains that Milyutin supported his proposal that the Bulair lines, Gallipoli, and the heights commanding Constantinople and the Bosphorus must be occupied, that the Tsar accepted this, and that the Grand Duke was correspondingly instructed by telegraph (see also below, p. 372, note 1). He does not give the date or text of any such telegram. He does give the text, correctly, of the telegram of 24 Jan.: he states that he drafted it himself, but he admits that Milyutin subsequently made certain alterations in it.

[1] Tsar to the Grand Duke, tel., 24 Jan., disp. 10.30 a.m. (Ignatyev gives 8.0 a.m.), rec. 2 p.m., 29 Jan.; text in *Hasenkampf*, pp. 389–90; *Skalon*, vol. ii, pp. 189–90; *San Stefano*, pp. 9–11. The words 'under the walls of Constantinople', a literal translation of the Russian text, imply that the Russians were to remain outside, and Ignatyev so interpreted them, though with the essential addition that the Russians were to occupy the heights commanding Constantinople and the Bosphorus.

[2] Gorchakov to the Grand Duke, tel., 26 Jan., rec. afternoon 30 Jan., repeating tel. of 24 Jan. from Shuvalov; the Tsar to the Grand Duke, tel., 1 Feb., rec. 3 Feb. (the Tsar did not receive news of the signature of the armistice until 2 Feb.); texts in *Skalon*, vol. ii, pp. 197, 211; *Hasenkampf*, pp. 393–4, 413.

tians or the foreign representatives to enter Constantinople, draw up a formal record of the request and enter; (iv) as regards Gallipoli, on no account go back upon our declaration to England that we do not intend to extend military operations to the peninsula: England has promised not to occupy Gallipoli and we ought not to give her an excuse for intervention even if Turkish troops are on the peninsula: it is sufficient to move an observation detachment to the isthmus, but not to the peninsula itself. These instructions as to Gallipoli went farther than the engagement given to England on 15 January (see above, p. 351), which had laid down two conditions; the Turks were not to concentrate regular troops there, and the British were not to occupy it. The former condition was now implicitly dropped, for nothing was said as to any distinction between Turkish regular and non-regular troops in the Gallipoli garrison. Thus only in the case of a British attempt at occupation was the Grand Duke to act likewise.

By some series of mishaps, of course unexplained, this telegram broke all records in transit. Dispatched from St. Petersburg at 10.40 a.m. on 24 January it did not reach Adrianople until 2.0 p.m. on the 29th. The provision as to the ultimatum with a three days' time-limit was by then largely nullified, and there was much discussion among the staff as to from when it was to be computed to run. The difficulty proved in fact to be of no consequence, for hardly had Nelidov delivered the ultimatum to Server and Namyk than a long cipher telegram arrived for them. It contained the Sultan's instructions to sign. It too had suffered every mishap in transit, having been sent from Constantinople likewise on the 24th, having missed the Turkish delegates at Kazanlik, and then having been held up in the impartial chaos of the Russian lines of communication. On the morning of 30 January the Turks formally announced to the Grand Duke their acceptance of the terms. 'Your arms are victorious; your ambition is satisfied; but Turkey is lost. We accept all that you desire.' On the following day the actual signature of the armistice and the bases of peace took place.[1]

---

[1] *Skalon*, vol. ii, pp. 191, 195; Nelidov's memoirs, in *I.V.*, vol. xci, pp. 78–9; *Hasenkampf*, pp. 391–2. It is stated in Bamberg, *Geschichte der orientalischen Angelegenheit...*, p. 588, that the Turkish plenipotentiaries received instructions to accept any conditions on 27 Jan. The Russian sources cited above imply that it was the 29th, and give no indication of any previous attempt of the Turkish plenipotentiaries to accept the terms in full. The date of the dispatch from Constantinople of

The detailed terms of the armistice had been left to the Grand Duke's staff, but strangely enough no alteration had been made in the requirement laid down in St. Petersburg in December that only the Danube fortresses still held by the Turks must be evacuated, although the Grand Duke had suggested to the Tsar, after the passage of the Balkans, that the evacuation of Shumla should also be demanded.[1] Neither it, nor Varna, nor Batum were mentioned in the armistice. Hence they remained in the hands of the Turks, and were to prove later a great stumbling-block. On the other hand, the fortresses of Widdin, Rustchuk, Silistria, Belgradchik, Razgrad, and Bazardzhik were to be evacuated, though the Turks were granted the right of removing their munitions and stores. They were to raise the blockade of the Black Sea ports, and the Russians were to occupy Burgas and Midia with the right of revictualling their army through them.

The demarcation line before Constantinople was so drawn that the Turks were to retire from the Chekmedje line and the Russians to advance somewhat from the positions they occupied on 31 January as far as the Chataldja line, a neutral zone about ten miles broad being left between the two forces. This provision was of the greatest importance. The Buyuk–Chekmedje line is a ridge, some twenty-five miles from Constantinople, from 400 to 700 feet in height, stretching from the Black Sea to the Sea of Marmara (here only twenty miles apart), and for the most part protected in front by lakes, swamps, or almost impenetrable thickets. The natural strength of this position was increased by the earthworks in process of construction. Even

the instructions is given by Layard as about 2 p.m. on 23 Jan., Layard to Derby, 29 Jan., in *A. and P.*, 1878, lxxxi, C. 1924; so too in Raschdau, *Ein sinkendes Reich*, p. 138; but the Sultan's telegram to the Tsar of 30 Jan. gives the date as the 24th; text in *Hasenkampf*, p. 410. Layard in his memoirs, British Museum, Add. MSS. 38936, f. 64, states that it had been decided to accept the Russian conditions only after an appeal had been made through Musurus, the ambassador in London, asking whether the British government would prevent a Russian occupation of Constantinople if the armistice conditions were refused, and after Derby had replied negatively.

[1] The Grand Duke to the Tsar, tel., 14 Jan., text in *Hasenkampf*, p. 318. In the same telegram he suggested that for Serbia there should be 'territorial acquisitions' instead of a 'rectification of frontiers'. I can find no further reference to this point or to Shumla prior to the signature of the Adrianople terms. The text of the armistice, in French and Russian, is given in *Hasenkampf*, appendix 5: the French text of the armistice is also in Martens, *Nouveau recueil général des traités . . .*, second series, vol. iii, pp. 241–4.

MAP 4

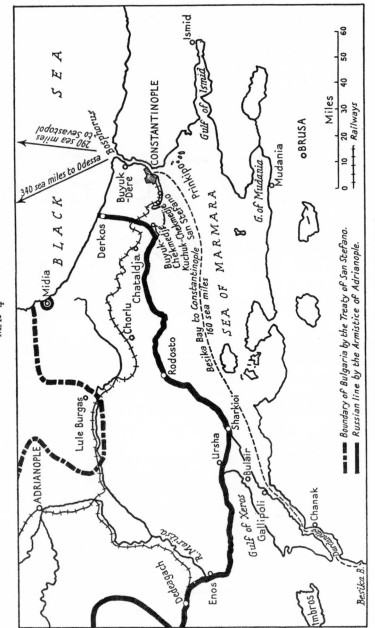

CONSTANTINOPLE AND THE STRAITS

B L A C K   S E A

340 sea miles to Odessa

290 sea miles to Sevastopol

Bosphorus

Midia

Derkos

Chorlu

Chataldja

Buyuk-Dere

Buyuk-Chekmedje
Chekmedje
Kuchuk-Chekmedje
San Stefano
Prinkipo

CONSTANTINOPLE

ADRIANOPLE

Lule Burgas

Rodosto

Besika Bay to Constantinople 160 sea miles

S E A   O F   M A R M A R A

G. of Mudania

Mudania

BRUSA

Gulf of Ismid

Ismid

R. Maritsa

Dedeagach

Gulf of Xeros

Ursha

Sharkioi

Bulair

Gallipoli

Chanak

Dardanelles

Enos

Imbros

Besika B.

Miles

0 10 20 30 40 50 60

Railways

━ ━ ━ Boundary of Bulgaria by the Treaty of San Stefano.
━━━ Russian line by the Armistice of Adrianople.

though uncompleted, they represented with a garrison of about 30,000 men immediately available an extremely formidable obstacle to the Russians; and they were accounted the last line of defence for Constantinople. The abandonment of these lines by the Turks, together with the advance of the Russians to the Chataldja position, inspired Layard and his government with the decisiveness of consternation. On the other hand, Russian extremists belaboured the Grand Duke first for granting any armistice at all, when the prize of Constantinople was within his grasp, and secondly, if armistice there must be, for not insisting that the Chekmedje lines be occupied by him. Such indeed had been his original intention, but in the face of the desperate opposition of the Turkish delegates he finally agreed that they should be left in the neutral zone between the two armies.[1]

Almost equal alarm was caused by the demarcation line from Sharkioi to Ursha which brought the Russians within easy striking-distance of the Bulair lines, and allowed of their prompt occupation of Rodosto on the Sea of Marmara. The cessation of hostilities was to apply to all fronts, but the actual armistice terms for the Asiatic front were to be fixed by the two local commanders. The evacuation of Erzerum, in any case, was specified in the bases of peace. On the Serbian front the armistice provided for Djuma, Kustendil, and Vranja to be in Serbian or Russian occupation, Priština in Turkish, the demarcation line running from Djuma by Vranja to the frontier of Novi Bazar. No definite line was laid down on the Montenegrin front. It, like the other lines, was to be demarcated at once by mixed commissions.

The armistice was readily accepted by Milan and Nicholas, although they had had no voice whatever in its conclusion. The Serbs in their six weeks' war had captured Pirot and Trno, but had been less successful in Old Serbia. Nish had fallen to them, and after severe fighting Vranja, but they had been held up by the defiles to the south. The Montenegrins, after an unsuccessful summer, had wound up with resounding triumphs. Nikšić, the key stronghold on the north-west, had at last been

[1] *Skalon*, vol. ii, p. 198; Nelidov's memoirs, in *I.V.*, vol. xci, p. 80 (mistaking the Chataldja for the Chekmedje line); Dukmasov, *Vospominaniya o russko-turetskoi woine...*, p. 299. For the Chekmedje line see especially Greene, *The Russian army and its campaigns in Turkey in 1877–1878*, p. 363, and Nemirovich-Danchenko, *God voiny*, vol. ii, pp. 232–4.

captured on 8 November. Ten days later Spizza had been occupied, and Prince Nicholas duly celebrated Montenegrin access to the sea by the composition of a stirring poem. On 18 January the citadel of Antivari had fallen and the Montenegrins entered Dulcigno. But in the Morača valley they had been unable to make much ground or to take Podgorica, which was to be an insuperable obstacle in the demarcation negotiations.

The attitude of Prince Charles was very different. He had demanded of the Grand Duke participation in the armistice negotiations, and the Roumanian government had dispatched a representative to Kazanlik to insist on sharing in these, as well as in the negotiations for a preliminary peace. Their choice of a representative, Heraclius Arion, was not a fortunate one, for he was an unimposing and entirely ineffective officer. He was to demand the occupation by the Roumanians, until the definitive peace, of Widdin, Rahova, Nicopolis, and Lom Palanka. The Russians had not the slightest intention of admitting the Roumanians to the negotiations. Arion was treated with the scantest courtesy, left completely in the dark, and told that his government must address themselves to St. Petersburg; where their approaches met with equal failure. He remained helpless at G.H.Q., unable even to extract an exact copy of the armistice terms a fortnight after they had been signed, and plaintively begging to be replaced. The Roumanian government, furious at the conclusion of the armistice without any consultation with them, announced their intention of occupying Widdin (which they had failed to capture) and other Danube towns, as gages for the payment by the Turks of a war indemnity, and probably with ulterior designs in the Widdin district. Relations had already become very strained; as a later chapter will show, the Roumanian reaction to the Adrianople and later to the San Stefano terms was to lead to an almost complete break with the Russians.[1]

---

[1] Prince Charles to the Grand Duke, tel., 9 Jan., text in *Aus dem Leben König Karls* . . . , vol. iii, p. 429; Iorga, *Correspondance diplomatique roumaine sous le roi Charles Ier*, nos. 542 (dispatch and instructions of Arion, 14 Jan.), 546, 555 (reports of Arion; he reached G.H.Q. 20 Jan.); Ghica (St. Petersburg) to Kogălniceanu, tel., 26 Jan., text in *Corespondenţa Generalului Iancu Ghica*, pp. 125–6; Prince Charles to the Grand Duke, tel., 4 Feb., text in *Hasenkampf*, pp. 416–17; *Skalon*, vol. ii, p. 217; *San Stefano*, pp. 39–40 (Ignatyev arrived in Bucarest 31 Jan.), 46, 56, and *Aus dem Leben König Karls* . . . , vol. iii, pp. 469, 484 (Widdin).

The political terms set out in the bases of peace had undergone no change despite the overwhelming Russian victories of the past month. On the other hand, as also already pointed out, they had been deliberately drawn up so as to give the widest scope in the subsequent peace negotiations, which had now been entrusted to Ignatyev—not a man to whom any scope could be given with impunity. Their provisions may conveniently be again stated.[1]

Bulgaria, 'dans les limites déterminées par la majorité de la population bulgare', which limits were in no case to be smaller than those indicated by the Constantinople conference, was to be erected into an autonomous, tributary principality, with a national, Christian government and an indigenous militia. No Turkish troops were to be quartered in it.

The independence of Montenegro was to be recognized. She was to receive an increase of territory at least equivalent to her conquests. The definitive frontier was to be fixed later.

The independence of Roumania and Serbia was to be recognized. The former was to gain 'un dédommagement territorial suffisant'; the latter 'une rectification de frontière'.

Bosnia and Herzegovina were to receive an autonomous administration with adequate guarantees. Analogous reforms were to be introduced into the other Christian provinces of Turkey in Europe.

Turkey engaged to reimburse Russia for her war expenses and losses. The manner of payment of this indemnity, whether in money or by cession of territory, was to be regulated by subsequent agreement.

The Sultan was to concert with the Tsar so as to safeguard the rights and interests of Russia as regards the Bosphorus and the Dardanelles.

Negotiations were to be opened immediately at the Grand Duke's head-quarters for the conclusion of preliminaries of peace.

The inevitable effect of these very general and far-reaching provisions was to aggravate intensely both British and Austrian hostility. In the foreign office the permanent under-secretary was so far stirred from the routine which Disraeli so much despised as to address a memorandum to the cabinet in which, while characterizing the terms as 'a peace which can be little

[1] Text in Appendix VI.

more than an armed truce, since it will leave behind it the smouldering embers of war', he argued that it was henceforth impossible to continue the traditional British policy of maintaining the Ottoman empire by strengthening it through internal reforms and that 'the question now to consider is how to protect Europe from the consequence of the downfall of that Empire . . .'.[1] In the Ballplatz Andrássy, disgusted at Russian deception, now regarded war as an imminent possibility and was determined to maintain the Austrian position to the utmost. January 1878 closed with the storm-clouds thickly packed.

[1] Observations by Lord Tenterden on Russian conditions of peace, 29 Jan., printed for the use of the cabinet, 30 Jan., in *F.O.* 65/1023.

XIII

CONSTANTINOPLE

WHILE Adrianople provided no respite to the suspicions and hostility of the English and the Austrians, it did mark a turning-point in the state of mind both of the Russian headquarters and, though less immediately, of the Turks in Constantinople. With the cessation of the Russian advance before the last defences of Constantinople had been seized the Turks were given at the least a breathing-space in which to recover some confidence in themselves, above all in their capacity to entangle Russia fatally with the other powers, and to hurry on their defensive measures. The situation still, however, remained chaotic, and might at any moment again degenerate into the state of panic which had marked the month of January. The wildest rumours gained instant circulation; not the most strange being that the conclusion of the armistice had been purposely delayed as a result of a secret compact between the Russians and the Sultan, who desired their advance upon his capital so that they might save him from the constitution he had granted a year before.

The new chamber of deputies, set up in accordance with this constitution, was indeed for some six weeks a power to reckon with, until on 14 February 1878 it was prorogued—never to meet again. Its violent attacks on the conduct of the war helped to produce the ministerial crisis as a result of which at the beginning of February the post of grand vizier was abolished in favour of that of prime minister, and various changes were made in the direction of ministerial responsibility which soon broke down and only added to the general confusion. On the other hand, the new prime minister, Akhmet Vekif Pasha, had shown great ability as president of the chamber and was an accomplished and honest man: strongly anglophil (he was well known as a close friend of Layard), he acted in concert with Said, still minister of marine, and Mavroeni, the Sultan's doctor, as the mainspring of the anti-Russian party. Against them were ranged all those who, like Server Pasha, the foreign minister, were disabused at what they considered the selfish desertion of England and believed that nothing remained but, at all costs, to placate Russia and enter into the closest contact with her.

From this babel of cross-purposes and intrigue there gradually emerged a growing spirit of resistance of which the Sultan in particular did not fail to take advantage. Abd ul-Hamid himself, at the end of January in fear for his throne and his life, was a prey to the general panic prevailing; but as February wore on he began to nourish hopes that if the Russians gave him time he might again dominate his capital, repel at least the most exorbitant of their demands, and secure through some form of foreign intervention a heavy whittling down of the final peace terms. Ultimately he succeeded far beyond anything he could have dreamed of on the dark thirty-first of January, when the Adrianople terms were signed and Ignatyev was hurrying to the scene of action. For the Russians, despite Ignatyev and despite the Tsar, gave him ample time.[1]

Nothing is less easy to recapture than the psychological, or physical, momentum of a long, break-neck advance brought to a halt. The effect of the armistice at Russian head-quarters was immediate. The will to victory vanished. Difficulties that had but a few days before been discounted or overridden now loomed as obstacles possibly to be overcome but only after cautious planning and prolonged reorganization. All attention was now concentrated on the slenderness and exhaustion of the Russian forces, only some 40,000 in all, stretched out between Adrianople and Constantinople; on their almost complete lack of supplies and munitions; on the absence of any heavy artillery, the nearest a hundred and fifty miles and more beyond the Balkans; on the chaotic condition of the lines of communication stretching back to the Danube; on the necessity of bringing up and re-equipping the Guards and other formations of Gurko's army, itself almost as worn out and disorganized as the advance corps. To all the higher command, with the exception of Skobelev the younger, some considerable pause at least seemed now essential. To the troops—the men who had fought and marched and ridden like men possessed—nothing could be more welcome than the armistice, unless it were a final peace.[2]

[1] For this and the preceding paragraphs: Drummond Wolff, *Rambling Recollections*, vol. ii, pp. 148–9 (rumours); de Moüy, *Souvenirs et causeries d'un diplomate*, pp. 70–3 (on the chamber); Raschdau, *Ein sinkendes Reich*, pp. 120–1, 143–5 (on the chamber; critical of Akhmet Vekif); Layard's memoirs, in *British Museum, Add. MSS.* 38936, ff. 6–7, 26–8, 92–3, 103, 163 (favourable to the chamber); ff. 59–61 (on the Sultan, Akhmet Vekif, and Said); 39131, f. 22 (on Akhmet Vekif). *The Times* during January (especially 21 and 25) had full reports on the chamber.

[2.] Ignatyev on arrival at Adrianople typically believed the troops to be eager to

The pause which the armistice brought also gave time for the Turks to make the capture of Constantinople, or the Bosphorus heights, or the Gallipoli peninsula, seem in the eyes of the Russian staff a very different proposition from that presented when all was rose-lined during the Turkish panic. The change in atmosphere at the Grand Duke's head-quarters is sharply illustrated by the fact that, whereas as January drew to a close he was busy with wildly optimistic plans for a descent from Sevastopol on the Asiatic shore of the Bosphorus, when February came, and with it Ignatyev making the same proposal, this plan was cursorily dismissed as a 'poetical fantasy'.[1]

Yet, while the Grand Duke quickly relapsed into a mood of jaded indecision at the prospect of having to force his way against Turkish resistance backed by the British, St. Petersburg and London vied with each other in interpreting in the worst sense every action taken by the other. To the one England was doing her utmost to stiffen Turkish resistance while she hurried on preparations for an expeditionary force and in the same breath tried to extract the most damaging concessions. To the other Russia was on the point of seizing Constantinople and both Straits while she sent Ignatyev, the arch-foe of Turkey, to extort a preposterous peace and in the same breath tried to lull suspicion with worthless scraps of paper. Both views were in large part well founded, but the most dangerous factor was the intensity of suspicion with which each regarded the other. Thereby not only was the inevitable crisis itself rendered more acute, but the difficulties of any exit from it were greatly increased. They were only overcome in the last resort owing to a third party, Austria-Hungary. For all her slowness and vacillation, she did ultimately take up a stand side by side, if not linked, with England. The probability of a war with her, combined with England and Turkey, forced Russia to waver so unsteadily that it gave the opportunity for fear to replace suspicion as the dominant note in the ruling circles in St. Petersburg, and for those who stood for peace to gain a decisive hearing. Whereas suspicion breeds failure, fear can provide a basis

press on and give the Turks a final beating; *San Stefano*, p. 79. Vereshchagin, the painter, who was at the time with the advance cavalry and heroized Skobelev, gives a description, bearing the stamp of truth because from him unexpected, of officers and men having no regrets at the armistice and being delighted at the prospect of peace and a speedy return home; *Na Voine*, pp. 269–73.

[1] *San Stefano*, pp. 141–2; cf. above, p. 355.

for an agreement, even though its after-effects continue long to disturb.

The main field of the suspicions of Russia and England lay immediately in the intricate and shifting military situation in and around Constantinople and the Straits, and it was upon this that hinged the diplomatic struggle of February, March, and April. The simultaneous struggle between Russia and Austria-Hungary was not in the same way directly bound up with the problem of Constantinople and the Straits, but it will be necessary to treat first of the rival efforts to forestall possession of them, reserving for the next two chapters the making of the treaty of San Stefano and the contest with Vienna.

A word of further explanation is required as to the question of communications during these months. As already stated (p. 349), the Grand Duke before the armistice was solely dependent on his erratic field telegraph, via Kazanlik across the Balkan range to the Danube, which had to be largely supplemented by relays of mounted orderlies: at the Danube there was a break; then there was a line continuing to Bucarest and the main Russian system. About the middle of February the delays of this route were somewhat shortened by the laying of a cable across the Danube. But within a week of the signature of the armistice new communication was established by reopening the Adrianople–Constantinople line and by the resumption of the Constantinople–Odessa cable service, and the bulk of the Russian telegrams went this way. It was normally much quicker, though also subject to delays (possibly deliberate) and to leakage in Constantinople. The fact that the cable service was operated by a British company caused additional suspicion, but the Russians were in a strong position at the Odessa end, where they claimed to have held up and deciphered Layard's telegrams sent by this route.[1]

The week immediately following the signature of the Adrianople terms was relatively calm, but it was the uneasy swell

---

[1] *Skalon*, vol. ii, pp. 238, 241, 288; *Hasenkampf*, pp. 401, 439–40. Ignatyev maintains that the British company operating the Odessa cable delivered copies of the telegrams to the British embassy and deliberately delayed or mutilated them; *San Stefano*, pp. 137–8, 150. Additional difficulties at G.H.Q. were caused by none of the telegraphists knowing French; *Skalon*, vol. ii, p. 246. There was also some communication between Adrianople and St. Petersburg by a line via Dedeagach and Valona; *Nouvelle Revue*, 1880, p. 769; *San Stefano*, p. 84; Layard to Derby, tel., no. 229, 17 Feb., copy in *F.O.* 65/1024, suspecting the Valona line of being worked in connivance with the Russians.

between one storm and a greater one at hand. The Russians had more than enough to do in taking up the demarcation line and beginning to get their troops and supply service into some semblance of order. The Grand Duke Nicholas, while he pondered anxiously the Tsar's reply of 24 January as to Constantinople and Gallipoli in the event of English action, could find comfort in the approval of the armistice implied in his brother's final instructions to hasten its conclusion, and in the injunction that an approach to Constantinople should not enter into his views as soon as the conditions had been accepted.[1]

At this moment there was a flurry from the side of Greece. The fall of Plevna, the re-entry of Serbia into the war, and then the trans-Balkan campaign drove the Greeks to believe that, as Giers broadly hinted to them, they had better go to war if they were to gain anything from the victors. Early in January a royal decree called up 10,000 men of the second reserve, and the Greeks counted on putting 30,000 troops into the field. The danger was that the war might be over before they could effect anything. King George was in steady correspondence with the Grand Duke Nicholas, but events were now far outpacing correspondence.[2] 'Roi veut guerre immédiate', Saburov telegraphed on 1 January, 'oserai-je demander si probabilités sont pour continuation de guerre?' The usual methods were being intensified; the government were actively fomenting insurrections in Thessaly and Epirus; more and more arms were being shipped over to Crete; open war would probably follow the outbreak of the insurrections (Saburov, tel. to St. Petersburg, 22 Dec.). During January excitement grew intense in Athens culminating in the formation of a war ministry headed by Coumoundouros. Trusting to the, all too vague, Russian declarations in the preceding summer, believing the Turks to be too panic-stricken for any action, hoping that the armistice might be yet further delayed, the order was given on 1 February for Greek troops to cross the frontier. That evening a Havas report appeared in Athens that the armistice had been signed, but no official confirmation came till the 3rd, and the troops were not recalled.[3]

---

[1] Tsar to the Grand Duke, tel., 1 Feb., rec. 3 Feb.; text in *Skalon*, vol. ii, p. 211; *Hasenkampf*, p. 413. The Tsar did not receive his brother's telegram announcing the signature of the armistice until about midday 2 Feb.; ib., p. 215, p. 415.

[2] Driault et Lhéritier, *Histoire diplomatique de la Grèce de 1821 à nos jours*, vol. iii, p. 447.

[3] Driault et Lhéritier, op. cit., pp. 427-32, 439, 444, 447-53; Lascaris,

The Greeks had rushed in without any adequate diplomatic preparations in St. Petersburg, and without regard to their helplessness at sea. A Turkish squadron and reinforcements to Thessaly were promptly under orders. Russia immediately joined the other powers in demanding that the Greek troops should be withdrawn behind the frontier. Coerced by these minatory measures the Athens government complied. By 7 February the troops were back where they had started from. The Russians, though willing for Epirus, Thessaly, and Crete to be handed over eventually to Greece, were far too hard pressed to add to the Balkan broil by actively assisting the Greeks to acquire these lands. The Tsar did not hesitate to put the strongest pressure upon King George. Only Ignatyev was anxious to forestall the armistice and utilize Greek intervention and risings among the Greek Christians for the destruction of Turkish rule in Europe. But he was at that moment in Bucarest on his way to Adrianople, and hence was powerless. Russia made no move to support her Orthodox brothers—who were not Slavs. The Greeks in reaction turned more and more attentive ears to the overtures which now came to them from London and which seemed to spell the defence of Hellenism against Slavdom. They could not abandon the furtive fomenting of insurrections, but British consuls in Epirus and Thessaly kept them within bounds, and the British government constrained Athens to keep the peace at least formally. After San Stefano laid open the Russian designs on the Aegean and Macedonia, Greek and British interests seemed more than ever to go hand in hand, anti-Slav feelings flared out unconstrainedly, and Russian influence at Athens sank to zero.[1]

Hardly had the Greek escapade collapsed when Ignatyev reached Adrianople (8 Feb.). He was of course too late: the armistice was more than a week old. Rumours of its signature had reached him while still in Bucarest, then fuller news while with the Tsarevich, in the congenial atmosphere of whose headquarters he found enmity towards the Grand Duke Nicholas

---

La politique extérieure de la Grèce avant et après le congrès de Berlin, p. 96 (for Giers, 12 Jan.).

[1] Driault et Lhéritier, op. cit., pp. 456–9, 466, 471–2, 484; *Hasenkampf*, p. 423; *Skalon*, vol. ii, pp. 228–9; Ignatyev to Gorchakov, from Bucarest, tel., 2 Feb. (rumours only had as yet reached him of the signature of the armistice), text in *San Stefano*, p. 48; Radowitz, *Aufzeichnungen und Erinnerungen*, vol. ii, p. 6 (Radowitz was in Athens at the time).

enough and to spare. The Tsarevich already in the preceding autumn had lost all shreds of confidence in G.H.Q. and had agreed with his friend and adviser Pobedonostsev as to the urgent necessity of removing the Grand Duke from the command. Over the New Year intrigues had been spun to displace Gurko by the Tsarevich and to bring into action as his new chief of staff Obruchev, a *bête noire* of G.H.Q. and a man whose sweeping ambition might possibly have given the Russians Constantinople. The Grand Duke had angrily refused to sacrifice the hero of the army, Gurko. The relations between the two head-quarters were worse than ever: the Tsarevich was kept completely in the dark: there had been no consultation as to the demarcation line; there was to be no evacuation of Shumla and Varna, the two fortresses which barred the way to the Tsarevich's army. Ignatyev was thus encouraged in his schemes for himself going direct to Constantinople and there conducting negotiations over the head of G.H.Q. According to his own account, he was only dissuaded by the Tsarevich in person from returning to Bucarest and wiring for new instructions to that effect.[1]

Ignatyev arrived at Adrianople in the worst of tempers. He expected to find G.H.Q. hostile and obstructive, and he was right. The only bright spot was the effusive welcome given him by Cherkasky, the civil governor for Bulgaria, himself at daggers drawn with G.H.Q.; but Cherkasky was already sickening and within a month he was dead. G.H.Q. as a whole was tired, weak, and eager for peace, the very opposite of Ignatyev himself. They had dreaded his arrival in advance: now his imperious conduct, his unconcealed bitterness at their failure to break off the armistice negotiations, his reduplicated intrigues intensified their dislike and their fear of a man incontestably far superior to any of them in resourcefulness and experience. To none was Ignatyev more antipathetic than to the Grand Duke himself, who was temperamentally distrustful of, and in any case quite unable to follow, the rapid and intricate combinations of the diplomatist's mind. From the first

---

[1] Letter of Pobedonostsev to the Tsarevich, 29 Sept. 1877, text in *Pisma Pobedonostseva k Aleksandru III*, vol. i, p. 71; letter of Tsarevich to Pobedonostsev, 12 Nov., text in *K. P. Pobedonostsev i ego korrespondenty*, vol. i, pt. 2, p. 1021; *Skalon*, vol. ii, pp. 74–5, 97–103, 134, 168, 170, 222, *Hasenkampf*, pp. 249, 281, and *Pisma Pobedonostseva k Aleksandru III*, vol. i, p. 111 (on the Tsarevich–Obruchev intrigue); *San Stefano*, pp. 67–9.

the two men quarrelled violently. On the very day of Ignatyev's arrival he directly tasked the Grand Duke with not having carried out the Tsar's instructions to occupy the heights commanding Constantinople before concluding an armistice.[1] The importance of this mutual hostility during the following month was great, since it meant that to a considerable extent the influence and ability of Ignatyev were counteracted by his own countrymen. The Grand Duke and his staff considered Ignatyev's demands extravagant and his methods impolitic, and the Turks did not fail to play upon this divergence in their enemy's camp. The one Russian on the spot, who had the capacity and was straining every nerve to combine force and diplomacy so as to present Europe with a series of *faits accomplis*, by his alienation of his own head-quarters failed to change its psychological atmosphere and hence failed to overcome the technical objections to which his bold, forward policy was open. For in the last resort the force which Ignatyev required to use lay in the hands of the Grand Duke: he alone could issue the decisive orders—which never came. The effect of Ignatyev at Adrianople was but to accentuate by reaction the indecision of the military.

Such was not the moment for any divergences to impair unity of action by the Russians. On the same day as Ignatyev reached Adrianople (8 Feb.) the British fleet was ordered from Besika Bay to Constantinople. This time there were no countermanding orders to delay the over-ripe crisis. Disraeli and the war party in the cabinet, urged on by the Queen, had triumphed. They had clutched at the belief that the Russians, as if the enormity of their bases of peace and their commanding military position were not enough, had violated the armistice and were continuing to advance. On 4 February Queen Victoria anxiously retailed news from Berlin that the Russians were only trifling with the Turks and despite the armistice were

---

[1] According to Ignatyev these instructions had been telegraphed on either 23 or 24 Jan. After heated argument and much browbeating of the signals officers Ignatyev claims to have extracted the admission that such a telegram had been received, but only on 31 Jan., when it was impossible, declared the Grand Duke, to go back upon his acceptance of the Turkish agreement to sign the armistice. *San Stefano*, pp. 77–81. Ignatyev presumably was referring to the telegram of 24 Jan., but this was received on 29, not 31 Jan., and was not a direct order to occupy the Bosphorus heights (see above, pp. 357–9). Ignatyev represents Gurko and Skobelev the younger (apart from Cherkasky) as alone being eager for energetic action. He succeeded in getting his protégé Tseretelev transferred from the army to the diplomatic staff at head-quarters.

pushing on to Constantinople. This was followed by the same news arriving from Constantinople itself. The Turkish government, still ignorant of the exact details of the armistice, on 5 February begged Layard to inform London that the Russians in advancing as far as Chataldja and demanding the evacuation of the Buyuk–Chekmedje lines were ignoring the demarcation line. Layard telegraphed: 'Armistice does not stop Russian advance. Porte in great alarm. . . . The conduct of the Russians is inexplicable, and treachery is suspected.' This was decisively sufficient for the cabinet. On the 8th Hornby was ordered with six ships to pass the Dardanelles and proceed to Constantinople, 'for the protection of British life and property'. There was considerable delay, since the Sultan refused to compromise himself by issuing a *firman* for the passage of the Straits either to the British or to the Austrians, who also applied, and since Layard was averse from sending up the fleet, in violation of the Straits convention, without the Sultan's consent and declared (10 Feb.) that 'there is no reason to apprehend at present any danger to British subjects or property here'. Hornby was ordered, nevertheless, to pass through the Dardanelles and to return fire if necessary.[1]

The Turks, feeling certain that the appearance of the British fleet would be followed by a Russian occupation, were in a condition of frenzied despair. The Sultan believed that it would cost him his throne and his life: the impetuous Akhmet Vekif rained protests upon Layard against a passage of the Dardanelles: only Said Pasha, at the admiralty, preserved some measure of coolness and worked unswervingly for a compromise. After three days of incessant parleyings Layard could telegraph (10 Feb.) that, if the British government considered it essential to send up the fleet, the Turks would probably make only a formal protest to save their face against the Russians.[2]   On

---

[1] Queen Victoria to Derby, tel., from Osborne, 4 Feb., in *F.O.* 65/1023; memorandum by Mr. Currie, 4 Apr., reviewing the events of these days and admitting that the Russians had not in fact violated the neutral line laid down in the armistice; in *F.O.* 65/1024. For the Austrian application: Derby to Elliot, tels., 8 and 12 Feb., drafts in *F.O.* 7/922 (urging the Austrians to act as the British); *San Stefano*, pp. 102–3; private letter of Layard to Hornby, 19 Feb., copy in Layard Papers, *British Museum, Add. MSS.* 39131, f. 32. The French and Italian governments also decided to apply for *firmans*, but their representatives at Constantinople did not actually do so; Derby to Loftus, tels., 8 Feb., in *F.O.* 181/565; private letter of Layard to Hornby, 19 Feb., as above.

[2] Layard's memoirs, in *British Museum, Add. MSS.* 38936, ff. 133–7, 144–58, 162.

13 February Hornby steamed up the Dardanelles, meeting with no resistance, but in response to the entreaties of the Sultan he did not anchor off Constantinople itself, but within sight off the island of Prinkipo (15 Feb.).[1] At the same time a £6,000,000 vote of credit was passed by the House of Commons and military and naval preparations were pressed on with yet more urgent haste. Napier of Magdala was summoned from Gibraltar to take command of the expeditionary force, Wolseley selected to act as his chief of staff.

The acute crisis to be prolonged for the next ten weeks was now reached. The effect of the British actions was immediate in Russia. The Tsar did not require to be urged along by the outburst of fury into which the whole of the Russian press broke, demanding immediate retaliation by seizing the Dardanelles and the Bosphorus. His armies had in one month swept from triumph to triumph, yet he had still offered the enemy the terms of December. He had not broken faith even when all resistance seemed to have been overcome and Constantinople and Gallipoli to lie at his mercy. The Turks accepted his terms; hostilities ceased; peace at least appeared on the near horizon. And then the English, on the mere rumour that he had broken the armistice, *which he had not*, showed their true colours, without the slightest regard of treaty obligations forced the Dardanelles in defiance of the Sultan, and obviously designed to dominate Constantinople and the Bosphorus and to force the Turks to renew the war. Thus for once passionately stirred the Tsar felt convinced that the English could never again be trusted, that they meant war, and that they must be forestalled by immediate action.

On the arrival of the news of Hornby being ordered to Constantinople the powers were at once informed that the Russian government were in consequence obliged 'to contemplate the

---

Layard thought that the fleet should have been sent two or three months earlier, that its dispatch at this juncture would make inevitable a Russian entry into Constantinople, and that the ostensible reason for sending it was preposterous. What he really wanted was a fleet and an expeditionary force frankly pledged to support the Turks to the full. The Russians believed, with substantial correctness, that the passage of the Dardanelles had been arranged between Layard and Akhmet Vekif, who had not, however, dared to urge an actual invitation; *San Stefano*, p. 152.

[1] Egerton, *Admiral Sir Geoffrey Phipps Hornby*, pp. 237–45; private letter of Layard to Hornby, 13 Feb., copy in Layard Papers, *British Museum, Add. MSS.* 39137, ff. 19–20; so too in copy of private letter to Derby, 15 Feb., ib., 39131, f. 30.

entry of a portion' of their troops into Constantinople, and the Sultan was told that measures must be concerted for the entry of some Russian troops, with the similar aim of protecting life and property![1] In the week following the Sultan multiplied appeals to the Tsar not to occupy his capital, but the latter insisted that a temporary occupation was inevitable unless the British retired through the Dardanelles.[2]

The Tsar's feelings were fully revealed in the telegram he sent his brother on 10 February, directing him to arrange with the Turks for a Russian entry into Constantinople with the same aim as the British, but adding: if the Turks object, we must be prepared to occupy Constantinople by force; 'I leave to you the numbers and moment to occupy.' This was the telegram which subsequently caused such altercation as to whether or not the Tsar had ever given an unqualified order to occupy Constantinople. At the moment at any rate it seemed such to Gorchakov and Milyutin, who thought that it would inevitably mean war with England. They therefore persuaded the Tsar to stop that telegram and to substitute for it one drafted by Milyutin: the entry of British ships into the Bosphorus will absolve us from our former obligations as to Gallipoli: if the British land anywhere, immediately occupy Constantinople; in such case I give you full freedom of action as regards the Bosphorus and the Dardanelles, except that you are to avoid a direct clash with the British as long as they do not commit hostile acts. This was dispatched on 11 February. The day after, the Tsar told Milyutin that he had after all sent the first telegram, as well as the second![3]

The second telegram only reached the Grand Duke on 13 February, but even so a day before the first, and as a final addition to his perplexity it was extremely difficult to decipher.

[1] Gorchakov's circular of 10 Feb., in *A. and P.*, 1878, lxxxi, C. 1951, no. 1 (published on 12 Feb.); Tsar to Sultan, tel., 11 Feb., text in *Tatishchev*, p. 449.

[2] Texts in *Tatishchev*, pp. 452–3, and *Skalon*, vol. ii, pp. 234–5.

[3] *Tatishchev*, pp. 447–8, citing Milyutin's diary for 12 Feb.; Tsar to the Grand Duke, tels., disp. 12.30 p.m. 10 Feb., rec. 14 Feb., disp. 5.40 p.m. 11 Feb., rec. 13 Feb., texts in *Skalon*, vol. ii, pp. 230, 232–3, and *Hasenkampf*, pp. 428, 430. It is not clear that the first telegram, though bearing 12.30 p.m. as the time of dispatch, was actually dispatched then. *Skalon*, vol. ii, pp. 364–6, writing after his return to St. Petersburg in defence of the Grand Duke against the Tsar's contention that his telegram of 10 Feb. was a categorical order to occupy Constantinople, gives much the same account of the two telegrams as does Tatishchev, but he does not give his source, which may well have been Milyutin again. See also the very much later account, supporting the Grand Duke, in Lamsdorff, *Dnevnik 1891–92*, p. 92.

What exactly *did* his brother want him to do? Actually there seems no doubt that the Tsar hoped the Grand Duke would act on his own and promptly seize Constantinople and the Bosphorus, with or without an agreement with the Turks. But the Grand Duke and his staff were more and more impressed by the probable strength of Turkish resistance and by the relative weakness of their own troops, who were now suffering severely from sickness; and the contradictions and uncertainties in the Tsar's instructions supplied sufficient ground for shirking the responsibility of interpreting them in the sense of drastic action. He therefore delayed replying to his brother till the 15th, when he assured him in vaguely optimistic terms that all would be carried out according to his instructions. On the following day, however, he sounded the keynote which was to be repeated in varying tones in his subsequent telegrams: every day the occupation of Constantinople by us becomes more difficult owing to increasing strength of Turkish forces, if they do not agree to our entry: do not think occupation of Constantinople so easy as a fortnight ago. He added that the British fleet was at Prinkipo (not at Constantinople or in the Bosphorus as his instructions had envisaged), and asked how he was to regard that action.[1]

In the meantime he continued to press the Turks for an agreement as to the entry of Russian troops into Constantinople; while Ignatyev was simultaneously hurrying on the peace negotiations with Safvet Pasha, the new plenipotentiary, who had arrived at Adrianople on 12 February. Ignatyev was also applying all possible pressure to induce the Grand Duke to take decisive action to ensure Russian control of Constantinople and both Straits. On 17 February, in view of sharp complaints from St. Petersburg as to G.H.Q. muddling their telegrams, he had prolonged conferences with Nicholas Nicholaevich and Nepokoichitsky, the chief of staff, in which all the Tsar's instructions were re-examined. These had by now been increased by the receipt of a telegram stating that the British government had been informed that in view of the British fleet having passed the Dardanelles and entered the Bosphorus (which in fact it had not) the temporary entry of a Russian detachment into Constantinople was inevitable, but that as a final concession Russia had promised not to occupy Gallipoli provided that no British troops

[1] The Grand Duke to Tsar, tels., 15 and 16 Feb., texts in *Hasenkampf*, pp. 432-3, 435-6; *Skalon*, vol. ii, pp. 236-7.

were landed on either shore of the Dardanelles. The telegram concluded by ordering vigilant action to prevent the British entering the Bosphorus, and, if they attempted to do so, occupation, if possible with the consent of the Sultan, of some of the fortifications on the European shore.[1]

It is not surprising that there was the utmost perplexity at G.H.Q. The Grand Duke thought that they could not make up their minds in St. Petersburg what to do and that Gorchakov was confounding matters. Ignatyev threw all the blame on Gorchakov: he never could give clear orders. The position now was that the following instructions one after the other had been received:

1. If the British fleet came up (not stated exactly where), the Russians must enter Constantinople (only with consent of Sultan?) (Gorchakov's circular of 10 Feb.).
2. The Sultan must concert measures for a Russian entry into Constantinople: a temporary occupation was inevitable unless the British retired through the Dardanelles (Tsar's telegrams to the Sultan, repeated to Grand Duke).
3. If the Sultan refused to allow occupation, the Grand Duke must be ready to effect it by force, the choice of time and numbers being left to him (Tsar's telegram of 10 Feb.).
4. If the British landed anywhere, Constantinople must be immediately occupied (Tsar's telegram of 11 Feb.).
5. In that case, full freedom of action was granted as regards the Bosphorus and the Dardanelles (ditto):
6. Except that a direct clash with the British must be avoided, unless they committed hostile acts (exact meaning?) (ditto).
7. The entry of British ships into the Bosphorus would cancel the previous Russian commitments in regard to Gallipoli (ditto).
8. Provided no British troops landed on either shore of the Dardanelles, the Russians were not to occupy Gallipoli (Tsar's telegram of 15 Feb.).
9. Vigilant action must be taken to prevent the entrance of British ships into the Bosphorus (ditto).

[1] Tsar to the Grand Duke, tel., disp. 10.40 p.m. 15 Feb., rec. night 16 Feb. and concluding portion morning 17 Feb., text in *Hasenkampf*, p. 437; *Skalon*, vol. ii, p. 238.

10. In the event of any British attempt on the Bosphorus the fortifications on the European shore must be occupied if possible with the consent of the Sultan (and otherwise without his consent?) (ditto).

11. Since the British fleet had passed the Dardanelles and entered the Bosphorus (but it had not), a temporary occupation of Constantinople was inevitable (ditto).

Certainly there was ample excuse for doubt and hesitation. In the evening of the 17th, during one of the conferences with Ignatyev, the last point at least was cleared up by the arrival of a telegram stating that in view of the British having anchored off Prinkipo (which was correct, though by the 17th they had just moved into the Gulf of Mudania farther away from Constantinople) a temporary occupation of Constantinople was inevitable.[1] But it was evident from 9 and 10 that a complete misapprehension existed in St. Petersburg as to the possibility of the Russians, on the line they then occupied, keeping a close watch on the British fleet or forestalling its action in the Bosphorus.[2] The demarcation line, from which the Russians had not advanced, was too far from the Bosphorus for that, and they had neither ships nor (at that moment) mines, and nothing but field artillery very poorly supplied with ammunition.

The Grand Duke Nicholas, thoroughly exasperated with the British and not believing that they would declare war (he had just learnt that there was no landing force with the fleet), was finally brought by Ignatyev to the conclusion that the Tsar did mean that Constantinople must be occupied in any event, but the fears of his chief of staff reinforced his own timidity, and he still recoiled from an actual break with the Turks. Thus Ignatyev fell back upon the suggestion that, as the negotiations with the Turks for an entry into Constantinople were being wrecked by the violent hostility of the British and Austrian embassies, arrangements should immediately be made with the Turks for the occupation by the Russians of San Stefano and certain barracks and suburbs on the west and south-west of Constantinople. After prolonged conference in the evening of 17 February

[1] Gorchakov to the Grand Duke (repeating tel. of the Tsar to the Sultan), tel., disp. 15 Feb., rec. about 5.0 p.m. 17 Feb., text in *Hasenkampf*, p. 440; *Skalon*, vol. ii, p. 241. It was believed at G.H.Q. that this telegram had been intentionally delayed in Constantinople; ib., and *San Stefano*, pp. 137–8.

[2] This was pointed out to the Tsar by the Grand Duke, tel., 17 Feb., text in *Hasenkampf*, pp. 439–40.

it was decided to act accordingly, and that night Onou, ex-first dragoman at the Russian embassy, who had just returned from a week of negotiating in Constantinople, was sent back with requisite instructions.[1]

Having followed through from the angle of the Russian G.H.Q. the intricacies of the new situation created by the sending of the British fleet to Constantinople, we must now turn back to the diplomatic struggle simultaneously being fought out between St. Petersburg and London. In this struggle the attitude of Shuvalov was crucial. Subsequently, when the failure of the Russians to occupy Constantinople and the substitution of the treaty of Berlin for that of San Stefano required a scapegoat, Shuvalov was singled out as the man who was guilty of persistent truckling to the English and above all of urging that Constantinople should not be entered. Against this last charge in particular Shuvalov countered privately in his memoirs with an indignant defence, in which he maintained that throughout the crisis of February he assumed from the Russian circular of 10 February that the Tsar was decided upon a temporary occupation of Constantinople and that in his conversations with Derby he accordingly represented such an occupation as virtually a *fait accompli*. His telegrams and private letters to Gorchakov at the time bear out the subsequent statements in his memoirs, with one important qualification, and his contention that it was Gallipoli and the Dardanelles and not Constantinople which he regarded as the real danger-point is substantiated. It is fair to say that Shuvalov, after 11 February, neither wished to contribute nor did contribute anything towards the failure of the Russians to enter Constantinople.

At the same time it is true that Shuvalov was bent upon preventing a rupture and that he was therefore ready enough to make certain concessions, at a time when any concession was anathema to the Tsar and his entourage. In contrast with their prevailing mood, he believed that the essential was the retention of Derby at the Foreign Office. 'La seule chose dont je me suis occupé depuis trois jours', he wrote privately to Gorchakov on 17 February, 'c'est d'ajourner une explosion de la part des Ministres anglais. Gagner un jour, une heure, c'est

---

[1] *Skalon*, vol. ii, pp. 241–2; *Hasenkampf*, pp. 440–1; *San Stefano*, p. 102. The Tsar was informed of the proposed move to San Stefano that same night, 17 Feb.

peut-être prévenir la rupture entre les deux pays.'[1] The one means of averting the explosion lay in his intimate relations with Derby, in whose personal veracity he entirely believed and whom he consistently represented to St. Petersburg in the most favourable light. 'Plus d'hésitations, de défaillances chez lui; il est calme, résiste aux incitations passionnées de l'opinion publique et croit encore à la possibilité de voir les choses s'arranger. Je dois ajouter que bien peu de monde partage à Londres cet espoir. . . .'[2] This last statement alone met with agreement from Shuvalov's superiors; they had no confidence whatever in Derby, and they could feel themselves justified in their belief that London was beyond hope or calculation from Shuvalov's own description of the political chaos:

'Confusion générale, totale, absolue! — c'est le mot de la situation et l'on pourrait se demander si nous sommes à Londres sous un Gouvernement régulier ou une "convention". La Reine et ses princes interviennent sans cesse dans les affaires publiques; ils crient bien haut que si l'humiliation de l'Angleterre devait durer quelques jours de plus, ils pendraient Lord Derby au premier arbre de Hyde Park. Les clubs signent des pétitions pour que le Comte soit renvoyé de son poste; l'on se croirait vraiment à Constantinople!'[2]

The ambassador did indeed, in conspiracy almost with the foreign secretary, succeed in weathering the immediate storm, but it was at the cost of tying himself more closely than ever to Derby and of antagonizing further the dominant circles in St. Petersburg. Shuvalov was not in general policy particularly anglophil, but neither he nor Derby was swayed by the violent nationalist feelings which were uppermost in England and Russia. That was enough to stamp them with opprobrium. Derby paid the penalty at the end of March. Shuvalov fell into marked disfavour at once: the Tsar and he moved in different worlds in the struggle over Gallipoli: at first intending him for the projected conference at Baden-Baden, now the Tsar would not have him even as the second Russian representative.[3] Yet in the end the course of events and the flexibility of the man himself were to bring him, for two fateful months, into the first rank among Alexander's counsellors. And meanwhile in February he secured his immediate aim; there was for the moment no actual break between Russia and England.

[1] Shuvalov to Gorchakov, letter, 17 Feb., text in *Seton-Watson MSS.*
[2] Shuvalov to Gorchakov, lettre particulière, 14 Feb., text in *Seton-Watson MSS.*
[3] Gorchakov to Shuvalov, letter, 21 Feb., text in *Seton-Watson MSS.*

The first reaction of Shuvalov to the news of the decision of the British cabinet to send the fleet to Constantinople left nothing to be desired in the eyes even of perfervid Russian nationalists: he warned Derby emphatically (9 Feb.) that, if the decision were carried out, all engagements in respect of Constantinople and Gallipoli would cease to be of effect. But on the next day Shuvalov wavered, for he telegraphed twice (10 Feb.) advising indeed an energetic declaration that Russia was now freed from her previous obligations but adding the condition that if the British landed even one single man Russia would be obliged to enter Constantinople; and on the 11th, when asked by Derby whether the Russians would enter Constantinople if the British fleet came up to the Bosphorus or only if the British landed, he answered that he must ask for instructions, and proceeded to warn Gorchakov that the former alternative would mean a rupture but that the latter would probably not, as the British would refrain from landing. Shuvalov was almost certain that the fleet had no troops on board to disembark (Derby explicitly assured him of this on the 15th), so that the only possibility was a very small naval landing-party. Therefore Shuvalov's suggestion was tantamount to tying the hands of the Russians without any substantial corresponding concession. Immediate rupture was in the air in London, and Shuvalov was struggling at all costs to avoid receiving his passports.[1]

St. Petersburg, however, was quite unmoved. Gorchakov tartly replied (12 Feb.) that the nuance, as he styled it, between a British entry into the Bosphorus without a landing and an entry with a landing made no difference. Four days later he countered the British pretext for the dispatch of their fleet with the rejoinder that the Russian occupation of Constantinople would last only as long as the security of the Christian inhabitants was menaced, only as long as the fleet should not have repassed the Dardanelles.[2] Shuvalov from now (12 Feb.) onwards assumed a Russian occupation to be inevitable, steadily impressed this upon Derby, and succeeded in shifting the diplomatic struggle from Constantinople to the Dardanelles. It was essential from the British point of view that the communications of their fleet in the Sea of Marmara should not be further

---

[1] Shuvalov to Gorchakov, tels., 9, 10, 11, and 15 Feb., texts in *Seton-Watson MSS.*
[2] Gorchakov to Shuvalov, tels., 12 and 16 Feb., texts in *Seton-Watson MSS.*

threatened by the Russians, and Shuvalov concentrated on bringing home to his government the seriousness of any threat to the Dardanelles: that, as even the pacific Derby declared, would mean war, though he significantly did not mention an occupation of Constantinople as similarly providing a *casus belli*. Shuvalov therefore counselled (13 and 14 Feb.) giving a promise not to occupy Gallipoli or the Bulair lines provided that the British did not land at any point on the European or Asiatic shores.[1]

The immediate effect of Shuvalov's telegrams was merely to exasperate the Tsar. His minutes on them reveal the full depths of his exasperation. 'Me fondant sur ce télégramme, j'ai donné l'ordre à mon frère d'accélérer la marche de mes troupes tant sur Constantinople que sur Gallipoli.' 'Et c'est pour cela [to endanger the safety of the British fleet by a movement on Gallipoli] que nous devons le faire.'[2] Yet Alexander was not in the last resort prepared to sweep aside the arguments of his foreign office and give full rein to his desires. On 15 February he sanctioned an instruction to Shuvalov to inform the British government that a temporary Russian entry into Constantinople was inevitable but that, as a final concession, the Russians would maintain their promise not to occupy Gallipoli provided that no British were landed on either shore of the Dardanelles.[3] When later on the same day (15 Feb.) Loftus, in accordance with urgent instructions, pressed for explicit assurances, he found Gorchakov 'calm and anxious; but very determined', curtly replying that he 'would take no further engagements or give any more assurances' in regard to Gallipoli, and that 'he could only view it [the order to the fleet] as an act of political demonstration against Russia'. 'Faites ce que vous voulez' were his final words.[4]

Loftus's telegram recounting this interview reached London on the 16th. 'Grand émoi', Shuvalov wrote next day, 'convocation immédiate du Conseil, et je reçus l'avis que les choses tournaient au plus mal.' He felt certain that if he communicated, as instructed, the reply of 15 February the bomb would

---

[1] Shuvalov to Gorchakov, tels., 13 and 14 Feb., texts in *Seton-Watson MSS*.

[2] Tsar's minutes on Shuvalov's tels. of 13 and 14 Feb., in Goriainow, *Le Bosphore et les Dardanelles*, pp. 364–5.

[3] Gorchakov to Shuvalov, tel., 15 Feb., rec. that same night, text in *Seton-Watson MSS*.

[4] Loftus to Derby, tel. and disp., no. 217, 15 Feb., in *F.O.* 65/999.

burst: for he interpreted it as a repetition of the engagement given a month before, on 15 January, and that engagement did not explicitly cover the Bulair lines and also was dependent on the Turks not concentrating any regular forces on Gallipoli, where in fact Suleiman was still in command of a considerable regular force. Shuvalov therefore hurried to Derby (16 Feb.) and informed him that the reply from Gorchakov was satisfactory, but in parts undecipherable and that he had wired for a repetition. The 16th was a Saturday: Parliament would not meet until the Monday: Derby was sufficiently appeased by the ambassador's explanation to conclude a new 'armistice' until then; and Shuvalov at once implored Gorchakov to modify his reply by adding the words 'ni entrer dans lignes de Bulair'.[1] His appeal was successful. On 17 February the Tsar empowered his ambassador formally to communicate assurances in the terms formulated in the embassy, and on the following day Shuvalov did so. Russia promised not to occupy Gallipoli and not to enter the Bulair lines provided that no British forces were landed on the European or Asiatic shores of the Dardanelles. Derby responded by undertaking that no British troops would be landed on the European shore of the Straits, and offering to give the same assurance as regards the Asiatic shore, if the Russians would do likewise (19 Feb.). On the 21st they did so, but Gorchakov refused to substitute the word 'Straits', so that the undertaking applied only to the Dardanelles.[2]

This engagement represented a decided success for the English, but, since neither side trusted the other, the tension was but slightly relieved. Hornby was immediately again ordered to assist the Bulair lines if seriously attacked,[3] and the situation round Constantinople itself continued to arouse the

[1] Shuvalov to Gorchakov, letter, 17 Feb., and tel., 16 Feb., texts in *Seton-Watson MSS.*; Derby to Loftus, disp., most conf., no. 150, 16 Feb., in *F.O.* 181/565. Shuvalov was at the same time much perturbed by reports as to the Austrian negotiations with the British. Derby, on 16 Feb., immediately after a long interview with Beust, said to Shuvalov: 'Je vous conjure, faites Votre possible pour éviter une guerre européenne. Je puis Vous le dire *aujourd'hui*, ne vous fiez pas à l'Autriche, car dans le cas d'une guerre, elle sera contre Vous.' Shuvalov to Gorchakov, letter, 17 Feb., text in *Seton-Watson MSS.* Shuvalov, however, followed this up with more reassuring information and on the 20th reported the failure of the loan negotiations; letter, 18 Feb., tels., 18 and 20 Feb., ib. Cf. below, p. 433.

[2] Gorchakov to Shuvalov, tel., 17 Feb., text in *Seton-Watson MSS.*; *A. and P.*, 1878, lxxxi, C. 1954, nos. 1 and 2.

[3] Derby to Layard, tel., 22 Feb., in *F.O.* 78/2766.

worst fears of the English. From St. Petersburg Loftus urged on his government the extreme desirability of requiring from Russia a similar engagement in respect of the Bosphorus.[1] In London Derby warned Shuvalov (21 Feb.) that, if Russian troops entered Constantinople without the consent of the Sultan, Loftus would be withdrawn and England would decline to enter into the proposed conference. He did not, however, actually threaten war, and Hornby, in contrast with his orders relative to Bulair, was instructed not to attempt armed resistance to a Russian entry into Constantinople.[2] Derby had asked that his warning of the 21st should be kept secret, but Gorchakov promptly communicated it to the other powers, and to Shuvalov gave pompous vent to his feelings: 'Il [the British government] fera ce qu'il voudra. L'histoire et peut-être même les contemporains porteront leur verdict sur cette conduite complètement illogique et sur ce dédain pour la paix générale.'[3]

From the British side the distrust of the Russians was being powerfully reinforced by the alarmist reports of their naval commanders on the spot. Hornby spoke of nearly 50,000 Russians being but twelve miles from Bulair and of their having a feasible plan for crossing the gulf of Xeros and taking the Bulair lines in the rear, and he recommended certain measures to oppose any such attack. Smith, in charge of the admiralty, approved and added that the Russian commander was to be warned that any attempt to land on the Gallipoli peninsula would be opposed by force. Further telegrams followed, giving an impression of the improbability of any effective resistance by the Turks or of their collaboration with the English, and emphasizing the position at Gallipoli as most critical. Clearly the cabinet, with their fears thus intensified, would take all possible steps lest the Russians should break their engagements.[4]

[1] Loftus to Derby, tel., private and conf., no. 43, and disp., no. 245, 20 Feb., in *F.O.* 65/999.

[2] Shuvalov to Gorchakov, tel., 21 Feb., communicating memorandum of Derby of that date, text in *Seton-Watson MSS.*; Derby to Layard, tel., 22 Feb., in *F.O.* 78/2766.

[3] Shuvalov to Gorchakov, tel., 22 Feb.; Gorchakov to Shuvalov, tels., 22 and 24 Feb., texts in *Seton-Watson MSS.*

[4] Hornby (from Gallipoli) to W. H. Smith, tel., 14 Feb.; W. H. Smith to Hornby, tel., 15 Feb.; Rear-Admiral Commerell (from Gallipoli) and Hornby (from Prinkipo) to W. H. Smith, tels., 15 and 17 Feb.; texts in Maxwell, *Life of W. H.*

On the other hand, Shuvalov's difficulties were equally increased by his own government's ineradicable conviction that the English would stick at no duplicity. St. Petersburg was in possession of secret information (which in fact was substantially accurate) that Layard was negotiating with the Porte for the purchase of four of the best Turkish warships and for permission to occupy the Chanak forts, on the Asiatic side of the Dardanelles, with a promise to restore them on the conclusion of peace (but was it likely that the promise would ever be fulfilled?). Shuvalov at first tried to discountenance this information, on the strength of assurances from Derby, but Gorchakov insisted that the information was correct, and Shuvalov had to admit that Layard was probably pursuing a personal policy, perhaps in secret correspondence with Disraeli, without the knowledge of the foreign secretary.[1] A few days later St. Petersburg was listening disgustedly to the rumours, loudly buzzing

Smith, vol. i, pp. 324–6; Hornby to W. H. Smith, private letter, 19 Feb., text in Egerton, *Admiral Sir Geoffrey Phipps Hornby*, pp. 252–4. The earlier reports of Capt. Fife from Gallipoli, at the end of January and the beginning of February, emphasized the necessity of removing Suleiman from command there, but represented the Turkish strength of 19,000 at Bulair as sufficient for its defence; *F.O.* 78/2883. Hornby was equally anxious to get rid of Suleiman, and was constantly urging the necessity of occupying the Bulair lines by British troops; Egerton, op. cit., pp. 216–18, 234–6, 253, 260.

[1] See also p. 407. Gorchakov to Shuvalov, tels., 18, 19, and 20 Feb.; Shuvalov to Gorchakov, tel., 19 Feb., and letter, 20 Feb.; texts in *Seton-Watson MSS.* Derby to Loftus, disp., no. 159, secret, 19 Feb., in *F.O.* 181/565, recounts Shuvalov's private explanation to him as to Russian insistence on a British undertaking not to land on the Asiatic shore. Derby admitted only that negotiations were on foot for the sale of three warships under construction in England for Turkey; he apparently did not deny the rumour as to the Chanak forts. According to Shuvalov Derby assured him that Layard had had no pourparlers with the Porte as to an occupation of the Asiatic forts of the Dardanelles; that the British had no troops to disembark; and that Layard had only been authorized to press the Porte to take fully adequate measures for the defence of the Dardanelles; Shuvalov to Gorchakov, letter, 20 Feb., text in *Seton-Watson MSS.* In fact Derby had instructed Layard on 14 Feb. to secure the purchase of the four best Turkish warships, but Layard had found the Sultan and the government extremely averse to any such action and, after consultation with Hobart Pasha, had dropped the matter; Derby to Layard, tel., most secret, 14 Feb., copy in Layard Papers, *British Museum, Add. MSS.* 39137, f. 25 (cf. 39131, f. 37); Layard's memoirs, ib. 38936, ff. 181–2, 193–4. On the other hand, Layard, acting on instructions, had by 19 Feb. secured the consent of the Sultan to an occupation of the Asiatic shore of the Dardanelles should the Russians force the Bulair lines; private letters of Layard to Hornby, 17 and 19 Feb., copies in Layard Papers, ib. 39131, ff. 32–3, and cf. Layard's memoirs, ib. 38936, ff. 183, 186–7. The Russians had probably learnt of these negotiations through the foreign minister himself, Server Pasha, who was removed from his post only on 19 Feb., largely owing to the accusations of Layard.

in London, that the British were about to seize some Turkish island or islands.[1] Thus the Russians regarded any British protestations as worthless scraps of paper, unless they took all possible counter-measures in advance.

On either side, the diplomatic struggle was subsidiary to the moves and counter-moves in and around Constantinople, and here the third week of February saw, not indeed a Russian entry into Constantinople, but a forward step almost as serious, the advance of Russian head-quarters and troops to San Stefano and neighbouring suburbs. The first reports as to this made the British government believe that it had been made without any agreement with the Turks, and, since they were also favoured with harrowing accounts from Layard as to the enormity of the peace terms demanded by Ignatyev, Shuvalov still had more than enough to do to keep them within bounds.[2]

The Russian peace terms naturally were severe. Onou, the Russian official sent to Constantinople to negotiate an entry, reported that the Sultan and his ministers would rather flee from the capital to Asia than accept them. Server Pasha, the russophil foreign minister bitterly denounced by Layard, was removed on 19 February in favour of Safvet, who received new instructions at Adrianople and withdrew all the concessions he had made (20 Feb.).[3] The Turks were being faced as well with the Russian demand for an agreement to advance to San Stefano, which as has already been seen had been decided upon on 17 February. Since, however, this represented a whittling down of the original demand for an agreement to enter Constantinople itself, might not Akhmet Vekif and the war party successfully stand by their guns and procure a still greater diminution in the demands of the Russians? They attempted to do this, but their efforts to checkmate Ignatyev by sending Namyk Pasha as a special ambassador direct to St. Petersburg

---

[1] Derby to Loftus, cancelled disp., no. 189, 26 Feb., in *F.O.* 65/994, reporting a warning from Shuvalov as to the seriousness of any seizure of Turkish islands; Shuvalov to Gorchakov, tel., 27 Feb., text in *Seton-Watson MSS.*, reporting possible occupation by the British of Mytilene or Crete, or both, and his warning to Derby that the Russian government would in that event be freed of all previous obligations.

[2] Shuvalov to Gorchakov, tel., 21 Feb.; Gorchakov to Shuvalov, tel., 22 Feb.; the Grand Duke to Shuvalov, tel., 24 Feb.; texts in *Skalon*, vol. ii, pp. 263–4, *Hasenkampf*, pp. 458–9.

[3] Onou's report of 19 Feb. from Constantinople, paraphrase in *San Stefano*, p. 148; *Hasenkampf*, p. 448; and *Skalon*, vol. ii, pp. 251–2, under date 20 and 21 Feb. For Server Pasha's dismissal, see also below, p. 400.

were stultified by the absolute refusal of the Tsar to receive him before peace had been signed and ratified.[1]

The Grand Duke Nicholas for once was not less resolute. Instructed by his brother to give the briefest possible time-limit for the consent of the Sultan to the forward move and at the same time sharply rebuked for his perpetual reference to the Tsar for his decisions, the Grand Duke on the morning of 21 February presented Safvet with an ultimatum: if by 6 a.m. on the 23rd he had not received an invitation to advance to San Stefano he would without further ado occupy it and such other points as he considered necessary. This was sufficient. Reouf Pasha, the Seraskier, negotiated the details with Onou and Russian officers: Akhmet Vekif was overborne: the ultimatum was accepted, and on the 22nd the Porte gave the required written declaration, though 1,500 was substituted for 10,000 as the strength of the force to occupy San Stefano, a provision to which the Russians paid no attention. On the 23rd G.H.Q. moved by rail from Adrianople, and after a dramatic hold-up in the night reached San Stefano in the early hours of the 24th. Thanks to the friendliness of Reouf, who had come out to meet them, the Russians took up their new positions unopposed.[2]

This was not the occupation of Constantinople which the Russians ten days before had been declaring was essential; and Ignatyev could bewail the unhealthiness of San Stefano and the failure to occupy the heights commanding Constantinople itself and the Bosphorus.[3] Yet the results of the advance were by no means negligible. San Stefano, on the Sea of Marmara,

---

[1] Sultan to Tsar, tel., 18 Feb.; Tsar to Sultan, tel., 19 Feb.; Grand Duke to Tsar, tels., 20 and 21 Feb.; texts in *Hasenkampf*, pp. 448, 451–3.

[2] *Skalon*, vol. ii, pp. 251–9; *Hasenkampf*, pp. 450–6, 465, 468; *San Stefano*, pp. 157–62; Nemirovich-Danchenko, *God voiny*, vol. ii, pp. 235–8.

[3] *San Stefano*, pp. 164–5. Despite Ignatyev's strong criticisms of the new positions occupied, Hasenkampf (p. 441) is probably right in ascribing to Ignatyev the original idea of the move to San Stefano. For Ignatyev any advance was better than none, and he hoped that the details of the new line would be much more favourable to the Russians than they actually were. He is throughout very critical of Onou (who, he states, had long been on very friendly terms with Akhmet Vekif), representing him as toning down the Russian demands and putting the best interpretation on each move of the Tur. · *San Stefano*, pp. 166–7. Reuss, the German ambassador, received the same impression, letter of 1 Mar. to Radowitz, *Aufzeichnungen und Erinnerungen*, vol. ii, p. 3. Cf. Kartsov, *Sem let na Blizhnem Vostoke*, p. 15, for Onou's reputed turkophilism. Onou was Roumanian by birth, had married a daughter of Jomini, and occupied the very influential position of first dragoman at the Russian embassy.

was but six miles from the walls of Constantinople. The Turks were yet more tightly squeezed. The Russians were now able to intrigue and threaten in Constantinople with greater effect, and they could keep some sort of watch on the movements of the British warships. Above all, for the first time since the armistice, they had imposed their will effectively upon the Turks. They had failed hitherto, despite their strong language, to enter Constantinople by agreement with the Turks. They had not, despite the Tsar, attempted to enter by force. Now at last they had compelled the Turks, by the direct threat of force, to consent to their advancing to the very outskirts of Constantinople, even though they did not occupy the key points.

But the Tsar at least had no intention that the move to San Stefano should be a substitute for an occupation of Constantinople, or of the Bosphorus heights. He was more than ever convinced that the British deliberately intended to break with him; that would probably entail a rupture also with Austria-Hungary; but his honour forbade further concessions: hence his brother must occupy Constantinople, by force if the Turks would come to no agreement, and must use his existing superiority to seize the Bosphorus and bar the entry of the British into the Black Sea.[1] This now became for two months the main burden of the Tsar's more and more insistent communications to the more and more reluctant Grand Duke. Both shores of the Bosphorus should be seized, if possible in concert with the Turks; their guns would be a most valuable addition to the insufficient Russian field artillery. (Heavy guns there were none; plans were only begun at the end of March for shipping them from Black Sea ports.) He was sending one of his general adjutants, Vice-Admiral Popov, who would be invaluable as a naval expert. But the arrival, on 27 February, of that ingenious officer could not alter the fact that Russia had no fleet.[2]

---

[1] Letter of Tsar to the Grand Duke, 23 Feb., rec. 4 Mar., text in *Skalon*, vol. ii, pp. 287–8. In this letter the Tsar definitely states that he had ordered the Grand Duke to occupy Constantinople, if possible with the consent of the Turks, otherwise by force. Presumably he was referring to his telegram of 10 Feb.; see above, p. 375.

[2] Tsar to the Grand Duke, tel., 25 Feb., rec. 26, text in *Skalon*, vol. ii, p. 269, *Hasenkampf*, p. 464. For Popov, ib., p. 270, and p. 469. The British were perturbed by reports as to the Russians being supplied with the newest type of Whitehead torpedoes; *The Times*, 19 Mar., report from its naval correspondent at Constantinople, 7 Mar.: see also his very informative article in *The Times*, 3 Apr., on the technical possibility of the Russians mining the Bosphorus.

Ignatyev's success in extracting the signature of the treaty of San Stefano on 3 March and in securing its ratification a fortnight later made no difference to the war plans of the Tsar except to render them yet more urgent. The reception of the peace terms in London and Vienna was emphatic and determined. The English refused to come to any conference which did not allow of the possibility of completely recasting the treaty of San Stefano. Meanwhile they continued arming, and at the end of the month called up the reserves and decided to bring a contingent of Indian troops to the Mediterranean (27 Mar.). Derby, unable to swallow what he understood to be a cabinet decision to occupy Alexandretta and Cyprus or some other strategic centre, at last resigned, and Salisbury entered the foreign office, 'picking up the china that Derby had broken'. The Russians felt certain that he would fling it violently at their heads. No definite answer from Vienna, wired the Tsar to his brother; Derby has retired: Salisbury in his place; very hostile to us.[1]

The Austro-Hungarians, despite their internal dissensions, were spurred on by the San Stefano terms, and by the knowledge that Germany would not support the Russian claims, to insist that their interpretation of Reichstadt and the secret conventions must be accepted, and that a conference in which England would take part must be held. Meanwhile they pushed on ambiguous troop movements; the delegations on 21 March voted Andrássy's 60,000,000 florins credit (about £6,000,000), and further overtures were made to London for financial assistance.[2]

The Roumanians, in the centre of the Russian lines of communication, were swept by the news of San Stefano into uncompromising hostility and renewed appeals for Austrian and British help. The situation seemed so serious that April was ushered in by a Russian ultimatum threatening the complete occupation of the country and demanding the disarming of the Roumanian army.

Thus the month of March, though not actually marked by

[1] Tsar to the Grand Duke, tel., 29 Mar., text in *Skalon*, vol. ii, p. 320, *Hasenkampf*, p. 538. For the cabinet crisis of 27 Mar., see *Disraeli*, pp. 1134–49, and *Salisbury*, pp. 218–23. The calling up of the reserves was publicly announced. News as to reinforcements from India was telegraphed by Shuvalov on 31 Mar.; paraphrase in *Seton-Watson MSS*.

[2] Elliot (Vienna) to Derby, tel., no. 88, 27 Mar., in *F.O.* 7/929.

any such tense incidents as those of February around Constantinople and the Straits, saw St. Petersburg convinced that war with England was inevitable, with Austria-Hungary probable, and that both must be forestalled by decisive measures. Gorchakov, unable to stem the tide even had he tried, was abandoning both the hope of and the desire for achieving a settlement through a congress, and did not hide even from Langenau that Russia was reckoning on the possibility of war not only with England but also with Austria-Hungary.[1] The panslavs were at the height of their influence in the governing circles, with the ministry of marine hurrying forward naval preparations, with Obruchev back at the war office straining for action, and in mid-March Ignatyev back from Constantinople, determined to spare no effort to finish what he had begun at San Stefano. March and April therefore were occupied with serious preparation for the army on the Austrian frontier as well as for the seizure of the Straits, the fitting out of commerce-destroyers, and a diversion from Central Asia towards India. The denial of the Black Sea to the British fleet was now of still greater consequence, for the new formations against Austria-Hungary were in part to be transported by sea from the Balkan and Caucasus fronts. Hence the Bosphorus continued to be the vital point for the military extremists in command at St. Petersburg. Their ideas were admirably illustrated by a memorandum of Obruchev which served as the guiding line for the Tsar's instructions to the Grand Duke.[2]

Starting from the assumption of the prime necessity of preventing the British fleet entering the Black Sea, Obruchev emphasized as the first essential the attitude of the Turks. The Sultan might either declare himself in favour of Russia or against her or neutral. The third possibility would be extremely unsatisfactory for Russia, and indeed impossible unless the Turks agreed to make obstruction by her military and naval forces out of the question. At the moment the predominating strength at Constantinople lay in the hands of the Russians. They must use it to force the Porte to send the British fleet back into the Aegean: they must ask the Turks, Will you and can you do this

---

[1] Gorchakov to Shuvalov, letter, 18 Mar., text in *Seton-Watson MSS*.

[2] A paraphrase of the memorandum is in *Tatishchev*, pp. 474–5, who does not, however, give its date, which must at latest be about the middle of March. For later confirmation as to the influence of Obruchev, see *Hasenkampf*, p. 507.

yourselves? If you cannot, will you agree to do it in conjunction with us? If the Turks refused, the immediate surrender must be demanded of all the fortifications of the Bosphorus and the Dardanelles, as well as the disbandment of the army and the disarming of the fleet. If the Turks again refused to comply, both shores of both Straits must be seized by force and the channels mined.

The first requirement in this plan was, if possible, to force an agreement upon the Turks for some kind of common action. Such was equally the aim of Ignatyev. He had striven hard during the peace negotiations to include in the treaty an article sanctioning the transport home of part of the Russian army from Buyuk Dere, on the Bosphorus, close to the Russian summer embassy, which would have given the Russians their desired strategical hold on the Bosphorus, and in addition would have placed at their mercy the water-supply of Constantinople. Though the Turks successfully resisted the insertion of any such commitment in the treaty of San Stefano, Ignatyev returned to the charge during the five days which he spent in Constantinople after the treaty had been signed (5–10 Mar.). Whether, as he claims, he then succeeded in winning over the Turks to the use of Buyuk Dere is extremely doubtful. In any case, after his departure for St. Petersburg (10 Mar.) the further negotiations collapsed before the definitive refusal of the Sultan to allow any such embarcation (18 Mar.).[1] This was a fatal blow to the Grand Duke Nicholas, since he regarded embarkation at Buyuk Dere as the only means of getting to the Bosphorus: action by force was daily becoming more difficult in the face of the growing Turkish strength, which he estimated at about 100,000, and it would lead to an immediate break with England: in case of such a break it would be quite impossible to secure any Turkish co-operation.[2]

---

[1] *San Stefano*, pp. 261, 264, 318; Layard to Derby, private letter, 20 Mar., copy in Layard Papers, *British Museum, Add. MSS.* 39131, f. 55.

[2] The Grand Duke to the Tsar, tels., 17 and 18 Mar., texts in *Hasenkampf*, pp. 502–3, 507, *Skalon*, vol. ii, pp. 297–8. G.H.Q. probably exaggerated the Turkish strength. Layard at this time estimated the Turkish strength in Constantinople at 80,000, but believed that the Russians could at any moment seize the European shore of the Bosphorus; private letters to Derby and Beaconsfield, 20 Mar., copies in Layard Papers, *British Museum, Add. MSS.* 39131, ff. 53, 55. The Sultan told Layard on 29 Mar. that he could have 100,000 troops within a fortnight for the defence of Constantinople and the Bosphorus; Layard to Tenterden, for Disraeli, tel., no. 341, most secret and personal, 31 Mar., in *F.O.* 78/2810.

Ignatyev's ambitious scheme for an alliance with Turkey fell to the ground. It would certainly have required all Ignatyev's powers of cajolery and intimidation to have concluded such an alliance. After his departure from Constantinople, on 10 March, in the company of Reouf Pasha, there was little or no chance that either Nelidov, left without instructions and without credentials, or the Grand Duke Nicholas would be able to forward matters. When after prolonged battlings over prestige and etiquette a meeting finally took place between the Sultan and the Grand Duke on 26 March, the latter's suggestions for a combined defence of the Bosphorus against England met with courteous, but obvious, evasion: if Russia required Turkey to do more than maintain neutrality, a price must be paid in the shape of modifications in the San Stefano treaty (already by then ratified): only in that case might a new direction be given to Turkish policy and an offensive and defensive alliance be concluded. But the Tsar would not hear of any modifications. The end of March marked the high-water mark of his desire for extreme action.[1]

Hitherto the Tsar had been urging on the Grand Duke to have everything in readiness for the occupation of the shores of the Bosphorus in case of a break with England. But he had not quite gone to the length of instructing his brother actually to precipitate the break himself by effecting the occupation. To this point he gradually moved during the course of March. On hearing of the refusal to allow embarkation at Buyuk Dere he telegraphed: 'I hope fully that all measures will be prepared for rapid seizure of Bosphorus when that appears necessary: how quickly can you effect it?' To this Nicholas Nicholaevich replied evasively and yet again did not dare report the real opinion of G.H.Q.: that no advance to the Bosphorus could be made if the Turks opposed.[2] Four days later (24 Mar.) a letter arrived from the Tsar which marked clearly the growing

---

[1] *San Stefano*, pp. 257–60, 263–4; Nelidov's memoirs in *Revue des deux mondes*, 15 Nov. 1915, vol. xxx, pp. 242–3; *Tatishchev*, pp. 477–8, citing two memoranda of Onou recording the meeting between the Sultan and the Grand Duke; the Grand Duke to the Tsar, tel., 26 Mar., and his reply, tel., 27 Mar., texts in *Hasenkampf*, pp. 535–6, *Skalon*, vol. ii, p. 314. The Russian version as to what took place at the meeting is in general corroborated by Layard's evidence, based on what the Sultan told him; disp., no. 436, most secret, 28 Mar., in *F.O.* 78/2783, and private letter to Hornby, 30 Mar., copy in *British Museum, Add. MSS.* 39131, f. 64.

[2] Tsar to the Grand Duke, tel., 19 Mar., the Grand Duke to Tsar, tel., 20 Mar.; texts in *Hasenkampf*, pp. 509–10, *Skalon*, vol. ii, p. 304.

power of Obruchev. Since the British were obviously aiming at war and seeking every means to put off the proposed congress, Alexander considered it essential to seize the Bosphorus by force if the consent of the Porte could not finally be obtained. As to Austria-Hungary he could say nothing positive, but England was certainly pushing her against Russia, and preparations must be made for the worst eventualities. This letter likewise was answered by nothing but vague generalities.[1]

For a moment now renewed efforts were made to take advantage of Reouf Pasha's return to Constantinople (24 Mar.) by insisting on the Turks' requiring the withdrawal of the British fleet from the Sea of Marmara. The Grand Duke had already discussed this with the Turks, and on 30 March after another visit to the Sultan and his ministers he reported that he had duly insisted on this, and that the Sultan, Reouf, and even Akhmet Vekif promised to invite the British government to remove their fleet from the Sea of Marmara: in return he had decided to withdraw certain troops from San Stefano and Bulgaria: meanwhile, until the receipt of an answer from London it was impossible to negotiate further with the Turks for the occupation of the Bosphorus. If this was the Grand Duke's idea of insistence it was not St. Petersburg's. He was sharply ordered to withdraw no troops (31 Mar.), and meanwhile had just received instructions which showed the full triumph of Obruchev and the extremists.[2]

The arrival in St. Petersburg of the news of Salisbury succeeding Derby and of the further war measures drove the Tsar to the decision that not only was a rupture inevitable, but that it was now immediately imminent. If the Russians delayed action against the Bosphorus until the rupture had actually occurred, they would be too late. Therefore they must strike in advance,

---

[1] Letter of the Tsar to the Grand Duke, 18 Mar., rec. 24 Mar., text in *Tatishchev*, pp. 476–7; for telegraphic reply to it, *Skalon*, vol. ii, p. 306, *Hasenkampf*, p. 517. It was not until 28 Mar. that the Grand Duke emphasized the extreme difficulty of controlling the Bosphorus in despite of the Turks, and even so he went on to say that all was ready for an immediate move forward to the Bosphorus and for the mining of it; letter of 28 Mar. to the Tsar, extract in *Tatishchev*, pp. 478–9. Five days later he admitted that it would be extremely difficult to mine the Bosphorus or to occupy the Asiatic shore of the Bosphorus; report of 2 Apr. to the Tsar, text in *Hasenkampf*, pp. 549–53.

[2] Gorchakov to the Grand Duke, tel., 28 Mar.; Grand Duke to Gorchakov, tel., 29 Mar.; Grand Duke to Tsar, tels., 30 and 31 Mar.; Tsar to the Grand Duke, tel., rec. 8 p.m., 31 Mar. (countermanding withdrawal of troops); texts in *Hasenkampf*, pp. 538–9, 541, 543, *Skalon*, vol. ii, pp. 321, 323.

and thereby themselves cause the rupture. Only thus could they secure the key to their house.

This was the assumption, though not the actual substance, of the Tsar's instructions dispatched in the night of 30 March: prepare everything for decisive action: when everything is ready, demand categorical answer from the Porte; how do you intend to act in case of hostile action by England? if openly with us, then Turks must immediately put Bosphorus forts into our hands, at least on European shore, and concert with us disposition of their troops: if Turks think themselves too weak to join in war against England, they must hand over forts specified by us, cease all armaments, disband or remove troops, disarm fleet in Black Sea, and send ships to ports specified by us: in either case, we must not enter into Constantinople itself, but must occupy strongly points on shores of Bosphorus: do not begin decisive negotiations and action until everything is ready, and do not expose undertaking to any risk; meanwhile advance your troops as near Bosphorus as possible. Within twenty-four hours the Tsar telegraphed again: do not lose any time in forestalling approach of British expeditionary force.[1]

Thus, the prospect of anything more than passive co-operation from the Turks having been abandoned, neutrality of the most impossible kind was to be demanded. If it were refused, the Tsar intended that force should be used to attain his object. He did not, it is true, actually order the Grand Duke to fight his way through to the Bosphorus, but for the past month he had been insisting on the urgency of being prepared for this necessity, and the Grand Duke had been trying so to prepare. What the Grand Duke evidently still shrank from was taking any action against the Turks which would bring about the break with England without express orders from the Tsar, and the seizure by force of the Bosphorus he considered certain to do so. And further, he was at one and the same time ordered to have everything ready for decisive action and warned not to expose the undertaking to any risk. How was it possible to seize the Bosphorus heights without the risk (in fact the probability) of meeting with resistance from the Turks? Of the virtual certainty indeed of such resistance he was becoming more and

---

[1] Tsar to the Grand Duke, tel., disp. 11.55 p.m. 30 Mar., rec. 2.40 p.m. 31 Mar., and tel., disp. 6.30 p.m. 31 Mar., rec. 8 p.m. same day; texts in *Hasenkampf*, pp. 541–3, *Skalon*, vol. ii, pp. 322–3.

more persuaded, but it was this third alternative—neither active Turkish co-operation with Russia, nor neutrality, but active co-operation with England—which was not squarely faced by St. Petersburg.

The Grand Duke decided to reply (31 Mar.) to the Tsar that his telegram of 30 March 'for information' had been received and that he would act according to circumstances. When the Tsar telegraphed in fury, *en clair*, that his telegram was 'for action', he expounded all his military difficulties, emphasized the extreme probability that the Turks would actively assist the British, and pressed for clear and definite orders. No such orders came. Instead arrived a direct request to know whether his health was sufficiently good for him to continue in command (1 Apr.).[1]

Alexander was always most unwilling to nerve himself for the unpleasant task of removing any nominees of his own. Within the imperial family itself the task was naturally still more distasteful, and in this particular case the decision could not but be a national, and even an international, event. That the Tsar was becoming more and more dissatisfied with his brother is abundantly clear from the growing asperity of his letters and telegrams. He had probably for some time been intending his supersession, and Ignatyev on his return to St. Petersburg did his best to hasten it. By the end of March Alexander could no longer, either personally or on grounds of policy, suffer the continued inaction and vacillation of G.H.Q. The Grand Duke had in fact been increasingly unwell and had mentioned it seriously to the Tsar at the beginning of March. He was worn out by the responsibilities of his position, for which he was in any case quite unfitted. Illness provided a convenient excuse for his recall, which was almost as welcome to the Grand Duke as it was to the Tsar. By 14 April all was arranged for him to be relieved of his command by Totleben.[2]

Apart from the (very likely) possibility of some explosive

[1] The Grand Duke to Tsar, tel., disp. 6 p.m. 31 Mar., rec. that night; Tsar to the Grand Duke, tel., *en clair*, disp. 10.20 a.m. 1 Apr., rec. 12.30 p.m. same day; the Grand Duke to Tsar, tels., 1 Apr.; Tsar to the Grand Duke, tel., disp. 6.30 p.m. 1 Apr., rec. that night; texts in *Hasenkampf*, pp. 543, 547–9, *Skalon*, vol. ii, pp. 323–6.

[2] Grand Duke to Tsar, tels., 5 Mar., 2 and 8 Apr., letter of 8 Apr.; Tsar to the Grand Duke, tel., rec. 14 Apr.; texts in *Skalon*, vol. ii, pp. 290, 326, 335–6, 344, *Hasenkampf*, pp. 549, 562–3, 582–3; *San Stefano*, p. 315 (for Ignatyev). *Aus dem Leben König Karls* . . . , vol. iv, p. 4, under date 9 Mar., already speaks of Totleben as intended as successor to the Grand Duke in a short time.

incident, no energetic action by the Russian army was to be expected until the arrival of the Grand Duke's successor. Thus was avoided the renewal of an intense crisis at Constantinople which the Tsar's telegram of 30 March if acted upon would have produced, and there now seemed a chance for less extreme influence to be exerted in St. Petersburg. This showed itself initially in the acceptance of the suggestion that negotiations should be attempted for the simultaneous withdrawal of the Russians and of the British from before Constantinople. Abd ul-Hamid had approached the British cabinet in this sense, and Salisbury decided to secure the good offices of Bismarck, who reluctantly undertook the task after Gorchakov, pleased enough that at last Bismarck should take some definite action, but highly suspicious of British instigation, had agreed to negotiate through Berlin (8 April).[1] Any progress was bound to be slow, given the inherent difficulties of estimating what constituted an equal handicap for a fleet and for an army and of negotiating through a third party, with continual reference required to Constantinople and San Stefano. When to this was added the maximum of suspicion on all sides it was improbable that arrangements for a simultaneous withdrawal would materialize.

Although these April negotiations ended in failure and thereby sharpened to some extent mutual hostility, yet they did at first have the effect of slightly clearing the thunderous atmosphere of March. Salisbury for his part by the end of April found himself unable to obtain satisfaction from Vienna, and came to the conclusion that it was necessary to make a real effort at direct discussions with St. Petersburg. There the predominance of Ignatyev and the military and naval extremists, almost unchallenged since February, was becoming more and more questioned during April. More sober views began to make some headway against the exaggerated calculations as to what Russia could achieve unaided against England, Austria-Hungary, Turkey, and probably Roumania, combined. An opportunity was given for the moderates to obtain some hearing, with the result that by the end of April Shuvalov from London could interpose with his rival bid for the direction of Russian policy in a sense favourable to peace. During the month a marked change occurred in the tone of much of the Russian

[1] *Hasenkampf*, pp. 561–2; *Skalon*, vol. ii, pp. 334–6. For the question of a simultaneous withdrawal see below, pp. 473, 477–8 and n.

press. Already at the beginning of April even the *Russky Mir* was explaining that it would be necessary for Russia to stave off the opposition of Europe by making some concessions. Financial and commercial interests were expressing their nervousness as to the consequences of a war with England. A long article in their organ *Birzheviya Vedemosti*, 9 April, openly avowed that the effect of such a war on the economic and financial condition of Russia would be disastrous.[1]

The *coup de grâce* to the hopes of the extremists was given by the new commander-in-chief himself, though possibly his appointment did not in the first instance seem a setback to their hopes.[2] Totleben arrived at San Stefano on 27 April, had a stormy meeting with the Grand Duke, and set to work with cleansing vigour to restore discipline, to transform the utterly inadequate supply and medical services, and to create rapidly an efficient fighting force of between 80,000 and 90,000 which faced the Turks and the British before Constantinople throughout the summer.[3] But his army thus reorganized was to remain strictly on the defensive. On 9 May he sent to the Tsar a report on the strategical situation, which, reaching St. Petersburg at the same time as Shuvalov on his peace-making visit from London, was of decisive importance in the defeat of the war party.[4] He declared that it was not possible to mine the Bosphorus and that therefore an attempt to occupy its shores would be without point, since without a mine-field it would be impossible to prevent the British fleet entering the Black Sea. The capture by storm of Constantinople would be a very difficult

---

[1] Loftus to Derby, disp., nos. 388 and 402, 7 and 10 Apr., enclosing extracts from the Russian press, in *F.O.* 65/1001.

[2] For Totleben's appointment and views, Shilder, *Graf E. E. Totleben*, vol. ii, pp. 862–3, but the evidence is unsatisfactory.

[3] *Skalon*, vol. ii, pp. 357–8, under date 27 Apr.; Shilder, op. cit., vol. ii, pp. 878–9, 882–3, 892, and appendixes, pp. 332–7, 339–40; Pfeil, *Experiences of a Prussian officer in the Russian Service*, pp. 334–7, 352 (he was with the Guards at San Stefano). The figure of 80,000 to 90,000 represents only the fighting strength (May to early Aug.) immediately in front of Constantinople. The total strength of the Russian forces south of the Pruth was estimated by Wellesley, in St. Petersburg, as being in Apr. about 600,000, of whom 400,000 were combatants, and of whom about one-third respectively were between the Pruth and the Danube, between the Danube and the Balkans, and between the Balkans and the Sea of Marmara; report of Wellesley to Loftus, 23 Apr., copy in the *Simmons Papers*, *F.O.* 358/2. 120,000 seems to have been accepted in London as the total strength south of the Balkans at this time; Home to Tenterden, 10 Apr. (Home thought this figure much exaggerated), copy in Layard Papers, *British Museum*, Add. *MSS.* 39137, f. 51.

[4] A summary of the report is in Shilder, *Graf E. E. Totleben*, vol. ii, pp. 866–78.

and risky operation in the face of 80,000 Turks, well armed, well fortified, and increasing in numbers. Even if it were captured, that would not be the end of war, and it would be necessary to retire if the Russian communications were not to be cut. If an attack upon Constantinople failed, the whole position of the Russians at San Stefano would be jeopardized. Totleben closed by advising as the best course a withdrawal to Adrianople and a defence of Bulgaria based on Adrianople, coupled with the demand for the Turkish evacuation of Shumla and Varna, and Batum. Only in such circumstances could he detach reinforcements which were being demanded for the Austrian frontier.

This damning delineation of the military situation ruined the chances of further ebullitions of war-fever proving effective and assured the success of those who believed that peace, and therefore concessions, were essential in the true interests of Russia. That the wheel was moving full circle from the heady days of February and March was evidenced clearly enough when on 15 May the Tsar approved Totleben's suggested measures, though their carrying out was to be dependent on the evacuation of the three Turkish fortresses, which in fact was not begun until after the signature of the treaty of Berlin. Totleben, therefore, remained in front of Constantinople, strictly on the defensive.[1]

In the meantime, the Grand Duke Nicholas had returned to St. Petersburg, with the formal consolation of a field-marshal's baton. As his train drew in he found an unexpected honour prepared for him. The Tsar in person had driven to the station to welcome the generalissimo who had captured Plevna, Sofia, the Shipka, Philippopolis, Adrianople—but not Constantinople. Alexander dryly explained that he had done so in order that his brother should not be hissed by the crowd.[2]

---

[1] Shilder, op. cit., vol. ii, pp. 878, 888–9.

[2] *Skalon*, vol. ii, pp. 354, 363–4. Eckardt, *Russia before and after the War*, p. 352, asserts that the Tsarevich refused to take part in the festivities given in honour of the Grand Duke. For Loris-Melikov's version of the interview between the Tsar and the Grand Duke, 'the Emperor storming at' him 'for his failure to take Constantinople', see Simpson, *The Saburov Memoirs*, p. 47.

XIV

SAN STEFANO

THE triumphs that brought the Russian army from Plevna to the outskirts of Constantinople brought Ignatyev to the crest of his career. Now, if ever, was the chance of remodelling the Ottoman empire according to his taste, and he did not fail to seize it. In the preceding chapter devoted to the dominating military aspect of Russian policy some stress has been laid upon the fact that Ignatyev failed to procure his dispatch to Constantinople direct instead of to Adrianople, failed to forestall the armistice, and failed to drag the Grand Duke Nicholas into decisive action; and it will shortly be seen that he also failed to impose certain of his most important conditions upon the Turks. But the recognition of these failures must not obscure the fact that for the first three months of 1878 Ignatyev exercised far more decisive positive influence on Russian foreign relations than any other single individual. The treaty of San Stefano, which was almost solely his handiwork, combined with the Russian military threat to Constantinople on the one hand to raise nationalist feeling in Russia to its highest pitch, on the other to inspire England and, after much hesitation, Austria-Hungary with the determination to stand resolutely across the path of panslavism in action.

Ignatyev, at the zenith of his power, marked down as Gorchakov's successor, left St. Petersburg for the south on 25 January, hampered by the minimum of instructions save that he was to proceed via Bucarest to Adrianople. He reached Bucarest on 31 January, charged with the task not of negotiating with the Roumanians, but of 'elucidating' the various delicate questions which would arise out of the peace treaty. The demand now at long last definitely put forward for the return of the districts of Bessarabia ceded in 1856 produced a prolonged crisis in Russo-Roumanian relations, from the start yet further embittered, as has already been seen (p. 362), by Roumanian disgust at the Grand Duke's armistice. From Bucarest Ignatyev started on 3 February for the Tsarevich's head-quarters, whence, at last abandoning any hope of extracting permission to go direct to Constantinople and certain now that an armistice was already concluded, he drove on at breakneck speed for Adrianople, where he arrived early in the morning of 8 February.

For the moment there was no one with whom to negotiate, since Server and Namyk after the signature of the armistice had returned to Constantinople, where confusion was rendered worse confounded by the orders for the British fleet to pass the Dardanelles. After insistent telegrams from Adrianople, Safvet Pasha arrived on the 12th, a slippery customer, who multiplied excuses to evade Ignatyev's brusque tactics. A second delegate, Sadullah Bey, the ambassador to Germany, was to arrive later (he did so on the 25th), but the negotiations started at once. Ignatyev pushed ahead with his usual vigour, but his demands were so exorbitant that the Sultan and the war party, backed by Layard, brought matters to a deadlock, and on 20 February Safvet went back upon the concessions to which the Russians understood he had agreed. The day before, a ministerial crisis had come to a head: Server Pasha at the foreign office was being violently accused by Layard of playing the traitor and of publicly calumniating him. The Sultan and Akhmet Vekif were forced, probably not unwillingly, to dismiss him, and Safvet took his place, though he remained for the time being at Russian head-quarters.[1] This coincided with the ultimatum of the Grand Duke Nicholas demanding an advance to San Stefano (see above, pp. 386-7).

When the advance had taken place, negotiations were resumed. Safvet was stiffened now by Sadullah and by Mehemet Ali, the ex-commander-in-chief, who had been called in to assist with his detailed knowledge of the western regions of Bulgaria particularly in dispute. The Turks were given 3 March as a limiting date for the conclusion of the treaty, but a final breakdown was threatened after a violent scene between Ignatyev and Mehemet Ali, when the former threatened denouncement of the armistice and renewal of hostilities unless his new demands in regard to the frontiers of Bulgaria were accepted (28 February). That night, according to Ignatyev's unsupported statement, he urged the Grand Duke to carry out the threat in

[1] Layard's memoirs, *British Museum, Add. MSS.* 38936, ff. 188–95; private letter of Layard to Derby, 20 Feb., copy in Layard Papers, ib. 39131, ff. 33–4. An additional reason for Layard's hostility to Server was the latter's very close relations with Reuss. For Server's exuberantly russophil interview with the special correspondent of the *Daily News*, published on 7 Feb., see Thompson, *Public Opinion and Lord Beaconsfield 1875–1880*, vol. ii, p. 377.

IGNATYEV

earnest. The Grand Duke protested angrily that the occupation of Constantinople and the Bosphorus heights would mean war with England, while Nepokoichitsky insisted on the military impossibility of such action. All that they were prepared to do was to make a demonstration as if an advance was to take place, and next morning the demonstration was accordingly staged. The Turks promptly sent word that they accepted Ignatyev's demands (1 March). Even then they continued to struggle over the indemnity and the Transcaucasian frontiers, until after securing some concessions they were induced by the intervention of the Grand Duke to yield on the remaining points. On the following day, 3 March, the peace was signed.[1]

Such is the bare outline of the making of the treaty of San Stefano. The framework of its terms was supplied by the bases of peace signed at Adrianople a month before, which had been carefully designed to leave ample scope in the subsequent process of filling in the picture. Hardly less ample scope appears to have been given Ignatyev in the instructions with which he left St. Petersburg. The final decisions as to Ignatyev's mission were taken at an imperial council held on 24 January, which approved the draft for a treaty which he had drawn up after written consultation with Gorchakov.[2] The main points in connexion with Ignatyev's proposals may be summarized as follows:

1. The draft was in the form of a treaty. Gorchakov had

[1] This and the preceding paragraphs are based primarily on Ignatyev's own account in San Stefano. The crisis of 28 Feb.–1 Mar. is described by him on pp. 215–21. Hasenkampf, pp. 472–3, and Skalon, vol. ii, pp. 272–3, have no mention of Ignatyev pressing the Grand Duke to denounce the armistice and to advance, but they recount in detail the demonstration, which in turn is not mentioned by Ignatyev. I have not been able to use Pancho Dorev's San Stefanska Blgariya (Sofia, 1929), cited by K. Krachunov, in Slavyanski glas, 1932, Sofia, vol. xxvi, p. 39, as being based on the Turkish archives.

[2] Ignatyev gives in San Stefano, pp. 16–18, the original text (in French) of a memorandum entitled 'Questions à résoudre' which he put to Gorchakov on 22 Jan. before drawing up his draft treaty; pp. 26–8, the text (in Russian, presumably a translation) of Gorchakov's reply; pp. 22–6, a full summary of his original draft treaty. He does not give the text as approved by the council, but implies that only one alteration was made by it, on Giers's suggestion, viz. the insertion of provisions for compensation to be paid by the Turks for damages to shipping on the Danube (p. 29). He gives (p. 22) as present at the council: the Tsar, Gorchakov, Milyutin, Giers, Jomini, Hamburger, and himself. According to the anecdotal reminiscences of Giers everything was hurried through in utmost haste, Gorchakov giving no detailed attention to the proposed terms and objecting only to the inclusion of Adrianople and Salonika in the new Bulgaria; Bartholomei, 'Extrait des mémoires d'un diplomate russe', Revue d'histoire diplomatique, vol. xlviii, pp. 103–4.

suggested that, in order to obviate the difficulties in connexion with an alteration of the treaties of 1856 and 1871, it should be in the form of a protocol outlining the conditions of a subsequent treaty to be negotiated in concert with the powers. In accordance with his assurances already given to them, he made it quite clear that the peace conditions could only be preliminary, in so far as they dealt with matters of general concern, though he did not abandon to the powers the decision as to which were matters of general concern. Ignatyev strongly objected to the idea of a protocol, claiming Nikolsburg as a precedent for Russia, but was prepared to consider favourably a combination of a protocol and a treaty, reserving certain enumerated articles for the approbation of the powers.

2. Roumania was to be independent and was to receive part of the delta of the Danube, including the Sulina mouth (the main artery of communication), but this was in the first instance to be ceded by the Turks to the Russians, who would exchange it for the Bessarabian districts ceded in 1856. The Dobrudja was to form part of Bulgaria, as provided for by the Constantinople conference. Bulgaria would thus be separated from Russian territory only by the Delta, and would receive the port of Constanza and the railway thence to the Danube. Ignatyev, with whom the problem of Russian communications with Bulgaria was always uppermost, further proposed a defensive alliance with Roumania which would ensure the passage of Russian troops to the Balkan peninsula, and which should take the place of the guarantee of the Principalities provided for in the treaty of Paris. Gorchakov, however, refused to be drawn into any alliance, and the proposal was dropped.

3. Montenegro was to receive in Herzegovina Nikšić, Stolac, Gacko, and Nevesinje, and in the Morača valley the key points of Podgorica, Spuž, and Žablyak. Of these only Nikšić and Gacko had actually been conquered by the Montenegrins. Ignatyev almost certainly must also have intended Montenegro to acquire the strip of sea-coast (Spizza, Antivari, and Dulcigno which she had already occupied), though he makes no mention of it in his original draft. On the north-east the frontier was to extend to the Lim, where it would be contiguous with the enlarged Serbia.[1]

4. Serbia was to be independent and to acquire the greater

[1] For the Montenegrin frontiers see map facing p. 412.

part of Novi Bazar, joining Montenegro along the Lim, including in particular Prjepolje and Mitrovica, and some further portion of Old Serbia, but not the *sanjak* of Nish.[1] In regard to both Serbia and Montenegro Gorchakov said that it was impossible to define the fróntiers in Herzegovina and Novi Bazar until agreement had been reached with the Austrians, but he appears to have made little effort to face Ignatyev squarely with the Reichstadt agreement and the secret conventions or to insist to the full that the utmost caution was required in view of the hostile attitude of Vienna.

5. Bulgaria within limits not less than those of the Constantinople conference was to form one autonomous vassal principality. Its boundaries were to be delimited by a Russo-Turkish commission before the Russian evacuation and on the basis of a map signed by the Russian and Turkish peace plenipotentiaries. Ignatyev's original idea of an independent Bulgaria and of the inclusion in it of Adrianople was abandoned as certain to meet with insuperable European opposition, but Bulgaria was to be extended to the Aegean and might include Salonika (as Ignatyev observed, admittedly not Bulgar in population, but hallowed in the eyes of Slavdom by the apostles St. Cyril and St. Methodius), if Turkish opposition was not too extreme.

6. A Russian army of not less than 50,000 was to remain in Bulgaria until the formation of a sufficiently strong and reliable Bulgarian army. This formula was considerably wider than Nelidov's original suggestion of a two years' occupation, and Gorchakov declared that the term must be fixed.

7. The remainder of the Russian army was to evacuate European and Asiatic Turkey within three months of the ratification of the treaty, and if desired via Varna, Burgas, Constantinople, and Buyuk Dere.

8. The reforms proposed for Bosnia and Herzegovina at the first sitting of the Constantinople conference were to be immediately introduced there, together with further regulations as to arrears and fixation of taxes.

9. Epirus, Thessaly, and those portions of Macedonia and Thrace to be left under direct Turkish rule were to have the

---

[1] That Nish was originally to be included in Bulgaria is expressly stated by Ignatyev in *San Stefano*, p. 105. It had been included in the Constantinople conference Bulgaria. See maps between pp. 240–1 and 410–11.

same reforms, adapted to local needs, as those worked out by the Constantinople conference for Bosnia. Ignatyev had wished to hand over Thessaly, part of Epirus, and Crete to Greece, but this solution was ruled out on the ground that it would arouse too much hostility from the powers as being tantamount to the complete disruption of the Ottoman rule in Europe. Crete, instead, was to be given a reformed version of the 1868 organic statute.

10. The three Russian monasteries on Mount Athos, always of close concern to Ignatyev and the Asiatic department, were to be expressly safeguarded by the recognition of the same rights and privileges as those promised to the other monasteries in Turkey. There were to be similar provisions for the recognition by the Porte of the rights and privileges of Russian Orthodox clergy and monks in the Turkish empire and of Russian protection of Russian pilgrims and religious and charitable institutions in the Holy Places and elsewhere.

11. Full satisfaction was to be accorded as regards debts, etc., of Russian subjects in Turkey.

12. The Porte, while preserving intact the traditional principle of the closure of the Straits to warships, was to allow the passage of up to ten Russian men-of-war a year (excluding the light vessels used for embassy communications): they would pass one at a time and would not stop in the Bosphorus.

13. There was to be an additional and secret article, to which Ignatyev attached the greatest importance. If the powers insisted on opening the Straits, the Black Sea was to be declared open in time of peace and closed in time of war between European powers for all warships of non-riverain powers: Russia and Turkey were to bind themselves to enter into an agreement for combined measures to guarantee the defence of the Straits against any foreign undertaking, and with this object in view they were to conclude a defensive treaty by which Russia would bind herself in case of need to support the Sultan with all her military and naval forces against any attempt to pass through or seize the Dardanelles.

14. As a war indemnity a total sum of 1,410,000,000 silver roubles (not less than £235,000,000) was to be demanded, but a part of this was to be paid in the form of the cession of southern Bessarabia, Ardahan, Kars, Batum, Kagizman, and part of Lazistan and Armenia up to Saganluk (the frontiers to be

delimited by a Russo-Turkish commission on the spot),[1] and part of it was to be paid in the form of the handing over of six men-of-war to be selected by the Russian admiralty. The remainder, representing a sum of 40,000,000 Turkish pounds (not less than £36,000,000 stg.), was to be paid in cash, guaranteed on the Turkish revenues, and as to one-fifth on those of Egypt, the details to be fixed by a mixed commission of Russian financial experts and representatives of the Ottoman Bank.

This was a programme formidable enough to tax beyond measure the skill and determination of its versatile progenitor. Engendered in an atmosphere intoxicated with the swirl of the January triumphs, it required first to be imposed upon the Turks, secondly upon the powers, and particularly upon Austria-Hungary. England, as long as Disraeli remained in power, would in any case strongly oppose any Russian terms likely to be dictated after such a campaign, whereas Austria-Hungary might perhaps have been won over by a skilful carrying out of the policy embodied in the Reichstadt agreement and the subsequent conventions. Ignatyev had only in this January been informed of the conventions, and he regarded them as a treacherous pandering to Vienna and Buda-Pesth. Backed by the chorus of jubilant panslavs he won the day for a reversal of Reichstadt and thereby assured the maximum of hostility from Austria-Hungary.[2] The hopes of assistance from Germany were found to be misplaced, since Bismarck consistently refused to put anything even savouring of pressure on Vienna to come to terms with St. Petersburg. Finally, the two allies most essential to Ignatyev were both lacking—a determined foreign office, and a determined army command. The last chapter has shown the

---

[1] For the Asiatic frontiers, see map between pp. 540-1.

[2] Ignatyev states, *San Stefano*, p. 7, that the content of the convention of 15 Jan. 1877 was hidden from him by Gorchakov until his dispatch to Adrianople, and that it was then shown to him on the express command of the Tsar after expostulations by Ignatyev as to Gorchakov's secrecy. He does not specifically state that the text was communicated to him. In *San Stefano*, p. 337, he maintains that it was not until Mar. 1878, just before his mission to Vienna, that the text of this convention, 'until then hidden', was shown to him by Gorchakov, very unwillingly, and on the Tsar's orders. Ignatyev always refers to the conventions as treaties, and in the singular, and nowhere alludes to the antedating of the political convention. His interpretation of its provisions as regards the Austrian occupation of Bosnia and Herzegovina (pp. 17, 178, 191, 267) suggests that he may not have been able, or may not have chosen, to study it closely. Although he frequently alludes to the Reichstadt agreement he never mentions having seen the text of it and from internal evidence does not seem to have done so. See also above, p. 176, and below, pp. 450-3.

fatal consequences for Ignatyev's policy of the indecision and
hostility of the Grand Duke Nicholas. Hardly less disastrous
to it were the tortuous waverings of Gorchakov, insistent on
retaining at least the nominal direction of affairs, and, in spasmodic bouts, capable of putting awkward spokes in Ignatyev's
wheels. The old chancellor still had his tolerably faithful satellites in key places at the foreign office. At the major embassies
Novikov and Shuvalov were bitterly hostile both to Ignatyev
personally and to his policy, while Oubril at Berlin, though a
man of straw, was an old henchman of Gorchakov. Never was
the almost invariable feature of Russian foreign policy during
these years, its lack of unified direction, more crucially illustrated than during the period between January and June 1878.

On the other hand, Ignatyev had initially to back him the
Tsar, the greater part of the war office headed by Obruchev,
and the whole excited mass of nationalist opinion, which for the
time dominated the entire press and which could see no difference between the unity of Italy or Germany, achieved without
the interference of a European conference, and the disruption
of Turkey in Europe similarly to be achieved. For three months
this was sufficient for Ignatyev: then in April the support of the
Tsar began to be withdrawn: his opponents took heart: by the
beginning of May it was Shuvalov's star that was rising fast: by
the end of May Ignatyev had withdrawn to his Kiev estates.

His initial task, to impose the terms on the Turks, proved
harder than had appeared in St. Petersburg when hopes ran
high that the armistice might be yet further delayed. It is true
that Safvet at first professed to attribute little practical importance to negotiations the result of which would be overhauled
by a congress of the powers, but in fact, as the Turks well knew,
the scope of the congress was as yet quite undetermined, and
even in the most favourable circumstances the extent of their
concessions to the Russians would be of the utmost importance
at the congress if and when it was held. And there were limits
beyond which the Sultan could not go without fear of the
fanatical mob of his capital or jeopardy to British aid. Thus
Abd ul-Hamid and his new prime minister Akhmet Vekif
fought their hardest to spin out negotiations and cut down the
demands of Ignatyev.

Two of these, in particular, if conceded would at once fatally
compromise the military and naval situation. To allow the

embarkation of Russian troops in Constantinople and Buyuk Dere would be equivalent to handing over to the Russians all that they missed obtaining by the armistice. The Turks successfully stood out against any such provision appearing in the treaty, just as they successfully withstood the Grand Duke's equivalent attempt to negotiate an entry into Constantinople and an occupation of the Bosphorus heights apart from the treaty (see above, pp. 391–2). To yield to the demand for a cession of six men-of-war would be a humiliation equally detrimental to their two chief assets, command of the sea and support by the British. None of Ignatyev's requirements met with more stubborn refusal from the Sultan.

The idea of remedying the Russian powerlessness in the Black Sea by acquiring a portion of the Turkish fleet had been well aired in the Russian press during the winter,[1] and was pressed to the uttermost by Ignatyev. He was the more insistent since he had news that the British were negotiating for the sale of certain Turkish warships, constructed in England, but not yet fully paid for or delivered, and for the requisition of four of the best ships in the Turkish fleet.[2] The alarm of the Turks at Ignatyev's demand for six of the best units of their fleet was from the first only too evident, and they declared that they would sink their fleet rather than suffer it to fall into the hands either of the Russians or of the English.[3] By 24 February Ignatyev found the opposition of the Sultan and Akhmet Vekif so extreme that he inquired of Gorchakov whether cession should still be insisted upon, but he did not immediately comply with Gorchakov's reply that the demand should be withdrawn, preferring not to reveal the abandonment of the condition until quite certain that the Turks could not be browbeaten into

---

[1] It had been first mooted by Prince Vasilchikov, (see above, p. 189, n. 1), in an article in *Severny Vestnik*, 12 Nov. 1877, and thereafter the Russian press was filled with varying demands for guaranteeing 'our exclusive right over the Black Sea', including in particular the permanent occupation of strong points on the Dardanelles and Bosphorus; Loftus to Derby, disp., no. 648, incl., 21 Nov. 1877, in *F.O.* 65/970, and disp., no. 79, incl., 23 Jan. 1878, in *F.O.* 65/997.

[2] Cf. above, p. 385. Gorchakov to Ignatyev, tel., 17 Feb. (paraphrase); Ignatyev to Gorchakov, tel., 19 Feb. (text); in *San Stefano*, pp. 122, 150–1. Ignatyev notes that in Apr. 1876 he had made efforts to purchase these ships for Russia.

[3] Derby to Loftus, tel., 21 Feb. (repeating news from Layard), in *F.O.* 181/565. Cf. private letter of Layard to Lyons, 1 May, emphasizing the personal determination of the Sultan not to yield on this, or on the question of a Russian occupation, or that of the evacuation of Shumla, Varna, and Batum; Lord Newton, *Life of Lord Lyons*, vol. ii, pp. 137–8.

yielding. Nothing, however, would induce the Sultan to give way, and Ignatyev had to console himself by pointing out that since Hobart was in command of the Turkish navy and the ships had British engineers in them they would probably have joined the British squadron rather than give themselves up to the Russians, or would have been seized by Hornby.[1]

The third demand of Ignatyev which the Turks successfully resisted was his proposal in regard to the Straits, with which was linked that for some form of alliance. Here his failure was as much due to Gorchakov as to the Turks themselves. It has been explained that hardly had Ignatyev left St. Petersburg than the acute tension with England led Gorchakov to give an assurance that the question of the Straits would be reserved for European settlement (26 Jan.), an assurance which he formally repeated on the 29th (see above, p. 356). Gorchakov confessed to the British ambassador that the last article of the bases of peace (which had been communicated to the British government on 25 Jan.) was 'vague and unnecessary', denied that it meant a separate Russo-Turkish understanding, and said that he had no objection to suppressing it. Derby very naturally asked him in that case to do so. But he learnt instead that the Adrianople terms as signed on the 31st still included the provision for the safeguarding of Russian interests in respect of the Straits by a separate agreement with the Turks.[2] Obviously Gorchakov's assurances seemed totally without value to the British government. Russia could not both declare that the question of the Straits was of European concern and at the same time bind Turkey to a bilateral agreement, publicly announced. Actually, Gorchakov was doing what he could to restrain Ignatyev. He repeated instructions at least six times, in slightly varying terms, that the Straits were to be reserved for an agreement in concert with the powers and that they should be passed over in silence in negotiating with the Turks.[3] The very need for such repeti-

[1] Ignatyev to Gorchakov, tel., 24 Feb.; Gorchakov to Ignatyev, tel., 25 Feb.; texts in *San Stefano*, pp. 173–4, and 222, 312.

[2] Loftus to Derby, tel., 30 Jan.; Derby to Loftus, tel., 31 Jan., in *F.O.* 65/998 and 181/564. The last article of the original bases of peace had provided for a revision of the regulations as to the Straits, by which the warships of all other powers should be prohibited from passing, while Russian warships might pass one at a time: this had been altered to the formula given above: see p. 341.

[3] Gorchakov to Ignatyev, tels., 25 and 30 Jan., 2, 9, and 28 Feb., disp., 1 Feb.; Goriainow, *Le Bosphore et les Dardanelles*, pp. 358–6q, 362, 368; *San Stefano*, pp. 65–6, 88–9, 93, 212.

tion shows the degree to which Ignatyev was out of hand, and in fact he did not spare himself to obtain a secret agreement along the lines of his original proposals (see above, p. 404). The Turks took immediate alarm, particularly at any idea of an alliance à la Unkiar-Skelessi. Finally (27 Feb.) Ignatyev suggested a secret separate article which, while recognizing that the question of the Straits would come before the conference and while reaffirming the principle of their closure to foreign warships, made allowance for the special position of Russia and bound the Sultan to allow the passage of Russian warships both for embassy communication purposes at Constantinople and Athens, and 'for other naval needs'. Gorchakov, however, refused to countenance this and in the end was successful in insisting that the question of the Straits must be left entirely to the conference.[1] It was his one victory over Ignatyev. In consequence of this the treaty of San Stefano merely stated that the Straits were to remain open, in time of war as well as in time of peace, to neutral merchant ships bound for or from Russian ports; and there were no secret articles which went behind this.

As an offset to this rebuff Ignatyev devised at the last moment a supplementary article whereby the Turks were explicitly to admit that they would be fully bound by the articles of the treaty once ratified, and whereby both signatory powers were to be obliged to support each other to preserve the treaty unchanged. He further suggested to the Turks a separate and secret article binding Turkey yet more closely to Russia to prevent any changes without mutual agreement. This was tantamount to a repudiation of the idea of the treaty as a preliminary treaty, and naturally aroused extreme opposition from the Turks, who interpreted it as again amounting to an offensive and defensive alliance, for the maintenance of the treaty against the powers. Their resistance was successful and the project was abandoned.[2]

Ignatyev, thus, was unable to impose on the Turks his proposals for embarkation at Buyuk Dere, for cession of cruisers, for the Straits, for some form of alliance, and for securing the validity and carrying out of the treaty; but the rest of his

[1] Ignatyev to Gorchakov, tel., 27 Feb.; Gorchakov to Ignatyev, tel., rec. 28 Feb.; texts in *San Stefano*, pp. 210–12.

[2] Ignatyev to Gorchakov, tel., 27 Feb., and disp., 6 Mar.; text and extract in *San Stefano*, pp. 210, 239–41.

programme he carried through with the minimum of concessions.[1] Among these other conditions Turkish opposition was especially concentrated upon the provisions as to Bulgaria and as to the partition of Novi Bazar between Serbia and Montenegro. In regard to the former they were in the end obliged to agree that a Russo-Turkish commission should fix the trace of the boundary in detail before the Russian evacuation, and they had to accept in the treaty Bulgarian frontiers so specified as to go beyond even those of the Constantinople conference in two vital directions.

To the south-east, Ignatyev left Adrianople in Turkish hands, but did his best to nullify this advantage by bringing the Bulgarian frontier as close as possible to it and by drawing the boundary in such a way as to include in Bulgaria a salient running down to the Orient railway at Lule Burgas. Thereby Constantinople itself was gravely threatened and the line to Adrianople cut.

To the south-west, the Turks succeeded in excluding Salonika from the new Bulgaria, but the new frontier line ringed in the town closely, and they had to abandon a large strip of the Aegean coast, including Kavalla and the mouth of the Struma, while the whole of Macedonia, with Monastir and Okhrida, likewise fell within Ignatyev's far-flung principality.

To the north-west, the acquisition by Serbia of Nish and half its *sanjak*, originally intended for Bulgaria, was no gain for the Turks save to the extent that the Serbs were incensed by the smallness of what they received from the hands of the Russians.

To the north-east, another change in the Russian plans, diminishing the extent of Bulgaria, brought no profit to Turkey. Here Ignatyev had first intended to demand the cession of the Delta only (together of course with southern Bessarabia), to be used to compensate Roumania, while the Dobrudja would be included in Bulgaria. But in view of the extreme hostility of the Roumanians and of his fears of an Austro-Roumanian combination against the Russian lines of communication, he decided to demand the cession of the Dobrudja as well, both it and the Delta to be available for Roumanian compensation for the loss of the Bessarabian districts.[2]

[1] The text of the treaty of San Stefano is given in Appendix VII. For the Bulgarian frontiers proposed at the Constantinople conference see the map between pp. 240–1.

[2] *San Stefano*, p. 276. For the Roumanians and the treaty see below, Chapter XVI. For the importance of Russian land communications with Bulgaria, cf. above, p. 326 and p. 402.

THE BALKAN PENINSULA ACCORDING T

TREATIES OF SAN STEFANO AND BERLIN

The internal provisions for the government of the principality
f Bulgaria represented a great success for Ignatyev: full autonomy; a Prince freely elected, but not to be a member of the
reigning house of any of the great European states, to be confirmed by the Sultan with the assent of the powers; a Bulgarian
assembly to work out an administrative statute, before the
election of a prince; a Russian commissary for two years to
supervise the introduction of the new régime; a national militia;
no Turkish troops to be quartered in Bulgaria; their passage
through Bulgaria to be strictly limited to certain roads according to conditions to be laid down in a convention between the
Porte and the Bulgarian administration (i.e. the Russian commissary) within three months of ratification; no irregulars
(Bazi Bazouks or Circassians) to be allowed in or to pass
through Bulgaria; a Russian army of occupation not more than
50,000 in strength for not more than two years. The only
vestige of Turkish control was that the Sultan was to be technically the suzerain of the Prince and that the principality was to
pay tribute.

Here again Ignatyev intended that the domination of Russia
over her new protectorate should be amply safeguarded. The
amount of the tribute was not specified in the treaty, but this
omission was carefully planned by Ignatyev so as to provide for
the possibility of linking up the Bulgarian tribute with the
Turkish indemnity to Russia. His scheme was that among the
guarantees for the indemnity which the Turks were to furnish
should figure the handing over to Russia of the right to receive
the Bulgarian tribute, which would place Bulgaria in the position of full, practical independence of Turkey and, on the other
hand, in one of financial dependence on Russia.[1]

While the only substantial concession which the Turks could
extract on the question of Bulgaria was the exclusion of Salonika,
they were slightly more successful in their struggle over the
partition of Novi Bazar between Serbia and Montenegro.
According to Ignatyev's original programme these two states,
the independence of which the Turks had to recognize in the
San Stefano treaty, were to be contiguous along the river Lim
and thus to divide Novi Bazar between them. Although such
a redrawing of the map would have cut off Bosnia and Herzegovina, not yet lost to the Turks, from any land communication

[1] *San Stefano*, p. 285. Cf. below, p. 548.

with the rest of Turkey, Safvet Pasha in the first instance was apparently induced to give his consent to the Montenegrin frontier marching with the Serbian along the Lim as far as Prjepolje (19 Feb.), but on the next day he was overruled from Constantinople and withdrew all his concessions. This was due to the crisis caused by his replacement of Server as foreign minister and by the Russian demand to advance to San Stefano. In view of the continued Turkish refusal to agree to Serbia and Montenegro joining in Novi Bazar and of further instructions from St. Petersburg Ignatyev gave way and granted a narrow strip running from Mitrovica to the Drina, but with the heights dominating it left in Serbian or Montenegrin hands.[1]

The Turks similarly began by raising little objection to the other new Montenegrin frontiers, but later stoutly opposed the acquisition of any sea-coast, though in the end they were compelled to cede Spizza, Antivari, and Dulcigno, all of which had already fallen to Montenegrin arms. In the Morača valley they were likewise compelled to cede Podgorica, Spuž, and Žablyak, none of which had thus fallen, but they were successful in resisting the extension to the Drin proposed by Ignatyev.

On the side of Herzegovina, where he was specially anxious to include in Montenegro the places most prominent in the rebellion, little difficulty was encountered from the Turks, but much from St. Petersburg in fear of Vienna. Ignatyev seems to have acted on the assumption that the Russians had undertaken with the Austrians not to pass the line Trebinje–Bilek–Gacko. He drew the line accordingly, thereby keeping for the Montenegrins their conquest of Niksić and the Duga pass.[2]

Throughout he had considerable, but not serious, difficulties with Prince Nicholas's envoy at Adrianople, Radonić, who put in a claim to all southern Herzegovina up to the Narenta, the Lim as frontier with Serbia, and Scutari and a large slice of Albania up to the Drin. Ignatyev expounded to him the extreme difficulty of the Albanian and Scutari claims, and thought it prudent not to keep him informed of the details of his negotiations with Safvet. But Radonić appears to have been satisfied with the resultant gains set down in the treaty of San Stefano, which approximately tripled the size of Montenegro, though

[1] *San Stefano*, pp. 135–6, 147, 151, 190–1.
[2] Ib., pp. 114, 265.

MAP 6

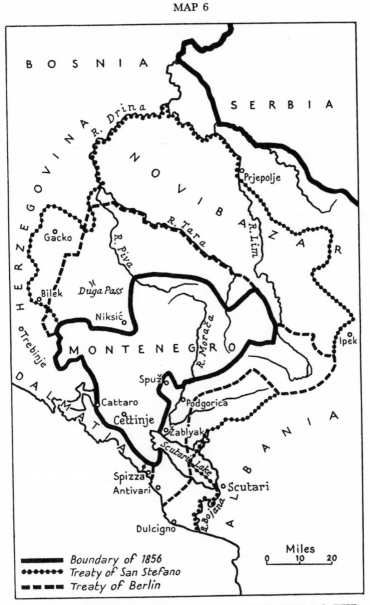

THE FRONTIERS OF MONTENEGRO ACCORDING TO THE
TREATIES OF SAN STEFANO AND BERLIN

only about a quarter of them were already in Montenegrin hands.[1]

As was to be expected, the attitude of the Serbian envoys, Catardzhi, Prince Milan's uncle by marriage, and Lešjanin, lately in command of the Morava corps, was very different.[2] It was inevitable that Ignatyev should meet with heated opposition from the Serbs, for his large Bulgaria shut the door on Serbian hopes of future absorption of any of the Macedonian lands, included the much contested western strip from Vranja to Widdin, and even took in as originally planned the whole of the upper Morava valley with Nish itself, just captured by Lešjanin's troops. Ignatyev added insult to injury by the offensive contempt with which he treated Catardzhi, who in return poured out vehement accusations behind his back. Ignatyev drew very unfavourable comparisons between the military performance of the Serbs and that of the Montenegrins, and maintained that the reason why it was not possible to do more for the Serbs was that they had succeeded in conquering so very little territory on the side of Novi Bazar and Old Serbia. This was true, but it was at least in part due to the desire of the Russian command that the Serbs, when they re-entered the war at the end of 1877, should co-operate on the Russian right wing with as strong forces as possible. The Serbs had complied in so far as they were able to spare troops from their main offensive against Nish, which they took on 10 January, and then against Vranja in the upper Morava valley. They were therefore unable to spare forces for any effective move against the Turks who remained strongly posted in Novi Bazar. But, in any case, action in this area had been more or less ruled out by threats from Vienna against any offensive not only in Bosnia but in the *sanjak* as well.[3]

The Serbs began by making very wide demands. Ignatyev refused to deprive his Bulgaria of the strategical advantages of Pirot, Trno, or Vranja, even though all three were occupied by

---

[1] *San Stefano*, pp. 104–5, 247–8.

[2] Lešjanin only arrived at G.H.Q. on 22 Feb., just after Ignatyev had abandoned his Novi Bazar programme; ib., p. 192.

[3] *Hasenkampf*, pp. 469–72, and *San Stefano*, pp. 105, 187–90, and Ristić, *Diplomatska istorija Srbije . . .* , vol. ii, pp. 120–1 (for Catardzhi's disgust with Ignatyev and Nelidov); Bobrikov's memoirs in *R.S.*, vol. clii, pp. 520 ff. (for the Serbian campaign); Jovanović, *Vlada Milana Obrenovića*, vol. i, pp. 403–4 (for Austrian warnings).

the Serbian army. His allocation of Nish to Bulgaria aroused the Serbs to violent protests, both at G.H.Q. and in St. Petersburg: they denounced Cherkasky's manufacturing of petitions against incorporation in Serbia and declared that they would fight for it rather than yield. Their protests were successful: Ignatyev was brought to recognize that it was impossible to deprive the Serbs of Nish and he accordingly cut it out of his Bulgaria. Elsewhere the Turks stubbornly fought against any Serbian acquisitions, combining the argument that they would not cede what had not been conquered with insistence on the text of the Adrianople bases of peace, which, as Ignatyev had previously complained, contained the formula 'rectification of frontiers' and not 'territorial acquisitions'. As has just been seen, Ignatyev, who was genuinely anxious to placate the Serbs with Novi Bazar, had to give way and concentrate his energies on keeping the Turkish route through it as narrow and difficult to defend as possible. On the side of Bosnia the long-standing claim of Serbia to Little Zbornik, on the right bank of the Drina, was settled in her favour. Finally, Turkey recognized in the treaty Serbian independence.[1] These gains for the Serbs fell far short of their expectations. They never forgave Ignatyev; they were convinced that St. Petersburg thought of no one but the Bulgars;[2] in bitter disillusionment with Russia they began to consider whether more might not be obtained from Austria-Hungary, who at least might be counted upon

[1] For the Serbian frontiers see map between pp. 410–11, and map facing p. 412. The Serbs originally claimed the *vilayet* of Kossovo (which would have given them Prizren, Skoplje, and the greater part of Novi Bazar), the *sanjak* of Nish (which included Nish, Leskovac, Vranja, Trno, and Pirot), and the greater part of the *sanjak* of Widdin, including the fortress of Widdin. In respect of this last Ignatyev contended that the population was indubitably Bulgar. Nish had been included in the Constantinople conference Bulgaria. *San Stefano*, pp. 104–5, 187–94, 271–2; Ristić, op. cit., vol. ii, pp. 111–13, 120 (for Serbian claims), 116–20 (for Serbian protests); Liegnitz's diary, under date 12 Feb., *Aus drei Kriegen*, p. 273 (for Cherkasky). Ristić seems to have believed that Nish was only given to Serbia by the treaty of San Stefano thanks to the personal intervention of the Tsar against Cherkasky and his violent bulgarophils; Busch's diary under date 12 June, in *Deutsche Rundschau*, vol. cxli, p. 368, and cf. Ristić's speech in the Skupština 25 July, *Revue d'histoire diplomatique*, 1891, p. 484. Cherkasky, who was even more anti-Greek than he was anti-Serb, wanted an independent Bulgaria which should include Nish, Priština, and Prizren, as well as Salonika, the Aegean littoral, and Adrianople; see two reports of his in Ovsyany, *Russkoe upravlenie v Bolgarii . . .*, vol. i, pp. 172–83, 286–7, and Bobrikov's memoirs in *R.S.*, vol. cliii, p. 61.

[2] See particularly the memorandum of 14 Mar. of Protić, Serbian envoy in St. Petersburg, on Russian opinion and the views of Giers and Jomini, text in Ristić, op. cit., vol. ii, pp. 122–7.

to assist them in pushing back the western frontiers of the new Bulgaria.

Ignatyev was able to carry out the remainder of his programme for the treaty without over-great difficulty or substantial alterations. The Turks finally consented to cede Batum and the neighbouring part of Lazistan, although neither had been conquered by the Russians, whereas the remainder of their acquisitions by the treaty were already in their hands. (See map between pp. 540 and 541.) At least the Turks might count on strenuous British opposition to such an increase of Russian power in Asia Minor.

Two further articles require closer notice: that on the indemnity, and a new one relating to the Armenians. The treaty as finally signed corresponded with Ignatyev's draft in that it linked up the indemnity with the territorial acquisitions of Russia. A total sum was named; then in consideration of cessions of specified territory a smaller sum was fixed for actual payment. Thus, if subsequently the Russians were compelled to reduce their territorial acquisitions, they could demand an increase of the money-payment to be made. Article XIX named the preposterous figures of 900,000,000 silver roubles for war costs and 510,000,000 for various damages—a total of 1,410,000,000 roubles (not less than £235,000,000). Reutern, the finance minister, declared that three to four hundred million roubles were amply sufficient to cover the expenses of the war, and the actual amount required to be paid by the Turks was accordingly laid down in the treaty as 310,000,000 roubles. The all-important details as to method of payment and securities were to be regulated by a subsequent agreement. Ignatyev immediately proposed to his government that the payment of the indemnity should be secured by an international loan floated under Russian auspices, guaranteed by the Sultan leasing the Heraclea coal-mines to a Russian organization and pledging the revenues of his silver- and copper-mines in Asia Minor, of the Smyrna and Salonika customs, and of the Bulgarian tribute. He plunged into negotiations with the officials of the Ottoman Bank, French financiers, and Decazes, with the threefold object of obtaining the indemnity from Turkey as rapidly as possible, of linking up the new syndicate for his international loan with the Ottoman Bank in such a way as to obtain Russian representation on it, and of pushing the French into sponsoring his scheme so that the opposition of the bond-holders of Ottoman loans to the Russian demands might be mollified. None of his financial schemes, in part ingenious, in part ingenuous, came to anything. In any case, neither Reutern nor Gorchakov would move. By the time that the Berlin congress met nothing had been settled, and the indemnity provisions of San Stefano lay open to the attacks of western financial interests.[1]

The Armenians had not been mentioned in the Adrianople bases of peace, but they now received their first international recognition (upon which Ignatyev greatly plumed himself) in Article XVI of the San Stefano treaty. The language used was as vague as in similar articles in previous treaties professing to protect other Christians in Turkey. Reforms (unspecified) were to be introduced into the provinces (unspecified) inhabited by Armenians, and there were to be guarantees (unspecified) against attacks by Kurds and Circassians. There was no actual mention of Russian surveillance or rights of intervention, but the article was intended to be used as a lever for the promotion of Russian influence in Turkish Armenia. Behind its stereotyped form of words lay much hard intriguing, tangled beyond even Levantine measure by the division of the Armenians into Orthodox, Gregorian, and Catholic communities. According to Ignatyev's version, he was approached at San Stefano by Narses, the Gregorian Patriarch, and other leading Armenians in Constantinople asking for a grant of autonomy for the *vilayets* of Sivas, Van, Mush, and Erzerum, and for their occupation by Russian troops for a certain length of time. The latter request may perhaps have contributed to the fixing of a longer time-limit (six months) for the evacuation of Asiatic Turkey than that for the evacuation of European Turkey (three months), but there was no parallel in Turkish Armenia to the two years' occupation of Bulgaria by Russian forces. The request for autonomy was transformed by Ignatyev, thoroughly distrustful of the Turkish Armenians, in such a way as almost to ensure in

---

[1] *San Stefano*, pp. 292–3, 229, 236–7; Ignatyev's memoirs in *I.V.*, vol. cxliv, pp. 39–44, where the details are cursory or confused, but his general aims clearly stated. Layard was thus right in suspecting that the Russians had their eyes on the Heraclea coal-mines as one of the guarantees for the indemnity: later he encouraged a project for acquiring the mines by a British company; private letters to the Duke of Sutherland, 22 May and 12 July, copies in Layard papers, *British Museum, Add. MSS.* 39131, ff. 103, 120; see also Lee, *Great Britain and the Cyprus Convention policy of 1878*, p. 135.

advance its refusal. After consultation with St. Petersburg, he proposed an article according to which the reformed *vilayet* system was to be applied, in agreement with the Russian government, to the four *vilayets*; but the article also directly recognized the Catolikos of Echmiadzin, the head of the Orthodox Armenians and accounted a tool of Russia, as the supreme representative of the Armenian people as a whole. The Turks, doubtless egged on by the Gregorians and the Catholics, stubbornly opposed any mention of the Catolikos, and Ignatyev eventually abandoned his draft article and substituted that which figured in the treaty. That was quite sufficient to arouse the worst suspicions of the British as to Russian designs.[1]

One final explanation must be made in regard to the making of the treaty. The discussions in St. Petersburg before Ignatyev's departure for Adrianople showed that Gorchakov wanted the results of the peace negotiations to take the form of a protocol or protocols, while Ignatyev successfully insisted upon the advantages of a treaty. This technical question of form involved a very important difference of view as to what Ignatyev was to accomplish. He himself aimed at binding Turkey as tightly as possible by a detailed treaty and facing Europe with accomplished facts: if it did become necessary to yield somewhat before western opposition, the more stringent the terms were the more possible it would be to find some tolerable concessions. Gorchakov, on the other hand, aimed at making only general arrangements with Turkey and at leaving the ground clear for his negotiations with the powers, particularly those with Austria-Hungary: if detailed provisions were imposed upon Turkey, the maximum of European opposition would be encountered. The question was directly bound up with the personal struggle between the two men: a treaty would give the real power to Ignatyev, a protocol would save much for Gorchakov. The latter lost the first bout when his rival started for the south with his draft treaty as the basis of his instructions, but won the second bout when, a week later, in view of changes in the diplomatic situation, Ignatyev's instructions were to be changed (1 Feb.). The preliminary peace should be in the form not of

---

[1] *San Stefano*, pp. 108–9, 174, 203–5, 289. For Layard's violent warnings as to these and other Russian intrigues over Armenia, see Layard to Derby, disp., conf., no. 401, 25 Mar., copy in *British Museum, Add. MSS*. 39148, ff. 12–13, and private letters to Derby and Beaconsfield, 20 Mar. and 3 Apr., ib. 39131, ff. 56, 54, 66.

a treaty but of a protocol or protocols as far as possible avoiding details.[1] These instructions did not reach Ignatyev until just before the move to San Stefano. In the meantime the Austrians were proving dangerously obdurate, the British had sent their fleet to Constantinople, the outlook for a conference was exceedingly black, and the Tsar was completely under the sway of the extremists. Consequently, whether partly because Gorchakov had now genuinely come to believe that he would be unable to manœuvre a conference into accepting a peace satisfactory to Russia, or solely because he was unable to stand out against the strength of nationalist feeling, he reversed his instructions of 1 February and again gave Ignatyev virtually a free hand, except as regards the Straits.[2] Ignatyev thus was able to make a treaty entering into sufficient detail for him to proceed apace with the forestalling of effective counter-measures by the hostile powers. Preliminary in name, it was intended to be as final as he could make it.

The signature of the treaty must be accounted a great success for Ignatyev, but its ratification and carrying out were the essentials, and he knew well enough that now would be fought the crucial battles. It was precisely those proposals which aimed at ensuring the maximum chance of the application of the treaty which he had failed to impose upon the Turks. It was, also, the validity of his whole treaty which was at this time being challenged by England in the struggle now raging over the terms of reference of the conference proposed by Andrássy (see below, pp. 434–8). Undaunted, Ignatyev plunged forward with more energy than ever.

He hastened to take up his quarters in Constantinople itself, where for five days, 5 to 10 March, he bombarded the Turkish ministers with plans for the rapid putting into effect of the treaty, and for securing the embarkation of Russian troops at Buyuk Dere. He claimed to have secured Safvet Pasha's agreement to the immediate appointment of Turkish commissioners to delimit the new frontiers of Bulgaria, to the evacuation by the

---

[1] Gorchakov to Ignatyev, disp., 1 Feb., text in *San Stefano*, pp. 85–9. The dispatch was apparently sent by special courier, but he did not leave St. Petersburg until either 6 or 10 Feb., probably the latter date, and did not arrive until 21 or 22 Feb.; *Hasenkampf*, p. 423, *Skalon*, vol. ii, p. 228; *San Stefano*, pp. 84, 150, 190.

[2] Gorchakov to Ignatyev, tels., 15 and 18 Feb.; Ignatyev to Gorchakov, disp., 16 Feb.; texts in *San Stefano*, pp. 118, 126, 116, and cf. pp. 92–3.

Turks of each frontier district as soon as delimited, and to the instalment of temporary Russian commissaries. His primary object was to force the pace in the most contentious portions of his new Bulgaria, the Lule Burgas salient and the western and south-western Macedonian regions. The latter were of especial concern in that the armistice had left them still in Turkish hands. To this end Ignatyev obtained from the Grand Duke Nicholas the appointment of General Imeretinsky as general commissary for the delimitation and taking over from the Turkish officials, and of Khitrovo, a man with great experience of the Balkans and for many years consul at Monastir, as civil commissioner in Macedonia. Skobelev was to be sent there with a full division and a cavalry brigade; Russian officers (among them notably Tseretelev) were selected to take over the administration; a proclamation to the new Bulgaria was prepared. Everything should be ready by the time the treaty was ratified. Here Ignatyev scored his second big success, making ratification a certainty by securing that Reouf Pasha, the russophil Seraskier, should accompany him at once to St. Petersburg for the exchange of ratifications.[1]

He failed, however, in his efforts to gain time by preventing the Turks from communicating to the powers the complete text of San Stefano before ratification. It was received in London on 16 March, and it had been preceded by full summaries of the main provisions. It was inevitable that the terms should create the worst impression and bring both England and Austria-Hungary to the verge of open rupture: the 'whole Treaty amounts to the destruction of Turkish rule in Europe and to the partition of Turkey amongst the Slav race under

---

[1] *San Stefano*, pp. 245, 249, 256–7, 278, 348. Ignatyev ostentatiously did not call upon either Layard or Fournier, the new French ambassador, whom he accused of bitter opposition, largely on the score of the size of the indemnity prejudicing the interests of the French holders of Ottoman stock; ib., pp. 252, 198–200, 234. Ignatyev was probably correct in believing Fournier to be very hostile to him; Layard's memoirs, *British Museum, Add. MSS.* 38936, f. 198; private letters to Derby and Tenterden, 27 Mar., to Salisbury, 17 Apr., copies, ib. 39131, ff. 61, 78. Raschdau bears testimony to the hostility of the Grand Duke Nicholas to Fournier, and to the close relations of the latter with Layard and Zichy; *Ein sinkendes Reich*, p. 162. Tseretelev, as one of Ignatyev's favourites, had been recalled from the army and had assisted him in working out the San Stefano Bulgaria. He was appointed Russian representative in Eastern Rumelia and, later, consul-general at Philippopolis, where he remained the centre of Russian activities until illness caused his retirement and early death in 1882; see the biographical sketch by Popruzhenko in *Slavyanski glas*, 1932, vol. xxvi, no. 1–2, pp. 65–6.

Russian protection'.[1] It was almost equally fatal in British eyes in its effect upon Asiatic Turkey. Layard, always a prolific writer, was moved to exceed himself in thirty-two pages of denunciation.[2] To Ignatyev this reception mattered little, for he had nursed no illusions as to the British attitude to his handiwork. He could view with content opinion at home. 'History can show but few such instances of moderation . . .', *Novoe Vremya* declared; 'the sole acquisitions which we must sooner or later make in the Balkan Peninsula are the Bosphorus and the Dardanelles, but the moment for this step, we are sorry to say, has not yet arrived.'[3] As long as Ignatyev was assured of such backing from nationalist opinion he might still dominate Russian foreign policy and carry through to a successful conclusion what had been signed at San Stefano.

Meanwhile he was bringing Reouf Pasha to St. Petersburg. They arrived on 14 March. On the 17th ratifications were exchanged. Two days later Reouf left for Constantinople, seemingly pledged to the fullest co-operation with Russia. Ignatyev was at the height of his power. He would return promptly to Constantinople as ambassador and there cajole and intimidate the Turks into carrying out the treaty which he had forced them into both signing and ratifying. But at this decisive moment Ignatyev's star failed him. He was never again to rule or struggle for rule on the Golden Horn.

First, he was sent to Vienna to confront Andrássy personally in battle over the Reichstadt agreement and the secret conventions. In anticipation the Vienna mission did not run counter to Ignatyev's own plans: it would give him an inside view of the situation in Austria-Hungary; it would give him opportunities to intrigue for the removal of Andrássy; he would speak in a very different tone and with very different effect from Novikov, tied hand and foot to the Ballplatz; he might return with all the elements hostile to Andrássy strengthened and with Russian firmness both feared and respected. But, in fact, he returned to St. Petersburg, early in April, with nothing accomplished save the yet more hostile alienation of Vienna. This failure immediately shook his prestige, and during the next few weeks of

[1] Loftus to Derby, tel. and disp., no. 339, 21 Mar., in *F.O.* 65/1001.
[2] Layard to Derby, disp., no. 343, 13 Mar., in *F.O.* 195/1176.
[3] *Novoe Vremya*, 19 Mar., Loftus to Derby, disp., no. 340, incl., 21 Mar., in *F.O.* 65/1001.

drift and confusion an obscure struggle ensued to prevent his control of policy whether from St. Petersburg or from Constantinople. By the end of the month it was decided that the new ambassador to Turkey should be not Ignatyev, but Prince Lobanov-Rostovsky, the very man whom he had succeeded fourteen years before, when he first took up his post at the Russian legation on the Bosphorus.[1]

The blow was complete. Lobanov, a great nobleman, later ambassador in London and Vienna and for a twelve-month to direct Russian policy as the successor of Giers in 1895, was Gorchakov's choice. He had had twenty years of diplomatic experience, but for the last ten years had been assistant minister of interior: conciliatory and lacking in energy, he would be certain to effect no adequate pressure on the Turks to carry out the terms of San Stefano. When he arrived at Constantinople in the middle of May, he made little secret of his disbelief in panslav foreign policy and proceeded to send home severe criticisms of the treaty and to urge the necessity of large concessions. It was small consolation to Ignatyev that the new first secretary was one of his own men, Bazili, with many years of service in Turkey behind him. Ignatyev himself attributed the decision that he was not to return to Constantinople mainly to the fear of adding to the international antagonism to Russia and the fear and dislike of Russian general head-quarters. The former owed much to the violent hostility of Layard and to the opposition of Reuss, the German ambassador. The latter took shape, not only according to Ignatyev's account, in a network of intrigues between the Grand Duke, Imeretinsky, Nelidov, and Onou to prevent at all costs his return as ambassador, which culminated in the dispatch of Imeretinsky to St. Petersburg with this express object.[2] Probably at least equal influence

---

[1] The decision to appoint Lobanov was taken prior to 1 May, when Loftus reported it, adding that Ignatyev had openly been speaking of his approaching return to Constantinople; Loftus to Derby, disp., no. 475, 1 May, in *F.O.* 65/1003. The official date of appointment is given as 4 May in Teplov, *Knyaz A. B. Lobanov-Rostovsky*, p. 24. Later in the summer Gorchakov favoured Lobanov as his eventual successor, private letter of Langenau to Andrássy, cited by G. Wittrock, *Gorčakov, Ignatiev och Šuvalov*, pp. 116–17.

[2] Raschdau, *Ein sinkendes Reich*, p. 205; Reuss (Constantinople) to Radowitz, 23 May, extract in Radowitz, *Aufzeichnungen und Erinnerungen*, vol. ii, p. 8; Lobanov to Gorchakov, 20 and 23 May, extracts in *Tatishchev*, pp. 512–13; *San Stefano*, pp. 302–9. Polovtsov's diary, under date 29 Apr., attributes the supersession of Ignatyev to the Grand Duke's violent warnings; *Krasny arkhiv*, vol. xxxiii, pp. 191–2. Polovtsov was a friend of Lobanov.

should be attributed to the fact that moderate counsels were greatly strengthened by the failure of Ignatyev's mission to Vienna: for this pointed unmistakably to the impossibility of patching up a reconciliation without his San Stefano treaty undergoing considerable modification.

Meanwhile there was a virtual interregnum in Russian diplomacy in Constantinople which was quite as prejudicial to the chances of success for Ignatyev's policy as the appointment of Lobanov. For two months, from 10 March, when Ignatyev departed with Reouf for St. Petersburg, until 14 May, when Lobanov took up his post, Russia had no effective diplomat on the spot. Just as April saw military stagnation in the Russian head-quarters while the Grand Duke's successor was being awaited, so it saw diplomatic inaction while the embassy was unfilled. Nelidov, the sole representative of the foreign office, was at first left without instructions or credentials. At the beginning of April he was appointed chargé d'affaires; a galling disappointment, for he coveted ambassadorial rank. Thereupon he took to his bed, begged to be recalled, and abandoned himself to the gloomiest predictions and to intrigues against Ignatyev. Clearly nothing could be expected of him in the shape of vigorous action.[1] Nor could it be expected of Onou, the first dragoman, with his turkophil moderation. Thus Ignatyev had no one at hand on whom could devolve the task of hurrying into effect the San Stefano provisions, while on the other hand the field was left clear for Turkish recalcitrance and Layard's stiffening.

The Turks took heart in the absence of Ignatyev to refuse positively any Russian embarkation at Buyuk Dere, and Reouf Pasha on his return from St. Petersburg on 24 March proved either unwilling or unable to lead the Sultan and his co-ministers along the path of a russophil policy.[2] This attractive and able Circassian appears to have played a double role with considerable skill. He had throughout been on good terms with the Russians, and was regarded by Ignatyev as his most valuable ally among the Turks. On the other hand, Layard, who was on 'very friendly and indeed intimate terms' with him, believed

[1] Nelidov's memoirs, in *Revue des deux mondes*, 15 Nov. 1915, vol. xxx, pp. 243–54; letter of Nelidov to Ignatyev, late Apr., text in *I.V.*, vol. cxliii, pp. 676–7.

[2] Ignatyev states in his memoirs that he had made much headway in his discussions with Reouf for an occupation of the Bosphorus heights and for some kind of Russo-Turkish alliance; *San Stefano*, pp. 299–300.

in his honesty and doubted the correctness of the warnings which reached him that Reouf had been won over by the Russians.[1] As *persona grata* to the Russians he had been selected for the exchange of ratifications in St. Petersburg in the hope that some last-minute modification of the San Stefano terms might be obtained there, but he was unable to gain anything beyond an undertaking that Bayazid might ultimately be retroceded.[2] Despite this, he received the impression that the Russians would, if pressed, make important concessions in order to avoid a break with England.[3]

By the end of March any hopes that the Russians might be able to obtain control of the Bosphorus with the connivance of the Turks or might even be able to coerce them into an alliance were extinguished, and nothing of Ignatyev's schemes for Macedonia or the other frontiers was being put into effect. The energetic support of England, so long expected and so tardily forthcoming, was now at last at hand to overbear those Turks who had, with much ground, held that Russia's bite was worse than England's bark. The Sultan was convinced that time was on his side and that the British government were in earnest. At the same time he was the more encouraged by the signs of Andrássy's heightened opposition to the San Stefano treaty and the failure of Russian efforts to win over Vienna. Thus even the removal from the ministry, owing to palace intrigues, of the two pillars of British influence, Akhmet Vekif and Said (18 Apr.), was not followed by any change of policy in a sense favourable to Russia, and Safvet remained at the Porte, working more and more closely with Layard. It is true that Sadyk Pasha, the new prime minister, was a shady individual, suspected (justly) of jobbery with Galata bankers, but the Sultan's assurances that the ministerial changes would have no anti-British effect proved correct.[4]

So the treaty of San Stefano remained signed, ratified—and not carried out. Ignatyev, unsupported by either G.H.Q. or his diplomatic subordinates on the spot, and cross-countered by his

---

[1] Layard's memoirs, *British Museum, Add. MSS.* 38936, f. 255.
[2] Ib., and Layard to Derby, tel., no. 351, 5 Apr., copy in Layard papers, *British Museum, Add. MSS.* 39148.
[3] Layard to Derby, disp., no. 399, secret, 25 Mar., copy, ib.
[4] Layard papers, *British Museum, Add. MSS.* 38936, ff. 311–18; 39131, ff. 79–80. The strength of Layard's influence is confirmed by Raschdau, *Ein sinkendes Reich*, pp. 173, 176–7.

foreign office, had failed to drive home victory at Constantinople before the international situation could harden into the
alternatives of a war with England and perhaps with Austria-
Hungary, or of a conference at which Russia would be required
to accept heavy sacrifices. The whole policy of which he was
the main instigator and the conductor rested on the view that
Turkey was of primary, England and Austria-Hungary of
secondary, consequence; that, if accounts could be settled with
satisfactory swiftness with Turkey, the other powers would be
unable to modify seriously a Russian settlement. This policy
failed because, for all its backing in Russian national opinion,
its execution was too great a task for any one man and required
a unity of aim and decision which was conspicuously absent
both in the head-quarters of the Grand Duke Nicholas and in
the foreign office at St. Petersburg; because the Turks clung
desperately, if at moments waveringly, to their belief that foreign
intervention in some form would in the end save them; finally,
because England, despite the internal divisions in the cabinet
and in public opinion upon which the Russians set such store,
moved more rapidly and decisively than expected, and because
Austria-Hungary refused to be browbeaten into acceptance of
the overriding of the Reichstadt policy which was the assumption underlying that of San Stefano.

XV

VIENNA

IN the three preceding chapters attention has been mainly concentrated on the military and diplomatic efforts of the Russians to impose their will upon the Turks, since these, and not the contemporaneous negotiations with the other powers, were the essential feature of the nationalist policy, hailed, after Kars and Plevna and the triumphs of the mid-winter trans-Balkan campaign, with frantic acclaim by the Russian press, and carried through by Ignatyev and Obruchev in reckless disregard of reactions upon England and Austria-Hungary. It was natural that Russians should feel passionately that their sacrifices had made possible the liberation of the Christians from the Moslem yoke and had called the Balkan peoples to a new life. But that did not alter the other fact that the future of the Ottoman empire was regarded by the powers as of general concern. The Europe of the eighteen-seventies was not the Europe of the eighteen-twenties. A Russo-Turkish war could not be concluded by a purely Russo-Turkish peace. This was recognized by the Russian government, if not by Russian public opinion. In the last resort the problem was, therefore, how to ensure that the inevitable European conference should be reduced to as much of a formality as possible. Ignatyev and his like gambled on the fear inspired in Constantinople by the military might of Russia and on the inability of the English and the Austrians to counter Russian predominance by a recourse to arms. It was necessary, indeed, while Russia by herself was settling accounts with Turkey, to hold discussions with London, with Berlin, and particularly with Vienna; but these were regarded by Ignatyev and in part by the Tsar as of secondary importance, as designed to spin out time until the situation of Russia in the Balkans was so strong as to render opposition fruitless, unless pushed to extremes which would be impossibly costly and dangerous.

On the other hand, Gorchakov and most of the Russian diplomats were too thoroughly imbued with the dangers and uncertainties of the international situation and too little captured by the idea of Russia's mission in the Balkans to regard the negotiations with England and again particularly those with Austria-Hungary as of anything but first-rate consequence. To them Vienna, Berlin, and London were the vital centres, not Constantinople. And it was in their hands and not Ignatyev's that lay the actual conduct of relations with these powers. Nor was the Tsar himself, despite his backing of Ignatyev's policy, in real agreement with Ignatyev's postulate of the irreconcilability of Russian and Austrian interests. His personal relations with the Emperor Francis Joseph and with the Emperor William, his belief in the *Dreikaiserbündnis* as a support for the principles of autocracy, his memory of the Crimean War, his apprehensions in regard to the alarming spread of revolutionary feeling and to the whole internal situation in his own country, finally his own policy of collaboration with Austria-Hungary in the Balkans sketched out at Reichstadt and specified in some detail in the secret conventions—all these factors weighed in the scales against his only too frequent feelings of disgust at or contempt for Vienna and prevented him from steadily viewing his relations with his brother emperor on the Danube in the same light as Ignatyev.

The outcome of these divergencies among the small group of men with whom the fortunes of Russia rested was that the negotiations with Vienna which were begun in December 1877 had a double character. They were in part an attempt to keep Austria-Hungary separated from England by coming to an agreement with her in regard to the peace terms, and in part an attempt to keep her quiet while Russia was pushing through her main designs in the Balkan peninsula. When in February 1878 the scope of the negotiations was extended by Andrássy's proposal for a European conference, they also assumed the character of manœuvres to place Russia in as favourable a position as possible when the conference should meet. Throughout they were overclouded by the fact that Andrássy with justice regarded Russian policy as in the main dominated by his most dangerous enemies, Ignatyev and the panslavs, who were quite unconstrained by the shackles laboriously forged in the secret conventions.

Within the Dual Monarchy, even before the final successes of the Russian arms caused consternation, there were powerful currents of russophobia. In Hungary, especially, these currents swelled during the summer and autumn of 1877 into alarming proportions. The Magyars hailed every Russian reverse with vociferous applause. Klapka, one of the revolutionary heroes of 1848–9, addressed demonstrations in undiluted hostility to Russia and friendliness to Turkey.[1] The ostentatious gift of the Turkish government to the Hungarian nation of the Corviniana (the loot from the library of Matthias Corvinus) and the return visit of a deputation of Turkish *softas* to Buda-Pesth aroused immense enthusiasm, in despite of Andrássy's attempts to moderate the outbreak of anti-Russian feelings.[2] How notoriously inflamed these became is well illustrated by a small incident in October 1877, when the readiest credence was given at the Russian head-quarters on the Danube to reports that a band of 1,500 Magyars had sallied across the Transylvanian frontier to cut the railways and harry the Russian communications; though in fact the project had been nipped in the bud by the government.[3] When Plevna at last succumbed, the news was greeted in Pesth by a mass meeting clamouring for the Russians to be stopped if necessary by force of arms.[4]

The Magyars no doubt went too far for Andrássy's liking, and they continued to cause him great difficulty by their dislike of any increase of the Slav weight in the Dual Monarchy by the annexation of Bosnia and Herzegovina, which, in addition, would run counter to their sympathies for Turkey. But it is questionable whether Andrássy did not in fact share the hostility to Russia of his countrymen to a larger extent than is admitted by his biographer. It seems that, just as Andrássy had reacted in a very unfavourable sense to the Russian successes of July, so in the face of the full tide of Russian victories following the surrender of Plevna and of what he regarded as their unpardonable deception of him over their peace terms he worked for a policy of armed resistance to Russian overbearingness. There is evidence that already in December 1877 he was striving to win over his Emperor to a policy of decisive action,[5]

[1] *A. and P.*, 1878, lxxxi, C. 1905, nos. 156 and 182–3. A good example of his views is supplied by the pamphlet *General Klapka on the Eastern Question* (London, 1877), giving a translation of a speech of his at Pressburg in Aug. 1877.

[2] Plener, *Erinnerungen*, vol. ii, p. 103; Przibram, *Erinnerungen eines alten Oester-reichers*, vol. ii, pp. 62–3; *Wertheimer*, vol. iii, pp. 10–13.

[3] Botkin, *Pisma iz Bolgarii*, pp. 257, 268; *Aus dem Leben König Karls . . .*, vol. iii, pp. 299–300; Plener, op. cit., p. 109. The British consul-general at Warsaw suspected the two English intriguers, Butler-Johnstone and the Earl of Denbigh, of having had a hand in 'the Transylvanian plot', as also of attempting to incite the Poles to revolt; Maude (Warsaw) to Derby, disp., pol., conf., no. 22, 5 Oct. 1877, in *F.O.* 65/976. [4] Havas report in *Hasenkampf*, pp. 224–5.

[5] Przibram, op. cit., vol. ii, p. 67. Wertheimer's 'peace interpretation' of Andrássy's

and it will be seen shortly that there is further evidence that in January and February 1878 he was deeply engaged in a struggle to carry through this policy against the russophil or passive tendencies of the court, the Archduke Albert, a number of the army leaders, and the politicians of Herbst's Austrian German party. Yet here again there was a further complication; for the Emperor's military chancellery and the army leaders (several of them Croat generals), though they opposed a specifically anti-Russian policy, were the advocates of the acquisition of Bosnia and Herzegovina which Andrássy, whatever his earlier vacillations, was now equally determined to bring about as an offset to inevitable Russian gains, even though it would require very difficult manœuvring on the home front. At any rate it is certain that the Russian peace conditions made the worst impression in Vienna as being tantamount to a repudiation of the Reichstadt agreement and the subsequent conventions. This was naturally the keynote of the Austrian reaction to Russian policy.

Since July no communications had passed between Vienna and St. Petersburg in regard to the issues of the war: while the military situation hung in the balance discussion of them seemed unprofitable. Then, on 9 December, when the fate of Plevna was sealed, Alexander wrote to both his brother emperors enclosing a sketch of the peace terms he had in mind, and enjoining the strictest secrecy particularly as regards the English. His letter to the Emperor Francis Joseph was uncommonly disturbing, and its effect could not be assuaged by his hearty assurances through Prince Alexander of Hesse that the *Dreikaiserbündnis* was the basis of his policy and that he fully trusted Andrássy.[1] The only reference in his letter to his engagements with Austria-Hungary was in the following form: 'Je les [his annexed views as to conditions of peace] crois dans l'esprit sinon dans la lettre de nos arrangements, auxquels je resterai fidèle. Une coopération de Ta part les aurait rendues aussi complètes que je l'eusse désiré.' The terms which he outlined

---

policy is strongly criticized by Sosnosky, *Die Balkanpolitik Oesterreich-Ungarns seit 1866*, vol. i, pp. 164–5, mainly on the basis of the evidence of Beck, the head of the Emperor's military chancellery; see also below, p. 433. Plener in his memoirs takes approximately the same view as Sosnosky.

[1] *Wertheimer*, vol. iii, p. 57, citing letter of Prince Alexander of Hesse, from St. Petersburg, to Archduke Albert, 23 or 24 Dec.: the letter was communicated to Andrássy.

were stated to be not definitive, but only 'des bases dont le développement dépendra des événements de la guerre, et des nécessités et des droits qu'elle aura créés'. These bases were closely similar to those drawn up by Nelidov and approved by the Tsar on the same date, 9 December.[1]

This communication was intended to open confidential discussions without, however, tying the hands of the Russians.[2] It met with a cautious reply from the Emperor William and in the first instance only a formal acknowledgement from the Emperor Francis Joseph (21 Dec.), whose views were not forthcoming until 8 January, by which date Gurko's sweeping advance had aroused the worst fears in Vienna.[3] In contrast with the Tsar's abrupt evasion of the past, his reply was a lengthy reminder of the Austrian attitude in 1876 and an almost menacing plea for a moderate and immediate peace.[4]

At the outset the Emperor laid it down: 'Il va sans dire que j'ai pris pour principale gouverne (sic) les arrangements auxquels ont abouti nos laborieuses négotiations.' Alarmed and stung by Alexander's reference to Austrian non-participation in the war, Francis Joseph harked back to his letters of 3 and 23 October 1876 (see above, pp. 209–10 and 276), and renewed his defence of non-participation on the ground that he was unable to follow the Tsar in forestalling 'le procès naturel de dissolution de l'Empire ottoman'. The Tsar before the opening of hostilities had rejected 'toute pensée d'acquisition et désigné comme seul but de la guerre la réalisation des réformes demandées par les Puissances et des garanties d'exécution'; now that his military honour was so amply satisfied, conditions of peace should be immediately communicated to the Turks. The alternative course of pressing on hostilities was described as being unlikely in the extreme to bring about a situation

'plus satisfaisante pour Toi ou plus rassurante pour la paix de l'Europe, en tant qu'à moins d'un cas imprévu elle aurait peu de

---

[1] Copy of letter of the Tsar to the Emperor Francis Joseph, 9 Dec., in *Seton-Watson MSS*. The annex containing the sketch of peace terms is word for word the same as that sent by Gorchakov to Shuvalov on 2 Dec. and printed in *S.R.*, vol. vi, pp. 427–8. For the Nelidov peace terms see above, pp. 340–1.

[2] Gorchakov to Shuvalov, letter, very secret, 2 Dec., text in *S.R.*, vol. vi, pp. 427–8.   [3] *G.P.*, p. 169, note; *Wertheimer*, vol. iii, p. 58.

[4] Copy of letter of the Emperor Francis Joseph to the Tsar, 8 Jan., in *Seton-Watson MSS*. The annexed memorandum containing Andrássy's detailed criticisms is paraphrased in *Wertheimer*, vol. iii, pp. 58–9, and *Tatishchev*, pp. 430–1, but its text is not in the *Seton-Watson MSS*.

chances d'aboutir à une solution définitive. . . . Il m'est donc permis, maintenant que Tes armées victorieuses se sont couvertes de gloire sur les deux théâtres de la guerre, de T'exposer avec d'autant plus d'abandon mes appréhensions sur la situation. Elles partent toutes de la conviction que le moment de la dissolution de l'Empire otto-man n'est pas encore arrivé et que par conséquent l'organisation de la Presqu'île des Balcans ne pourra pas aboutir cette fois à un résultat définitif tel que nous l'avions prévu à Reichstadt. Il est bien possible d'achever la Turquie par la force des armes, mais non pas de faire naître la conviction dans l'opinion publique de l'Europe qu'elle se soit éteinte d'une mort naturelle, faute de vitalité. Ce point de vue qui est décisif pour l'opinion publique de mes États a dû me diriger dans l'examen des propositions renfermées dans les notices annexées à Ta lettre. Toi-meme Tu ne les considères pas comme définitives. Je soumets en toute confiance mes remarques à Ton équitable et loyale appréciation.'

These 'remarks' took the form of a detailed criticism by Andrássy of the Russian terms, from which it was additionally evident that Vienna had no intention of allowing the Russians to reap the fruits of victory without a severe diplomatic, and perhaps an even grimmer, struggle. He objected to the bases of peace being linked up with the armistice; he objected with especial emphasis to the big Bulgaria as being contrary to Reichstadt and the secret political convention; he objected to a Russian occupation of Bulgaria; he accused the Russians of breaking their obligation, under Article III of the political convention, not to decide issues in the Balkans without previous agreement with Austria-Hungary; he insisted that Austria-Hungary was entitled to annex Bosnia and Herzegovina in the event of territorial changes in the Ottoman empire or of the retrocession of Bessarabia; finally, he declared that Austria-Hungary would recognize as valid only such peace conditions as might be consonant with her own interests, and in the case of those which touched the general interest of Europe only such conditions as might be confirmed by all the signatories of the treaty of 1856.

This cold douche from Vienna was far from damping the blaze of nationalism in St. Petersburg, where Ignatyev had just been rewarded with a countship. The Tsar reacted with pained but decidedly bellicose deplorance of what he termed his brother em-peror's serious threat to the *Dreikaiserbündnis*.[1] All that Austrian

---

[1] Corti, *Alexander von Battenberg* . . . , p. 28, citing from the Vienna archives

pressure effected at the moment was an admission that questions affecting general interest should be settled by a European conference to follow a separate Russo-Turkish peace. In a long letter dated 16 January[1] the Tsar insisted that, after such an outpouring of blood and unchaining of passions, the decisions of the Constantinople conference were entirely insufficient for the protection of the Christians in Turkey. Public opinion in Russia refused to allow Christians to be replaced under the direct authority of the Moslems. There must, therefore, be complete autonomy for Bulgaria, linked to the Sultan only by the payment of tribute. 'Toute autre transaction serait une œuvre bâtarde, menteuse, illusoire. Je ne m'y associerai point, la Russie l'envisagerait comme incompatible avec les devoirs qu'elle s'est imposés, les sacrifices qu'elle a portés et le martyre des populations dont elle a fait la défense.' A temporary Russian occupation of Bulgaria was inevitable; immediate evacuation after the signature of peace was impossible; 'ce serait s'exposer à y créer une sanglante anarchie et à faire renaître la guerre à bref délai.' He insisted, with direct mention of Buol's stab in the back, that his honour imperatively required the retrocession of the Bessarabian districts, the effacement of 'ce souvenir incompatible avec les relations qui nous unissent'. Thus the complete autonomy of Bulgaria, a temporary Russian occupation of it, and the retrocession of southern Bessarabia were laid down as conditions sine quibus non; but the extent of Bulgaria, though implicitly assumed to be that of his letter of 9 December, was not directly stated to be outside discussion. In regard to the other points raised in Andrássy's memorandum of 8 January Alexander merely declared that a mutual agreement could be easily reached. Having thus stated in the most categorical terms his absolute requirements, he offered to examine what could be done to render these requirements inoffensive to the interests of Austria-Hungary. He was prepared to give Francis Joseph a free hand as regards the temporary occupation and, if he preferred it, the ultimate annexation of Bosnia and Herzegovina, even though the Russian occupation of Bulgaria would in any case be only temporary. He warned his brother emperor

Langenau's reports, 12 and 15 Jan., of Prince Alexander of Hesse's conversations with the Tsar.
[1] Copy of letter of the Tsar to the Emperor Francis Joseph, 16 Jan., in *Seton-Watson MSS.*; rec. 19 Jan., *Wertheimer*, vol. iii, p. 63.

that reports had reached him that this acquisition had been offered him by the Porte. 'Mais cette offre n'a pas été faite à titre gratuit. Si elle avait en vue une alliance avec la Turquie c'était une insulte à Ta loyauté et je conçois que Tu l'aies refusée.' He also warned him that 'si Tu renonçais à l'avantage que nos arrangements T'ont réservé et que je maintiens, Tu comprendras, j'espère, que je ne saurais subordonner ce qui pour moi est une nécessité à ce qui n'est pour Toi qu'une question de convenance'. Thus, even to the limited degree in which Alexander did recognize Reichstadt and the secret conventions, he intended to take the lead in their application. His letter closed with a firm defence of the necessity of separate peace preliminaries, which alone could supply a practical basis for a collective examination of the questions touching European interests. That such a meeting must subsequently be held was admitted. The object of his confidential communications to Vienna and Berlin was 'd'établir un accord préalable sur ces questions. Une fois cet accord établi, Ton gouvernement sera d'autant plus à même de faire valoir les intérêts de l'Autriche-Hongrie dans une délibération collective.'

On the same day (16 Jan.) Gorchakov wrote privately to London:

'. . . le point culminant de la situation réside dans nos pourparlers actuels avec l'Autriche et l'Allemagne. La moindre fissure dans l'entente des trois Cours Impériales rendrait à l'Angleterre toute son audace, et les provocations anglaises réagissant à leur tour sur Vienne et Pesth, les plus grandes complications seraient à craindre. Sans vouloir faire de conjectures, je crois qu'on peut espérer que les tergiversations du Cabinet de Vienne ne tiendront pas devant la netteté du langage ferme et conciliant de Notre Auguste Majesté, s'il est appuyé à Berlin, comme l'assurance nous a été donnée.'[1]

Neither Berlin nor Vienna were to realize such hopes: the latter in particular could see alarming firmness but no conciliatoriness in this ukase, as Francis Joseph termed Alexander's letter. It arrived in Vienna (19 Jan.) at a moment when it could act on Andrássy as a strong incentive to his efforts to prepare for extreme measures against the ambition of Russia. Four days previously at a ministerial conference he had argued the necessity of being prepared to fight Russia, though he admitted

<hr />

[1] Gorchakov to Shuvalov, letter, 16 Jan., text in *Seton-Watson MSS.*

that immediate war was impossible. Long discussions followed, during which at one point Andrássy, owing to divisions of opinion among the military as to a war with Russia, apparently went so far as to cffer his resignation. The more powerful section among the military were averse from any such war, emphasizing the danger of an Italian attack, and they received full support from Bechtolsheim, the military attaché in St. Petersburg, who returned on leave at the beginning of February and depicted the dangers of an armed struggle with Russia in glaring colours. In addition, the financial situation was very difficult. The British government offered to guarantee a loan (16 Feb.), but at the price of immediate mobilization, and the resultant negotiations came to nothing. Andrássy contrasted the stakes involved for the two countries in case of war with Russia; partly misled by Beust, he was suspicious of being pushed forward to bear the full weight of Russian strength by land, while England with impunity secured her interests in and around Constantinople and, a matter of no concern to Vienna, in Asia Minor. Contemporaneously with these negotiations, further conferences (12 to 23 Feb.) took place in Vienna, examining the possibilities of war (which Andrássy now considered near at hand) and making ready for mobilization; but again he did not carry the day for decisive measures. St. Petersburg was not the only capital to display vacillation or confusion. Andrássy was determined to resist the Tsar's ukase to the utmost on the diplomatic field of battle, but he was unable to assure for himself unequivocal backing should he in the last resort be faced with the alternative of a real field of battle.[1]

Meanwhile the alarm created in Vienna by the Tsar's letter of 16 January had been heightened by the communication on the 26th by Novikov of the peace terms as incorporated in the instructions sent to the Grand Duke Nicholas, terms which went considerably beyond the thirteen points sent to Francis Joseph on 9 December (see above, pp. 340–1 and 428–9). Andrássy refused to be left with the empty formality of a mere ratification

---

[1] *Wertheimer*, vol. iii, pp. 60–3, 77–9; von Glaise-Horstenau, *Franz Josephs Weggefährte: das Leben des Generalstabchefs Grafen Beck*, pp. 196–202, 186; Stolberg to Bülow, 12 Feb., in *G.P.*, p. 191; Busch's diary, under date 28 Feb., in *Deutsche Rundschau*, vol. cxli, p. 219. The Anglo-Austrian financial negotiations, 16 to 26 Feb., are in *F.O.* 7/922 and 928. For Shuvalov's reports on them see above, p. 383, note 1. For my interpretation of Andrássy's policy, cf. above, pp. 427–8.

by the powers of the peace conditions: it was now a question of 'Konflikt mit Russland oder Konferenz'.[1] Langenau in St. Petersburg was instructed to make it clear that Austria-Hungary insisted upon a conference, if 'la ligne de conduite concertée' were to be continued.[2] This was tantamount to declaring the acceptance of a conference a condition of further negotiations with Russia. The prospects for these were not improved by the Emperor Francis Joseph's insistence that it was quite impossible for him to consent to a Russian occupation of Bulgaria after the peace, though he agreed to raise no difficulties as to Bessarabia and grudgingly admitted the creation of some form of autonomous Bulgaria.[3]

As a result of the Austrian attitude and of British demands the question of a conference was brought into the foreground. It was impossible for Gorchakov to decline the proposal for a conference, which he again (29 Jan.) admitted would ultimately be necessary to confirm the conditions of peace which were of European interest.[4] A refusal would in any case merely drive the Austrians into the arms of the English. But it was a very different question whether any agreement could be reached as to its character (was it to be a conference or a congress?), as to the place and time of meeting, and above all as to its terms of reference. By the time that the Adrianople terms had been signed, Gorchakov let it be known that he would accept a conference in Berlin, but not one held in Vienna or London, and its competence was not defined.[5] Thereupon Andrássy, on 3 February, issued a formal proposal for a conference of the signatories of the treaty of Paris, but held to Vienna as the place of meeting. Gorchakov accepted a congress (not a conference) which should be composed of the leading statesmen of all the powers and which should deal with all questions of a general European character; but he refused Vienna and suggested instead Baden-Baden or Dresden.[6]

---

[1] Andrássy to Károlyi, 28 Jan., copy in *G.P.*, pp. 169–71.
[2] Andrássy to Langenau, tel., 28 Jan., copy in *G.P.*, pp. 171–3.
[3] Copy of letter of the Emperor Francis Joseph to the Tsar, 26 Jan., in *Seton-Watson MSS.*
[4] Langenau to Andrássy, tel., 29 Jan., in *Actenstücke*, ii, no. 92.
[5] Schweinitz to Bülow, 1 Feb., in *G.P.*, p. 175.
[6] Circular tel of Andrássy, 3 Feb., in *Actenstücke*, ii, no. 94; Gorchakov to Novikov, 5 Feb., cited in *Tatishchev*, p. 459; Andrássy to Langenau, tel., 13 Feb., recording Novikov communicating on previous day dispatch from Gorchakov, in *Actenstücke*, ii, no. 103.

The issue as to the proposal for a conference was soon found to lie primarily with Russia and England, and not with Russia and Austria-Hungary. Gorchakov himself was anxious to shine resplendent on the glittering stage of a European congress, and therefore opposed the idea of a conference at which only subordinates would appear. More important, no Russian could accept as the place of meeting any of the major capitals save Berlin. Andrássy agreed to the conversion of the conference into a congress and to Baden-Baden as its meeting-place, and, forcing the pace against Ignatyev, proposed that it should meet early in March.[1] But the Russians were now more deeply embroiled than ever with the English and more anxious than ever not to tie their hands; hence Gorchakov, on the plea that Bismarck would not attend a congress, shuffled back to the idea of a preliminary conference, to be held at Baden-Baden.[2] Ten days later, by the opening of March, anxious above all to secure German support, the Russians veered again and succeeded in persuading the reluctant Bismarck to agree to summon a congress, not a mere conference, at Berlin, though of course he reserved to himself the decision as to when to issue invitations and would make no definitive move until assured of a satisfactory result.[3] For this the outlook at the moment seemed bleak enough, when the conclusion of the San Stefano treaty had further exasperated the Austrians and seemed likely to drive the English rapidly to war, and certain to render them adamant on the question of the competence of the congress.

This was the crucial point. On it the British, but not the Austrian, government took up an attitude of the most intractable suspicion. Andrássy had without much difficulty agreed to the conference being transformed into a congress and to its meeting in Berlin instead of Baden-Baden, and on 6 March he had correspondingly circularized the powers. Further, he accepted Gorchakov's assurances that it was for the congress to decide what were the articles of the preliminary treaty which affected the interests of Europe, and that all the points which were found to be of European interest would be discussed by the congress and could not be considered as valid until they

---

[1] Andrássy to Langenau, tel., 18 Feb., in *Actenstücke*, ii, no. 106.
[2] Langenau to Andrássy, tel., 19 Feb., ib., no. 107.
[3] Gorchakov to Oubril, tel., 28 Feb., and Oubril to Gorchakov, tel., 2 Mar., cited in *Tatishchev*, p. 464; Bülow to Stolberg, tel., 3 Mar., in *G.P.*, p. 207.

obtained the assent of all the powers. This declaration Andrássy considered met the requirements both of Austria-Hungary and of England.[1]

The British government thought otherwise. Was it certain that the provisions in the treaty of San Stefano as to Asiatic Turkey or as to the indemnity would be regarded as of general European interest? What of the chances of Ignatyev forcing into immediate application the most dangerous of the articles of his treaty? In any case not the slightest loophole must be given for Russian lack of good faith: it was monstrous that the Russian government should refuse to communicate the terms of San Stefano until after ratification (a course adhered to despite Shuvalov's warnings). The British government therefore accepted the Austrian proposal of 6 March only on the conditions that 'no alteration in the condition of things previously established by Treaty' should be acknowledged as valid until assented to by the powers, and that every article of the treaty should be laid before the congress and no territorial change be sanctioned which was not also submitted to it (9 Mar.). A week later (16 Mar.) it was demanded 'that every Article in the Treaty between Russia and Turkey . . . be placed before the Congress, not necessarily for acceptance, but in order that it may be considered what Articles require acceptance or concurrence by the several Powers, and what do not'. Until these requirements were met no congress could assemble.[2]

They were regarded in St. Petersburg as a deliberate attempt to humiliate Russia or to wreck the conference in advance and drive her into war. The proposal, renewed by Bismarck in the middle of March, that a preliminary conference of ambassadors should be held to prepare the ground for the congress itself was now received with embittered discomposure. Gorchakov suspected that it was an entanglement originally devised in London, until he discovered that the British government were equally suspicious and had refused to accept the suggestion.[3] St. Peters-

---

[1] Derby to Elliot, 14 Mar., communicating Andrássy's statement of the same date through Beust, in *A. and P.*, 1878, lxxxi, C. 1977, no. 9.

[2] Derby to Beust, 9 Mar., and to Shuvalov, 16 Mar., in *A and P.*, 1878, lxxxi, C. 1977, nos. 6 and 12; Beaconsfield to Queen Victoria, 8 Mar., *Disraeli*, pp. 1126–8.

[3] Schweinitz to Bülow, 15 and 17 Mar., in *G.P.*, pp. 220–1, 230–1; Schweinitz, *Denkwürdigkeiten*, vol. ii, pp. 14–15; Gorchakov to Shuvalov, letter, 18 Mar., text in *Seton-Watson MSS.*; Derby to Russell, 16 Mar., in *A. and P.*, 1878, lxxxi, C. 1977, no. 13.

burg in fact was heading away from a congress towards the arbitrament of war. The Tsar was feeling convinced that the aim of England was merely to play out negotiations until such time as her military preparations were ready. Even from his ambassador in London he had the avowal that the cabinet were seeking a pretext to avoid Berlin: Derby was thoroughly set against a congress and kept harping on Bismarck's desire to drag England into war with Russia; the cabinet were distrustful of the whole idea of a congress at Berlin as being of Russian origin, were fearful that Bismarck would hand over the presidency to Gorchakov, and were putting the worst interpretations on the refusal to communicate the San Stefano terms until after ratification: one phrase could sum up the real cause of animosity—'la Russie victorieuse'.[1] The Tsar, with Ignatyev now back on the Neva (14 Mar.), had no need of the discredited Shuvalov to confirm him in his resistance to any humbling of victorious Russia. He answered the British demand of 16 March with the bald statement that as the other powers reserved to themselves 'pleine liberté d'appréciation et d'action', so did Russia (19 Mar.). Pressure from London took a week to extract the elucidation that the powers could raise what questions they liked at the congress, but that Russia reserved to herself 'la liberté d'accepter ou non la discussion de ces questions' (26 Mar.). The deadlock seemed complete: the final crisis of March was reached.[2]

The struggle had now assumed the most dangerous of forms, that of national honour. 'Ce ne sont plus des intérêts qui sont en jeu', wrote Gorchakov to Shuvalov, 'mais des questions d'amour-propre et de prestige. Cela peut mener fort loin. . . . Actuellement après une guerre sanglante et victorieuse nous ne saurions même pour la forme abaisser la dignité de la Russie devant le prestige de l'Angleterre.' He closed this letter still more ominously: 'Notre Auguste Maître se prépare pour toutes les éventualités, et je n'ai pas caché au Baron de Langenau que parmi ces éventualités nous rangions une guerre possible non seulement avec l'Angleterre mais encore avec l'Autriche-Hongrie.' To Loftus he insisted that Russia would not hear of 'submitting'

---

[1] Shuvalov to Gorchakov, tel., 14 Mar.; letter, 7 Mar., rec. by 18 Mar.; disp., 4 Mar.; texts in *Seton-Watson MSS.*

[2] Shuvalov to Derby, 19 and 26 Mar., in *A. and P.*, 1878, lxxxi, C. 1937, Nos. 15 and 19.

anything to the congress as if it were a tribunal before which
she were to be summoned for public humiliation. 'Either . . .
the question raised by His Majesty's Government is one of
perfect insignificance (enfantillage) the purport of which is
incomprehensible to me, or it has a much weightier meaning,
namely, the humiliation of Russia which I should reject with
indignation.'[1]

On this one question the Austrian attitude was substantially
the same as the Russian. Francis Joseph much disliked what
he regarded as British attempts to force a war by preventing a
conference from meeting. Andrássy spoke out to the same effect
to the British ambassador: he strongly objected to the stand
made against the holding of any congress until assurances as
to the right of examining every article of the treaty of San
Stefano had been extracted from the Russians: of course that
would be so; he, not Gorchakov, had summoned the congress,
and Gorchakov would have no right to exclude consideration
of any article in a treaty which had now been communicated
to the powers: but how, after both England and Austria-
Hungary had said that they could not be bound by a majority
in the congress, could England insist that Russia alone should
bind herself in this way in advance?[2] The English were not to
be moved by such appeals, though Derby finally admitted to
Shuvalov that he had taken a mistaken line.[3] Nor would the
Russians for their part give way. March closed with England
seemingly decided on war, with the Tsar prepared to precipitate
what he regarded as now inevitable by ordering the Grand
Duke Nicholas to seize the Bosphorus at all costs. It closed also
with the crisis of the negotiations with Austria-Hungary—the
Ignatyev mission to Vienna.

While the struggle over the congress occupied in the public
eye the diplomatic stage, in the wings was being played what
was in reality Act I. For it was not possible for Russia to come
to a congress without attempting some kind of agreement either

---

[1] Gorchakov to Shuvalov, letter, 18 Mar., rec. by 26 Mar., text in *Seton-Watson
MSS.*; Loftus to Derby, disp., no. 365, 27 Mar., recording an interview with Gorchakov on that day, in *F.O.* 65/1001.

[2] Prince Alexander of Hesse (then in Vienna) to the Tsar, letter, 18 Mar.,
extract in Corti, *The Downfall of Three Dynasties*, p. 244; Elliot to Derby, disp., no.
241, 24 Mar., in *F.O.* 7/929. Bismarck was likewise clear that there could be no
departure from the invariable diplomatic rule requiring unanimity; to Münster,
15 Mar., *G.P.*, p. 219.

[3] Shuvalov to Gorchakov, letter, 28 Mar., text in *Seton-Watson MSS.*

with England or with Austria-Hungary. Of attempts to reach agreement with the former there was as yet no question. The inheritance of Reichstadt, hopes of German support, the general political and strategical situation made it almost inevitable that St. Petersburg should advance from the uncompromising communications which had been exchanged with Vienna in December and January to definite negotiations, which might at the least serve to determine the points upon which Vienna was really determined not to yield. Hence it was in part true that the Russians deliberately subordinated the question of the congress to that of their negotiations with the Austrians.

The analysis already given of the correspondence between Alexander and Francis Joseph has shown that the outlook for such negotiations was unpromising, but the Tsar and Gorchakov had hopes of assistance from Germany. The old Emperor's letters were as warm-hearted and reassuring as ever, and he had brusquely told the Austro-Hungarian ambassador in Berlin that in 1870 no one had contested his right to demand an occupation of French territory until the treaty was executed and that he did not see why Alexander should be required to act any differently.[1] He also put forward a practical suggestion (23 Jan.); might not the best initial course be to enter into confidential *pourparlers à trois* in Vienna? Andrássy was simultaneously approached in the same sense, and replied favourably. After considerable hesitation the Russian government followed suit.[2] Gorchakov was extremely desirous of gaining Bismarck's help in bringing about an understanding with the Austrians, but the suggestion of conversations in Vienna could not have been pleasing to the extremists in St. Petersburg, since it was likely to give fuller scope to the austrophil influence of their adversary Novikov. What St. Petersburg wanted from Berlin was direct pressure upon Vienna to come to an agreement. This, as Andrássy rightly calculated, was precisely what Bismarck refused to supply.

On 19 February he delivered his 'honest broker' speech in the Reichstag, designed in part to aid Andrássy and prevent an

[1] Gorchakov to Shuválov, letter, 5 Feb., text in *Seton-Watson MSS.*
[2] Copy of letter of the Emperor William to the Tsar, 23 Jan., in *Seton-Watson MSS.*; *Wertheimer*, vol. iii, p. 72, citing Károlyi to Andrássy, 25 Jan., and Andrássy to Károlyi, 25 Jan.; pro memoria of Bülow, 8 Feb., recording a communication made by Oubril, in *G.P.*, pp. 187–8; Gorchakov to Shuvalov, tel., 5 Feb., text in *Seton-Watson MSS.*

Austro-Russian rupture,[1] in part as a reply to a fiery speech of Windhorst, who had argued that the eastern question was of the utmost importance to Germany since it raised the question as to which of two forces, Germanism or Slavdom, would dominate Europe; designed above all to represent German policy as aiming solely at a pacific agreement satisfactory to all the powers. The ability of Bismarck has been judged by the fact that this famous speech was interpreted favourably by all parties. But there is evidence that the official or officially inspired approval of the speech by the Russian government and the Russian press did not represent the real opinions of St. Petersburg and Moscow.[2] Much more had been hoped for; in particular there was no hint of that support against Austrian pretensions which Russians claimed as their due. Bismarck was at the same time privately using language to Oubril which made it quite clear, with his usual carefully calculated *brusquerie*, that he refused to be pushed into the position of opting between the two other members of the *Dreikaiserbündnis*: if you want to take Constantinople, do so; Germany will not oppose: but if you do not want war the only alternative is a conference: in that case do all that you can to satisfy Austria; England by herself cannot do you any harm: Germany in any case will remain neutral; if she moved France would take action against her: Germany will assist a Russo-Austrian understanding in Vienna; but she will not put pressure upon Austria to yield to Russia.[3]

But such pressure was exactly what the Russians required of Bismarck: without it conversations *à trois* in Vienna would be extremely difficult. They had delayed entering upon these, partly in the hope of securing the preliminary support of Bismarck, partly because of the preoccupation with the crisis caused by the dispatch of the British fleet to Constantinople, partly because of the desire to achieve a *fait accompli* by getting the peace treaty with Turkey signed, partly—and perhaps chiefly—because of the absence of any driving control from the foreign office in St. Petersburg. Hence it was not until the end of February that Andrássy, Novikov, and Stolberg, the German

---

[1] St. Vallier to Decazes, tel., 15 Feb., and disp., 16 Feb., in *D.D.F.*, pp. 253–5. The text of the 'honest broker' speech is in Bismarck, *Gesammelte Werke*, vol. ii, pp. 520–9.

[2] Loftus's reports in *F.O.* 65/1000, particularly disp., no. 281, 27 Feb., enclosing a memorandum on Russian opinion on Bismarck's speech.

[3] *Tatishchev*, p. 463, citing Oubril to Gorchakov, tels., 17, 20, and 21 Feb.

ambassador, met together. By then the chances of a satisfactory outcome had been further diminished by a very unaccommodating justification of Russian policy, which dealt at length with five points to which objection had been raised.[1]

It was based not on the secret convention, but on the necessity of going far beyond the half-measures of the Constantinople conference ('ces replâtrages inefficaces'), and on the peace conditions of Adrianople as being the irreducible minimum applicable to the new circumstances. It was, however, definitely allowed that the question of the Straits was reserved for a European agreement. Otherwise the memorandum was in substance little more than a recapitulation of the requirements laid down a month before in the Tsar's letter of 16 January to the Emperor Francis Joseph. Here again figured the *sine quibus non*: complete autonomy of a large, compact Bulgaria, which was to pay tribute but to be freed of Turkish garrisons; a temporary occupation of it by Russian troops; the retrocession of the ceded districts of Bessarabia. Here again there was no treatment of Novi Bazar or of Montenegrin and Serbian frontiers. Here again figured, as the one sop, the abandonment of Bosnia and Herzegovina, but this was not squarely admitted as being required by the secret convention, which was throughout either ignored or twisted out of shape by the argument that it required application in the light of the situation produced by the war.[2] St. Petersburg roundly declared that the objections of Vienna to the creation of a new and compact Slav state could not be reconciled with this new situation. It was a question of the powers' either condemning the Bulgarian nationality to irrevocable death or recognizing its imprescriptible right to exist.[3] It was not possible for Vienna or for Europe to take the former course. 'Quant à nous nous devons persister dans nos résolutions

[1] The text of this notice confidentielle, dated 12 Feb., is printed by Gauld in *Cambridge Historical Journal*, vol. i, pp. 328–33, from the copy in the Berlin foreign office communicated by Oubril on 15 Feb. It was probably not communicated to Andrássy until 23 or 24 Feb.

[2] It was, however, stated that if events led on to the necessity of more radical solutions the Russian government would hold to the Reichstadt arrangements; but one alteration was put forward: the provision that Constantinople might be a free city would expose it too much to internal jealousies and disorders and to the influence of the Turks across the Bosphorus: it was therefore now suggested that the Turks should be left in Constantinople as the mandatories of Europe for the guardianship of the Straits.

[3] Underlined by Bismarck with the comment 'and Poland?'

sur ce point essentiel du programme pour l'accomplissement duquel la Russie a fait la guerre,[1] c.-à-d. une Bulgarie entière compacte autonome et tributaire.' Minor changes in regard to the extent of the new Bulgaria were allowed for, and some concessions over the Russian occupation and some participation by the powers in the setting up of Bulgaria were foreshadowed, but the language used was studiously vague, and the news from Constantinople (where the Russians had by now advanced to San Stefano) suggested that the negotiations required to translate into effect these slender admissions of the Russians were more than likely to be outpaced by the march of events in the Balkans.

As would be expected, Andrássy was incensed at this 'Orthodox Slav sermon', which with its overbearing tone 'might have been dictated by Aksakov himself', and which still, despite a month of expostulation, treated the written agreements between Austria-Hungary and Russia 'as if they had never existed'. He declared it to be plainly unacceptable.[2] With the text of the secret convention in his hands he insisted to Novikov and Stolberg that the project of a big Bulgaria was contrary to its provisions: Russia had done too much and too little: one of two things was possible; either, as the secret convention envisaged, there might be full independence for the European subjects of Turkey, which would mean new independent Christian states, with Greece acquiring Epirus and Thessaly, and Constantinople being converted into a free city; or the Turkish empire in Europe might remain, in which case Bulgaria should be confined to the north of the Balkans, since otherwise irreconcilable counter-claims would be raised by the Greeks and Albanians. Such at least was Novikov's version of what occurred at the first meeting à trois on 25 February. Novikov, pleading that he could not budge from his instructions, switched over from the question of the extent of Bulgaria to that of the Russian occupation, but could make no headway with Andrássy.

---

[1] 'fait la guerre' was underlined by Bismarck with the comment 'sic'.

[2] Stolberg to Bülow, 26 Feb., in G.P., p. 201; Andrássy to Károlyi, 24 Feb., quoted in Wertheimer, vol. iii, pp. 75–6. The following account of the negotiations à trois is based on Stolberg's reports to Bülow, 25, 26, and 28 Feb. and 2 and 3 Mar., in G.P., pp. 197–8, 200–4, and on a report of Novikov to Gorchakov, 6 Mar., extracts and paraphrase in San Stefano, pp. 337–41. These negotiations are not dealt with in Wertheimer. There were apparently only two meetings, on 25 Feb. and 2 Mar.

Thus the first day's meeting ended in failure and fog. It seems evident that Novikov did not understand what Andrássy intended, though it is not clear how far he was to blame for this, for the German ambassador's reports suggest that Andrássy was in fact far from being specific. Andrássy had told Stolberg in advance that he was prepared to have, instead of a tributary Bulgaria, an entirely independent Bulgaria with a southern frontier to the south of the Balkans, but not drawn so far southward as to include non-Bulgar Christians, and that he proposed for the region thus cut off from Bulgaria the formation of a Greek province ('Land'). Whether he meant such a province also to be independent, whether he meant that the new Bulgaria should not touch the Aegean at any point, whether he was thinking primarily of the creation of some sort of Macedonia, why he mentioned only the southward and not as well the westward extension of Bulgaria, is not clear. Nor were matters made clearer by the suggestion which, according to Stolberg, Andrássy threw out to Novikov on the 25th that there might be independent states instead of one large tributary Bulgaria. Andrássy indeed himself recognized that there was misunderstanding, for he spoke of the Russians' being mistaken in thinking that he proposed that the southern portion of Bulgaria should be placed under Turkish rule.

Nothing, however, seems to have been done to clear up this fog when the three met for the second, and last, time on 2 March. Andrássy maintained a thick reserve as to the extent of Bulgaria, and in fact added to the confusion by observing that if Russia proposed to leave the western regions of the Turkish empire under Turkish suzerainty the southern frontier of Bulgaria ought not to be pushed so far to the south as to make communications from Constantinople to the west almost impossible. On the question of occupation he suggested as a compromise that its length should be cut down from two years to three or six months, together with certain guarantees including that of a European commission to supervise the introduction of the new constitution. He did not apparently at this stage mention any requirements as to a reduction of the strength of the occupying army. Nor did he disclose to Novikov his idea of making the compromise as to the occupation conditional upon the agreement of the Russians to abandon their communications with Bulgaria through Roumania.

In the midst of this unresolved tangle the negotiations *à trois* abruptly terminated. On 3 March the treaty of San Stefano was signed. Although it was officially not communicated to the Austrian government until after its ratification on 17 March, its main terms promptly became known in Vienna. Ignatyev and the panslavs seemed more than ever in the saddle. Andrássy, furious at the conclusion of peace without his consultation, turned once more to England, pushed forward preparations on the home front for the meeting of the delegations and a vote of 60,000,000 florins, and for the time being waited for St. Petersburg to declare itself as regards his proposals concerning Bulgaria and the occupation. The Russians, thoroughly confused as to what exactly Andrássy demanded, were concentrated now on their duel with England as to the competence of the congress and on the ratification of the San Stefano treaty. No definite steps to clear up relations with Vienna were likely until after Ignatyev's return from Constantinople in the middle of the month. Thus almost the whole of March elapsed before the next stage in the struggle between the two countries—the dramatic confrontation of Ignatyev with Andrássy.

On 22 March the Tsar, acting apparently on his own initiative, decided to send Ignatyev to Vienna in an attempt to unravel the situation, which he could not understand from the reports of Novikov. The mission was optimistically described by Gorchakov as 'une tentative suprême pour ranimer et reserrer l'entente des trois Cours Impériales qui est aujourd'hui l'unique chance de préserver la paix générale, et de contenir la prépotence anglaise'.[1] Ignatyev left St. Petersburg on 24 March, arrived in Vienna on the evening of 26 March, left on the morning of the 31st, and was back in St. Petersburg on the evening of 2 April. There had been no previous sounding of the ground: Andrássy only learnt of this perturbing mission on the 24th: Berlin was equally taken by surprise, and was kept in the dark as to its precise object.[2] This was soon openly described in

---

[1] *San Stefano*, pp. 336–7; Schweinitz, *Denkwürdigkeiten*, vol. ii, p. 16; Gorchakov to Shuvalov, letter, 29 Mar., text in *Seton-Watson MSS.*

[2] *Wertheimer*, vol. iii, p. 90, citing Andrássy to Károlyi, 24 Mar., and Károlyi to Andrássy, 25 Mar. Elliot's information, derived from Calice, that the news was only received on 25 Mar. was mistaken; Elliot to Derby, tel., no. 83, 26 Mar., in *F.O.* 7/929. Shuvalov likewise was only informed on 24 Mar.; Gorchakov to Shuvalov, tel., 24 Mar., text in *Seton-Watson MSS.*

Vienna as being the prevention of an Austrian understanding for common action with England.[1]

When the leader of the panslavs arrived in his enemy's capital, the situation there was radically different from what it had been a month earlier. The ministerial crisis was over: Andrássy had been fully reassured as to his emperor's confidence. He had just faced the delegations successfully and secured his 60,000,000 florins vote of credit (21 March). The treaty of San Stefano was generally regarded as exorbitant, and its signature had eased his internal difficulties, had confirmed the necessity for the most vigilant action, and in particular had brought to the forefront the whole problem of the future of the western Balkans. During the conversations *à trois* it was upon the southern frontiers of Bulgaria and upon the occupation that all the emphasis apparently had been placed. Beyond a general expostulation by Andrássy against the Russian violation of the previous agreement to settle the Serbian and Montenegrin frontiers in conjunction with Austria,[2] nothing definite either in this respect or as regards the western extent of Bulgaria seems to have been demanded. Now, however, Ignatyev was to find Austrian policy above all concerned with these problems of the western Balkans, but comparatively little with the extension of Bulgaria to the Rhodope Mountains or even to the Aegean Sea.

During March the alarm created by San Stefano was being successfully exploited by those interests which regarded as essential the expansion of Austrian commercial development and the strengthening of Austrian prestige in the western Balkans. In the Ballplatz itself the head of the commercial section, Baron Schwegel, an ex-consul-general at Constantinople and a recognized Balkan expert, was a very assiduous and able exponent of these views. He inveighed to the Russian ambassador against the fantastic character of the big Bulgaria provided for in the treaty of San Stefano: not only was it contrary to the secret convention; not only would it cripple the Ottoman empire in Europe; the ethnographic basis for it claimed by the Russians was non-existent; there were not more than 3,000,000 Bulgars in all, instead of the Russian claim of between five and six millions; even if the Struma valley might

---

[1] Elliot to Derby, disp., no. 262, 29 Mar., in *F.O.* 7/929.
[2] Novikov to Gorchakov, 6 Mar., paraphrase in *San Stefano*, p. 339.

be claimed as Bulgarian by population, the Vardar basin could not be so claimed and belonged to what Schwegel termed the Albanian system: in any case, as Novikov had already learnt from Andrássy himself, the Mitrovica–Salonika railway could not be included in Bulgaria since Austro-Hungarian commercial interests would thereby be destroyed.[1] In addition, San Stefano had pushed the military into no longer contenting themselves with the occupation of Bosnia and Herzegovina. Beck, the highly influential chief of the Emperor's military chancellery, was now insisting that in addition Novi Bazar must be occupied: this was essential in order to keep Montenegro and Serbia divided: the Montenegrin and Serbian frontiers as laid down in the treaty of San Stefano must be pushed back, Serbia receiving compensation to the east: Bulgaria must not be allowed to extend farther west than the line of the Struma: only thus, by securing Austrian occupation as far as Mitrovica and by cutting off from Bulgaria the Vardar watershed and Old Serbia, could the Dual Monarchy secure the route to Salonika and sway Albanians, Greeks, and Moslems against Jugoslavs.[2]

The result of this powerful coalescence of interests was evident in the programme placed before Ignatyev by Andrássy. This programme proved to be the central feature and the one definite result of the Ignatyev mission, and it was to be maintained by Andrássy, with almost complete success, throughout the following months until its incorporation in the treaty of Berlin. Its contents were as follows:[3]

1. Austria-Hungary would remain faithful to the entente of the three empires. In the event of war between Russia and England she would maintain benevolent neutrality towards the former.

2. Austria-Hungary was to occupy Bosnia and Herzegovina

[1] Novikov to Gorchakov, 17 Mar., summarized in *San Stefano*, pp. 319–20.

[2] Čubrilović, *Bosanski ustanak*, p. 287, paraphrasing from the Vienna archives a memorandum by Beck, dated 24 Mar., 'Militärische Betrachtungen über die durch den Frieden von St. Stefano geschaffenen neuen Grenzen auf den Balkan-Halbinsel'.

[3] The text, in the original French, in the form of a pro memoria drawn up by Ignatyev and dated 29 Mar., is in *G.P.*, pp. 273–5; it was communicated by Oubril to Bülow on 14 Apr. The text in Russian is printed in Ignatyev's memoirs, *I.V.*, vol. cxliii, pp. 369–71: it agrees with the French text, except for the (probably accidental) omission of Montenegrin freedom of navigation on the Boyana and the lake of Scutari. The copy in the Vienna archives is paraphrased in *Wertheimer*, vol. iii, p. 93; in so far as it is possible to judge from the brevity of the paraphrase it agrees with the above. For the following pages, see maps 3, 5, and 6.

after warning the Porte and arranging for the withdrawal of the Turkish troops there. The date of occupation could not at the moment be fixed, if the congress was going to be held: if it was not, occupation would take place immediately. In view of the creation of Bulgaria and of future railway requirements, the occupation of the *sanjak* of Novi Bazar and the consequent modification of the secret convention were also demanded. (It is not clear whether annexation as well as occupation was claimed.)

3. Andrássy withdrew his previous assent to the frontier of Montenegro being extended to the Lim and proposed a line excluding any of the *sanjak* of Novi Bazar from Montenegro. Austria-Hungary was to annex the coast-line as far as the mouth of the Boyana and the lake of Scutari.

4. Andrássy proposed to cut down the acquisitions of Serbia on the west, and to give her Vranja and Trno in exchange. Austria-Hungary reserved to herself the right to occupy Ada Kale[1] and to impose on Serbia the obligation to allow a through railway with the same rates as those in force on Austro-Hungarian lines.

5. Austria-Hungary recognized the Russian right to regain the ceded districts of Bessarabia and declared her readiness to support this claim diplomatically against Roumania and the powers.

6. Austria-Hungary, while admitting the provisions in the treaty of San Stefano as regards the organization of Bulgaria,[2] proposed: (i) that on the south-east the frontier proposed at the Constantinople conference should be maintained, so that the Lule Borgas salient and part of the Black Sea littoral should be excluded from Bulgaria;[3] (ii) that on the west the general

[1] Ada Kale was a Turkish island in the Iron Gates of the Danube opposite Orsova.

[2] Ignatyev must certainly have misinterpreted, whether deliberately or not, Andrássy's views. According to Stolberg, who reported on 1 Apr. Andrássy's verbal communication to him on that day as to his conversations with Ignatyev, Andrássy demanded that the administrative organization of Bulgaria should be worked out by an assembly of Bulgarian notables with the assistance of the powers, instead of by Russian and Turkish commissions; *G.P.*, p. 256. Andrássy held the same language to Elliot on the same day; Elliot to Derby, disp., no. 269, 1 Apr., repeating tel., no. 94, of the same date, in *F.O.* 7/930. Ignatyev himself indirectly bears this out in his report to Gorchakov of 4 Apr., text in *I.V.*, vol. cxliii, p. 364:

[3] According to what Andrássy told Elliot the coast-line of the new Bulgaria on the Black Sea was not to go farther south than Sizepoli; Elliot to Derby, disp., no. 269, 1 Apr., in *F.O.* 7/930.

trace of the frontier should be a line from the middle of the gulf of Rendina towards Vranja, and that everything west of this (i.e. the Vardar and part of the Struma watersheds) should be formed into an administratively autonomous Macedonia entirely independent of Bulgaria.

7. Austria-Hungary required the Russian occupation of Bulgaria to last for not more than six months and the occupying strength to be not greater than 20,000.

If Russia accepted these proposals, Austria-Hungary would be prepared to support the remainder of the Russian programme at the congress; if the congress did not meet, she would continue the entente of the three empires which could act as a pacific restraint upon England.

In examining this programme of Andrássy it must first be observed that the terms of its formulation which have just been given were not his but Ignatyev's. They were set down in a pro memoria drawn up by Ignatyev on the basis of his discussions with Andrássy and submitted to him on 29 March. But Andrássy, though admitting that it represented in general his standpoint, refused to commit himself to Ignatyev's invitation that he should make such alterations in the text as he thought necessary. He would take no responsibility for the document, and hence avoided tying his hands. He thereby also avoided glossing over a fundamental difference between his position and that of Ignatyev: the latter had so drawn up his pro memoria as to produce the effect that it was Austria-Hungary which was ignoring her previous commitments with Russia, whereas for Andrássy it was Russia which had created a completely new political situation through the treaty of San Stefano. He was emphatic in explaining that he took his stand upon the secret convention and that it was only in the attempt to reach an agreement upon the new basis created by Russia that he was compelled to go outside the convention.[1]

This attitude was almost inevitable since on the one hand Andrássy was appealing to the secret convention as ruling out a big Bulgaria, while on the other hand he was himself ignoring the convention in his two new demands, for the occupation of Novi Bazar and of the sea-coast claimed by the Montenegrins. Ignatyev naturally insisted that the former demand was inadmissible inasmuch as the secret convention had ruled out any such

<hr>

[1] *Wertheimer*, vol. iii, pp. 93–4, citing Andrássy to Langenau, 2 Apr.

occupation and expressly reserved the question of Novi Bazar for a future agreement between the two signatories: it had merely stipulated, in complete reversal of the Reichstadt agreement of the summer of 1876, that Novi Bazar was not to be divided between Serbia and Montenegro: this stipulation, Ignatyev maintained, was duly observed in the treaty of San Stefano, by the terms of which Serbia and Montenegro were not contiguous. Against this, however, it could be argued that the treaty had not left the whole of the *sanjak* of Novi Bazar to Turkey, but only a narrow and indefensible corridor. Andrássy, if Ignatyev is to be believed, allowed that at the time of the signature of the secret convention he had not envisaged any annexation of Novi Bazar, but he maintained that the Russian creation of a big Bulgaria contrary to the convention now justified Austrian annexation up to Mitrovica, and that in any case the San Stefano frontiers were impossible since they would interrupt the railway route to Salonika via Novi Bazar and Mitrovica.[1]

The second new demand of the Austrians, that they should annex the coast-line as far south as the Boyana river, raised equally bitter conflicts. The claim to the sea-coast was all the more severe in that the Montenegrins were already in possession of Spizza, Antivari, and Dulcigno, whereas the bulk of the remaining gains allotted to them at San Stefano were still in Turkish hands. Ignatyev represented Andrássy as insisting that the coastal strip must not fall to Montenegro: the inhabitants were in part Catholic and desired to come under Austrian rule; Montenegrin access to the sea would put a premium on contraband, and would afford direct communication with Italy. It could also have been added that Andrássy professed to regard Antivari as already a focal point for panslav agents and as designed by them for sinister future developments. Inland, he would not allow more than the increase of territory suggested at the Constantinople conference, less the Herzegovina districts, which meant the abandonment by the Montenegrins of the grimly contested Nikšić and the Duga pass. To all this emasculation of the new Montenegro Ignatyev presented an unqualified opposition.[2]

[1] Text of report of Ignatyev to Gorchakov on his Vienna mission, 4 Apr., in *I.V.*, vol. cxliii, pp. 56–7. On Novi Bazar, see above, pp. 284 and 411–12.

[2] Text of report of Ignatyev to Gorchakov, 4 Apr., in *I.V.*, vol. cxliii, pp. 57–8; de Vogüé (Vienna) to Waddington, disp., 30 Apr., reporting Andrássy's exposition to him of his policy, in *D.D.F.*, p. 303 (on Antivari).

The main battle, however, raged over the big Bulgaria. Here Ignatyev was forced to the wall. How could he make his San Stefano provisions harmonize with the terms of the secret convention? How could he counteract the effect of the avowals brought back from St. Petersburg by Prince Alexander of Hesse, the Tsar's brother-in-law, that the Russian interpretation of the convention was unsound?[1] What could he reply to Andrássy when he read over to him the text of Article III of the political convention? 'En cas d'un remaniement territorial ou d'une dissolution de l'empire Ottoman l'établissement d'un grand état compact slave ou autre est exclu; en revanche la Bulgarie, l'Albanie et le reste de la Roumélie pourraient être constituées en états indépendants.' Ignatyev's answer was that the exclusion of a large Slav state applied only to an enlarged Serbia or Montenegro (but then what was the meaning of 'ou autre'?), and that the semicolon showed that the words which followed and which dealt with regions not previously mentioned in the convention were not governed by the opening clause of the article. Andrássy insisted that such an interpretation was entirely inadmissible, and confidently offered to refer it to the judgement of the Emperor William or even of the Tsar. And he inquired why there was no recognition in the treaty of San Stefano of the 'reste de la Roumélie' mentioned in the convention. To this Ignatyev could but expatiate, with some effective use of an Austrian memorandum at the Constantinople conference, on the vagueness and variety of meanings of the word Rumelia, but he apparently did not make play with the argument that the secret convention had spoken of 'états indépendants', whereas the San Stefano treaty spoke only of very wide autonomy. Ignatyev in his turn could produce no effect upon Andrássy when he emphasized that the frontiers of his Bulgaria were substantially the same as those agreed upon at the Constantinople conference. The Magyar brushed this aside by reiterating that the conference Bulgaria was to have been divided and to have far less autonomy. On the other hand, he did not maintain his opposition to the frontiers of Ignatyev's Bulgaria between the Struma and Adrianople, which not only brought Bulgaria far to the south of the Balkans but also gave

---

[1] Ignatyev's memoirs in *I.V.*, vol. cxliii, pp. 36–7, and text of his report of 4 Apr., ib., p. 365. There is no confirmation of this in Corti, *The Downfall of Three Dynasties*, based on the papers of Prince Alexander. He was in Vienna 12–25 Mar.

her a strip of the Aegean coast: on both these questions Andrássy
decided to leave it to the English to do the fighting.

Ignatyev's main defence of his Bulgaria was not based on the
conventions, but on quite different grounds. At Christmas time
1876 General Obruchev had been in Vienna, engaged in the
negotiations for the secret conventions, and had brought with
him a map of the Balkans upon which were marked the boundaries desired by the Russians for the new states and which the
Russians intended to annex to the convention when signed,
though in fact it was not so annexed and was not referred to in
the conventions (see above, p. 283). According to Ignatyev, the
Russians based the subsequent negotiations upon this Obruchev
map; and there figured on it a red line drawn roughly from
Salonika to Serbia, which represented the western frontier of
a new Bulgaria and was almost exactly followed in the treaty of
San Stefano. The Austrians, he said, had had this map for
more than a year and lengthy discussions had taken place as to
the frontiers of Montenegro marked on it, yet they had raised
no question as to the frontiers of Bulgaria; the Russians therefore were fully justified in supposing that Vienna accepted in
general the proposed Bulgarian frontiers, and he had in consequence received a copy of this map from his government in
January 1878 to serve as the basis for negotiating the boundaries
of Bulgaria with the Turks. Against this Andrássy countered,
that there was no explanation on the map to show what the red
line meant, and that he had taken it as roughly showing the
eastern limit of what might go to the Greeks or Albanians,
leaving a Rumelia between this line and Bulgaria; that in any
case Novikov had made no reference whatever to the Obruchev
map, though he had held long conversations with him on the
frontiers of Bulgaria; that similarly there had been no mention
of the map in the correspondence between the two monarchs
and the two governments; and finally, that it was not his concern if Ignatyev was supplied by his government with untenable
instructions. He continued to demand that Bulgaria must not
extend farther west than the Struma, and that the Vardar
valley must be reserved for the political and commercial influence of Austria. He did not make clear how this Macedonian
region was to be constituted, except that it could receive only
administrative and not political autonomy.[1]

[1] For this and the preceding paragraph: Andrássy to Langenau, 2 Apr.,

These heated discussions produced no *détente*. Ignatyev terminated his mission incontinently. He himself described its object as being to clear up the misunderstandings over the treaty of San Stefano and the secret convention and to agree upon joint action at the congress, or, if the congress were not to meet owing to the hostility of England, to agree as to the means of strengthening the *Dreikaiserbündnis* by a special treaty regulating the eastern question. If this were so its failure was pronounced. Having received Andrássy's requirements, he declared that they went far beyond the secret convention and that his instructions empowered him to negotiate only on that basis: departure was the only course.[1]

How far his arguments as to the compatibility of the San Stefano treaty with the secret convention were anything more than juggling improvisations may well be doubted. He had always been opposed to the general lines of the Reichstadt policy. He had not been informed of the contents of the secret conventions until January 1878, and it is possible that even then he was not furnished with the text. He himself maintained in his memoirs that the text was hidden from him until just before his departure for Vienna. But in any case Ignatyev was from the first determined to drive through a policy of his own which, regardless of any previous commitments to Austria-Hungary, would result in as large a Bulgaria as possible and maximum gains for Montenegro and Serbia (except to the east and south). In defending his handiwork at home he did not plead that, had he been aware of the text of the secret conventions at an earlier date, he would have modified his San Stefano programme.[2]

---

paraphrased in *Wertheimer*, vol. iii, pp. 91–2; Stolberg to Bülow, 1 Apr. (giving Andrássy's version), in *G.P.*, p. 253; Andrássy to Beust, tel., 1 May, communicated to Salisbury 3 May (for Aegean coast), in *F.O.* 7/944; text of report of Ignatyev to Gorchakov, 4 Apr., in *I.V.*, vol. cxliii, pp. 360–7; Schweinitz to Bülow, disp., 4 Apr. (recording conversation with Ignatyev), in *G.P.*, pp. 259–62.

[1] Text of Ignatyev's report of 4 Apr., in *I.V.*, vol. cxliii, pp. 41, 49. Ignatyev in a footnote (p. 49) accuses Gorchakov of doing what he could to make his success in Vienna difficult and as pressing for his early return in fear of his intrigues against Andrássy.

[2] Text of memorandum by Ignatyev justifying his big Bulgaria, in *I.V.*, vol. cxliii, pp. 670–2. It was written about the middle of Apr., partly in reply to Bismarck's strictures as reported by Oubril, and was sent by Gorchakov to the Russian diplomatic representatives abroad on 22 Apr. For Ignatyev's knowledge of the secret conventions see p. 405, note. I cannot agree with M. Onou's arguments against the view that the treaty of San Stefano constituted a violation of the Reichstadt agreement and the secret convention of Mar. 1877, although his emphasis on

On the contrary, no mention was made of the Reichstadt agreement or the secret conventions, and his main argument was based on the agreement of the powers as to Bulgarian boundaries in December 1876 at the Constantinople conference, which boundaries, in turn, were approved in the Tsar's instructions in January 1878 and in the Adrianople bases of peace. The only change in those boundaries to the advantage of Bulgaria made by the San Stefano treaty was the inclusion of parts of the Aegean coast-line, and these were offset by the allocation to Serbia of the *sanjak* of Nish and the reservation of the Dobrudja for Roumania. After the Tsar's proclamation, on crossing the Danube, promising the Bulgars freedom from the Moslem yoke and calling them to a new life, after so triumphant a war, how could Russia demand less for the Bulgars than the powers had agreed upon before the war? If the Russians on their own initiative had cut down the frontiers of Bulgaria, the powers would have demanded a still greater diminution, and the difficulties to be faced would have been even greater. The uniting of the Bulgars into one principality and its much greater degree of autonomy compared with that outlined at the Constantinople conference were justified on the same line of argument. In fact Ignatyev's policy amounted to the creation of a maximum Bulgaria by isolated action on the part of Russia: if, as now in April seemed probable, that maximum could not be obtained, then the concessions which might prove necessary ought still to

the change in Andrássy's views on the convention seems to me sound: see his 'Graf N. P. Ignatyev i San Stefano', in *Slavyanski glas*, 1932, Sofia, vol. xxvi, no. 1–2, pp. 50–4. M. Onou seems to defend Ignatyev on two main grounds. Firstly, the Reichstadt agreement and the secret convention only came into application in the event of the dissolution of Turkey or the capture of Constantinople; neither of these eventualities had occurred; therefore there could be no question of incompatibility with the treaty of San Stefano. Yet M. Onou on the same page allows that in Article III of the political convention occur the words 'en cas de remaniement territorial ou d'une dissolution de l'Empire Ottoman', and he does not explicitly deny that the treaty of San Stefano involved a 'remaniement territorial'. Secondly, the same Article III excluded the creation of a large compact Slav state, but allowed of the setting up of Bulgaria, Albania, and the rest of Rumelia as independent states: the treaty of San Stefano did not set up a large compact Slav state, but an independent Serbia, an independent Montenegro, and a vassal Bulgaria: this Bulgaria was a compact state, but not an independent one; hence all Andrássy's argumentation fell to the ground. This argument seems to assume that the San Stefano Bulgaria could not be called a large compact Slav state, but only a compact state, and that the fact that it was not to be independent meant that the secret convention was not applicable to it: it also seems to assume that the words 'le reste de la Roumélie' need not be taken into account.

result in a Bulgaria substantially larger and freer than if he had never tried to impose on Austria-Hungary and England the *fait accompli* of his San Stefano treaty.

Ignatyev, however, was not immediately prepared to give ground. On his return to St. Petersburg he professed himself as well pleased with his reception from all in Vienna except Andrássy, whom he depicted as impossible to negotiate with; and he urged that pressure should be put upon Francis Joseph to substitute at the Ballplatz Potocki, the governor-general of Galicia, or Mollinary, the Croat general—a suggestion which the Tsar refused absolutely to entertain. Ignatyev contended that it was out of the question to accept Andrássy's proposals as a basis of negotiation: everything must be done to press forward with the full carrying out of the treaty of San Stefano, particularly as regards the occupation and organization of Bulgaria: if necessary the Greek question should be raised, as a counter-weight to the Anglo-Austrian bogy of Slavdom, by suggesting the annexation of Epirus, Thessaly, and the islands of the Archipelago: military concentration against Austria should be hurried on. But he did not believe that it would come to war; neither England nor Austria was prepared; the latter in any case could not be ready before three months: they would come to some deal with Russia if only she acted with resolution. Such was the burden of Ignatyev's exhortations to the Tsar and Gorchakov (3 April). Still, San Stefano or nothing.[1]

He did not win the day. An imperial council, held on either 6 or 7 April, showed that the current was at least beginning to turn against him and that some attempt was to be made to negotiate on the basis of Andrássy's programme.[2] The foreign office was bent upon discrediting Ignatyev to the utmost. The breach between him and Gorchakov was complete: by the end of the month they were literally not on speaking-terms. While preparations for the worst were pressed forward, negotiations with Vienna were not abandoned. After all, there seemed a chance that England might not fight without Austria-Hungary, whereas she certainly would if the latter did; and, in particular, it could well be argued that the Austrian modifications of San Stefano might prove to be less severe than those demanded by the English. They would presumably demand a heavy cutting

---

[1] Ignatyev's memoirs, in *I.V.*, vol. cxliii, pp. 371–2, 376–7.
[2] Ib., pp. 656–7.

down of Russian gains in Asia, revision of the indemnity clause, no change in the regulation of the Straits which might benefit Russia; they might even require no retrocession of Bessarabia. The Austrians had no interest in Asiatic Turkey or in the indemnity; they were far less concerned in the problem of the Straits; they had admitted the retrocession of Bessarabia, and the annexation of Batum and adjacent territory. The English would probably require that the new Bulgarian principality should not extend to the south of the Balkans, and hence that not only the Vardar valley, 'Macedonia', should be excluded, but also the Aegean sea-coast and the Maritsa and Struma valleys. The Austrians were insisting that 'Macedonia' should be excluded; but otherwise, except as regards the Lule-Borgas salient, they seemed prepared to accept the San Stefano boundaries of Bulgaria. Both would raise great difficulties as to the occupation and organization of Bulgaria, but the Austrians, if satisfied on the west, might be somewhat less unaccommodating. Finally, the English put Bosnia-Herzegovina, Novi Bazar, and Montenegro entirely in the background, whereas the Austrians stated that they were going to annex Bosnia-Herzegovina (which had been conceded by the Russians), and demanded the annexation of Novi Bazar and the littoral as far as the Boyana, as well as a further reduction of the enlarged Montenegro and Serbia. Thus, in summary, if Russia were compelled to compromise on the treaty of San Stefano, she stood to gain only in Novi Bazar and Montenegro by reaching an agreement with England, while she stood to gain in Asiatic Turkey and Bulgaria by reaching an agreement with Austria-Hungary.

The Andrássy programme was indeed not far short of the solution always recommended by Bismarck, the western Balkans in the exclusive sphere of Austria-Hungary, the eastern Balkans in that of Russia. This involved the abandonment by Russia of Serbia, but she had already sacrificed the possibility of a greater Serbia on the side of Bosnia and Herzegovina by agreeing to their occupation by Austria-Hungary, and had discarded this possibility on the side of 'Macedonia' by the enormous westward extension given by Ignatyev to his Bulgaria. There remained in consequence only Nish (reluctantly conceded) and parts of Novi Bazar and Old Serbia wherewith to satisfy the ambitions of Belgrade. This was entirely inadequate in the eyes of the Serbs, who by the beginning of April were in effect already lost to Russia, largely through Ignatyev's own policy. On the other hand, Andrássy's demands in respect of Montenegro certainly would have to be heavily reduced if Russia were to come to an agreement: the exclusion of Montenegro from the sea-coast especially was inadmissible. But Andrássy had pitched his requirements so high that it seemed likely that they were intended in part for bargaining purposes. It is significant that the Germans, who took this view, thought that the prospects of an understanding between Russia and Austria-Hungary were fairly hopeful provided that the latter did not mean to insist on vetoing a port for Montenegro.[1]

In broad perspective it might thus be claimed that, if San Stefano had to be revised, the balance of disadvantages inclined in favour of attempting an arrangement with Vienna. But only rarely does broad perspective take shape until after the event. The lack of a single directing centre of policy was never more seriously felt. Novikov in Vienna was ardent for a settlement, but he did not carry the weight or possess the energy to make up for the confusion at home. Shuvalov in London, who had energy and eventually weight, was urgent for an agreement with England, and if anything confused still further the issue of negotiations with Austria-Hungary. In St. Petersburg the Tsar was vacillating, gloomily obsessed with the feeling that war or humiliation, or both, were being forced upon him; Gorchakov was a wreck; Giers had prudence but no assured position and no drive; Jomini, twisting this way and that, was never more than a skilful permanent official. Ignatyev was the only man who combined strength of will, energy, and first-class ability. But he was the man of San Stefano; he could not walk in company with Andrássy. So throughout April Russian policy drifted between San Stefano, Vienna, and London, and the opportunity to clear the decks by an agreement with Andrássy was lost.

Yet the Austrians were not anxious for such an outcome. Andrássy, for all his negotiations with London, placed no full reliance on the intentions of the British government: he doubted whether they really intended to fight; he was not impressed by

[1] Stolberg to Bülow, disp., 1 Apr., Schweinitz to Bülow, disp., 4 Apr., and Bülow to the Kaiser, 15 Apr., in *G.P.*, pp. 257, 262, 273; Oubril to Gorchakov, 17 Apr. (giving Bismarck's views), summarized in Ignatyev's memoirs, *I.V.*, vol. cxliii, p. 669.

their military preparations; he feared they might leave him in the lurch.[1] Russian troop movements were highly disquieting, and, even apart from financial difficulties, as late as June influential military opinion was advising him that a successful campaign could not be contemplated before the spring of next year.[2] But his hopes of receiving a prompt and clear answer from the Russians to his proposals of the end of March were disabused. By the middle of April, nothing satisfactory having arrived from St. Petersburg, Novikov on Andrássy's request agreed to open negotiations, in the form of a confidential exchange of views subject to the condition that concessions made on the part of Russia were dependent upon a successful conclusion to the negotiations. Novikov himself was quite ready to comply with the Austrian requirements, save as regards Montenegro. He was, with good reason, nervous that, if the Russian concessions proved insufficient, Andrássy would reserve for himself freedom of action and return to demanding the Balkans for the southern boundary of Bulgaria, which meant going hand in hand with the English and the Turks. Hence he urged the importance of conceding the substance of the demands for Novi Bazar and the cutting off from Bulgaria of 'Macedonia', emphasizing that adequate guarantees of trade routes to the Aegean were of first-class importance to the Dual Monarchy, and arguing that such concessions might bring Andrássy to compromise on the Montenegrin sea-coast.[3]

Such pleadings for conciliation went much too far for St. Petersburg. Ignatyev, it is true, had been forced on to the defensive, and was by now fighting a losing battle. But he could still be dangerous. Struggling to maintain influence, he had to accommodate himself in some fashion to the growing strength of moderate counsels. Throughout April he surpassed himself in elaborating diverse ingenious combinations, as the month closed, more and more marked by compromise, but his concessions to Vienna were both inadequate and tardy. All that he would countenance in the last resort was a reduction in the duration of the occupation of Bulgaria and in the strength of

---

[1] *Wertheimer*, vol. iii, pp. 95–6.

[2] Ignatyev's report of 4 Apr., text in *I.V.*, vol. cxliii, pp. 47–8; Novikov to Gorchakov, tel., 17 Apr., text, ib., p. 668; *Wertheimer*, vol. iii, p. 107, citing a memorandum of the Archduke Albert, 7 June.

[3] Novikov to Gorchakov, tels., 10, 15, 16, 17 Apr., texts in *I.V.*, vol. cxliii, pp. 663–9.

the occupying army, and the formation of a fully autonomous western Bulgaria with the same rights and institutions as those laid down for the San Stefano Bulgaria. He would not yield on Novi Bazar or the Montenegrin sea-coast, save possibly Dulcigno. He urged that Bulgarian delegates should be heard at the congress, and, seizing on a remark of Andrássy, that the Emperor William be appealed to as regards the interpretation of the secret convention. As a result of this obstruction the negotiations with Vienna made no real headway. Nor, as usual, could the Russians gain help from Berlin, even though what was stated to be the complete correspondence between St. Petersburg and Vienna was communicated to the German government 'en l'invitant à se prononcer sur la manière dont le Gouvernement de l'Autriche-Hongrie comprend et pratique l'entente à trois'. By the end of April the only concessions which the Russians had made were relatively minor, and the essential questions remained in dispute; the Austrians were still demanding the cutting off of 'Macedonia', but refusing its organization as an autonomous principality, still demanding the annexation of Novi Bazar up to Mitrovica, still refusing any coastal strip to Montenegro, save possibly Antivari under very onerous conditions.[1]

At this moment the situation was suddenly transformed. In mid-April Wellesley, the British military attaché, had returned to St. Petersburg. As will be seen later (pp. 479–82), within a fortnight the idea of a direct Russian approach to London gained the field. On 3 May St. Petersburg agreed to Shuvalov's suggestion that he should pay a flying visit home to make ready for direct negotiations with Salisbury. This marked the ruin of the negotiations with Vienna, and the final defeat of Ignatyev.

Yet Ignatyev was not ousted without an effort on his part to play the chief role in negotiations with the British if such there had to be. When, at the end of April, the swing towards an understanding with England became so pronounced that he

---

[1] Texts of Ignatyev's memoranda of 7, 9, 27 Apr. and one undated but shortly before 27 Apr., in *I.V.*, vol. cxliii, pp. 657–62, vol. cxliv, pp. 34–5, 44–52; Gorchakov to Shuvalov, letter, 13 Apr., and copy of Gorchakov to Oubril, 21 Apr., texts in *Seton-Watson MSS.* (for appeal to Berlin); Čubrilović, *Bosanski ustanak*, p. 289, citing from the Vienna archives pro memoria handed to Andrássy by Novikov, 17 Apr.:—a free hand to Austria in Serbia as regards economic and railway questions, Ada Kale to Austria, withdrawal of the Montenegrin frontier from the Lim in return for compensation elsewhere, acceptance of the principle of a revision of the Serbian frontier in Novi Bazar.

could not afford to ignore it, he hastily began to trim his sails accordingly. Either, he said, secure the mediation of the Emperor William and through him an agreement with Austria-Hungary; or approach England through Italy. This latter suggestion was an ingenious manœuvre to save his position; for Corti, now the Italian foreign minister, had been on good terms with Ignatyev and with Salisbury at the Constantinople conference, and it was Ignatyev's intention that he himself should be entrusted with the negotiations through Corti. This would effectually prevent Shuvalov from being the central figure of any Anglo-Russian negotiations. In despite—more probably in consequence—of Gorchakov's express disapproval of any broaching of the subject to Nigra, the Italian minister in St. Petersburg, Ignatyev did so approach him, but Corti refused to budge from his publicly announced attitude of strictest reserve.[1]

In any case the possible concessions to England which Ignatyev had suggested were not promising. Bayazid and the Alashkert valley might be given up, so that the Trebizond–Tabriz caravan route should not be cut, but on condition that the fortresses of Bayazid and Erzerum were razed: a small strip in Bessarabia (but not including Kilia or Ismail) might, in the last resort, be left to Roumania, but the Dobrudja should then go to Bulgaria: European commissaries might be substituted for Russian in the delimitation of boundaries: the Turkish war debt

[1] Text of memorandum of Ignatyev, 27 Apr., in *I.V.*, vol. cxliv, pp. 34–5; Ignatyev's memoirs, ib., pp. 337–8; Paget (Rome) to Salisbury, tel., no. 34, conf., 4 May, in *F.O.* 45/338. It appears that Nigra was a firm supporter of the idea of a Russo-Italian entente. In January and February King Victor Emmanuel and Pope Pius IX had died. In March the Cairoli ministry, all but two members of which were new to office, was formed, with marked irredentist sympathies (though not in the case of Corti), and a strong irredentist agitation began, which added to the Austrian fears of some combination between Italy and Russia; Haines, 'Italian irredentism during the Near Eastern crisis, 1875–78', in *Journal of Modern History*, vol. ix, pp. 36–8. Corti himself, however, on becoming foreign minister, had shown that he would not favour any kind of active policy by refusing the overtures of England for some form of Mediterranean league against Russia; Lee, 'The proposed Mediterranean league, 1878', in *Journal of Modern History*, vol. iii, pp. 33–45. The Consulta had no particular objection to Russian expansion in the eastern Balkans or to Russian predominance at the Straits; another flag in the Mediterranean would offset the predominance of the British and the French; Bosnia and Herzegovina were its primary interest, but it would not abandon a policy of cautious waiting; extract from memorandum of Malvano, secretary-general at the Italian foreign office, June 1878, in M. Rosi, *I Cairoli* (Bologna, 1929), vol. ii, pp. 270–2.

might be regulated by a European syndicate, with Russian participation in it. The remaining concessions were not of much substance. On the vital question of the extent of Bulgaria he would not go farther than admit in the very last resort a longitudinal division, on the lines put forward at the Constantinople conference, but the frontiers were to be those of San Stefano and each portion was to receive the same autonomous rights provided for at San Stefano. His final suggestion is of special interest: if England insisted on the cession to her of Mytilene or Chios, Russia should not unconditionally oppose this, but if she demanded the occupation of some point on the Dardanelles Russia could yield only if she received in return the right to occupy and fortify positions on either shore of the Bosphorus.[1]

The maker of San Stefano was not, however, destined to be its reviser. In the inner circle round the Tsar his decisive influence was now gone. Unable to press home the immediate fulfilment of his treaty, unable to make headway against Andrássy, he was not to be given the chance of extricating Russia from the position in which he was so largely responsible for placing her by trying his charms again on Salisbury. That task was entrusted to his most dangerous rival, Shuvalov. Yet at the same time as the turn towards England a final effort to intimidate Vienna was made, in which the hand of Ignatyev was apparent.

On 2 May instructions were sent to Novikov which contained the maximum Russian concessions. An Austrian annexation, not merely occupation, of Bosnia and Herzegovina was conceded, and the San Stefano Bulgaria might be divided longitudinally as planned at the Constantinople conference, both portions receiving identical institutions as provided for by the treaty of San Stefano. Ignatyev calculated that such a western Bulgaria, as contrasted with his previous idea of an autonomous 'Macedonian' principality, would, by including more Bulgars, offset Austrian influence, and that the union of the two halves could be engineered more easily in the future. Since Andrássy had steadily refused to countenance the prospect even of a politically autonomous 'Macedonian' principality, it was impossible to expect that this new Russian device could receive any consideration in Vienna, unless fears of an Anglo-Russian

---

[1] Text of memorandum of Ignatyev on possible concessions to England, 28 Apr., in *I.V.*, vol. cxliv, pp. 36–9.

understanding were to lead to a precipitate abandonment of Austrian requirements. The Russians also demanded that Novi Bazar should be divided between Serbia and Montenegro, and that the latter should keep what she had conquered on the Adriatic coast. Not even the treaty of San Stefano had gone so far. Apart from the 'Scheinkonzession' of a longitudinally divided Bulgaria, almost the only other concessions were freedom for Austria-Hungary to conclude commercial, tariff, and railway agreements with Serbia, Montenegro, and the new western Bulgaria (though even so Novi Bazar was hedged about with a specially dangerous formula), and evacuation of Russian troops and officials from the two Bulgarias immediately after the installation of the new Bulgarian authorities and the formation of the militia and national police. On this concession Bismarck pertinently minuted 'et à quand cette installation'; as to the former concession Andrássy exclaimed that it meant nothing at all, since he already possessed such freedom without needing Russian consent. Finally, Austria-Hungary was to bind herself in writing to adopt a common diplomatic front with Russia in defence of the remaining articles of the treaty of San Stefano, and to bind herself to benevolent neutrality in case of a renewal of the war 'et quelle que soit l'extension qu'elle prendrait'.[1]

These Russian requirements were totally unacceptable to Andrássy, who regarded them as involving that the Balkans should be hermetically sealed against Austria-Hungary.[2] It is not clear how far the Russians seriously believed it possible to reach an agreement on such bases, but they did at least appeal yet again to Berlin, and the Tsar wrote personally to the Emperor William begging him to back up the Russian proposals in Vienna.[3] Bismarck declined as usual to take up the cudgels:

[1] Copy of Giers to Novikov, disp., and pro memoria, 2 May (handed to Andrássy on 8 May), and Stolberg to Berlin, tel., 9 May, in *G.P.*, pp. 298–303; text of undated memorandum of Ignatyev, shortly before 27 Apr., in *I.V.*, vol. cxliv, p. 51; *Wertheimer*, vol. iii, p. 98, citing Andrássy to Károlyi, 9 May. Ignatyev had always held that the only excuse for not dividing Novi Bazar between Serbia and Montenegro was the necessity for providing the Turks with safe land communication with Bosnia and Herzegovina; since these two provinces were to pass to Austria, the *raison d'être* for not dividing the *sanjak* had disappeared.

[2] Stolberg to Berlin, tel., 9 May, reporting conversation with Andrássy that day, in *G.P.*, p. 303.

[3] Memorandum of Bülow, 6 May, recording conversation with Oubril that day, in *G.P.*, p. 297; Oubril had laid before him the instructions to Novikov and pro memoria of 2 May. The text of the Tsar's letter is not given.

'no breach with Austria, no breach with Russia' remained his watchword. He agreed with the latter that the Austrian claims against Montenegro to the sea-coast were unjustified: he agreed with the former that there could be no question of German support for Russian attempts to cut off Austria-Hungary from her legitimate sphere in the East, and that, if Bulgaria were to be divided longitudinally, the western portion must be placed more under Austrian influence.[1]

As before, the Russians found that Bismarck, though anxious for some Austro-Russian agreement to be reached, and in fact much perturbed by the breach between the two countries, would not 'opt' to the extent of meeting the Russian requirements by pressure on Vienna. He was at this moment all the less likely to take any such step in view of Andrássy's agreement, given secretly on 13 April, to the long-desired abrogation of Article V of the treaty of Prague, which had committed Prussia to an eventual plebiscite in the northern districts of Schleswig. Without Bismarck's aid the Russians could scarcely hope for success. It only remained for them to attempt revenge against Austria-Hungary by isolating her through coming to an agreement with England. Meanwhile, throughout May Andrássy held his ground—in great anxiety.

[1] Bismarck to Bülow, tel., 10 May, in *G.P.*, p. 303 (p. 296, marginal comment on Montenegro and sea-coast).

XVI

BUCAREST

WHILE Russia was at grips with Austria-Hungary and the long crisis with England was dragging itself to the edge of war, alarums and excursions in Roumania, coming to a head at the dark close of March, caused yet further confusion and dissension. Though the Bucarest crisis in itself was secondary, the strategical situation of Roumania was bound to make events there of ominous importance to the Russians

Mention has already been made (see above, p. 362) of the anger of the Roumanians at the Adrianople negotiations having been conducted without their participation and at the terms themselves. Relations between the two countries became more and more acrimonious until they culminated in the Russian ultimatum of the beginning of April. The Roumanian government were vainly struggling to share in the negotiations for the treaty of San Stefano; vainly demanding that their war indemnity be fixed at a definite, and of course large, sum; vainly hoping that some form of guaranteed neutrality for the future might be obtained. They were multiplying their appeals to the powers for diplomatic support in upholding the 1856 treaty of Paris, as interpreted by Bucarest, for admission to the congress, and for financial or military assistance. Above all, they were refusing to agree to give up Bessarabia. In secret they feared that Reichstadt had settled that it should be returned to Russia, or, worse still, that some partition of Roumania herself had been arranged between Russia and Austria-Hungary.

The Russian attitude was one of uncompromising severity. No participation in the San Stefano negotiations was possible, since Roumanian independence could only be recognized as a result of the final congress. The Russians would support Roumanian participation at the congress, but not as full members. Any suggestion as to Roumanian neutrality was ruled out of court 'comme une offense directe'.[1] On Bessarabia St.

---

[1] Ghica to Kogălniceanu, tel., 26 Jan., recording interview with the Tsar and Gorchakov that day, text in *Corespondenţa Generalului Iancu Ghica*, p. 126: cf. private letter of Jomini to Kogălniceanu, 29 Jan., text in Kogălniceanu, *Acta şi documente din corespondenţa diplomatică . . .*, pp. 10–11: 'Ne vous laissez pas non plus illusionner par le *humbug* de la neutralité. Celle de la Belgique, qu'on vous prêche comme

Petersburg would not hear of any compromise. A few days before the signature of the armistice and bases of peace on 31 January, the Tsar and Gorchakov informed Iancu Ghica, the envoy of Roumania in St. Petersburg, that she would have to give up her portion of Bessarabia, but might receive in compensation the Delta and the Dobrudja, as far as Constanza; the reacquisition of Bessarabia was 'une question d'honneur et dignité nationale . . . une décision inébranlable'.[1] Immediately after the receipt of this information Ignatyev arrived in Bucarest (31 Jan.), *en route* for the Grand Duke Nicholas's head-quarters. He was charged with letters from the Tsar and Gorchakov to Prince Charles and his foreign minister, and with the task of elucidating Roumanian views as to the peace terms, though not of conducting any actual negotiations.[2] Bucarest could no longer pretend to doubt the determination of Russia to take back Bessarabia, but it still remained uncertain exactly how she proposed to do so, and exactly what she would offer in return. Gorchakov found ample excuse for indefiniteness in the argument that it would be dangerous to set out in detail the compensations for Roumania or to put them in the form of any engagement until the diplomatic situation became clearer.[3]

The visit of Ignatyev and the declarations from St. Petersburg brought the Bessarabian question to a head. The news of the Russian demand leaked out, and feeling against a voluntary cession ran fever-high. Ignatyev represented Prince Charles, after an initial refusal to consider the idea of cession, as anxious that public opinion should be gradually prepared for the inevitable sacrifice. This was perhaps also the view of Kogălniceanu,

modèle, ne repose pas du tout sur des traités, car de nos jours ce sont hélas! des chiffons de papier.' Two days later Ghica had another interview with Gorchakov, who inveighed against Roumanian efforts to wage an anti-Russian campaign 'tant par envoi de représentants *ad hoc* à l'étranger que par des pétitionnements à Ismail, Cahoul . . .' (i.e. in Roumanian Bessarabia); Ghica to Kogălniceanu, tel., 28 Jan., text in *Corespondența Generalului Iancu Ghica*, pp. 130–1. Ignatyev was complaining of Roumanian authorities at Ismail engineering petitions in favour of retention by Roumania: the local Russian consul seems to have countered with similar intrigues in the opposite sense; *San Stefano*, p. 54; *Corespondența Generalului Iancu Ghica*, p. 133.

[1] Ghica to Kogălniceanu, tels., 26 and 28 Jan., text ib., pp. 128, 130–1.

[2] Ignatyev's account of his visit to Bucarest is in *San Stefano*, pp. 31–64. He arrived on 31 Jan., and left in the early morning of 3 Feb. The text of the Tsar's and Gorchakov's letters are in *Aus dem Leben König Karls . . .*, vol. iii, pp. 456–7.

[3] Gorchakov's instructions to Ignatyev, *San Stefano*, p. 33, text given in the original French.

the foreign minister, who in strict privacy considered that the Dobrudja would be of the greatest importance to Roumania and that the offer of exchange should be accepted, at least if it could be greatly extended so as to include Varna. For the moment Prince Charles appears to have thought it more prudent to appeal to the Tsar in the hope of reconsideration and to wait somewhat longer until the attitude of the powers should be evident. On the other hand, Brătianu, the prime minister, probably in fear of his political life, professed to regard voluntary cession as impossible and swam with the tide of russophobia.[1]

In consequence, on the one hand the government officially adopted an indignant attitude of *non possumus*, appealed to the powers to uphold the treaty of Paris, and insisted that Russia had solemnly guaranteed by the convention of 16 April 1877 the possession by Roumania of the Bessarabian districts. On the other hand Kogălniceanu, continuing soundings which had been made to Ignatyev during his visit, instructed Ghica to discover unofficially whether St. Petersburg would agree to the Dobrudja extending to the line Silistria–Mangalia.[2] Ghica reported (7 Feb.) some initial hopes of success, perhaps due to confidential information that Gorchakov himself had never set much store by the retrocession of Bessarabia and had merely bowed to the Tsar's insistence on it.[3] But he soon found that no headway could be made.

The Russians in fact had far too much on their hands in this crowded month of February to spend time bargaining with such small fry, even though their suspicions of Roumanian negotiations with Vienna showed that under certain circumstances Bucarest might become of first-rate importance. They were the more incensed by heated debates in the Roumanian Chamber

---

[1] Extract from Stuart to Gorchakov, 4 Feb. (recording Ignatyev's account), printed by Adamov in *Le Monde slave*, 1928, no. 1, p. 103; M. C. Kogălniceanu (son of the foreign minister), in *Le Monde slave*, 1928, no. 4, p. 149; *Aus dem Leben König Karls* . . . , vol. iii, pp. 457–8, 464 (text of Prince Charles's letter to the Tsar, 3 Feb.).

[2] *San Stefano*, pp. 46–7, 55–6; Kogălniceanu to Ghica, tels., 30 Jan. and 5 Feb., text in *Corespondenţa Generalului Iancu Ghica*, pp. 132, 137.

[3] Ghica to Kogălniceanu, tel., 7 Feb., text, ib., p. 139. Ghica's information was probably derived from Jomini: cf. Jomini deploring the personal insistence of the Tsar on regaining the whole of Bessarabia; Polovtsov's diary, under date 10 Apr. 1878, in *Krasny arkhiv*, vol. xxxiii, p. 189. Similarly, Loftus believed that it was the Tsar who insisted on the retrocession and that Gorchakov after trying to dissuade him was now resigned to it; Loftus to Derby, disp., no. 301, 11 Mar., in *F.O.* 65/1000.

and Senate, on 4 and 6 February, when both houses unanimously decided not to accept any change of frontiers, and by the private expostulations of Kogălniceanu that the Russians had never previously formulated the demand for the retrocession of the Bessarabian districts.[1] Gorchakov brushed aside his appeal to the treaty of Paris with the argument that by it the Bessarabian districts had been ceded to Turkey, and had later been ceded to Moldavia, not to a non-existent Roumania, and he slipped out of the guarantee of territorial integrity contained in the Russo-Roumanian convention by the shameful contention that the guarantee was valid only as against Turkey.[2] In short, if the Roumanians would not truckle, so much the worse for them.

Meanwhile Ignatyev was driving through his negotiations at San Stefano. The news of the signature of the treaty caused a further outburst in Bucarest. The fate of Bessarabia was sealed by Article XIX, which provided for the cession by Turkey to Russia of the Delta and Dobrudja up to the Rasova–Mangalia line (which did not include Silistria), Russia reserving the right to hand over to Roumania these acquisitions in exchange for the Bessarabian districts. Article VIII provided for the maintenance of Russian communications through Roumania with the army of occupation in Bulgaria for two years. The treaty did not specify any definite sum to be paid Roumania as a war indemnity; the amount was to be settled by subsequent negotiations. The only crumb of comfort was that Turkey was to recognize the independence of Roumania.

These terms had been dictated over the head of the Roumanian government, who had not been even formally consulted. They were first known in Bucarest, through Havas, on 6 March,

---

[1] Letter of Kogălniceanu to Gorchakov, text in *Aus dem Leben König Karls . . .*, vol. iii, p. 474, under date 14 Feb., in which Kogălniceanu protested that Gorchakov had only once mentioned Bessarabia to him, and that in only very general terms. According to E. Adamov and M. C. Kogălniceanu, in *Le Monde slave*, 1928, no. 1, p. 103, and no. 4, p. 148, the letter also contained the statement: 'ni le tsar, ni le grand duc Nicolas, ni personne d'autre, n'avait jamais fait cette prévision' (that Bessarabia would be required to be ceded); against which the Tsar minuted, 'Mensonge effronté! Bratiano me l'a entendu dire plus d'une fois.' Kogălniceanu had to admit in the course of an arduous debate in the Senate that Gorchakov had mentioned to him Russian claims to Bessarabia in June 1877; *Aus dem Leben König Karls . . .*, under date 26 Feb., vol. iii, p. 495.

[2] Ghica to Kogălniceanu, tel., 13 Mar., text in *Corespondența Generalului Iancu Ghica*, p. 161. The Russians had elaborated the same argument a month before to the Austrians in their notice confidentielle of 12 Feb.; see above, p. 441.

and the ministry were not in possession of the full text until its publication in the *Journal de St Pétersbourg* after ratification. How did the Russians intend to retake possession of Bessarabia? By separate agreement with Roumania? By agreement reached at the congress? Simply by force? This was the immediate task of Ghica in St. Petersburg to discover. From the Tsar he received a 'dressing down' before the whole diplomatic corps (10 Mar.).[1] After much delay he forced himself upon Gorchakov. 'Inutile de vous faire illusion. Jamais l'Empereur ne reviendra sur cette demande. Sa résolution est inébranlable. . . . Je ne pense pas soumettre cette question à la décision du Congrès. . . . Si rien ne peut vous faire fléchir, alors nous vous prendrons le territoire demandé et vous n'aurez aucune compensation. Que ferez-vous? Nous opposer par les armes? Ce serait inutile et dangereux pour vous.'[2] On 15 March Ghica telegraphed his complete abandonment of any hopes of compromise.[3] It was clear beyond doubt that Russia intended to act by main force if Roumania would not negotiate a separate agreement with her.

Yet, though Prince Charles and Kogălniceanu urged that the cession could not be avoided and that a new direction must be given to their foreign policy, Brătianu still clung to the hope that Bessarabia might be saved, and the general feeling in political circles, further incensed by the requirement as to Russian communications through their country, was still obdurate. The news from Vienna and Buda-Pesth, where Ion Ghica and Dimitrie Sturdza were intriguing hard for support, seemed more hopeful. Might not Austro-Hungarian opposition to San Stefano go to extreme lengths? Might not British aid as well be available? On 28 March Kogălniceanu, his hand forced by political pressure, and meditating resignation, announced in the Chamber that Roumania could not accept the treaty and would not agree to any arrangement in respect of Bessarabia. On the same day it was decided to send Brătianu on a special mission to Vienna and Berlin.[4]

---

[1] Extract from diary of Gontaut-Biron (then on a visit to St. Petersburg), under date 12 Mar., in Dreux, *Dernières années de l'ambassade en Allemagne de M. de Gontaut-Biron*, p. 377.

[2] Ghica to Kogălniceanu, tel., 12 Mar., reporting interview with Gorchakov on the previous day, text in *Corespondenţa Generalului Iancu Ghica*, pp. 160–1.

[3] Ghica to Kogălniceanu, tel., 15 Mar., text ib., p. 163.

[4] *Aus dem Leben König Karls* . . . , under various dates throughout Mar., vol. iv,

The reply of St. Petersburg was immediate and drastic. On 1 April Gorchakov furiously threatened Roumania in the name of the Tsar with occupation and with the demand for the disarmament of her army if she did not accept the requirements of San Stefano. Prince Charles, all his pride in his army aroused, stung to the quick by the threat of this indignity, immediately answered that his army would only be disarmed after it had been defeated, and hurried on its concentration in Little Wallachia, where it could be in direct contact with the Austro-Hungarians. The Russians retaliated by continued concentrations in Roumania and Roumanian Bessarabia and seemed about to carry out their threat of occupation. A complete rupture was imminent.[1]

But in fact Gorchakov had overshot the mark. The Roumanian declaration of 28 March had coincided with the substitution of Salisbury for Derby at the British foreign office and the further turn of England towards war; with the extreme tension with Austria-Hungary and the Ignatyev mission to Vienna; and with the Tsar's final effort to induce the Grand Duke Nicholas to force the Bosphorus heights and his belated decision to recall his brother. The Tsar, in fear for the communications of his army in the Balkans, may have been determined to take forcible action against Roumania when such became necessary, but that could hardly be until he was more certain of the course to be taken by Austria-Hungary. And, further, the threat to Roumania, besides being couched in intolerably humiliating form, was rash; for it seems that the Russian troops available might well not have been sufficient to carry it out.[2] At any rate,

pp. 1, 4–7, 9, 12–14; Dimitrie Sturdza to Kogălniceanu, disp., 13 Mar., from Pesth, text in Kogălniceanu, *Acta și documente din corespondența diplomatică* . . ., pp. 30–1; Kogălniceanu to Ghica, tels., 29 Mar., text in *Corespondența Generalului Iancu Ghica*, pp. 169–70. The only specific reference to Austro-Roumanian relations during these months in *Wertheimer*, vol. iii, is the statement (p. 103) that Roumanian delegates came to Vienna to offer Andrássy in case of a war with Russia the support of the Roumanian army, 50,000 strong, and the occupation of Widdin. No authority is cited, nor is any date given, but if the reference is to the mission of Ion Ghica and Dimitrie Sturdza to Vienna it would be in March.

[1] Ghica to Kogălniceanu, tel., 1 Apr., and disp., 8 Apr., text in *Corespondența Generalului Iancu Ghica*, pp. 171–2, 197–202; *Aus dem Leben König Karls* . . . , vol. iv, pp. 19–23, 25, 28, 30, 38, 40: on p. 20, under date 7 Apr., mention is made of a suggestion of Stuart that Brătianu should return from Berlin via St. Petersburg, a suggestion which Stuart would hardly have put forward without the approval of his government: it was not acted upon.

[2] British investigations estimated the total number of Russian troops in Roumania during April as between 40,000 and 50,000, though one estimate was as low

Gorchakov having delivered himself of his spleen in this dangerous fashion did nothing further. The Roumanian tangle was
left to Giers and Stuart, the Russian representative in Bucarest.
Within a fortnight the crisis was on the wane. On 10 April
Giers proposed officially the negotiation of a new military convention to regulate Russian communications during the occupation of Bulgaria, and the Tsar urged this on Prince Charles in
a personal letter which was not unfriendly in tone. On the
15th Brătianu returned from his mission; Vienna had been not
discouraging, except the Emperor himself; but Berlin had been
very reserved, and Bismarck had emphasized that Bessarabia
was a *sine qua non* for Russia and that opposition to its cession
should be abandoned. The news from London was not very
hopeful. On the whole, it was clear that the powers would do
nothing for Roumania, if they could settle their own differences
with Russia, and, as far as Bucarest could judge, this seemed
by no means unlikely. Opinion began to veer towards recognizing that some compromise was necessary if Roumania were
not to go empty-handed. Ghica, just back from St. Petersburg
on 26 April, reported that pacific influences now had the upper
hand there and were likely to be strengthened if the Roumanians could show themselves accommodating. The month, so
stormily opened, closed with an official Roumanian celebration
of the Tsar's birthday.[1]

Although the immediate danger of an armed clash disappeared, feelings were still running very high; mutual suspicions
continued to thrive; military preparations on either side continued uneasily. The negotiations between the two governments
did not proceed far. St. Petersburg was immersed in the final
grapple of Ignatyev, Gorchakov, and Shuvalov: England and
Austria-Hungary filled the horizon: there was still no time yet

as 20,000; Mansfield (Bucarest) to Derby, disp., conf., nos. 70 and 71, 23 and
24 Apr.; Ward (acting consul-general) to Derby, disp., nos. 80 and 81, 2 May,
in *F.O.* 78/2833. The Roumanian foreign office professed to accept the estimate
of 40,000. The total strength of the Roumanian army at that time was about the
same. Mansfield, a military man, less badly informed on military than on other
affairs, telegraphed on 12 Apr. that 'there are no indications of a regular military
occupation'; *F.O.* 78/2834. For a much higher estimate see above, p. 397, note 3.
[1] Ghica to Kogălniceanu, tel., 10 Apr., text in *Corespondența Generalului Iancu
Ghica*, p. 181; *Aus dem Leben König Karls* . . . , vol. iv, pp. 27–8 (text of Tsar's letter
of 13 Apr.), 19 and 25–7 (on Brătianu's mission), 34 (on Ghica's return and celebration of Tsar's birthday); E. Adamov, in *Le Monde slave*, 1928, vol. i, p. 104, citing
Stuart to Gorchakov, 19 Apr. (on change in opinion).

for small principalities struggling towards independence. Thus Bessarabia and the question of communications remained left on one side. No settlement, other than a precarious military convention, was reached with Bucarest prior to the meeting of the Berlin congress.[1]

[1] *The Times*, 6 June, reported from Bucarest (2 and 4 June) that the opposition press had revealed full details of a Russo-Roumanian convention signed by Brătianu, Kogălniceanu, and Drenteln, the Russian general in charge of lines of communication, and that it was violently attacking the government for omitting any time-limit for the continued presence of Russian troops in Roumania. The Russians naturally would have refused to specify a time-limit until the duration of their occupation of Bulgaria was definitely fixed.

XVII

LONDON

IGNATYEV had played his hand, and he had not won. Andrássy would make no substantial concession. Rumoured troop movements to Galicia, though explicitly denied by Francis Joseph, pointed towards an armed struggle. The Roumanians would join it if they could, and the long line of communications from Constantinople to the Dniester was in jeopardy. Before Constantinople some 90,000 Russians faced 80,000 Turks, well armed, in strong positions, growing in numbers and in confidence. For not only was the British fleet still there; British military preparations were being pushed ahead, and England was publicly committed to the support of Turkey. At home the month of April saw the internal crisis quickened by the popular acquittal of Vera Zasulich by a St. Petersburg jury, her successful escape abroad, and serious student outbreaks in Kiev.

By the end of April a firm stand on San Stefano could hardly be maintained by St. Petersburg, and the pressure on Vienna desired from Bismarck was definitely not forthcoming. Ignatyev himself was busy now with memoranda on concessions, and, sensing the new wind, on possible negotiations with England. After all, it seemed highly doubtful whether Austria would fight without England; but the reverse was not the case: if some agreement could be reached with the most determined opponent of Russia, would not Vienna find herself compelled eventually to come into line? This moment of inclination towards London was ably used by the rival who had always been opposed to Ignatyev's designs in the Balkans and was now convinced of the seriousness of British preparations for war and of the necessity of a retreat from the position in which Ignatyev's ambition and Gorchakov's indecisiveness had placed Russia. Shuvalov, in his strategic vantage-post at the London embassy, seized the opportunity to mitigate the disfavour of his master and to make a successful bid for the lead in Russian policy. The outcome was his agreement with Salisbury, the congress of Berlin, and peace with or without honour.

In the eyes of Shuvalov the treaty of San Stefano was 'the greatest act of stupidity that we could have committed. . . .

Ignatyev's Bulgaria is nonsense.'[1] Its effect on Vienna was serious enough, but naturally for the ambassador in London it was the intensification of British hostility upon which his fears were concentrated. Just before the decisive cabinet meeting of 27 March Disraeli had completely severed personal relations, believing Shuvalov to be hand and glove with the opposition.[2] The definite ascendancy in the cabinet of extreme measures was an overwhelming blow to him. He lost everything through the departure of Derby, which he described in despairing terms as paralysing his action, and he wrote home almost impassionedly that it was *solely* due to Derby's efforts that peace had been maintained and that Russia had been able to crush Turkey before any British intervention.[3] Now the resolute tone of the British seemed to Shuvalov to make war 'almost unavoidable'.[4]

So it seemed also in St. Petersburg, where, in addition to war preparations in the Balkans, on the Austrian frontiers, and in Central Asia, plans for privateering or cruiser raids on British commerce were from this moment being pushed forward with all possible speed. Since January efforts had been made to secure approval for the purchase of fast, up-to-date liners in the United States, and their fitting out as armed cruisers. A naval officer, Semechkin, who had been with Lesovsky's squadron in American waters in 1863 when operations against the British mercantile marine had similarly been worked out, was the heart and soul of the venture. An inter-departmental committee on it in St. Petersburg had wrangled inconclusively, but now, when war with England was felt to be almost a certainty, the Tsar decided in favour. On 13 April 660 officers and men of the Russian navy, followed by Semechkin and a small staff, sailed for the United States, where the acquisition and arming of four American steamers were proceeded with and detailed

[1] Corti, *Alexander von Battenberg*, pp. 43-4.

[2] *Disraeli*, pp. 1134 and 1142, where Shuvalov categorically denies ever having had private conversations on pending negotiations with members of the opposition, particularly Harcourt. In a letter to Gorchakov, 29 Mar., text in *Seton-Watson MSS.*, he indignantly denied the accusation of Disraeli that he had communicated to the opposition the last Russian answer three days before communicating it to the government. From Shuvalov's own correspondence and from the Granville papers it is certain that he had earlier been in close touch with members of the opposition (see above, p. 356, note 1), and this is also shown to be the case by Gardiner, *Life of Sir William Harcourt*, vol. i, pp. 320-4, 328, though no date later than 5 Mar. is mentioned.

[3] Shuvalov to Gorchakov, letter, 28 Mar., text in *Seton-Watson MSS.*

[4] Münster's report of 2 Apr., in *G.P.*, pp. 258-9.

SHUVALOV

plans for the destruction of English commerce prepared. The fact that the British government (and from the end of April the press) were being kept amply informed of these, and other, naval activities of the Russians inevitably led to increased tension.[1]

While both governments were hastening forward naval and military preparations, Salisbury himself, after issuing his famous circular of 1 April, directed his first efforts to the prevention of a clash between the British and Russians around Constantinople by their simultaneous retirement. 'Stratégie oiseuse', Shuvalov termed it in retrospect;[2] nevertheless it remained one of the main features of British policy for the next two months. At the same time Salisbury was attempting to secure from Andrássy a concerted policy in the Balkans. But he found that the Magyar was slow to move and still slower to pin himself down to anything. Each was distrustful of the other, and Beust in the London embassy added to the difficulties. Andrássy was still continuing his negotiations with the Russians, and his proposals to Salisbury for the modification of the treaty of San Stefano (14 Apr.) were not satisfactory: nothing was said as to Asiatic Turkey, and above all Andrássy would not bind himself to demand the Balkan range as the southern frontier of the new Bulgaria, a requirement which had assumed major importance with Salisbury.[3]

In the latter part of April, uncertain of securing fully satisfactory co-operation with Austria, Salisbury was more and more convinced that the demand for a drastic revision of the treaty must be put to the Russians themselves by undertaking direct negotiations with Shuvalov, and that compensation in some shape for any large Russian gains in Asia must be sought by secret agreement with the Turks.[4] He already agreed with

---

[1] Butkovsky, 'Tainstvennaya ekspeditsiya v Ameriku v 1878 g.', in *I.V.*, vol. xi, pp. 604–15; additional information from American archives is in Strakhovsky, 'Russia's privateering projects of 1878', in *Journal of Modern History*, vol. vii, pp. 21–40. See also below, p. 486.

[2] Shuvalov's memoirs, quoted in Hanotaux, *Histoire de la France contemporaine*, vol. iv, p. 337.

[3] For the Anglo-Austrian negotiations during April; Andrássy to Beust, 14, 21, 23, and 29 Apr., all communicated to Salisbury, in *F.O.* 7/944; *Salisbury*, pp. 245–50; Stojanović, *Serbia in international politics: from the insurrection of Herzegovina (1875) to the Congress of Berlin (1878)* (MS.), based on the British and Austrian foreign office papers.

[4] For Salisbury's approach to the Cyprus convention, see *Salisbury*, pp. 214–15, and his private letters to Layard of 4 and 18 Apr., 2, 9, and 10 May, in Layard Papers,

Bismarck in thinking that it would be essential for England and Russia to come to some general agreement as to the chief points at issue if the congress were not to break up in failure.[1] The time for attempting such an agreement had now arrived.

Already, a month earlier (26 Mar.), Shuvalov had pressed on Gorchakov the possibility of staving off war by means of verbal negotiations carried on in London, and even immediately after Derby's resignation Shuvalov had forwarded Derby's private advice to attempt a direct entente, advice which had been coupled with the warning that any Russian movement towards the Bosphorus or Gallipoli would be equivalent to a declaration of war and with the suggestion that the bait not of Egypt but of some naval station in the Aegean might be held out.[2] Such advice, coming when the Tsar was desperately stirring on the Grand Duke Nicholas to seize the Bosphorus and when anti-British feeling was at its height, could have no effect. Any idea of a direct entente was curtly rejected.[3] To the news of Derby's resignation Gorchakov reacted with a castigation of his (and consequently Shuvalov's) conciliatory policy as being but a mournful replica of that of Aberdeen.[4] To the publicly announced news (28 Mar.) of the calling up of the Reserve was added on 31 March secret information as to renewed Austrian parleys in London and as to reinforcements being summoned from India.[5] Everything went to confirm the Russian belief that a rupture was intended. When Salisbury, at his first interview with Shuvalov on 3 April, spoke of a pacific solution being dependent on no Russian movements on the Bosphorus and Gallipoli taking place, the immediate rejoinder came that no assurance as to the Bosphorus and Dardanelles could be given unless the British fleet withdrew from the Sea of Marmara and from proximity to Gallipoli.[6]

The one point on which Shuvalov and St. Petersburg appear

British Museum, Add. MSS. 39137, ff. 39–40, 60–3, 73–6, 82–97; and particularly the analysis in Lee, Great Britain and the Cyprus Convention Policy of 1878, pp. 72–82.

[1] Münster's report of 18 Apr., in G.P., p. 279.

[2] Shuvalov to Gorchakov, letter, 26 Mar., tels., 29, 30, and 31 Mar., texts in Seton-Watson MSS., and Goriainow, Le Bosphore et les Dardanelles, p. 372. Cf. Disraeli, p. 1132.

[3] Gorchakov to Shuvalov, tel., 31 Mar., text in Seton-Watson MSS.

[4] Gorchakov to Shuvalov, letter, 29 Mar., text ib.

[5] Shuvalov to Gorchakov, tels., 31 Mar., paraphrase ib.

[6] Shuvalov to Gorchakov, tel., 3 Apr.; Gorchakov to Shuvalov, tels., 5 and 6 Apr.; texts ib.

to have been in agreement in the closing days of March was their marked dislike of a congress. Gorchakov, on hearing of Derby's retirement, at once telegraphed that the only service which the British government could render Russia would be to refuse to attend the congress, for it was obviously better that England rather than Russia should bear the responsibility for its break-down. Shuvalov heartily agreed that a congress would be contrary to Russian interests, in that it would deliver Russia into the hands of an Anglo-Austrian entente.[1] But if there were to be no congress, what then? The practicable alternatives were either an agreement with Austria-Hungary, or an agreement with England, or war. With the failure of the Ignatyev mission to Vienna and with the war party apparently in full power in England this last alternative, that of war, seemed the most probable to St. Petersburg. Even as late as 22 April Gorchakov continued to believe that, sooner or later, war with England would come.[2] The first alternative, an agreement with Vienna, was still during April gropingly attempted, even despite the failure of Ignatyev, but no accommodation was reached. Instead, the close of the month brought what at its opening had been debarred: direct negotiations in London. Some of the considerations which help to explain this volte-face on the part of Russia have been put forward in previous chapters; it now remains to examine it from the angle of Shuvalov and London.

At the beginning of April the only asset which Shuvalov had was negative, the defeat of Ignatyev in Vienna and the resultant decline of his influence in St. Petersburg. The dominating factor for Shuvalov was the advent of Salisbury at the foreign office. Inevitably he found Salisbury personally very reserved; appearing to fear frequent or intimate visits; pacific and conciliatory in private, but refusing to take him into his confidence.[3] The contrast with Derby could not be more marked: instead of the old easy and confident approaches he now had to feel his way mainly in the dark. Earlier, Shuvalov had professed to regard war with Austria-Hungary as more dangerous than war with England, and he had correspondingly favoured concessions

---

[1] Gorchakov to Shuvalov, tels., 28, 29, 31 Mar.; Shuvalov to Gorchakov, letter, 28 Mar.; texts in *Seton-Watson MSS*.

[2] Gorchakov to Shuvalov, letter, 22 Apr., text ib.

[3] Shuvalov to Gorchakov, tels., 3, 8, 19 Apr., text and paraphrase ib.

being made to the former.[1] But now that the negotiations with Vienna appeared to have so slender a chance of success, now that the odds seemed to be inclining towards war with both countries, Shuvalov seems to have decided that the right course to aim at was an agreement with England. Such a policy, if successful, would save his country from an impossible struggle and eventual humiliation, and might at the same time win for himself a decisive victory over Ignatyev and Gorchakov, win for himself the chancellorship. For he knew that, if direct negotiations for an agreement were to be entered into between Russia and England, they would never be entrusted to Loftus; and he assumed that a special envoy would not be sent to St. Petersburg: hence they would be carried on between himself and Salisbury. His proposal for direct verbal negotiations in March, as has been seen, had been sharply rebuffed by Gorchakov, and they could indeed hardly be started until Salisbury had had some time in which to accustom himself to the suspect ambassador. But as April wore on the chances in favour of Shuvalov's alternative improved.

Salisbury's opening move had been his circular of 1 April. This stated comprehensively the British objections in detail to the treaty of San Stefano, and most emphatically to 'the instrument as a whole. A discussion limited to Articles selected by one Power in the Congress would be an illusory remedy for the danger to English interests and to the permanent peace of Europe, which would result from the state of things which the Treaty proposes to establish.' In so far as the circular killed for the time being the congress, it was, secretly, satisfactory to the Russians. In so far as it harped on the sacrifice of Greek to Slav interests, it added to Russian fears of an Anglo-Greek offensive combination. In so far as it challenged the total effect of San Stefano as depressing 'almost to the point of entire subjection, the political independence of the Government of Constantinople', it was anathema to the panslavs and the dominant governmental circles. In so far as it did not explicitly specify any provisions of the treaty as excluded from possible accommodation, it could be said to offer scope for very wide negotiation and to that extent to be adaptable to Shuvalov's ideas.[2]

---

[1] Shuvalov to Gorchakov, 28 Feb. and 23 Mar., extracts in *Seton-Watson MSS.*

[2] The text of the Salisbury circular of 1 Apr. is published in, e.g., *British and*

The Russian reply, which followed on 9 April, emphasized the fact that the British government had stated what they did not want, but not what they did want: here was a pointer towards possible subsequent negotiations. It also left the door open to possible concessions in Europe, but scarcely in Asia; here was a pointer towards accommodation with Austria-Hungary at the expense of England. Otherwise Gorchakov's pro memoria was a recriminatory defence of the treaty of San Stefano, in which the most novel point was the argument that the intention of the Russian government in regard to the provisions concerning Bulgaria was substantially to repeat what had been done for Moldavia and Wallachia in 1830, and that the autonomy of these two principalities showed how little Russian predominance at the expense of the powers need be feared. This reading of Roumanian history of the last half-century was scarcely likely to be accepted either by Roumania or by the powers which had won the Crimean war. In regard to the congress Gorchakov still clung to his formula, 'une pleine liberté d'appréciation et d'action': here the deadlock continued.

The initial effect of both circulars was somewhat further to embitter Anglo-Russian relations, but Salisbury's immediate preoccupation was with the explosive situation in and around Constantinople, and his main endeavours were directed towards securing a retirement of the Russian troops approximately to Adrianople, in return for which there would be a concurrent withdrawal of the British fleet.

From the first the Russian government were extremely suspicious of negotiations for concurrent withdrawal, into which they agreed to enter (9 Apr.) only because the ostensible initiative for them came from Berlin. That Bismarck should take a direct hand might be all to the good, but they, rightly, believed that his action had been concerted with Salisbury.[1] 'C'est un parti pris', the Tsar said to Schweinitz, 'ils [the English] ne sont pas prêts et ils veulent gagner du temps.' From the Russian standpoint it would be no real gain for the British fleet to be withdrawn outside the Dardanelles at the price of a Russian withdrawal to Adrianople if at the same time troops were being

Foreign State Papers, vol. lxix, pp. 807–14; that of the Russian reply of 9 Apr. on pp. 815–22.

[1] Gorchakov to Shuvalov, tel., 11 Apr., text in Seton-Watson MSS. For the negotiations as to concurrent withdrawal, see also below, pp. 482–3, 492–3, 499, and 514–16. For the German evidence see G.P., pp. 262–72, 276–80, 289, and 292–3.

hurried from India and the other military and naval preparations against Russia were given time to be completed. Shuvalov
on this point was in substantial agreement with his government:
of what use was it to agree to disadvantageous military movements before knowing whether a pacific solution would in the
end be likely? On no account should the army be withdrawn
before a settlement was assured.[1] He was perhaps the more
biased against the negotiations in that he himself was partially
side-tracked, and was not, at any rate at first, any too fully
au courant with their confused twists and turns.[2] On the other
hand, his very friendly relations with Bismarck and his grasp
of the obvious fact that any counter-crossing would prejudice
him in Bismarck's eyes made him chary of any move towards
direct conversations in London as long as Berlin was prepared
to continue mediatory efforts. In fact, by 27 April Bismarck,
disgusted with the confusion reigning among the Russians,
abandoned his task as intermediary. Yet although these negotiations for concurrent withdrawal were not destined even ultimately to achieve their initial object, they did have the very
important effect of paving the way for direct Anglo-Russian
conversations upon the real issues involved.

Shuvalov, for all his objections to any Russian retirement,
considered that the situation would be rendered far worse if
pourparlers were broken off. He also considered it regrettable
that Bismarck was dealing only with the military question.
Hence he was eager to press upon his government a suggestion
put forward by Salisbury on 18 April, that the object to be
aimed at was an 'accord préalable sur points principaux soit
directement soit par entremise de Berlin'. At the moment he
thought that the Berlin wire should continue to be used.[3] Two
days later Shuvalov and Salisbury went over the same ground
and moved somewhat nearer each other. Shuvalov expressed
the hope that, if the German government declined to continue
mediation, the British would not on that account consider the
negotiations for the congress broken off; while Salisbury urged

[1] Shuvalov to Gorchakov, tels., 15, 16, and 20 Apr., texts in *Seton-Watson MSS.*
[2] This reason for Shuvalov's attitude to the negotiations for concurrent withdrawal appears implicitly in the telegrams to and from St. Petersburg in *Seton-
Watson MSS.*, and was explicitly surmised by *Salisbury*, p. 252.
[3] Shuvalov to Gorchakov, tels., 15, 16, and 18 Apr., texts in *Seton-Watson MSS.*
I cannot find any record of this conversation in the British foreign office documents
in the Public Record Office.

the danger of a break-down of a congress and 'that the best hope of coming to an agreement was to be found in a more accurate apprehension on both sides of the essential points on which each side was inclined to insist or to give way'. Shuvalov still, however, admitted that negotiations through a third power such as Germany were more likely to succeed than direct pourparlers.[1]

Within a fortnight the final advance was made. It was due to the effect in London of the reports received from St. Petersburg and to the adroit handling of the situation by Shuvalov. On 29 April arrived a batch of dispatches from Loftus, but it was the enclosures to them that counted. Wellesley had returned as military attaché by 13 April and he set to work at once to explore the situation. He saw the chancellor on the 15th, the Tsar and Ignatyev on the 17th. He found them convinced that England was aiming at war with Russia. His efforts to disabuse them of that belief could not have been assisted by the announcement on the 17th of the dispatch of Indian troops to Malta, and the Tsar in fact, though he did not tell Wellesley so, was very apprehensive that England might be able to count on the armed support of Austria-Hungary.[2] At the same time he was sanctioning measures in Central Asia which might confront the English with a hostile Afghanistan and a Russian diversion against India.[3] Yet to Wellesley the Tsar appeared as sincerely anxious to maintain peace if that could be done without

[1] Salisbury's memorandum of a conversation with Shuvalov on 20 Apr., in *F.O.* 65/994. It was embodied in disp., no. 288, to Loftus of the same date, though not sent until 26 Apr., by post. Cf. extract from Salisbury to Lord Odo Russell, letter, 20 Apr., in *Salisbury*, p. 252.

[2] Le Flô to Waddington, 26 Apr., in *D.D.F.*, p. 301.

[3] According to Loftus, *Diplomatic Reminiscences, 1862–1878*, second series, vol. ii, pp. 267–8, the first instructions to Kaufmann, the governor-general of Turkestan, to send a mission to Kabul, were sent on 25 Apr. During April London was receiving a number of reports from Russia (in *F.O.* 65/1029) as to designs for an expedition from Turkestan and the Caspian against the North-West Frontier, and the Indian government were more than usually alarmed as to Russian intrigues in Afghanistan. These reports, which were not very circumstantial, do not seem to have unduly disturbed Salisbury. Wellesley himself did not, so far as I can find, send any information regarding Central Asia until 28 Apr.; copy of disp. of Kaufmann to Milyutin, 2 Apr., translation enclosed in Wellesley's report, no. 27, secret, in *F.O.* 65/1030, in which Kaufmann stated that he might have to take preventive action against Bokhara since, egged on by England, she seemed to be preparing for war. Cf. p. 498 and pp. 513–14, and note 1. At the beginning of May Milyutin suggested to Giers an expedition to Tibet to afford 'political and moral support' against the British, but Giers argued in favour of one of the usual 'scientific' expeditions, to be led by Przevalsky; Popov, 'Ot Bosfora k Tikhomu okeanu', in *Istorik Marksist*, vol. xxxvii, p. 15, citing the Russian foreign office archives.

humiliation, which meant that on Bessarabia, Batum, and Kars he would not yield. He added that the Russians were much impressed by the firm attitude of England: 'Any concession on the part of England would be regarded as a sign of weakness and would lead to corresponding high talk on the side of Russia.' These words were not lost upon Disraeli and the Queen. A long conversation with Ignatyev, besides revealing his spite against Shuvalov, brought the admission that Russia had placed far too much trust in the strength of the opposition party in England, and protestations, closely reminiscent of the Russian pro memoria of 9 April, that Ignatyev had purposely left much that was vague in his treaty of San Stefano so as to allow loopholes for subsequent modification. Characteristically enough, after pointing out the desirability of a frank interchange of views between England and Russia, he suggested that he might himself pay an incognito visit to Belgium for this purpose, an idea that was sternly nipped in the bud by Wellesley.[1]

All this information pointed to the fact that St. Petersburg was preparing to seek peace, but the confusion that reigned there made progress slow. When Wellesley saw Gorchakov on 15 April he had intimated to him, with Salisbury's full subsequent approval, that the foreign secretary might be ready to negotiate with Russia either directly or indirectly through Berlin, perhaps preferably the latter: to this Gorchakov made very little response, merely approving in general terms the second alternative.[2] On 24 April the Tsar was still desiring Bismarck as intermediary, but Shuvalov was informed that if difficulties arose on that score he might enter into direct explanations with Salisbury: it was added that no military arrangement could be concluded until after an accord upon the points in dispute had been reached and the holding of the congress thus assured. By the 27th Bismarck had abandoned his attempts

---

[1] Wellesley's reports, nos. 2, 3, 4, and 5 of 15, 17, and 23 Apr., all rec. 29 Apr., in *F.O.* 65/1002.

[2] So reported by Wellesley, no. 2, 15 Apr. According to Gorchakov, tel. to Shuvalov, 23 Apr., text in *Seton-Watson MSS.*, this took place at an interview with Loftus on 22 Apr. Loftus's account of this interview, disp., no. 462, 23 Apr., in *F.O.* 65/1002, does not mention any such sounding. Gorchakov, tel., to Shuvalov, 15 Apr., text in *Seton-Watson MSS.*, speaks only of Wellesley expressing Salisbury's extreme desire for peace and of discussions as to a formula for the congress, in which Gorchakov repeated his usual remarks as to refusing to allow Russia to be cited before a tribunal. Since the *Seton-Watson MSS.* are not complete, I have followed provisionally the English version.

to arrange a concurrent withdrawal, whereupon Shuvalov was to declare to Salisbury that Russia was ready to enter into direct pourparlers; and, although Shuvalov's instructions (27 Apr.) contained very dangerous stipulations as to Russian military conditions, they closed with emphasizing the desirability of an 'accord général'.[1] On the same day Loftus reported that a council had just been held (the Tsar, Ignatyev, Giers, Milyutin, and Jomini), at which Alexander had shown himself much more conciliatory. Bayazid and the Alashkert valley would be given up, thus freeing the Trebizond–Erzerum–Tabriz caravan route—'even the cession of Batum would apparently be no longer insisted upon'. Loftus continued: 'I am told that this suggestion [for direct Anglo-Russian negotiations] is approved here, and it is thought that the Treaty of San Stefano might be confidentially discussed in London between Count Schouwalow [sic], and it is confidently hoped that by these means a direct understanding may be arranged between the two Governments of a nature to ensure the meeting of an European Congress.'[2]

The receipt of this telegram and of Wellesley's reports coincided with an interview of Shuvalov with Salisbury on the 29th. The ambassador suggested that verbal pourparlers should be entered upon as to the British *sine quibus non* and that, to avoid misunderstandings, he should ask permission to bring in person to St. Petersburg the British requirements and return with the imperial answer. This suggestion was warmly welcomed by Salisbury.[3] As he reported to the Queen, the best thing was 'that we should state to him what were the points on which we insisted most, and that he should go back to St. Petersburg to counteract, as he hinted, sinister influences there. [Shuvalov thought that] the only points on which Russia would fight were Bessarabia—Kars—Batum—and Antivari for Montenegro.'[4] Two days later (1 May) Disraeli and Salisbury agreed to the course suggested by Shuvalov, who at once strongly pressed his government to spin out the military questions in dispute and to

[1] Giers to Shuvalov, tels., 24 and 27 Apr., texts in *Seton-Watson MSS.*
[2] Loftus to Salisbury, tel., no. 100, conf., and disp., no. 468, conf., 27 Apr., in *F.O.* 65/1002. The quotation is taken from the dispatch which is an extender.
[3] Shuvalov to Gorchakov, lettre très confidentielle, 30 Apr., text in *Seton-Watson MSS.*, which do not appear to contain any telegram or other report as to the interview on 29 Apr. This letter is a continuation of a previous letter, of either 30 or 29 Apr., which is not available in *Seton-Watson MSS.* Shuvalov's memoirs, in *Krasny arkhiv*, vol. lix, p. 95, are in general agreement.
[4] Salisbury to Queen Victoria, 29 Apr., text in *Salisbury*, p. 254.

sanction the proposal.[1] He urged as an additional reason the fact that England was still unbound as regards Austria-Hungary.[2] In reply, on 3 May, Giers, who already the day before had been urging on Loftus the desirability of confidential negotiations, telegraphed the imperial authorization; 'un dernier essai', in the words of the Tsar.[3] Shuvalov had nicely anticipated Alexander's veering mood, for his telegram of 1 May had crossed with an agitated instruction from the Tsar to extract if possible direct from Salisbury the fundamental British requirements, or failing that to concert personally with Bismarck to the same end.[4]

Shuvalov had won the first round. He had seized exactly the right moment, when Bismarck had withdrawn, to make use of the suggestions for direct negotiations which had come from both Salisbury and his own government in such a way as to displace the military by the political issues and to formulate precisely what the vague expression 'direct negotiations' should mean. He had done so, in his interview with Salisbury on 29 April, in terms which guarded him as far as was possible from jealous and conflicting interventions from St. Petersburg. At the same time, on his own initiative, he had taken an equally essential step if his plans were to be realized: he had refused to act on the instructions of his government as to concurrent retirement from the neighbourhood of Constantinople.

---

[1] Shuvalov to Gorchakov, tel., 1 May, text in *Seton-Watson MSS*. If it is the case that Shuvalov did not telegraph his proposal made to Salisbury on 29 Apr., but was waiting for it to be put forward by the English, this telegram is vital. I cannot find any record of the meeting on 1 May in the British foreign office papers, and it is not mentioned in *Disraeli* or *Salisbury*.

[2] Shuvalov to Giers, tel., 2 May, text in *Seton-Watson MSS*.

[3] Giers to Shuvalov, tel., 3 May, text ib.; Loftus to Salisbury, tel., no. 104, and disp., no. 481, 2 May, and Wellesley, no. 26, 5 May, in *F.O.* 65/1003. Loftus's later account, in which he claimed to have initiated on 2 May the idea of a confidential exchange of views in London, is incorrect; *Diplomatic Reminiscences, 1862-1879*, second series, vol. ii, pp. 249-51. Giers's telegram of 3 May ran: 'Pensons comme Vous préférable faire traîner question militaire et élucider question d'avenir. Si recevez des Ministres anglais communication confidentielle sur leurs vues au sujet du traité, S.M. Vous autorise la porter Vous-même à Pétersbourg en passant si trouvez possible par Friederichsruhe où ne devez Vous arrêter que le moins de temps possible.'

[4] Giers to Shuvalov, tel., 1 May, text in *Seton-Watson MSS*. 'L'Empereur trouve urgent déjouer calcul anglais de gagner du temps et amener Salisbury à formuler sine qua non britannique, si pouvez l'obtenir par explication directe. Sinon, Bismarck pourrait y aider. S.M. consent à ce que Vous lui fassiez visite à Friederichsruhe si croyez possible une très courte absence, pour le mettre au fait de la situation à Londres. S.M. Vous réserve apprécier opportunité et choix du moment.'

The entangled deadlock over this question very nearly caused a break-down. When Giers telegraphed on 27 April that Bismarck recommended direct pourparlers with London and that Shuvalov was to declare to Salisbury that St. Petersburg was ready to enter upon them, he had primarily in mind negotiations for the mutual withdrawal of the army and the fleet, and he formulated new conditions for the retirement of the Russian troops to the demarcation-line provisionally agreed upon. These conditions, which were to be communicated to Salisbury, included the requirement that the Porte should in advance hand over Shumla, Varna, and Batum, in accordance with the treaty of San Stefano. Shuvalov was aghast; he felt that this new requirement, in particular that of Batum, would cause a rupture, and immediately (28 Apr.) asked that Batum should not be mentioned. On the following day, *The Times* having reported, correctly, from San Stefano the Russian demands, Shuvalov learnt that Salisbury had declared to the German ambassador that if these were true he would consider the negotiations terminated. He immediately wired that he was suspending the communication to Salisbury of the Russian conditions until further orders. On the same day (29 Apr.) St. Petersburg yielded and sanctioned the omission of any mention of the three fortresses, substituting a dangerously vague but less provocative formula. Shuvalov was thus able to tide over the vital days of 29 April to 3 May.[1]

A bridge had been constructed; how much weight it would carry remained to be seen. Shuvalov left London on 8 May, after several interviews with Salisbury, armed with a copy of a cabinet memorandum setting out the British objections to San Stefano. Throughout these conversations he was careful to maintain that he was without instructions from St. Petersburg and that he was not telegraphing their substance to his government.[2] It seems, therefore, that St. Petersburg in sanctioning his overtures was leaving open the possibility of a subsequent

---

[1] Giers to Shuvalov, tel., 27 Apr. (cf. p. 481, note 1); Shuvalov to Giers, tels., 28 and 29 Apr.; Gorchakov to Shuvalov, tel., 29 Apr.; texts in *Seton-Watson MSS.*

[2] Salisbury to Loftus, disp., no. 305, 7 May, in *F.O.* 181/567 (so too Shuvalov's memoirs in *Krasny arkhiv*, vol. lix, p. 95); see the text given in Appendix VIII, p. 637. The rest of this chapter, except where otherwise stated, is based on documents printed in this appendix. Shuvalov made a detailed abstract of these conversations which unfortunately is not available. It evidently differed from Salisbury's version in certain particulars (probably as regards acquisitions in Asia), though its general tenor was admitted by Salisbury to be correct.

disavowal. Shuvalov gave Salisbury the impression that Russia would lay especial stress on the retention of Batum, Kars, and Bessarabia, and of Antivari by Montenegro, but might agree to a division of the big Bulgaria, provided that the southern portion received a very large measure of administrative autonomy which would curtail the political and military rights in it of the Sultan. Here was foreshadowed what was shortly to grow into the violent struggle over Turkish strategical control of Eastern Rumelia.

The cabinet memorandum objected to the treaty of San Stefano on three main grounds: '(1) That it admits a new naval Power to the coast of the Aegean. (2) That it threatens with extinction the non-Slav populations of the Balkan peninsula. (3) That it places the Porte so much at the mercy of Russia, that it is no longer able to discharge with independence political functions which are still assigned to it, and which deeply interest other nations.' As a remedy for the first two evils the pushing back of Bulgaria from the Aegean and Macedonia was declared to be essential for any agreement. In regard to the third objection the British statement required such modifications of the treaty as taken together should effectively reduce the pressure exerted upon the independence of Turkey. The points mentioned, in the relative order of their importance, were: the extension of Bulgaria to the neighbourhood of Constantinople and the degree of Russian influence on the new Bulgaria provided by its form of government and the period of Russian occupation; the annexations in Asia; the vagueness of the indemnity clause; the acquisition of Bessarabia; the augmentation of territory given to the tributary states. If concessions were made as to the most important of these points, it would not be necessary to make such large changes in the less important. It seemed that British opposition was to be concentrated above all on Bulgaria, and in particular on obtaining 'the restriction of the Slav State to the north of the Balkans, together with a limitation of the time of occupation'. Salisbury enlarged to Shuvalov upon the apprehensions of the government as to Russian annexations in Asia, though he 'did not exclude the possibility of an understanding with respect to them'; but Shuvalov seems to have gained the impression that the British did not mean seriously to dispute the acquisitions obtained in Asia, and that they directed far more attention to a division of

Bulgaria than to Kars, or even Batum.[1] Finally, an important statement as regards the Straits was made by the foreign secretary. After pointing out the inadmissibility of excluding warships in all cases during war while admitting merchant ships, he expressed the preference for the Straits being treated 'as an open water-way, like the Sound, to be free to all vessels at all times'. If this were not accorded, Great Britain could not agree to abandon the right of blockading the Dardanelles.

Shuvalov on his departure for St. Petersburg was warned by Disraeli that the British war preparations must of necessity continue.[2] It was understood that the strictest secrecy was to be preserved as to the negotiations except as regards Germany, and Shuvalov broke his journey at Friedrichsruhe and Berlin to see Bismarck and the Emperor (9 and 10 May). He found the former much disturbed that Russia was negotiating with England before having concluded any arrangement with Austria-Hungary, and extremely surprised on learning that the British had agreed to the cession of Kars and Batum. 'Le prince crut même à un malentendu; je dus, pour le convaincre, lui redire deux fois les notes que j'avais prises pendant mon entretien avec le *foreign secretary*.'[3] Bismarck was right: there was a misunderstanding, if Shuvalov thought that Salisbury had committed himself in any event to not contesting seriously the Russian annexations in Asia. Although the foreign secretary may have gone farther than his colleagues in the cabinet, he could not bind himself until some 'key of Western Asia' was secured for England, and that was not obtained until the end of the month, in the shape of Cyprus. Where Shuvalov was correct was in interpreting British views as aiming not so much at cutting down Russian Asiatic gains as at counteracting their effect by other means.

On 12 May Shuvalov arrived in St. Petersburg—to find a chaos of irresolution and intrigue. Schweinitz has left a vivid contemporary picture of these May days, clouded ominously with fears of anarchy at home and the effects of Vera Zasulich's acquittal.

---

[1] Hanotaux, *Histoire de la France contemporaine*, vol. iv, p. 339, quoting Shuvalov's memoirs: full text of these, in Russian translation, in *Krasny arkhiv*, vol. lix, p. 96.

[2] *Disraeli*, pp. 1164–5.

[3] Shuvalov's memoirs, quoted in Hanotaux, op. cit., vol. iv, pp. 339–40. There is nothing in *G.P.* directly on this visit, but from pp. 312, 314, it is clear that Germany was very anxious lest England and Russia should come to an agreement and leave Austria-Hungary stranded.

Gorchakov had taken to his bed, in a stuffy little room without light or air: irritable after sleepless nights and incapable of keeping closely in touch with affairs, he was not ill enough and was too obstinate to give up altogether. He had nobody upon whom he could rely as personal adherents except Jomini and Hamburger, the latter of no consequence, the former always shifting his views. Giers had knowledge and good political sense, but lacked the necessary weight to play a big part in the councils against the Grand Dukes and the generals. Ignatyev was still powerful but losing ground to Shuvalov: the one-eyed among the blind, Ignatyev was the only person with geographical and ethnographical knowledge, and used his power accordingly.[1]

Shuvalov was greeted on the very day of his arrival with a passionate appeal in the papers, official as well as non-official, for subscriptions to be sent to the Tsarevich for the fitting out of volunteer cruisers as British commerce destroyers. This was the culmination of the campaign for privateers and a volunteer fleet which for six weeks past had been preached vociferously from Moscow, and now, thanks largely to Pobedonostsev, had captured the Tsarevich's circle. 'The Almighty has a new trial in store for us:' ran the Moscow committee's appeal, prominently inserted in the official gazette, 'our irreconcilable foe threatens us with war. . . . We may, however, do him sensible injury on the high seas. All must know that the interests of our foe consist merely of profit and gain.' Such incitement of bellicose patriotism, coupled with the jubilant assertion of imperial sanction for the movement, reacted dangerously on Shuvalov's efforts for peace. He himself at once protested to the British embassy that the government wholly deplored the publication of the appeal in the official press; which was probably true, since it was the work of Pobedonostsev. But Russian naval activities continued to claim close attention from the British and rendered mutual concessions additionally difficult.[2]

[1] Schweinitz to Bülow, disp., 19 May, in *G.P.*, pp. 307–10; Ignatyev in his memoirs, in *I.V.*, vol. cxliv, pp. 53–4, states that he was side-tracked and laid low with fever during Shuvalov's mission. This is his only mention of the Shuvalov mission: Schweinitz confirms that he was ill.

[2] Polovtsov's diary, under date 25 May, in *Krasny arkhiv*, vol. xxxiii, p. 195; Ignatyev's memoirs, in *I.V.*, vol. cxliii, pp. 654–5 (on possible Russian soundings of the United States); Loftus's reports from 27 Mar. onwards, in *F.O.* 65/1001 and 1002, and particularly during May, in *F.O.* 65/1003, containing numerous references to naval preparations, the fitting out of privateers in the United States, torpedo

Despite this hostile atmosphere, and despite the fact that Shuvalov was very anglophil in his outlook and very critical of Russian policy, he was able to achieve substantial success in St. Petersburg and to win the day against the nationalists. He was only too ready to be impressed by the violent criticism of all those who opposed the panslavs and by the lugubrious picture of financial, military, and political disaster, if peace were not secured, which was drawn in the best-informed circles. The Tsar struck him as greatly surprised by, and highly suspicious of, the reported British concessions in Asia, but as wearied to death with Bulgaria, declaring that it was a matter of indifference to him whether there were one, two, or three Bulgarias. Shuvalov held that a division of Bulgaria, even with the Balkan passes in the hands of the Turks, could only be factitious— 'l'une la Bulgarie satisfaite, l'autre la Bulgarie mécontente'— and apparently urged compliance with the British view as to the passes being so controlled. This was too much for Alexander, who refused to abandon his opposition to Turkish military control of southern Bulgaria, but approved the remainder of Shuvalov's proposals.[1]

Before this was done, one reference back to London was required: to ask whether, if the proposed modifications of San Stefano were accepted, Salisbury would agree not to contest the advantages gained by the treaty for Serbia and Montenegro. Loftus had been strictly instructed by Salisbury not to intervene in the negotiations unless directly appealed to, in which case he was to support Shuvalov fully. In forwarding Shuvalov's

equipment, and activities in connexion with the volunteer fleet movement. The subscriptions for this were nominally voluntary, but were reported to be levied in some places under government pressure; consul-general Stanley (Odessa) to Salisbury, disp., no. 28, pol., 23 May, in *F.O.* 65/1015, and Vice-Consul at Taganrog, in *F.O.* 65/1016. There is much information about the volunteer fleet, from 18 May onwards, in Pobedonostsev's letters to the Tsarevich: they are mainly concerned with questions of finance and administration, and they are nearly all subsequent to the Berlin congress. Four ships were purchased from the Hamburg-Amerika line, one of them at Leith. *Pisma Pobedonostseva k Aleksandru III*, vol. i, pp. 121 ff. There is further information as to Russian naval preparations in *F.O.* 64/905, 181/566 and 567, and 65/1004. See also above, p. 472.

[1] Schweinitz to Bülow, disp., 19 May, in *G.P.*, p. 309 (criticizing Shuvalov for being too harshly anglophil); private letter of Langenau to Andrássy, 17 May, (recording Giers's admiration of Shuvalov's outspoken language to the Tsar), cited in Wittrock, *Gorčakov, Ignatiev och Šuvalov*, p. 71; Shuvalov's memoirs in *Krasny arkhiv*, vol. lix, pp. 97–8, and quoted in Hanotaux, *Histoire de la France contemporaine*, vol. iv, p. 339. Shuvalov states that the Tsar gave way in regard to Turkish military rights in southern Bulgaria, but this as the sequel shows is incorrect.

inquiry he expressed much suspicion of it as being intended to separate England from Austria-Hungary, but Salisbury was not impressed by his ambassador's misgivings and replied by giving the requisite assurance.[1]

The concessions which Shuvalov extracted from St. Petersburg were far-reaching and ultimately decisive. The Tsar regarded the proposals of the British government as offering a basis for an entente for the coming congress on the following points. Bulgaria was not to extend to the Aegean coast; its western frontier was to be so rectified as to exclude non-Bulgarian populations; it was to be divided into two provinces, one to the north of the Balkans with political autonomy under a prince, the other to the south of the Balkans with a large measure of administrative autonomy ('tracée par exemple sur celle qui existe dans les Colonies Anglaises') and a governor-general nominated with the consent of the powers for a period of five to ten years:

'L'Empereur attache une importance toute particulière au retrait de l'armée Turque de la Bulgarie méridionale. Sa Majesté ne verrait aucune securité ni garantie pour l'avenir de la population Bulgare si des troupes Ottomanes y étaient maintenues. Il appartiendrait au Congrès de statuer sur les cas où le Sultan pourrait y envoyer des troupes, en se guidant sur le principe établi au Congrès de 1856 pour le cas d'une intervention militaire ottomane dans les principautés Danubiennes.'[2]

The Tsar agreed to alter Article XV of the treaty of San Stefano so as to allow a consultative voice to the other powers, as well as to Russia, in regard to the future organization of Epirus, Thessaly, and the other Christian provinces remaining under Turkish domination. The Tsar stated that he had never had the intention of converting the war indemnity into territorial compensation and that he did not refuse to give assurances in this respect. Finally, the Tsar agreed to restore to the Turks the

---

[1] Loftus to Salisbury, tels., nos. 113 and 115, and disp., no. 530, 14 May, in *F.O.* 65/1003; Salisbury to Loftus, tel., 11 May, in *F.O.* 65/994 (instructing him not to take part in the negotiations); Salisbury to Loftus, tel., 15 May, in *F.O.* 181/567 (the draft in *F.O.* 65/994 is marked approved by the Queen); Loftus to Salisbury, tel., no. 116, and disp., no. 540, 16 May, in *F.O.* 65/1003.

[2] Article 27 of the treaty of Paris ran: 'Si le repos intérieur des Principautés se trouvait menacé ou compromis, la Sublime Porte s'entendra avec les autres Puissances contractantes sur les mesures à prendre pour maintenir ou rétablir l'ordre légal. Une intervention armée ne pourra avoir lieu sans un accord préalable entre ces Puissances.'

Alashkert valley and Bayazid in return for the consent given by the Porte to the handing over of the district of Khotur to the Shah. In consideration of Russia having thus met the principal British objections to the treaty of San Stefano, it was expected that England would not contest at the congress the other parts of the treaty. If agreement were reached with the British government as to these proposals, they would serve as an engagement at the congress between the two countries. A supplementary plea (a vestige of Ignatyev's influence) was added in favour of returning to the idea of a longitudinal division of Bulgaria, with two governors-general, with the exclusion of Ottoman troops, but without the Aegean littoral or so great an extension westward.

Such were the Russian offers with which Shuvalov left St. Petersburg on 18 May. In addition, it was understood that he was to be first plenipotentiary at the congress; Oubril second: Ignatyev was ruled out: Gorchakov was too unwell. Shuvalov halted again in Berlin and at Friedrichsruhe to confer with Bismarck. They arranged a formula for the invitations to the congress which should allow of the complete admission of a free discussion of the whole San Stefano treaty. This particular obstacle was henceforth out of the way, Salisbury readily accepting the formula, and the French *caveat* that Egypt, Syria, and the Holy Places must be excluded raising no difficulties;[1] but during the next fortnight the summoning of the congress still remained in suspense, since the British were continuing to press hard for a Russian withdrawal from before Constantinople prior to its assembly.

Bismarck was very friendly and seemed ready enough to do his utmost at the congress for Shuvalov. But the wind veered when the news came that the Tsar had reversed his decision and was sending Gorchakov: Shuvalov would be only second plenipotentiary. 'Tout est changé,' said Bismarck; 'nous resterons personnellement amis pendant le congrès; mais je ne permettrai pas au prince Gortschakoff de monter une seconde fois sur mes épaules pour s'en faire un piédestal.'[2] The memory of

---

[1] *G.P.*, pp. 313, 317; *D.D.F.*, p. 325, and cf. pp. 269–70.
[2] Shuvalov's memoirs, quoted by Hanotaux, *Histoire de la France contemporaine*, vol. iv, pp. 342–3, and by J. F. Baddeley, *Russia in the Eighties*, pp. 369–70, adding that Shuvalov had tried to secure Milyutin as the other plenipotentiary with him. There seems to be some confusion between Shuvalov's visit to Berlin and Friedrichsruhe on 20 May (*G.P.*, p. 317) and his visit to Berlin on 3–4 June on his way

1875 had burnt deep. In any case, Bismarck had no illusions as to the difficulties that still confronted the congress, and he even attempted to plead grounds of health as preventing him from presiding over it. Only the express request of the Tsar himself conveyed through Shuvalov inclined him to yield.[1] However friendly the personal relations between Bismarck and Shuvalov may have been, the moment was far from opportune for the approach which Shuvalov at this time may have made for a Russo-German alliance. Bismarck refused to be drawn and replied by lauding the virtues of the *Dreikaiserbündnis*.[2]

Late on 22 May Shuvalov arrived back in London. Next day he communicated to Salisbury the Russian concessions just summarized, in the form of two memoranda signed by him. At the same time, in explaining the views of the Tsar, he added that his master consented in principle to the period of Russian occupation in Bulgaria being more closely limited and did not object to European machinery being to some extent substituted for Russian in organizing the administration of Bulgaria. As Shuvalov confessed to Salisbury, he had bluntly told the Tsar that no concessions were to be expected from the British as regards provisions having for their object the extension of Russian influence in Bulgaria. He also declared explicitly, what was implicit in his first memorandum, that Russia adhered to the retrocession of Bessarabia, the acquisition of Kars and Batum, and the accession of territory for Montenegro.

The memoranda were immediately submitted to the cabinet,

back to St. Petersburg. Presumably it was on the latter occasion that advance news of Gorchakov's appointment arrived; although the Tsar does not seem to have taken the final decision to send Gorchakov to Berlin until after a personal visit to his sick chancellor on 4 June; extract from report of Schweinitz, 5 June, quoted by Müller, *Die Bedeutung des Berliner Kongresses für die deutsch-russischen Beziehungen*, p. 18; Schweinitz to Bülow, disp., 5 June, in *G.P.*, p. 333. Schweinitz had seen Gorchakov on 3 June and he had expressed lively hopes of being able to come to Berlin; Schweinitz to Bülow, disp., 4 June, in *G.P.*, pp. 331–2: presumably this dispatch was the extender of a telegram, which could have reached Berlin before Shuvalov's departure (night of the 4th). Giers had telegraphed to Shuvalov on 30 May that, in view of the uncertainty as to whether Gorchakov would be well enough to go to Berlin, the Tsar had decided on Shuvalov and Oubril as plenipotentiaries; text in *Seton-Watson MSS*.

[1] Radowitz, *Aufzeichnungen und Erinnerungen*, vol. ii, p. 17; Bismarck to the Emperor William, 7 Sept. 1879, in *G.P.*, vol. iii, p. 52; cf. Bismarck's speech in the Reichstag, 6 Feb. 1888.

[2] Bismarck, *Reminiscences and Reflections*, vol. ii, pp. 242–3, 246–7, but without indicating any precise date. Despite *Tatishchev*, pp. 487–8, Shuvalov's memoirs, as printed in *Krasny arkhiv*, vol. lix, do not mention any such sounding of Bismarck.

where they met with much opposition, particularly from Disraeli, as also from the Queen. The maintenance of Turkish military rights in southern Bulgaria was insisted upon, and great uneasiness was expressed as to the Asiatic settlement, while the continued refusal of the Russians to come to terms on a simultaneous withdrawal from before Constantinople caused additional suspiciousness.[1] In fact the immediate object of the British was now to make certain of Cyprus. On 24 May Salisbury telegraphed final instructions to Layard to demand of the Sultan acceptance of the defensive alliance which would ensure Cyprus and an adequate English counterweight to the Russian gains in Asiatic Turkey, threatening that refusal would result in 'the capture of Constantinople and the partition of the Empire'. On the morning of 26 May the required acceptance reached London. Thereafter the negotiations with Shuvalov could be pushed to a conclusion, though the British were still careful to hedge themselves around with reserves, since the actual convention on Cyprus was not signed until 4 June and even then there might well follow a slip betwixt cup and lip.[2] Salisbury, on 24 May, expounded to Shuvalov the British views on the memorandum in terms closely similar to the final agreement reached a week later. A first draft of the proposed engagements was then prepared, which after considerable stiffening in detail attained its final form on 28 May. The cabinet approved and on 30 May signatures were exchanged. The Anglo-Russian agreement was achieved.

From the Russian side its achievement had needed great pressure by Shuvalov upon his government, who were distrustful

[1] *Disraeli*, pp. 1166–7; *Queen Victoria's Letters, 1862–1878*, vol. ii, p. 622; Shuvalov to Gorchakov, tels., 24 and 26 May, texts in *Seton-Watson MSS*.

[2] Headlam-Morley, *Studies in diplomatic history*, particularly pp. 199–200; Temperley, 'Disraeli and Cyprus', in *English Historical Review*, vol. xlvi, pp. 274–9, 457–60, 694; Seton-Watson, *Disraeli, Gladstone, and the Eastern Question*, pp. 421–30; Lee, *Great Britain and the Cyprus Convention policy of 1878*, pp. 83–5, 98–100. Layard had the utmost difficulty in extracting the consent of the Turks and keeping them to it. The Sultan was obsessed with the idea that his life was being conspired against, and his mental delusions had the effect, amongst others, of perpetual changing of his officials (see particularly the detailed account in Raschdau, *Ein sinkendes Reich*, pp. 188–97). Layard, with his influence much imperilled by the publication of the Shuvalov–Salisbury agreements and by the handing over of Bosnia and Herzegovina by the congress, on British initiative, to Austria-Hungary, had a hard struggle to force the Turks to issue the necessary *firman* for the immediate occupation of Cyprus, which they only did on 7 July: Layard's private letters, *British Museum, Add. MSS*. 39137, especially ff. 143–6, 179–81; and 39131, especially ff. 112–13, 122–3.

as to the extent of the concessions he might allow. Shuvalov, now seriously perturbed by the British alarm at Russian acquisitions in Asia, and not aware of Salisbury's simultaneous negotiations over Cyprus, depicted the opposition in the cabinet as very strong and begged for permission to conclude immediately an engagement with Salisbury, fearing that otherwise further concessions would be demanded and final agreement rendered impossible (24 May). The Tsar, however, refused to give him *carte blanche*, demanded explanations as to the proposed frontiers, and ordered the full text of the proposed engagements to be telegraphed to St. Petersburg (26 May). Shuvalov replied with an almost despairing appeal for his master's confidence (26 May), but, on finding that Salisbury was no more ready than the Tsar to commit himself over-hurriedly, he complied and transmitted the three memoranda (28 May). Next day Giers telegraphed the Tsar's authorization to sign them.[1]

Throughout this week of 23–30 May, as during the end of April and the beginning of May, the military and naval situation around Constantinople had caused extreme difficulty. The British position still was that the congress should not meet until concurrent withdrawal had been effected. St. Petersburg and G.H.Q. at San Stefano still were insistent that there should be no withdrawal until Shumla, 'Varna, and (less emphatically) Batum had been handed over. Shuvalov frankly subordinated the military question to the paramount importance of reaching a political agreement with England and was ready in the last resort to agree to retirement before the opening of the congress, but his pleadings to be empowered to give such an undertaking had no effect.[2]

Fortunately, however, the ambassador and his government did see eye to eye on one major issue. 'Très désirable', telegraphed Giers on 25 May, 'que réussissiez à séparer entièrement question militaire de celle du Congrès.' Shuvalov heartily agreed. The Russians were not binding up the surrender of the fortresses with agreement to the congress: they wanted the

---

[1] Shuvalov to Gorchakov, tels., 23, 24, 26, 28 May; Giers to Shuvalov, tels., 26, 29, and 30 May; texts in *Seton-Watson MSS*. It should be mentioned that during this week Shuvalov had the assistance at the embassy of a special Balkan expert, Col. Bogolyubov, three weeks later one of the Russian military experts at the Berlin congress.

[2] Shuvalov to Gorchakov, tels., 24 and 26 May; Giers to Shuvalov, tels., 25 and 27 May; texts in *Seton-Watson MSS*.

fortresses if possible before the congress met, but they did not want any retirement: if they could separate this question from that of the congress, so much the better. Shuvalov therefore devoted his utmost energies to securing from Salisbury acceptance of the memoranda and of the congress without insisting on previous withdrawal. By 29 May he had succeeded in the former task, but Salisbury was still holding to retirement as a necessary preliminary to the congress, encouraged, so Shuvalov learnt, by some rash remark of the wearied Tsar to Wellesley to the effect that he would, after all, accept retirement without the handing over of the fortresses. It was only after protracted efforts that Shuvalov could send word (2 June) that Salisbury accepted the congress without laying down conditions as to withdrawal. The Russians, thanks to their ambassador, had scored a decided success.[1]

On the other hand, the Anglo-Russian agreement itself was far from constituting a decided success, even though it went far towards ensuring peace. As is now to be seen, the price was very severe. The main basis of the agreement was provided by Shuvalov's memorandum of 23 May, which, with important additions and modifications from the British side, constituted the first memorandum signed on 30 May. A second set out the points upon which the British reserved full liberty of action at the congress. A third, signed on 31 May, represented the Russian attempt to reassure the British government as to the acquisition of Batum and Kars by offering to negotiate a secret engagement to the effect that Russia had no intention of extending her conquests in Asia beyond the limits assigned in the treaty of San Stefano, as modified by the retrocession already conceded of Bayazid and the Alashkert valley. Certain explanations and supplementary points were made in four letters exchanged between the two negotiators.

The most notable feature of the first memorandum, which professed to record the points of agreement between Russia and England, was the treatment of the question of the Sultan's military rights in the southern portion of Bulgaria. Involved language thinly veiled the failure to reach any real compromise,

---

[1] Giers to Shuvalov, tels., 25, 27, 30, and 31 May; Shuvalov to Gorchakov, tels., 26, 29, 30, and 31 May, 2 June; texts in *Seton-Watson MSS.* See also Bülow to Bismarck, 1 June (repeating news from St. Petersburg); Münster to Bismarck, 2 June; Schweinitz to Bülow, 4 June; in *G.P.*, pp. 322–5. See also below, pp. 514–16.

and it was apparent that, unless further negotiations cleared the ground before the meeting of the congress, there would be a hard struggle as between the Russian thesis of minimum military rights and the British thesis of maximum military rights. A second problem which would obviously provide much difficulty at the congress was that of the boundaries of the two Bulgarias, since nothing was specified about them in detail. One main point was, however, clear: Bulgaria was to be divided into a northern and a southern portion. The English put out of court the Russian resurrection of the idea of a longitudinal division, which had never been seriously entertained by Shuvalov and as to which he made a purely formal reserve. The Balkan range was to be the boundary between the two Bulgarias, but the question was not raised as to what exactly constituted that range. The western frontier of Bulgaria was in principle not to extend farther westward than the rough line Novi Bazar–Seres, a concession to the Russians which suggests that Salisbury was not using large-scale maps. The southern part of Bulgaria was to be removed from the Aegean coast to the line proposed at the Constantinople conference, but its frontier around Adrianople and to the Black Sea was left in dispute. The third main problem, that of Asiatic Turkey, was resolved by Russia giving up Bayazid and the Alashkert valley and Turkey transferring Khotur to Persia, by the engagement that Russia would make no further acquisitions in Asiatic Turkey, and by the statement of the British that they would not contest by arms the Russian territorial gains there. They also stipulated that there must be no exclusive Russian claims on behalf of the Armenians, and that the Russian indemnity must not in any way jeopardize the prior claims of British creditors of Turkey. Reluctant consent to the retrocession of Bessarabia was formally given.

In view of agreement to the above modifications of the treaty of San Stefano the British government undertook not to contest its remaining articles, if after full discussion at the congress Russia persisted in maintaining them. But this engagement was immediately limited by the second memorandum consisting of six points upon which Salisbury reserved full freedom of action, and four of these were of great importance—European participation in the organization of the two Bulgarias, the duration and character of the Russian occupation of Bulgaria and communications through Roumania, the navigation of the Danube, and the question of the Straits. In regard to the last, the British entirely reserved their action at the congress, while Shuvalov, calling attention to Derby's declaration of 6 May 1877 on the desirability of maintaining the *status quo*, recorded his intention to insist upon that at the congress. The precaution was taken of making quite clear that the Dobrudja, if refused by Roumania, should not remain in the hands of Russia. Strict secrecy again, except towards the German government, was to be maintained in respect of the memoranda and letters exchanged.

The whole constituted a very notable success for British diplomacy. Salisbury had agreed to Bessarabia going back to Russia—which had never been seriously disputed. He had agreed to the acquisition of Batum and Kars, but had saved the Trebizond–Erzerum–Tabriz caravan route, and had secretly countered with the Cyprus convention, at the time regarded as of extreme value. He had agreed to the northern Bulgaria becoming a politically autonomous principality—which again had never been seriously disputed. He had agreed not to contest the Montenegrin and Serbian boundaries, except by implication in so far as the latter marched with Bulgaria, but he had said nothing of any kind of support for the Russian desires in this quarter against Austria-Hungary. On almost every other question arising from the treaty the net result of the British additions and reservations was to provide the maximum possibility of amendment, particularly when account is also taken of the Austrian demands, which were not to any appreciable degree cross-countered by the agreement. It is probably fair to say that Shuvalov, convinced that the British government meant to fight for the maintenance of Turkey as an independent political power, was aiming at peace at any price, save that of Bessarabia, Antivari for Montenegro, Kars and Batum. Feeling sure almost from the beginning of the negotiations that the British yielded those acquisitions, he was prepared to meet them more than half-way on the remainder of the treaty. It is also fair to add that there is no evidence that Shuvalov might have induced the British to accept less than what they obtained by the agreements. Salisbury in sending them to Lyons at the Paris embassy summed them up: 'The upshot of the matter has been that the Czar yields substantially all we want in Bulgaria and as to the Greek provinces, but sticks to his text as to

Montenegro, Bessarabia, and the Armenian conquests, except Bayazid.'[1]

Russia had virtually sacrificed the essentials of the Balkan settlement of San Stefano, for she still had come to no terms with Austria-Hungary, without which the fate of Serbia, Novi Bazar, and Montenegro remained in the balance; and her agreement with England did not mean the isolation of Austria-Hungary. On the contrary, during the final period of conversations with Shuvalov, Salisbury not only secured his agreement with the Sultan to offset Kars and Batum, but also renewed his negotiations with Vienna and brought them to a conclusion with the signature on 6 June of what Andrássy styled 'a general agreement as between gentlemen'. By this the northern Bulgaria was not to extend south or south-west of the Balkan range nor westward of the Morava; the Russians were to be pressed to evacuate Bulgaria within six and Roumania within nine months and to cut down their army of occupation to 20,000; European commissaries were to be substituted for Russian in the relevant articles of San Stefano; the Sultan was to be ensured adequate political and military control of the southern portion of Bulgaria; and finally England would support any proposal on Bosnia brought forward by Austria-Hungary at the congress. Andrássy had tried to obtain British support on Herzegovina and Novi Bazar, but Salisbury had not been prepared to add Herzegovina to Bosnia without a qualification that he did not bind himself to contest definitely the boundaries assigned to Montenegro and Serbia, whereupon Andrássy preferred to sign with the omission of any reference to Herzegovina.[2]

Against this the Russians had nothing to set. Their maximum concessions to Vienna were totally unacceptable, and after 8 May no effective steps had been taken in that quarter. They had, indeed, in the negotiations with Salisbury, given way on their demand to Vienna for a longitudinal division of Bulgaria, and they had already consented to an Austrian occupation of Bosnia

---

[1] Letter of Salisbury to Lyons, 29 May, quoted in Lord Newton, *Lord Lyons*, vol. ii, p. 142.

[2] *Wertheimer*, vol. iii, pp. 113, 115–16; Gauld, 'The Anglo-Austrian Agreement of 1878', in *English Historical Review*, vol. xli, pp. 108–12, utilizing the foreign office papers in the Public Record Office. The latter prints the text of the agreement which Elliot was instructed on 27 May to sign, and which was finally signed on 6 June in the same form, save for an additional clause providing against any possibility of the Dobrudja being left in Russian hands.

and Herzegovina, but as June opened they still maintained their opposition to Austrian designs on Novi Bazar together with insistence on Montenegrin access to the sea. In no respect perhaps was the lack of any dominating hand at the helm of Russian foreign policy more fatal than in the complete failure to co-ordinate negotiations in London and in Vienna, and to prevent the Serbian and Montenegrin problems drifting into an incoherent impasse. Here Shuvalov, London-centred, with his lack of Balkan knowledge and interest, had done nothing to remedy the indecision and confusion of his government, but he did at least know his own mind: a definitive peace treaty must be obtained.

He did not need the promptings of Salisbury to hurry once more to St. Petersburg to counteract last-minute hostility to his policy and to make final preparations for the congress. Leaving London late on 2 June he was back on the Neva on the 6th. Although the war party was again dangerous, the situation was less tense than a month before. Ignatyev had disappeared from the scene of action: on 23 May he had had a farewell audience with the Tsar, and then had retired to his Kiev estates.[1] Not till the Tsarevich succeeded his murdered father was he recalled to power, for a brief spell striving to direct the internal fortunes of his country as earlier he had struggled to control her fate abroad. The riddance of Ignatyev was to some extent offset in Shuvalov's eyes by the unwelcome news that Gorchakov was after all to represent Russia at the congress.[2] The old chancellor, fired by the news that Disraeli would be coming to Berlin, was determined now, despite his ailments, to appear on a gala stage for a final *nunc plaudite*. Two days before Shuvalov's arrival the Tsar had paid a personal visit to his sick-bed and accorded him his desire.[3]

The more immediately awkward affair was the Baryatinsky campaign, then at its height in St. Petersburg. Field-Marshal Prince Baryatinsky had gained his reputation as the final subduer

---

[1] Ignatyev's memoirs, in *I.V.*, vol. cxliv, p. 53.

[2] Shuvalov in his memoirs, in *Krasny arkhiv*, vol. lix, p. 100, described Gorchakov as by then an absolute nullity who would be certain to irritate Bismarck to the detriment of Russian interests. But he also made a show of representing himself as determined to drag Gorchakov to Berlin to defend his handiwork; Károlyi to Andrássy, 5 June, cited in *Wertheimer*, vol. iii, p. 118.

[3] Schweinitz to Bülow, disp., 4 June, in *G.P.*, pp. 331–2; extract from report of Schweinit 5z, June, quoted by Müller, *Die Bedeutung des Berliner Kongresses* . . ., p. 18. See also above, p. 489, note 2.

of the Caucasus. He was a great, Russian nobleman; eccentric and blindly self-confident; a long-standing opponent of Milyutin, and in close touch with the panslavs, especially through his friend Fadeyev, whose slogan 'the way to Constantinople lies through Vienna' he heartily echoed. During the war there was much talk as to why he was not employed. Now, when the Grand Duke Nicholas so miserably belied the hopes of all good Russians for Constantinople and an ignominious peace seemed to be at hand, Baryatinsky was to come to the rescue. Having lived for sixteen years in retirement, with much bad health, out of touch with affairs, out of favour with the Tsar, and at odds with the government, he was in fact very unlikely to be able to fill the role which nationalist opinion assigned to him. Ignatyev, returning from Vienna at the beginning of April, carefully arranged a meeting *en route* and primed him with the latest news. At the end of that month he, very characteristically, addressed a letter to the Tsar offering his services as commander-in-chief. The offer was declined. But powerful influences were at work, and the Tsar ended by calling him to St. Petersburg, where he plunged into a network of intrigues and plans, elaborating his favourite ideas of a war against Austria-Hungary and an advance, in alliance with Persia, into Afghanistan. Exactly at the time of Shuvalov's arrival the Baryatinsky campaign reached its climax with the most circumstantial reports of a great massing of troops on the Austrian frontier and Baryatinsky in command. Almost the first action of Shuvalov had to be to deny the truth of the appointment, which Loftus had already reported to London; just as the month before he had had to try to explain away the volunteer fleet campaign.[1]

The real significance of Baryatinsky was as an emblem of all that proudly nationalist opinion which, whether labelled panslav or not, repudiated or ignored the bonds of western forging which shackled Russia; which was demanding that Russia should act alone, break loose from old dynastic ties and the mental assumptions of Romanov diplomacy, and, a world to herself, should look out upon the divided world of Europe with the eyes of Moscow, not of St. Petersburg. Russian national-

[1] Zissermann, *Feldmarschal Knyaz Aleksandr Ivanovich Baryatinsky, 1815–1879*, especially vol. iii, pp. 271–3; Ignatyev's memoirs, in *I.V.*, vol. cxliii, p. 377; Loftus to Salisbury, tels., 7 and 8 June, in *F.O.* 65/1004; Polovtsov's diary, under date 6 June, in *Krasny arkhiv*, vol. xxxiii, p. 195; Anuchin's diary, in *R.S.*, vol. cl, p. 4, recording Shuvalov's talk of Baryatinsky expounding to him his plans for a war with Austria.

ism in this sense was already a potent force, but it had not yet
gained a strong enough influence among the directing bureaucracy around the Tsar. Under his son it was to make decisive
advances, but in this summer of 1878 it failed finally to make a
capture of Alexander II.

If Shuvalov is to be at all trusted, and with full allowance
for his concern to defend his own policy, the Tsar was convinced
that he was threatened with war with England, and probably
also with Austria-Hungary, and that concessions, however much
against the grain, were necessary. Milyutin was emphatic as
to the technical impossibility of war and as to the imperative
necessity of the congress not breaking down. Gorchakov for his
part declared that his desire for peace was exceeded only by
Milyutin's.[1] In this prevailing atmosphere in the key positions
Shuvalov could gain the day. Two imperial councils were
held, on 8 and 9 June, which debated the situation and laid
down the lines of action for the delegation to the congress. The
unsolved problem of the simultaneous retirement of Russians
and British from before Constantinople remained acute, but
the council would not offer more than the giving up of the
Chataldja lines and the restoration of Turkish prisoners of war
in exchange for Turkish abandonment of Shumla. Thus the
matter rested in uneasy suspense, to cause an initial storm a
week later in Berlin.[2]

How far the questions arising out of the Anglo-Russian agreement gave rise to prolonged discussions in the imperial councils
is not clear, but the unresolved differences with Vienna were
certainly very prominent. It was decided not to oppose even
annexation of Bosnia and Herzegovina, but to insist on the San
Stefano terms for Montenegro, and as a last resort, if the Austrians and Turks pushed matters to extremes, to appeal to the
congress to prevent war. If for any reason the Austrians did not
take the expected action in Bosnia and Herzegovina and were
to oppose the retrocession of Bessarabia, the Russian plenipotentiaries were to stand firm and declare that Russia would

---

[1] Nelidov's memoirs, in *Revue des deux mondes*, 15 Nov. 1915, vol. xxx, p. 260 (and
cf. p. 263), Anuchin's diary, in *R.S.*, vol. cl, p. 4, Schweinitz, *Briefwechsel*, p. 141
(all recording Shuvalov's subsequent statements, perhaps overcoloured, as to the
desire of the Tsar and particularly Milyutin for peace); Schweinitz, *Denkwürdigkeiten*, vol. ii, p. 32 (on Gorchakov).

[2] Salisbury to Loftus, disp., no. 353, 3 June, in *F.O.* 181/567; Loftus to Salisbury,
disp., nos. 598, 599, 600, 8 June, and nos. 603, 604, 9 June, in *F.O.* 65/1004.

fight for it. If the Turks refused to evacuate Batum (a possibility which much exercised the Russians), they were to declare that Russia would carry out the decisions of the congress only if the Sultan handed it over, and that in the last resort she would use force. The question of Austrian claims on Novi Bazar, which had an important bearing on the Montenegrin boundaries, seems to have been left in confusion. Milyutin and Shuvalov in this case argued against concessions, but apparently no decided policy was adopted. On Bulgaria evidence is lacking, but the Russian attitude at Berlin shows at least that Turkish military rights in southern Bulgaria were to be combated to the full.[1]

On the whole it may be said that the course of action laid down lacked both clarity of purpose and decision as to means. Shuvalov possessed the former, but his control was disputed and uncertain. He, like Ignatyev, had played his hand—a very different hand—and so far he had won. It remained for him to fight his last and most arduous battle, almost unaided, in the congress of Berlin.

[1] *Tatishchev*, pp. 490–1; Anuchin's diary, for 17 June, in *R.S.*, vol. cxlix, p. 244 (for Novi Bazar). Tatishchev uses, very unsatisfactorily, the journal of the imperial council of 9 June. He enumerates a long series of questions put by Shuvalov, but gives no indication of the answers elaborated, merely stating that the answers and the decisions of the council served as instructions for the congress. Perhaps the account given by Shuvalov in his memoirs is substantially right, though he was writing two years later (*Krasny arkhiv*, vol. lix, p. 100): only one council with the Tsar was held; it lasted less than two hours; at it the instructions for the congress, very hastily drawn up on the same day, were approved; most of the essential points had not been considered when the council was declared closed; Gorchakov was so ailing that he understood nothing of what was said. Later, p. 102, he definitely states that the Russian plenipotentiaries had explicit instructions not to yield on Novi Bazar; so too in Baddeley, *Russia in the Eighties*, p. 372.

KARÓLYI   GORCHAKOV   BEACONSFIELD   ANDRÁSSY   BISMARCK   SHUVALOV   BÜLOW   MEHEMET ALI
HAYMERLE   DE LANNAY   WADDINGTON   RADOWITZ   OUBRIL   BUCHER   SADULLAH BEY   CARATHÉODORY PASHA
HOHENLOHE   MOÜY   DEPREZ   HOLSTEIN   H. BISMARCK   RUSSELL   SALISBURY
CORTI   ST. VALLIER   BUSCH

THE CONGRESS OF BERLIN

From the painting by A. Werner

XVIII

BERLIN

'JE ne veux pas m'éteindre comme une lampe qui file, je veux me coucher comme un astre.' 'Je ne veux pas paraître devant Dieu sans avoir présidé au moins un congrès en Europe.' Duly the congress was assembled which was to accomplish the most important settlement of the century in regard to the Ottoman empire. Duly Gorchakov was present at the head of the Russian delegation.

He was almost eighty, and much enfeebled; very senile, in his wheel-chair; very vain, sitting in a first-floor window of the Russian embassy in full view of the crowds in the street; very petulant, flinging his paper-knife about the congress table.[1] Like Disraeli, he left most of the real work to his second in command, was hazy as to particular points at issue, and was lamentable with maps. His experts soon found that he could not be trusted with anything secret. To one sitting (which was not concerned with Asiatic frontiers) he brought along an extremely confidential map showing the limits of the Russian concessions in Asia and spread it out before the curious eyes of Odo Russell, until Shuvalov succeeded in removing it. Thereafter all secret maps were, so far as possible, kept from him. Talking with the Montenegrin delegates just before the opening of the congress, he amazed them by his complete ignorance in urging them to give Podgorica or Spuž to Serbia—thinking that they were in Novi Bazar. When they expostulated, Gorchakov summed up: 'Well, you must give up something: I am weak in the geography of these parts. I am only concerned with the broad lines.'[2] Somewhat similar tales are told of Fiume and Teschen of a far abler man than Gorchakov at a far more momentous conference than Berlin. It is not the business of statesmen to carry in their heads the precise location of Monte-

---

[1] The Russians at Berlin differ as to Gorchakov's illness. Nelidov, *Revue des deux mondes*, 15 Nov. 1915, vol. xxx, p. 259, directly accuses him of feigning illness in absenting himself from the three humiliating sittings which unmade the San Stefano Bulgaria. Anuchin, *R.S.*, vol. cl, pp. 12, 231, 234–5, emphasizes that he only missed three out of the twenty sittings, and accepts the story that he really was ill, though not seriously.

[2] Anuchin's diary in *R.S.*, vol. cl, p. 9, vol. cxlix, pp. 55–6.

negrin villages, but they lose in effectiveness if they do not prime themselves adequately in advance with geography.

With Shuvalov Gorchakov was on the worst of terms, and he did not scruple to criticize his conduct of negotiations in the most damaging terms in private letters to St. Petersburg. Shuvalov's disgust was all the more violent, when he learnt of this a month later, since he had attempted to forearm himself against any such intrigues by extracting a promise from Gorchakov and Oubril at the beginning of the congress that none of them should send home any reports which had not first been seen by the other two.[1] During the critical second week of the congress, when the tension between the Russians and the British was at its height and Shuvalov's nerves were more than usually on edge with his superior's inconsistencies and desire to escape responsibility, Shuvalov talked of resigning if a new first plenipotentiary were not appointed.[2] Salisbury used to give a description of an outburst, which is typical of their relations, when Gorchakov completely lost his temper and flung out of the room repudiating all the concessions made in the Anglo-Russian agreement. Shuvalov, a silent spectator of the scene, followed him out, whispering to Salisbury: 'Attendez-moi,—je reviens. Faites pas attention—ce sont là un tas de bêtises.' A little later he returned and resumed as though nothing had occurred.[3]

Probably Gorchakov was in large part deliberately manœuvring so as to cast upon Shuvalov the onus of the losing battle which Russia fought at Berlin. All at the congress agree that Shuvalov played his most thankless part with the utmost skill. Bismarck considered him and Disraeli the two principal figures of the congress. Disraeli himself described him as fighting 'a

[1] Radowitz to Bismarck, 8 Aug. 1878 (repeating a long conversation with Shuvalov), *G.P.*, vol. iii, p. 3: so too Shuvalov's memoirs, in *Krasny arkhiv*, vol. lix, p. 101, where Shuvalov adds that he had armed himself with the war office cipher in case of need for personal communication with Milyutin, though in fact he did not use it.

[2] Anuchin's diary, referring to 17 June, in *R.S.*, vol. cxlix, p. 244. He states later, vol. cl, p. 227, that on 23 June Shuvalov sent a very pessimistic report to St. Petersburg, asking, if possible, for the appointment of Milyutin in the place of Gorchakov. This is not borne out, though it is not contradicted, by Hohenlohe, *Memoirs*, vol. ii, p. 215, diary entry 25 June, who records Shuvalov telling him that on 23 June he had prevented Gorchakov telegraphing to the Tsar that he was ill and could not accept responsibility for the last resolutions by threatening, if that telegram were sent, to telegraph himself asking the Tsar to appoint some one in his place: Gorchakov's telegram was therefore stopped.

[3] *Salisbury*, p. 284.

difficult and losing battle with marvellous talent and temper. He is a first-rate parliamentary debater, never takes a note, and yet in reply never misses a point.'[1] Always the polished, charming *grand seigneur*; holding his own against every one; 'like a stag under pursuit that shows its horns when too hard pressed'; a tireless worker, struggling to find an honourable exit for his country; he was the model diplomatist.[2] A youthful member of the British delegation wrote of him: 'Schouvaloff has gained immense prestige here for his ability and conciliatory manner. He has been indefatigable in Congress, Committee of Delimitation, Committee of Redaction, Private Conferences, etc. and he has also managed to pay his usual attentions to the women and the wine.'[3] But the most striking testimony to Shuvalov's skill comes from other members of the Russian delegation. Nelidov, Anuchin and Bobrikov (two of the military experts) scarcely knew him at all previously: Baron Frederiks, the courtier, did, and disliked him strongly. All of them were fiercely hostile to his policy of extreme conciliation. Yet all ungrudgingly praise him for his great abilities, his power of hard work, his friendliness, and the dignity with which he represented Russia. He won the hearts of the military experts by fully admitting his ignorance about the Balkans and then proceeding to be coached by them with assiduous rapidity. He spoke French, German, and English excellently, besides Russian, but quick and ready though he was he never trusted his own gifts too far and was scrupulous in fully getting up his case, usually with Nelidov and Anuchin, before every important meeting.[4]

He received little or no help from the third Russian plenipotentiary, Oubril. He may perhaps have exercised more influence than was supposed in acting as a link between Shuvalov and Gorchakov, with both of whom he kept on good terms,[5]

[1] Letter of Disraeli to Lady Bradford, 26 June, Marquis of Zetland, *The Letters of Disraeli to Lady Bradford and Lady Chesterfield*, vol. ii, p. 175.
[2] Blowitz, *My Memoirs*, pp. 164–5 (recording a conversation with Bismarck); Radowitz, *Aufzeichnungen und Erinnerungen*, vol. ii, pp. 24–5.
[3] Private letter of Bertie (later Lord Bertie) to Tenterden, 14 July, in *Tenterden Papers, F.O.* 363/1.
[4] Nelidov's memoirs in *Revue des deux mondes*, 15 Nov. 1915, vol. xxx, p. 257; Bobrikov's memoirs in *R.S.*, vol. cliii, p. 284; Anuchin's diary in *R.S.*, vol. cxlix, pp. 241, 242 (including Jomini's praise of Shuvalov), 253–4 (Baron Frederiks's); vol. cl, pp. 12, 231; vol. clii, p. 486.
[5] De Moüy, *Souvenirs et causeries d'un diplomate*, p. 115, is alone in speaking well of Oubril.

but his main asset was his kitchen. Of the excellence of that there was no possible doubt. It was said of him: 'Parmi les choses que je jugerais absolument idéales, serait de pouvoir me payer Oubril comme maître d'hôtel.'[1] This summing up represented the general opinion of the man who had been for almost sixteen years in charge of the Russian embassy in Berlin.

The advisers and experts who made up the remainder of the Russian delegation were unable, in any case, to bring to Shuvalov's assistance that weight and prestige which could belong only to plenipotentiaries. Jomini, Gorchakov's most trusted confidant on the permanent staff of the foreign office, was experienced enough on the diplomatic stage and could always be relied upon with his pen, but he contributed nothing of special value. Nelidov, with his knowledge of Constantinople and the making of the treaty of San Stefano, seemed an obvious choice, but in fact he had only been added to the delegation as a second string at the last moment. He had left Constantinople in the middle of May, depressed and disappointed, on Lobanov's arrival as ambassador, and had retired to join his wife and family at Heidelberg without travelling through Russia. Thence he was suddenly summoned to join the delegation in Berlin, where he arrived unprepared, and sore and angry both with his foreign office and with Shuvalov.[2]

The three military experts were competent and experienced men: Colonel Bogolyubov for the Montenegrin frontiers, Major-General Bobrikov for the Serbian, Colonel Anuchin for the Bulgarian. They knew their ground well and were all three fresh from the Balkans. Anuchin had been one of Cherkasky's right-hand men in administering the infant Bulgaria: like Nelidov, he had been summoned to Berlin at the last moment and arrived without papers or maps. Bobrikov was almost as much at home in Roumania, Bulgaria, and Montenegro as he was in Serbia, where he had been the Grand Duke Nicholas's representative since September 1877. He was much perturbed by the clumsiness of Russian policy in antagonizing the Serbs with the Bulgars, and realized that compact solidarity not size was the essential; hence he did not regard a big Bulgaria

[1] Radowitz, *Aufzeichnungen und Erinnerungen*, vol. ii, p. 25.
[2] Nelidov's memoirs, in *Revue des deux mondes*, 15 Nov. 1915, vol. xxx, pp. 254–6. Gorchakov had wished to take to Berlin the consul-general in Paris, Cumani, Nelidov's predecessor at Constantinople and a recognized Balkan expert, but this proved impossible, so Nelidov was called in at the last moment to take his place.

stretching to the Aegean as necessary, but did so regard a linking up of the Serbian and Montenegrin frontiers.[1] Strong in
technical knowledge of the Balkans, the Russians with the
carelessness they so often showed in regard to the Caucasus
front did not provide themselves with a single Asiatic expert.
They fell back on the singularly ineffective expedient of impressing the services of an ex-consul at Aleppo, Nicholas Ivanov,
partly under the impression, it seems, that he had been at
Erzerum.[2]

   This was not a powerful team, even had they worked together
as such, with which to oppose the British and the Austro-
Hungarians. Disraeli at the head of the British delegation was
the lion of the congress. 'Der alte Jude, das ist der Mann.'
Prime Minister and literary light combined, Berlin devoured
his novels and crowded invitations and favours upon him, the
Crown Princess naturally leading the way. Disraeli was delighted with them. He was seventy-three and at the end very
unwell, but he never flinched either from social routs or from
emphatic battling for British interests. His letters and diary for
the Queen were as sparkling and judicious as ever. To another
correspondent he summed up the situation, at the beginning of
July, with all his accustomed verve: 'Gorchakov is not dying,
but very lively and always talking; Schou: has shown considerable ability in his management of business; Andrassy is an
English convert; and P. Bismarck, with one hand full of cherries,
and the other of shrimps, eaten alternately, complains he cannot
sleep and must go to Kissingen.'[3] He opened badly with Bismarck, but they soon became very friendly. Bismarck never
failed to appreciate courage and decision. In the work of the
congress no doubt Salisbury found it hard to keep him straight.
'What with deafness, ignorance of French, and Bismarck's
extraordinary mode of speech, Beaconsfield has the dimmest
idea of what is going on—understands everything crossways—
and imagines a perpetual conspiracy.' His 'perfect disregard

---

[1] Bobrikov's memoirs, in *Russky vestnik*, Dec. 1889, pp. 5–7.
[2] Anuchin's diary, in *R.S.*, vol. clii, p. 496; Nelidov's memoirs, loc. cit., p. 268.
The other members of the delegation were Arapov and Butenev, from the Berlin
embassy; Baron Frederiks, Count Adlerberg (from the London embassy), Kotzebue,
and Sorokin. Gorchakov's son Michael, the minister at Berne, was also present
as a factotum for his father. Shuvalov's private secretary was A. Raffalovich,
through whom Hanotaux obtained access to Shuvalov's unpublished memoirs.
[3] Disraeli to Tenterden, private letter, 2 July, in *Tenterden Papers*, F.O. 363/1.

for facts', his confusion over details, his muddles with maps
added heavily to Salisbury's difficulties with 'the labouring oar'.
None the less it was Disraeli who provided the decisive weight
and the ascendancy of personality. Though Gorchakov beat
him in the confused wrangle over Batum, he had his way in
what he regarded as essential: Bulgaria, Eastern Rumelia, and
Turkish military control of the Balkan passes. He may have
been short-sighted and miscalculating, but he knew what he
wanted and he secured it.

Salisbury has left in his private letters an incisive view of the
congress and particularly of his working difficulties with his
chief. There is no doubt that, as with Shuvalov, the main brunt
of the detailed work fell on him. Such work was of a kind in
which neither then nor later Salisbury excelled. For at an
international conference it involved a suppleness, a tactfulness,
a capacity for 'talking things over', which were not qualities
which he possessed or gave foreign observers the impression of
possessing. Preferring himself to work alone, almost unaided,
behind the double doors of Hatfield, Berlin represented the
opposite extreme of what was congenial to him. 'Heat here is
extreme—the place detestable. At Potsdam there are mosqui-
toes—here there are minor Powers. I don't know which is
worst.' In any case, he had a heavy and ungrateful part to play.
His agreements with Shuvalov had eased but had not removed
Anglo-Russian divergences. Their publication in the *Globe* on
the very opening of the congress created an unpleasant sensa-
tion in England, which for some weeks could not be countered
by the announcement of the acquisition of Cyprus. The cabinet
were nervously pressing the British plenipotentiaries. The
general situation was one in which the British at Berlin showed
themselves unbending and provocative. Disraeli quite rightly
confined himself in the main to broad essentials: it fell to Salisbury to fight persistently in detail and to raise secondary issues.
Hence it is not surprising that he encountered much dislike,
however much his competence and industry were recognized.
The Germans did not think well of him; he made too much of
details, was awkward or rude in discussion, and did not get on
well with Bismarck.[1] He began gratingly enough when at the

---

[1] Radowitz, *Aufzeichnungen und Erinnerungen*, vol. ii, pp. 26, 47. Caratheodory
Pasha has a typical story of Bismarck's angry impatience with Salisbury over the
Lazes: 'My lord, je ne doute pas que les Lazes ne fassent partie des intéressantes

second sitting of the congress he defended the British proposals as not entirely annihilating the results of the war; whereupon Shuvalov brusquely retorted that Russia had come to Berlin to co-ordinate the treaty of San Stefano with the general interests of Europe, not to annihilate the results of her victories. He was regarded as the tactician of the British delegation and earned correspondingly unfavourable criticism. His frequent appeals to humanitarian feelings, when it suited the English case, rang hollow. Nelidov disgustedly wrote him off as a 'born liar and unabashed double-dealer'.[1]

The third British plenipotentiary, Lord Odo Russell, produced a completely different effect. Very popular as ambassador in Berlin, both with the foreign office and in society, he was on excellent, confidential terms with the other diplomats and played his secondary role with calmness and effect. He and his charming wife were the opposite numbers to the Károlyis in the Austro-Hungarian embassy, with whom they vied in the brilliance of their *soirées*.

As Károlyi's leader had come of course Andrássy; to Salisbury's eye, 'thinner and gypsyer than ever'; to Anuchin's, 'evil and lean, with shaggy hair and hideous hands always clasped in front of him'. With an assortment of marvellous uniforms and an air less of a negotiator than of 'un artiste ardent ou d'un capitaine héroïque', he bargained domineeringly with the Serbs and Turks, was on cordial terms with Bismarck, played in closely with the English, and got, almost, all that he wanted. 'Andrassy, très cordial, jouant en chevalier dans ses tête-à-tête avec moi', Shuvalov wrote privately, 'devient tout différent, lorqu'il est en présence des Anglais et se fait le servile admirateur de chacune des paroles qui tombent des lèvres de Beaconsfield

populations orientales. Seulement, je me demande si ça vaut réellement la peine qu'on leur consacre son temps, surtout aux approches de la canicule.' Bareilles, *Le rapport secret sur le Congrès de Berlin adressé . . . par Carathéodory Pacha*, pp. 71–2. Another incident as to Salisbury and the Lazes, though doubly vouched for, smacks of elaboration. Salisbury was proposing to the congress a frontier alteration to protect 'les intérêts d'une vaillante nationalité mussulmane qui se refuse à la domination russe'. Shuvalov ironically asked if he might be informed of the name of this interesting people who enjoyed the noble lord's protection. There was a long and awkward pause. Salisbury had mislaid his notes and could not remember the name. Then Odo Russell came to the rescue and Salisbury belatedly produced the Lazes. Busch's diary, under date 6 July, in *Deutsche Rundschau*, vol. cxli, p. 377; Radowitz, *Aufzeichnungen und Erinnerungen*, vol. ii, p. 56.

[1] Private letter of Nelidov to Ignatyev, in Ignatyev's memoirs, *I.V.*, vol. cxliv, p. 333.

et de Salisbury.'[1] However opportune it was for the Austrians to range themselves behind the English in their sustained opposition to the Russians, it was by no means due merely to such tactics that they came so well out of the congress. Taken as a whole they had the strongest delegation of any of the powers. To Andrássy's prestige and authority and Károlyi's social gifts and seventeen years' knowledge of Berlin were added Haymerle's expert diplomatic skill and the technical backing of a group of first-rate and excellently prepared assistants. Haymerle —'a little snake' and the worst of Russia's enemies, as Nelidov dubbed him—was indefatigable in details and did the main work for Austria-Hungary behind the scenes, with conspicuous success. Coming from the Rome embassy he had also had earlier experience of Constantinople. To back him admirably he had Baron Schwegel, the very influential director of the commercial section at the Ballplatz; Baron Mayr, formerly in the St. Petersburg and Constantinople embassies; Kosjek, an ex-dragoman from Constantinople; and Thömmel, just back from Cettinje, military specialist on the western Balkans. Fully armed with knowledge, hard-working, hard to move, they proved a formidable combination.

The two Latin powers, for obvious reasons, remained in the background. The French, ill at ease in Berlin but treated with marked friendliness by the Germans, played a difficult role with dignity and skill. Waddington won high praise, save from Disraeli, who misjudged him badly, describing him as a grocer and thinking him weak and sly. St. Vallier, the new ambassador, much liked by Bismarck (delighted to be rid of Gontaut-Biron), was tireless and faultless, even though racked by an incurable liver disease. Desprez, from the Quai d'Orsay, 'l'homme du protocol et du bureau', was given the major share in the technical drafting of the treaty. 'Quand on touche le directeur politique de France,' the gibe ran, 'comme un bouton électrique, il en sorte une note diplomatique.'[2]

---

[1] *Salisbury*, p. 279; Anuchin's diary, in *R.S.*, vol. cl, p. 231; de Moüy, *Souvenirs et causeries d'un diplomate*, p. 102; extract from letter of Shuvalov to Giers, 19 June, in Goriainow, *Le Bosphore et les Dardanelles*, p. 378.

[2] Du Chastel, *Les événements d'Orient et le Congrès de Berlin*, p. 50. *D.D.F.*, p. 279, reveal that in mid-March a private suggestion was made by Bismarck to Waddington that he should preside over the conference. It is not clear whether Bismarck hoped thereby that the conference would be transferred to Paris. For Waddington's favourable impression of Bismarck see extract from a letter to his wife, 11 June,

Of the two Italians one was a sugary, old-style diplomat, de Launay, for many years ambassador in Berlin. The other, Corti, the foreign minister, was the reverse. 'A small ugly man who looked like a Japanese', with his little, piercing eyes and his flattened nose, he made no showing in a set speech, but nothing escaped him: he was active and ingenious, and was caustically to the point in private gatherings. As has been seen, he knew Salisbury and the Turks from the Constantinople conference eighteen months before, and if Ignatyev could have had his way he would have been used as a bridge between Russia and the western powers. Though himself a man of the right, he had accepted the portfolio of foreign affairs in the new ministry formed by Cairoli in March, but only under strong pressure and after insisting that he should be free to pursue a policy of dignified pacificness. By that he meant a reaction from Crispi's angling and an acceptance of an Austrian occupation (though not annexation) of Bosnia and Herzegovina without compensation for Italy. The Germans feared that Corti would press claims at the congress for some *quid pro quo* in Albania, but he immediately assured Bismarck that he would not do so, and would work for peace. 'That's a very sensible little man; he must be treated well', Bismarck instructed Radowitz.[1]

The Turkish trio counted for nothing. Caratheodory Pasha, an experienced foreign office official, for the occasion raised to ministerial rank, was a cultivated Greek, who won considerable sympathy by his tact and intelligence; but he was too tied and kept in the dark by Constantinople to have any real scope, and in any case nobody intended to pay any attention to the Turkish delegates, save the British. Mehemet Ali, the second plenipotentiary, was almost an insulting choice for a congress in Berlin.

printed by F. Waddington, 'La France au congrès de Berlin', in *Revue politique et parlementaire*, vol. clvi, p. 458.

[1] Hohenlohe, *Memoirs*, vol. ii, p. 208; de Moüy, *Souvenirs et causeries d'un diplomate*, p. 106; Corti, 'Il conte Corti al Congresso di Berlino', in *Nuova Antologia*, vol. ccxl, pp. 352–4, and *Historische Vierteljahrsschrift*, vol. xxiii, pp. 458–60; Radowitz, *Aufzeichnungen und Erinnerungen*, vol. ii, p. 30. For Crispi's soundings in the autumn of 1877 as to an alliance with Germany and as to a possible compensation for Italy if Austria acquired Bosnia, see his memoirs, vol. ii, pp. 7–91; G. Salvemini, *La politica estera di Francesco Crispi* (Rome, 1919), pp. 7–32; and his article 'Alla vigilia del Congresso di Berlino', in *Nuova rivista storica*, 1925, fasc. 1. Both Bismarck and Derby had at various times broached the possibility of something in Albania serving as a *quid pro quo* for Italy; L. Chiala, *Pagine di storia contemporanea*, vol. i, pp. 272–92. Bülow during the congress threw out a hint as to Tunis; *Nuova Antologia*, ib., p. 354.

He had first seen the light in a Magdeburg back street under the name of Detroit, and was a deserter from the Prussian service, a Moslem convert, and a military careerist under Ali Pasha. He was treated by Bismarck with ferocious rudeness. Sadullah Bey, the third Turkish representative, and minister in Berlin, was a nullity, who had been jobbed into the legation by palace intrigue and ended shortly afterwards by drinking himself to death. Nothing went right for the Turks, except their official banquet which every one thought would be a very poor affair, but turned out to be admirable, especially the *pilaffe*; Waddington asked for a second helping. At the congress sittings Bismarck insulted and shut them up with almost unfailing regularity. In committee they meekly took shelter under the British wing. 'The Turks sit and speak—like logs', noted Anuchin. They had come with verbal instructions only: to obtain the line of the Balkans, to keep Varna, to hold back Montenegro and Serbia from Albania, to secure the retrocession of Batum and the Alashkert valley, to rid themselves of the indemnity; above all they were to pin themselves to the British as regards Bulgaria and Eastern Rumelia. They did not fail to keep in close relations with the British delegation, for whom Caratheodory had almost nothing but praise. The British, though they revealed to the Turkish delegates the general lines of their agreement with the Russians, were extremely reserved as to Asiatic questions, wishing to discover whether they knew of the Cyprus convention, of which in fact they were not informed by their government until as late as 4 July.[1]

Over the congress, not merely over the Turks, Bismarck towered, in both senses. Inevitably he was president. He ruled the plenary sittings with military brusqueness; hastened on the work unsparingly; threatened retirement to his Kissingen baths if proceedings did not move faster. But he was at the outset extremely cautious. During the first ten days only three meet-

---

[1] Raschdau, *Ein sinkendes Reich*, pp. 55, 205–6 (on Caratheodory); Radowitz, *Aufzeichnungen und Erinnerungen*, vol. ii, p. 31; *Disraeli*, p. 1202; Anuchin's diary, in *R.S.*, vol. cl, p. 231; Bareilles, *Le rapport secret sur le Congrès de Berlin adressé . . . par Carathéodory Pacha*, pp. 83, 104, 76–7, 162, and Layard to Salisbury, tel., no. 579, 16 June, in *F.O.* 78/2907 (on instructions). Layard originally thought Caratheodory able and 'trustworthy for a Greek'; tel. to Salisbury, draft, 9 June: Salisbury later came to have a low opinion of him: he 'is a poor weak frightened creature and when not frightened is not wholly trustworthy': and Layard then agreed. Salisbury to Layard, tel., private, 12 Aug., and reply of Layard, 13 Aug., Layard papers, *British Museum, Add. MSS.* 39137, f. 186, and 39138, ff. 69, 74.

ings of the congress were held, and the agenda were as far as possible confined to formalities or minor questions. It was essential for Bismarck that the congress under his presidency should not break down. At the opening the British and Russians were still far apart, and Disraeli's attitude highly alarmed him. Private negotiations were imperatively required. He arranged for these, and also that the Germans should avoid being deeply committed on the crucial difficulties of Bulgaria by themselves not being a party to these negotiations. He left them to the British, the Russians, and the Austrians, himself only intervening to prevent a deadlock. As he was careful to impress upon Shuvalov, he could not support the Russians more insistently against the combined opposition of the British and Austrians, lest they should disrupt the congress and leave.[1] With Shuvalov he preserved the same close and cordial relations as before, but his violent dislike of Gorchakov was only sharpened by the Russian's 'colère sénile' and 'caprices de vieille femme'. In public he maintained the politic balancing of a well-wisher of Russia, supporting her effectively in several major questions and inclining prominently to her side on minor points. At the time Bismarck's honest brokership was scarcely called in question by the Russian press: only later in the year the campaign began which laid the blame for the treaty of Berlin upon his deliberate refusal to give his backing to the Russian delegates.

On the task of the congress, the settlement of the Ottoman empire, Bismarck made no disguise of what he had always expounded as the German point of view. Caratheodory Pasha correctly summed up: '. . . le prince Bismarck ne manque aucune occasion de faire voir qu'à son avis la question orientale, en tant que se rapportant à des peuples et à des formes de gouvernement placés en quelque sorte en dehors du cercle de la civilisation européenne et n'ayant aucun avenir, ne doit intéresser l'Europe que par les conséquences qu'elle peut avoir sur les relations des grandes puissances européennes entre elles'. In undiplomatic language: 'Bismarck has shaved,—and sits upon the Turks mercilessly. . . . He never loses an opportunity of informing us that he does not care two straws for the "bonheur de ces gens là-bas" (the Bulgars).' When, in a discussion of Article VII of San Stefano, the name of the Kutzo-Vlachs

---

[1] Extract from private letter from Shuvalov to Giers, 19 June, in Goriainow, *Le Bosphore et les Dardanelles*, p. 378.

appeared in a list of non-Bulgar peoples whose rights ought to be guaranteed: 'Coutzo-Valaques, dit-il, voilà un mot qu'on a le droit d'effacer, et aussitôt il passa le crayon là-dessus.'[1]

In his own capital, Bismarck naturally had available all his Wilhelmsstrasse men. His son Herbert acted as general liaison officer for him. Bülow, the secretary of state for foreign affairs, and Hohenlohe, from the Paris embassy, were the other two plenipotentiaries, the latter especially active during the second half of the congress as chairman of the most important committee. Radowitz, high in Bismarck's favour, was secretary-general of the congress, with de Moüy, the French diplomat from Constantinople, and C. A. Busch as joint secretaries. There were no Russians on the secretariat. French was used by all the delegates, except Disraeli. Holstein tried to impose himself on Radowitz as an assistant secretary, but was relegated to keeping touch with the foreign journalists. This secretariat worked efficiently and discreetly. The protocols, like all of their kind, covered up more than they revealed. They were not read at the beginning of each sitting, and important modifications were inserted in them. The most appreciated feature of the congress was the sumptuous buffet, just off the conference hall. It was Radowitz's idea, originally frowned upon by Bismarck; and he justly plumed himself on it.[2]

At the buffet not the least assiduous were the representatives of the Balkan states, anxiously gleaning all they could of prospects of being admitted in some capacity to the congress and of decisions fateful for their homelands. For Greece, Delyannis, minister for foreign affairs, and Rangabe, minister in Berlin, poet and archaeologist; for Roumania, the prime minister and the minister for foreign affairs, Brătianu and Kogălniceanu; for Serbia, likewise the minister for foreign affairs, Ristić; for Montenegro, Petrović and Radonić. No Bulgars came: the Russians preferred to represent them in absence.[3]

[1] Bareilles, *Le rapport secret sur le Congrès de Berlin adressé . . . par Carathéodory Pacha*, pp. 71–2; *Salisbury*, pp. 286–7.

[2] There is much inside information on the working of the secretariat from its three principal members, Radowitz, de Moüy, and Busch. The young Bülow had been recalled from Athens for the congress, but was ill for the first fortnight, and his account of the congress is either second-hand or anecdotal; Bülow, *Denkwürdigkeiten*, vol. iv, pp. 437, 439.

[3] The Bulgars had made belated efforts to send petitions to Berlin representing their case and some kind of a deputation to Berlin, but the Russians prevented any action; S. Radev, *Stroitelite na svremenna Blgariya* (Sofia, 1911), vol. i, pp. 6–8.

A third circle formed an outer ring of interested parties of diverse colouring: Count de Kératry, the publicist, briefed for the French holders of Ottoman bonds; Guedalla, Hammond, and Landon briefed for the English; Baron Hirsch with his involved railway interests; working with him Count Franz zu Solm-Reifferscheidt, strongly supported by the Austrians; Mr. J. T. Barkley, vice-chairman of the Constanza–Cernavoda railway company, an English venture with long scores against the Turks and anxious fears as to the Roumanians; M. Kann, from Paris, delegate of the *Alliance Israélite*, a highly influential and successful body. From the Eastern churches: Archimandrite Sava from Belgrade; Gerasimos, the Archbishop of Philadelphia, representative of the Patriarch of Jerusalem; two Turkish Armenians, the ex-Patriarch Magnardich Kherimian, and Khorene Nar-Bei, Archbishop of Beschikatash, all too well known in Constantinople, heavily laden with memorials, and signing himself, as descendant of the Kings of Jerusalem and Cyprus, Narbey de Lusignan. A deputation of three Constantinople Greeks joined Delyannis to voice the dreams of their unredeemed compatriots. A Bosnian rebel leader struggled fruitlessly with his hastily acquired western costume and the refusal of any one to pay any attention to his precious memorandum on Bosnian desires.

At farthest remove from the turmoil of all these delegations, deputations, and hangers-on, the one figure before whom each would have made his deepest bow was never to be seen. Away in the great palace the old Emperor remained secluded by Nobiling's bullet.

The congress opened amid lowering clouds. Not only did alarums and excursions continue around Constantinople; Crete was in revolt; the Greek bands in Thessaly and Epirus were chafing at the British attempts to prevent a renewal of their efforts at insurrection; the Pomaks in the Rhodope mountains were still struggling desperately against large Russian forces. And in Central Asia events were working up towards a crisis. British fears of Russian designs were mounting steadily. Simla was adding heavily to the increasing stream of ominous reports that came in to London; the Russians were planning an expedition to Merv; Chernyaev (name to kindle the worst suspicions) was busy at Krasnovodsk; the Shah's visit to St. Petersburg in May meant the Atrek for Russia. The reports from Persia, in part confirmatory, in part conflicting, did nothing to allay alarm. Then, exactly a week before the congress opened, the Viceroy telegraphed news of an approaching Russian mission to Kabul. Thereafter the Afghan danger loomed larger and larger on the near horizon. In Berlin Disraeli and Salisbury might not at first take the alarmist reports of Simla at their face value, but these did not exactly contribute to make a sunny atmosphere, and they stiffened the cabinet at home in their anxiety that their two colleagues should bring home a treaty as unfavourable as possible to Russia.[1]

Of all these storm-clouds the most threatening seemed the situation at Constantinople. The continued importance attached by the British to a withdrawal of the Russians had been made abundantly clear by Salisbury during his final negotiations with Shuvalov, and he had explicitly reserved the right to bring the matter before the congress if Shuvalov failed to persuade his government to begin retiring at once. Accordingly, the cabinet instructions for the British plenipotentiaries, drafted by Salisbury in his own hand, included as the first of two preliminaries simultaneous withdrawal from before the Turkish capital. The instructions did not, however, go beyond an emphatic reminder to the congress of the danger of the existing position. By the

[1] Cf. p. 479, note 3, and p. 498. *F.O.* 181/567 shows the increasing British fears of Russian activities in Central Asia, leading up to the Viceroy's telegram of 7 June giving the first definite report of a Russian mission to Kabul. *F.O.* 181/568 becomes fuller and fuller of the Russo-Afghan question. The reports from Loftus and others in Russia for April to July are in *F.O.* 65/1029 and 1030. Loftus himself was assured by the Persian foreign minister that there had been no question during the Shah's visit of any exchange of territory, only of the retrocession of Khotur (disp., no. 588, conf., 5 June), and he was also assured by Giers on 2 July that no mission 'had been or was intended to be, sent to Cabul either by the Imperial Government or by General Kauffmann' (disp., no. 623, 3 July, rec. 11 July). Loftus felt certain that the Russians had been preparing a military expedition towards India, but he believed that since the meeting of the congress these preparations had been abandoned. It was not until 19 Aug. that Salisbury addressed a protest to St. Petersburg against the reported movement of General Kaufmann to the Afghan frontier and the mission to Kabul; *F.O.* 65/995. Shuvalov maintained later to Salisbury that during the Berlin congress he knew nothing whatever as to the mission to Kabul; *Salisbury*, p. 345. In fact Stoletov left Tashkent on his mission to Kabul on 13 June; and in fact the visit of the Shah was followed next year by the formation of the Persian Cossack Brigade, one of the main arms of Russian influence in Persia during the next forty years; see particularly the article based on the diary of General Kosagovsky, the organizer of the brigade, in *Novy Vostok*, Moscow, 1923, nos. 3 and 4. For British counter-projects for an alliance with Persia see J. G. Allen, 'Sir Ronald Thomson and British policy towards Persia in 1879', in *Journal of the Royal Central Asian Society*, 1935, vol. xxii, pp. 601–16.

time the delegations assembled the Russians had made no adequate move.[1]

Disraeli arrived in Berlin late on 11 June; Salisbury on the 12th; Shuvalov that same evening; Gorchakov on the morning of the 13th; and that afternoon at 2 o'clock the first sitting took place. There was little enough time for private soundings, though Bismarck had a tête-à-tête with Disraeli in which he urged successfully the necessity of tackling at the outset the thorniest problem, Bulgaria, and Salisbury had some amicable converse with Shuvalov, without apparently mentioning the question of withdrawal. Thus the Russians were all the more perturbed at the opening sitting to hear Disraeli orate (in English, without warning, an additional aggravation) in stiff terms on the menace of the Russian troops before Constantinople as a question of extreme urgency. Gorchakov, who did not have the presence of mind to reply in Russian and was too proud to admit his ignorance of English, coined a few vapid phrases and threw the onus of answering on Shuvalov. Bismarck hastily intervened to the effect that the question was not within the competence of the congress and should be settled privately by the two parties.[2] This was agreed to, but Bismarck remained very anxious lest it should again be brought up at the next sitting. He even visited the Turks himself, urging them to give up Varna to the Russians or at least agree to its prompt evacuation, but the Turks did not dare override their instructions. Finally, he armed himself in advance of the second sitting with a very russophil proposal, drawn up by Radowitz, that the Russians should evacuate the country between Constantinople and

---

[1] Shuvalov to Giers, tels., nos. 50 and 51, 2 June, text in *Seton-Watson MSS.*; Salisbury to Loftus, disp., no. 353, 3 June, in *F.O.* 181/567; Salisbury to Russell, draft disp., no. 308, 3 June, in *F.O.* 64/905, asking for German pressure on St. Petersburg and showing extreme suspicion of the Russian refusal to withdraw; cabinet instructions of 8 June, original draft in *F.O.* 78/2898, published in *A. and P.*, 1878, lxxxiii, C. 2083, no. 2. For the recurrent incidents around Constantinople: private letter of Layard to Hornby, 19 June, copy in Layard Papers, *British Museum, Add. MSS.* 39131, f. 109; Raschdau, *Ein sinkendes Reich*, pp. 209–11; Tenterden to Salisbury, tel., 24 June, in *F.O.* 78/2905.

[2] Anuchin's diary, in *R.S.*, vol. cxlix, pp. 238–9; Nelidov's memoirs in *Revue des deux mondes*, 15 Nov. 1915, vol. xxx, p. 258; Radowitz, *Aufzeichnungen und Erinnerungen*, vol. ii, pp. 37–8; Busch's diary, under date 15 June, in *Deutsche Rundschau*, vol. cxli, p. 369. The well-known story, given in *Disraeli*, p. 1183, of Odo Russell dissuading Disraeli from speaking in his appalling French by telling him that everybody was looking forward to listening to a master of English parliamentary oratory speaking in his own tongue is unfortunately open to doubt.

Adrianople, and the Turks Shumla and Varna, it being understood that an agreement would be reached as to the British fleet. In fact this was not required, for the British yielded to Bismarck and let the matter drop, but this opening to the congress served the more to embitter the struggle which was now being waged over Bulgaria.[1]

A further aggravation was immediately supplied by the publication in the *Globe* of 14 June of the full text of the first two Salisbury–Shuvalov memoranda. A summary of the engagements had appeared in the same paper on the very day after their signature, and the summary was a correct one save that it made England concede entire exclusion of Turkish military forces from Eastern Rumelia. This had been sufficient for Salisbury to assure the House of Lords that the report was 'wholly unauthentic and not deserving of the confidence of your Lordships' House'. The new revelation in full could not be brushed aside, for the text was accurate save for the omission of a few unimportant words. It made a bad impression in England, and gave another handle to Shuvalov's enemies in Russia. Batum became a new catchword in England, linked with Kars, the traditional bulwark against Russian expansion southwards. No offset was yet possible in the shape of making public the Cyprus agreement, and the government were very uneasy at the prospect of any concessions to Russia. In Berlin the British and Russians showered mutual accusations on each other. Salisbury agreed with his department that the communication was 'evidently Russian'; but the leakage proved to be due to the carelessness of the foreign office in employing a temporary, and underpaid, copyist for such secret work.[2] The reaction of the disclosure on the impending negotiations was at

---

[1] Radowitz, *Aufzeichnungen und Erinnerungen*, vol. ii, pp. 42–3; Bareilles, *Le rapport secret sur le Congrès de Berlin adressé . . . par Carathéodory Pacha*, pp. 83–9. Carathéodory's account of Bismarck's visit to the Turks is confirmed by the Berlin foreign office archives; Müller, *Die Bedeutung des Berliner Kongresses für die deutsch-russischen Beziehungen*, p. 22.

[2] *Salisbury*, p. 282. Tenterden pointed out that the signature of Shuvalov preceded Salisbury's and suggested that it was therefore a Russian copy; Tenterden to Salisbury, tel., 14 June, in *F.O.* 78/2901. The temporary clerk was the journalist Charles Marvin, who was also responsible for communicating to the press the earlier summary of the agreements. Next year he published his own account of the affair in his book *Our public affairs*, which though quite unreliable as to details leaves no doubt that the foreign office was culpably lax. The texts as published in the *Globe* are printed in *Staatsarchiv*, vol. xxxiv, no. 6749, and Martens, *Nouveau Recueil des traités . . .*, 2nd series, vol. iii, p. 296.

once shown by Disraeli emphasizing to Shuvalov the bad effect produced on English opinion and stating that, though he would not go back upon the concessions, he would have to insist to the full on the other points which had been left open; and two days later Salisbury expatiated in strict secrecy to Bismarck on the difficulties presented by Batum and on the probability of England requiring some alteration of the Straits convention of 1871 if Russia kept that port.[1]

The atmosphere in which the discussions on Bulgaria began was thus dangerously charged. These almost monopolized the first fortnight. The congress had begun by requiring unanimity for its decisions other than those on procedure. The rule was conspicuously overridden to the disadvantage of the Turks, but in respect of the Russians it necessarily involved preliminary compromise negotiations outside of the congress sittings or in committee. They took the form first of a private interchange of views; then, at the second sitting of the congress, which did not take place until 17 June, the British formally put forward two proposals on Bulgaria and Eastern Rumelia which were referred to private meetings of the Russian, British, and Austrian delegates. Four such meetings were held during the ensuing week. By 22 June the Russians had yielded sufficiently for the question to come up again at a plenary sitting, when Waddington was deputed to find a basis of agreement in respect of the points of difference still outstanding. By 26 June these and certain other points were settled, partly by the mediation of Waddington and Corti, partly in the congress itself. Detailed decisions as to the frontiers of the new Bulgaria remained to be taken, for which purpose the congress set up a boundary committee, assisted by a committee of the military experts, each composed of representatives from all the delegations. The discussions here almost culminated in another deadlock, so that the Bulgarian frontiers, in part because their western trace involved disputes over Serbia, were not finally completed by the congress until 9 July. When all was done Bulgaria and Eastern Rumelia occupied twenty-two out of the sixty-four articles of the treaty.

---

[1] Goriainow, *Le Bosphore et les Dardanelles*, p. 379, citing letter of 14 June (apparently of Shuvalov to St. Petersburg); Salisbury to Cross, disp., no. 10, most conf., 19 June, in *F.O.* 78/2899. The draft of this dispatch, in *F.O.* 78/2904, shows that it was initialled by Beaconsfield as well as by Salisbury. According to Shuvalov's memoirs, *Krasny arkhiv*, vol. lix, p. 106, Bismarck intervened energetically with Disraeli on behalf of the Russians.

Three main groups of questions in regard to the Bulgaria of San Stefano may be distinguished: its extent, its form of government and administration together with the duration of the Russian occupation, and Turkish military rights. Since Russia had yielded, with only formal reservations, on the division of the big Bulgaria into a politically autonomous Bulgaria north of the Balkans and an administratively autonomous Eastern Rumelia south of the Balkans, the first two groups of questions affected equally Bulgaria and Eastern Rumelia, while the third concerned only Eastern Rumelia. The formal reservations by which Russia had preserved the right to urge the desirability of a longitudinal division of the big Bulgaria, in accordance with the Constantinople conference, though shorn of the Aegean sea-coast and certain other areas, were utilized by Shuvalov in the private talks and again in the congress on 17 June, but they were not seriously meant and were thereafter dropped. Nor was there any real difficulty over the name to be given to the province south of the Balkans; the British had their way with 'Eastern Rumelia', and the Russians abandoned 'Southern Bulgaria', which had encountered the obvious objection that it would encourage dangerous aspirations for unity.

The struggle was concentrated above all on the extent of Bulgaria and Eastern Rumelia and on the Turkish military rights in the latter province. This second problem was immediately brought to the fore with great vehemence by Disraeli. On the morning of the 14th he gave Shuvalov 'what he calls a dusting', holding forth at length on Turkish military and political control in Eastern Rumelia. In reporting to the Queen, he styled the Russian refusal to allow the Sultan to employ his army in the province as 'outrageous . . . monstrous and a gross insult to England. Lord B. spoke thunder about it. It will be given up by St Petersburg.'[1] And so it was; but not before continued thunder. The week-end soundings did not clear the air. Bismarck, much disturbed at the high tone of the British, conversed deeply with all the principals in turn. Shuvalov could extract nothing whatever from the Turks and henceforth,

---

[1] Letter to Lady Salisbury, 14 June, extract in *Salisbury*, p. 280; letter to the Queen, 14 June, text in *Disraeli*, p. 1191. Shuvalov in private conversation with Salisbury immediately on arrival, 12 June, had given him the impression that neither he nor his military advisers personally supported strongly the Tsar's insistence against Turkish garrisons in Eastern Rumelia; letter to Lady Salisbury, 12 June, extract in *Salisbury*, p. 279.

considering them tied to the British, made no further efforts to deal with them. Andrássy, on the other hand, obtained Gorchakov's consent to the acquisition of Novi Bazar; behind the back of Shuvalov, who was correspondingly infuriated with his leader. The Austrians, and still more the British, were demanding a heavy cutting down of the western frontiers of Bulgaria and Eastern Rumelia, and it became apparent that the ideas of the latter as to what constituted the Balkan range differed vitally from those of the Russians and involved the *sanjak* of Sofia being included in Eastern Rumelia. The British opposition to the frontier of Eastern Rumelia cutting the Adrianople–Constantinople railway was so strong that the Russians agreed among themselves to abandon the San Stefano line here and fall back upon that outlined by the Constantinople conference. Shuvalov also gathered from Salisbury that there were likely to be serious difficulties over the war indemnity from Turkey. The outlook for the second sitting of the congress on the Monday (17 June) was gloomy in the extreme.[1]

The sitting was opened with the question of the admission of Greece: then followed Bulgaria. Salisbury proposed the examination of two questions: first, the confinement of the tributary autonomous principality of Bulgaria to the north of the Balkan range; secondly, the placing of the province of Rumelia and all else south of the Balkans under the direct political and military authority of the Sultan, due regard being paid to the welfare of the inhabitants by sufficient guarantees of administrative autonomy or by other means. Some general discussion followed, in which Andrássy prominently supported Salisbury in principle, and then Bismarck suggested that the latter's proposals should first be discussed in detail at private meetings between the British and Russians. Thereupon Andrássy interposed to demand the presence of the Austrians at these meetings, which of course was accepted.[2] Bismarck had thus avoided himself proposing that the Russians should be outnumbered. The Turks said nothing and were ignored.

The Austrians had hitherto been disinclined to pin themselves

---

[1] For maps illustrating the frontiers of Bulgaria see those between pp. 410–11 and facing p. 653. Bareilles, *Le rapport secret sur le Congrès de Berlin adressé . . . par Carathéodory Pacha*, p. 89; Anuchin's diary in *R.S.*, vol. cxlix, pp. 240–5; *Disraeli*, p. 1191; *Salisbury*, pp. 282–3, and disp., no. 10, 19 June, most conf., to Cross, in *F.O.* 78/2899.

[2] *Wertheimer*, vol. iii, pp. 113–14. The protocol of this second sitting on 17 June does not reveal this point.

down to the demand for the Balkans as the southern frontier of Bulgaria, possibly with a view to extending their occupation to Mitrovica if Bulgaria in her turn extended to the Maritsa, but they now accepted the British standpoint.[1] On 18 June (Waterloo day, as Disraeli did not fail to remind the Queen), the first of the private meetings was held; a very wearing tussle of four hours between Disraeli and Salisbury, Shuvalov and Oubril, Andrássy and Haymerle. Disraeli opened at length in decided language, manfully backed up by the Austrians to the consternation of the Russians. He presented as a virtual ultimatum the demand for wide military rights for the Turks in Eastern Rumelia, for the line of the Balkans as its northern frontier, and for the inclusion in it of the *sanjak* of Sofia unless Varna or the upper Mesta and Struma valleys were given up. The frontier of Eastern Rumelia around Adrianople and to the Black Sea was also to be drastically redrawn. The Russians accepted the Balkan range as the southern frontier of Bulgaria, though with their own interpretation of what was meant by that range, but their instructions did not allow them to agree to more than what amounted to a Turkish right to observation-posts on the Balkans or to accept definitely the proposals as to the *sanjak* of Sofia. There was privately, however, prompt agreement among the Russian representatives that it was far preferable to consent to cutting off the upper Mesta and Struma valleys from Eastern Rumelia than to consent to excluding Varna and its surroundings from Bulgaria, in return for the inclusion of the Sofia *sanjak* in Bulgaria. This they believed (rightly) the Austrians would support, since their especial aim was to keep Russian influence as far removed as possible from the Vardar valley, while it was the British alone who pressed the Turkish claim to Varna. The day closed with the dispatch of Bogolyubov to St. Petersburg for personal report and further instructions, with the deferment until 21 June of further discussion of the Bulgarian question at a plenary sitting, and with instructions to the military experts to discuss in detail the frontiers.[2]

The 19th was, as Disraeli described it, an 'anxious day'. He

[1] Salisbury to Elliot, no. 1, 15 June, in *F.O.* 78/2908; *Disraeli*, p. 1189.
[2] *Disraeli*, pp. 1194–5, recording also, but without any details, an important conversation after the meeting with Gorchakov at his desire; *Salisbury*, p. 282; Salisbury to Cross, disp., no. 7, 18 June, in *F.O.* 78/2899; Anuchin's diary in *R.S.*, vol. cxlix, pp. 461–2, 464; Bobrikov's memoirs, in *R.S.*, vol. cliii, p. 285, and *Russky vestnik*, Dec. 1889, p. 13.

was beginning to spread about his intention to break up the congress if the Russians did not yield, and there was a passage of arms between him and Shuvalov in the congress sitting when the latter asked for a further postponement, until the 22nd, of the discussion of Bulgaria in the congress. Meanwhile, a seven-hours' fight between the Russian and British military experts had left the former in furious indignation. Simmons, the British military representative, proposed to include Varna and a wide rayon in Eastern Rumelia, and to exclude both from that province and from Bulgaria any of the Mesta and Struma watersheds; he insisted on tracing a line for the northern frontier of Eastern Rumelia which did not follow the crest of the Balkans but came well down on the northern side so as to ensure to the Turks full strategical control; and he further gave the Russians to understand that, even if the Turks secured Varna, the British demanded that a large portion of the *sanjak* of Sofia (at the least that falling within the watershed of the Maritsa) should be in Eastern Rumelia. Here the divergence between the Russian and the British views as to what constituted the Balkan range was fully revealed, since Simmons based his argument on the agreement in the Salisbury–Shuvalov memorandum, reaffirmed by Shuvalov during the congress, that the line of the Balkans should be the southern boundary of Bulgaria. How far due west did this range extend? The British were anxious to secure for the Turks against the Bulgars and Serbs as much as possible of the main route, soon to be the Orient railway line, from Philippopolis over the Ikhtiman pass to Sofia, Tsaribrod, Pirot, and Nish, and they declared in consequence that the mountains in the north of the Sofia *sanjak* were the western continuation of the Balkan range and that they were therefore justified in claiming that *sanjak* as cut off from Bulgaria.

The Russians, fully primed in advance, countered by arguing that it was the mountains running south-west and south to the great knot of the Rila Dagh and dividing the *sanjaks* of Sofia and Philippopolis which formed the true extension of the Balkan range, and that thus the Sofia *sanjak* had been assigned to Bulgaria. The conflict between the military ended in an embittered deadlock, and on the report of the Russians to Shuvalov and Oubril it was agreed that the British trace of the frontier on the northern side of the Balkans was entirely inadmissible and that, if this were persisted in, the private negotiations would have to cease and the dispute be threshed out in full congress. Shuvalov's apprehensions could not have been appreciably diminished when on appealing to Disraeli against the extremism of Simmons, he was told not to take the general too seriously.[1]

The telegrams from St. Petersburg were neither encouraging nor helpful. Bogolyubov had not yet arrived, and Giers could extract no adequate decisions; but it was clear that the Tsar was extremely put out by the demand for Turkish troops to be allowed in Eastern Rumelia, and was insistent that Varna should remain in Bulgaria: as to the Sofia *sanjak* he was hesitant and was awaiting information from Bogolyubov. In consequence, nothing could be effected at the second private meeting between the three powers on 20 June, and they adjourned until five o'clock on the following day, when a definitive answer from the Tsar was expected to have arrived.[2]

This Friday, 21 June, was a decisive day. Disraeli was confidently standing his ground and threatening to leave by special train, while Bismarck was making great personal efforts with Disraeli and Shuvalov separately to prevent a rupture.[3] But the deciding factor was the receipt that day of new instructions from the Tsar, dispatched after Bogolyubov's arrival in St. Petersburg. When the third private meeting took place at five o'clock, Shuvalov was able to accept the exclusion of the Macedonian portion of the Mesta and Struma valleys from Bulgaria

[1] For this and the preceding paragraph: Anuchin's diary, in *R.S.*, vol. cxlix, pp. 464–70, vol. cl, p. 3, reporting the meeting in great detail; Simmons's report to Salisbury, 19 June, in *F.O.* 78/2909, similarly in great detail, and agreeing substantially with Anuchin's version of the frontiers proposed; Bobrikov's memoirs, in *Russky vestnik*, Dec. 1889, pp. 11–14, and *R.S.*, vol. cliii, pp. 282–3. General Sir Lintorn Simmons had had Crimean experience of Turkey and was now Inspector-General of Fortifications. Captain Ardagh, another engineer officer and just back from eighteen months in the eastern Balkans, was his assistant. According to Anuchin, the Austrian experts, Schwegel and Thömmel, thought that Simmons went much too far. For the geographical areas in dispute, see map facing p. 653.

[2] Anuchin's diary, in *R.S.*, vol. cl, pp. 3, 9; Salisbury to Cross, disp., no. 20, 20 June, in *F.O.* 78/2899.

[3] Radowitz, *Aufzeichnungen und Erinnerungen*, vol. ii, p. 45; *Disraeli*, pp. 1195–8, including the original version of the story of Corry, his private secretary, as to the special train, in a letter to Lady Ilchester dated 2 July. Twenty years later Corry, then Lord Rowton, had greatly expanded his account, as given in the very unreliable article by Cumming, 'The secret history of the treaty of Berlin, being a talk with the late Lord Rowton', in *The Nineteenth Century and after*, 1905, vol. lviii, pp. 83–90. In *Disraeli*, p. 1197, it is stated, without the source being cited, that Disraeli instructed Corry as to ordering a special train during a morning walk on 21 June.

and Eastern Rumelia in return for Varna and the *sanjak* of Sofia going to Bulgaria, and in particular to accept the British proposals as to the Turkish military occupation of the frontiers of Eastern Rumelia subject to two reservations. A European commission was to decide which strong places might be occupied by the Turks and in what strength; and the congress was to lay down the conditions in which the governor-general of Eastern Rumelia could summon Turkish troops into the interior of the province if internal security were gravely menaced. The British required time for consideration of these reservations, and a further meeting was to be held next day before the congress sitting in the afternoon. At this, the fourth private meeting, Disraeli objected to the reservations and was supported by Andrássy, who had on the 21st successfully urged the British to give way on Varna and the Sofia *sanjak* subject to strategical rectifications of the frontier; but the Russians held firm and announced that they would bring their reservations before the congress as amendments to the British resolutions. Disraeli even before this meeting telegraphed home that Russia had surrendered. This, though somewhat exaggerated, was sufficiently near the truth, and, taken as a whole, the crisis was past. Salisbury more accurately summed up to his wife on the same day: 'The Russians have very nearly given way on all material points.'[1]

In the afternoon of the 22nd the congress duly heard the British proposals. In consideration for the Russians yielding on the Mesta and the Struma the British abandoned Varna to Bulgaria, to the disgusted surprise of Caratheodory whose ineffectual protest only called forth offensive threats from Bismarck.[2] The British agreed also to the incorporation of part of the *sanjak* of Sofia in Bulgaria, though how much remained uncertain, and the time-honoured formula 'rectification straté-

---

[1] Salisbury to Cross, disp., nos. 24, 27, and 29, 21 and 22 June, recording the third and fourth private meetings, on 21 and 22 June, in *F.O.* 78/2899; Anuchin's diary in *R.S.*, vol. cl, pp. 10–11; *Disraeli*, p. 1196; *Salisbury*, p. 286. Salisbury's no. 24 speaks of the first Russian reservation as stating that it was the Turks who were to decide which strong points they intended to garrison, but the Russian reservation as made in the congress next day was quite clear that this decision was to be taken by a European commission.

[2] Bareilles, *Le rapport secret sur le Congrès de Berlin adressé . . . par Carathéodory Pacha*, pp. 94–7, 103. The version given in the protocol was of course ultra-discreet. Caratheodory after this sitting asked his government, without success, to replace him.

gique des frontières' suggested a stiff struggle still to come over
the detailed boundaries. The question as to where the southern
boundary of Eastern Rumelia should meet the Black Sea was
also left for further discussion. Finally, they proposed that
Eastern Rumelia should be placed under the direct political
and military authority of the Sultan, who should have the right
to provide for the defence of its frontiers by fortifying them and
maintaining troops on them, while internal order should be
maintained by a militia, whose officers should be appointed by
the Sultan, taking into account the religion of the population:
in addition, the governor-general should have the right to call
upon Turkish troops in the event of internal insecurity or
the frontiers being threatened. Against this the Russians put
forward the two reservations already stated. Andrássy ranged
himself behind the British. Bismarck, studiously conciliatory
towards the Russians, proposed that Waddington should be
deputed to find a formula which would meet the Russian
objections. He had prepared his ground carefully in advance
with the French and the Italians, and the congress readily
assented.[1]

Waddington had two busy days before he could report an
agreed text to the congresss on 25 June. He was at one with
the British in regarding any attempt at binding the Turks to
fixed places and fixed numbers on the frontier as impossible,
and this point was abandoned. On the other hand, he was in
agreement with the Russian contention that the use of Turkish
troops in the interior of Eastern Rumelia in exceptional circumstances must be more strictly safeguarded, and with a Russian
proposal forbidding any use of irregular troops. The British
had already conceded that in normal times there should be no
Turkish troops in the province except those stationed on the
frontier, internal order being maintained by the proposed local
militia. The Turks strongly objected to a militia, and Mehemet
Ali was urging that there should only be a gendarmerie, thereby
hoping to avoid the sanctioning of what he quite correctly
regarded as inevitable cadres for a subsequent revolt. Waddington combined the two proposals and the congress duly voted
the creation of a gendarmerie and of a militia, the officers of
both being appointed by the Sultan, taking into account the

---

[1] Radowitz, *Aufzeichnungen und Erinnerungen*, vol. ii, p. 46; Protocol of the fourth
sitting, 22 June.

religion of the inhabitants according to the locality. Here Salisbury had been careful to secure that the words 'de la majorité', which had figured in Waddington's original text, should be eliminated. He was also insistent on making less binding on the Sultan Waddington's initial draft regulating the passage of Turkish troops to their posts on the frontier, and the final agreement recorded only that, in time of peace, the troops moving through the province to their frontier posts were not to stop *en route* for any length of time, that they were prohibited from being billeted, and that none but regular troops could be employed. The right to employ Turkish troops within the province if its internal or external security might be threatened was maintained, with the proviso that in such a case the Porte was to justify its action to the ambassadors at Constantinople. All this Shuvalov accepted, saving reference to St. Petersburg on the complete elimination of any European commission to tighten control of the Turks. Three days later the agreement of St. Petersburg was formally announced.[1]

Thus, in effect the dispute over Turkish military rights in Eastern Rumelia was settled by Waddington's report to the sixth sitting of the congress on 25 June. As often happens in a tangled network of problems, one single question had been given an over-emphasized importance, figuring as a symbol of prestige and carrying a charged weight of personal feeling. From a Russian standpoint, it could well seem that it had been largely an academic question, purposely made much of to humiliate Russia; for had the Turks either the men or the resources to put into effective use the military rights secured them by the British? And if they had not, would Eastern Rumelia remain long separated from Bulgaria? Within a decade these doubts were to be proved only too well founded.[2]

The struggle had been so largely concentrated on the Turkish military rights that the two equally important problems of the duration of the Russian occupation and of the Russian control of administration in Bulgaria received far less than their due share of attention. The former problem was settled with surprising rapidity in one single sitting of the congress on 24 June;

[1] *D.D.F.*, pp. 339–42; F. Waddington, 'La France au Congrès de Berlin', in *Revue politique et parlementaire*, vol. clvi, pp. 470–1; *A. and P.*, 1878, lxxxiii, C. 2083, no. 13; Simmons to Salisbury, 21 June (urging Mehemet Ali's objection to a militia), in *F.O.* 78/2909; Protocol of the sixth sitting, 25 June.

[2] Anuchin's diary, in *R.S.*, vol. clii, p. 232.

the latter after somewhat greater difficulties on 26 June. The treaty of San Stefano had provided for a Russian occupation of the big Bulgaria by not more than 50,000 troops for not more than two years. Austrian and British objections to this had been made evident from the first, and at Berlin Shuvalov attempted to meet them by offering to Andrássy that one-third of the Russian forces should evacuate immediately after peace, one-third after a fixed period, and the last third when the peace and security of Bulgaria were assured. Andrássy strongly objected to this last condition, and countered it by suggesting that if conditions were gravely troubled some kind of European occupation should succeed Russian evacuation.[1] He accordingly proposed to the congress on 24 June that the Russians should evacuate Bulgaria and Eastern Rumelia within six months of the conclusion of peace, and Roumania within eight or nine months, and that, if after the six months it was agreed that troops were still required in Bulgaria, these should be provided to the number of 10,000 to 15,000 by the great powers under the orders of the European commission. This was immediately welcomed by Disraeli, who declared that England was quite prepared to furnish her share of a European force. Shuvalov followed by expounding the obvious objections to any such joint contingents, and, emphasizing the difference between Eastern Rumelia and Bulgaria, demanded a longer period of occupation at any rate of the latter. He was supported by Bismarck, and after confused discussion agreement was reached on nine months for the occupation of both Bulgaria and Eastern Rumelia, and one year for the complete evacuation of Roumania, to run from the exchange of ratifications of the treaty. The figure of 50,000 was left unaltered as the maximum number of Russian troops. The suggestion of a European occupation, which Andrássy had probably only brought forward as a tactical move, was abandoned, and he was well enough pleased at securing the nine months.[2]

It was Andrássy again who led the way in revising the San Stefano provisions whereby a Russian commissary was to control for two years the internal administration of Bulgaria and

---

[1] Report of Andrássy to Francis Joseph, 23 June, cited in *Wertheimer*, vol. iii, p. 116.

[2] Protocol of the fifth sitting, 24 June; Andrássy to Francis Joseph, tels., 24 and 25 June, cited in *Wertheimer*, vol. iii, p. 117.

the working out of its constitution. As regards that portion
of the San Stefano Bulgaria which was now to form Eastern
Rumelia there was no difficulty. The Russians accepted a
European commission, which was to work out its organization
within three months in accord with the Porte and was to
administer its finances, again in accord with the Porte, until
the new régime was functioning. For the new Bulgaria, the
San Stefano provision for the free election of a prince by the
population, to be confirmed by the Sultan, with the assent of
the powers, did not require alteration, for the treaty had added
that the prince could not be a member of any of the reigning
houses of the great powers, and Salisbury's efforts to insert
'with the assent of a majority of the powers' were overruled.
Nor did the question as to whether the prince should be hereditary create difficulties: it had been left open in San Stefano on
the express request of the Turks, so the Russians stated, and as
the Turks were still divided among themselves it still remained
unspecified. But the Russian commissary for Bulgaria was
strongly attacked. Andrássy opened with a motion that the
functions assigned in the treaty of San Stefano to Russian or
Russo-Turkish commissaries or commissions should everywhere
be transferred to European commissaries or commissions. This
was discussed in the congress on 25 June and received the strong
support of Salisbury; but it was stubbornly opposed by Shuvalov
who would not do more than suggest that the ambassadors at
Constantinople might exercise a watching brief over the Russian
commissary in Bulgaria through their consuls on the spot. To
avoid an impasse Corti, on his own suggestion, was appointed
to find a solution. Accordingly, on the following morning Corti
met the Russians, British, and Austrians, the Turks as usual
being disregarded. The Russian delegation had decided to
hold fast to their refusal to accept the Austrian proposal, and
at the meeting they substantially gained their point: Shuvalov's
compromise put forward in the congress on the previous day
was elaborated, and formally confirmed by the plenary sitting
in the afternoon (26 June). The Russian commissary in Bulgaria was maintained, for nine months, but a Turkish commissary and the consuls of the powers were to assist in the
control of the provisional administration: in case of disagreement among the consuls a majority was to decide: in case of
disagreement between the consuls and the Russian commissary

the ambassadors of the powers at Constantinople were to decide.[1]

At the same time, three important economic questions affecting Bulgaria were decided. The Austrians secured, through the medium of the French, that the Turkish commercial treaties should remain in force in Bulgaria: no transit duties could be levied, and the way was barred to the according of any special commercial favours to Russia. After private discussions between Oubril, Nelidov, Haymerle, and Schwegel, the congress agreed that the Turkish obligations, financial and other, in respect of railways in Bulgaria should be taken over by the new principality. The Austrian interests in the Orient railway, as well as the British interests in the Rustchuk–Varna line, were thus safeguarded. Thirdly, the amount of Turkish public debt to be taken over by Bulgaria was to be fixed in relation to its annual revenue and the tribute to be paid to the Porte. Here Waddington was prominent in defence of the interests of the foreign bondholders. This affirmation of principle clearly did not come to grips with the real difficulties of apportionment, which were left to be settled by the signatories of the treaty at the end of a year, but it did destroy the Russian contentions that since Bulgaria was not severed from Turkey it should not have to take over any portion of the Ottoman debt, and that the claims of the foreign bondholders should be protected only by a certain portion of the tribute being earmarked on their account.[2]

Thus, by the end of the first fortnight of the congress the Russian Bulgaria had more than half disappeared and little more remained beyond settling in detail its boundaries, a task, however, which was to prove extremely arduous. An important change was now made in the organization of the congress. The three consecutive meetings on Bulgaria on 24, 25, and 26 June had exhausted the temper of Bismarck, who had been none too successful in handling the complicated and ill-prepared details which were being threshed out in the full sittings of the congress. At every conference there comes a point when emphasis on

[1] Protocols of the fifth, sixth, and seventh sittings, 24, 25, and 26 June; Anuchin's diary, in *R.S.*, vol. cl, p. 234; *A. and P.*, 1878, lxxxiii, C. 2083, no. 14; Bareilles, *Le rapport secret sur le Congrès de Berlin adressé . . . par Carathéodory Pacha*, pp. 123–5 (on the Prince of Bulgaria being hereditary).

[2] Protocols of the fifth, sixth, and seventh sittings, 24, 25, and 26 June; *D.D.F.*, p. 343; Anuchin's diary, in *R.S.*, vol. cl, p. 234.

time becomes dominant. Bismarck was determined, now that Bulgaria seemed safely out of the way, that the tempo should be quickened. He presented the conference with a definite programme for its future work, and decreed that all detailed discussions of frontiers should be referred to a boundary committee, on which each of the delegations was to have one representative. A drafting committee, similarly constituted, was also set up, with Desprez as its chairman. Upon the boundary committee was to fall the main weight of the contentions to follow. It was composed of Hohenlohe (chairman), Haymerle, St. Vallier, Odo Russell, de Launay, Shuvalov, and Mehemet Ali. To assist it the sub-committee of military experts was reconstituted to include a member from each delegation: the Russians thus ensured that they would not again have to face alone the British and Austrian officers.[1]

The first new problem to be tackled, Bosnia and Herzegovina, was not, however, a matter for the boundary committee. The situation save as regards Novi Bazar was sufficiently clear. Occupation, not annexation, had been decided upon, in part so as to make it somewhat easier for the Sultan to yield and to placate the Italians, but the Austrian efforts to reach a previous agreement with the Porte had failed. At Berlin the Turks strove in vain to extract concessions and to secure help from Salisbury. It was obvious that they would be overruled. The British were now prepared to propose in the congress the Austrian occupation and administration of both Bosnia and Herzegovina. There was no fear of danger from the Italian delegation: Corti had explained amicably to Andrássy that considerations of home politics would require him to record the protest of Italy, but that this was merely formal and was not intended to raise difficulties. In fact, his conciliatory policy was felt to be far too mild by a section of his cabinet and by popular opinion, and he resigned four months later in the face of the outburst of irredentism which swept Italy. Bismarck cared nothing for Bosnia and Herzegovina, but much for the prearranged details of the congress sitting at which occupation was to be decided. The Russians had long since washed their hands of the two provinces, though they were unpleasantly surprised by the British initiative. On 28 June the Austrian occupation was agreed upon by

[1] Hohenlohe, *Memoirs*, vol. ii, p. 216; Radowitz, *Aufzeichnungen und Erinnerungen*, vol. ii, pp. 47–8; Bobrikov's memoirs, in *Russky vestnik*, Dec. 1889, p. 14.

the congress, a decision which left the Turks in isolated opposition.[1]

This decision took no account of feelings in the two provinces, which were sharply divided. Austria had gained the day in Berlin, but it was only after many months and much blood that the occupation became an accomplished fact. Andrássy had done his best to multiply his connexions with the Catholics,[2] but the Moslems and many of the Orthodox were determined to resist, and they had as usual some encouragement from unofficial Russian circles. Vasilevich, the panslav agent at Cettinje, was working hard to draw together Orthodox and Mussulman in Herzegovina in common resistance to an Austrian occupation, though Prince Nicholas stood against any action that would put a further strain on his relations with Vienna. In Belgrade, in the summer, the irrepressible Fadeyev appeared yet again, attempting to organize rebel committees and to subsidize armed opposition to an Austrian entry into Bosnia. It was given out (very improbably) that he came with the Tsar's approval and on a secret mission from the Russian war office. Ristić from Berlin urged that nothing should be done to prejudice Serbia in Austrian eyes, and neither Milan nor the government would have any dealings with so dangerous an adventurer. Despite Fadeyev's failure, there was serious enough anti-Austrian feeling among the Bosnian Orthodox. Already in March a group of rebels and refugees had been planning how to avert the threatened Austrian occupation. Three memoranda were drawn up, for St. Petersburg, for Belgrade, and for the congress when it met, the gist of which was that, if union with Serbia were impossible, Bosnia desired autonomy more or less

---

[1] Čubrilović, *Bosanski ustanak 1875–1878*, pp. 292–302 (for the previous Austro-Turkish negotiations; mainly based on the Vienna archives); Bareilles, *Le rapport secret sur le Congrès de Berlin adressé . . . par Carathéodory Pacha*, pp. 131–42; *Wertheimer*, vol. iii, pp. 125–6, 128–30; Haines, 'Italian irredentism during the Near Eastern crisis, 1875–78', in *Journal of Modern History*, vol. ix, pp. 39–47; Radowitz, op. cit., vol. ii, p. 50. For the subsequent extraction by the Turks from the Austrians at Berlin of the recognition of the Sultan's rights of sovereignty in Bosnia and Herzegovina and of their occupation as only provisional, see Bareilles, pp. 150–90, *Wertheimer*, vol. iii, pp. 132–4, Čubrilović, pp. 307–13. For the final settlement in the protocols and convention of 21 Apr. 1879, see Fournier, *Wie wir zu Bosnien kamen*, pp. 81–2; Čubrilović, pp. 379–83; Noradounghian, *Recueil d'actes internationaux de l'empire ottoman*, vol. iv, pp. 209–22; *D.D.F.*, pp. 509–10; Przibram, *Erinnerungen eines alten Oesterreichers*, vol. ii, pp. 94–103.

[2] Čubrilović, *Bosanski ustanak 1875–1878*, p. 328, citing telegrams of 8 and 10 Mar. 1878, from Andrássy to Vasić (Sarajevo).

on the Bulgarian model, and in no case occupation, still less annexation, by Austria-Hungary. Two delegates (prominent rebel leaders, Vaso Vidović and Mileta Despotović) were sent to Berlin to urge these claims. Inevitably, since they received no support from the Russians, or from Ristić, their efforts were entirely in vain: the congress paid not the slightest heed and their memorandum was filed unread in the archives of the secretariat.[1]

If from the point of view of the congress as a whole Bosnia and Herzegovina provided little difficulty, the same could not be said of Novi Bazar. Andrássy joined to his statement on the occupation of Bosnia and Herzegovina a declaration that he reserved the Austrian right to garrisons and to commercial and military routes in the whole of the *sanjak*, though he disclaimed any desire to take over its administration from the Turks. Here was cast the heavy shadow of von Schwegel's Sarajevo–Mitrovica–Salonika railway plans, and here was made apparent Andrássy's determination that Serbia and Montenegro should be kept as far apart as possible and that there must therefore be a revision of the treaty of San Stefano, which had given most of the *sanjak* of Novi Bazar to Serbia and Montenegro and had left to the Turks only a narrow corridor into Herzegovina, with the key positions dominating it in the hands of their enemies. No clear understanding with the Russians as to Novi Bazar had yet been reached, to the undisguised disgust of Bismarck. According to Shuvalov, they had definite instructions not to yield on Novi Bazar. To his fury 'this impossible Gorchakov' on arrival in Berlin at once openly told Andrássy that he should have the much-disputed *enclave*, although the day before (15 June) Shuvalov himself had strongly opposed Andrássy on it. Confusion continued to reign, even though the Austrians offered, owing to Shuvalov's insistence, not to occupy Novi Bazar provided that they were allowed certain military rights and that the Russians would not oppose an Austrian occupation

[1] Čubrilović, op. cit., pp. 370–3, 314–17, based on Serbian printed and MS. sources, the Vienna archives, and oral account by Vidović. Despotović, a Serb by birth, may have been chosen because he had previously served for a long time in the Russian army; but I know of no evidence of his relations with the Russians at Berlin. The most illustrious of living Jugoslavs, Bishop Strossmayer, had tentatively suggested that he should appear before the congress to plead for the complete autonomy of Bosnia; Seton-Watson, *The Southern Slav question and the Habsburg Monarchy*, p. 127. His presence would have made no difference to the result but it would have provided a remarkable confrontation.

some years later: in return the Austrians would be more amena-
ble on other frontier questions. By 28 June the Russians were
still unsquared; no answer had come from St. Petersburg, and
the situation as regards the boundaries of Montenegro and
Serbia was desperately obscure. Accordingly, in the congress
the Russians reserved their acceptance of Andrássy's proposal
on Novi Bazar. Three days later they gave way and formally
accorded acceptance (1 July). It appears that Nelidov, who
had been sent to St. Petersburg to report, had aroused alarms
as to Austria possibly opposing the retrocession of Bessarabia
and had persuaded the Tsar reluctantly to agree to Austrian
designs upon Novi Bazar, 'si l'attitude du Cabinet de Vienne
à notre égard justifiait une pareille concession'. The outcome
of this was that before the end of the congress Andrássy gained
a further success by securing Gorchakov's signature on 13 July
to a convention whereby Russia declared that she would not
object if Austria-Hungary, in consequence of Turkish mal-
administration of Novi Bazar, were compelled to occupy it
definitively; Austria-Hungary promised in return diplomatic
assistance in all difficulties which might arise out of the execution of the Berlin treaty.[1]

Lack of concerted policy or firm decisions on the part of the
Russians had enabled Andrássy to gain his ends in Novi Bazar
before the congress discussed Serbia and Montenegro, thus
largely prejudging their frontiers in this direction. The frontiers
of Montenegro indeed were settled with but little difficulty. The
Russians, having given way on Novi Bazar, came to a private
agreement with the Austrians at the expense of Turks and
Montenegrins alike. The San Stefano boundary was to be
pushed well back from the middle Lim so as to broaden the
Novi Bazar corridor, and to be drawn on the east so as to exclude some of the Albanian clans included by San Stefano.
Montenegro was to receive the border insurgent districts in
Herzegovina (above all Nikšić and the Duga pass), Spuž and
Podgorica (neither conquered from the Turks), and the coveted

---

[1] *Wertheimer*, vol. iii, p. 131; Anuchin's diary, in *R.S.*, vol. cxlix, pp. 243–4,
vol. cl, p. 9; Shuvalov's memoirs, in *Krasny arkhiv*, vol. lix, p. 102; Protocols of the
eighth and tenth sittings, 28 June and 1 July; Nelidov's memoirs, in *Revue des deux
mondes*, 15 Nov. 1915, vol. xxx, pp. 262–4; Fournier, *Wie wir zu Bosnien kamen*, p. 74,
and *Wertheimer*, vol. iii, pp. 134–5 (on the convention of 13 July). For Austrian
difficulties with the Turks and their actual occupation of a portion of Novi Bazar
see Sosnosky, *Die Balkanpolitik Oesterreich-Ungarns seit 1866*, vol. ii, pp. 17–29.

access to the sea at Antivari. This last acquisition was a *sine qua non* with the Russians, which the Austrians accepted, but only on their own terms. Not only was Dulcigno, which had been taken by the Montenegrins, to be given back to the Turks but their third occupied seaport, Spizza, was also lost to them. It was to be annexed to Dalmatia. Haymerle openly avowed that, since it commanded Antivari, its possession was necessary in order to control the diminutive Montenegrin littoral. To make trebly sure of this, the Montenegrins were also saddled with a series of restrictions and prohibitions which ensured that they should possess no ships of war and should be as heavily handicapped as possible in smuggling. All these provisions, together with recognition of independence, had been arranged with the Russians before the question of Montenegro came before the congress on 1 July, and the Turks were left in isolation to protest that Montenegro must be much further diminished. The detailed line of the frontier was referred to the boundary committee, which agreed without difficulty, so that by 4 July Montenegro was out of the way.[1]

The Serbian frontiers, on the contrary, involved prolonged controversy. Only on the side of Novi Bazar was there no question but that the new line must be pushed back from the commanding hills, from the fortress of Novi Bazar itself, from Mitrovica and Priština. In return for this the Austrians were ready to allow to the Serbs Little Zvornik, the fortress on the Drina, and to press the Serbian claims to the south and the east against Ignatyev's big Bulgaria, but exactly how far the new Serbia should extend in these directions was very uncertain. Four places became the storm-centres of the struggle, Vranja, Trno, Tsaribrod, and Pirot, all Bulgarian by the treaty of San Stefano; Vranja and its neighbouring defiles controlling the main route to Skoplje and the Vardar valley from Nish and the Morava valley; Pirot and Tsaribrod (with the Dragoman pass) on the main Sofia–Nish road; Trno on a secondary flanking route threatening Sofia. The Russians were prepared to give up Vranja to the Serbs with alacrity, for otherwise it would fall to Turkey, but not Pirot, and they stood for Tsaribrod and Trno as necessary for the defence of Bulgaria. The British fought

---

[1] For the Montenegrin frontiers see map facing p. 412. *Wertheimer*, vol. iii, pp. 124–5; Annexes to protocol of eighth sitting, 28 June; Protocols of tenth and twelfth sittings, 1 and 4 July.

for the Turks keeping as much as possible of the upper Morava valley, but on the eastern side backed Serbia against Russia's Bulgaria. For the Serbs the vital factor was the Austrian attitude.

Andrássy was prepared to support reasonable Serbian territorial claims at a price: Novi Bazar must be out of the question; and the Serbs must bind themselves by commercial and railway agreements. This Ristić had learnt on 7 June in Vienna on his way to Berlin, and was relieved that no customs union or military convention was included in the price. As to what was meant by reasonable territorial claims Andrássy would not commit himself further than Vranja and Pirot.[1] It was made threateningly clear that if Serbia did not thus bind herself to Austria she could expect no support at the congress. San Stefano had profoundly disabused the Serbs of Russia, and Prince Milan and Ristić looked to Vienna to give them their revenge. But Grujić, the other leading minister, was russophil, and it was inadvisable for Serbia to fling herself into the arms of Austria before seeing whether, with the changed situation of mid-June, something might not be gained by attempting to play off Russia against Austria. Whether Ristić made serious approaches to the Russians at Berlin is doubtful, for his own version naturally paints his policy in the most favourable colours. He reported to Belgrade that Shuvalov counselled him to agree with the Austrians on all points and to take no step which would give umbrage to Andrássy.[2] This meant that there was no alternative for the Serbs but to purchase Austrian support by signing the railway and commercial agreements required, and thus Ristić could present his policy of close accord with Vienna as forced upon him by the Russians.[3]

The Russian attitude is far from clear. St. Petersburg still concentrated almost solely on the Bulgars, and the instructions

---

[1] Georgévitch, 'La Serbie au Congrès de Berlin', in Revue d'histoire diplomatique, vol. v, pp. 485–98.

[2] Ristić to Belgrade, tel., 19 June, and Ristić to Gruić, letter, 20 June, extracts in Georgévitch, loc. cit., pp. 503–5.

[3] There were two conventions, signed on 8 July: a railway convention by which Serbia engaged to build the Belgrade–Nish–Sofia line within three years and to agree with Austria as to a uniform exploitation of these lines; a commercial convention by which Serbia engaged to enter into a commercial treaty immediately and to examine a customs union. It appears from Ristić's account that he had himself given his agreement to these by 3 July, although the Austrians would not in return make any detailed promises as to Serbian acquisitions. Georgévitch, loc. cit., pp. 524–7, 532–3, 538.

to Berlin were unyielding to the Serbs on the Serb-Bulgarian frontier. Shuvalov knew neither Ristić nor Serbia. Bobrikov, his expert at Berlin, did, and though he mistrusted Ristić he was in general friendly to the Serbs and did not approve of Ignatyev's sacrifice of them to the Bulgars. Vranja and Pirot he thought should go to the Serbs on strategical grounds, though he held that Pirot was Bulgar by population, but Tsaribrod and the Dragoman defile were necessary for the defence of Bulgaria. Anxious to calm down Serb-Bulgarian rivalry, he had looked to satisfy the Serbs in Novi Bazar and Old Serbia.[1] A further complication was caused in Berlin by the fact that the question of the eastern frontiers of Serbia to march with the new Bulgaria was linked with the final decisions to be taken on the *sanjak* of Sofia. The British proved so obstinate on the southern and particularly on the eastern boundaries of the *sanjak* that the Russians could the less afford to yield on its western boundaries to Serbian claims. Thus the one line of Serbian extension which could receive Russian support was to the south in the Vranja district at the expense of the Turks.

The struggle began with the reference of Serbian frontiers to the boundary committee on 29 June, and to the reinforced sub-committee of military experts. It continued with confused embitterment for the next ten days, the sittings of the military sub-committee proving especially arduous and provocative. The first round was fought over the Vranja salient and resulted in substantial success for the Russians in support of Serbian claims. The stubbornness of the British could not prevent Vranja from going to Serbia. The second round was fought over the Serb-Bulgarian boundary and especially Pirot, Tsaribrod and the Dragoman defile, and Trno. Here the Austrians, backing the Serbs, were the main opponents of the Russians. In the end, the latter could not save Pirot for Bulgaria. The third round, overlapping with the second, was fought over the southern and eastern boundaries of the *sanjak* of Sofia. The British did their utmost to recede from their earlier concession that the *sanjak* should be included in Bulgaria, and at one point it seemed as if the whole Bulgarian settlement might be thrown back into the melting-pot. The deadlock was resolved only after Gorchakov, on 6 July, had shown a conciliatory attitude over Batum and Asiatic acquisitions. The British then felt that they could give

[1] Bobrikov's memoirs, in *Russky vestnik*, Dec.1889, pp. 21–5; see map facing p. 653.

way in Bulgaria. The defences of Eastern Rumelia were safeguarded by the allotment to it of the Ikhtiman pass, on the
Philippopolis–Sofia highway, but otherwise Bulgaria kept
almost all that was in dispute. The congress sanctioned these
arrangements on 8 July, and the other frontiers of Eastern
Rumelia and Bulgaria were at the same time approved. Thus
at last the new Bulgaria, since its northern boundary had already
been fixed, took final shape—for seven years.[1]

This northern boundary was part of the problem of Roumania, in that it involved the Dobrudja. The return of the Bessarabian districts was the one point upon which the Russians
were absolutely decided to insist at all costs: in return, they
offered the Roumanians the Dobrudja. They had made this
attitude quite clear to the other powers, and England had given
reluctant but explicit consent, Austria virtual consent. They
raised no incriminating difficulties as to the international régime
on the Danube, nor as to the Delta and the isle of Serpents being
included with the Dobrudja. In consequence, despite the tension between St. Petersburg and Bucarest and despite the very
suspect relations between Bucarest and Vienna, the Roumanian
delegation in Berlin found no serious encouragement in any
quarter. The two delegates did not see eye to eye with each
other. Kogălniceanu, agreeing with Prince Charles, believed
that, since none of the powers would assist, Bessarabia was lost
and that the wisest course would be to come to a direct understanding with Gorchakov and Shuvalov and obtain as much
compensation as possible. (He dreamed of the Rustchuk–Varna
line and even more.) His prime minister, Brătianu, persisted
that Roumania must not give way save before a decision of
Europe, and his politician friends at home continued to endorse
this policy of no last-minute agreement with the Russians.
Prince Charles, with his usual sanity of judgement, was wiser.
'I consider', he wrote to his father during the congress, 'that the
friendship of an entire people is of more value than one bit of
land.' With equal wisdom he did not overrule Brătianu and the
ministerial council.[2]

Roumania did at least achieve the honour, and very doubtful

[1] The details, and authorities, for the very complicated struggle over the Serb-
Bulgarian frontiers and the *sanjak* of Sofia are given in Appendix IX, together with
a map.

[2] *Aus dem Leben König Karls* . . ., vol. iv, pp. 59–60, 64, 66–7, 72; White (Bucarest)
to Salisbury, tels., 25 and 26 June, in *F.O.* 78/2908.

advantage, of being heard by the congress. Greece, which had just been heard, was not strictly a precedent, for Roumania was technically a vassal of Turkey, not an independent state; and Serbia, also a vassal, had been refused a hearing. However, on Salisbury's motion, opposed only by Bismarck and Gorchakov, it was decided that the Roumanians should be allowed to state their case.[1] They did so on 1 July, while the congress slept ostentatiously. They demanded that Bessarabia should not be torn from them, that the Russians should not evacuate their army in Bulgaria through their territory, that they should receive the Delta and a war indemnity, and that Roumanian independence should be recognized and neutrality guaranteed. Then they withdrew.

The congress gave them satisfaction on none of their demands, which were in any case designed primarily for home consumption. Recognition of independence was accepted, but with it was coupled the condition of civil, political, and religious equality for the Jews, a requirement hotly contested by Roumanian politicians of all shades. They also received the Delta, but this was coupled with the Dobrudja, for they were of course to lose the Bessarabian districts. In the Dobrudja they obtained more than they would have under the San Stefano treaty, which drew the frontier from Rasova to Mangalia. The French had in private urged the Russians to give more of the Dobrudja to Roumania, and proposed in the congress, after previous agreement with Andrássy, that the frontier should run from Silistria to Mangalia. This line had three advantages: it pushed the boundary farther to the south of the Constanza–Danube railway; it included in the Dobrudja almost the only Roumanian villages there; it threatened the stronghold of Silistria, and, in its immediate environs, gave to Roumania what was claimed to be the necessary site for a bridge across the Danube. Shuvalov was ready to accept this line, but he specified that it must exclude Silistria itself. There was some contest over this (Shuvalov afterwards declared that if the congress had insisted he would have abandoned Silistria), and it was only decided a week later that the line should run from a point to the east of Silistria to a point on the Black Sea just south of Mangalia, the exact trace to be determined later by the European commission which was

[1] Protocol of ninth sitting, 29 June. For the following see map between pp. 410 and 411.

to delimit the boundaries of Bulgaria on the spot. Subsequently there was a violent conflict within the commission over Silistria, which ended in the Roumanians securing the commanding heights.[1]

Allied with the question of Bessarabia and the Dobrudja was that of the freedom of navigation of the Danube: as Disraeli tartly reminded the congress, the cession of the Delta and the Bessarabian districts in 1856 had been expressly stated in the treaty of Paris to have been required in order to assure this end: now that the Russian frontier was again to extend to the Danube (to the northern, Kilia, mouth, though not to include the Delta), the problem of securing free navigation required renewed consideration. It did not, however, cause serious difficulty at Berlin. In an earlier chapter it has been pointed out (see above, pp. 121–2) that the European commission in the twenty years of its functioning had built up a strong position for itself by its efficient conversion of the central mouth—the Sulina channel—into an artery of international commerce, and that it would be extremely difficult, if not impossible, for the Russians to re-acquire control of the mouths. During the war both the Russians and the Turks, who had a powerful river flotilla in action, had on the obvious plea of military necessity temporarily suspended neutral navigation. The Russians had sunk stone-laden ships to block the Sulina channel and had even bombarded Sulina and sunk a Turkish gunboat there. Lengthy protests had come from the Austrians and English, but they were designed rather against any permanent suspension than against temporary stoppage which was inevitable in the circumstances of the campaign. The Russians had given assurances acknowledging the principle of the international control of the Danube, and at Berlin they were prepared to accept the continuance of the European commission, though they made some show of opposing the proposals put forward by Haymerle (2 July) for an extension of its powers, and in secret would have preferred its supersession by a commission of the riparian powers, of which they were

---

[1] Protocol of the tenth sitting, 1 July; *D.D.F.*, pp. 346–8; Waddington, 'La France au Congrès de Berlin', in *Revue politique et parlementaire*, vol. clvi, pp. 479–80; *Wertheimer*, vol. iii, p. 136; Protocol of the fifteenth sitting, 8 July. On the delimitation of the Dobrudja boundary, 1878–9, see particularly *Aus dem Leben König Karls . . .* , vol. iv, pp. 119, 124, 128, 162 ff. For other difficulties with the Russians and over the recognition of independence see Medlicott in *S.R.*, vol. xi, pp. 354–72, 572–89.

now again one. They likewise accepted the neutralization of the river up to the Iron Gates (which now was made to cover the exclusion of Turkish warships) and a provision for the razing and non-erection of fortresses on either bank. Bismarck was determined that the congress should not become enmeshed in the detailed proposals elaborated by the Austrians, and the Danube was discussed only in two sessions (2 and 4 July), most of the work falling to Haymerle and Oubril in private conclave. The upshot was highly satisfactory to the Austrians, and the Russians seem to have regarded the whole question as of quite minor interest. In particular they did not raise any awkward demands in regard to the Kilia mouth, which remained under the control of the European commission, even though the northern bank of it was now Russian and its final course into the sea entirely within Russian territory.[1]

Though by the opening of July the Danube was out of the way and Bessarabia was safe for the Russians, their Asiatic claims seemed gravely jeopardized. Left to the last, the Asiatic problem, which produced the reactions already mentioned on the negotiations over the boundaries of Bulgaria, raised the final struggle in Berlin between Russia and England. Bismarck had not been wrong in his misgivings in the middle of May as to the English so easily giving way on frontier questions in Asia. It was true that by the first Salisbury–Shuvalov memorandum Salisbury had agreed not to make a *casus belli* of the Russian acquisition of Batum and her other territorial gains in Asia under the treaty of San Stefano, in view of Russian retrocession to Turkey of Bayazid and the Alashkert valley, while the Turks were to hand over the district of Khotur to Persia. This seemed to give security to Russia, but the British cabinet accepted it only with uneasiness, for they remained in great anxiety as to the carrying into effect of the secret Cyprus convention, and

---

[1] Subsequently, in the 1883 London conference on the Danube, Russia succeeded in securing sole control of that portion of the Kilia mouth which ran wholly within her territory, but the fears that were thereby aroused that this would prove the first step in the transformation of the Kilia channel into a Russian preserve to the detriment of the Sulina mouth were not in the event justified. Ignatyev, with his usual attention to detail, had been careful to draw the frontier in the treaty of San Stefano (which was not changed in Berlin) precisely so as to allow of this possibility; *San Stefano*, p. 291. For the above paragraph: Protocols of the ninth, eleventh, and twelfth sittings, 29 June and 2 and 4 July; Avril, *Négociations relatives au traité de Berlin*, pp. 398–400, 447–51; Chamberlain, *The Régime of the International Rivers: Danube and Rhine*, pp. 63–6.

the outcry in England upon the publication of the Salisbury–Shuvalov agreement (14 June) spurred Northcote and his colleagues into agitated exhortation that Batum at least should be saved for the Turks. Immediately in Berlin the difficulty arose of meeting what Salisbury privately termed 'the extravagant nonsense talked at home about Batum. . . . Its real importance is not very large, but the mass of the people are so ignorant about it that a few strenuous Jingoes have contrived to persuade the world it is a great matter. We shall make what efforts we can, either to get it back or to have it converted into something of the nature of a free port.'[1] And further, under the second Salisbury–Shuvalov memorandum, the former had reserved his rights at the congress as regards any question affecting the Straits, while Shuvalov had stated that Russia would demand the *status quo*. It could be argued that changes in Russia's position in the Black Sea affected the question of the Straits and that a Russian naval harbour at Batum would constitute such a change.

Hence from the very beginning of the congress Batum and the Straits figured much in secret conclaves. Already on 16 June Salisbury had confidentially expounded to Bismarck the dangers as regards Batum and had intimated the probability of England requiring some alteration of the treaty of 1871 if Russia obtained it.[2] The day before he had telegraphed to Layard a proposal that the Porte should sign with England an agreement whereby, in case Russia having acquired Batum the British government considered the presence of a British fleet in the Black Sea to be expedient with a view to protecting the Sultan's interests in respect of his territories as laid down in the treaty of peace, the Sultan would not oppose by force the passage of a British fleet through the Straits for that purpose. Such an agreement, Salisbury argued, would probably prevent the Russians insisting on Batum, or, if they did gain it, it would provide for the security of Turkey without putting the Sultan in the difficult position of summoning the British fleet to his aid

---

[1] Salisbury to Lady Salisbury, extracts from letters of 23 and 22 June, in *Salisbury*, pp. 287, 286. So, too, in writing to Layard, private, 25 June, in *British Museum, Add. MSS.* 39137, ff. 256–7: 'Batum is little more than a flag. . . . It will bring little real advantage to Russia: without a very large expenditure of money, it will not enable her to threaten or injure Turkey. To Turkey the port is of the smallest possible value.' For Batum and the question of the Straits see particularly Lee, *Great Britain and the Cyprus Convention policy of 1878*, pp. 91–103.

[2] Salisbury to Cross, disp., no. 10, most conf., 19 June, in *F.O.* 78/2899.

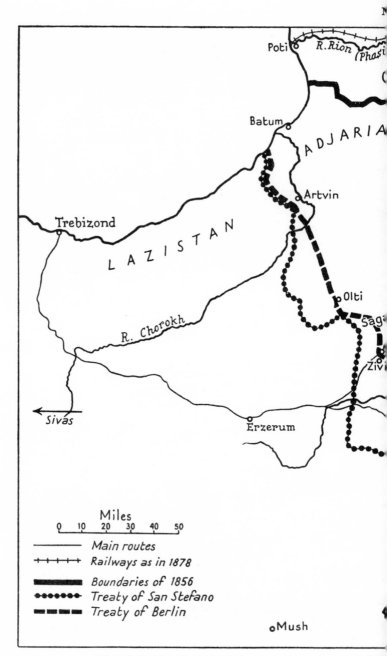

Poti · R.Rion (Phasi

Batum

ADJARIA

Artvin

Trebizond

L A Z I S T A N

R. Chorokh

Olti

Sag

Ziv

Sivas

Erzerum

Miles

| 0 | 10 | 20 | 30 | 40 | 50 |

———— Main routes
+++++ Railways as in 1878
▬▬▬ Boundaries of 1856
●●●●●● Treaty of San Stefano
▬ ▬ ▬ Treaty of Berlin

oMush

THE ASIATIC FRONTIERS OF TURKEY ACCORDIN

THE TREATIES OF SAN STEFANO AND BERLIN

according to the terms of the treaty of 1871. The Turks were willing to give a verbal undertaking, but declined to enter into a written agreement, on the score of the impossibility of keeping it secret.[1] In London the cabinet, though anxious to do something to save Batum, disliked Salisbury's proposal. In consequence he propounded a somewhat different course: England would declare, if Russia obtained Batum as a future naval station, that she interpreted the previous treaties regarding the Straits as involving an agreement with the Sultan alone and that she reserved the right of assisting him with her fleet if she thought his independence threatened. This proposal, which amounted to a unilateral declaration in the sense of what had just been proffered as an agreement with the Porte, had, in Salisbury's view, the same advantage that it would either serve to bring the Russians to terms on Batum, or, if it failed to do so, would in itself prove a wise policy to pursue. It was sanctioned by the cabinet, with a few verbal changes, on 29 June.[2]

By this time the English and Russians had come to grips with Batum. The position of the latter was awkward. They had not conquered Batum nor the Lazes territory to the south. Batum itself was strongly held by the Turks, and the wild Moslem mountaineers around were quite capable of requiring a long and costly subjugation. Constantinople was making the utmost of the Lazes; engineered a deputation coached in the verbiage of an unoffending little nation struggling to remain free; and was putting all possible pressure on the English in Berlin.[3] On the other hand, for Russia secure possession of Batum and the routes to Kutais and Tiflis were of the utmost importance for her whole position in Transcaucasia. Capable of being made into the one adequate port on that coast, Batum in Russian hands would ensure relatively rapid and easy communications by sea with Georgia and Armenia; in Turkish hands it would remain a persistent threat and a dangerous block.

Shuvalov, realizing the seriousness of the coming struggle, had sent Nelidov on 26 June to report fully to St. Petersburg

[1] Salisbury to Layard, copy of tel., 15 June; Layard to Salisbury, tels., drafts, 17 and 24 June, in *British Museum, Add. MSS.* 39137, ff. 204–5, 251.

[2] Cross to Salisbury, draft of secret and personal tel., 25 June, in *Tenterden Papers, F.O.* 363/4; Salisbury to Cross, disp., no. 39, secret, 26 June, in *F.O.* 78/2899; Cross to Salisbury, draft tel., 29 June, in *F.O.* 78/2901. Salisbury's original draft of his memorandum enclosed in his no. 39 is in 78/2911.

[3] Good samples of petitions from the Lazes will be found in the reports of the British vice-consul at Trebizond, in *F.O.* 195/1187.

and to extract definite decisions from the Tsar.[1] The next day Salisbury, by direction of Disraeli, opened negotiations with him for an independent Khanate of the Lazes to include Batum, offering in return immediate evacuation by the Turks of Varna and Batum, and a Russian military road through the Khanate to link up with her frontier. This would involve also consent to the *status quo* as regards the Straits, for Salisbury's suggestion as to this new Lazistan was preceded by a frank warning that if 'some intermediate arrangement with respect to Batoum' were not found the British government would reserve themselves the right of sending warships into the Black Sea to protect the Sultan's interests. Very naturally, from his standpoint, Shuvalov felt that this withdrawal of British consent to the Russian acquisition of Batum was tantamount to a dishonourable repudiation of the Anglo-Russian agreement, and he dryly stated that he must communicate with St. Petersburg. The suggestion as to an independent Khanate of the Lazes had, however, to be promptly dropped, since Gorchakov maintained that Disraeli had expressed himself as perfectly satisfied if Batum were declared a free port, and Gorchakov had telegraphed this to St. Petersburg.[2] Shuvalov was next met with the threat that the English would demand the freedom of the Straits if his final instructions from St. Petersburg were not satisfactory, and if some modification of the San Stefano frontier to the south of Batum were not made. By 5 July there was still no definite answer from the Tsar, and Disraeli was again rumoured to be angrily talking of departure if the Russians did not immediately declare Batum to be a free port and pledge themselves not to fortify it: whereupon Shuvalov privately promised Salisbury to arrange a retrocession of territory to Turkey with a population of 90,000, mainly Lazes.[3] One asset of the greatest importance to the Russians during these difficult days was the support of Bismarck, who appears to have worked hard to bring pressure to bear in their favour.[4]

[1] Anuchin's diary, for 26 June, in *R.S.*, vol. cl, p. 234; Nelidov's memoirs, in *Revue des deux mondes*, 15 Nov. 1915, vol. xxx, p. 262, which, however, misdate his departure by five days.

[2] Salisbury to Cross, disp., no. 55, 28 June, in *F.O.* 78/2899 (original draft in 78/2904); extract from private letter of Salisbury to Cross, 10 July, in *Salisbury*, pp. 291–2.

[3] Anuchin's diary, for 3 and 5 July, in *R.S.*, vol. clii, pp. 234, 238; Hohenlohe, *Memoirs*, under date 7 July, vol. ii, pp. 221–2; extract from private letter of Salisbury to Cross, 10 July, in *Salisbury*, p. 292.

[4] Hohenlohe, *Memoirs*, under date 2 July, vol. ii, p. 219; Bismarck, *Gesammelte*

On Saturday the 6th, in the afternoon, the congress was to discuss the Asiatic frontiers. By the early morning the Russian delegation had still received no definitive answer from St. Petersburg. When it did arrive, it appears to have been to the effect that Batum should not be insisted on at all costs.[1] But Gorchakov scored a success in the congress. The Russians announced that they gave back to Turkey Bayazid and the valley of Alashkert, in consideration of Turkey ceding Khotur to Persia, and that the Tsar would declare Batum a free port. The English, after a cryptic forewarning of the Cyprus convention, accepted the Russian statement but requested an alteration of the boundary line to the south of Batum to the advantage of the Lazes. It was agreed that the two delegations should come to a private agreement as to this amongst themselves. The English also declared that, since Batum was to be a free port and solely commercial, they would not raise any question as to the treaty of 1871 respecting the Straits, and Bismarck carefully recorded the unanimous agreement of the congress to the maintenance of the *status quo*.[2] Salisbury seems to have thought that the Lazes districts to be given back to Turkey had been already as good as settled between Disraeli and Gorchakov, though actually this was not the case, and he therefore allowed the question of the Straits to be settled in the congress without more ado.[3] He appears also to have taken the declaration of the Russians on Batum as binding them to keep it as a purely commercial port, yet in fact they had not stated in the congress more than that it should be a free port, merely enlarging without specific commitments on its commercial importance.

In consequence, though the sitting of 6 July did mark the end of the acute tension on the question of Batum, there remained another four days of sharp and extremely confused struggle. The sharpness was accentuated by the official publication on 8 July of the Cyprus agreement, which could not fail to add to

Werke, vol. viii, p. 32; *G.P.*, vol. iii, p. 4 (Shuvalov in Aug. 1878, emphasizing Bismarck's services to Russia during the congress), p. 8 (Bismarck in Aug. 1879, specifying Batum).

[1] So Anuchin states in his diary for 6 July, in *R.S.*, vol. clii, pp. 486–7. It is not clear from Anuchin exactly when the instructions from St. Petersburg arrived, nor what were their full contents. The account given by Nelidov in his memoirs as to his mission to St. Petersburg and the question of Batum is so vague as to be almost useless.

[2] Protocol of fourteenth sitting, 6 July. See also below, p. 546.

[3] Extract from private letter of Salisbury to Cross, 10 July, in *Salisbury*, p. 292.

Russian hostility, and also made the worst impression on the French and Italian delegations.[1] The confusion was greatly aggravated by the fact that Gorchakov and Disraeli largely took the negotiations into their own hands. Disraeli was ill. Neither could read a map: in any case the maps were very inaccurate and contradictory; nor was there any expert in Berlin who even claimed to know the country. The inevitable result was heavy floundering.

To the formula of Batum as a free port Salisbury pressed hard to add the words 'exclusively commercial' and at one moment he had secured this, but Gorchakov succeeded in catching Disraeli when he was very unwell and persuading him that 'essentiellement' and 'exclusivement' were the same. And so it was announced to the congress on 9 July. 'We have tried to wriggle in words', as Salisbury put it privately to Cross, 'to make it also a "disarmed" port, but we have not got more than the words "essentiellement commercial".'[2] Eight years later the Russian government threw aside any restraints that 'essentiellement' might impose upon them, and announced that they intended to fortify Batum.

On the Lazes boundary there was a recriminatory muddle during three days (7, 8, and 9 July) of constant interchanges in private between Gorchakov, Disraeli, Salisbury, and Shuvalov. On the morning of the 9th Gorchakov proposed privately a line which gave back some 90,000 souls to the Turks, and was accepted by the English. In the afternoon the congress met and he then, according to Salisbury, 'produced the map marked with a totally different line, not giving half the population, and swore it was the right one'. There was a heavy squall. The two old gentlemen each swore that the other had tricked him. There was nothing for it but to call upon the boundary committee to

[1] Waddington had been accurately informed as early as 4 June through the French naval attaché in London of the contents of the Shuvalov–Salisbury agreement and (though without specific mention of Cyprus) of an English counterstroke in the shape of a special position in Asiatic Turkey and some territorial cession; extract from report of Minister of Marine to Waddington, 4 June, in *Revue politique et parlementaire*, vol. clvi, pp. 463–6. Salisbury did not reveal the Cyprus convention to Waddington until the evening of 6 July, whereupon the French naturally displayed extreme disquiet and Salisbury was immediately led to point the way to Tunis; *F.O.* 78/2909; *D.D.F.*, pp. 352–3; Hanotaux, *Histoire de la France contemporaine*, vol. iv, pp. 384–91; Newton, *Life of Lord Lyons*, vol. ii, pp. 151–9; Langer, 'The European Powers and the French occupation of Tunis', in *American Historical Review*, vol. xxxi, pp. 58–73 (and also for the Italian reaction).

[2] Extract from private letter of Salisbury to Cross, 10 July, in *Salisbury*, p. 292.

straighten out matters. Bismarck insisted that the committee should decide by majority votes if required, and that no recourse should be had to the military sub-committee. The congress had had enough of the experts' wrangles. The committee set to work that evening. 'After a long search,' Hohenlohe noted in his diary, 'we found a small piece which we could take away again from the Russians; some mountain-ridges out of which we made a so-called *ligne de conciliation*, which was then accepted. None of us knew whether it was a sensible frontier.' Nor, of course, did the plenary sitting of the congress which adopted the committee's line on the next day without further discussion.[1]

There still remained one further Asiatic boundary question, and here the military experts did have another chance of falling out. The Turks, after an agreement reached with the Russians prior to the congress, had formally assented to the cession of Khotur to Persia, and the Russian retrocession of Bayazid and the Alashkert valley was therefore operative. This Alashkert boundary required to be laid down and was passed on by the boundary committee to the military sub-committee. It met on 10 July, fortified but not pacified by Oubril's superb official dinner, and fell out lustily, while Mehemet Ali regaled the impatient boundary committee with a recitation of his own poems. The Russians did not know their ground, but they knew enough to hold out for Zivin which commands the most important pass on the Erzerum–Kars main road. Unable to reach agreement, the sub-committee reported that a mixed boundary commission, Russian, Turkish, and British, should be set up to settle the questions at issue in delimiting the frontier on the spot. The boundary committee agreed; likewise the congress next day (11 July).[2] Yet frontier details again cropped up, and the last working sitting of the congress was adjourned in the middle,

[1] Nelidov's memoirs, in *Revue des deux mondes*, 15 Nov. 1915, vol. xxx, pp. 267–9 (an unsatisfactory version which more or less confirms Salisbury's belief that Gorchakov had deliberately tricked Disraeli); extract from private letter of Salisbury to Cross, 10 July, in *Salisbury*, pp. 292–3; *Disraeli*, p. 1209; Shuvalov's memoirs quoted by Hanotaux, *Histoire de la France contemporaine*, vol. iv, pp. 356–8, and cf. Baddeley, *Russia in the Eighties*, p. 371; Hohenlohe, *Memoirs*, under date 10 July, vol. ii, p. 224. The dispute ranged round the Chorok and Olti valleys, with the little towns of Artvin and Olti (twice captured by the Russians). Shuvalov seems finally to have given up hope of keeping Olti, but Gorchakov was the more encouraged to score a notch against his rival. He succeeded: the line agreed upon left Olti in Russian hands.

[2] Anuchin's diary, for 10 July, in *R.S.*, vol. clii, pp. 495–6; Hohenlohe, *Memoirs*, under date 10 July, vol. ii, p. 225; *A. and P.*, 1878, lxxxiii, C. 2083, no. 38.

to the buffet, while Shuvalov, Salisbury, and Mehemet Ali settled a final point as to the Alashkert boundary (12 July).[1] Even then, Desprez, in dictating as chairman of the drafting committee the finishing touches to the final text of the treaty, omitted by mistake an important word intended to save Zivin for the Turks. The commission to delimit the Asiatic frontier of the treaty, when it began its work later in the year, was to rival even Russo-Afghan frontier commissions in the protracted acerbity of its disputes. But Berlin, at least, was finished with Asiatic frontiers.[2]

It was also finished with the Straits, and without a battle. Salisbury had let this question go by in the congress sitting of 6 July, but he returned to the charge on the 11th, after the Batum question had been settled. Reverting to his project already approved by the cabinet, he read out a formal declaration to the effect that his government considered that their obligations in regard to the closure of the Straits were limited to an engagement towards the Sultan to respect in that regard the independent determinations of the Sultan conformable to the spirit of existing treaties. Shuvalov countered in the next sitting with an official statement of the Russian government's view that the principle of the closure of the Straits was a European one, and that each power was bound in respect of the treaties concerning the Straits both to the Sultan and to the other signatories. The congress, with the end of its labours almost reached, was not prepared to enter upon a new controversy, and in neither case was there any discussion raised. Both statements figured in the protocols, but the treaty itself contained only an article reconfirming the treaties of 1871 and 1856 in so far as they were not altered by preceding articles. In fact the British declaration was of great consequence, for it was,

[1] Radowitz, *Aufzeichnungen und Erinnerungen*, vol. ii, p. 59; Hohenlohe, *Memoirs*, under date 12 July, vol. ii, p. 226.

[2] Salisbury to Russell (Berlin), tel., no. 365 A, 21 July, in *F.O.* 64/900; Salisbury to Loftus, disp., no. 412, 24 July, enclosing memorandum of Simmons, in *F.O.* 181/568; Russell to Salisbury, disp., no. 448, 29 July, in *F.O.* 64/906; Dering (Berlin) to Salisbury, tel., no. 43, and disp., no. 471, 7 Aug., in *F.O.* 64/907. The signed text of the treaty, Article LVIII, ran: 'D'un point à l'Ouest du village de Karaougan, la frontière se dirige sur . . . .' The text as agreed between Salisbury, Shuvalov, and Mehemet Ali on 12 July ran: 'D'un point à l'Ouest près du village de Karaougan, la frontière se dirige sur . . . .' The wording 'près du village de Karaougan' was meant to secure Zivin for the Turks. There is much information on the working of the Asiatic delimitation commission in the *Simmons Papers, F.O.* 358/2: and see Tenterden's memorandum of 28 Apr. 1880, in 358/3.

rightly, taken by the Russians as tantamount to a fundamental alteration of the situation in regard to the Straits, and it was looked upon by St. Petersburg during the following years as a very grave menace to Russian interests.[1]

The most arduous questions arising out of the treaty of San Stefano were thus settled. The other articles caused far less contention. In Asia the Armenians were rescued from the threat of Russian assistance and given the mock comfort of a promise by the Porte to introduce reforms and protect them from the Circassians and Kurds. The San Stefano clause regulating the Russian evacuation of Anatolia had appeared to subordinate withdrawal to the effective introduction of reforms for the Armenians, and Salisbury secured the renewal of the offending article (XVI).[2] He had, however, provided in his Cyprus convention for that special protection of the Armenians which he was so careful to deny to the Russians, and he did his best, while he remained in office, to carry out an active policy of penetration of Anatolia in connexion with Armenian reforms.

In Europe the old fears of Russian religious claims and influence were not forgotten. The wording of San Stefano was carefully scanned; Mount Athos and Russian pilgrims meticulously watched; the *status quo* in regard to the Holy Places explicitly reconfirmed. But these were in the main echoes of the past; far more potent were the new fears as to Turkey's finances, yet more heavily burdened by the Russian demand for an indemnity of some £32,000,000 stg. The danger of Russia obtaining territorial cessions in lieu of a money payment had been removed by the Tsar's undertaking in the Anglo-Russian agreement, an undertaking formally renewed in the congress, but the claims of the foreign holders of Ottoman bonds needed vigilant safeguarding, and were not exactly likely to be lessened by the experience of two years of default. It does not appear that at the time the Russians set great store on the indemnity itself. Reutern told Shuvalov that he did not count on it, believing payment to be impossible, and Shuvalov told Salisbury that he was prepared in principle to abandon half of it. Salisbury had expressed his apprehensions as to the Russian financial demands

[1] Salisbury to Cross, disp., no. 99 A, 11 July, in *F.O.* 78/2900; Protocols of the eighteenth and nineteenth sittings, 11 and 12 July. See further below, pp. 571–3.
[2] Protocols of twelfth, fourteenth, and fifteenth sittings, 4, 6, and 8 July; Article LXI of treaty of Berlin.

and had put forward the strange suggestion that Russia should forgo the indemnity and that instead Bulgaria should be recognized as fully independent and should pay to Russia the tribute which she would pay to Turkey if she were not independent. Shuvalov did not have full powers to deal with this, and the sounding came to nothing.[1]

In the full congress, on 2 July, the Russian delegation had to face a lengthy offensive led by Waddington on behalf of the foreign bondholders. They escaped with the promise that they would make no arrangement with the Turks as to the payment of the indemnity which would injure the interests of the holders of Ottoman bonds, whether guaranteed or not. Their declarations were of so general a character that sharp criticism was levelled at Salisbury in the English press for not having insisted that anterior rights should be unreservedly acknowledged. In the treaty of Berlin itself the indemnity did not figure, and it was left to be regulated by the Russians and Turks alone in their definitive treaty of peace.[2]

The Russians were faced also with a proposal that, in addition to Roumania, Serbia, and Montenegro taking over a portion of the Ottoman debt proportionate to their increase of territory, the two former should pay a sum equal to the capitalized value of the tribute which they had up till now paid. This was urged by Salisbury specifically on the ground that this tribute formed part of the guarantees of the creditors of the Porte. Shuvalov, hotly urged by Ristić to stand out against this imposition, was ready enough to achieve something for the Serbs, and he had found support in Hohenlohe, Andrássy, and even the French, tender towards the young Roumania. With this backing he opposed successfully the Anglo-Turkish draft, which disappeared into the waste-paper basket.[3]

On the same day (11 July) the congress took the most important of all its decisions affecting the finances of Turkey, in the form of a modest declaration, instigated by the Anglo-French committee of bondholders and presented for insertion

---

[1] Anuchin's diary, under date 15 June, in *R.S.*, vol. cxlix, pp. 244–5. Cf. Ignatyev's almost identical suggestion; see above, p. 411.

[2] Protocol of eleventh sitting, 2 July; *The Economist*, 27 July and 31 Aug., pp. 886, 916. For the definitive treaty of peace between Russia and Turkey, signed 8 Feb. 1879, see below, p. 564: the text is printed in Appendix XI.

[3] Protocol of eighteenth sitting, 11 July; Georgévitch, in *Revue d'histoire diplomatique*, vol. v, pp. 548–51; Hohenlohe, *Memoirs*, under date 12 July, vol. ii, p. 225.

in the protocol by Corti, in the name of England and France as well, which recommended to the Porte the creation of an expert financial commission at Constantinople to examine the claims of the Ottoman bondholders and recommend satisfactory measures for their being met. The Austrians and the Germans adhered to this without demur: so too the Russians who had no bondholders. Thus the infant was born which after three tortuous years grew into the Administration of the Ottoman Public Debt.[1]

One final question, actually among the very first to be raised in Berlin, caused but little difficulty for the Russians, though in advance it had seemed a likely danger to be combated. The cause of Hellenism could serve as a useful antidote to the panslav reconstruction of the Balkans at San Stefano. Early in March the British government had been to the fore in urging that Greece should be represented at the congress, and in May they had worked hard to keep the peace in Thessaly, to draw Greeks and Turks together, and to arrange some cession of territory to Greece.[2] Gorchakov, hostile to a Greek entry into the congress, yielded so far as to allow of a Greek representative being admitted to plead his cause, if the members of the congress so decided and if the same right were accorded to the other Balkan states.[3] But with Germany and Austria similarly arguing that the admission of Greece must be settled by the congress itself, any serious fear of the Russians finding themselves faced on arrival in Berlin with another vote against them in the shape of a Greek delegation bound to England was removed. In fact by June the British official attitude had changed. Layard ardently discountenanced any further weakening of Turkey by seeking to gain something for the Greeks,[4] and this view was

---

[1] Protocol of eighteenth sitting, 11 July. For the Anglo-French committee, consisting of Guedalla, Hammond, Landon, and Kératry, and their pressure on Corti, see Guedalla to Granville, 15 July 1880, in *A. and P.*, 1880, C. 2709, no. 110.

[2] Driault and Lhéritier, *Histoire diplomatique de la Grèce depuis 1821 à nos jours*, vol. iii, pp. 474, 486–7, utilizing the Greek foreign office papers; private letters of Salisbury to Layard, 18 Apr. and 30 May, in Layard Papers, *British Museum, Add. MSS*. 93137, ff. 60, 138–40.

[3] Driault and Lhéritier, op. cit., p. 476, citing tel. of Greek minister at St. Petersburg to Athens, 10 Mar.; Loftus to Derby, tel., no. 61, 12 Mar., and extender no. 307, 13 Mar., in *F.O.* 65/1000 (but not mentioning other Balkan states).

[4] Layard Papers, *British Museum, Add. MSS*. 39131, *passim*, and particularly copies of Layard's private letters to Tenterden, 27 Mar., to Wyndham (Athens), 27 Mar., to Beaconsfield, 3 Apr.; and in 39137 to Salisbury, 12 June. Layard's general attitude to the Greeks (which was only one degree less violent than his

now accepted by Disraeli and Salisbury, anxious for the carrying out of the Cyprus convention and at the rapid changes in the Turkish ministry. It was the French, not the British, who showed themselves in Berlin eager to do all that was possible for the Greeks, and French support was clearly far less dangerous for the Russians. This was all the more the case since Waddington, though from his early years a philhellene, was not the man to proceed except with circumspection.

He left it to Salisbury to open for the Greeks. This he did, in the second sitting of the congress, in the widest terms, proposing that Greece be admitted to take part in the deliberations as the representative of Hellenism or at least to the sittings at which questions touching the interests of the Greek race were to be discussed. This opened the field so indiscriminately that it is difficult to believe that Salisbury regarded his motion very seriously and that he had not mainly in mind the philhellenes among the opposition in England. The French were ready with an amendment: the Greeks should be heard by the congress when dealing with the 'provinces limitrophes du royaume'. This whittled the field down to Thessaly and Epirus. A long discussion followed in the next sitting. Gorchakov stated that Russia would accept any proposal made in the congress in favour of Epirus, Thessaly, and Crete, and accepted the French amendment, but made it quite clear that he had done so in order to restrict the opportunities of the Greek delegates. Bismarck led the way in favour of the French; but Salisbury, after proposing to substitute 'des provinces grecques' for 'des provinces limitrophes', secured the votes of Andrássy and Corti. The Turks abstained. Thereupon Bismarck declared the British amendment lost as having divided the votes equally: the French proposal carried the day, and nothing more was heard of Greece in the congress for ten days. 'La Grèce sera entendue, mais pas écoutée.'[1]

The Russians, thus relieved, had little to fear from any backing of the Greeks. Feeling towards them was cooling fast in Berlin, and the French, despite initial hopes and despite some help from Corti, found no practical encouragement from other

attitude to the Bulgars) is summed up in his remark: 'The Greeks are only waiting for the moment to fall upon the carcase—jackal like'; private letter to Lytton, 2 Jan., copy in 39131, f. 5.

[1] Protocols of second and third sittings, 17 and 19 June; de Moüy, *Souvenirs et causeries d'un diplomate*, pp. 137-9.

quarters. Salisbury was very discouraging, and Disraeli made it clear to Delyannis that the Turks could not be forced to give way and that the principal task of the congress was to strengthen Turkey. The Turks for their part had instructions to persist to the last in refusing any annexation of Thessaly and Epirus, and their government complained unceasingly of Greek provocation on the frontier. On 29 June Delyannis pleaded before the congress for the annexation of Crete, Thessaly, and Epirus, but he had no real hopes of gaining anything beyond a possible frontier rectification or some autonomy for the bordering provinces and Crete. When the Greek question at last came up for discussion on 5 July, Waddington could not do anything more positive than propose that the congress should invite the Porte to come to an agreement with Athens for a frontier rectification along the line of the Salamyrias and Kalamas rivers (which meant most of Thessaly and Epirus), and that the powers should offer their mediation if the two parties failed to come to terms. Disraeli indulged in a harangue on the misfortunes of the Turks and the necessity of doing nothing further to weaken them, but he ended by giving reluctant assent to the French motion, which was then adopted. The Turks gave a foretaste of the difficulties they were going to raise in the negotiations that subsequently took place by declaring themselves without any instructions and reserving their opinion entirely. More important to the Russians was the decision taken previously to substitute European for the Russian surveillance, provided in the treaty of San Stefano, of reforms which the Sultan undertook to put into execution in Crete and the other Turkish provinces in Europe.[1]

Here lay the real care of the congress, to eliminate or cut down exclusive Russian influence. With the partial exception of Russia, the powers showed no sympathy whatever with the

[1] Driault and Lhéritier, *Histoire diplomatique de la Grèce de 1821 à nos jours*, vol. iii, pp. 503–4, citing Delyannis, tels., to Athens, 29 June and 3 July; Salisbury to Layard, disp., no. 2, conf., and tel., 18 June, in *F.O.* 78/2906; Layard to Salisbury, tel., no. 594, 19 June, in *F.O.* 78/2907; *D.D.F.*, pp. 347, 350–1, 357; Corti, 'Il conte Corti al Congresso di Berlino', in *Nuova Antologia*, vol. ccxl, p. 355, and *Historische Vierteljahrsschrift*, vol. xxiii, p. 462; de Moüy, *Souvenirs et causeries d'un diplomate*, pp. 133–7; Protocols of ninth and thirteenth sittings, 29 June and 5 July. According to F. Waddington, 'La France au Congrès de Berlin', in *Revue politique et parlementaire*, vol. clvi, pp. 475–6, Waddington shortly before the sitting of 5 July approached Shuvalov with the suggestion that the Russians should abandon their insistence on the cession by the Turks of Batum in return for the Turks accepting an immediate and satisfactory settlement of the question of Greek frontiers. Shuvalov would not look at such a suggestion.

strivings of the Balkan peoples to build up a new life for themselves. The Turks, though beaten, still seemed capable of
resistance to Russia in the future, and the British government
were determined to combat the panslav danger in the Balkans
from Constantinople. Hence they refused to strengthen Athens,
the centre of Hellenism, as a counterpoise to Slav Bulgars. On
the Russian side, Ignatyev's dominance earlier in the year combined later with vacillation in St. Petersburg and russophobia
in Athens removed any chance of Russia boldly standing out as
champion of Greeks and Bulgars alike at the expense of the
Turks. Thus with both British and Russians negative the Greek
problem in Berlin proved entirely subordinate. Very justifiably Gladstone, Argyll, and the opposition in England made
the most of the Conservative government's treatment of the
Greeks.[1]

The congress had laboured apace and the sixty-four articles
of the treaty were ready for signature on 13 July. By the treaty
of Paris in 1856 the powers had given their solemn adhesion
to another attempt to settle the problems presented by the
Ottoman empire and an eastern war. Infractions of this settlement had begun almost immediately. What security was there
that the treaty of Berlin would be more honoured in the obser-
vance than the treaty of Paris had been? With direct allusion to
this, Gorchakov at the closing sessions in Berlin staged a double-
edged discussion of a guarantee for the treaty about to be signed.
In 1856, as he well knew, a guarantee had indeed been undertaken, but by England, France, and Austria alone, in secret,
directed solely against Russia. On 8 July he inquired of the
congress what were the principles and the mode by which it
intended to ensure the execution of its solemn decisions. On
the three following days long discussions took place in part to
elucidate, in part to evade, the Russian proposals. It is not clear
how far Gorchakov may have been actuated by a desire for a
taste of revenge in watching the other delegations wriggling out
of an undertaking to guarantee the treaty collectively, or how
far he seriously hoped to achieve the insertion in the treaty of
an article which would engage the powers to control closely
the execution of reforms in Turkey and the carrying out of the
treaty as a whole. The Germans at least believed that he was

[1] See particularly Argyll, *The Eastern Question*, vol. ii, pp. 157–70, 206–7: it was
first published in 1879.

very sore at his failure to secure any such article.[1] Bismarck from the outset rejected any idea of a collective guarantee of an engagement to use force, but announced that he was not opposed to an article laying down the right of the powers to control by their representatives in Turkey the execution of the treaty. He continued in cautious support of the Russians, and when it came finally to voting upon the modified Russian formula he was the only one to accept it—knowing that its defeat was certain. The Austrians were critical and negative, but left the brunt of the opposition to the English who were emphatic in their hostility, as also, of course, were the Turks, since no question arose as to a guarantee covering the integrity and independence of their empire. The French and Italians were coolly opposed. Hence Gorchakov's effort, whether serious or not, to secure some species of guarantee failed.

On the day after, 13 July, the treaty was signed, and the usual valedictory encomia were pronounced. As the assembled delegates were bidding each other good-bye, the Englishmen jestingly appealed for sympathy in their task of defending their action in Parliament—'aux Chambres'. 'J'ai devant moi', Shuvalov replied with a grim shrug, 'une tâche bien autrement difficile, — me défendre dans une chambre.'[2]

---

[1] Radowitz, *Aufzeichnungen und Erinnerungen*, vol. ii, p. 59; Hohenlohe, *Memoirs*, under date 12 July, vol. ii, p. 225. De Moüy, *Souvenirs et causeries d'un diplomate*, pp. 142–4, represents Gorchakov as aiming only at putting the other powers in a quandary. For the discussion of his guarantee proposal see the protocols of the fifteenth, sixteenth, seventeenth, and eighteenth sittings.

[2] *Salisbury*, p. 285.

XIX

AFTER BERLIN

Twenty-two years earlier Tsar Alexander II had begun his reign in defeat by receiving from Paris a treaty which was for him a humiliation and a nightmare, for Russia the proof of her internal weakness and of her inability to prevent the other powers treating the eastern question as one of European concern, for Turkey a breathing-space and perhaps a new lease of life. Now in July 1878 the Tsar, thanks to the victories of his armies, received from Berlin a treaty which restored the cession wrung from him in Bessarabia, gave him most valuable acquisitions in Asiatic Turkey, recognized the full independence of Roumania, Serbia, and Montenegro, enlarged their territories, provided forms of organized national life for the great majority of the Bulgars, promised far-reaching reforms for the Christians elsewhere in the Ottoman empire, saddled the Turks with a heavy indemnity, and left them beaten and disrupted, with but a tattered patchwork of empire in Europe, with their finances ruined, and with their prestige at its lowest ebb.

Inevitably the treaty of Berlin spelt defeat for the Turks, and defeat due to Russian victories. Yet it did not spell victory for Russia. Opinions might differ as to what should have been done, by arms and by diplomacy, and as to what now should be done, but there was in Russia an almost unanimous feeling that the congress of Berlin marked the all too successful completion of a six months' campaign on the part of Europe to deprive her of the rewards due to her efforts. Already while the congress was still sitting Aksakov had delivered himself of the vials of his wrath against the western powers, 'Germany at their head', and against the governing circles in St. Petersburg.[1] For this speech the government removed him from Moscow, but the effect of his outburst, for all its exaggeration, was great in Russia and not less so abroad, notably in Germany. Aksakov was voicing the passionate disillusionment of Russians, all the more

---

[1] Speech of 4 July to the Moscow Slavonic Benevolent Society; text in Aksakov, *Slavyansky vopros*, pp. 297–308. Katkov did not take a line against Germany until the end of July, and then in cautious terms; see the summary of his views, March–July 1878, in Nolde, *L'alliance franco-russe*, pp. 203–6.

profound after the intoxicating triumphs of Gurko and Skobelev had not been consummated by the prize of all prizes, the capture of Constantinople. The press, without exception, minimized to the utmost the gains preserved to Russia in the treaty and intensified denunciation of Austria-Hungary and England emerging from the congress with Bosnia, Herzegovina, and Cyprus calmly pocketed. Only in regard to the role of Bismarck and Germany Aksakov's lead was not at the moment representative: some months were yet to elapse before the Russo-German press campaign was to be unloosed.[1]

The spirit of disillusionment was rendered immensely more serious by the intensity of the internal strain which was gradually absorbing all the energies of the government and was to increase without respite until the murder of Alexander II in 1881 was followed by iron reaction under Alexander III. The fundamental struggle of Tsardom lay not with foreign powers but with the mass of seething discontent at home ranging in every hue from ideas of pre-Petrine, Muscovite oligarchy to the dynamite of *Narodnaya Volya*. The discontent was broad-based upon the complex economic dislocation inherent in the agrarian results of the emancipation of the serfs, upon the disastrous financial situation occasioned by the war, and upon the chaotic inefficiency of a bureaucracy which combined at one and the same time the most hated and the most ridiculed vices both of routine and of arbitrariness. What more natural than that governmental circles, beset with fears of terrorism and collapse at home, should attempt to unload the failures of Russian diplomacy upon the foreigner, or that Gorchakov in particular should point in senile self-defence first to Shuvalov, then to Bismarck, as the scapegoats?

Shuvalov returned from Berlin to find the Tsar embittered against the treaty (largely through the agency of Gorchakov himself, the ambassador suspected), styling the congress 'the European coalition against Russia under the leadership of Prince Bismarck', and regarding Shuvalov as from the beginning Bismarck's dupe. He defended both himself and Bismarck hotly before his master, declared that it was only thanks to the German chancellor that the congress had not broken up in war, and argued strongly that Russia still required the *Dreikaiserbündnis*,

[1] Grüning, *Die russische öffentliche Meinung und ihre Stellung zu den Grossmächten, 1878–1894*, pp. 56–62, analysing the Russian press July–December 1878.

and, above all, good relations with Germany.[1] In the face of the general resentment against Shuvalov as the sponsor of the treaty the hopes of the last four months that he might replace Gorchakov or at least take over the Berlin embassy were dashed to the ground. During the autumn he struggled hard to prevent a break with Berlin and even to revive some understanding with Vienna along the old lines of the three imperial courts, and he and Giers succeeded, while Gorchakov was abroad for his health, in persuading the Tsar to sanction overtures through Shuvalov in person. But Andrássy put no trust in Shuvalov's manoeuvrings and continued to stand in line with Salisbury insistent on the full execution of the treaty.[2] Gorchakov's return to St. Petersburg in December completed the triumph of Shuvalov's adversaries. From his London post he struggled unavailingly against them, and in May 1879 went on long leave. He never returned for effective duty; and was never again employed, save for one brief interlude in the negotiating of the 'reinsurance treaty' eight years later.

Gorchakov remained in nominal charge of foreign affairs, but sufficiently active during the winter of 1878–9 to spur on the Russian press against Bismarck and Germany, and to add to the alarm of Berlin and Vienna by favouring a policy of wounded, but truculent, isolation: 'Inutile de vous dire', he wrote to Novikov, 'qu'à nos yeux l'alliance des trois empereurs est de fait déchirée par les agissements de nos deux alliés. À présent il ne nous reste qu'à terminer la liquidation du passé et à ne chercher dorénavant notre appui qu'en nous-mêmes.'[3] Recognition of the international isolation of Russia was, at any rate by the end of 1878, inescapable, but it was a long step farther thus to aim at the perpetuation of this isolation. Gorchakov's attitude was in substance—and here lay its true impor-

---

[1] Private letter of Radowitz to Bismarck, 8 Aug., reporting confidential communications of Shuvalov, in *G.P.*, vol. iii, pp. 3–6; Berchem (St. Petersburg) to Bismarck, disp., 22 July, reporting conversation with Shuvalov, in *G.P.*, pp. 336–7; private letter of Reuss (Vienna) to Bülow, 13 Sept., reporting conversation with Shuvalov, in *G.P.*, vol. iii, pp. 6–7.

[2] Medlicott, 'Diplomatic relations after the Congress of Berlin', in *S.R.*, vol. viii, pp. 74–9, using especially Giers to Shuvalov, 1 Nov., and Elliot to Salisbury, 16 Nov. Giers had thought that the results of Berlin should mean a great gain to Russia and bemoaned the attacks in the Russian press; extracts from his letters to Jomini, 30 June and 5 July, in Nolde, *L'alliance franco-russe*, p. 208.

[3] Extract from Gorchakov to Novikov, disp., 14 Feb. 1879, in E. Cyon, *Histoire de l'entente franco-russe* (Paris, 1895), p. 21; and in Skazkin, *Konets avstro-russko-germanskogo soyuza*, vol. i, p. 70.

tance—the same as that of Katkov and his Moscow papers with their predilection for 'the policy of free hands'. It involved the repudiation of his whole policy since 1870. At the same time he did not seriously propose (and still less did Katkov at this period) to renew the close ties with France which he himself had for a time woven with the Second Empire after the Crimean war: in his eyes the Third Republic was a suicidal prey to democratic anarchy; and the hostility of her ambassador at Constantinople and of her representatives on the commissions set up under the Berlin treaty was not readily to be forgiven. The fears which Bismarck professed in the autumn of 1879 as to Russian soundings for an alliance with France were much exaggerated and probably based on little but rumours, originating with Andrássy as a means of overcoming the Emperor William's opposition to the Austro-German alliance.[1]

By the close of 1878 the animus of the Russian press began to be turned against Germany, and from February 1879 onwards 'the war of the two chancellors' was in full swing. In this the leading role was played not by the nationalist press of Moscow but by the liberal *Golos* and semi-official St. Petersburg papers directly inspired by Gorchakov and Jomini.[2] The former was spurred on by an interview given some months earlier by Bismarck to *The Times*, in which the German had vented all his old scores of 1875 against the Russian. He had ample additional ammunition for an embittered press campaign. The new German duties aimed specially at Russian corn, timber, and cattle; the German quarantine measures against an outbreak of plague in Russia; the publication on 4 February 1879 of the Austro-German treaty abrogating the provisions for a plebiscite in northern Schleswig contained in the 1866 treaty of Prague— each in turn added fuel to the fire, which was stacked higher and higher by the inevitable counter-attacks in German newspapers and pamphlets. In the Russian foreign office especial offence was given by the attitude of the German representatives

---

[1] Skazkin, *Konets avstro-russko-germanskogo soyuza*, vol. i, pp. 107–8, note: his examination of the Russian archives reveals no clear evidence as to Russian approaches to Paris; Langer, *European Alliances and Alignments, 1871–1890*, p. 182; Koerlin, *Zur Vorgeschichte des russisch-französischen Bündnisses 1879–1890*, pp. 46–51; Simpson, *The Saburov Memoirs*, pp. 106–9.

[2] Skazkin, op. cit., pp. 71–8; Grüning, *Die russische öffentliche Meinung und ihre Stellung zu den Grossmächten 1878–1894*, pp. 63–79, analysing the Russo-German press campaign during the years 1878 to 1882; Busch, *Bismarck, some secret pages of his history*, vol. ii, pp. 391–6.

on the various commissions set up to execute the treaty of Berlin. On the Rhodope commission and as regards the handing over of Batum by the Turks the Russians had indeed been backed by the Germans, but from October 1878 onwards German policy occasioned a long series of recriminations. Bismarck's claim that the German representatives on the commissions had usually voted with the Russians was in fact unsubstantial, and his instructions to adopt an attitude of cautious observation and waiting upon Austria-Hungary and England together with his refusal, despite overtures from Giers, to take any step to- wards drawing Russia and Austria-Hungary together caused the Russians to redouble their attacks on the dishonesty of 'the honest broker' and finally produced the thunder-clap of the Tsar's letter of 15 August 1879 to the Emperor William.[1]

Bismarck, on his side, sounded what was almost a trumpet of alarm at the movements of Russian cavalry to Poland and other military preparations, which he finally asserted meant the massing of more than half the Russian army in Poland and Lithuania, with an additional concentration on the side of Galicia and Bukovina. It is unlikely that he was really con- vinced that an attack on Germany by Russia was probable, at a time when she was exhausted by her war with Turkey and was, as he himself described her, 'en complète décomposition'. But by the spring of 1879 he was undoubtedly anxious as to Austria-Hungary, nervous as to the impossibility of forecasting what Russia might do, incensed against Gorchakov, Milyutin, and the violence of the Russian press, and very dubious as to the reliability of the Tsar himself. Early in April he disclosed to Schweinitz 'entirely new and terrible horizons' involving the sacrifice, if necessary, of the uncertain friendship of Russia in favour of a closer understanding or even alliance with Austria. By June he was expounding to St. Vallier that Gorchakov had now secured the complete disgrace of Shuvalov through an unholy alliance with Katkov, Milyutin, Ignatyev, and female influence around the Tsar; that Giers was not more than a confidential valet, enfeoffed to Gorchakov; that he, Bismarck, was faced with 'la politique d'aventures remise en honneur à Pétersbourg', against which 'nous avons dans les Autrichiens des

---

[1] Muller, *Die Bedeutung des Berliner Kongresses für die deutsch-russischen Beziehungen*, pp. 61–73, and 74–104 printing texts of previously unpublished documents in the Berlin foreign office.

alliés qui peuvent compter sur un instant appui, un ferme concours, une solide alliance de notre part'. 'L'alliance des Trois
Empereurs a malheureusement cessé d'exister; je le regrette
et je voudrais la faire revivre, mais j'en reconnais l'impossibilité . . .': meanwhile the existence and integrity of the Dual
Monarchy remained for Germany the first condition of security.[1]

Doubtless this long outburst was specially intended for French
ears; and Bismarck was astray in his judgement on what was
happening in Russia. Giers, it was true, had little personality
but he was pertinacious, and so far from following Gorchakov
he remained faithful to the idea of good relations with Germany
as the corner-stone of Russian policy. Milyutin was not the
aggressive panslav that Bismarck imagined. Ignatyev did not
return to power as Bismarck feared. His alarms as to panslavism, well reflected in Treitschke's articles in *Preussische Jahr-
bücher* of that autumn, proved exaggerated. Yet, when all these
reservations have been made, Bismarck's confidences to St. Vallier may still be taken as correctly reflecting his exasperation
with Gorchakov and Russia and his intention to guard himself
by alliance with Austria-Hungary if possible before Andrássy's
resignation became effectual. Two months later the 'box on
the ear', the Tsar's letter of 15 August, was received with its
warning that circumstances had become so grave that he could
not hide from his uncle the fears that preoccupied him, the
consequences of which might become disastrous for both countries. This letter, according to Giers written by the Tsar '*ab
irato* without consulting anybody',[2] marked the climax of Russo-
German tension. It supplied Bismarck, though he could not
prevent the meeting of the two sovereigns at Alexandrovo, with
much-needed assistance in wearing down the old Emperor's
resistance to the alliance with Austria-Hungary. On 7 October
the *Zweibund* was concluded. Russia was completely isolated.

---

[1] Chanzy (St. Petersburg) to Waddington, disp., 28 Mar. 1879, in *D.D.F.*,
pp. 459–60; Schweinitz, *Denkwürdigkeiten*, vol. ii, pp. 60–1; St. Vallier to Waddington, dépêche particulière, 27 June 1879, in *D.D.F.*, pp. 518–24. St. Vallier's well-
known dispatch from Varzin of 14 Nov. 1879, recounting Bismarck's defence of
the Austro-German treaty and his attack on Gorchakov, the Tsar, and Russian
foreign policy, is republished in *D.D.F.*, pp. 580–9.
[2] Simpson, *The Saburov Memoirs*, p. 63, under date 17 Aug. 1879. This is substantially confirmed by what the Tsar told the Emperor William at Alexandrovo,
see *G.P.*, vol. iii, p. 37, and by Giers's much later account given in *G.P.*, vol. v,
p. 102. The text of the Tsar's letter of 15 Aug. to the Emperor William is in *G.P.*,
vol. iii, pp. 14–16.

The alienation of Russia from her two partners was precisely what Disraeli plumed himself on having attained at the Berlin congress. 'Next to making a tolerable settlement for the Porte, our great object was to break up, and permanently prevent, the alliance of the three Empires, and I maintain that there never was a great diplomatic result more completely effected.'[1] But at the time when Disraeli was writing thus—it was November 1880—the triumph of which he boasted was already revealing its impermanence. Giers was doing his best to repair the links between St. Petersburg and Berlin, and the detested Oubril had been replaced by Saburov. Already during the last four months of 1879 the turn was made towards 'finding the necessary support in a close Entente with Germany'.[2] From that summer Gorchakov counted for almost nothing. His health henceforward kept him mainly abroad and his interventions became increasingly spasmodic and ineffectual. Out of the confusion which continued as usual to be the most characteristic feature of the conduct of Russian foreign policy there emerged a renewal of the league of the three emperors, thanks to three men, Saburov, Giers, and Milyutin. After protracted negotiations, which had originated from St. Petersburg with the idea of a defensive agreement with Berlin alone, the tripartite treaty was at length signed on 18 June 1881. Ten months later Gorchakov formally resigned the office which in fact Giers, now appointed his successor, had been filling for the past three years. In 1883 he died, at the age of eighty-five.

Ostensibly Russia stood *vis-à-vis* the other two empires much as she had ten years before, when Gorchakov had welcomed an entente with Austria-Hungary and had joined with Germany in the first league of the three emperors. But that of 1881 owed nothing to Gorchakov, and it was formulated much more specifically in treaty provisions. Despite the appearance of renewed amity there remained unforgettable the spectre of the rupture of 1878 and 1879 and the shadow of the new Austro-German alliance, all the darker for not yet being known in detail by St. Petersburg. For this fundamental change in the relations of the three eastern powers Gorchakov himself was only in part re-

[1] Text of letter of Beaconsfield, 4 Nov. 1880, to Drummond Wolff, in his *Rambling Recollections*, vol. ii, p. 265.

[2] Extract from instructions given to Saburov by the Tsar, 20 Sept. 1879, in Simpson, *The Saburov Memoirs*, p. 67. For Giers see the extracts from his private correspondence in Nolde, *L'alliance franco-russe*, pp. 219–20, 231, 241–2, 245.

sponsible, but since he insisted on clinging to office despite his age and failing powers he must bear his share. The most powerful single influence was the growth in Russia of what Saburov described as 'the anti-German reaction . . . the spontaneous expression of a national feeling, indifferent to the calculations of politics'.[1] The upheavals in the Balkans gave to the panslavs and, above all, to Ignatyev the chance of working upon this Russian nationalism, which the war raised to a fever-heat. Then it was forced to yield by England, Austria-Hungary, and (in Russian eyes) Germany.

The Balkan question had raised the storm, and, just as it had raised Gorchakov twenty years earlier from the stepping-stone of Stuttgart to the direction of foreign affairs in St. Petersburg, so it now cast him down in impotence and dotage. Gorchakov at his best was a very clever diplomatist in the narrow sense of the word, but he had never been a statesman, and he was past sixty when for the first time he began to be faced with the problem of co-ordinating foreign policy and public opinions in Russia. Quite naturally, he never really tackled the problem. He continued with the traditions and technique of an age which was passing away. Though he used the press and was more aware of the economic forces struggling for expansion than might have been expected, his mind worked almost exclusively in terms of court intrigues, chancellery formulae, and the weekly report to the Tsar. If the bearing of old age be one of the tests of a man's true greatness Gorchakov must be severely judged, for advancing years brought out in sharpest relief all his vices and all his weaknesses. 'Le Prince Gortschakow nous a fait alors', Giers said of the late seventies and the congress of Berlin, 'le plus grand mal, il était complètement éteint et ramolli, ses mauvais instincts seuls avaient survécu.'[2] But, to do him justice, it must be allowed that fate dealt hardly in calling upon him when nearly eighty to weather the full complexity of a Near Eastern crisis.

Until the outbreak of the war Gorchakov had, on the whole, played his cards adroitly: Russia in April 1877 was well enough placed diplomatically. Thereafter he lost all grip, while still retaining sufficient intermittent energy to render confusion worse confounded. Always repelled by panslavism, but swept

---

[1] Simpson, *The Saburov Memoirs*, p. 36.
[2] Bülow (St. Petersburg) to Bismarck, 24 Dec. 1886, in *G.P.*, vol. v, p. 101.

along in the racing tide of nationalism after December 1877, he succumbed before his most dangerous rival, Ignatyev. Yet he was too much committed to working in terms of the grouping of the European powers and too well aware of Russia's weakness before a hostile combination to swallow the new policy of reckless isolation, even if his personal jealousy of Ignatyev had not acted as a sharp enough spur. Whilst almost completely prostrated in April and May 1878 he saw his other rival, Shuvalov, secure Ignatyev's discomfiture. Then his insatiable vanity lured him to the congress of Berlin, whence he returned with an intensely unpopular treaty. The aged invalid, acutely sensitive to the imprecations of outraged national feeling, did not scruple to cast all the blame upon Shuvalov, the more obnoxious to him in that he was the friend of Bismarck. The two chancellors, since 1875 mutually antagonistic and suspicious, were from now on at open war. The jettisoning of Shuvalov was insufficient either to appease the rancour of the Russian chancellor or to stem the reactions of Russian nationalism against the treaty of Berlin. Thus Gorchakov, in his last year of activity, intermittent though it was, not only went with the tide of xenophobia, but gave rein to his personal hatred of his last and greatest rival and did what he could to saddle Germany even more than England and Austria-Hungary with responsibility for the incubus of the treaty and for the failure of Russia to settle the Balkan question as she wished. The antagonism in Russia towards England and Austria-Hungary was too powerful not to be reflected in any case by the St. Petersburg foreign office, but hostility to Germany, though rising, was probably not powerful enough to have prevented Gorchakov from maintaining tolerably harmonious relations with Berlin, had he so determined. To this extent he was responsible for the aftermath of the congress which in any event was bound to be highly unpalatable to Russia.

The Tsar ratified the treaty on 27 July 1878. His dissatisfaction was only too apparent in the closing words of the official commentary which followed a fortnight later. 'The congress of Berlin was only a breathing-space, a halt on this difficult path [the final settlement of the eastern question]. Evaluating it from this point of view, Russia finds in the past faith in the future.'[1] However that might be, the immediate future held in

---

[1] *Pravitelstvenny Vestnik* (the official government gazette), 8 Aug., quoted in *Tatishchev*, p. 510.

store difficulties over the carrying into effect of the treaty even more embittering and prolonged than those encountered after the Crimean war.

Batum was the most pressing anxiety. The Russians, doubly suspicious after the struggle over it with the English at Berlin and after the Cyprus convention, were in fear lest the Turks might be stiffened into obstructing its actual cession.[1] They were intensely relieved when on 6 September it finally passed into their hands. The evacuation of eastern Thrace was thereupon begun and Totleben's head-quarters were moved from San Stefano to Adrianople on 27 September; but the further fulfilment of the Berlin treaty now met with opposition from all quarters and the three-months time-limit for the Russian occupation of eastern Thrace proved to be a dead letter. A horde of Turkish refugees had been spreading ghastly tales of Russian cruelty; the Moslem inhabitants of the Rhodope mountains were in open revolt—almost intolerable birth-pangs for the new Eastern Rumelia; Macedonia was seething, thanks to Russian encouragement; Albania was in ferment and the northern clans were leagued together to oppose by arms the cessions due to Montenegro under the treaty; the Turks could thus cling obstinately to Podgorica; in the reoccupied areas accusations of Turkish outrages were at once rife. In Bulgaria itself Dondukov-Korsakov was in command; he and his satellites openly defied the Berlin treaty as an 'Offenbachiad'; on the various commissions set up under the treaty the British, Austrian, and Turkish members retaliated with the stiffest opposition. Soon a similar struggle was waged on the commissions dealing with the frontiers in the Caucasus and around Silistria.[2] In Con-

---

[1] Loftus to Salisbury, disp., nos. 656a, conf., and 659, 20 and 22 July, recording interviews with Shuvalov and Gorchakov, in *F.O.* 65/1005. Shumla had been handed over on 18 July; Varna on 8 Aug.

[2] On Russian conduct and the commissions in Eastern Rumelia and Bulgaria there is much information in Raschdau, *Ein sinkendes Reich*, particularly pp. 223–53, 275–94, 310–13. Raschdau was closely connected with the Rhodope commission. It was widely believed that the excesses of the Russian military, which led to a wholesale flight of the Moslem inhabitants, were in part deliberately intended to procure an Eastern Rumelia and a Bulgaria which should be solidly Bulgarian. The reports of the British members of the commissions are in *F.O.* 78/2912 to 2924, and 358/2 and 3 for the Caucasus. For the Bulgarian boundary commission see also Lady Ardagh, *The Life of Major-General Sir John Ardagh* (the British commissioner), pp. 56–111. For the struggle over Silistria see particularly *Aus dem Leben König Karls . . .*, vol. iv. Hertslet, *Map of Europe by Treaty*, vol. iv, reproduces valuable maps showing the final boundaries both in European and in Asiatic Turkey.

stantinople repeated changes among the Sultan's ministers served to increase procrastination. Off Constantinople there still rode the British squadron, the effective symbol in Russian eyes of British dominance at the Porte. Layard and his government were accounted, as usual, the fountain-head of anti-Russian intrigues; to persuade the Roumanians, if a rupture with Turkey occurred, to refuse passage to the Russians; to urge the Turks on to rapid occupation and fortification of the line of the Balkans; by every means to confuse and retard the separate negotiations for a final peace treaty which Lobanov was conducting with the Porte.[1]

These negotiations were of primary concern to St. Petersburg. San Stefano, in any case, was but a preliminary treaty: such of it as had not been abrogated or modified at Berlin remained to be confirmed or supplemented by definitive peace terms. Legal and commercial relations and, above all, the question of the indemnity required a final settlement. Only with the signature of a definitive treaty of peace could the Russians feel somewhat reassured lest the Turks should abandon themselves to recalcitrance. At last, in February 1879, the Turks agreed to sign, but only after having succeeded in postponing a final agreement on the payment of the indemnity.[2] Within a month the Russian troops had evacuated eastern Thrace. But there remained the army of occupation in Eastern Rumelia and Bulgaria, which under the treaty of Berlin was due to withdraw on 3 May. Here was 'the great question . . . , Will they evacuate on the 3rd May all the territories south of the Danube,—or rather of Roumania? If not, I do not see how peace can be preserved. . . .' So Salisbury wrote six months in advance, castigating 'the usual duality of Russian policy', fearing the trickery and resistance of the military, but on the whole hopeful that the Tsar would abide by the

---

[1] Extracts from the Tsar to Totleben, 15 Nov. 1878, and 7 Mar. 1879, quoted in *Tatishchev*, pp. 515, 521.

[2] For the text of the definitive treaty of peace signed 8 Feb., see Appendix XI. The payment of the indemnity, amounting in all to 802,500,000 francs (about £32,000,000 stg.), was finally regulated by the Russo-Turkish convention of 14 May 1882; see text in Noradounghian, *Recueil d'actes internationaux de l'empire ottoman*, vol. iv, pp. 301–4. The indemnity was to be paid in annual instalments of £T. 350,000 (about £320,000 sterling), guaranteed on certain taxes. The Russians waived their claim to interest payments on the total sum. The payments, which began in 1883, were in fact not regularly made, the Russians only from time to time bestirring themselves for fulfilment; Ch. Morawitz, *Die Turkei im Spiegel ihrer Finanzen* (Berlin, 1903), pp. 116–20.

treaty.[1] He did so: for he was able to induce the powers to account 3 May as the date for the beginning, not the completion, of evacuation, and to score a signal success in being empowered to announce to the Bulgars that the Sultan did not intend, at any rate for the time being, to exercise his right of garrisoning the Balkan passes.[2] By 3 August evacuation was duly completed.

If the intention of the Sultan were persisted in (as in fact it was), the eventual union of the two provinces would clearly be all the easier. Union was the ultimate aim of Russian policy, the immediate object of Bulgarian aspirations. But, although the conduct of the Russian administrators on the spot gave ample ground for European accusations, the Tsar, for all the confused waverings of his Bulgarian policy, felt that the only course was to fulfil the Berlin treaty and wait judiciously for time to prove its impracticability. Time, aided by Russian agents supplying arms and money, proved him right. Seven years later the revolution in Philippopolis broke out which secured union, but at the same time ushered in the crisis that completely alienated Alexander II's successor from the one Balkan country which in 1878, despite the efforts of Disraeli, had been left predominantly under Russian influence. Salisbury was right in his belief, expressed at the very end of that year, 'that we shall get the Russians out and set up a rickety sort of Turkish rule again South of the Balkans. But it is a mere respite. There is no vitality left in them.'[3] The congress of Berlin, as the congress of Paris in dealing with the Roumanians, failed to keep the Bulgars disunited, though it had the better excuse in that Bulgarian nationalism was more of an unknown quantity. Ultimately the problem of Macedonia, where Austria-Hungary and England only too successfully checkmated the solution of San Stefano, was of more serious consequence than that of Bulgaria and Eastern Rumelia. Whereas the Austrians themselves had never set great store by the separation of Bulgaria and Eastern Rumelia and by 1881 were ready to admit the principle of union in the *Dreikaiserbund*, they insisted in the same treaty on guarding themselves amply against any alteration to their disadvantage of the *status quo* in Macedonia. In fact, after the

[1] Extract from letter of Salisbury to Loftus, 16 Oct. 1878, in *Salisbury*, pp. 344–5; and see pp. 359–60.

[2] *Tatishchev*, p. 521, citing Lobanov to Gorchakov, 7 May 1879.

[3] Minute of Salisbury on a memorandum of Tenterden, 29 Dec. 1878, in *Tenterden Papers, F.O.* 363/5.

summer of 1878 the Russians scarcely looked west of the Struma, and confined their energies almost exclusively to the two eastern Bulgarian regions.

There, Eastern Rumelia was for nine months under Russian control, beset by armed insurrection in the Rhodope mountains and the prying intervention of the European commissions. Notwithstanding all difficulties, the new autonomous régime, based on an inordinately lengthy organic statute, was installed in May 1879 and the Russians departed. Besides their success in at least delaying any military occupation by the Turks, they had also secured the appointment as governor-general of an Orthodox Bulgaro-Greek, Aleko Pasha (Alexander Vogorides), in place of Rustem Pasha, a Catholic of Dalmatian origin, who had originally been agreed upon by the other powers.[1] More important, they had made good progress with the formation of the gendarmerie and militia, and had distributed arms widespread. The armed Bulgarian nation was to be the advanced post of any Russian action in the Balkans which the all too dubious future might require.[2]

North of the Balkans in the principality of Bulgaria universal military service, more or less on the Russian model, was instituted; equipment and armament on a lavish scale were provided; some 400 Russian officers and 2,700 noncommissioned officers were left to train and command the Bulgarian levies: a Russian general, Parensov, well acquainted with the country, acted as minister of war, in strict accordance with the instructions of Milyutin.[3] Substantially this was the

[1] Aleko's appointment was denounced by Layard as 'the very worst that could be made. He is a weak, silly fellow, very disloyal to the Sultan and a mere tool in the hands of the Russians and Bulgarians.' Private letters of Layard to Hammond (formerly permanent under-secretary for foreign affairs), 7 June and 1 July 1879, in Layard Papers, *British Museum, Add. MSS.* 38962, ff. 5, 8.

[2] Most of the higher administrative posts in Eastern Rumelia were filled by foreigners but not Russians, except in the militia: for details, and an encomium on Tseretelev as consul-general at Philippopolis, see Tatishchev, *Iz proshlago russkoi diplomatii*, pp. 399–401.

[3] P. A. Mateyev, 'Bolgariya i Vostochnaya Rumeliya posle Berlinskogo Kongressa', in *I.V.*, vol. xxiv, pp. 349–51. Parensov was recalled in Mar. 1880 after Prince Alexander's personal expostulations in St. Petersburg that he refused to carry out the Prince's orders without the previous sanction of Milyutin; Corti, *Alexander von Battenberg . . .* , pp. 82–3; Parensov, *Iz Proshlago*, vol. iv, pp. 232–50, 266, 274–8, 283–9. But the four succeeding ministers of war were also Russian generals. Parensov was hard-working and effective, but most of the Russian officers were of poor quality and very unpopular; Nemirovich-Danchenko, *Posle voiny*, pp. 133–6, 214.

quid pro quo for the democratic radicalism of the Tirnovo constitution, which, to the disgust of men such as Aksakov and Leontyev, was in full contradiction with the principles and practice of Russian Tsardom.[1] Provided the Russian military controlled the armed forces, the Bulgarian 'liberals' might have their western constitution with its maximum obstacles in the path of the oligarchical 'conservatives' and of Prince Alexander. The prince had been elected by the national assembly, under Russian direction, in April 1879. A favoured nephew of the Tsar, a volunteer in the Russian army during the war, a Battenberg and well connected with Germany and Austria, a relative of Queen Victoria (and soon to win her warmest feelings), he started with much in his favour; but he quickly showed that, unlike the Hohenzollern at Bucarest, he did not possess the qualities, in truth exceptional, that were needed in the cockpit, both national and international, of Sofia.

If, under Alexander II, the official Russian policy in Bulgaria was primarily concentrated, thanks to the influence of Milyutin, upon strategical considerations, there was at the same time such confusion in St. Petersburg and such division of aim among the Russian officers and agents in Bulgaria that, even without the action of Prince Alexander, there was every likelihood of prolonged tension with Austria-Hungary and England and of disastrous embroilments with the little groups of Bulgarian politicians. The seven years following the treaty of Berlin were the history of the complete collapse of Russian hopes that in Bulgaria something at least might be achieved to offset the humiliations suffered through the congress; a collapse so ironically complete that the very union of Eastern Rumelia with Bulgaria was a blow in the face of Alexander III. Politically the dominance of a Tsarist Russia was impossible, save by force, over a peasant people ruggedly individualist and ardently nationalist. The Russians in the end were anxious to impose a viceroy in the position of a military dictator, but they delayed too long and were reduced to fomenting a series of military plots and conspiring against Ferdinand, the new prince,—without success.[2]

---

[1] For a spirited, contemporary Russian defence of the Bulgarian radicals, see Nemirovich-Danchenko, *Posle voiny*, pp. 5, 81, 255–9.

[2] See particularly the documents from the Moscow archives published in *Avantyury russkogo tsarizma v Bolgarii*, edited by P. Pavlovich.

Economically there were still no links which might serve to bind Bulgaria to Russia in semi-colonial vassalage. The tentative efforts of Moscow firms such as the Morozovs towards effecting the commercial conquest of their brother Slavs were soon abandoned: Prince Gagarin's Black Sea–Danube shipping company collapsed after five ignominious years: banking and insurance schemes remained mere paper projects. Muscovite capitalism showed itself too weak to compete with its English and Austrian rivals; and indeed Bulgaria, and the Balkan peninsula in general, never captured the serious attention of the main Russian commercial and industrial interests. This general statement remains true even though one of the chief issues in the struggle for Bulgaria was the Russian railway programme. This involved a line from Rustchuk to Sofia and Kustendil and called forth the most determined opposition from the Austrians intent on the completion of the Orient railway and armed with their treaty rights extracted at Berlin. The Russian project was the work of the two notorious St. Petersburg Jewish entrepreneurs Polyakov and Günzberg, but Russian financiers were not deeply engaged, and most of their funds seem to have come from Paris. They belonged to the international class of financiers of the type of Strousberg and Hirsch (their rival of the Orient railway with whom, nevertheless, they were in the closest relations) and were not bound up with Muscovite nationalism. The real importance of the battle over the Bulgarian railways lay less in any economic expansion of Russia in Bulgaria than in their strategical significance. The diplomatic support which the Polyakov–Günzburg combination received from the St. Petersburg foreign office was in the last resort dictated by the military considerations of the war office, not by the pressure of economic interests.[1]

Inevitably the Bulgars were the main centre of the diplomatic struggle following the treaty of Berlin, for they alone might serve as a secure base for Russian influence in the Balkan peninsula. Elsewhere Austria-Hungary and England had already gained the day, and the former within a few years very successfully consolidated her position. Montenegro remained true to Russia, but she was too closely hemmed in by Austrian power and too much weakened by the struggle for her Berlin gains with the Albanians and Turks to count alone. Her frontiers

---

[1] Skazkin, *Konets avstro-russko-germanskogo soyuza*, vol. i, pp. 214, 254–5, 261; Popov, 'Ot Bosfora k Tikhomu okeanu', in *Istorik Marksist*, vol. xxxvii, pp. 12–13.

were finally settled only at the end of 1880, when she received Dulcigno in place of the territory in dispute.

Greece, persistently hostile to Russia as the creator of the Bulgarian nation, followed in the wake of Austria-Hungary or England: she was extremely dissatisfied with the Berlin treaty, but was too weak to take independent steps; and where else could she look for active help? The negotiations for frontier rectification, which had been promised in the treaty, were rendered wholly nugatory by the Turks. The return of Gladstone to power in April 1880 seemed to presage some success for Hellenism, but in point of fact his Berlin conference of that summer failed utterly, and it was only the intervention at Constantinople of Bismarck, for reasons quite unconnected with Greece herself, that at long last secured for her some small gains in Thessaly and Epirus.

Serbia, indignant and disabused with Russia, had to put up with the only other alternative. She was helpless before Austria-Hungary, and once Ristić was forced out of office in 1880 she passed into the vassalage of Austria-Hungary for the rest of Prince Milan's reign. The railway convention of 1880 for the Belgrade–Nish and Nish–Vranya lines, the Orient railway agreement of 1883, the tariff and commercial treaty of 6 May 1881, and the political treaty of 28 June of the same year combined to reduce Serbia to a virtual protectorate of Vienna. The irredentist feelings incipient in Bosnia and Herzegovina, once these had been occupied after violent resistance, went underground or were divided, and a generation was to pass before the vacillation of Vienna, the obstinacy of Buda-Pesth, the restoration of the Karageorgević dynasty, and the incitement of more solid revolutionary movements confronted the Dual Monarchy with the Jugoslav menace in acute form.

Roumania, with her *irredenta* in Transylvania, was reluctant enough to revolve in the orbit of Austria-Hungary. But the national revival across the Carpathian border was scarcely begun and still looked to Vienna rather than Bucarest; and Russia, the betrayer, spoliator, and tyrant, also had unredeemed Roumanians, in Bessarabia, as well as her protégés the Bulgars. The hatred of Russia was further increased by the struggle on the Dobrudja boundary commission, which in the end failed to allot Silistria to Roumania, and by continued disputes over the passage of Russian troops and other matters arising out of the

Berlin treaty. The wonder is that the Roumanians did not come
to terms with Vienna sooner than they did. A close agreement
was retarded by quarrels over the working of the commercial treaty of 1875, over the Danube navigation and railway
concessions, and over the position of the Jews in Roumania,
an article in the treaty of Berlin which caused the utmost difficulty. Above all, Bismarck for some time was driving Roumania
hard in the intermixed tangle of railway financing and Jewish
rights, and Roumania was not definitely won over into the
camp of the Triple Alliance until the German attitude had
changed (1883). Thereafter Austria-Hungary if attacked by
Russia (or Serbia) was assured of Roumanian assistance, while
Roumania in case of attack from any quarter was to be supported by Austria-Hungary. Russia's land route to Bulgaria
was blocked. Politically Roumania was tied to the two central
powers; economically they had the lion's share of her trade.

Thus the Dual Monarchy emerged from the Near Eastern
crisis with her position in the Balkans transformed. Bosnia and
Herzegovina were hers, though their subjection in 1878–9 was
unexpectedly costly and in 1881–2 she had to suppress a last
revolt, owing something to Russian agents in Sofia.[1] Her garrisons in the *sanjak* of Novi Bazar separated Serbia from Montenegro, and they were there with the written concession by the
Russians that eventual permanent occupation and administration might take place.[2] Further territorial extension to the
south-east was certainly not contemplated by Andrássy or his
successors, Haymerle and Kálnoky. Magyar opposition was by
itself sufficient to frustrate any such aims. A political preponderance in the western Balkans which would ensure economic
control, above all in the Morava and Vardar valleys, and a
through railway route to Constantinople were the main objects

[1] For the violent resistance put up in 1878–9, see Sosnosky, *Die Balkanpolitik
Oesterreich-Ungarns seit 1866*, vol. i, pp. 187–286. For Russian intrigues in 1881–2:
Skazkin, op. cit., pp. 207–12, using the Russian archives; and cf. nos. 15, 16, 18,
19, 21–4, 26–30, 32, and 39 in the, probably genuine, '*Occupationsfonds*' documents,
German translation in R. Leonow, *Geheime Dokumente der russischen Orient-Politik
1881–1890* (Berlin, 1893). Sosnosky, op. cit., vol. ii, pp. 30–42, describes the revolt
in 1882, but without referring to Russian intrigues.

[2] See above, p. 532. In the final stages of the negotiations for the *Dreikaiserbund*,
in June 1881, Alexander III refused to recognize annexation of Novi Bazar, though
he accepted annexation of Bosnia and Herzegovina in the protocol to the treaty;
Simpson, *The Saburov Memoirs*, pp. 247–8. For Andrássy's views on Novi Bazar and
his failure to secure Turkish consent to complete occupation by the Austrians see
Wertheimer, vol. iii, pp. 269–77, and Sosnosky, op. cit., vol. ii, pp. 17–29.

of the Ballplatz. Their successful attainment, coupled with similar success in Bucarest and Alexander III's fiasco in Bulgaria, marked the temporary extinction of Russian panslav dreams and the nadir of Russian influence in the peninsula.

For Russia, on the other hand, the Balkans had always meant both the problem of the Balkan peoples, whether looked upon primarily as Orthodox or primarily as Slavs, and the problem of Constantinople and the Straits. The latter problem strategically and economically was paramount. It was not so for Austria-Hungary; but in the eyes of Russian statesmen, as of British, it occupied the first place in the Near Eastern question. For two generations Constantinople had figured as the crucial point of Anglo-Russian hostility. In 1878 it had brought the two countries almost to war again. The congress of Berlin relaxed the immediate tension of impending hostilities, but so far from allaying the fears of the Russians it added materially to their suspicions of British designs upon the Straits, and in the following years the influences that dominated Russian policy in the Near East were above all concentrated on the defensive problem of denying the Bosphorus and the Black Sea to the British fleet.

The treaty of Berlin itself (Art. LXIII) had not done more than renew the treaty of 1871. It gave international sanction to the closure of the Dardanelles and the Bosphorus to all warships, other than Turkish, so long as Turkey was at peace, except that the Sultan was accorded the right to open the Straits in time of peace to the warships of friendly and allied powers if considered necessary by him for the maintenance of the 1856 treaty of Paris in so far as it was still in force. By 1878 the treaty of Paris was even more of a dead letter than in 1871, but this provision might have dangerous consequences for Russia, who was still without a fleet in the Black Sea and without a maritime ally, and was concerned to prevent ingress into the Black Sea rather than to secure egress into the Aegean. What, with good cause, caused the gravest alarm to the Russians was not the wording of Article LXIII but the interpretation officially given to it by Salisbury at the congress. His declaration that the obligations of Great Britain in respect of the closure of the Straits were limited to respecting the independent decisions of the Sultan in conformity with the spirit of existing treaties was taken in Russia to mean that the whole principle of the closure of the Straits was reduced to a nullity. Shuvalov's counter-declaration to the congress placed on record the Russian point of view but could do nothing to change the gravity of the situation.

Even after Batum had been handed over and the British fleet had repassed the Dardanelles, which was not until March 1879, the further execution of the Berlin treaty and the chronic instability of the Turkish government were in the eyes of St. Petersburg all too likely to lead to conflagration or collapse which would be seized upon by the British to their fullest advantage. The Cyprus convention, the continuous struggles with the British on the treaty commissions, Layard's threatening activities as retailed by Lobanov-Rostovsky, the miniature army of British instructors, consuls, and agents in Asia Minor—all combined to persuade the Russians that the British were aiming at establishing a position of such predominance in Turkey that at the required moment they could make certain of controlling the Straits. Salisbury's active intervention in Asia Minor was especially disturbing. At Alexandrovo Milyutin spoke out openly to the Emperor William. 'England is organizing and arming Asia Minor; the country is flooded with her officials, generals, and officers disguised as consuls—that means hostile intentions against our possessions in the Caucasus. We must be armed on all sides; we are not yet strong enough. The clash in the East is at hand.'[1] The Afghans and the Tekke Turkomans added to the likelihood of the clash. The winter of 1878–9 brought to a head the whole Afghan problem, and although Gladstone's return to power in 1880 was followed by abandonment of the Conservative government's Anatolian policy the Middle East remained a battle-ground in Russian policy, always closely linked with that of the Near East. If England were at war with Russia, would not Turkey be forced to take part, or in any event to deliver the Straits to England?

The degree of Russian preoccupation with the defence of the Straits can be judged from the views of Giers and Milyutin, the two men who from the summer of 1879 until the close of Alexan-

---

[1] Text of the report of the Emperor William on the Alexandrovo meeting, 9 Sept. 1879, in *G.P.*, vol. iii, p. 64; cf. extract from report of Lobanov-Rostovsky to Giers, 12 Dec. 1878, in Nolde, *L'alliance franco-russe*, pp. 222–3. The Russians were not unjustified in their alarm over Salisbury's policy in Asia Minor; see *Salisbury*, pp. 304–24, and Lee, *Great Britain and the Cyprus Convention policy of 1878*, pp. 125–65.

der II's reign exercised the greatest influence on foreign policy. Both were deeply alarmed at the isolation of Russia; both feared the worst from the British declaration on the Straits at the Berlin congress; both were convinced that Russia, in view of her financial exhaustion, of her internal situation, and of her lack of a Black Sea fleet, could only stand on the defensive. Giers, with his bureaucratic conservatism and close attention to the Tsar, looked upon Germany as the natural support for autocratic Russia against internal and external foes alike and felt that Russia's international position could be safeguarded only by an entente or even an alliance with Germany. The conversations with Bismarck inaugurated by Saburov as early as July 1879 were only too welcome as the first step in this direction, but from the very first both Giers and Milyutin, as against Saburov, insisted on the problem of the Straits figuring as the predominant question in the long negotiations with Berlin that were to follow. It was essential to obtain German adhesion to the Russian view on the principle of the closure of the Straits and at least diplomatic support for Russian resistance to any attempt by the British to implement their completely opposite interpretation of the treaty of Berlin. When agreement with Bismarck was finally reached in accordance with Russian desires and the draft treaty was presented to Haymerle, his amendments whittling down the article on the Straits were brusquely and successfully pushed aside:— 'Nous insistons sur le maintien de la rédaction primitive' — 'Maintenir le texte primitif'. Article III of the *Dreikaiserbund* was the Russian reply to the British declaration on Article LXIII of the treaty of Berlin.[1]

This was a none too effective reply, for it could not alter the

[1] Skazkin, *Konets avstro-russko-germanskogo soyuza*, vol. i, particularly pp. 120–32, based on the Russian archives; Simpson, *The Saburov Memoirs*, pp. 294–5, giving the Russo-German draft, the Austrian amendments, and the Russian replies. The text of Article III as finally signed ran: 'Les Trois Cours reconnaissent le caractère européen et mutuellement obligatoire du principe de la fermeture des détroits du Bosphore et des Dardanelles, fondé sur le droit des gens, confirmé par les traités et résumé par la Déclaration du second Plénipotentiare de Russie à la séance du 12 juillet du Congrès de Berlin (protocole 19). Elles veilleront en commun à ce que la Turquie ne fasse pas d'exception à cette règle en faveur des intérêts d'un Gouvernement quelconque, en prêtant à des opérations guerrières d'une Puissance belligérante la partie de son Empire que forment les détroits. En cas d'infraction, ou pour la prévenir si une pareille infraction était à prévoir, les trois Cours avertiront la Turquie qu'Elles la considèreraient, le cas échéant, comme s'étant mise en état de guerre vis-à-vis de la partie lésée, et comme s'étant privée, dès lors, des bénéfices de sécurité assurés par le Traité de Berlin à son statu quo territorial.'

fact that the British had a fleet and the Russians had not, and that neither Germany nor Austria-Hungary would give actual material support against England over the Straits. Only as the Black Sea fleet was re-created in the later eighties and Russia moved more and more closely towards France was the naval defencelessness of Russia remedied. A risky *coup de main* on the Bosphorus was a possibility, but that, at any rate between the congress of Berlin and the assassination of Alexander II, would not be attempted *unless* the Tsar was forced to attempt it in order to forestall British action. Milyutin, the most consistently influential of the Tsar's advisers in his last three years, looked at the problem of Constantinople and the Straits from a strictly defensive angle. For him even ultimate acquisition by Russia was not essential: all that Russia needed was the assurance that the entrance into the Black Sea did not pass into the hands of a great power, and that no other great power acquired the predominance in the Balkan peninsula. It is true that Milyutin, while ridiculing the political aberrations of Russian panslavs, recognized that the growth of nationalism among the Slavs outside Russia was full of danger for Austria-Hungary and Germany and that it was a force which inevitably inspired sympathy and assistance in Russia; and it is also true that he sketched as an eventually desirable solution the formation of a Balkan federation, composed of Turkey (reduced to Constantinople and Thrace with Adrianople), Greece, Albania, Bosnia-Herzegovina (represented by Austria), Montenegro, Serbia, Roumania, Bulgaria, and if insisted upon by Austria-Hungary a separate Macedonia, with the Straits and the Sea of Marmara neutralized under an international commission, backed by warships of each of the six great powers. Such views were undoubtedly in complete opposition to the interests of Austria-Hungary (though not necessarily to those of England), but Milyutin did not propose that Russia should aggravate the burning question of panslavism, and his idea of a Balkan federation related to a distant future not to the immediate present, for which it was obviously impracticable. The most striking feature of his attitude was the relative moderation displayed in regard to Constantinople and the Straits. For Milyutin plans for an annexation of Bulgaria by Russia or for a seizure of Constantinople were extravagant adventures which were utterly distasteful. He regarded the Bulgars simply as a possible armed ally against

Turkey and England, *if* the latter showed her hand at the vital point for Russia—the Straits. It was necessary for the Russians to use all possible means, however unreliable or however indirect, which might assist to prevent the seizure by England of the keys to their house; and here Central Asia could play a role; but the very last of the means of defence that Milyutin countenanced was the gamble of trying to put the keys in their own pocket.[1]

In the earlier years of Alexander III there was no material change from the defensive role which was forced upon Russia, even though the 'liberal' Milyutin immediately left the ministry of war and Ignatyev returned to favour for a year at the head of the ministry of the interior. The new Tsar, who acted much more effectively as his own foreign minister than his father had done in his failing years, held firmly to the necessity of being prepared in advance and certainly was explicit enough as to the final end of Russian policy in the Near East. 'In my view', he wrote to Obruchev, since 1881 chief of the general staff, 'we ought to have one principal aim—the occupation of Constantinople, so that we may once for all maintain ourselves at the Straits and know that they will remain in our hands.' But, as his comments on Nelidov's proposals of 1882 showed, he had few illusions as to the likelihood of any early attainment of this aim. He went on to say: 'That [the occupation of Constantinople] is in the interests of Russia and it ought to be our aspiration; everything else in the Balkan peninsula is secondary for us. There has been enough propaganda to the detriment of the true interests of Russia. The Slavs must now serve Russia, and not we them.'[2] Nothing could bring out more clearly the primacy of the problem of the Straits and the complete transformation of the panslav sentiments which had played such a part in 1876 and 1877. Alexander himself at that time had appeared to share them, but he had frowned privately upon the excesses of the Slavonic committees and had ended by recoiling in alarm before 'the national movement'. Years later, as Tsar, he was credited appropriately enough with the saying: 'Our mistake in 1876 and 1877 was that we went with the masses and

---

[1] Skazkin, *Konets avstro-russko-germanskogo soyuza*, vol. i, particularly pp. 143–7 (analysing two memoranda of Milyutin, Nov. 1879 and 17 Oct. 1880) and p. 227.

[2] Text of letter of Alexander III to Obruchev, 24 Sept. 1885, in *Krasny arkhiv*, 1931, vol. xlvi, pp. 180–1. The text of Nelidov's 1882 memorandum on the occupation of the Straits, and the Tsar's comments, are given loc. cit., pp. 182–7.

not with the governments. A Russian emperor ought to deal only with governments.'[1]

Such a feeling was of all the greater force in the years immediately following the Berlin congress when Russian autocracy was at grips with Russian terrorism. The mass propaganda of 'the going to the people' and *Zemlya i Volya* were succeeded by the conspiratorial organization *Narodnaya Volya*. The shot fired by Vera Zasulich at the chief of police in St. Petersburg in January 1878 began the campaign of terrorism against the government which was finally concentrated on the life of the Tsar. Thanks to the crass inefficiency of police and body-guard his assassination was eventually accomplished in March 1881, just when the personnel and material means of the tiny group that composed *Narodnaya Volya* were all but exhausted. At no period were 'the masses' more suspect in the eyes of those in authority. To many, indeed, it seemed that Russia was all but undermined by 'nihilist' conspiracies, that the war had quickened and unloosed revolutionary forces which might rapidly bring about a complete break-down. Bismarck, for one, could wonder whether 'the ramshackle empire' was not the Habsburg but the Romanov.

The situation during the closing years of Alexander II's reign was probably less revolutionary than appeared at the time to the government and to many foreign observers. The war could not have anything of the direct social and political effect of the disasters either of the Crimea or of Manchuria (though it did have the effect, literally of vital importance, of introducing certain of the terrorists to the latest types of mines and bombs).[2] The peasantry, for all their dark mutterings as to what emancipation ought to mean, were in great part somewhat better off than before 1861: there were no such outbreaks among them as occurred after the Crimean war;[3] the experiences of those who 'went to the people' in the seventies had been utterly disillu-

---

[1] *G.P.*, vol. v, p. 53.

[2] See particularly Pokrovsky, *Russkaya istoriya s drevnyeshikh vremen*, vol. iv, pp. 209–10. Of the ten attempts or plans to assassinate Alexander (1878–81) only one was with a revolver.

[3] There were, however, serious agrarian outbreaks in 1878–9 among the Moslems in Kazan and Samara governments. To judge from the reports of officials, events in the Balkans, as in 1854, had only a minor effect on the Volga Moslems. See the collection of documents, *Materialy po istorii Tatarii vtoroi poloviny xix veka*, vol. i; *Agrarny vopros i krestyanskoe dvizhenie 50–70–kh godov xix v.* (Akademiya Nauk, 1936).

sioning. The factory workers were still too few and too un-
developed for any revolutionary movement to have yet found
a firm basis among them. The revolutionary groups, largely
recruited from the poverty-stricken student class, and from 1878
more than usually divided amongst themselves, had the character of a staff without an army. But to contemporaries and above
all to the government the situation appeared almost catastrophic.
All the energies of the latter were concentrated on police
measures, and a large part of European Russia was put under
the equivalent of a state of siege. The experiment of Loris
Melikov's 'dictatorship of the heart' meant little relaxation.
His greatest task was to win over the general mass of the public
from indifferentism or even sympathy with the revolutionaries.
The war had revealed, as usual, gross incompetence, or even
worse, on the part of the authorities. The peace had shown
them, in the opinion of most, as unable to defend the honour
or interests of Russia. The continuance of the terrorist campaign
was showing that they were equally ineffective on the home
front. The atmosphere was electric, even though the temperature was not comparable to that of the opening of the reign. By
1880 talk of a 'constitution' was a commonplace. It is true that
such talk, in most of the very diverse quarters in which such
ideas were being canvassed, was a sign not of any desire to
weaken authority but, on the contrary, of a desire to strengthen
it through providing some effective means of official collaboration with 'sound opinion'. Still, in Russia as it then was, talk
of a 'constitution' meant that a crisis of confidence had been
reached and that Tsardom must devote the best part of its
efforts towards some satisfaction of its mainstay, the great and
medium-sized landowners.

As the internal problems of Russia became more and more
acute, as the immediate post-war boom in certain industries,
notably cotton, revealed its insecure basis (a close parallel to
the years 1855–7), as the financial chaos created by the war
became more generally apparent, so foreign affairs were forced
into the second place. The beginnings of a return to high protection were in part the reflection of that nationalist disgust
with the West which was now compelled to turn inwards instead
of attempting new foreign ventures. Only in Central Asia the
dominant military circles, backed with increasing force by
economic interests, were able to press forward. There at least,

if the worst came to the worst, it would be England alone that would have to be faced. Elsewhere Russia was on the defensive, essentially even in Bulgaria. The Balkans soon lost nearly all their emotional appeal, and panslavism as such became too discredited and too overborne by the internal crisis to continue as a power. In 1878 at the height of its influence Russia had almost been carried into a struggle with the West, but once peace had been obtained, however violent the disillusionment might be, the possibility of fending off internal transformation by a national summons to renew the armed conflict on a vastly more dangerous scale was almost out of the question. It could not be said to be entirely out of the question as long as Skobelev was alive. The power of his magnetic personality and his semi-legendary reputation, particularly among the rank and file of the army, had won for him a unique position in Russia. After his mercilessly successful campaign against the Tekke Turkomans in 1880–1 he reached the pinnacle of his fame and influence. Both Alexander II and Alexander III, and almost all the authorities, disliked him; but they also feared him. He was a leader who might stampede millions. His Paris speech, in which he denounced Germany as the enemy of Slavdom and proclaimed war with her to be inevitable and imminent, had prolonged international repercussions. Suddenly, four months later, in the summer of 1882, he died. Twenty-five years were to pass before panslavism again bulked as one of the major influences in Russia.

Meanwhile the Great Russian nationalism which was the real core of strength behind Skobelev and the panslavs was far from suffering decline. Closely identified with the person of Alexander III himself it intensified russifying measures at home and was a preponderant factor in the relations of the great powers. The Bulgarian crisis of 1885–7 brought about Katkov's last, and most dangerous, nationalist campaign and his final espousal of France as the ally for Russia against Germany; and it also brought Russia again within measurable distance of war. Yet the feeling was different from that of ten years earlier, and Russia in the end proved prepared to abandon Bulgaria in disgust, though not the future of Constantinople and the Straits. Thereafter Armenian massacres, Crete, and Macedonia kept the problem of Turkey in the foreground of Russian foreign relations, but the pressure of other problems prevented Russia from taking the lead. The ever heightening protectionist wall, the railway and industrial expansion, the French loans and the French alliance, the persistent fall in wheat prices, the effects of the famine of 1891, the increasing plight of all engaged in agriculture, the engrossing claims of the Far East—symbolized by the beginning of the Trans-Siberian railway in 1891—these became the dominating features of the internal and the external position of Russia for the rest of the century.

Hence, with the initial exception in Bulgaria, there was no sustained effort from the side of Russia during the thirty years that followed the Near Eastern crisis of 1875–8 to undo its results. The Franco-Russian alliance produced concrete results against England rather than Germany, who was not yet committed to economic expansion in Turkey and was improving her relations with Russia. From 1897 a period of uneasy but substantial accommodation with Austria-Hungary in the Balkans showed how much Russian interest in her 'Slav brethren' had cooled. No important Russian initiative was seriously to be expected there unless Turkish control of the Straits was about to collapse. England, though her traditional concern for them actually was changing, now that her rivalry with Russian imperialism was extended from Teheran and Kabul to Pekin was far more the enemy than Austria-Hungary. It was only after the shipwreck of the Manchurian venture, only when the very continuance of the Dual Monarchy seemed to be dependent on some speedy solution of its Slav problems, above all that of the Jugoslavs, only when the very continuance of Turkish rule in Europe seemed at last about to be successfully challenged by the growth of nationalism among the Balkan peoples, that Russian policy swung again to the Near East as the pivot of her international relations. By then their whole setting had been entirely altered since the days of Reichstadt and the Berlin congress; in the place of the *Dreikaiserbündnis* stood the Dual Alliance and the Triple Entente on the one hand, the *Zweibund* and the *Dreibund* on the other. And in the place of the *narodniki* and the terrorists there was the revolution of 1905–6, already spoken of as a dress rehearsal.

RUSSIAN INFLUENCE ON THE REVOLT
IN HERZEGOVINA

THE Russians originally had on the spot Ionin, consul-general at Ragusa and diplomatic agent at Cettinje, and his staff. There was also a Russian vice-consulate at Mostar, as to which I have no information for 1875, and a consulate at Sarajevo (see above, p. 141, note 1). Towards the end of 1875 Ionin was joined by Col. Bobrikov from the war office and Col. Monteverde and his wife acting as agent for the St. Petersburg Slavonic Benevolent Committee and correspondent of the extreme nationalist paper *Russky Mir*. In October Wesselitsky-Bojidarovich arrived; he left for St. Petersburg in January 1876, and returned in March (see above, pp. 157–60). In the early months of 1876 numerous other Russian agents appeared at Ragusa. Professor Temperley's researches confirm the view that the originators of the revolt were the semi-independent clans in southern Herzegovina, and not Russian agents or Prince Nicholas: see his *The Bulgarian and other Atrocities, 1875–8, in the light of Historical Criticism*, pp. 4–8, 43–4. Taylor, the British consul at Ragusa, who had only been there a few months and was not well informed, attributed the continuance of the revolt in the autumn of 1875 mainly to the aid and sympathy of the Dalmatian Slavs and the Montenegrins: he made little reference to Russian intrigues beyond general condemnation of Ionin, 'a thorough and celebrated Pan Slav' (Taylor's political reports, in *F.O.* 7/860). It is worth noticing that as far as can be judged from the rebel sources published in *Spomenica o hertsegovačkom ustanka* direct Russian influence was very much in the background during the incubation and opening stages of the rebellion.

But by the beginning of 1876 there seems little doubt that the effect of Russian agents and money was very considerable. Koetschet (*Aus Bosniens letzter Türkenzeit*, p. 23), who was at Ragusa in January 1876, depicted Ionin as by then holding in his hands the threads of the revolt and Ragusa as filled with refugees, bandit leaders, and international adventurers, all receiving help from him. W. J. Stillman, *The Times* correspondent at Ragusa, who was on very good terms with the Russians and underrated their activities, allows that their influence increased from the new year. At the same time, he still considered that Elliot was only too ready to pass on from Constantinople to London anti-Russian versions largely emanating from the Turkish consul-general at Ragusa: see e.g. his refutation in *Herzegovina and the Late Uprising*, pp. 111–12, of Elliot's denunciation of Ionin for attending in person the funeral of one of the insurgent chiefs, Maksim Bacović, and flying the consulate flag at half-mast, in *A. and P.*, 1876, lxxxiv, C. 1531, nos. 11, 23, and 29; 1877, xci, C. 1738, no. 292. Holmes, the British consul at Sarajevo, who was himself only once very briefly in Ragusa, and never in Cettinje, early in 1876 began plying Elliot with denunciations of Ionin as directing the actions of Montenegro and of Stillman as being hand in glove with him: Elliot to Derby, disp., conf., no. 84, 23 Jan., and no. 194, 14 Feb.; copies in *F.O.* 181/536 (omitted from the blue-books); and Holmes's memorandum on Herzegovina in *A. and P.*, 1876, lxxxiv, C. 1531, no. 67 incl., and his no. 11, to Elliot, 20 April 1876, in *F.O.* 195/1101. Disraeli (p. 907) accurately reflected these views when he wrote to the Queen that the insurgents were 'not natives of any Turkish province but are simply an invasion of revolutionary bands, whose strength lay in the support afforded to them by Servia and Montenegro, acting on the instigation of foreign agents and foreign committees'. Holmes's pro-Turkish bias was the subject of a violent attack by (Sir) Arthur Evans on his second journey as *Manchester Guardian* correspondent in 1877 to Bosnia and Herzegovina: *Illyrian Letters*, pp. 45–7, 84–91, and see Seton-Watson, *Disraeli, Gladstone, and the Eastern Question*, pp. 213–16. The result of Holmes's accusations against the Russians was that Derby instructed Loftus to protest verbally to Gorchakov as to Ionin encouraging the insurgents, and did so himself to Shuvalov: Derby to Loftus, 16 and 29 Feb. 1876, in *A. and P.*, 1876, lxxxiv, C. 1531, nos. 17 and 23.

Derby also sent Monson, first secretary at the Vienna embassy, to Ragusa in March 1876, to watch and report on the situation at first hand. In October 1876, and from February to April 1877, Monson was, on his own suggestion, at Cettinje as diplomatic agent. He was not previously acquainted with these lands and did not know the language, but his judgement and opportunities for acquiring information were good, and his reports, which are in *F.O.*7/882–4, 911–12 (not many of them appear in the blue-books), are of much value in estimating the character and degree of Russian influence. Monson was confident that more than half the money received from Russia had been expended in aid of the combatants, and not of the actual refugees (no. 79, 9 July), and he was confirmed in this opinion by the later avowals of Shchatokin, Ionin's deputy (no. 162, 20 Sept.). Ionin was absent from 9 May until 30 June in Berlin, Ems, and Vienna, but Monson did not believe that his connexions with the rebels and with the Montenegrins were any the less close (no. 60, 20 June; no. 71, 30 June). After Montenegro and Serbia had declared war in July 1876, Ionin more or less admitted complicity in the insurrection: 'I did not create the situation,' he told Monson, 'but I profited by it. It began as a small stream, which might have been lost for want of direction; so I put up a stone here, and a stone there, and kept the water together' (no. 132, 23 Aug.). A month later Shchatokin admitted: 'As for the Insurrection itself during the whole of the winter it was perfectly fictitious;—was sustained by artificial means [mainly Russian money];—and might have been suppressed by the simple withdrawal of those means' (no. 162, 20 Sept.). Durando, the Italian consul-general at Ragusa, a very well-informed and judicious observer, who had 'never been inclined to attribute to Russia any other complicity in the Insurrection than a desire to profit by its various chances . . . admitted to me [Monson] yesterday that, although he remained of the opinion that the Russian Government was not directly responsible for the outbreak, the movement must have collapsed long ago, had it not been for Russian money, and Russian supervision' (no. 130, 22 Aug.). Durando was informed by Prince Nicholas's private secretary 'that if the Czar could inspect the letters which His Highness had received, His Imperial Majesty would send not only Mr. Jonine, but Prince Gortchakow also to Siberia' (no. 170, 28 Sept.). Monson fully shared Holmes's views on the very biased attitude of Stillman as to the non-connivance of Russia; while entirely agreeing as to the encouragement given by the local Austrian officials to the insurrection, he strongly attacked Stillman's disclaimers of the complicity of Russian officials, and sent home a lengthy recital of 'the notorious facts' as to 'the insincerity of Russian neutrality . . . and the extent of the encouragement necessarily given by the conduct and attitude of Russia's official representative . . .' (Ionin) (no. 162, 20 Sept.).

While making allowance for the fact that Monson's evidence for what occurred before the end of March 1876 is second-hand, it may be concluded that Russian semi-official and unofficial support for the insurgents was from the beginning of 1876 (but probably not earlier) of very great importance, although Ionin, Wesselitsky, and other Russian agents by no means saw eye to eye as to the ultimate objective. At the same time it must be allowed that this Russian support would not have been as effective as it was had it not been for the readiness of the Austrian Slavs, including most of the officials, to make the utmost of the rebellion.

THE REICHSTADT AGREEMENT AND THE CONVENTIONS WITH AUSTRIA-HUNGARY

THE Austrian version of the Reichstadt meeting and a full summary of Andrássy's copy of the 'Résumé des pourparlers secrets de Reichstadt du 8 juillet 1876', also referred to as an aide-mémoire, were first given in *Wertheimer*, pp. 320–5. The full text of this, in the original French, was first published in 1919 in Pribram's *Die politische Geheimverträge Oesterreich-Ungarns*. This Austrian version, according to Wertheimer, was written down at Andrássy's dictation by Novikov immediately after the meeting at Reichstadt and given to Novikov for communication to his government, a copy marked 'from the original' being kept by Andrássy.

The Russian version of the agreement was first revealed in 1903 in *Tatishchev*, pp. 315–16, and then, not quite in the same terms, by Goriainow in 1907 (*Le Bosphore et les Dardanelles*, p. 318). The full text of the Russian version in the original French was first published in 1921 in *Krasny Arkhiv*, vol. i, republished in *Russko-germanskie otnosheniya* (Moscow, 1922). This version is headed, 'très secrète. Reichstadt, le 26 juin [i.e. 8 July, new style] 1876: Il a été convenu . . .', and then follow on the right-hand side of the page the various points of the agreement, on the left-hand side certain explanations by Gorchakov. Both are written in the same hand, that of an unknown confidential clerk of Gorchakov, but the date at which this copy, from which the text in *Krasny Arkhiv* is printed, was made is not known. The editors of *Krasny Arkhiv* state that the original document is not in the Russian foreign office archives, implying that the text which they print is a copy of the original document. This copy must have been made at least prior to 25 July/6 August 1878, since there is a pencil note on it stating that the Tsar sent it back to the foreign office on that date.

N. V. Tcharykow, who entered Gorchakov's chancellery in December 1876, devotes an unsubstantial chapter in his *Glimpses of High Politics* (1931) to the Reichstadt agreement and the subsequent secret conventions with Austria-Hungary. He prints the text, in the original French, of the agreement (pp. 103–4). It is not clear what is the origin of his text. He makes no mention of the text published in *Krasny Arkhiv*, though the two are identical in wording, save for the heading in Tcharykow, 'Arrangements pris à Reichstadt le 26 juin [8 July, new style] 1876'. Tcharykow states (p. 98): 'Its essential points were noted down by Prince Gortchakoff in a very secret memorandum, which, with his accompanying comments, was inscribed in his *Book* (*Le Livre*), in which a confidential secretary copied out all his writings.'

There is also printed in *Krasny Arkhiv*, vol. i (republished in *Russko-germanskie otnosheniya*) the text, in the original French, of a second Russian document, styled a pro memoria and dated 28 June [10 July, new style] 1876, in which are set out certain general considerations of Gorchakov in regard to the agreement.

There is a useful comparison of the Austrian and Russian versions of the Reichstadt meeting by G. H. Rupp in the *American Historical Review*, 1925, vol. xxx, pp. 503–10.

1. *The Austrian Version of the Reichstadt Agreement*

Text reprinted from A. F. Pribram, *The Secret Treaties of Austria-Hungary*, English edition by A. C. Coolidge (Harvard, 1921), vol. ii, pp. 188–90.

Résumé des pourparlers secrets de Reichstadt du 8 juillet 1876. The following remark by Andrássy in his own hand: 'Niedergeschrieben gleich nach Reichstadt nach meiner Dictée durch Nowikoff und dem russischen Cabinet mitgetheilt.'

On a raisonné dans deux hypothèses: celle où les Turcs sortiraient victorieux de la lutte et celle où ils seraient vaincus.

Dans le premier cas l'on est convenu de ne pas les laisser aller au delà de certaines garanties qui ne seraient pas exagérées. On s'efforcerait d'empêcher que la guerre ne devienne une lutte d'extermination; on maintiendrait la Serbie et le Monténégro dans les circonscriptions territoriales que ces deux principautés ont actuellement et l'on s'opposerait à l'idée d'un rétablissement des forteresses turques en Serbie.

On ne reconnait pas à cette dernière le caractère d'un état indépendant; mais on est tombé d'accord de le reconnaître au Monténégro quelle que fût l'interprétation que d'autres puissances voudraient donner à la position politique de la Montagne Noire. Par suite de cette indépendance, le gouvernement austro-hongrois s'est déclaré prêt à fermer les deux ports de Klek et Cattaro à toute importation d'armes et de munitions pour les parties adverses, bien qu'il prévoie de la part du gouvernement turc, de très graves objections à la fermeture du premier de ces ports.

Pour ce qui est des insurgés, l'on est convenu, toujours dans le cas d'une victoire des Turcs, de faire des efforts communs pour leur garantir les libertés et les réformes qui ont été demandées à la Porte et promises par elle.

Dans toutes les éventualités susmentionnées il ne serait pas question d'un remaniement territorial quelconque, ni d'un côté ni de l'autre.

En passant à la seconde hypothèse, celle d'une défaite des Turcs, voici les idées sur lesquelles on est tombé d'accord:

L'Autriche-Hongrie ayant déclaré ne pouvoir admettre que la Serbie occupe et garde par droit de conquête l'enclave comprise entre la Dalmatie, la Croatie, et la Slavonie, attendu que cela impliquerait un danger pour les provinces de la monarchie, surtout pour son littoral dalmate lequel, s'étendant comme un mince ruban, devrait évidemment ou être annexé à la nouvelle Serbie ou placer le gouvernement I. et R. dans la nécessité de s'annexer la Serbie même, ce qui est exclu du programme: L'on est convenu que la Serbie obtiendrait une extension de territoire du côté de la Drina en Bosnie, en même temps que du côté de Novi-Bazar dans l'ancienne Serbie et dans la direction du Lim. De son côté le Monténégro serait arrondi par l'annexion d'une partie de Herzégovine adjacente; il obtiendrait le port de Spizza ainsi qu'un agrandissement du côté du Lim, de manière à ce que la langue de terre, qui s'étend au-jourd'hui entre la Serbie et le Monténégro fût partagée entre les deux principautés par le cours de ce fleuve.

Le reste de la Bosnie et de l'Herzégovine serait annexé à l'Autriche-Hongrie. La Russie reprendrait ses frontières naturelles d'avant 1856 et pourrait s'arrondir du côté de la Mer Noire et dans la Turquie d'Asie autant que cela serait nécessaire pour lui con-stituer de meilleures frontières dans cette direction et pour servir d'équivalent à la partie du territoire à être annexé à l'Autriche-Hongrie.

La Bulgarie, la Roumélie et l'Albanie pourraient former des états autonomes.

La Thessalie, l'île de Crète devraient être annexées à la Grèce.

Constantinople avec une banlieue à déterminer, deviendrait ville libre.

L'on est également convenu que toutes ces idées seraient gardées secrètes entre les deux empereurs et leurs ministres respectifs: qu'elles ne seraient pas communiquées aux autres puissances et plus spécialement encore aux Serbes et Monténégrins jusqu'à ce que le moment de leur réalisation soit arrivé.

With the above there is also a 'Note by Prince Gorchakov con-cerning the meeting at Reichstadt': 'Les deux empereurs se sont séparés dans le meilleur accord, décidés à proclamer le principe de la non-intervention dans le moment actuel. Ils se réservent une entente ultérieure avec les grandes puissances chrétiennes, si les circonstances en démontrent la nécessité.' In pencil.

2. *The Russian Version of the Reichstadt Agreement*

Text reprinted from *Krasny Arkhiv*, vol. i, pp. 36–8.

Très secrète.

Reichastadt [*sic*], le 26 juin 1876.

Il a été jugé nécessaire de ne pas proclamer le principe de non-intervention *absolue* afin de ne pas se lier les mains d'avance en vue de certaines éventualités. Nous avons insisté sur la fermeture du port de Klek, sans laquelle la non-intervention ne serait pas sincère et effective. De notre côté, nous ne pourrions pas nous y croire liés et, en ce cas, l'Angleterre ne l'observerait pas. Le Comte Andrássy y a ajouté la fermeture de Cattaro qui a été réclamée par les Anglais, afin de donner à cette mesure le caractère de l'impartialité. Toutefois, le Cabinet de Vienne prévoit l'impossibilité d'empêcher l'assistance privée de venir en aide aux Chrétiens vu les vives sympathies des populations Dalmates.

Il a été convenu:

1° *Quant au présent:*

Les Puissances observont le principe de non-intervention dans le moment actuel, se réservant de s'entendre ultérieurement si les circonstances l'exigeaient. Les ports de Klek et de Cattaro seront fermés aux deux parties. En aucun cas on n'assistera les Turcs contre les Chrétiens.

2° *Quant à l'avenir:*

a. En cas de succès des Turcs, les Puissances s'entendront pour les arrêter s'ils se livrent à des violences excessives contre les Chrétiens.

Elles exigeront le rétablissement du *status quo ante* en Serbie, y compris l'abolition des forteresses turques.

Quant à la Bosnie et à l'Herzégovine, les Puissances insisteront à Constantinople pour qu'elles soient organisées sur la base du programme tracé par la dépêche du 30 Décembre et le Mémoire de Berlin ou, du moins, d'après le règlement crétois.

b. Si les Chrétiens sont victorieux: Les Puissances agiront d'accord pour régler les conséquences de la guerre.

Elles ne favoriseront pas l'établissement d'un grand Etat Slave, mais le Monténégro et la Serbie pourront s'annexer: le

Le Cabinet de Vienne considère cette compensation comme une condition vitale sans laquelle elle ne pourrait admettre un agrandissement des Principautés Slaves voisines.

Si le Gouvernement Russe le jugeait possible et utile, il lui est réservé de s'annexer le port de Batoum.

premier l'Herzégovine et un port sur l'Adriatique, la seconde quelques parties de la vieille Serbie et de la Bosnie.

Mais, en pareil cas, l'Autriche aura la faculté de s'annexer la Croatie Turque et quelques parties de la Bosnie contiguës à ses frontières, d'après un tracé à convenir.

De son côté, la Russie aurait alors la faculté de reprendre la partie de la Bessarabie cédée par le Traité de 1856.

Si, enfin, les conséquences d'un succès des Chrétiens devraient amener l'entier écroulement de l'Empire Ottoman en Europe, la Bulgarie et la Roumélie pourraient former des Principautés indépendantes dans leurs circonscriptions naturelles.

L'Epire et la Thessalie seraient libres de s'annexer à la Grèce.

Constantinople pourrait être érigé en ville libre.

3. *Gorchakov's Pro memoria of 10 July 1876*

Text reprinted from *Krasny Arkhiv*, vol. i, pp. 40–2.

Pro memoria

28 Juin, 1876

Il me semble utile de préciser quelques-uns des points indiqués dans la précédente notice.

Ad. I. En aucun cas une intervention directe ou indirecte en faveur des Turcs contre les Chrétiens ne saurait être admise.

Ad. II. Le port de Klek devrait être fermé aux troupes turques dès la proclamation du principe de non-intervention.

Dans le cas où cette fermeture n'aurait pas lieu, il serait impossible de refuser aux Serbes et aux Monténégrins le transit des armes et munitions destinées à les renforcer. Mais il est très désirable qu'on puisse éviter cette nécessité qui pourrait donner lieu à des interprétations malveillantes de la part de quelques Puissances.

Ad. III. On ne saurait prévoir le moment ni la mode que les Cabinets pourraient choisir pour s'interposer entre les deux parties.

Le moment peut être indiqué soit si les succès et revers étant partagés, l'épuisement de la lutte amenait les deux parties à prêter l'oreille aux transactions, soit si les Turcs ayant brisé la résistance militaire, la poursuite des opérations prenait un caractère de cruauté inutile et de vengeance. Le mode d'interposition dépendrait alors de l'accord entre les Cabinets.

Ad. IV. Les suites possibles de la lutte ouvrent la porte aux plus graves combinaisons.

Si les Turcs ont le dessus, les Puissances ont le droit, le devoir, et l'intérêt d'exiger que la position assurée par les traités à la Serbie ne soit pas altérée et que les forteresses turques ne soient pas rétablies. Les mesures de précaution que la Porte pourrait prendre pour sa sécurité à venir ne devraient pas enfreindre ces limites.

Quant aux provinces sujettes, on devrait insister pour que leur sort à venir soit réglé d'après les conditions du programme de Berlin ou d'après le règlement Crétois suggéré par le Cabinet de Londres, ou, enfin, s'il est possible, sur une base plus large d'autonomie administrative.

L'Angleterre ayant admis ce principe, si l'Europe agit d'accord, le Gouvernement Turc ne pourrait pas se refuser à un vœu unanime justifié par l'intérêt de la paix générale et la sécurité des pays voisins. C'est pourquoi il serait nécessaire de s'entendre sur un programme à poursuivre en commun.

Si la victoire se déclarait en faveur des Chrétiens, le principe convenu d'abandonner les choses à leur cours naturel semble impliquer l'obligation de laisser les diverses nationalités se développer et s'organiser selon leur propre vitalité et dans leurs limites naturelles.

En aucun cas on ne saurait admettre une intervention de l'Europe au profit de la domination turque que la force des choses aurait irrévocablement condamnée. Mais une entente des Cabinets peut être nécessaire pour organiser l'état des choses que présenterait alors la presqu'île des Balkans, soit:

(1) Que les Turcs chassés de la région montagneuse se maintiennent dans les plaines de Bulgarie, Roumélie, Thessalie et Macédoine ainsi qu'à Constantinople;

(2) Que, s'ils succombent définitivement, un conflit éclate entre les diverses nationalités appelées à fonder leur existence indépendante.

(3) Que la révolution fasse prévaloir ses tendances anarchiques.

A l'égard de ces éventualités on ne peut se tenir qu'aux lignes principales.

L'Autriche-Hongrie excluant un grand Etat Slave et la Russie un Empire Grec, il semblerait que la solution la plus rationnelle serait la création de petits Etats indépendants, chacun dans les circonscriptions territoriales où l'histoire les a placés, avec un lien fédéral.

4. *Austro-Russian Negotiations, 1876–7*

The four following documents are reprinted from G. Wittrock, *Gorčakov, Ignatiev och Šuvalov* (Stockholm, 1931), pp. 106–7, 109–13, from copies in the Berlin foreign office archives.

PRINCE GORCHAKOV *to* NOVIKOV

St Petersburg 15/27 dec. 1876.

Monsieur l'Ambassadeur,

L'expédition confiée par V.E. au Gal Obroutchew a été mise sous les yeux de notre A.M.

Après l'examen attentif du projet de convention sorti de Vos pourparlers avec le Cte Andrassy, S.M. a daigné Vous autoriser à la signer.

En prenant cette décision, L'Empereur ne meconnait pas l'importance des divers points sur lesquels V. avez présenté à Mr le Comte Andrassy des objections, que S.M. a trouvées parfaitement fondées.

Toutefois n. A.M. prend acte des bonnes dispositions témoignées par l'Empereur F. Joseph, et par Mr le Cte Andrassy et des assurances verbales qui V. ont été données quant à l'interprétation de ces divers points.

Ainsi il reste convenu que si, après l'armistice la Turquie poursuivait la guerre en Serbie ou continuait à occuper le territoire de cette Principauté, les troupes russes ne sauraient être empêchées de combattre l'ennemi sur ce territoire.

Il reste également convenu qu'en cas de nécessité militaire absolue, les troupes russes auraient la faculté de s'y replier.

En un mot, il reste entendu que le Cab^et Impl. ayant égard aux intérêts politiques de l'Autriche-Hongrie, assurera autant qu'il sera possible la neutralité du territoire Serbe, sans préjudice de la participation active de l'armée Serbe à nos opérations militaires hors de la Principauté; que dans les cas où il serait absolument obligé de transgresser les limites du territoire Serbe, il s'abstiendrait de donner à ces transgressions le caractère d'un mouvement combiné en vue d'une occupation de la Principauté; et que de son côté, le Cabinet de Vienne appréciera équitablement et amicalement les nécessités militaires éventuelles, auxquelles il nous serait impossible de nous soustraire.

Les mêmes considérations s'appliquent au Monténégro, et il reste entendu que le Gt. Austro-Hongrois apportera toute la tolérance possible afin de permettre à cette Principauté de puiser en Autriche les moyens d'armements qui seuls peuvent rendre son concours militaire efficace.

C'est le principe et l'esprit de cette convention plutôt que sa lettre qui en constituent la valeur aux yeux de l'Empereur.

S.M. a le désir et conserve l'espoir qu'elle n'entrera pas en vigueur quant à présent. Mais elle restera pour l'avenir comme le premier jalon d'une entente qui portera en tout cas de bons fruits.

C'est là surtout ce qui détermine n. A.M. à y donner Son assentiment.

Veuillez le dire à Mr. le Comte Andrassy en ajoutant que l'Empereur lui sait personellement gré des efforts qu'il a faits pour mener à bonne fin cette importante négociation.

Recevez, etc., etc.

COUNT ANDRÁSSY *to* BARON LANGENAU

Budapest, 24 jan. 1877.

Monsieur le Baron,

M. Novikow m'a donné communication de la dépêche ci-jointe en copie du P^ce Gortschacow en date du 15 décembre dr. v. st. Elle reproduit exactement l'entretien que j'ai eu avec Monsieur l'Ambassadeur de Russie, à l'exception d'un seul point.

Tandis que le Prince Chancelier écrit: 'Ainsi il reste convenu que si, après l'armistice, la Turquie poursuivrait la guerre en Serbie ou continuait à occuper le territoire de cette Principauté, les troupes russes ne sauraient être empêchées de combattre l'ennemi sur ce territoire,'— M. Novikow convient que j'avais décliné d'insérer cette clause dans la convention.

Un surcroît d'occupations ne m'a pas permis jusqu'ici de signaler cette nuance au Prince Gortschacow. D'ailleurs cela ne me paraissait pas urgent, M. Novikow m'ayant assuré d'avoir bien saisi et fidèlement rendu notre point de vue. Si aujourd'hui je crois devoir appeler l'attention du Prince sur la différence entre les deux versions, ce n'est pas par méfiance. Son Altesse voudra bien en voir une preuve dans le moment que je choisis pour l'entretenir de ce sujet, et qui est précisément celui où le rappel des volontaires témoigne de l'intention du Gouvernement Impérial de ne pas faire de la Principauté la base de ses opérations militaires. Mais le Prince comprendra que je doive tenir à ce que des assurances données avec l'autorisation de Sa Majesté l'Empereur et Roi, mon Auguste Maître, ne puissent un jour être sujettes à des divergences d'interprétation. J'ai en outre à cœur de me prémunir personnellement pour l'avenir, — que je sois ou non dans le Conseil de Sa Majesté — contre l'apparence même d'avoir manqué à une promesse écrite ou verbale. Si dans mes pourparlers avec Monsieur l'Ambassadeur de Russie j'ai cru devoir maintenir invariablement l'impossibilité de l'occupation de la Serbie par les troupes russes, c'était uniquement pour obvier, conformément aux vœux des deux Empereurs et des deux Gouvernements, à la possibilité d'une collision entre les intérêts des deux Empires. D'autre part, mais dans ce même ordre d'idées, voulant tenir compte dans la mesure du possible des nécessités militaires de la Russie, j'ai déclaré verbalement à M. Novikow que, si les événements imprévus de la guerre ou, ce qui est peu probable, un revers amenaient les troupes russes à transgresser momentanément les frontières de la zone neutre formée par la Serbie, l'Empereur et Roi et le Gouvernement Impl. et Royal apprécieraient cette éventualité équitablement et amicalement et ne la considéreraient pas, dans ces conditions, comme un acte hostile envers l'Autriche-Hongrie.

En revenant sur ce point, je le répète, aucune pensée de méfiance n'est entrée dans mon esprit. Je me suis surtout inspiré d'un sentiment personnel, que le Prince appréciera, j'en suis certain. Il me semblait aussi que la cordialité de notre entente exigeait la plus grande clarté et qu'il répondait le mieux à nos intérêts mutuels d'écarter d'avance tout ce qui dans le cours des événements pourrait causer peut-être un malentendu.

Vous êtes autorisé a placer cette dépêche sous les yeux du Prince Chancelier et à lui en laisser une copie s'il le désire. Recevez, Monsieur le Baron, l'assurance de ma considération la plus distinguée.

PRINCE GORCHAKOV *to* NOVIKOV

St Petersburg 26 janvier 1877.

L'expédition de Votre Excellence du 7/19 janvier[1] a été placée sous les yeux de S.M. l'Empereur. Elle a été de notre part l'objet d'un examen attentif.

Je m'empresse de Vous en transmettre le résultat que je Vous prie de communiquer à M. le Comte Andrassy.

Ce n'est pas un contre-projet que nous lui soumettons, mais de simples nuances que nous lui signalons afin de mettre notre accord à l'abri de tout malentendu.

1. A la page 2, 5e ligne du projet, nous voudrions supprimer les mots: 'la guerre' à propos des éventualités en vue desquelles la convention secrète aurait à entrer en vigueur. Il nous semble plus conforme à la pensée de M. le Comte Andrassy lui-même de limiter cette éventualité au cas d'une dissolution de l'Empire Ottoman. Il est possible, peut-être même probable, que la guerre, si elle éclatait entre la Russie et la Porte, aurait pour conséquence un écroulement plus ou moins complet de l'Empire Ottoman, lors même que nous serions loin de le désirer. En pareil cas l'éventualité de cette dissolution qui, dans l'opinion de M. le Comte Andrassy, devrait seule amener l'application des remaniements territoriaux convenus entre nous, se trouverait réalisée. Mais le fait n'est pas

---

[1] Not printed by Wittrock, but see below, p. 597 and pp. 600–1, notes.

certain et par conséquent il nous semble que la guerre à elle seule ne doit pas être mentionnée comme un des cas devant entraîner ce résultat.

La même suppression devrait, par les mêmes motifs, être faite à la page 6, 15ᵉ ligne du projet.

2. A la page 4, ligne 13, les mots: *'y compris l'Herzégovine'* demanderaient à être précisés. Qu'entend-on par la dénomination d'Herzégovine? La contrée connue sous le nom de vieille Serbie peut-elle être envisagée comme en faisant partie? La Porte a fait entrer la vieille Serbie dans la circonscription de l'Herzégovine pour des motifs politiques et administratifs qui lui sont propres, mais qui ne répondent ni à l'origine, ni aux intérêts, ni aux vœux de la population. Il est donc essentiel que la délimitation de la partie de l'Herzégovine qui devrait être annexée à l'Empire d'Autriche-Hongrie soit indiquée d'une manière plus exacte à l'exclusion de la vieille Serbie.

Nous proposerions de rediger cet article de la manière suivante:

'L'Empereur d'Autriche et Roi de Hongrie, etc. etc. . . à la Bosnie et à l'Herzégovine à l'exclusion de la partie comprise entre la Serbie et le Monténégro, au sujet de laquelle les deux Gouvernements se réservent de se mettre d'accord lorsque le moment d'en disposer serait venu.'

3. A la page 5, la partie de l'article concernant les acquisitions éventuelles de la Russie devrait être modifiée en ce sens que les six premières lignes précisant ces acquisitions *en Europe* seraient seules maintenues et que celles relatives aux acquisitions en Asie seraient entièrement supprimées.

Nous n'avons pas en vue d'autre annexion que celle de Batoum et d'un territoire adjacent nécessaire à une bonne délimitation. Mais les intérêts de l'Autriche-Hongrie et de la Russie ne sont pas en contact en Asie. C'est pourquoi les extensions ou rectifications éventuelles de frontières que la Russie pourrait être amenée à faire de ce côté en cas de guerre ne peuvent relever que du jugement qu'elle porterait elle-même sur les circonstances et les intérêts créés par les résultats de la guerre. — Il suffit que l'esprit même des conventions conclues entre les deux pays établisse le principe d'un bon-vouloir mutuel dans l'appréciation de leurs intérêts réciproques, même là où ils ne seraient pas en contact direct.

4. Par ces motifs, à la page 6, l'article 2 devrait être remanié de la manière suivante:

'Les Hautes Parties Contractantes s'engagent à se prêter un mutuel concours sur le terrain diplomatique, si les remaniements territoriaux résultant d'une guerre qui aménerait le démembrement ou la dissolution de l'Empire Ottoman, devaient donner lieu à une délibération collective des Grandes Puissances.'

5. A la page 7, ligne 16, nous proposons de dire:

'En cas d'un remaniement territorial résultant d'une dissolution de l'Empire Ottoman.'

Cette rédaction nous semblerait plus conforme à la pensée de M. le Comte Andrassy.

6. A la page 8, ligne 8, les mots *Etats autonomes* ne répondent pas à la situation prévue puisqu'il n'y aurait plus de pouvoir même suzerain.

Dans l'éventualité dont il s'agit, il a été convenu à Reichstadt que ces diverses nationalités pourraient former des Etats *indépendants*.

7. A la même page, ligne 9, nous croyons juste d'ajouter une partie *de l'Epire* aux territoires qui pourraient être annexés à la Grèce.

Telles sont, Monsieur, les nuances de rédaction que nous proposons à M. le Comte Andrassy. Elles précisent mieux l'accord sans en altérer le fond ni les bases.

Nous ne prévoyons pas qu'elles puissent soulever d'objections. Toutefois, par un sentiment de délicatesse que Son Excellence appréciera, S.M. l'Empereur a cru devoir suspendre la ratification de la convention militaire jusqu'à ce que l'entente se soit complètement faite sur cette politique.

Aussitôt que Vous nous en informerez par le télégraphe, cette formalité sera accomplie.

Recevez, etc.

COUNT ANDRÁSSY to BARON LANGENAU

Wien 28 febr. 1877

Monsieur le Baron,

M. l'Ambassadeur de Russie m'a communiqué la dépêche ci-jointe en copie du Prince Gortschakow en date du 26 janvier dernier. Elle renferme certaines remarques du Prince sur le projet de convention additionnelle, relative aux arrangements de Reichstadt, que nous avions soumis à l'examen du Cabinet de St. Pétersbourg. J'ai cru nécessaire de faire part à M. Nowikow des observations qu'elle me suggère. Vous en trouverez ci-après le résumé. Il vous mettra au fait de la phase actuelle des négociations. Je n'ai pas besoin de relever son caractère confidentiel. En substance, voici le langage que j'ai tenu à l'Ambassadeur russe.

Le Prince Chancelier n'a pas l'intention de nous soumettre un contre-projet. Il nous propose des nuances de style, une précision plus serrée de rédaction, pour mettre notre accord à l'abri de tout malentendu. Nous sommes pénétrés de la haute importance de l'entreprise que nous poursuivons en commun. Elle est destinée à assurer aux peuples des deux Empires les bienfaits de la paix, non pas pour le présent seul, mais pour l'avenir, à travers des générations,

Cependant, à notre avis, la garantie de ce but élevé doit être recherchée moins dans la lettre que dans l'esprit des conventions, et il suffit qu'elles établissent entre les deux pays, comme le Prince relève avec justice — le principe d'un bon-vouloir mutuel dans l'appréciation de leurs intérêts réciproques. Tous les mots, quelque soin que l'on mette à les choisir et à les grouper, se prêtent plus ou moins à des nuances d'interprétation, quand même l'esprit des arrangements exclut toute divergence d'opinion. Le mot de la bible: 'verbum occidit, spiritus vivificat' ne me paraît pas hors de propos à cette place. Pour ma part je pense que notre projet, même s'il avait été accepté tel quel par le Cabinet de St Pétersbourg, n'aurait donné lieu à aucun malentendu. Mais le Prince ayant manifesté le désir d'y apporter quelques changements, je ne veux pas élever des difficultés et je suis prêt à entrer dans le détail des modifications proposées.

Ad. 1. Dans le préambule du projet, le Prince voudrait supprimer les mots: 'la guerre'. Selon Son Altesse cette suppression serait indiquée pour limiter les éventualités, en vue desquelles la convention additionnelle aurait à entrer en vigueur, au seul cas de la dissolution de l'Empire Ottoman. Cette rédaction semble aussi au Prince plus conforme à ma pensée. Le Gouvernement Impérial de la Russie connaît le point de vue, auquel nous n'avons cessé d'envisager la perspective de changements éventuels en Orient. Tant que le maintien de l'intégrité territoriale en Turquie est possible, nous n'avons aucun intérêt ni aucun désir de faire des annexions. Toute altération du statu quo par contre porterait atteinte à l'équilibre et à la sécurité de la Monarchie austro-hongroise. Plusieurs de nos provinces, la Dalmatie nommément, en ressentiraient le contre-coup. Une éventualité pareille seule et non pas le désir d'un agrandissement pourrait nous amener, pour la sauvegarde de nos intérêts en Orient, à annexer la Bosnie et l'Herzégovine.

Après avoir rempli sa mission en Bulgarie, après avoir pacifié cette province et l'avoir dotée d'institutions nationales, la Russie pourrait l'évacuer sans préjudice pour son autorité. La Bulgarie possède les conditions nécessaires à une existence indépendante. Sous une forme nouvelle, elle restera toujours la Bulgarie.

Il n'en est pas de même de la Bosnie et de l'Herzégovine. Les éléments nécessaires à une vie propre leur font défaut. Livrées à elles-mêmes, elles deviendraient d'un côté un objet de convoitise, de l'autre un centre de compétitions et de rivalités en vue de la formation d'un grand état slave du midi, enfin un foyer permanent d'intrigues révolutionnaires. Si l'Autriche-Hongrie, intéressée en première ligne comme Puissance limitrophe, occupait ces contrées, sans y établir un état de choses définitif elle aurait l'air d'admettre la légitimité des aspirations en vue de la création d'un état compact slave et de considérer un pareil dénoûment comme la seule solution possible. Sous un autre aspect, une occupation de la Bosnie et de l'Herzégovine par les troupes de Sa Majesté proclamée d'avance comme transitoire, ne nous donnerait-elle pas l'apparence d'avoir voulu nous assurer un gage contre la Russie, d'avoir suivi à son égard — contrairement à l'esprit de la convention, contrairement à nos vœux et à nos intentions — une politique de méfiance et d'opposition?

Néanmoins le fait *seul* de la guerre qui viendrait à éclater entre la Russie et la Porte n'aménerait pas, dans notre opinion, l'application des remaniements territoriaux convenus entre nous. Mais de même il nous est impossible de faire dépendre exclusivement de la dissolution de l'Empire Ottoman la mise à exécution des stipulations respectives. Comment en effet la définir? Il en est comme de la calvitie. Quand commence-t-elle? Quand est-ce qu'elle s'achève? Un Empire ne se dissout pas en un jour. Dès lors comment préciser le degré de décomposition auquel la dissolution deviendrait effective? Tel pourrait la croire réelle à la première, tel autre à la dernière atteinte qui serait portée au statu quo. En résumé. Dans notre pensée la réalisation de nos arrangements ne dépend pas du fait seul de la guerre, mais des remaniements territoriaux que la guerre ou la dissolution de l'Empire Ottoman pourrait avoir pour résultat. Tel a été notre point de vue à Reichstadt, tel il est encore. Notre rédaction, à notre avis, l'exprime fidèlement. C'est pourquoi je dois prier le Prince Chancelier de vouloir bien la maintenir.

Ad. 2. Dans notre pensée la vieille Serbie n'a pas été comprise dans la dénomination de l'Herzégovine qui ne devait s'appliquer qu'à l'Herzégovine proprement dite. Quant à la portion de l'Herzégovine, entre la Serbie et le Monténégro au sujet de laquelle les deux Gouvernements Impériaux se réservent de se mettre d'accord lorsque le moment d'en disposer serait venu, Sa Majesté l'Empereur et Roi, convaincu que le Gouvernement Impérial de Russie apprécierait équitablement, le cas échéant, nos intérêts — relatifs surtout à la liberté de nos communications commerciales, — a daigné m'autoriser à adhérer à la modification proposée par le Prince.

Ad. 3. Les traités de 1856, en tant qu'ils se réfèrent à la garantie de l'intégrité de l'Empire Ottoman, n'établissent pas de différence entre les possessions du Sultan en Asie et ses possessions en Europe.

Comme une des Puissances garantes nous ne pouvons pas nous considérer comme tout-à-fait désintéressés en présence de la perspective d'une altération du statu quo territorial en Asie. C'est pour ces motifs qu'il a été fait mention à Reichstadt des territoires à être annexés par la Russie en Asie. D'un autre côté, nous en convenons, en Asie la Russie est intéressée en première ligne, de même que sur nos frontières nos intérêts sont plus directement en jeu que ceux de la Russie. Néanmoins nous inspirant du désir de témoigner au Cabinet de St Pétersbourg notre bon vouloir dans l'appréciation de ses intérêts, nous n'hésitons pas à consentir à la suppression de la partie de l'article 1 concernant les acquisitions éventuelles en Asie. Il demeure toutefois entendu que cette omission n'altère en rien ni l'esprit de la convention ni les droits et obligations réciproques.

Ad. 4. Bien que je ne me rende pas compte des motifs qui portent le Prince à désirer une autre rédaction pour la première partie de l'article 2, nous y consentons, à condition toutefois que ce changement n'altère pas la solidarité des deux Hautes Parties Contractantes sur le terrain diplomatique, si les acquisitions territoriales respectives stipulées dans la convention, devraient donner lieu à une délibération collective des Puissances.

Quant au changement proposé par le Prince pour la seconde partie de ce même article, nous ne saurions l'accepter pour les raisons développées tout à l'heure.

Voici quelle devrait être en conséquence la teneur de cet article:

'Les Hautes Parties Contractantes s'engagent à se prêter un mutuel concours sur le terrain diplomatique si les remaniements territoriaux résultant d'une guerre ou de la dissolution de l'Empire Ottoman devaient donner lieu à une délibération collective des Grandes Puissances.'

Ad. 5. Pour les motifs précédemment exposés nous ne pouvons pas consentir à substituer le mot 'résultant' au mot 'ou'.

Ad. 6. Nous partageons l'avis du Prince que les mots 'Etats autonomes' ne répondent pas à la situation prévue et nous consentons à les remplacer par les mots 'Etats indépendants'.

Ad. 7. Nous nous empressons de même accéder au désir du Prince d'ajouter 'une partie de l'Epire' aux territoires qui pourraient être annexés à la Grèce.

Je regrette de n'avoir pas été à même d'accepter toutes les modifications proposées par le Prince Chancelier. Mais j'espère qu'il appréciera nos objections. Quoique je suppose que Son Excellence M. Nowikow les aura déjà portées à la connaissance du Prince Vous voudrez néanmoins lui donner lecture de cette dépêche et en laisser, s'il le désire, une copie entre ses mains.

Recevez, Monsieur le Baron, l'assurance de ma considération la plus distinguée.

5. *The Secret Austro-Russian Conventions of 15 January 1877*

The texts are reprinted from E. Wertheimer's article 'Neues zur Orientpolitik des Grafen Andrássy, 1876–1877', in *Historische Blätter*, Heft 3, 1921–2, pp. 454–6, 458–60. They are also printed in A. F. Pribram, *The Secret Treaties of Austria-Hungary*, vol. ii, pp. 190–203.

Wertheimer in addition prints in footnotes to the second convention differences between Andrássy's first draft and Gorchakov's counter-proposals and the final text, which are reproduced here. As explained above, p. 278, the second convention (*convention additionnelle*) was antedated to 15 January though it was in reality signed on 18 March.

Sa Mté l'empereur de toutes les Russies et Sa Mté l'empereur d'Autriche, etc. roi apostolique de Hongrie considérant que dans le cours des négociations diplomatiques pendantes il pouvait surgir des dissentiments de nature à amener une rupture entre la Russie et l'empire Ottoman, ont jugé conforme à l'étroite amitié qui les lie et à l'urgence d'obvier à la possibilité d'une collision des intérêts de leurs Etats respectifs de s'entendre en prévision de cette éventualité.

A cet effet leurs dites majestés ont nommé pour leurs plénipotentiaires:... Andrássy ... Novikow....[1] Lesquels après avoir échangé leurs pleins-pouvoirs trouvés en bonne et due forme sont convenus des articles suivants:

Article I

Les hautes parties contractantes considérant que les populations chrétiennes et musulmanes en Bosnie et dans la Herzégovine sont trop entremêlées pour qu'il soit permis d'attendre d'une organisation autonome seule une amélioration réelle de leur sort, sont convenues entre elles de ne demander pour ces provinces dans la conférence de Constantinople qu'un régime autonome ne dépassant pas trop la mesure fixée par la dépêche du 30 décembre 1875 et les garanties du memorandum de Berlin. La Bulgarie étant placée dans des conditions plus favorables à l'exercice d'institutions autonomes, elles s'engagent à réclamer pour cette province dans la conférence une autonomie plus large, entourée de sérieuses garanties.

Article II

Pour le cas où les négociations ne devraient pas aboutir et qu'il dût en résulter une rupture suivie d'une guerre entre la Russie et la Turquie, le gouvernement impérial et royal prend l'engagement formel d'observer en présence de l'action isolée de la Russie une attitude de neutralité bienveillante et de paralyser autant qu'il dépend de lui par son action diplomatique les essais d'intervention ou de médiation collective que pourraient tenter d'autres puissances.

Article III

Si le gouvernement de l'empereur et roi est invité à concourir à la mise en exécution du traité du 15 avril 1856, il déclinera sa coopération pour le cas prévu dans la présente convention et, sans

[1] Their titles are here omitted.

contester la validité du dit traité, proclamera sa neutralité. De même, il ne prêtera pas son concours actif à une action effective qui pourrait être proposée sur la base de l'article VIII du traité du 30 mars de la même année.

Article IV

Considérant que les nécessités du passage du Danube pour les troupes russes et le besoin de protéger ce passage contre les canonnières turques obligeront le gouvernement impérial de Russie à apporter des difficultés temporaires à la navigation du fleuve placée sous la garantie des traités, ce qui peut donner lieu à des protestations, le gouvernement austro-hongrois comme signataire de ces traités et principal intéressé dans la liberté du fleuve envisagera cette question comme incident de fait temporaire, inévitable en cas de guerre, mais ne touchant pas aux grands principes dont le maintien intéresse l'Europe. De son côté le gouvernement russe prend l'engagement formel de respecter les principes de la liberté de navigation et de la neutralité du Danube et de se mettre d'accord avec le gouvernement de sa Mté l'empereur et roi pour les rétablir aussitôt que faire se pourra.

Article V

Le gouvernement austro-hongrois prêtera dans les limites de la convention de Genève un concours bienveillant à l'organisation des ambulances provisoires russes sur les lignes de chemins-de-fer Cracovie–Léopol–Csernowitz (entre Granicza et Suczava) avec les embranchements de Woloczysk et Brody ainsi qu'au mouvement sur les lignes susmentionnées du matériel roulant nécessaire à ces ambulances. Il admettra dans ses hôpitaux civils et militaires sur le parcours des lignes susmentionnées les malades et blessés russes contre paiement d'après le tarif militaire autrichien en vigueur.

Article VI

Le gouvernement austro-hongrois ne mettra aucun obstacle à ce que les commissionnaires et agents du gouvernement russe effectuent dans les limites des Etats austro-hongrois les achats et commandes d'objets indispensables à l'armée russe à l'exclusion des articles de contrebande de guerre prohibés par les lois internationales. Toutefois le gouvernement de sa majesté impériale et royale s'engage à user dans l'application et dans l'interprétation de ces lois de la plus large bienveillance à l'égard de la Russie.

Article VII

Sa Mté l'empereur d'Autriche etc. roi de Hongrie se réserve le choix du moment et du mode de l'occupation de la Bosnie et de l'Herzégovine par ses troupes. Il demeure entendu que cette mesure sans assumer un caractère de solidarité avec l'occupation de la Bulgarie par l'armée russe ne devra présenter ni dans son interprétation par le gouvernement de sa Mté impériale et royale ni dans son exécution un caractère d'hostilité à l'égard de la Russie. De même l'intervention de l'armée russe en Turquie ne devra présenter ni dans son interprétation par le gouvernement impérial de Russie ni dans son exécution un caractère d'hostilité à l'égard de l'Autriche-Hongrie.

Article VIII

Les hautes parties contractantes s'engagent réciproquement à ne pas étendre le rayon de leur action militaire respective: sa Mté l'empereur d'Autriche, etc. et roi apostolique de Hongrie à la Roumanie, la Serbie, la Bulgarie et le Monténégro; sa Mté l'empereur de toutes les Russies à la Bosnie, l'Herzégovine, la Serbie et le Monténégro. La Serbie, le Monténégro et la partie de l'Herzégovine qui sépare ces deux principautés formeront une zone neutre continue que les armées des deux empires ne pourront pas franchir et destinée à préserver ces dernières de tout contact immédiat. Toutefois il demeure entendu que le gouvernement impérial et royal ne s'opposera pas à l'action combinée des forces serbes et monténégrines hors de leurs pays avec les troupes russes.

Article IX

Les conséquences de la guerre et les remaniements territoriaux qui résulteraient d'une dissolution éventuelle de l'empire Ottoman seront réglées par une convention spéciale et simultanée.

Article X

Les hautes parties contractantes s'engagent à tenir secrètes les stipulations de la présente convention. Elle sera ratifiée et les ratifications en seront échangées dans l'espace de quatre semaines ou plutôt si faire se peut.

En foi de quoi les plénipotentiaires respectifs l'ont signée et y ont apposé le sceau de leurs armes.

Fait à Budapest le 15 janvier 1877.

ANDRÁSSY. NOVIKOW.

Convention additionnelle, 15 Janvier 1877

Sa majesté l'empereur d'Autriche etc. et roi de Hongrie d'une part et Sa majesté l'empereur de toutes les Russies de l'autre en exécution de l'article IX de la convention secrète signée en date d'aujourd'hui ont jugé conforme à l'étroite amitié qui Les lie et à l'urgence d'obvier à la possibilité d'une collision des intérêts de leurs Etats respectifs de s'entendre sur les conséquences de la guerre et de conclure à cet effet une convention additionnelle destinée à régler d'avance les remaniements territoriaux que la guerre[1] ou la dissolution de l'empire Ottoman pourrait avoir pour résultat. A cet effet leurs dites majestés ont nommé pour leurs plénipotentiaires savoir: ... Andrássy ... Novikow ...[2] lesquels après avoir échangé leurs pleins-pouvoirs, trouvés en bonne et due forme, sont convenus des articles suivants:

Article I

Les deux hautes parties contractantes ayant pour but final l'amélioration du sort des chrétiens et voulant écarter tout projet d'annexions d'une étendue qui pourrait compromettre la paix ou l'équilibre européen — ce qui n'est ni dans leurs intentions ni dans les intérêts des deux empires — sont tombées d'accord de limiter leurs annexions éventuelles aux territoires suivants:

L'empereur d'Autriche, etc. etc. et roi de Hongrie: à la Bosnie et l'Herzégovine à l'exclusion de la partie comprise entre la Serbie et le Monténégro au sujet de laquelle les deux gouvernements se réservent de se mettre d'accord lorsque le moment d'en disposer serait venu.[3]

L'empereur de toutes les Russies: en Europe aux contrées de la Bessarabie qui rétabliraient les anciennes frontières de l'empire avant 1856.[4]

Article II

Les hautes parties contractantes s'engagent à se prêter un mutuel concours sur le terrain diplomatique si les remaniements territoriaux résultant d'une guerre ou de la dissolution de l'empire Ottoman devaient donner lieu à une déliberation collective des grandes puissances.[5]

[1] In Gorchakov's counter-draft 'la guerre ou' was struck out, but Andrássy would not agree.

[2] Their titles are here omitted.

[3] Andrássy's first draft ran: 'à la Bosnie y compris l'Herzégovine à l'exception toutefois de la partie de l'Herzégovine qui d'un commun accord entre les deux hautes parties contractantes serait cédée au Monténégro'. Gorchakov substituted for this the wording which became the final text.

[4] Andrássy's first draft included as well: 'En Asie au port de Batoum et à une partie du territoire adjacent nécessaire pour assurer à la Russie une meilleure délimitation et pouvant quant à l'étendue servir d'équivalent au territoire destiné à être éventuellement annexé à l'Autriche-Hongrie.' This was omitted on Gorchakov's demand.

[5] Andrássy's first draft ran: 'Les hautes parties contractantes se reconnaissent mutuellement solidaires des acquisitions territoriales respectives stipulées dans la présente convention et s'engagent à maintenir indissolublement cette solidarité en se prêtant...'. Gorchakov's counter-draft omitted this and substituted: 'Les hautes parties contractantes s'engagent à se prêter', which became the final text, Gorchakov adding 'territoriaux' after 'remaniements'. Andrássy's first draft read: '... résultant de la guerre ou de la dissolution...'. Gorchakov tried unsuccessfully to alter

Article III

Sa majesté l'empereur d'Autriche etc. et roi de Hongrie etc. et Sa majesté l'empereur de toutes les Russies sont tombées d'accord en principe dans l'entrevue qui a eu lieu entre elles à Reichstadt sur les points suivants: en cas d'un remaniement territorial ou[1] d'une dissolution de l'empire Ottoman l'établissement d'un grand état compact slave ou autre est exclu; en revanche la Bulgarie, l'Albanie et le reste de la Roumélie pourraient être constituées en états indépendants;[2] la Thessalie, une partie de l'Epire et l'île de Crète[3] pourraient être annexées à la Grèce; Constantinople avec une banlieue dont la circonscription reste à déterminer pourrait devenir ville libre. Leurs dites Majestés constatent n'avoir rien à changer à ces vues et déclarent de nouveau vouloir les maintenir comme bases de leur action politique ultérieure.

Article IV

Les hautes parties contractantes s'engagent à tenir secrètes les stipulations de la présente convention qui sera ratifiée et dont les ratifications seront échangées à Vienne dans l'espace de quatre semaines ou plus tôt si faire se peut.

En foi de quoi les plénipotentiaires respectifs l'ont signé et y ont apposé le sceau de leurs armes.

Fait à Budapest le quinzième jour du mois de janvier de l'an mil huit cent soixante dix sept.

ANDRÁSSY. NOVIKOW.[4]

this to ' . . . résultant d'une guerre qui aménerait le démembrement ou la dissolution . . .', the only change in the text as signed being 'une guerre' in place of 'la guerre'.

[1] This was also the wording of Andrássy's first draft. Gorchakov did not succeed in inducing him to substitute 'résultant' for 'ou'.

[2] Andrássy's first draft read 'autonomes'. Gorchakov proposed instead 'indépendants'.

[3] Andrássy's first draft mentioned only Thessaly and Crete; Gorchakov added 'une partie de l'Epire'.

[4] Autograph signatures.

THE IMPERIAL COUNCILS IN MID-OCTOBER 1876 AND MOBILIZATION

THE evidence which I have been able to use as to the imperial councils in mid-October 1876 and the measures taken for mobilization is unclear and in part conflicting. An imperial council was not a formally constituted institution, but simply a conference of whomever the Tsar chose to summon. It was particularly easy for there to be uncertainty both as to exactly at what point decisions were finally reached and as to the precise nature of those decisions. Mobilization requires of course a number of preparatory steps and is a technical term of varying meaning and frequent misuse.

1. Ignatyev in his memoirs, in *I.V.*, vol. cxxxvi, pp. 432–43, writes of two councils, 14 and 15 October, at which he mentions as attending—Gorchakov, Milyutin, himself, and the Tsar. At the council of 15 October Gorchakov's memorandum of 13 October was read and discussed, and his instructions for Ignatyev on his return to Constantinople were decided upon (see above, pp. 214–15).

2. *Tatishchev* (p. 328) records an imperial council held on 15 October, and implies the presence of the Tsar, the Tsarevich, the Grand Duke Nicholas, and Reutern; see above, p. 218. Ignatyev, *I.V.*, vol. cxxxvi, p. 447, states that the Grand Duke arrived at Livadia on 27 October, and does not mention him previously. This evidence by itself cannot be accepted as reliable, but it is borne out by Wellesley reporting on 25 October that the Grand Duke had been summoned from St. Petersburg to Livadia; Doria to Derby, no. 1, 25 October, in *F.O.* 65/941. He may perhaps have made two journeys to the Crimea.

3. Reutern records in his journal, under date 24 October, *R.S.*, vol. cxliii, pp. 40–1, that at an imperial council held on 16 October, and attended by the Tsar, the Tsarevich, Gorchakov, Milyutin, Ignatyev, Adlerberg, and himself, it was decided to send Ignatyev back to Constantinople, to mobilize part of the army on 13 November, and to cross the frontier about the middle of December if the Russian demands were not accepted at the forthcoming conference. This latter statement probably represents a too definite pinning down of Gorchakov's remarks.

4. Cyon, in *Nouvelle Revue*, 1880, vol. iv, pp. 480–1, has an account, based on subsequent hearsay from the Grand Duke Nicholas, of a special council at Livadia held on 30 October (new style; the date

given by Cyon, 18 October, I take to be old style), at which were present the Grand Duke, Gorchakov, Milyutin, and Obruchev (the Tsar is not mentioned), and as a result of which the Grand Duke, who had been pressing for immediate action against Turkey, gained his end and it was decided to present an ultimatum to Constantinople and draw up a manifesto announcing mobilization. The Grand Duke on 2 November left for St. Petersburg to make his final preparations: *en route* he received a telegram from the Tsar that the Turks had accepted his ultimatum and that the orders for mobilization would not be given until 14 November.

5. Ignatyev states, *I.V.*, vol. cxxxvi, p. 447, that mobilization was not decided upon until after the arrival of the Grand Duke Nicholas at Livadia on 27 October, and that he only learnt of this decision from the press announcements of 14 November.

Further evidence as to mobilization measures is supplied by the following sources:

6. *Tatishchev*, p. 337, without citing any authority, states that at the very beginning of October partial mobilization had been ordered in the Odessa, Kharkov, Kiev, and part of the Caucasus military districts, and on 24 October partial mobilization of four divisions of the Moscow military district.

7. This is in part confirmed by the information sent from St. Petersburg by the British military attaché Wellesley, on 11 October, no. 31, secret, enclosed in Loftus to Derby, disp., no 478, secret, 11 October, in *F.O.* 65/941: no symptoms of any real intention on[1] the part of the government to go to war were observable until 5 October, when a great change took place and the military departments had been working at full pressure since then; orders had been received from Livadia that preparation was to be made for immediate mobilization in the Kiev, Odessa, Kharkov, and Caucasus military circles and that unless counter-orders were received a manifesto declaring intended occupation of Turkish territory would be issued on the 7th; this manifesto was printed but not issued; heavy buying of forage, &c., was taking place; heavy guns were being sent to the Black Sea coast; all leave had been stopped; 'there is a general uneasiness and a conviction that war is inevitable'.[1]

8. In *La Guerre d'Orient en 1877–8*, p. 28 (Paris, 1879; an anonymous work by 'un tacticien' based on official documents published by the Russians and the Turks), it is stated that the movement of active troops had begun a fortnight before the issue of the manifesto of

---

[1] Wellesley had previously described Russia as too weak militarily and financially to think seriously of war: 'she is glad to bark, because she dare not bite. . . . I do not believe that the present Emperor of Russia is a man to rush headlong, in an unprepared state, into a war, which would compromise the work of a whole reign'; report no. 29, conf., 26 Sept., in *F.O.* 65/940.

13 November and that after the big manœuvres these had not taken up their winter quarters, but had remained at points close to the railway lines.

9. It is clear from *Skalon*, vol. i, p. 9, under date 7 December, that the Grand Duke Nicholas's staff calculated mobilization from 14 November.

DOCUMENTS CONCERNING THE LONDON PROTOCOL

1. *Ignatyev's Draft Protocol*

Translated from the Russian text as printed in Ignatyev's memoirs in *I.V.*, vol. cxxxvi, pp. 860–1.

The Powers, which have undertaken in common the pacification of the East and have with that view taken part in the conference of Constantinople, have entered into agreement as to their future actions consequential upon the refusal of the Porte to accept their pressing and unanimous proposals. First and foremost they have undertaken to maintain their close concert in this new phase of the question confronting them. The Cabinets have unanimously agreed to insist upon the carrying into execution of the reforms recognized by them as necessary for the improvement of the condition of the Christian populations of Turkey. In the event of the conclusion of peace with Serbia and Montenegro the Cabinets will take cognizance of it. If the peace negotiations with Montenegro shall not have been completed, the Cabinets will insist upon the decision of the Conference in regard to the extension of the frontiers of the principality and the reservation to it of the right of free navigation of the Boyana. The Cabinets, regarding the re-establishment of peace with the principalities as the first step towards the attainment of the end which they all desire, the pacification of the Balkan peninsula, invite the Porte to consolidate it by placing its armies on a peace footing and demobilizing its assembled forces, keeping under arms only the number of troops necessary for the maintenance of order, and also by putting into operation without any delay those reforms which were enumerated in the protocols of the Conference. The Cabinets have the more right to expect this in that the Turkish plenipotentiaries, and later the Porte, have already declared themselves ready to carry into execution the greater part of these reforms. The Powers take cognizance specially of the declaration of the Grand Vizier in regard to the immediate introduction of the following measures:

Prohibition of use of irregular forces except in the case of enemy forces having penetrated within the frontiers of Turkey.

Cessation of colonization of Caucasian natives in Christian districts.

Full freedom of religion.

Reorganization of police, and local autonomy.

Formation of commission of observation, to be presided over by a representative of the Porte.

Prohibition of the carrying of arms in those localities where risings have ceased.

New delimitation of territorial divisions on the basis of the demands of the Conference.

Remission of taxation arrears.

In view of such a disposition on the part of the Porte and of its evident interest to translate it into immediate effect, in order to put an end to a condition of affairs which is ruining it, the Cabinets believe that they have full grounds for hoping that the Porte will profit by the present calming down of feelings to carry into effect energetically all the measures devised by the Conference and destined for the improvement of the condition of the Christian populations. Effective improvement is unanimously recognized to be indispensable to the tranquillity of Europe. Having once entered upon this path, the Porte will understand that its honour and the realization of its own interests demand that it continue in this path honourably and effectively without a return to unsound actions which have brought upon it so many calamities and have necessitated the intervention of Europe.

The Powers intend to watch carefully by means of their representatives at Constantinople and their local agents the manner in which the promises of the Turkish Government are carried into effect.

If their hopes should be yet again deceived and if the condition of the Christian subjects of the Sultan should not be so improved as to prevent the return of the disorders which periodically disturb the peace of the East and of Europe, the Cabinets consider it necessary to declare that it would be impossible for them to tolerate longer a position of affairs incompatible both with their interests and with the rights of humanity. In such case the Powers reserve their right to consider in common and define the measures which may be deemed necessary by them to secure the well-being of the Christian populations and the interests of the general peace.

2. *Shuvalov's Draft Protocol*

Given by Shuvalov on 11 March to Derby. The text is taken from the copy in *F.O.* 65/986. The minutes given in the footnotes are by Tenterden. The words in italics are underlined in pencil.

Confidential

Draft Protocol

Les Puissances qui ont offert bons offices pour la pacification de l'Orient et ont participé dans cette vue à la Conférence de Constantinople, reconnaissent que le moyen le plus sûr d'atteindre le but qu'elles se sont proposé est de maintenir avant tout l'entente si heureusement établie entre elles et[1] *d'affirmer de nouveau* ensemble *les réformes qu'elles* ont signalées *comme indispensables* pour l'amélioration du sort des populations Chrétiennes de la Turquie.

Elles prennent acte de la conclusion de la paix avec la Serbie et le Monténégro.

(Dans le cas où la paix avec Monténégro n'aurait pas été conclue, rappeler que les Puissances considèrent[2] *comme nécessaires* la rectification des frontières et la libre navigation de la Boïana.)

Les Puissances considèrent les arrangements intervenus ou à intervenir entre la Porte et les deux Principautés comme une preuve de ses bonnes dispositions et comme un pas accompli vers l'apaisement qui est l'objet de leurs communs désirs.

Elles demandent à la Porte[3] *de le consolider* en *replaçant ses armées sur le pied de paix,* et en mettant en œuvre, *sans aucun délai*[4], les *réformes*[5] énumérées dans les *Protocoles de la Conférence* et dont les Plénipotentiaires Ottomans, et depuis la Porte elle-même se sont déclarés prêts à réaliser *la*[6] *plus grande partie.*

Elles prennent spécialement acte de la déclaration par laquelle le Gouvernement Ottoman a annoncé la résolution de les appliquer.

En présence de ces bonnes dispositions de la Porte et de son intérêt évident à y donner immédiatement suite, les Puissances se croient fondées à espérer que celle-ci profitera de l'apaisement actuel pour appliquer avec énergie les mesures conseillées par la Conférence et destinées à apporter à la condition des populations Chrétiennes l'amélioration effective unanimement réclamée comme indispensable à la tranquillité de l'Europe, et, qu'une fois entrée dans cette voie, elle comprendra qu'il est de son honneur, comme de son intérêt, d'y persévérer loyalement et efficacement.

Les Puissances se proposent de surveiller *d'une manière efficace*[7], par intermédiaire de leurs Représentants à Constantinople et de leurs agents locaux, la façon dont les promesses du Gouvernement Ottoman seront exécutées.

Si leur espoir se trouvait encore une fois déçu et si la condition des sujets Chrétiens du Sultan n'était pas améliorée de manière à

[1] These reforms shd be looked at in detail—some of them have been declared to be impracticable.

[2] Ought the Powers to insist on the grant of territory to Montenegro as *necessary* quite *advisable.*

[3] Surely a *reciprocal* engagement on the part of Russia shd be inserted.

[4] Is not this too stringent. How can these reforms (many of wh. require careful preparation) be carried out without any delay.

[5] See above as to the reforms. Shd not a clear definition be made of those to wh. the Porte had agreed and those wh. it had refused and it be decided how many of the latter shd be insisted upon.

[6] If these words were left out the matter wd. be simplified.

[7] This is inconsistent with the Treaty of Paris. Moreover the words imply both a general and local supervision of an inquisitorial character.

prévenir le retour des complications qui troublent périodiquement le repos de l'Orient et de l'Europe, elles croient devoir déclarer qu'un tel état de choses serait incompatible avec leurs intérêts et les droits de l'humanité. En pareil cas, elles se réservent d'aviser en commun à l'action qu'elles jugeront indispensable pour assurer le bien-être des populations Chrétiennes et les intérêts de la paix générale.[1]

3. *Shuvalov's Pro memoria*

Given by Shuvalov to Derby on 11 March. The text is taken from the original in *F.O.* 65/986.

Le but du voyage du Général Ignatiew a été de fournir des éclaircissements sur la pensée intime du Cab^t. Impérial et de faciliter la voie d'une solution pacifique.

Après les sacrifices que s'est imposée la Russie — la stagnation de son industrie et de son commerce, les frais énormes de la mobilisation de cinq cent mille hommes — elle ne peut se retirer, ni renvoyer ses troupes sans avoir obtenu quelque résultat palpable en vue de l'amélioration du sort des populations chrétiennes.

L'Empereur veut sincèrement la paix, mais non pas une paix à tout prix.

Les Cabinets Européens préparent en ce moment des réponses à la circulaire russe, nous ne les préjugeons pas, mais prévoyons qu'elles peuvent offrir un grand danger. Si ces réponses ne sont pas identiques quelle serait la situation du Cabinet Impérial? A l'opinion de laquelle devrait-il se ranger? L'accord européen, si heureusement établi à la Conférence, ne serait-il pas rompu par suite de nuances que les différents Cabinets établiraient dans leurs réponses? Enfin, si l'un des Cabinets proposait à la Russie de reprendre sa liberté d'action, ne serait-ce point une cause déterminante pour rechercher la solution, soit dans l'entente directe avec la Porte, soit par la voie des armes?

Dans ces conditions, il paraît au Cabinet Impérial que la solution la plus pratique, la meilleure pour assurer le maintien de la paix générale, serait la signature par les Puissances d'un protocole qui mettrait, pour ainsi dire, fin à l'incident.

Ce protocole pourrait être signé à Londres par les Représentants des Grandes Puissances et sous l'inspiration directe du Cabinet de St. James.

Ce protocole ne contiendrait rien d'autre que les principes et les bases dont s'inspirent les Gouvernements pour répondre à la circulaire russe. Il serait à désirer qu'il affirme le caractère européen de la situation et constate que l'amélioration du sort des chrétiens continuera à être l'objet de la sollicitude de tous les Cabinets.

[1] What is meant by *'action'*?

La Porte ayant déclaré à maintes reprises qu'elle s'engageait à introduire des réformes, il serait désirable de les énumérer sur la base de la circulaire de Safvet-Pacha. De cette manière, il n'y aurait pas de malentendu dans la suite sur les promesses de la Turquie.

Puisque un terme de quelques mois ne suffirait pas pour accomplir ces réformes, il serait préférable de ne point préciser de limites. Le terme d'un an ferait croire en Russie que l'armée n'est remise sur pied de paix que provisoirement et qu'elle doit se retrouver prête à l'expiration du terme. Il dépendra de l'accord de toutes les Puissances de déterminer si la Turquie avance dans son œuvre de régénération d'une manière satisfaisante.

Le protocole devrait mentionner que l'Europe continuera à veiller par l'organe de ses représentants diplomatiques à l'exécution progressive des réformes.

Si l'espoir des Puissances se trouvait encore une fois déçu et si la condition des sujets chrétiens n'était pas améliorée, elles se réservent d'aviser en commun à l'action qu'elles jugeront indispensable pour assurer le bien-être des populations chrétiennes et les intérêts de la paix générale.

L'Ambassadeur de Russie espère que Lord Derby appréciera la modération et l'esprit de conciliation dont s'inspire le Cabinet Impérial en énonçant ses pensées qui n'ont rien d'incompatible avec les principes de la politique anglaise. Leur application assurerait le maintien de la paix générale.

Chesham House,
le $\dfrac{\text{27 Février}}{\text{11 Mars}}$ 1877.

4. *Memorandum by Shuvalov*

Given by Shuvalov to Derby on 15 March. The text is taken from the copy in *F.O.* 65/986.

Copy

1. Il semblerait insuffisant de n'affirmer qu'une sympathie pour les Chrétiens; il faut qu'elle se manifeste aussi pour les Réformes. L'on pourrait dire en conséquence: 'et d'affirmer de nouveau ensemble l'intérêt commun qu'elles prennent à l'amélioration du reste des populations Chrétiennes de la Turquie, et aux réformes à introduire en Bosnie, Herzégovine et Bulgarie.'

2. Pour obvier à l'objection de L^d. Derby, l'on pourrait dire: 'Elles invitent la Porte le consolider en replaçant ses armées sur le pied de paix, sauf le nombre de troupes indispensable pour le maintien de l'ordre.'

3. Afin de ne point trop affaiblir la rédaction Russe, on pourrait dire 'Veiller avec soin'.

4. Le mot démarche a en Français une nuance humiliante. Faire des démarches semble solliciter.

On pourrait dire 'les moyens qu'elles jugeront les plus propres.' Le mot moyen ne peut pas être considéré comme coërcitif, enfin une dernière observation qui a été omise ce matin. Est-il bien nécessaire d'employer l'expression Les Puissances reconnaissent avec plaisir ou satisfaction? Ne vaudrait-il pas mieux dire simplement: reconnaissent ou constatent? L'insuccès de la Conférence est trop présent encore à l'esprit des Cabinets et plusieurs d'entre eux ne voudraient peut-être pas exprimer de la satisfaction.

Si l'énumération des réformes se fait d'après l'énumération de Safvet Pacha, j'indique le point 6 que l'Angleterre ne voudrait peut-être pas accepter; je propose de le remplacer par les deux mots: Amnestie partielle.

5. *Counter-alterations by the Russian Government*

Communicated by Shuvalov on 19 March. The text is taken from the original in *F.O.* 65/986.

Le Cabinet Impérial accepte le projet de protocole avec les modifications suivantes:

1. En place de:
Puissances qui ont offert leurs bons offices . . . .

> Les Puissances qui ont entrepris en commun la pacification de l'Orient.

Le résultat de toutes les modifications proposées par Lord Derby ayant très sensiblement affaibli la signification et la portée du protocole, le Cabinet Impérial propose à son tour quelques arrangements:

2. Au lieu de:
Affirmer l'intérêt commun . . .

> D'insister sur les réformes qu'elles ont jugé indispensables d'introduire en Bosnie, Herzégovine et Bulgarie pour l'amélioration du sort des populations Chrétiennes et que la Porte a acceptées sauf à les appliquer elle-même.

3. A l'article de la paix avec le Monténégro, ajouter:

> Sur la base des conditions proposées par la Conférence.

4. En place de:
De l'état desquels la Conférence s'est préoccupée. . . .

> Sur les bases suggérées par la Conférence.

En dernier lieu, le Cabinet Impérial croit préférable de substituer à:

	la phrase:
5. l'énumération des points . . .	Elles prennent spécialement acte des déclarations à ce sujet faites par le Gouvernement Ottoman, pendant la Conférence et depuis par l'entremise de ses représentants.

[*Signed*]   Cte SCHOUWALOFF.

6. *Text of the London Protocol as signed 31 March, 1877*

The text is reprinted from Martens, *Nouveau recueil général des traités*, second series, vol. iii, pp. 174–6.

Protocole.

Les Puissances qui ont entrepris en commun la pacification de l'Orient et ont participé dans cette vue à la Conférence de Constantinople, reconnaissent que le moyen le plus sûr d'atteindre le but qu'elles se sont proposé, est de maintenir avant tout l'entente si heureusement établie entre elles et d'affirmer de nouveau ensemble l'intérêt commun qu'elles prennent à l'amélioration du sort des populations chrétiennes de la Turquie, et aux réformes à introduire en Bosnie, Herzégovine et Bulgarie que la Porte a acceptées, sauf à les appliquer elle-même.

Elles prennent acte de la conclusion de la paix avec la Serbie.

Quant au Monténégro, les Puissances considèrent comme désirable, dans l'intérêt d'un arrangement solide et durable, la rectification des frontières et la libre navigation de la Boïana.

Les Puissances considèrent les arrangements intervenus ou à intervenir entre la Porte et les deux Principautés comme un pas accompli vers l'apaisement qui est l'objet de leurs communs désirs.

Elles invitent la Porte à se consolider en replaçant ses armées sur le pied de paix, sauf le nombre de troupes indispensable pour le maintien de l'ordre, et en mettant en œuvre, dans le plus court délai possible, les réformes nécessaires pour la tranquillité et le bien-être des provinces, de l'état desquelles la Conférence s'est préoccupée. Elles reconnaissent que la Porte s'est déclarée prête à en réaliser une partie importante.

Elles prennent acte spécialement de la circulaire de la Porte du 13 février 1876 [see above, p. 153, and note 1], et des déclarations faites par le Gouvernement ottoman pendant la Conférence et depuis par l'entremise de ses Représentants.

En présence de ces bonnes dispositions de la Porte et de son intérêt évident à y donner immédiatement suite, les Puissances se croient fondées à espérer que celle-ci profitera de l'apaisement actuel pour appliquer avec énergie les mesures destinées à apporter à la condition des populations chrétiennes l'amélioration effective unanimement réclamée comme indispensable à la tranquillité de l'Europe, et qu'une fois entrée dans cette voie, elle comprendra qu'il est de son honneur comme de son intérêt d'y persévérer loyalement et efficacement.

Les Puissances se proposent de veiller avec soin, par l'intermédiaire de leurs Représentants à Constantinople et de leurs Agents locaux, à la façon dont les promesses du Gouvernement ottoman seront exécutées.

Si leur espoir se trouvait encore une fois déçu et si la condition des sujets chrétiens du Sultan n'était pas améliorée de manière à prévenir le retour des complications qui troublent périodiquement le repos de l'Orient, elles croient devoir déclarer qu'un tel état de choses serait incompatible avec leurs intérêts et ceux de l'Europe en général. En pareil cas elles se réservent d'aviser en commun aux moyens qu'elles jugeront les plus propres à assurer le bien-être aux populations chrétiennes et les intérêts de la paix générale.

Fait à Londres, le 31 mars 1877.

> MÜNSTER.
> BEUST.
> L. D'HARCOURT.
> DERBY.
> L. G. MENABREA.
> SCHOUVALOW.

Procès-verbal.

Monsieur le Comte de Münster, Ambassadeur de l'Allemagne, Monsieur le Comte de Beust, Ambassadeur de l'Autriche-Hongrie, Monsieur le Marquis d'Harcourt, Ambassadeur de la France, Monsieur le Comte de Derby, Principal Secrétaire d'État de Sa Majesté Britannique pour les affaires étrangères, Monsieur le Général Comte Menabrea, Ambassadeur de l'Italie, et Monsieur le Comte de Schouvalow, Ambassadeur de la Russie, se sont réunis aujourd'hui au Foreign Office pour signer le Protocole proposé par la Russie, relatif aux affaires de l'Orient.

Monsieur le Comte de Schouvalow a fait la déclaration suivante en en remettant un pro memoria entre les mains du Secrétaire d'État de Sa Majesté Britannique:

Si la paix avec le Monténégro est conclue, et que la Porte accepte les conseils de l'Europe et se montre prête à se remettre sur le pied de paix et à entreprendre sérieusement les réformes mentionnées dans le Protocole — qu'elle envoie à St. Pétersbourg un Envoyé spécial pour traiter du désarmement auquel Sa Majesté l'Empereur consentirait aussi de son côté. Si des massacres pareils à ceux qui ont ensanglanté la Bulgarie avaient lieu, cela arrêterait nécessairement les mesures de démobilisation.

Monsieur le Comte de Derby a lu et remis à chacun des autres Plénipotentiaires une déclaration, dont copie est annexée au présent Procès-verbal.

Monsieur le Général Comte de Menabrea a déclaré que l'Italie n'est engagée par la signature du protocole de ce jour que pour autant que l'entente heureusement établie entre toutes les Puissances par le Protocole lui-même sera maintenue.

Il a été ensuite procédé à la signature du Protocole.

(Suivent les signatures.)

Déclaration de Lord Derby.

The Undersigned, Her Britannic Majesty's Principal Secretary of State for Foreign Affairs, makes the declaration following in regard to the Protocol signed this day by the Plenipotentiaries of Great Britain, Austria-Hungary, France, Germany, Italy and Russia:—

Inasmuch as it is solely in the interest of European peace that Her Britannic Majesty's Government have consented to sign the Protocol proposed by that of Russia, it is understood beforehand that in the event of the object proposed not being attained—namely, reciprocal disarmament on the part of Russia and Turkey and peace between them—the Protocol in question shall be regarded as null and void.

London, March 31, 1877.

DERBY.

Déclaration du Général Menabrea.

L'Italie n'est engagée par la signature du Protocole de ce jour que pour autant que l'entente heureusement établie entre toutes les Puissances par le Protocole lui-même, sera maintenue.

Londres, le 31 mars 1877.

REPORTS FROM WELLESLEY TO DERBY, JULY–OCTOBER 1877

THE following reports from Wellesley to Derby are in *F.O.* 65/985. They have not previously been published, except no. 11. They are marked for circulation to Queen Victoria and the Cabinet; nos. 5 and 14 also to St. Petersburg, nos. 11 and 22 to Constantinople, no. 11 to Vienna.

No. 5   Imperial Head Quarters
Most Confidential   Simnitza on the Danube
                                      July 11. 77.
My Lord, ...

General Ignatieff who is here has laid himself out to be especially civil to me, and loses no opportunity of endeavouring to persuade me that he is England's best friend.

In a conversation I had with him this morning he said how much he hoped that England would persuade the Turks to make peace before the Russians crossed the Balkans, adding that a victory in those mountains would have a most 'intoxicating' effect on the army, a result which he much dreaded and wished to avoid.

I asked His Excellency casually what terms would be exacted by Russia in the event of the Turks treating for peace, and whether she would be satisfied with the requirements of the Conference.

In reply His Excellency said that Russia would demand more efficacious guarantees and spoke of an occupation by Russian troops for some six or eight months; he also said that it was intended to organize a police force out of the Bulgarian Legion, and appeared to lay great stress on the fact of their having already a flag of their own, by which I understood him to imply that they must become completely independent.

To prove to me the ingratitude of the Turks, General Ignatieff informed me that in deference to England, and at his advice the Russian Army in Asia, which had advanced too rapidly, and threatened the Euphrates Valley, received orders to hold back, and that the Turks attributing this self-denial on the part of Russia to weakness, immediately reinforced their troops and endeavoured to advance! I am bound to say that I daily become more and more convinced of the intention of Russia, I do not say the Emperor, to go to Constantinople, nor have I much confidence in the power of the Emperor to restrain the military party if once the Russian Army arrives at Adrianople, or even crosses the Balkans.

Every one speaks of Constantinople as the objective, and the

Emperor appears so elated by the recent successes of his troops that I much fear he will give way to popular opinion.

I believe that the only chance of preventing an advance on the Turkish capital is the signature of peace north of the Balkans.

I have to-day heard from Colonel Mansfield that your Lordship has sanctioned his sending me a cypher, and I will not fail to communicate anything of importance which may occur during our advance.

I have the honor to be [&c.]

FRED. WELLESLEY.

[*Endorsed*] Rec^d July 19.

No. 6   Imperial Head Quarters
Most Confidential   Simnitza on the Danube
                                                July 13. 77.
My Lord,

. . . .

It must be remembered that the Emperor is now surrounded by men belonging to the War party, and that although at first averse to War, General Milutine has lately used all his influence in the direction of a warlike policy.

Count Adlerberg is perhaps the only man who sees the gravity of the situation, and appreciates the ruin which Russia is preparing for herself, and even he said to me two days ago 'le vin est tiré — il faut le boire'.

The presence of General Ignatieff at Head Quarters is a great evil.

Although he would have me think that he is doing all in his power to calm spirits which are becoming intoxicated with hitherto trifling military success, it is evident that on the contrary he is leaving no stone untouched in order to exasperate the Emperor's mind to the utmost against the Turks.

He endeavoured, for instance, to make His Majesty believe that the Naval officer lately made prisoner by the Turks, had been murdered in prison; and that the Turks had announced their intention of making no prisoners.

The harm done in this direction by General Ignatieff is incalculable, and will go far to render the present war a most savage one, for the Russians believing all these stories, will be more disinclined than ever to give quarter.

In conclusion I can only repeat that the military spirit is running so high at the Imperial Head Quarters, that I have little confidence in either the wish or the power of the Emperor to check his troops should a decisive victory open the road to Constantinople.

I have the honor to be [&c.]

FRED. WELLESLEY.

[*Endorsed*] Rec^d 30th.

No 9   Imperial Head Quarters
Most Confidential   Bjela. Bulgaria
                                              July 23. 77.

My Lord,

Your Lordship will have received my telegram of the 20th Inst.,
announcing the capture by the Russians of the Shipka Pass, and
giving an idea of the military operations which preceded it.

This important event, and especially the ease with which it was
accomplished, was hailed with the utmost delight by the Emperor
and his staff.

There was however one exception, namely General Ignatieff, who
was evidently alarmed at the unexpected rapidity of the Russian
advance.

I saw directly that His Excellency feared that so sudden and easy
a victory might lead to plain speaking, if not to immediate action
on the part of Great Britain.

He begged me to impress on Her Majesty's Government the fact
that if European complications are to be avoided the moment has
arrived for England to induce the Porte to make overtures of peace
—overtures, which if couched in suitable language, His Excellency
assured me the Emperor would be glad to entertain.

Again and again did General Ignatieff request me to telegraph
in this sense to your Lordship.

I told His Excellency that I could not take upon myself such a
responsibility without the orders of the Emperor, but that if His
Majesty were directly or through General Ignatieff to authorize me
to send a telegram in this sense to Your Lordship, I should be only
too happy to do so.

General Ignatieff then went to the Emperor's tent, and in about
20 minutes returned and authorized me in His Majesty's name to
inform Your Lordship that notwithstanding recent successes, the
Emperor was still of the same peaceful disposition and ready to
treat for peace, if 'suitable' propositions were made by the Sultan.

I embodied the substance of the above in a cypher despatch to
Your Lordship on the 20th Inst. [See above, p. 322.]

Now that the Russians are virtually masters of the Balkans, there
appear to be only two courses open to them, that is, if the Turks
refuse to make peace, and withdraw their field army to the walls of
Constantinople.

The one is to march on Constantinople at all hazards: and the
other to advance as far as Adrianople only, and from thence appeal
to Europe to force the Porte to come to terms, whereby Russia
would prove the sincerity of her protestations with regard to the
Turkish capital.

If Europe however, were, in the latter case, to fail in persuading the Turks to commence negociations, Russia would repudiate the responsibility of a march to Constantinople which would then become inevitable, provided of course, that Russian successes continue. Whether the Emperor would be powerful enough, or have the moral courage to stop a young and victorious army within so short a distance of the prize coveted by every Russian, it is impossible to say.

Judging however from the general spirit at Head Quarters I entertain great doubts on the subject.

Policy and respect for the interests of other countries appear to have vanished entirely from the mind of the Emperor who is entirely absorbed in military events of even daily occurrence.

In my humble opinion this is a danger which should not be lost sight of, for Russia is essentially a Military nation, and one in which under present circumstances, military honor has more weight than considerations of policy and solemn assurances.

Only yesterday General Ignatieff begged me again to impress on Your Lordship that the time had arrived when England should bring her influence to bear on the Porte in favour of peace, and added that the dream of the Grand Duke Nicholas and of those who surround him is 'de faire célébrer la messe dans l'église de Sainte Sophie'.

I have the honor to be [&c.]

FRED. WELLESLEY.

[*Endorsed*] Rec^d July 30.

See accompanying telegrams. We have no answer from Mr. Layard as to what has been done about peace overtures. Probably suspended by the Plevna battles.

T[ENTERDEN]

[The following report and the enclosure were printed in *A. and P.*, 1878, lxxxi, C. 1929, no. 3.]

No. 11   London
Secret   August 7. 77.

My Lord,

On taking leave of the Emperor of Russia at Bela (Bulgaria) on the 30th Ult., His Majesty was pleased to make certain remarks to me respecting the present political situation, with a view to their being communicated to Her Majesty's Government.

After my interview I made a short memorandum of His Majesty's observations which I have now the honor to submit to Your Lordship.

The Emperor was most anxious that my journey to England should not have the aspect of a diplomatic mission, and that it should not be thought that I proceeded to London by His Majesty's orders.

I was particularly requested by the Minister of War not to mention either to Prince Gortchakoff or to Count Schouvaloff the object of my journey, which is supposed to have been undertaken with the sole view of explaining to Your Lordship the true state of the case with regard to the alleged Russian atrocities.

I submitted the enclosed memorandum to the Emperor before my departure, and His Majesty informed me that it was correct.

At the Emperor's request I had the honor to furnish Him with a copy of it.

I have the honor to be [&c.]

FRED. WELLESLEY.

His Majesty the Emperor, in consequence of the false reports current in England respecting alleged Russian atrocities, thought it might be useful for me to report personally to H.M.'s Gov^t the true state of affairs.

In an interview which I had before my departure, His Majesty was pleased to make the following remarks to me, and at the same time authorized me to communicate them to my Government.

His Majesty repeated what he had already said to Lord A. Loftus at Livadia, and to myself at Simnitza.

The object of the present war was solely the amelioration of the condition of the Christian population of Turkey.

The conditions of peace required by the Emperor are those lately communicated to Lord Derby by Count Shouvaloff, and will remain the same as long as England maintains her position of neutrality; if however, England abandons that position, matters will have entered a new phase.

His Majesty has no ideas of annexation, beyond perhaps that of the territory Russia lost in 1856, and perhaps that of a certain portion of Asia Minor.

The Emperor will not occupy Constantinople for the sake of military honor, but only if such a step is rendered necessary by the march of events.

His Majesty is ready to enter into negotiations for peace, if suitable propositions are made by the Sultan; but mediation in favor of Turkey could not be entertained.

Europe will be invited to a Conference for the final settlement of the conditions of peace.

The Emperor has not the slightest wish or intention in any way to menace the interests of England either with regard to Constantinople, Egypt, the Suez Canal, or India.

With respect to India His Majesty not only considers it impossible to do so, but an act of folly if practicable.

His Majesty assured me that the Triple Alliance was formed for the preservation of peace and without any idea of aggression, or of offence to England, with which country His Majesty has every desire to remain on friendly terms.

A temporary occupation of Bulgaria will be necessary.

His Majesty has never entertained hostile feelings towards England nor has he desired to give her offence, but if one is determined to 'Chercher midi à quatorze heures', it is easy to take offence at anything.

The Emperor fears that the present policy of England only tends to encourage the Turks, and consequently to prolong the war, and considers that if English influence were brought to bear on the Porte, the Sultan would be ready to come to terms, and thus a war regretted and felt by all Europe, would be brought to a speedy conclusion.

Bjela, Bulgaria. July 17/29 1877.

[*Endorsed*] In Col. Wellesley's No. 11. Secret.

Copy   Gorny Stooden. Bulgaria
No. 14   Aug. 30. 77.
Most Confidential.

My Lord,

I have the honor to report my arrival at the Imperial Head Quarters on the evening of the 29th Inst., and to submit the following account of my interviews with His Majesty the Emperor since my return.

Soon after my arrival I was received by the Emperor who said that he had already heard from Count Schouvaloff of the conciliatory language I had held in London, and thanked me for the endeavours I had made to explain to Her Majesty's Government his views with respect to the relations at present existing between Russia and England.

I informed the Emperor in a few words of the substance of Your Lordship's memorandum of which I was the bearer, and of which I was authorized to give him a copy. [This is the cabinet reply of 14 August, see above, p. 323, and is printed in *A. and P.*, 1878, lxxxi, C. 1929, no. 4.]

His Majesty being anxious to know the judgment I had formed on the state of public opinion in England I took the opportunity of impressing on His Majesty's mind the advisability of ending the war this year, and the danger which would attend a renewal of hostilities in the Spring.

I was in a position to assure the Emperor from personal experience of the warlike tendency of a very great proportion of public opinion in England, and to shew how difficult it might become for Her Majesty's Government to restrain this feeling, should Russia determine to attack Turkey a second time with all the forces she could muster during the winter months.

I pointed out to His Majesty that the feeling of sympathy for the Turks among the English people increased in proportion to the brave resistance which they displayed in the defence of their country, and that if, after a campaign in which Turkey had been able more or less to hold her own Russia were to collect all the immense forces at her disposal for a renewal of the attack at the commencement of next year, I had grave apprehensions as to the effect such a policy might produce on the public mind in England.

The Emperor replied that the intelligence he received from Count Schouvaloff entirely bore out my words and added that he had himself foreseen the influence which Turkish successes would have on the friends of that nation in England.

I explained to His Majesty that although perfect tranquillity apparently reigns in England at the present time, His Majesty must not attribute this calmness to apathy on the part of the people, but rather to the confidence they have in the present Government, and to the conviction that it is prepared to act should the honor or interests of England be in any way menaced.

I endeavoured to disabuse the Emperor's mind of the idea prevalent in Russia that the Queen and Her Majesty's Government are desirous of engaging in war with Russia and assured His Majesty that on the contrary it was the sincere wish of the Queen and the British Government to remain on friendly terms with the Emperor, and that consequently everything was avoided which could in any way be construed as an act of encouragement to the Turks.

I further added my belief that any Russian successes which might enable the Emperor to obtain conditions of peace at once honorable and satisfactory would be welcomed in England with joy.

I likewise informed the Emperor that I had reason to believe that anti-Russian meetings and discussions in Parliament on the Eastern Question had been discouraged by Her Majesty's Government in order to avoid any semblance of encouragement to Turkey.

His Majesty appeared much pleased at this and said that he hoped sincerely to end the war this year, and above all to avoid a conflict with England, adding 'et pour quoi — Mon Dieu, pour quoi?'

I took this opportunity of begging the Emperor not to believe in the alleged weakness of the present British Government and in the absurd strength attributed to the Opposition, assuring His Majesty that faith in such reports could only lead to a false appreciation of the actual state of affairs.

As I left the room the Emperor thanked me sincerely for what I had told him and 'especially' said His Majesty 'for the frankness with which you have spoken'.

On the following morning the Emperor sent for me again, and I read to His Majesty the memorandum with which Your Lordship had charged me.

The Emperor interrupted me twice during the reading, once to say that although Her Majesty's Government might now be desirous of seeing the war brought to a close, it could not be denied that they had done much towards bringing it on; and again to give his approval to that portion of the memorandum which refers to the present not being a favorable opportunity for trying to obtain suitable conditions of peace from the Porte.

When I had finished reading, the Emperor said that he had been thinking a great deal about what I had said to him on the previous day, and that he could not but think that if I were correct in my idea that Russian successes would be welcomed in England, the fact must be attributed to the conviction that it is impossible for Russia to cross the Balkans this year.

I replied that I believed Her Majesty's Government earnestly desired to see the present war terminated in a manner honorable to the Emperor and his country, and that they would therefore receive with satisfaction the news of such Russian successes as would enable this result to be obtained.

The Emperor went on to say that he had commenced the war 'son corps défendant', and with the object of obtaining the execution of the recorded wishes of the Great Powers, and that glad as he would be to terminate the war even north of the Balkans, it would be impossible for him to do so otherwise than on conditions which would guarantee a solid and lasting peace.

With regard to the conditions of peace His Majesty said that of course if he continued to suffer reverses, he would be compelled to adapt himself to circumstances, but that if the Almighty were to bless his arms he could not give his sanction to 'une paix boiteuse'.

'God knows,' said His Majesty, 'I undertook this war mon corps défendant.—I had no wish for war, but now I am responsible to my country, and if, after the sacrifices in blood and money which I have called upon my subjects to make, I were to consent to an unstable peace, Russia would never forgive me. She has, as it is, been thrown back some 20 or 30 years and has a right to demand some substantial result for so great a sacrifice.'

'I have told you many times,' continued His Majesty, 'and I repeat it to you again in the most solemn manner, that I do not now, and never have entertained the slightest intention or wish to menace the interests of England in any way. I bear her no malice, and my sincere desire is to live on friendly terms with her. I trust most sincerely that there will never be a collision between our two countries, and feel sure que vous travaillerez vous même pour cela.

I have the same pacific intentions now which I have always entertained and should be only too delighted to end the war now, if I
saw my way to a durable peace.'

The Emperor also read to me a letter he had received from Prince
Gortchakoff relating to conversations which His Highness and Baron
Jomini had had with me when I passed through Bucharest, and in
which I had impressed upon them the desirability of a speedy peace.
I had stated, said Prince Gortchakoff, that the conditions as submitted by the Emperor were considered impossible in London,
especially the one which relates to the destruction of the fortresses,
to which it had been replied that after all the conditions presented
were only the expression of what Russia required, but liable of course
to modification according to the march of events.

As the Emperor did not disavow this answer, it may be supposed
that the Russian Government are already disposed to entertain great
modifications of the conditions as presented by Count Schouvaloff
to Your Lordship, and this idea is strengthened by a few words
which my Austrian Colleague was evidently asked to say to me,
to the effect that as Russia had proposed certain conditions it was
impossible for her to take the initiative in proposing modifications
of them, but that he believed that she would be ready to listen to
any counter proposals on the part of Her Majesty's Government.

Other proofs are not wanting of the disposition on the part of
Russia to be more reasonable in her demands.

Baron Jomini, for instance, told me that at the Grand Duke's
Head Quarters they had 'added a great deal of water to their wine',
and one of the Grand Duke's Aides de Camp, after saying what
dispositions should in his opinion be made for carrying on the war,
concluded by remarking 'that is my opinion as a soldier, but as a
man I say that having had advantages and reverses on both sides,
we ought to make mutual concessions and come to terms of peace'.

At the conclusion of my conversation with the Emperor, His
Majesty said that he was often told of British interests, but that it
must not be forgotten that Russia has interests also which as
Emperor it is his duty to protect.

I have the honor to be

                              [*Signed*]   FRED. WELLESLEY.
[*Endorsed*] Rec^d Oct. 8/77.

No. 22.   Bucharest
Most confidential.   Oct. 29. 77.

My Lord,

I arrived here from the Imperial Head Quarters the day before
yesterday in order to purchase winter clothes, etc.

The day after tomorrow I go to Poradim near Plevna to which village the Emperor and his staff moved yesterday.

This afternoon I called on Baron Jomini who seemed much depressed at the present state of affairs.

He did not appear to think that the victories which the Russians have lately gained in Asia Minor and to the west of Plevna have materially affected the position of Russia.

As he spoke to me with great frankness and apparently with little reserve, his opinions with regard to the prospects of peace may be interesting to your Lordship.

Alluding to the above mentioned victories, His Excellency said that although they somewhat brightened the hitherto sombre aspect of affairs it 'was not enough'.

'What we want,' said Baron Jomini, 'is the fall of Kars as well as that of Plevna, and should we be fortunate enough to take these two fortresses I see no reason why negotiations should not be commenced without at the same time putting an end to military operations.'

He said that the military party in Russia was far less pretentious than it was a few months ago, a fact which would diminish the difficulties of negociation. 'In fact,' said Baron Jomini, 'the military element has at last realized the truth of what we diplomatists told them at Ploeshti when the war first commenced.

'When I first arrived at that place, I had in my pocket the proposal of Count Schouvaloff that Russia should at once declare that her military operations should be limited to that portion of Bulgaria which lies north of the Balkans.

'This proposal was received with scorn on the part of the Grand Duke Nicolas and his staff, and during the discussion I made the following statement:

' " If you gentlemen consider the invasion of Turkey so easy, and will prove by your victories that such is the case, then we diplomatists will be very glad to be able to add a considerable amount of wine to our water, but if on the contrary you experience difficulties which render what you now consider a military promenade, a campaign fraught with danger, you will be compelled to add still more water to your wine." '

Baron Jomini considers that the military authorities, being now convinced of the difficulties attending an invasion such as Russia has undertaken, are ready and willing to be very moderate in imposing conditions of peace.

He believes that the only question of vital importance and the one which Russia will be compelled to insist on, is that of the destruction of the fortresses, which he thinks would be a sufficient guarantee for the liberty and better government of the Bulgarians.

He sincerely hoped that the Grand Duke Michael would succeed in capturing Kars before the winter puts an end to military operations, as he thought that Turkey might then agree to give up Batoum to Russia in exchange for the former fortress.

Baron Jomini thinks that the question of the Dardanelles will not be an obstacle to peace negociations, and that it is a matter which could hereafter be settled according to the general wish of Europe.

He told me that M. Nelidoff formerly first secretary of the Russian Embassy at Constantinople and at present attached to the staff of the Grand Duke Nicolas, is strongly of opinion that the question of the fortresses should not be insisted upon by Russia if by doing so a winter campaign would be rendered inevitable.

Baron Jomini however does not think that a durable peace can be obtained without the destruction of these fortresses, which as he naively said, would enable the Russians to march into Bulgaria without difficulty should the Turks recommence the oppression of the Christian subjects of the Porte.

The possible renewal of hostilities in the spring is evidently a matter of serious danger in the opinion of Baron Jomini, who fears that such an event would very probably lead to European complications on account of the excited state of Hungary, and the present attitude of England.

In conclusion His Excellency expressed his grave anxiety respecting future events in Russia at the termination of the present war.

'I believe, said His Excellency, that our serious troubles will only commence when the war ends.

'I look with great apprehension to the future — croyez moi nous aurons nos comptes à faire chez nous.'

The impression which this conversation made on me is that both the Government and the military party in Russia are most desirous of terminating the war, and would make great concessions were it to do so this year.

The Russians do not disguise the fact that they no longer consider the Bulgarians in this war, and General Greig the Controller of the Empire, lately at Head Quarters, himself told me that Russia was now fighting not for the Bulgarians, but for the re-establishment of her military honor.

In the Army, both officers and men are much discontented. They openly complain of having been deceived with regard to the alleged miserable condition of the Bulgarians, and the soldiers are particularly exasperated at being required to fight for the amelioration of the position of a people infinitely better off and more well to do than the peasantry of Russia.

I have the honor to be [&c.]

FRED. WELLESLEY.

[*Endorsed*] Rec^d Nov. 12.

THE BASES OF PEACE SIGNED AT ADRIANOPLE
31 JANUARY 1878

The text is reprinted from Noradounghian, *Recueil d'actes internationaux de l'empire ottoman*, vol. iii, pp. 507–8.

En vue d'un armistice à conclure entre les armées belligérantes russes et ottomanes, Leurs Excellences Server Pasha, Ministre des Affaires Etrangères de la Sublime Porte, et Namyk Pacha, Ministre de la Liste Civile de Sa Majesté Impériale le Sultan, se sont rendus au quartier général de Son Altesse Impériale le Grand-Duc Nicolas, Commandant en chef de l'armée russe, munis des pleins pouvoirs de la Sublime Porte, et les bases proposées par Son Altesse Impériale le Grand-Duc au nom de Sa Majesté l'Empereur de Russie ayant été acceptées par les Plénipotentiaires Ottomans, ont été établies d'un commun accord dans les termes suivants:

1° La Bulgarie dans les limites déterminées par la majorité de la population bulgare et qui, en aucun cas, ne sauraient être moindres que celles indiquées par la Conférence de Constantinople, sera érigée en Principauté autonome, tributaire, avec un gouvernement national chrétien et une milice indigène. L'armée ottomane n'y séjournera plus.

2° L'indépendance du Monténégro sera reconnue. Un accroissement de territoire équivalent à celui que le sort des armes a fait tomber entre ses mains, lui sera assuré. La frontière définitive sera fixée ultérieurement.

3° L'indépendance de la Roumanie et de la Serbie sera reconnue. Un dédommagement territorial suffisant sera assuré à la première et une rectification de frontière à la seconde.

4° La Bosnie et l'Herzégovine seront dotées d'une administration autonome avec des garanties suffisantes. Des réformes analogues seront introduites dans les autres provinces chrétiennes de la Turquie d'Europe.

5° La Sublime Porte s'engage à dédommager la Russie des frais de la guerre et des pertes qu'elle a dû s'imposer. Le mode, soit pécuniaire, soit territorial ou autre, de cette indemnité, sera réglé ultérieurement. Sa Majesté Impériale le Sultan s'entendra avec Sa Majesté l'Empereur de Russie pour sauvegarder les droits et les intérêts de la Russie dans les Détroits du Bosphore et des Dardanelles.

Des négociations seront immédiatement ouvertes au quartier général de Son Altesse Impériale le Grand-Duc, Commandant en chef, entre les Plénipotentiaires des deux Gouvernements pour arrêter les préliminaires de la paix.

Aussitôt que les présentes bases et une convention d'armistice auront été signées, les hostilités seront suspendues entre les armées belligérantes, y compris celles de la Roumanie, de la Serbie et du Monténégro, pour la durée des négociations de paix.

Les Commandants en chef des deux armées belligérantes en Asie en seront immédiatement avisés à l'effet de procéder entre eux à la conclusion d'un armistice qui mettra fin également aux opérations militaires. Le Gouvernement Impérial Ottoman donnera l'ordre aux troupes ottomanes d'évacuer, dès que l'armistice aura été signé, les forteresses de Viddin, de Roustchouk et de Silistrie en Europe et celle d'Erzeroum en Asie. En outre, les troupes russes auront la faculté d'occuper militairement pendant la durée des pourparlers certains points stratégiques spécifiés dans les conventions d'armistice.

En foi de quoi le présent protocole a été dressé et signé en double exemplaire à Andrinople le 19/31 Janvier 1878.

(*Signé*) NICOLAS. — SERVER. — NAMYK.

PRELIMINARIES OF PEACE SIGNED AT SAN STEFANO, 3 MARCH 1878

THE text is reprinted from Noradounghian, *Recueil d'actes internationaux de l'empire ottoman*, vol. iii, pp. 509–21. For maps showing the boundaries laid down by the treaty, see maps nos. 3–8.

Sa Majesté l'Empereur de Russie et Sa Majesté l'Empereur des Ottomans, animés du désir de rendre et d'assurer à leurs pays et à leurs peuples les bienfaits de la paix, ainsi que de prévenir toute nouvelle complication qui pourrait la menacer, ont nommé pour leurs Plénipotentiaires à l'effet d'arrêter, conclure et signer les préliminaires de la paix:

Sa Majesté l'Empereur de Russie d'une part — le Comte Nicolas Ignatiew [titles omitted],

Et Sa Majesté l'Empereur des Ottomans de l'autre — Safvet Pacha, Ministre des Affaires Étrangères [titles omitted],

Lesquels, après avoir échangé leurs pleins pouvoirs, trouvés en bonne et due forme, sont convenus des articles suivants:

ARTICLE 1er. — Afin de mettre un terme aux conflits perpétuels entre la Turquie et le Monténégro, la frontière qui sépare les deux pays sera rectifiée conformément à la carte ci-annexée, sauf la réserve ci-après, de la manière suivante:... [given in *A. and P.*, 1878, IV, lxxxiii, C. 1973: and see above, map facing p. 412. There follows a description of the frontier in some detail, which I omit.]

Une commission européenne, dans laquelle seront représentés la Sublime Porte et le Gouvernement du Monténégro, sera chargée de fixer les limites définitives de la Principauté, en apportant sur les lieux, au tracé général, les modifications qu'elle croirait nécessaires et équitables au point de vue des intérêts respectifs et de la tranquillité des deux pays, auxquels elle accordera de ce fait les équivalents reconnus nécessaires.

La navigation de la Boyana, ayant toujours donné lieu à des contestations entre la Sublime Porte et le Monténégro, fera l'objet d'un règlement spécial qui sera élaboré par la même commission européenne.

ART. 2. — La Sublime Porte reconnaît définitivement l'indépendance de la Principauté du Monténégro.

Une entente entre le gouvernement impérial de Russie, le gouvernement ottoman et la Principauté du Monténégro, déterminera ultérieurement le caractère et la forme des rapports entre la Sublime Porte et la Principauté en ce qui touche notamment l'institution d'agents monténégrins à Constantinople et dans certaines localités de l'Empire ottoman, où la nécessité en sera reconnue, l'extradition des criminels réfugiés sur l'un ou l'autre territoire et la soumission des Monténégrins, voyageant ou séjournant dans l'empire ottoman, aux lois et aux autorités ottomanes, suivant les principes du droit international et les usages établis concernant les Monténégrins.

Une convention sera conclue entre la Sublime Porte et le Monténégro pour régler les questions se rattachant aux rapports entre les habitants des confins des deux pays et aux ouvrages militaires sur ces mêmes confins. Les points sur lesquels une entente ne pourrait être établie seront résolus par l'arbitrage de la Russie et de l'Autriche-Hongrie.

Dorénavant, s'il y a discussion ou conflit, sauf les cas de nouvelles réclamations territoriales, la Turquie et le Monténégro abandonneront le règlement de leurs différends à la Russie et à l'Autriche-Hongrie, qui devront statuer en commun, arbitralement.

Les troupes du Monténégro seront tenues d'évacuer le territoire non compris dans la circonscription indiquée plus haut, dans le délai de dix jours à partir de la signature des préliminaires de paix.

Art. 3. — La Serbie est reconnue indépendante.

La frontière, marquée sur la carte ci-jointe, . . . [given in *A. and P.*, 1878, IV, lxxxiii, C. 1973: and see above, maps between pp. 410–11 and facing p. 653. There follows a description of the frontier in some detail, which I omit.]

Ada Kalé sera évacué et rasé.

Une commission turco-serbe établira sur les lieux, avec l'assistance d'un commissaire russe, le tracé définitif de la frontière, dans l'espace de trois mois, et réglera définitivement les questions relatives aux îles de la Drina. Un délégué bulgare sera admis à participer aux travaux de la commission lorsqu'elle s'occupera de la frontière entre la Serbie et la Bulgarie.

Art. 4. — Les musulmans qui possèdent des propriétés dans les territoires annexés à la Serbie, et qui voudraient fixer leur résidence hors de la Principauté, pourront y conserver leurs immeubles en les faisant affermer ou administrer par d'autres. Une commission turco-serbe, assistée d'un commissaire russe, sera chargée de statuer souverainement, dans le courant de deux années, sur toutes les questions relatives à la constatation des propriétés immobilières où des intérêts musulmans seraient engagés. Cette commission sera également appelée à régler, dans le terme de trois années, le mode d'aliénation des biens appartenant à l'État ou aux fondations pieuses (*vacoufs*) et les questions relatives aux intérêts des particuliers qui pourraient s'y trouver engagés. Jusqu'à la conclusion d'un traité direct entre la Turquie et la Serbie, déterminant le caractère et la forme des relations entre la Sublime Porte et la Principauté, les sujets serbes, voyageant ou séjournant dans l'empire ottoman, seront traités suivant les principes généraux du droit international.

Les troupes serbes seront tenues d'évacuer le territoire non compris dans la circonscription indiquée plus haut dans le délai de quinze jours à partir de la signature des préliminaires de paix.

ART. 5. — La Sublime Porte reconnaît l'indépendance de la Roumanie, qui fera valoir ses droits à une indemnité à débattre entre les deux parties.

Jusqu'à la conclusion d'un traité direct entre la Turquie et la Roumanie, les sujets roumains jouiront en Turquie de tous les droits garantis aux sujets des autres puissances européennes.

ART. 6. — La Bulgarie est constituée en Principauté autonome, tributaire, avec un gouvernement chrétien et une milice nationale.

Les frontières définitives de la Principauté bulgare seront tracées par une commission spéciale russo-turque avant l'évacuation de la Roumélie par l'armée impériale russe. Cette commission tiendra compte dans ces travaux, pour les modifications à introduire sur les lieux au tracé général, du principe de la nationalité de la majorité des habitants des confins, conformément aux bases de la paix, ainsi que des nécessités topographiques et des intérêts pratiques de circulation pour les populations locales.

L'étendue de la Principauté de Bulgarie est fixée, en traits généraux, sur la carte ci-jointe [see Article 3], qui devra servir de base à la délimitation définitive. . . .

ART. 7. — Le Prince de la Bulgarie sera librement élu par la population et confirmé par la Sublime Porte avec l'assentiment des Puissances. Aucun membre des dynasties régnantes des grandes Puissances européennes ne pourra être élu Prince de Bulgarie.

En cas de vacance de la dignité de Prince de la Bulgarie, l'élection du nouveau Prince se fera dans les mêmes conditions et dans les mêmes formes.

Une assemblée de notables de la Bulgarie, convoquée à Philippopoli (Plovdiv) ou Tirnovo, élaborera, avant l'élection du Prince, sous la surveillance d'un commissaire impérial russe et en présence d'un commissaire ottoman, l'organisation de l'administration future conformément aux précédents établis en 1830, après la paix d'Andrinople, dans les principautés danubiennes.

Dans les localités où les Bulgares sont mêlés aux Turcs, aux Grecs, aux Valaques (Koutzo-Vlachs) ou autres, il sera tenu un juste compte des droits et intérêts de ces populations dans les élections et l'élaboration du règlement organique.

L'introduction du nouveau régime en Bulgarie et la surveillance de son fonctionnement seront confiées pendant deux années à un commissaire impérial russe. A l'expiration de la première année, après l'introduction du nouveau régime, et si une entente à ce sujet s'établit entre la Russie, la Sublime Porte et les cabinets européens, ils pourront, s'il est jugé nécessaire, adjoindre au commissaire impérial de Russie des délégués spéciaux.

Art. 8. — L'armée ottomane ne séjournera plus en Bulgarie, et toutes les anciennes fortifications seront rasées aux frais du gouvernement local. La Sublime Porte aura le droit de disposer à sa guise du matériel de guerre et autres objets appartenant au gouvernement ottoman, et qui seraient restés dans les forteresses du Danube déjà évacuées en vertu de l'armistice du 19/31 Janvier, ainsi que de ceux qui se trouveraient dans les places fortes de Choumla et de Varna.

Jusqu'à la formation complète d'une milice indigène suffisante pour le maintien de l'ordre, de la sécurité et de la tranquillité, et dont le chiffre sera fixé plus tard, par une entente entre le gouvernement ottoman et le cabinet impérial de Russie, des troupes russes occuperont le pays et prêteront main-forte au commissaire en cas de besoin. Cette occupation sera limitée également à un terme approximatif de deux années.

L'effectif du corps d'occupation russe, composé de six divisions d'infanterie et de deux de cavalerie, qui séjournera en Bulgarie après l'évacuation de la Turquie par l'armée impériale, n'excèdera pas cinquante mille hommes. Il sera entretenu aux frais du pays occupé. Les troupes d'occupation russes en Bulgarie conserveront leurs communications avec la Russie non seulement par la Roumanie, mais aussi par les ports de la mer Noire, Varna et Bourgas, où elles pourront organiser, pour la durée de l'occupation, les dépôts nécessaires.

Art. 9. — Le montant du tribut annuel que la Bulgarie paiera à la cour suzeraine, en le versant à la Banque que la Sublime Porte désignera ultérieurement, sera déterminé par un accord entre la Russie, le gouvernement ottoman et les autres cabinets à la fin de la première année du fonctionnement de la nouvelle organisation. Ce tribut sera établi sur le revenu moyen de tout le territoire qui fera partie de la Principauté.

La Bulgarie sera substituée au Gouvernement Impérial Ottoman dans ses charges et obligations envers la Compagnie du chemin de fer de Roustchouk–Varna, après entente entre la Sublime Porte, le gouvernement de la Principauté et l'administration de cette Compagnie. Le règlement relatif aux autres voies ferrées qui traversent la Principauté est également réservé à un accord entre la Sublime Porte, le gouvernement institué en Bulgarie et l'administration des compagnies intéressées.

ART. 10. — La Sublime Porte aura le droit de se servir de la voie de la Bulgarie pour le transport, par des routes déterminées, de ses troupes, munitions et approvisionnements, dans les provinces situées au delà de la Principauté et vice-versa. Afin d'éviter les difficultés et les malentendus dans l'application de ce droit, tout en garantissant les nécessités militaires de la Sublime Porte, un règlement spécial en établira les conditions dans l'espace des trois mois après la ratification du présent acte, par une entente entre la Sublime Porte et l'administration de la Bulgarie.

Il est bien entendu que ce droit ne s'étendra qu'aux troupes ottomanes régulières et que les irréguliers, les bachi-bozouks et les Circassiens en seront absolument exclus.

La Sublime Porte se réserve aussi le droit de faire passer à travers la Principauté sa poste et d'y entretenir une ligne télégraphique. Ces deux points seront également réglés de la façon et dans le laps de temps sus-indiqués.

ART. 11. — Les propriétaires musulmans ou autres, qui fixeraient leur résidence personnelle hors de la Principauté, pourront y conserver leurs immeubles en les faisant affermer ou administrer par d'autres. Des commissions turco-bulgares siégeront dans les principaux centres de population, sous la surveillance de commissaires russes, pour statuer souverainement, dans le courant de deux années, sur toutes les questions relatives à la constatation des propriétés immobilières où des intérêts musulmans ou autres seraient engagés.

Des commissions analogues seront chargées de régler, dans le courant de deux années, toutes les affaires relatives au mode d'aliénation, d'exploitation ou d'usage pour le compte de la Sublime Porte, des propriétés de l'État et des fondations pieuses (*vacoufs*).

A l'expiration du terme de deux années, mentionné plus haut, toutes les propriétés qui n'auront pas été réclamées seront vendues aux enchères publiques et le produit en sera consacré à l'entretien des veuves et des orphelins, tant musulmans que chrétiens, victimes des derniers événements.

ART. 12. Toutes les forteresses du Danube seront rasées. Il n'y aura plus dorénavant de places fortes sur les rives de ce fleuve, ni des bâtiments de guerre dans les eaux des principautés de Roumanie, de Serbie et de Bulgarie, sauf les stationnaires usités et les bâtiments légers destinés à la police fluviale et au service des douanes.

Les droits, obligations et prérogatives de la Commission internationale du Bas-Danube sont maintenus intacts.

ART. 13. — La Sublime Porte prend à sa charge le rétablissement de la navigabilité du passage de Soulina et le dédommagement des particuliers dont les biens auraient souffert du fait de la guerre et de l'interruption de la navigation sur le Danube, en affectant à cette double dépense une somme de cinq cent mille francs sur celles qui lui sont dues par la Commission Danubienne.

ART. 14. — Seront immédiatement introduites en Bosnie et en Herzégovine les propositions européennes communiquées aux Plénipotentiaires ottomans dans la première séance de la Conférence de Constantinople, avec les modifications qui seront arrêtées d'un commun accord entre la Sublime Porte, le gouvernement de Russie et celui d'Autriche-Hongrie. Le paiement des arriérés ne sera pas exigé, et les revenus courants de ces provinces jusqu'au premier Marsmil huit cent quatre-vingt seront exclusivement employés à indemniser les familles des réfugiés et des habitants, victimes des derniers événements, sans distinction de race et de religion, ainsi qu'aux besoins locaux du pays. La somme qui devra revenir annuellement après ce terme au gouvernement central sera fixée ultérieurement par une entente spéciale entre la Turquie, la Russie et l'Autriche-Hongrie.

ART. 15. — La Sublime Porte s'engage à appliquer scrupuleusement dans l'île de Crète le règlement organique de 1868, en tenant compte des vœux déjà exprimés par la population indigène.

Un règlement analogue, adapté aux besoins locaux, sera également introduit dans l'Epire, la Thessalie et les autres parties de la Turquie d'Europe pour lesquelles une organisation spéciale n'est pas prévue par le présent acte.

Des commissions spéciales, dans lesquelles l'élément indigène aura une large participation, seront chargées dans chaque province d'élaborer les détails du nouveau règlement. Le résultat de ces travaux sera soumis à l'examen de la Sublime Porte, qui consultera le gouvernement impérial de Russie avant de les mettre à exécution.

ART. 16. — Comme l'évacuation, par les troupes russes, des territoires qu'elles occupent en Arménie et qui doivent être restitués à la Turquie, pourrait y donner lieu à des conflits et à des complications préjudiciables aux bonnes relations des deux pays, la Sublime Porte s'engage à réaliser sans plus de retard les améliorations et les réformes exigées par les besoins locaux dans les provinces habitées par les Arméniens et à garantir leur sécurité contre les Kurdes et les Circassiens.

ART. 17. — Une amnistie pleine et entière est accordée par la Sublime Porte à tous les sujets ottomans compromis dans les derniers événements et toutes les personnes détenues de ce fait, ou envoyées en exil, seront immédiatement mises en liberté.

ART. 18. — La Sublime Porte prendra en sérieuse considération l'opinion émise par les commissaires des Puissances médiatrices au sujet de la possession de la ville de Khotour et s'engage à faire exécuter les travaux de délimitation définitive de la frontière turco-persane.

ART. 19. — Les indemnités de guerre et les pertes imposées à la Russie, que S.M. l'Empereur de Russie réclame et que la Sublime Porte s'est engagée à lui rembourser, se composent de:

(a) Neuf cent millions de roubles de frais de guerre (entretien de l'armée, remplacement du matériel, commandes de guerre);

(b) Quatre cent millions de roubles de dommages infligés au littoral méridional du pays, au commerce d'exportation, à l'industrie et aux chemins de fer;

(c) Cent millions de roubles de dommages causés au Caucase par l'invasion;

(d) Dix millions de roubles de dommages et intérêts aux sujets et institutions russes en Turquie.

Total: mille quatre cent dix millions de roubles.

Prenant en considération les embarras financiers de la Turquie, et d'accord avec le désir de S.M. le Sultan, l'Empereur de Russie consent à remplacer le paiement de la plus grande partie des sommes énumérées dans le paragraphe précédent par les cessions territoriales suivantes:

(a) Le sandjak de Toultcha, c'est-à-dire les districts (cazas) de Kilia, Soulina, Mahmoudié, Isaktcha, Toultcha, Matchin, Babadagh, Hirsovo, Kustendjé et Medjidié, ainsi que les îles du Delta et l'île des Serpents.

Ne désirant pas s'annexer ce territoire et les îles du Delta, la Russie se réserve la faculté de les échanger contre la partie de la Bessarabie détachée par le traité de 1856 et limitée au midi par le thalweg du bras de Kilia et l'embouchure du Stary-Stamboul. La question du partage des eaux et des pêcheries devra être réglée par une commission russo-roumaine dans l'espace d'une année après la ratification du traité de paix.

(b) Ardahan, Kars, Batoum, Bayazid et le territoire jusqu'au Soganlough. En traits généraux, la ligne frontière, ... [There follows a description of the frontier in some detail, which I omit. See above, map between pp. 540–1.]

Les limites définitives du territoire annexé à la Russie, indiquées sur la carte ci-jointe [see article I], seront fixées par une commission composée de délégués russes et ottomans. Cette commission tiendra compte dans ses travaux tant de la topographie des localités que des considérations de bonne administration et des conditions propres à assurer la tranquillité du pays.

(c) Les territoires mentionnés dans les paragraphes a et b sont cédés à la Russie comme équivalent de la somme d'un milliard cent millions de roubles. Quant au reste de l'indemnité, sauf les dix millions de roubles dus aux intérêts et institutions russes en Turquie, soit trois cent millions de roubles, le mode de paiement de cette somme et la garantie à y affecter seront réglés par une entente entre le gouvernement impérial de Russie et celui de S.M. le Sultan.

(*d*) Les dix millions de roubles réclamés comme indemnité pour les sujets et institutions russes en Turquie seront payés à mesure que les réclamations des intéressés seront examinées par l'Ambassade de Russie à Constantinople et transmises à la Sublime Porte.

ART. 20. — La Sublime Porte prendra des mesures efficaces pour terminer à l'amiable toutes les affaires litigieuses des sujets russes pendantes depuis plusieurs années, dédommager ces derniers, s'il y a lieu, et faire exécuter sans délai les sentences rendues.

ART. 21. — Les habitants des localités cédées à la Russie, qui voudraient fixer leur résidence hors de ces territoires, seront libres de se retirer, en vendant leurs propriétés immobilières. Un délai de trois ans leur est accordé à cet effet à partir de la ratification du présent acte. Passé ce délai, les habitants qui n'auront pas quitté le pays et vendu leurs immeubles, resteront sujets russes.

Les biens immeubles appartenant à l'État ou aux fondations pieuses sises en dehors des localités précitées, devront être vendus dans le même délai de trois années, suivant le mode qui sera réglé par une commission spéciale russo-turque. La même commission sera chargée de déterminer le mode de retrait, par le gouvernement ottoman, du matériel de guerre, des munitions, des approvisionnements et autres objets appartenant à l'État, et qui existeraient dans les places, villes et localités cédées à la Russie et non occupées actuellement par les troupes russes.

ART. 22. — Les ecclésiastiques, les pèlerins et les moines russes, voyageant et séjournant dans la Turquie d'Europe et d'Asie, jouiront des mêmes droits, avantages et privilèges que les ecclésiastiques étrangers appartenant à d'autres nationalités. Le droit de protection officielle est reconnu à l'ambassade impériale et aux consulats russes en Turquie, tant à l'égard des personnes susindiquées, que de leurs possessions, établissements religieux, de bienfaisance et autres dans les Lieux-Saints et ailleurs.

Les moines du mont Athos d'origine russe seront maintenus dans leurs possessions et avantages antérieurs et continueront à jouir, dans les trois couvents qui leur appartiennent et dans les dépendances de ces derniers, des mêmes droits et prérogatives que ceux qui sont assurés aux autres établissements religieux et couvents du mont Athos.

ART. 23. — Tous les traités, conventions et engagements, antérieurement conclus entre les deux Hautes Parties contractantes relativement au commerce, à la juridiction et à la position des sujets russes en Turquie, et qui avaient été supprimés par l'état de guerre, seront remis en vigueur, sauf les clauses auxquelles il serait dérogé par le présent acte. Les deux gouvernements seront replacés, l'un vis-à-vis de l'autre, pour tous leurs engagements et rapports commerciaux et autres, dans la situation même où ils se trouvaient avant la déclaration de guerre.

ART. 24. — Le Bosphore et les Dardanelles resteront ouverts, en temps de guerre comme en temps de paix, aux navires marchands des États neutres, arrivant des ports russes ou en destination de ces ports. La Sublime Porte s'engage en conséquence à ne plus établir dorénavant, devant les ports de la mer Noire et de celle d'Azow, un blocus fictif qui s'écarterait de l'esprit de la Déclaration signée à Paris le 4–16 Avril 1856.

ART. 25. — L'évacuation complète, par l'armée russe, de la Turquie d'Europe, à l'exception de la Bulgarie, aura lieu dans l'espace de trois mois après la conclusion de la paix définitive entre S.M. l'Empereur de Russie et S.M. le Sultan.

Afin de gagner du temps et d'éviter le maintien prolongé des troupes russes en Turquie et en Roumanie, une partie de l'armée impériale pourra être dirigée vers des ports de la mer Noire et de celle de Marmara pour y être embarquée sur des bâtiments appartenant au gouvernement russe ou frétés pour la circonstance.

L'évacuation de la Turquie d'Asie s'opérera dans l'espace de six mois à dater de la conclusion de la paix définitive, et les troupes russes auront la faculté de s'embarquer à Trébizonde pour retourner par le Caucase ou par la Crimée.

Les opérations de l'évacuation devront commencer immédiatement après l'échange des ratifications.

ART. 26. — Tant que les troupes impériales russes séjourneront dans les localités qui, conformément au présent acte, seront restituées à la Sublime Porte, l'administration et l'ordre des choses resteront dans le même état que depuis l'occupation. La Sublime Porte ne devra y prendre aucune part durant tout ce temps et jusqu'à l'entière sortie de toutes les troupes.

Les troupes ottomanes ne devront entrer dans les localités qui seront restituées à la Sublime Porte, et cette dernière ne pourra commencer à y exercer son autorité, que lorsque, pour chaque place et province qui aura été évacuée par les troupes russes, le commandant de ces troupes en aura donné connaissance à l'officier désigné à cet effet de la part de la Sublime Porte.

Art. 27. — La Sublime Porte prend l'engagement de ne sévir d'aucune manière, ni laisser sévir contre les sujets ottomans qui auraient été compromis par leurs relations avec l'armée russe pendant la guerre. Dans le cas où quelques personnes voudraient se retirer avec leurs familles à la suite des troupes russes, les autorités ottomanes ne s'opposeront pas à leur départ.

Art. 28. — Immédiatement après la ratification des préliminaires de paix, les prisonniers de guerre seront rendus réciproquement par les soins de commissaires spéciaux nommés de part et d'autre, et qui se rendront à cet effet à Odessa et à Sébastopol. Le gouvernement ottoman paiera tous les frais de l'entretien des prisonniers qui lui seront restitués, en dix-huit termes égaux, dans l'espace de six années, d'après les comptes qui seront établis par les commissaires susmentionnés.

L'échange de prisonniers entre le gouvernement ottoman et ceux de la Roumanie, de la Serbie et du Monténégro, aura lieu sur les mêmes bases, en déduisant, toutefois, dans le décompte à établir, le nombre des prisonniers restitués par le gouvernement ottoman du nombre de prisonniers qui lui seront restitués.

Art. 29. — Le présent acte sera ratifié par Leurs Majestés Impériales l'Empereur de Russie et l'Empereur des Ottomans, et les ratifications seront échangées, dans quinze jours ou plus tôt, si faire se peut, à Saint-Pétersbourg, où l'on conviendra également du lieu et de l'époque à laquelle les stipulations du présent acte seront revêtues des formes solennelles usitées dans les traités de paix. Il demeure, toutefois, bien entendu que les Hautes Parties contractantes se considèrent comme formellement liées par le présent acte depuis le moment de sa ratification.

En foi de quoi les Plénipotentiaires respectifs ont revêtu le présent acte de leurs signatures et y ont apposé leurs cachets.

Fait à San-Stefano, le dix-neuf Février (trois Mars) mil huit cent soixante-dix-huit.

Paragraphe final de l'article 11 de l'acte des préliminaires de paix, signé aujourd'hui le 19 Février (3 Mars) 1878, qui a été omis et qui doit faire partie intégrante du dit article :

Les habitants de la Principauté de Bulgarie qui voyageront ou séjourneront dans les autres parties de l'Empire ottoman seront soumis aux lois et aux autorités ottomanes.

San-Stefano, le 19 Février (3 Mars) 1878.

(S.) Comte N. Ignatiew.　　　(S.) Safvet.
　　　L. S.　　　　　　　　　　　L. S.
(S.) Nélidow.　　　　　　　　(S.) Saadoullah.
　　　L. S.　　　　　　　　　　　L. S.

DOCUMENTS CONCERNING THE ANGLO-RUSSIAN AGREEMENT, MAY 1878

1. SALISBURY *to* LOFTUS, *dispatch, no. 305, 7 May 1878: in F.O. 181/567.*

My Lord,

I have had several conversations with Count Schouvaloff with respect to the present state of the negotiations upon the Eastern Question previous to his departure for St. Petersburgh.

Throughout these interviews he has stated that he was entirely without instructions from his Government, and that he had carefully refrained from communicating with them by telegraph as to the substance of our conversations. The general effect of his language has been to convey that Russia was likely to place especial stress on the retention of Batoum, Kars, Bessarabia, and of Antivari for Montenegro, but on the question of the new Bulgaria he did not appear to view with great aversion the idea of a division; nor did he press strongly the contention that the Southern portion (if a division was made) should be subjected to a tributary Prince, but he laid great emphasis on the demand for autonomy, which, as the discussion went on, he consented to define more closely as a 'large administrative Autonomy'. Under this phrase, he appeared to contemplate not only guarantees against mal-administration, such as were suggested, on behalf of Her Majesty's Government, at the Conference of Constantinople, but also arrangements limiting the political and strategic value to the Porte of the Province to be created South of the Balkans.

The language which I held to Count Schouvaloff will be sufficiently indicated to Your Excellency by the inclosed Confidential Memorandum drawn up for the consideration of the Cabinet and of which I gave to him a copy, on a pledge that the most absolute secrecy should be observed in respect of it. In addition to the considerations mentioned in this paper, I made one or two further observations. With respect to the annexations in Asia, while I did not exclude the possibility of an understanding with respect to them, I stated that Her Majesty's Government regarded any advance of the Russian frontier in that direction with grave misgiving, not only on account of the intrinsic value of the positions sacrificed, but because they would give facilities for further encroachments in the same region and would place both the Porte itself, and the Asiatic populations of the Ottoman Empire under the constant apprehension of such an advance.

With respect to the passage of the Straits, I pointed out to him that a proposal to exclude Ships of war and admit merchant Ships in all cases during war time was entirely inadmissible. Great Britain would prefer that the Straits should be treated as an open waterway, like the Sound, to be free to all vessels at all times. But if this were not accorded, this country could not agree to abandon on that account its ordinary right of Blockade. If Her Majesty's Ships were not allowed to pass through the Straits to exercise her belligerent rights, no choice would be left but to exercise those rights at the Mouth of the Dardanelles.

The Russian Ambassador made an abstract in more detail of the Conversations, according to his recollection, the substance of which I have communicated to Your Excellency. He read me these abstracts and I observed that while their general tenour was correct, there were some inaccuracies in various particulars. I declined however to correct them as it would have been difficult to do so quite satisfactorily, and I thought that some misapprehension might be caused if I accepted the responsibility for a report which I had not myself drawn up. I have made this observation in case they should be inadvertently quoted to your Excellency. In conclusion, I have to express my belief that Count Schouvaloff is undertaking the duty, with which he has charged himself, with the most pacific wishes and intentions, and I have no doubt your Excellency will second his endeavours by language not only courteous in form but as conciliatory in effect as is compatible with the substantial objects Her Majesty's Government have in view.

I am with great truth and respect
My Lord
Your Excellency's
most obedient humble servant
[*Signed*] SALISBURY.

2. *Enclosure sent with no. 1: headed, Printed for the use of the Cabinei.*
May 3, 1878.

MOST CONFIDENTIAL. (3596)

Memorandum for the Cabinet

The objections of Great Britain to the Treaty of San Stefano rest principally on three grounds:

(1) That it admits a new naval Power to the coasts of the Ægean.

(2) That it threatens with extinction the non-Slav populations of the Balkan peninsula.

(3) That it places the Porte so much at the mercy of Russia, that it is no longer able to discharge with independence political functions which are still assigned to it, and which deeply interest other nations.

The remedy for the first two of these evils, is to push the frontier of the Slav State back from the Ægean and Macedonia. This change is essential to any agreement between England and Russia. Due securities for good government must, of course, be provided for the populations of the region thus excluded from the autonomous State.

The remedy for the third evil is more complex, as the stipulations which cause it are of various kinds. The provisions which deprive the Porte of the independence necessary to its present position may be ranked in different categories according to the efficacy of their operation.

In the first rank of importance stands the configuration of the Slav State. It runs close up to Constantinople, is separated from it by no effective or defensible frontier, and severs it from communication with the remaining European provinces. These effects must be considered, together with the influence over this State conferred upon Russia by the provisions as to government and occupation. A remedy for this evil would be the restriction of the Slav State to the north of the Balkans, together with a limitation of the time of occupation.

In the second place come the annexations in Asia. They despoil the Porte of the only good harbour in the Black Sea; menace from the conquered line of fortresses the richest of the remaining provinces; and, by the acquisition of Kars, will alienate from Turkey the respect, and shake the fidelity, of the Mesopotamian and Syrian populations.

In the third rank stand the vague provisions of the indemnity Clause, which are capable of being converted either into further annexations, or into a compulsory alliance.

And, after these, stand such provisions as the alienation of Bessarabia, the augmentation of territory given to the tributary States, and some other less prominent stipulations.

It is important to note, with respect to the above observations, that the enumeration of these provisions, and the expression of an insuperable objection to the result towards which they converge, do not necessarily imply an expectation that they will all be abandoned. They may be upheld with more or less of modification. But what England claims is, that the modifications in them taken altogether and as a whole shall be sufficient to reduce effectively the pressure which, in combination, they exert upon the independence of the Porte. The relative importance of the several stipulations is indicated in the classification which has been given. If much is conceded in respect to the most important, it will not be necessary to change so largely those which are less important. As it is the operation of the instrument as a whole to which England objects, so it is the result of the modifications as a whole, and not the particular form they take, to which England looks as a condition of her assenting to any definitive Treaty founded on the Preliminaries of San Stefano.

3. *The Shuvalov Memoranda: in F.O. 65/567. Printed for the use of the Cabinet. May 23, 1878.*

CONFIDENTIAL. (3618)

No. 1

Memorandum communicated to the MARQUIS OF SALISBURY *by* COUNT SCHOUVALOFF, *May 23.*

Sa Majesté l'Empereur ayant pris connaissance des modifications que le Gouvernement de Sa Majesté Britannique propose d'introduire dans le Traité Préliminaire de San Stefano pour le rendre acceptable par le Cabinet Anglais, a jugé que ces modifications n'étaient pas en contradiction avec le but principal de la guerre, qui consistait à assurer la prospérité et la sécurité des populations Chrétiennes de la Péninsule des Balkans, en leur garantissant des institutions stables et un bon gouvernement.

Mon auguste Maître trouve en conséquence que les propositions du Gouvernement de Sa Majesté Britannique offrent pour le prochain Congrès les bases d'une entente qui porteraient sur les points suivants:—

1. La délimitation de la Bulgarie au sud serait modifiée de manière à l'éloigner de la Mer Egée.

2. Les frontières occidentales seraient rectifiées sur la base du principe des nationalités de manière à exclure de la Bulgarie les populations non-Bulgares.

3. Le Gouvernement de Sa Majesté Britannique se montrant disposé à accorder à la population Bulgare une large autonomie administrative, mais ayant refusé son consentement à ce que la Bulgarie au sud des Balkans fût gouvernée par un Prince, et dotée d'une autonomie politique, qui serait au point de vue Anglais une menace politique et stratégique contre l'indépendance du Sultan, Sa Majesté l'Empereur exprime son assentiment à ce que la Bulgarie, replacée dans les limites des deux points précédents, soit partagée en deux provinces, de la manière suivante:—

L'une au nord des Balkans serait dotée d'une autonomie politique sous le gouvernement d'un Prince, et l'autre au sud des Balkans recevrait une large autonomie administrative (tracée par exemple sur celle qui existe dans les Colonies Anglaises), avec un Gouverneur Chrétien nommé du consentement de l'Europe pour cinq à dix ans.

L'Empereur attache une importance toute particulière au retrait de l'armée Turque de la Bulgarie méridionale.

Sa Majesté ne verrait aucune sécurité ni garantie pour l'avenir de la population Bulgare si des troupes Ottomanes y étaient maintenues.

Il appartiendrait au Congrès de statuer sur les cas où le Sultan pourrait y envoyer des troupes, en se guidant sur le principe établi au Congrès de 1856 pour le cas d'une intervention militaire Ottomane dans les Principautés Danubiennes.

Le Gouvernement de Sa Majesté Britannique prenant un vif intérêt à la future organisation des provinces Grecques de la Péninsule des Balkans, Sa Majesté l'Empereur consent à modifier l'Article XV du Traité Préliminaire de San Stefano de manière à ce que les autres Puissances, et notamment l'Angleterre, aient, comme la Russie, une voix consultative dans la future organisation de l'Epire, la Thessalie, et les autres provinces Chrétiennes restées sous la domination de la Porte.

En ce qui concerne l'indemnité de guerre, Sa Majesté l'Empereur n'a jamais eu l'intention de la convertir en annexions territoriales, et il ne se refuse pas à donner des assurances à cet égard.

Quant à la vallée d'Alashkert et la ville de Bayazid, cette vallée étant la grande route du transit pour la Perse et ayant une immense valeur aux yeux des Turcs, Sa Majesté l'Empereur consent à la leur restituer, mais il a demandé et obtenu en échange l'abandon à la Perse du petit territoire de Khotour, que les Commissions des deux Cours Médiatrices ont trouvé juste de restituer au Shah.

Sa Majesté l'Empereur croyant avoir répondu ainsi aux principales objections que le Gouvernement de Sa Majesté Britannique a faites au Traité Préliminaire de San Stefano, il s'attend à son tour à ce que le Cabinet de St. James ne conteste pas en Congrès les autres parties du Traité.

Une entente préalable à ce sujet faciliterait au Congrès la solution pacifique si vivement désirée par le Gouvernement de Sa Majesté Britannique et le Cabinet Impérial.

Dans cet ordre d'idées le présent Memorandum, s'il était approuvé du Gouvernement de la Reine, devrait servir d'engagement au Congrès, pour les Plénipotentiaires Anglais et Russes.

(Signé) SCHOUVALOFF.

Londres, le 11/23 Mai, 1878.

No. 2

Memorandum communicated to the MARQUIS OF SALISBURY *by* COUNT SCHOUVALOFF, *May 23.*

Sa Majesté l'Empereur considère que la division longitudinale de la Bulgarie, prévue par la Conférence de Constantinople selon le tracé qu'elle avait proposé, est préférable à la séparation par la ligne des Balkans, en raison des arguments qui déjà à cette époque avaient été pris en considération et qui militent en faveur d'un précédent déjà consacré par une délibération Européenne.

La division longitudinale assure davantage la future administration de la Bulgarie, en ce qu'elle permet à la partie nord d'emprunter à la partie sud les contingents intellectuels qui y prédominent. C'est évidemment de la Bulgarie du sud que serait choisi le personnel des Tribunaux et les meilleurs employés administratifs.

Si la division longitudinale était acceptée, Sa Majesté Impériale ne s'opposerait pas à ce que les deux Bulgaries, Orientale et Occidentale, fussent administrées par deux Gouverneurs-Généraux, afin d'éviter les petites Principautés que l'Angleterre désapprouve en principe. Le retrait de l'armée Ottomane serait maintenu, sauf les cas à prévoir.

Il va sans dire que les rectifications de frontière à l'ouest et au sud que l'Angleterre demande, et qui sont mentionnées dans les points 1 et 2 du Memorandum ci-joint, s'appliqueront également à cette séparation longitudinale.

(Signé) SCHOUVALOFF.

Londres, le 11/23 Mai, 1878.

4. SALISBURY *to* LOFTUS, *dispatch, no. 332, 23 May 1878*: *in F.O. 181/567.*

My Lord,

Count Schouvaloff called to-day on his return from St. Petersburgh, and communicated the two Memoranda, of which copies are enclosed.

He proceeded to explain the views of the Emperor of Russia as to the terms to which Russia might accede, in order to secure the assembling of a Congress for the discussion of the stipulations of the preliminary Treaty of San Stefano.

His Majesty adhered to the provisions of the Treaty in regard to the retrocession of the Roumanian portion of Bessarabia, the accession of territory to Montenegro, and the acquisition by Russia of Kars and Batoum.

His Majesty was prepared to concede that the Western Boundary of the Bulgaria proposed in the Treaty should be modified so as to cut off from it all non-Slav populations, and that on the South the position should be removed from the Ægean Sea, and the continuity of the Turkish Empire with its Western provinces be thus fully restored.

He would agree that the remaining portion of the proposed Bulgaria should be divided, as suggested by Her Majesty's Government, into an autonomous State limited to the North of the Balkans, and that to the South of the Balkans should be constituted as a Turkish province with guarantees for the good government of the

Christian populations, or, as an alternative proposition, he was willing that the autonomous Principality should be altogether abandoned, and that two Turkish Provinces, under arrangements similar to those proposed at the Conference of Constantinople, and like them divided by a line from North to South, should be substituted for it.

His Majesty would further consent generally that the term of occupation by Russian troops should be more closely limited: and he did not object to the proposal that, in organizing the administration of Bulgaria, European should, to some extent, be substituted for Russian Machinery; that the Reforms in the Greek provinces should be submitted to Europe instead of to Russia alone; that Bayazid and the road from Trebizond to Persia should be given back to the Turks; and that security should be taken that the indemnity to be paid by Turkey should not be used as a pretext for further annexation of her territory.

Count Schouvaloff informed me that in describing the attitude taken up by Her Majesty's Government to the Emperor, he had said that on all proposals aiming at the good government of the populations they would be found ready to yield: but that no concessions were to be expected from them upon provisions having for their object the extension of Russian influence in Bulgaria.

I accepted this as a correct description of the policy of Her Majesty's Government.

I informed Count Schouvaloff that I would submit his communication to the Cabinet.

I am with great truth and respect,
My Lord,
Your Excellency's most obedient humble servant,
(*Signed*) SALISBURY.

5. SALISBURY *to* LOFTUS, *dispatch, no. 334, 24 May 1878: in F.O. 181/567.*

My Lord,

I discussed with Count Schouvaloff to-day the Memorandum which he had left with me yesterday: and pointed out to him several points in which, in the judgment of Her Majesty's Government, it was imperfect or inadequate.

In the first place the indication of the frontiers to be assigned to the new Bulgarian Provinces was too vague for the purposes of an understanding between Her Majesty's Government and that of Russia. It was necessary that they should be more precisely defined: and I suggested that for the South the boundary assigned to the Bulgarian Provinces proposed in the Conference of Constantinople would be suitable. To the West the line from Novi Bazar to the

Gulf of Rendina, which had been suggested some time ago by the Austrian Government, would indicate the Western limit of the region which under the application of the principle of nationalities Her Majesty's Government were prepared to see annexed to either of the Bulgarian Provinces.

I further pointed out to him that England was too deeply interested in the well being of the Asiatic Subjects of the Porte, to agree that exclusive promises in respect to the Armenians should be given to Russia.

Her Majesty's Government could not but protest against the excessive amount at which the indemnity was fixed: and in any case they would require that their own interests in Turkish Revenues should be protected: and that as creditors they should be placed in exactly the same position as that which they occupied before the war.

I observed that the withdrawal of the Ottoman Troops from the Southern Province of Bulgaria might be accepted by England in principle—so far as was necessary to effect the protection of the population in which Great Britain no less than Russia was deeply interested. But it would be necessary that Congress should define the mode and the emergencies in which the entry of troops to protect the province against either actual or threatened invasion or insurrection should be permitted: and England would contend for the right of the Sultan to place Garrisons in the passes of the Balkans and on the littoral of the Black Sea. To the first of these two reservations the Russian Ambassador assented: with respect to the second he reserved to himself full right of discussion.

In order the better to secure the Sultan against treasonable intrigues, I insisted on the part of Her Majesty's Government, that the superior officers of the local Militia should be named by the Porte with the consent of the Powers: and to this Count Schouvaloff offered no objection.

There were other matters which did not appear to Her Majesty's Government to be of that primary importance that it was necessary to insist on a preliminary condition respecting them, before entering into Congress: but on which, nevertheless, England would reserve her full right of discussion and decision in Congress. In this category would be included the time and the manner of Russian occupation: the employment of European instead of Russian Commissaries in the organization of the Bulgarian Provinces: the time during which the right of passage through Roumania should remain open: and the conversion of the Sultan's promise to Russia in favour of the Russian Monks on Mount Athos into a promise to Europe in favour of the Monks of all nationalities on Mount Athos.

I also stated that England would consider herself free in Congress with respect to any questions affecting the Bosphorus and Dardanelles. Count Schouvaloff, while taking note of this reservation, stated that Russia would contend for the *status quo*: and appealed in that behalf to the observations of Lord Derby on that subject in his Despatch of the 6th. of May 1877. Subject to these reservations, and on the assumption that these changes were accepted, I stated that England would undertake not to contest the points in the Treaty, not affected by the modifications above mentioned, if after full discussion in Congress, Russia should finally determine to abide by them. But I did not conceal from Count Schouvaloff my opinion that the retrocession of Bessarabia was a proceeding which could not be defended on principles of International Law: though, as it appeared that no other Power was prepared to contest it, the matter was not one in which England was so closely interested as to be justified in undertaking alone by force to maintain the provisions of the Treaty of Paris. The Armenian annexations were in themselves highly objectionable: and involved a menace to the future tranquillity of Turkey in Asia, which it was impossible to ignore. The protection of the Ottoman Empire from this danger would, however, in the judgment of Her Majesty's Government, be more effectually provided for by other means than by an appeal to arms.

    I am with great truth and respect
      My Lord
         Your Excellency's most obedient, humble servant
                     (Signed) SALISBURY.

6. *Letter of* SALISBURY *to* SHUVALOV, *28 May 1878*.

In *F.O.* 65/1002: marked 'Copy', and headed 'To Count Schouvaloff': undated: an earlier draft of this is dated 28 May, and the copy printed for the Cabinet, 29 May (in *F.O.* 181/567, enclosure to disp., no. 347, 3 June, to Loftus), which agrees with the text printed here, is dated 28 May.

    The origin of this letter was due to Andrássy's introduction of the question of the Dobrudja into the contemporaneous Anglo-Austrian negotiations: Elliot to Salisbury, tel., secret, 28 May, and Salisbury's reply, tel. and extender, 28 May, agreeing to insist at the congress that the Dobrudja should not become Russian; in *F.O.* 7/938 and 924.

Dear Count Schouvaloff,

    It has been suggested that a construction might possibly be placed on the XIXth. art. of the Treaty by wh. in certain events the Dobrudscha might remain Russian territory in perpetuity.

    I shd. not think of putting such a construction on the Treaty myself, but in order to prevent any misunderstanding, I think it right to tell you that in agreeing not to contest the article of the Treaty wh. concerns Bessarabia, H.M. Gt. must not be understood as agreeing that the Dobrudscha shall in any event become permanently Russian territory.

I have, &c.

(*Signed*) SALISBURY.

7. *The Anglo-Russian Agreement : copy in F.O. 65/1022.*

Memorandum No. 1 signed by the MARQUIS OF SALISBURY *and* COUNT SCHOUVALOFF, *May 30.*

Sa Majesté l'Empereur de Russie ayant pris connaissance des modifications que le Gouvernement de Sa Majesté Britannique propose d'introduire dans le Traité Préliminaire de San Stefano, pour le rendre acceptable par le Cabinet Anglais, a jugé que plusieurs d'entr'elles n'étaient pas en contradiction avec le but principal de la guerre, qui consistait à assurer la prospérité et la sécurité des populations Chrétiennes de la Péninsule des Balkans, en leur garantissant des institutions stables et un bon Gouvernement.

Le Cabinet de St. Pétersbourg trouve en conséquence que les idées exprimées par le Cabinet de St. James offrent pour le prochain Congrès les bases d'une entente qui porterait sur les points suivants:

1. L'Angleterre écarte la division longitudinale de la Bulgarie, mais le Représentant de la Russie se réserve d'en faire valoir les avantages au Congrès en promettant toujours de ne pas y insister contre l'opinion définitive de l'Angleterre.

2. La délimitation de la Bulgarie au sud serait modifiée de manière à l'éloigner de la Mer Egée selon la délimitation sud des provinces Bulgares proposée par la Conférence de Constantinople. Ceci ne concerne la question des frontières qu'en tant qu'elle se rapporte à l'exclusion du littoral de la Mer Egée, c'est-à-dire à l'ouest de Lagos. Depuis ce point au littoral de la Mer Noire la discussion de la frontière reste libre.

3. Les frontières occidentales de la Bulgarie seraient rectifiées sur la base des nationalités de manière à exclure de cette province les populations non-Bulgares. Les frontières occidentales de la Bulgarie ne devraient pas dépasser en principe une ligne tracée à peu près de Novi-Bazar au Koursha-Balkan [i.e. approximately Seres].

4. La Bulgarie replacée dans les limites qui sont mentionnées dans les points 2 et 3 sera partagée en deux Provinces, à savoir:—

L'une au nord des Balkans serait dotée d'une autonomie politique, sous le gouvernement d'un Prince, et l'autre, au sud des Balkans, recevrait une large autonomie administrative (par exemple, à l'instar de celles qui existent dans les Colonies Anglaises), avec un Gouverneur Chrétien nommé du consentement de l'Europe pour cinq à dix ans.

5. L'Empereur de Russie attache une importance toute particulière au retrait de l'armée Turque de la Bulgarie Méridionale. Sa Majesté ne verrait aucune sécurité ni garantie pour l'avenir de la population Bulgare si des troupes Ottomanes y étaient maintenues.

Lord Salisbury accepte le retrait des troupes Turques de la Bulgarie Méridionale, mais la Russie n'objectera pas à ce que le Congrès statue sur le mode et les cas où il serait permis aux troupes Turques d'entrer dans la Province Méridionale pour résister à l'insurrection ou à l'invasion, soit en état d'exécution ou à l'état de menace.

Toutefois l'Angleterre se réserve d'insister au Congrès sur le droit pour le Sultan de pouvoir cantonner des troupes sur les frontières de la Province Méridionale.

Le Représentant de la Russie se réserve au Congrès une complète liberté dans la discussion de cette dernière proposition de Lord Salisbury.

6. Le Gouvernement Britannique demande et la Russie accepte que les chefs supérieurs de la milice dans la Bulgarie Méridionale soient nommés par la Porte avec l'assentiment de l'Europe.

7. Les promesses pour l'Arménie stipulées par le Traité Préliminaire de San Stefano ne doivent pas être faites exclusivement à la Russie mais à l'Angleterre aussi.

8. Le Gouvernement de Sa Majesté Britannique prenant, ainsi que le Gouvernement Impérial, un vif intérêt à la future organisation des Provinces Grecques de la Péninsule des Balkans, l'Article XV du Traité Préliminaire de San Stefano sera modifié de manière à ce que les autres Puissances, et notamment l'Angleterre, aient comme la Russie une voix consultative dans la future organisation de l'Epire, la Thessalie, et les autres Provinces Chrétiennes restées sous la domination de la Porte.

9. En ce qui concerne l'indemnité de guerre, Sa Majesté l'Empereur n'a jamais eu l'intention de la convertir en annexions territoriales et il ne se refuse pas à donner des assurances à cet égard.

Il est entendu que l'indemnité de guerre n'enlèvera pas au Gouvernement Anglais ses droits de créancier, et il se trouvera sous ce rapport dans la même situation qu'avant la guerre.

Sans contester la décision définitive que la Russie prendra au sujet du montant de l'indemnité, l'Angleterre se réserve de faire valoir au Congrès les objections sérieuses qu'elle y voit.

10. Quant à la vallée d'Alashkert et la ville de Bayazid, cette vallée étant la grande route du transit pour la Perse et ayant une immense valeur aux yeux des Turcs, Sa Majesté l'Empereur consent à la leur restituer, mais il a demandé et obtenu en échange l'abandon à la Perse du petit territoire de Khotour, que les Commissions des deux Cours médiatrices ont trouvé juste de restituer au Shah.

11. Le Gouvernement de Sa Majesté Britannique croirait devoir constater son profond regret pour le cas où la Russie insisterait définitivement sur la rétrocession de la Bessarabie. Comme il est cependant suffisamment établi que les autres Signataires du Traité de Paris ne sont pas prêts à soutenir par les armes la délimitation de la Roumanie stipulée dans ce Traité, l'Angleterre ne se trouve pas assez immédiatement intéressée dans cette question pour qu'elle soit autorisée à encourir seule la responsabilité de s'opposer au changement proposé, et ainsi elle s'engage à ne pas contester la décision définitive de la Russie en ce qui concerne la rétrocession de la Bessarabie.

En consentant à ne pas contester le désir de l'Empereur de Russie d'acquérir le port de Batoum et de garder ses conquêtes en Arménie, le Gouvernement de Sa Majesté ne se cache pas qu'il soit probable que de graves dangers menaçant la tranquillité des populations de la Turquie en Asie puissent résulter dans l'avenir de cette extension de la frontière Russe. Mais le Gouvernement de Sa Majesté est d'avis que le devoir de sauvegarder l'Empire Ottoman de ce danger, qui dorénavant reposera d'une mesure spéciale sur l'Angleterre, pourra s'effectuer sans que l'Europe éprouve les calamités d'une nouvelle guerre. En même temps le Gouvernement de la Reine prend acte de l'assurance donnée par Sa Majesté Impériale que dans l'avenir la frontière de la Russie ne sera plus étendue du côté de la Turquie d'Asie. Le Gouvernement de Sa Majesté étant par conséquent d'opinion que les modifications du Traité de San Stefano agréées dans ce Memorandum suffisent à mitiger les objections qu'il trouve au Traité dans sa forme actuelle, s'engage à ne pas contester les Articles du Traité Préliminaire de San Stefano qui ne sont pas modifiés par les dix points précédents, si, après que ces Articles auront été dûment discutés au Congrès, la Russie persiste à les maintenir.

Il se pourrait que dans le cours des discussions au Congrès, les deux Gouvernements trouvent préférable d'introduire d'un commun accord de nouvelles modifications qu'il serait impossible de prévoir; mais si l'entente sur ces nouvelles modifications ne s'établissait pas entre les Plénipotentiaires Russes et Anglais, le présent Memorandum est destiné à servir d'engagement mutuel au Congrès pour les Plénipotentiaires de la Russie et de la Grande Bretagne.

En foi de quoi ce document a été signé par l'Ambassadeur de Russie à Londres et le Principal Secrétaire d'Etat de Sa Majesté Britannique.

Le 30 Mai, 1878

(Signé) Salisbury.
Schouvaloff.

Memorandum No. 2 signed by the MARQUIS OF SALISBURY *and* COUNT SCHOUVALOFF, *May 30.*

En dehors des stipulations du Memorandum précédent, le Gouvernement Britannique se réserve de faire valoir au Congrès les points suivants:—

(*a.*) Le Gouvernement Anglais se réserve de demander au Congrès la participation de l'Europe dans l'organisation administrative des deux Provinces Bulgares.

(*b.*) Le Gouvernement Anglais discutera en Congrès la durée et la nature de l'occupation Russe en Bulgarie et du passage par la Roumanie.

(*c.*) Le nom à donner à la province méridionale.

(*d.*) Sans toucher à la question territoriale, le Gouvernement Britannique se réserve de discuter les questions de navigation du Danube, ce à quoi l'Angleterre a des droits par les Traités.

(*e.*) Le Gouvernement Anglais se réserve de discuter au Congrès toute question touchant aux Détroits. Mais l'Ambassadeur de Russie à Londres prend acte de la communication verbale qu'il a faite au Principal Secrétaire d'Etat, à savoir que le Cabinet Impérial s'en tient à la Déclaration de Lord Derby du 6 Mai, 1877, et notamment:—

'The existing arrangements made under European sanction, which regulate the navigation of the Bosphorus and the Dardanelles, appear to them (the British Government) wise and salutary, and there would be, in their judgment, serious objections to their alteration in any material particular.'

Et le Plénipotentiaire Russe insistera au Congrès sur le *status quo.*

(*f.*) Le Gouvernement Anglais adressera à Sa Majesté le Sultan la demande de promettre à l'Europe de protéger également au Mont Athos les moines des autres nationalités.

Le 30 Mai, 1878.   (*Signé*)   SALISBURY.
                                               SCHOUVALOFF.

Memorandum No. 3 signed by the MARQUIS OF SALISBURY *and* COUNT SCHOUVALOFF, *May 31.*

Sa Majesté l'Empereur de Russie, ayant consenti à restituer à Sa Majesté le Sultan la vallée d'Alaschkert et la ville de Bayazid, et n'ayant pas l'intention d'étendre ses conquêtes en Asie au delà de Kars, Batoum, et des limites posées par le Traité Préliminaire de San Stefano, et rectifiées par la rétrocession susmentionnée, le Gouvernement Impérial ne se refuse pas à conclure avec le Gouvernement Britannique un engagement secret à l'effet de le rassurer à cet égard.

Le 31 Mai, 1878.   (*Signé*)   SALISBURY.
                                               SCHOUVALOFF.

The MARQUIS OF SALISBURY *to* COUNT SCHOUVALOFF.

Foreign Office, May 30, 1878.

Dear Count Schouvaloff,

Some ambiguity may arise with respect to the precise bearing of the first Memorandum upon the reservations contained in the second, and it being inconvenient to wait till the sanction of the Imperial Government can be obtained to a change in the language used, I desire to note that in signing the Memoranda as they stand, I reserve to the Government of Great Britain, while I recognize in that of Russia, entire liberty of action at the Congress in respect to the matters mentioned in the second Memorandum.

I have, &c.

(*Signed*)   SALISBURY.

COUNT SCHOUVALOFF *to the* MARQUIS OF SALISBURY.

Londres, le 18/30 Mai, 1878.

M. le Marquis,

Le Memorandum confidentiel No. 1 mentionne les assurances que Sa Majesté l'Empereur de Russie a donné de ne pas étendre les frontières de son Empire du côté de la Turquie d'Asie. L'engagement à cet égard, qui sera signé entre les Représentants des deux Gouvernements, constitue, ainsi que cela a été convenu entre nous, un acte secret. Je tiens donc à constater qu'en tout cas, et même si le Memorandum sus-mentionné venait à être livré à la publicité, l'acte même de l'engagement tel qu'il se trouve relaté dans le Memorandum secret et confidentiel No. 3, ne saurait être rendu public sans le consentement du Cabinet Impérial.

Veuillez, &c.

(*Signé*)   SCHOUVALOFF.

COUNT SCHOUVALOFF *to the* MARQUIS OF SALISBURY.

Londres, le 19/31 Mai, 1878.

M. le Marquis,

Conformément au désir que vous m'avez exprimé, je vous accuse réception de la lettre du 30 Mai, que vous m'avez adressée à l'effet d'établir que tout en admettant en Congrès une entière liberté d'action au Gouvernement Russe par rapport à tous les points spécifiés dans le second Memorandum du même jour, vous réservez à cet égard la même faculté au Gouvernement Britannique.

Veuillez, &c.

(*Signé*)   SCHOUVALOFF.

8. SALISBURY *to* LOFTUS, *dispatch, no. 347, 3 June 1878: in F.O. 181/567.*

My Lord,

I have to enclose to Your Excellency copies of memoranda and letters in respect to them which have recently passed between Count

Schouvaloff and myself. They have been communicated by him to the German Government but to no other.

I find that the German Ambassador, in reading the terms of the fifth article concerning the provisions as to the Ottoman troops in the Southern Province understood it as if the words 'la frontière' or 'la frontière méridionale' were substituted for 'les frontières'; in other words, as if the liberty which we propose to retain for the Sultan of placing his troops upon the frontiers of the Southern Province, referred to the Adrianople or Southern frontier of that Province only, instead of extending to all the frontiers, the Northern, the Eastern, and the Western, as well. Count Schouvaloff's attention was carefully drawn to the meaning of these words before the Memoranda were signed: and he inserted in consequence a special reservation of Russia's liberty of action in the question. But as the matter is one which Her Majesty's Government will press earnestly in Congress, I am anxious that Count Münster's misconception should not in any degree be shared at St. Petersburg and therefore I beg that you will, if necessary, point out to M. Giers that the words to which I refer must be construed literally.[1] Her Majesty's Government are as anxious as the Government of Russia that the Bulgarians should be protected from vexation or abuse on the part of the Musulman troops: but they at the same time attach the greatest importance to the maintenance of sufficient authority in the Sultan to secure his political supremacy and his safety from insurrection or invasion.

I am

With great truth and respect

My Lord

Your Lordship's most obedient and humble servant

(*Signed*)   SALISBURY.

[1] Giers took the obvious line and expostulated in reply: What then was meant by the words 'Lord Salisbury accepte le retrait des troupes Turques de la Bulgarie Méridionale'? Loftus to Salisbury, tel., no. 131, and disp., no. 602, 9 June, in *F.O.* 65/1004.

MAP 8

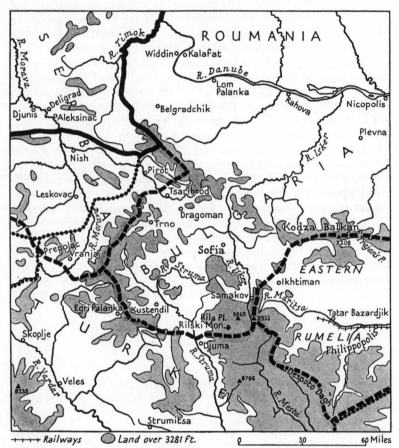

THE WESTERN BOUNDARIES OF BULGARIA AND THE
CONGRESS OF BERLIN

THE STRUGGLE IN THE CONGRESS OF BERLIN OVER VRANJA AND THE BOUNDARIES OF THE *SANJAK* OF SOFIA

THE account in the text (pp. 533–6) of the struggle in the Berlin congress over Serb-Bulgarian boundaries and the eastern and southern frontiers of the *sanjak* of Sofia gives only the barest outline owing to the extreme complexity of the negotiations, dependent as they were (or should have been) on detailed geographical knowledge. It is hoped that the fuller description given here, together with the accompanying map, will bring out the main points at issue.

The question of the Serbian frontiers was referred on 29 June by the congress to the boundary committee, and then to the reinforced sub-committee of military experts. The chairman of the latter body, Bluhme, was an able German general-staff officer on very good terms with the Russians, and the French and Italian officers were at times useful counterweights to the British, Austrian, and Turkish officers; but Simmons, though by now personally respected by Bobrikov and Anuchin, would not accept defeat, and Thömmel appeared in an aggressively rude and continuously hostile light.[1] The first question at issue was the Vranja salient. There was no question of its remaining in Bulgaria, so that the Russians did their best to secure it for the Serbs. In this they succeeded; but the British and Turks carried on their fight for Prepolac and the neighbouring defiles, the key to Vranja, in the boundary committee and finally in the congress itself. Vranja itself, however, remained allotted to the Serbs with adequate defensive positions around, though the British had their way in the end as to Prepolac.[2]

---

[1] Bobrikov's memoirs, in *R.S.*, vol. cliii, p. 289; Anuchin's diary, in *R.S.*, vol. clii, pp. 223–4.

[2] Porte to Caratheodory, tel., 30 June (do everything possible to keep Vranja), copy in Layard Papers, *British Museum, Add. MSS.*, 39137, f. 282; Anuchin's diary, for 30 June, in *R.S.*, vol. clii, pp. 226–9; Bobrikov's memoirs in *Russky vestnik*, Dec. 1889, pp. 16–17, and *R.S.*, vol. clii, p. 231; Hohenlohe, *Memoirs*, under date 9 July, vol. ii, p. 223; Protocols of the fifteenth and nineteenth sittings, 8 and 12 July. Ristić, while later declaring that Serbia owed Vranja to Andrássy, admits the Russian support and great difficulties with Thömmel; Georgévitch, in *Revue d'histoire diplomatique*, vol. vi, pp. 529–32, 539, 544–5. An English secretary's irreverent version of the Vranja wrangle is worth recording: 'There was a great dispute about whether Wrania was to be Turkish or Servian. At the wish of the Turks we held out but Mehemet Ali in committee said he was satisfied to let it go and so it was arranged, but up got Carathéodory in Congress and said his instructions were to hold out about Wrania and Mehemet Ali afterwards admitted that

With Trno and Pirot it was the Austrians who were the main opponents of the Russians and who began by proposing a line that gave Trno and Pirot to Serbia, including Tsaribrod and the Dragoman defile. To this the Russians replied with their full demands for Pirot and Trno to remain in Bulgaria. Bobrikov himself, with his more friendly views towards Serbia, seems to have been ready to put forward a compromise which would give Pirot to Serbia whilst keeping Tsaribrod, the Dragoman defile, and Trno for Bulgaria, but Anuchin, with his Bulgarian sympathies, was little inclined to give away to the Serbs what the Russian delegation agreed was ethnographically Bulgar. And in any case instructions from St. Petersburg insisted on Pirot. When the suggestion was made behind the scenes that there should be a plebiscite for those districts in dispute, Anuchin hotly contested the Serbian sympathies of the inhabitants, and, taxing Ristić with the arbitrariness of the Serbian authorities in occupation and with the kidnapping of the Metropolitan of Pirot, declared that a plebiscite would be a farce unless the Serbian occupying troops withdrew. Ristić, after consultation with Belgrade, was evidently quite uncertain how such a vote would go if the Serbs did withdraw; if the worst came to the worst a plebiscite might be consented to provided that it were held with a European commission on the spot to counter Bulgarian and Russian agitators. It did not come to that. In the face of Austrian and English opposition the plebiscite proposal disappeared, and in the sub-committee the original Austrian line, save for Tsaribrod and Dragoman, was forced upon the Russians (8 July).[1] This, however, did not settle the question, for Shuvalov in the boundary committee would not give way. He had declared to Ristić, according to the latter's account, that he would give the Serbs what they wanted if the British would give way on the other side of the Sofia *sanjak*. But the British would not yield sufficiently, and accordingly that same afternoon (8 July) in the congress itself Shuvalov pressed successfully for Trno to be left to Bulgaria in return for the concessions that he had made on the eastern frontier of the Sofia *sanjak*. And so the congress decreed: Pirot to Serbia; but Trno, Tsaribrod, and the Dragoman defile to Bulgaria.[2] As often happens in such cases, the ultimate factor in the decision was not anything in the

he had met a friend and had had a drop and had got confused. The question is therefore to be reopened.' Bertie (later Lord Bertie) to Tenterden, private letter, 9 July, in *Tenterden Papers*, F.O. 363/1.

[1] Georgévitch, in *Revue d'histoire diplomatique*, vol. vi, pp. 502, 516–19, and 523–4 (on the plebiscite), 541–3; Anuchin's diary, for 1 and 8 July, in *R.S.*, vol. clii, p. 230 (on the plebiscite), pp. 489–90.

[2] Hohenlohe, *Memoirs*, under date 8 July, vol. ii, p. 223; text of undated letter of Ristić to Grujić, in *Revue d'histoire diplomatique*, vol. vi, p. 543; Protocol of fifteenth sitting, 8 July.

merits of the dispute itself but the resolution of a different dispute, that over the eastern boundary of the *sanjak* of Sofia.

The British had agreed earlier to give Varna to Bulgaria in exchange for the return to Turkey of that portion of the valleys of the Struma and the Mesta which otherwise would have fallen within Eastern Rumelia and to include the *sanjak* of Sofia in Bulgaria subject to strategical rectifications of the frontier. These latter involved initially the eastern boundaries of the *sanjak*, and above all the Ikhtiman pass on the Philippopolis–Sofia highway, to which the Orient railway already nearly reached on the eastern side. But to the south also there were obstacles in the path of an agreement. The British appeared only tardily to realize the importance of the chief road linking Eastern Rumelia with the upper Vardar valley and running from Tatar Bazardjik, on the Orient railway, through the *sanjak* of Sofia via Samakov and Kustendil, to Egri Palanka and Skoplje.[1] They therefore raised contention as to the upper valley of the Struma, which itself rises far within the *sanjak* of Sofia, a few miles to the south of Sofia itself. The net result was that the British, perhaps harking back to a Turkish boundary proposal put forward at the time of the Constantinople conference, claimed to interpret strategical rectifications so as to leave only the basin of the Isker within the *sanjak*.[2] On the other hand, the Russians, while they had abandoned to Turkey Djuma on the Struma (though occupied by their troops), had not abandoned Kustendil (also in their occupation) and had reserved Bulgarian control of the Tatar Bazardjik–Skoplje road throughout its course through the *sanjak* of Sofia. Thus, when they had agreed to give up the upper valley of the Struma, they meant so much of the valley as was outside the limits of the *sanjak* of Sofia. They knew that there would be a fight over the Ikhtiman pass and that the British realized that they had been over-hasty in their concessions as to the *sanjak* of Sofia and would make large claims under the guise of strategical rectifications of the frontier, but how much they would demand back remained obscure.

The disagreement came to a head on 3 July, in the boundary committee, and lasted four acute days. Salisbury and Russell had not concealed from the Russians that they intended to fight hard to win back much of the *sanjak*,[3] and on 3 July Russell put forward extreme demands for the upper Isker and Struma valleys as well as

[1] Bareilles, *Le Rapport secret sur le Congrès de Berlin adressé . . . par Carathéodory Pacha*, p. 113.

[2] Gauld, 'The Making of Bulgaria', in *History*, new series, vol. x, p. 30, referring to a Turkish map in the Vienna archives; private letter of Bertie (later Lord Bertie) to Tenterden, 4 July, in *Tenterden Papers*, F.O. 363/1. Salisbury in the fifteenth sitting of the congress confessed that he had not originally realized that any of the Struma valley was within the *sanjak* of Sofia.

[3] Anuchin's diary, under dates 1 and 3 July, in *R.S.*, vol. clii, pp. 231, 234.

the Maritsa watershed, amounting to something like two-thirds of the *sanjak*, incorporating Kustendil, Samakov, and the Ikhtiman pass in Eastern Rumelia. This was 'strategical rectifications' with a vengeance. Shuvalov naturally refused what he termed large territorial alterations, whereupon Russell threatened to throw the whole previous agreement into the melting-pot by returning to the original British proposal that Varna should remain Turkish. Shuvalov retaliated by threatening withdrawal of the Russian concessions as to Turkish military rights in Eastern Rumelia. The committee adjourned in an atmosphere of crisis, with Hohenlohe instructing Bluhme to discover some compromise with the military experts and Bismarck furious at the unabashed conduct of the English.[1]

Compromise was not the strongest point of the military experts. Nor was their task made easier by the fact that Salisbury had given Simmons written instructions not to make any concessions on the *sanjak* of Sofia unless, in concert with Mehemet Ali, to gain a more favourable line for the Turks.[2] Thus, for two days, 4 and 5 July, the sub-committee wrangled inconclusively, not over the *sanjak* frontiers alone, but also over the whole southern trace of the Bulgarian boundary and the south-eastern trace of that of Eastern Rumelia. Simmons insisted on a prior settlement of the line along the Balkan range before deciding the eastern frontier of the Sofia *sanjak*. This involved the final struggle for a five-kilometre zone to the north of the Balkans, which would ensure to the Turks command of the passes, all the more necessary to the east if Shumla and Varna were to be out of their hands. Simmons would not yield to a French compromise on the *sanjak*, by which Ikhtiman was to go to Eastern Rumelia, and Samakov to Bulgaria. Bismarck was incensed at British extremism, and Hohenlohe did his best in private to induce Salisbury and Shuvalov to compromise, but there was really nothing further for the Russian to yield, and Salisbury was waiting for Batum. This was probably the decisive factor behind his stubbornness on Bulgarian frontiers. The crisis over these was linked with the simultaneous crisis over the Asiatic frontiers.[3]

In the afternoon of the next day, the 6th, daylight began to appear. Gorchakov's declaration in the congress on Batum and

[1] Busch's diary, under date 3 July, in *Deutsche Rundschau*, vol. cxli, p. 376; Hohenlohe, *Memoirs*, under date 4 July, vol. ii, pp. 219–20.

[2] Salisbury to Simmons, 3 July, in *F.O.* 78/2909.

[3] Simmons to Salisbury, 6 July, in *F.O.* 78/2898; memorandum of Lt.-Col. Home, 7 June, in *F.O.* 78/2909 (for the importance of the eastern passes); Anuchin's diary for 3, 4, and 5 July, in *R.S.*, vol. clii, pp. 235–7, 482–4; Hohenlohe, *Memoirs*, under date 6 July, vol. ii, p. 221. Shuvalov later told Radowitz that he had emphasized strongly to the Tsar that it was only through the personal intervention of Bismarck that the British had given way on the five-kilometre zone, the Sofia *sanjak*, and Batum; Radowitz to Bismarck, 8 Aug., 1878, in *G.P.*, vol. iii, p. 4.

some cession of territory in Asia to Turkey was satisfactory to the English. They were now prepared to give ground over Bulgaria. When the boundary committee met on the night of 7 July agreement was reached on the Bulgarian frontiers; next morning the sub-committee put into shape the detailed line; in the afternoon the congress adopted it. No five-kilometre zone to the north of the Balkans was allowed, though a form of words was found to give some satisfaction to the English. The Ikhtiman pass went to Eastern Rumelia, but only minor alterations were made in the southern frontier of the Sofia *sanjak*: Samakov and Kustendil went to Bulgaria, as well as the Rilski monastery which was the spiritual fountain-head of Bulgarian nationalism.[1]

[1] Hohenlohe, *Memoirs*, under date 8 July, vol. ii, p. 223; Anuchin's diary for 8 July, in *R.S.*, vol. clii, pp. 488–90; Protocol of fifteenth sitting, 8 July. According to figures based on Kiepert the population of the new Bulgaria was put at 1,773,000; that of Eastern Rumelia at 740,000; that of the San Stefano Bulgaria at 3,980,000; O.K., *Russia and England from 1876 to 1880*, p. 114. S. Gopčević, *Bulgarien und Ostrumelien mit besonderer Berücksichtigung des Zeitraumes von 1878–1886* (Leipzig, 1886), pp. 18–25, gives 2,000,000 for the new Bulgaria and 816,000 for Eastern Rumelia according to 1881 and 1880 figures; these, for what they are worth, show the Bulgars as constituting 67·5 per cent. of the population of the former, and 70·3 per cent. of that of the latter; the Turks as 26·2 and 21·4 per cent., but their numbers were being further diminished by continued migration. The statistical information supplied to the British delegation in Berlin is in the Simmons Papers, *F.O.* 358/4; it was mainly collected by Layard, and was mainly pro-Greek.

THE TREATY OF BERLIN, 13 JULY 1878

THE text is reprinted from Noradounghian, *Recueil d'actes inter-nationaux de l'empire ottoman*, vol. iv, pp. 175–92. For maps showing the frontiers laid down in the treaty see maps nos. 5–8.

S.M. l'Empereur d'Allemagne, S.M. l'Empereur d'Autriche-Hongrie, le Président de la République française, S.M. la Reine du Royaume Uni de la Grande-Bretagne, Impératrice des Indes, S.M. le Roi d'Italie, S.M. l'Empereur de toutes les Russies, S.M. l'Empereur des Ottomans, désirant régler dans une pensée d'ordre européen, conformément aux stipulations du Traité de Paris du 30 Mars 1856, les questions soulevées en Orient par les événements des dernières années et par la guerre dont le Traité préliminaire de San-Stefano a marqué le terme, ont été unanimement d'avis que la réunion d'un Congrès serait le meilleur moyen de faciliter leur entente. A cet effet Leurs Majestés et le Président de la République française ont nommé en conséquence pour leurs Plénipotentiaires, savoir (suivent les noms des Plénipotentiaires), lesquels, suivant la proposition de la Cour d'Autriche-Hongrie et sur l'invitation de la Cour d'Allemagne, se sont réunis à Berlin munis de pleins pouvoirs, qui ont été trouvés en bonne et due forme.

L'accord s'étant heureusement établi entre eux, ils sont convenus des stipulations suivantes:

ARTICLE PREMIER. — La Bulgarie est constituée en Principauté autonome et tributaire, sous la suzeraineté de S.M.I. le Sultan. Elle aura un Gouvernement chrétien et une milice nationale.

ART. 2. — La Principauté de Bulgarie comprendra les territoires ci-après:

La frontière suit, au Nord, la rive droite du Danube, depuis l'ancienne frontière de Serbie jusqu'à un point à déterminer par une Commission européenne à l'Est de Silistrie et, de là, se dirige vers la mer Noire au Sud de Mangalia, qui est rattaché au territoire roumain. La mer Noire forme la limite Est de la Bulgarie. Au Sud .... [There follows a detailed description of the course of the southern and western frontiers, which is omitted by me.]

Cette délimitation sera fixée sur les lieux par la Commission européenne où les Puissances signataires seront représentées. Il est entendu:

1° Que cette Commission prendra en considération la nécessité pour S.M.I. le Sultan de pouvoir défendre les frontières du Balkan de la Roumélie-Orientale.

2° Qu'il ne pourra être élevé de fortifications dans un rayon de 10 kilomètres autour de Samakow.

Art. 3. — Le Prince de Bulgarie sera librement élu par la population, et confirmé par la Sublime Porte, avec l'assentiment des Puissances. Aucun membre des dynasties régnantes des Grandes Puissances européennes ne pourra être élu Prince de Bulgarie. En cas de vacance de la dynastie princière, l'élection du nouveau Prince se fera aux mêmes conditions et dans les mêmes formes.

Art. 4. — Une assemblée de notables de la Bulgarie, convoquée à Tirnovo, élaborera avant l'élection du Prince le Règlement organique de la Principauté. Dans les localités où les Bulgares sont mêlés à des populations turques, roumaines, grecques, ou autres, il sera tenu compte des droits et des intérêts de ces populations en ce qui concerne les élections et l'élaboration du règlement organique.

Art. 5. — Les dispositions suivantes formeront la base du droit public de la Bulgarie. La distinction des croyances religieuses et des confessions ne pourra être opposée à personne comme un motif d'exclusion ou d'incapacité en ce qui concerne la jouissance des droits civils et politiques, l'admission aux emplois publics, fonctions et honneurs, ou l'exercice des différentes professions et industries, dans quelque localité que ce soit. La liberté et la pratique extérieure de tous les cultes sont assurées à tous les ressortissants de la Bulgarie aussi bien qu'aux étrangers, et aucune entrave ne pourra être apportée, soit à l'organisation hiérarchique des différentes communions, soit à leurs rapports avec leurs chefs spirituels.

Art. 6. — L'administration provisoire de la Bulgarie sera dirigée jusqu'à l'achèvement du règlement organique par un Commissaire Impérial russe. Un Commissaire Impérial ottoman, ainsi que les Consuls délégués *ad hoc* par les autres Puissances signataires du présent Traité, seront appelés à l'assister, à l'effet de contrôler le fonctionnement de ce régime provisoire. En cas de dissentiment entre les Consuls délégués, la majorité décidera; et en cas de divergence entre cette majorité et le Commissaire Impérial russe ou le Commissaire Impérial ottoman, les Représentants des Puissances signataires à Constantinople, réunis en Conférence, devront prononcer.

Art. 7. — Le régime provisoire ne pourra être prolongé au délà d'un délai de neuf mois à partir de l'échange des ratifications du présent Traité. Lorsque le règlement organique sera terminé, il sera procédé immédiatement à l'élection du Prince de Bulgarie. Aussitôt que le Prince aura été institué, la nouvelle organisation sera mise en vigueur et la Principauté entrera en pleine jouissance de son autonomie.

Art. 8. — Les Traités de commerce et de navigation, ainsi que toutes les conventions et arrangements conclus entre les Puissances étrangères et la Porte et aujourd'hui en vigueur, sont maintenus dans la Principauté de Bulgarie, et aucun changement n'y sera apporté à l'égard d'aucune Puissance avant qu'elle n'y ait donné son consentement. Aucun droit de transit ne sera prélevé en Bulgarie sur les marchandises traversant cette Principauté. Les nationaux et le commerce de toutes les Puissances y seront traités sur le pied d'une parfaite égalité. Les immunités et privilèges des sujets étrangers, ainsi que les droits de jurisdiction et de protection consulaires, tels qu'ils ont été établis par les Capitulations et les usages, resteront en pleine vigueur, tant qu'ils n'auront pas été modifiés du consentement des Parties intéressées.

ART. 9. — Le montant du tribut annuel que la Principauté de Bulgarie paiera à la Cour suzeraine, en le versant à la Banque que la Sublime Porte désignera ultérieurement, sera déterminé par un accord entre les Puissances signataires du présent Traité à la fin de la première année du fonctionnement de la nouvelle organisation. Ce tribut sera établi sur le revenu moyen du territoire de la Principauté. La Bulgarie devant supporter une part de la dette publique de l'empire, lorsque les Puissances détermineront le tribut, elles prendront en considération la partie de cette dette qui pourrait être attribuée à la Principauté, sur la base d'une équitable proportion.

ART. 10. — La Bulgarie est substituée au Gouvernement impérial ottoman dans ses charges et obligations envers la Compagnie du chemin de fer de Roustchouk-Varna, à partir du jour de l'échange des ratifications du présent Traité. Le règlement des comptes antérieurs est réservé à une entente entre la Sublime Porte, le Gouvernement de la Principauté et l'administration de cette Compagnie. La Principauté de Bulgarie est de même substituée, pour sa part, aux engagements que la Sublime Porte a contractés tant envers l'Autriche-Hongrie qu'envers la Compagnie pour l'exploitation des chemins de fer de la Turquie d'Europe par rapport à l'achèvement et au raccordement, ainsi qu'à l'exploitation de lignes ferrées situées sur son territoire. Les conventions nécessaires pour régler ces questions seront conclues entre l'Autriche-Hongrie, la Porte, la Serbie et la Principauté de Bulgarie, immédiatement après la conclusion de la paix.

ART. 11. — L'armée ottomane ne séjournera plus en Bulgarie. Toutes les anciennes forteresses seront rasées, aux frais de la Principauté, dans le délai d'un an, ou plus tôt, si faire se peut. Le Gouvernement local prendra immédiatement des mesures pour les détruire, et ne pourra en faire construire de nouvelles. La Sublime Porte aura le droit de disposer à sa guise du matériel de guerre et autres objets appartenant au Gouvernement Ottoman, et qui seraient restés dans les forteresses du Danube déjà évacuées en vertu de l'armistice du 31 Janvier, ainsi que de ceux qui se trouveraient dans les places fortes de Choumla et de Varna.

ART. 12. — Les propriétaires musulmans ou autres qui fixeraient leur résidence personnelle hors de la Principauté pourront y conserver leurs immeubles en les affermant ou en les faisant administrer par des tiers. Une Commission turco-bulgare sera chargée de régler, dans le courant de deux années, toutes les affaires relatives au mode d'aliénation, d'exploitation ou d'usage, pour le compte de la Sublime Porte, des propriétés de l'Etat et des fondations pieuses (*vacoufs*) et les questions relatives aux intérêts des particuliers qui pourraient s'y trouver engagés. Les ressortissants de la Principauté de Bulgarie qui voyageront ou séjourneront dans les autres parties de l'Empire Ottoman, seront soumis aux autorités et aux lois ottomanes.

ART. 13. — Il est formé au Sud des Balkans une province qui prendra le nom de 'Roumélie Orientale' et qui restera placée sous l'autorité politique et militaire directe de S.M.I. le Sultan, dans les conditions d'autonomie administrative. Elle aura un Gouverneur Général chrétien.

ART. 14. — La Roumélie Orientale est limitée au Nord et au Nord-Ouest par la Bulgarie et comprend les territoires inclus dans le tracé suivant. . . . [Remainder of article describing in detail the frontiers is omitted by me.]

ART. 15. — S.M.I. le Sultan aura le droit de pourvoir à la défense des frontières de terre et de mer de la province en élevant des fortifications sur ces frontières et en y entretenant des troupes. L'ordre intérieur est maintenu dans la Roumélie Orientale par une gendarmerie indigène, assistée d'une milice locale. Pour la composition de ces deux corps, dont les officiers seront nommés par le Sultan, il sera tenu compte, suivant les localités, de la religion des habitants. S.M.I. le Sultan s'engage à ne point employer de troupes irrégulières, telles que Bachi-Bozouks et Circassiens, dans les garnisons des frontières. Les troupes régulières destinées à ce service ne pourront en aucun cas être cantonnées chez l'habitant; lorsqu'elles traverseront la province, elles ne pourront y faire de séjour.

ART. 16. — Le Gouverneur Général aura le droit d'appeler les troupes Ottomanes dans le cas où la sécurité intérieure ou extérieure de la Province se trouverait menacée. Dans l'éventualité prévue, la Sublime Porte devra donner connaissance de cette décision, ainsi que des nécessités qui la justifient, aux Représentants des Puissances à Constantinople.

ART. 17. — Le Gouverneur Général de la Roumélie Orientale sera nommé par la Sublime Porte, avec l'assentiment des Puissances, pour un terme de cinq ans.

ART. 18. — Immédiatement après l'échange des ratifications du présent Traité, une Commission européenne sera formée pour élaborer, d'accord avec la Porte Ottomane, l'organisation de la Roumélie Orientale. Cette Commission aura à déterminer, dans un délai de trois mois, les pouvoirs et les attributions du Gouverneur

Général, ainsi que le régime administratif, judiciaire et financier de la Province, en prenant pour point de départ les différentes lois sur les vilayets et les propositions faites dans la huitième séance de la Conférence de Constantinople. L'ensemble des dispositions arrêtées par la Roumélie Orientale fera l'objet d'un firman impérial, qui sera promulgué par la Sublime Porte, et dont elle donnera communication aux Puissances.

ART. 19. — La Commission Européenne sera chargée d'administrer, d'accord avec la Sublime Porte, les finances de la Province jusqu'à l'achèvement de la nouvelle organisation.

ART. 20. — Les Traités, les Conventions et Arrangements internationaux, de quelque nature qu'ils soient, conclus ou à conclure entre la Porte et les Puissances Etrangères, seront applicables dans la Roumélie Orientale comme dans tout l'Empire Ottoman. Les immunités et privilèges acquis aux étrangers, quelle que soit leur condition, seront respectés dans cette province. La Sublime Porte s'engage à y faire observer les lois générales de l'Empire sur la liberté religieuse en faveur de tous les cultes.

ART. 21. — Les droits et obligations de la Sublime Porte en ce qui concerne les chemins de fer dans la Roumélie Orientale sont maintenus intégralement.

ART. 22. — L'effectif du corps d'occupation russe en Bulgarie et dans la Roumélie Orientale sera composé de six divisions d'infanterie et de deux divisions de cavalerie, et n'excédera pas 50,000 hommes. Il sera entretenu aux frais du pays occupé. Les troupes d'occupation conserveront leurs communications avec la Russie, non seulement par la Roumanie, d'après les arrangements à conclure entre les deux Etats, mais aussi par les ports de la Mer Noire, Varna et Bourgas, où elles pourront organiser pour la durée de l'occupation les dépôts nécessaires. La durée de l'occupation de la Roumélie Orientale et de la Bulgarie par les troupes impériales russes est fixée à neuf mois, à dater de l'échange des ratifications du présent Traité. Le Gouvernement impérial russe s'engage à terminer dans un délai ultérieur de trois mois le passage de ses troupes à travers la Roumanie et l'évacuation complète de cette Principauté.

ART. 23. — La Sublime Porte s'engage à appliquer scrupuleusement dans l'île de Crète le règlement organique de 1868 en y apportant les modifications qui seraient jugées équitables. Des règlements analogues, adaptés aux besoins locaux, sauf en ce qui concerne les exemptions d'impôts accordées à la Crète, seront également introduits dans les autres parties de la Turquie d'Europe pour lesquelles une organisation particulière n'a pas été prévue par le présent Traité. La Sublime Porte chargera des Commissions spéciales, au sein desquelles l'élément indigène sera largement représenté, d'élaborer les détails de ces nouveaux règlements dans chaque province. Les projets d'organisation résultant de ces travaux seront soumis à l'examen de la Sublime Porte, qui, avant de promulguer les actes destinés à les mettre en vigueur, prendra l'avis de la Commission Européenne instituée pour la Roumélie Orientale.

ART. 24. — Dans les cas où la Sublime Porte et la Grèce ne parviendraient pas à s'entendre sur la rectification de frontière indiquée dans le treizième Protocole du Congrès de Berlin, l'Allemagne, l'Autriche-Hongrie, la France, la Grande-Bretagne, l'Italie et la Russie se réservent d'offrir leur médiation aux deux Parties pour faciliter les négociations.

ART. 25. — Les Provinces de Bosnie et de l'Herzégovine seront occupées et administrées par l'Autriche-Hongrie. Le Gouvernement d'Autriche-Hongrie, ne désirant pas se charger de l'administration du sandjak de Novi-Bazar, qui s'étend entre la Serbie et le Monténégro dans la direction Sud-Est jusqu'au delà de Mitrovitza, l'administration Ottomane continuera d'y fonctionner; néanmoins, afin d'assurer le maintien du nouvel état politique, ainsi que la liberté et la sécurité des voies de communication, l'Autriche-Hongrie se réserve le droit de tenir garnison et d'avoir des routes militaires et commerciales sur toute l'étendue de cette partie de l'ancien vilayet de Bosnie. A cet effet les Gouvernements d'Autriche-Hongrie et de Turquie se réservent de s'entendre sur les détails.

ART. 26. — L'indépendance du Monténégro est reconnue par la Sublime Porte et par toutes celles des Hautes Parties Contractantes qui ne l'avaient pas encore admise.

ART. 27. — Les Hautes Parties Contractantes sont d'accord sur les conditions suivantes: Dans le Monténégro, la distinction des croyances religieuses et des confessions ne pourra être opposée à personne comme un motif d'exclusion ou d'incapacité en ce qui concerne la jouissance des droits civils et politiques, l'admission aux emplois publics, fonctions et honneurs, ou l'exercice des différentes professions et industries, dans quelque localité que ce soit. La liberté et la pratique extérieure de tous les cultes seront assurées à tous les ressortissants du Monténégro, aussi bien qu'aux étrangers, et aucune entrave ne pourra être apportée soit à l'organisation hiérarchique des différentes communions, soit à leurs rapports avec leurs chefs spirituels.

ART. 28. — Les nouvelles frontières du Monténégro sont fixées ainsi qu'il suit. . . . [Remainder of article describing in detail the frontiers is omitted by me.]

ART. 29. — Antivari et son littoral sont annexés au Monténégro sous les conditions suivantes: Les contrées situées au Sud de ce territoire, d'après la délimitation ci-dessus déterminée, jusqu'à la Boyana, y compris Dulcigno, seront restituées à la Turquie. La commune de Spizza, jusqu'à la limite septentrionale du territoire indiqué dans la description détaillée des frontières, sera incorporée à la Dalmatie. Il y aura pleine et entière liberté de navigation sur la Boyana pour le Monténégro. Il ne sera pas construit de fortifications sur le parcours de ce fleuve, à l'exception de celles qui seraient nécessaires à la défense locale de la place de Scutari, lesquelles ne s'étendront pas au delà d'une distance de six kilomètres de cette ville. Le Monténégro ne pourra avoir ni bâtiments ni pavillon de guerre. Le port d'Antivari et toutes les eaux du Monténégro resteront fermés aux bâtiments de guerre de toutes les nations. Les fortifications situées entre le lac et le littoral sur le territoire monténégrin seront rasées, et il ne pourra en être élevé de nouvelles dans cette zone. La police maritime et sanitaire, tant à Antivari que le long de la côte du Monténégro, sera exercée par l'Autriche-Hongrie au moyen de bâtiments légers garde-côtes. Le Monténégro adoptera la legislation maritime en vigueur en Dalmatie. De son côté l'Autriche-Hongrie s'engage à accorder sa protection consulaire au pavillon marchand monténégrin. Le Monténégro devra s'entendre avec l'Autriche-Hongrie sur le droit de construire et d'entretenir à travers le nouveau territoire monténégrin une route et un chemin de fer. Une entière liberté de communication sera assurée sur ces voies.

Art. 30. — Les musulmans ou autres qui possèdent des propriétés dans les territoires annexés au Monténégro, et qui voudraient fixer leur résidence hors de la Principauté, pourront conserver leurs immeubles en les affermant ou en les faisant administrer par des tiers. Personne ne pourra être exproprié que légalement pour cause d'intérêt public, et moyennant une indemnité préalable. Une Commission turco-monténégrine sera chargée de régler, dans le terme de trois ans, toutes les affaires relatives au mode d'aliénation d'exploitation et d'usage, pour le compte de la Sublime Porte, des propriétés de l'État, des fondations pieuses (*vacoufs*), ainsi que les questions relatives aux intérêts des particuliers qui s'y trouveraient engagés.

Art. 31. — La Principauté du Monténégro s'entendra directement avec la Porte Ottomane sur l'institution d'Agents monténégrins à Constantinople et dans certaines localités de l'Empire Ottoman, où la nécessité en sera reconnue. Les Monténégrins voyageant ou séjournant dans l'Empire Ottoman seront soumis aux lois et aux autorités Ottomanes, suivant les principes généraux du droit international et les usages établis concernant les Monténégrins.

Art. 32. — Les troupes du Monténégro seront tenues d'évacuer dans un délai de vingt jours, à partir de l'échange des ratifications du présent Traité, ou plus tôt, si faire se peut, le territoire qu'elles occupent en ce moment en dehors des nouvelles limites de la Principauté.

Les troupes Ottomanes évacueront les territoires cédés au Monténégro dans le même délai de vingt jours. Il leur sera toutefois accordé un terme supplémentaire de quinze jours, tant pour quitter les places fortes et en retirer les approvisionnements et le matériel, que pour dresser l'inventaire des engins et objets qui ne pourraient être enlevés immédiatement.

ART. 33. — Le Monténégro devant supporter une partie de la dette publique ottomane pour les nouveaux territoires qui lui sont attribués par le Traité de paix, les Représentants des Puissances à Constantinople en détermineront le montant, de concert avec la Sublime Porte, sur une base équitable.

ART. 34. — Les Hautes Parties Contractantes reconnaissent l'indépendance de la Principauté de Serbie en la rattachant aux conditions exposées dans l'article suivant.

ART. 35. — En Serbie, la distinction des croyances religieuses et des confessions ne pourra être opposée à personne comme un motif d'exclusion ou d'incapacité en ce qui concerne la jouissance des droits civils et politiques, l'admission aux emplois publics, fonctions et honneurs, ou l'exercice des différentes professions et industries, dans quelque localité que ce soit. La liberté et la pratique extérieure de tous les cultes seront assurées à tous les ressortissants de la Serbie, aussi bien qu'aux étrangers, et aucune entrave ne pourra être apportée soit à l'organisation hiérarchique des différentes communions, soit à leurs rapports avec leurs chefs spirituels.

ART. 36. — La Serbie reçoit les territoires inclus dans la délimitation ci-après:

La nouvelle frontière suit le tracé actuel en remontant le thalweg de la Drina depuis son confluent avec la Save, laissant à la Principauté le Mali-Zvornik et Sakhar, et continue à longer l'ancienne limite de la Serbie jusqu'au Kopaonik. . . . [Remainder of article describing the frontiers in detail is omitted by me.]

ART. 37. — Jusqu'à la conclusion de nouveaux arrangements, rien ne sera changé en Serbie aux conditions actuelles des relations commerciales de la Principauté avec les Pays étrangers. Aucun droit de transit ne sera prélevé sur les marchandises traversant la Serbie. Les immunités et privilèges des sujets étrangers, ainsi que les droits de juridiction et de protection consulaires, tels qu'ils existent aujourd'hui, resteront en pleine vigueur, tant qu'ils n'auront pas été modifiés d'un commun accord entre la Principauté et les Puissances intéressées.

ART. 38. — La Principauté de Serbie est substituée pour sa part aux engagements que la Sublime Porte a contractés tant envers l'Autriche-Hongrie qu'envers la Compagnie pour l'exploitation des chemins de fer de la Turquie d'Europe par rapport à l'achèvement et au raccordement, ainsi qu'à l'exploitation des lignes ferrées à construire sur le territoire nouvellement acquis par la Principauté.

Les Conventions nécessaires pour régler ces questions seront conclues, immédiatement après la signature du présent Traité, entre l'Autriche-Hongrie, la Porte, la Serbie, et, dans les limites de sa compétence, la Principauté de Bulgarie.

Art. 39. — Les musulmans qui possèdent des propriétés dans les territoires annexés à la Serbie, et qui voudraient fixer leur résidence hors de la Principauté, pourront y conserver leurs immeubles en les affermant ou en les faisant administrer par des tiers. Une Commission turco-serbe sera chargée de régler, dans le délai de trois années, toutes les affaires relatives au mode d'aliénation, d'exploitation ou d'usage, pour le compte de la Sublime Porte, des propriétés de l'État et des fondations pieuses (*vacoufs*), ainsi que les questions relatives aux intérêts des particuliers qui pourraient s'y trouver engagés.

Art. 40. — Jusqu'à la conclusion d'un Traité entre la Turquie et la Serbie, les sujets Serbes voyageant ou séjournant dans l'Empire Ottoman seront traités suivant les principes généraux du droit international.

Art. 41. — Les troupes Serbes seront tenues d'évacuer, dans le délai de quinze jours à partir de l'échange des ratifications du présent Traité, le territoire non compris dans les nouvelles limites de la Principauté.

Les troupes Ottomanes évacueront les territoires cédés à la Serbie dans le même délai de quinze jours. Il leur sera toutefois accordé un terme supplémentaire du même nombre de jours, tant pour quitter les places fortes et pour en retirer les approvisionnements et le matériel, que pour dresser l'inventaire des engins et objets qui ne pourraient être enlevés immédiatement.

Art. 42. — La Serbie devant supporter une partie de la dette publique ottomane pour les nouveaux territoires qui lui sont attribués par le présent Traité, les Représentants à Constantinople en détermineront le montant, de concert avec la Sublime Porte, sur une base équitable.

Art. 43. — Les Hautes Parties Contractantes reconnaissent l'indépendance de la Roumanie en la rattachant aux conditions exposées dans les deux articles suivants:

Art. 44. — En Roumanie, la distinction des croyances religieuses et des confessions ne pourra être opposée à personne comme un motif d'exclusion ou d'incapacité en ce qui concerne la jouissance des droits civils et politiques, l'admission aux emplois publics, fonctions et honneurs, ou l'exercice des différentes professions et industries, dans quelque localité que ce soit. La liberté et la pratique extérieure de tous les cultes seront assurées à tous les ressortissants de l'État roumain, aussi bien qu'aux étrangers, et aucune entrave ne sera apportée soit à l'organisation hiérarchique des différentes communions, soit à leurs rapports avec leurs chefs spirituels. Les nationaux de toutes les Puissances, commerçants ou autres, seront traités en Roumanie, sans distinction de religion, sur le pied d'une parfaite égalité.

ART. 45. — La Principauté de Roumanie rétrocède à S.M. l'Empereur de Russie la portion du territoire de la Bessarabie détachée de la Russie en suite du Traité de Paris de 1856, limitée à l'Ouest par le thalweg du Pruth, au Midi par le thalweg du bras de Kilia et l'embouchure du Stary Stamboul.

ART. 46. — Les îles formant le Delta du Danube, ainsi que l'Ile des Serpents, le sandjak de Toultcha, comprenant les districts (cazas) de Kilia, Soulina, Mahmoudié, Issaktcha, Toultcha, Matchine, Babadagh, Hirsovo, Kustendjé, Medjidié, sont réunis à la Roumanie. La Principauté reçoit en outre le territoire situé au Sud de la Dobroudja jusqu'à une ligne ayant son point de départ à l'Est de Silistrie et aboutissant à la Mer Noire au Sud de Mangalia. Le tracé de la frontière sera fixé sur les lieux par la Commission Européenne instituée pour la délimitation de la Bulgarie.

ART. 47. — La question du partage des eaux et des pêcheries sera soumise à l'arbitrage de la Commission Européenne du Danube.

ART. 48. — Aucun droit de transit ne sera prélevé en Roumanie sur les marchandises traversant la Principauté.

ART. 49. — Des Conventions pourront être conclues par la Roumanie pour régler les privilèges et attributions des consuls en matière de protection dans la Principauté. Les droits acquis resteront en vigueur, tant qu'ils n'auront pas été modifiés d'un commun accord entre la Principauté et les Parties intéressées.

ART. 50. — Jusqu'à la conclusion d'un Traité réglant les privilèges et attributions des consuls entre la Turquie et la Roumanie, les sujets Roumains voyageant ou séjournant dans l'Empire Ottoman, et les sujets Ottomans voyageant ou séjournant en Roumanie, jouiront des droits garantis aux sujets des autres Puissances européennes.

ART. 51. — En ce qui concerne les entreprises des travaux publics et autres de même nature, la Roumanie sera substituée, pour tout le territoire cédé, aux droits et obligations de la Sublime Porte.

ART. 52. — Afin d'accroître les garanties assurées à la liberté de la navigation sur le Danube, reconnue comme étant d'intérêt européen, les Hautes Parties Contractantes décident que toutes les forteresses et fortifications qui se trouvent sur le parcours du fleuve depuis les Portes-de-Fer jusqu'à ses embouchures seront rasées, et qu'il n'en sera pas élevé de nouvelles. Aucun bâtiment de guerre ne pourra naviguer sur le Danube en aval des Portes-de-Fer, à l'exception des bâtiments légers destinés à la police fluviale et aux services des douanes. Les stationnaires des Puissances aux embouchures du Danube pourront toutefois remonter jusqu'à Galatz.

Art. 53. — La Commission Européenne du Danube, au sein de laquelle la Roumanie sera représentée, est maintenue dans ses fonctions, et les exercera dorénavant jusqu'à Galatz dans une complète indépendance de l'autorité territoriale. Tous les Traités, Arrangements, Actes et Décisions relatifs à ses droits, privilèges, prérogatives et obligations, sont confirmés.

Art. 54. — Une année avant l'expiration du terme assigné à la durée de la Commission Européenne, les Puissances se mettront d'accord sur la prolongation de ses pouvoirs ou sur les modifications qu'elles jugeraient nécessaires d'y introduire.

Art. 55. — Les Règlements de navigation, de police fluviale et de surveillance depuis les Portes-de-Fer jusqu'à Galatz seront élaborés par la Commission Européenne, assistée de délégués des États riverains, et mis en harmonie avec ceux qui ont été ou seraient édictés pour le parcours en aval de Galatz.

Art. 56. — La Commission Européenne du Danube s'entendra avec qui de droit pour assurer l'entretien du phare sur l'Ile des Serpents.

Art. 57. — L'exécution des travaux destinés à faire disparaître les obstacles que les Portes-de-Fer et les cataractes opposent à la navigation, est confiée à l'Autriche-Hongrie. Les Etats riverains de cette partie du fleuve accorderont toutes les facilités qui pourraient être requises dans l'intérêt des travaux. Les dispositions de l'article VI du Traité de Londres du 13 Mars 1871, relatives au droit de percevoir une taxe provisoire pour couvrir les frais de ces travaux, sont maintenues en faveur de l'Autriche-Hongrie.

Art. 58. — La Sublime Porte cède à l'Empire Russe en Asie les territoires d'Ardahan, Kars et Batoum avec ce dernier port, ainsi que tous les territoires compris entre l'ancienne frontière russo-turque et le tracé suivant. . . . [Remainder of article describing the frontier is omitted by me.]

Art. 59. — S.M. l'Empereur de Russie déclare que son intention est d'ériger Batoum en port franc, essentiellement commercial.

Art. 60. — La vallée d'Alachkerd et la ville de Bayazid cédées à la Russie par l'article XIX du Traité de San-Stefano font retour à la Turquie.

La Sublime Porte cède à la Perse la ville et le territoire de Khotour, tel qu'il a été déterminé par la Commission mixte anglo-russe pour la délimitation des frontières de la Turquie et de la Perse.

Art. 61. — La Sublime Porte s'engage à réaliser, sans plus de retard, les améliorations et les réformes qu'exigent les besoins locaux dans les provinces habitées par les Arméniens et à garantir leur sécurité contre les Circassiens et les Kurdes. Elle donnera connaissance périodiquement des mesures prises à cet effet aux Puissances qui en surveilleront l'application.

Art. 62. — La Sublime Porte ayant exprimé la volonté de maintenir le principe de la liberté religieuse en y donnant l'extension la plus large, les Parties Contractantes prennent acte de cette déclaration spontanée. Dans aucune partie de l'Empire Ottoman la différence de religion ne pourra être opposée à personne comme un motif d'exclusion ou d'incapacité en ce qui concerne l'usage des droits civils et politiques, l'admission aux emplois publics, fonctions et honneurs, ou l'exercice des différentes professions et industries. Tous seront admis, sans distinction de religion, à témoigner devant les tribunaux. La liberté et la pratique extérieure de tous les cultes sont assurées à tous, et aucune entrave ne pourra être apportée soit à l'organisation hiérarchique des différentes communions, soit à leurs rapports avec leurs chefs spirituels. Les ecclésiastiques, les pèlerins et les moines de toutes les nationalités voyageant dans la Turquie d'Europe ou la Turquie d'Asie, jouiront des mêmes droits, avantages et privilèges. Le droit de protection officielle est reconnu aux Agents diplomatiques et consulaires des Puissances en Turquie, tant à l'égard des personnes sus-mentionnées que de leurs établissements religieux de bienfaisance et autres dans les Lieux-Saints et ailleurs. Les droits acquis à la France sont expressément réservés, et il est bien entendu qu'aucune atteinte ne saurait être portée au *statu quo* dans les Lieux-Saints.

Les moines du Mont Athos, quel que soit leur pays d'origine, seront maintenus dans leurs possessions et avantages antérieurs et jouiront, sans aucune exception, d'une entière égalité de droits et prérogatives.

Art. 63. — Le Traité de Paris du 30 Mars 1856, ainsi que le Traité de Londres du 13 Mars 1871, sont maintenus dans toutes celles de leurs dispositions qui ne sont pas abrogées ou modifiées par les stipulations qui précèdent.

Art. 64. — Le présent Traité sera ratifié et les ratifications en seront échangées à Berlin dans un délai de trois semaines ou plus tôt, si faire se peut.

En foi de quoi, les Plénipotentiaires respectifs l'ont signé et y ont apposé le sceau de leurs armes.

Fait à Berlin le treizième jour du mois de Juillet mil huit cent soixante-dix-huit.

Signé: Andrassy. — Karolyi. — Haymerle. — V. Bismarck. — B. Bulow. — Hohenlohe. — Waddington. — Saint-Vallier. — H. Desprez. — Beaconsfield. — Salisbury. — Odo Russell. — L. Corti. — Launay. — Gortschakow. — Schouvalow. — P. d'Oubril. — Al. Carathéodory. — Mehemed Ali. — Saadoullah.

PROTOCOL AND DEFINITIVE TREATY OF PEACE BETWEEN RUSSIA AND TURKEY, 8 FEBRUARY 1879

THE texts are reprinted from Noradounghian, *Recueil d'actes internationaux de l'empire ottoman*, vol. iv, pp. 204–9.

(Protocole.)

LL.EE. Messieurs les Plénipotentiaires de Turquie et de Russie, s'étant réunis au Ministère des Affaires Etrangères le 27 Janvier/ 8 Février 1879 pour procéder à la signature du Traité négocié entre eux, passent en revue article par article le texte de cet Acte, ainsi que le projet de Traité précédemment communiqué à la Sublime Porte par M. le Plénipotentiaire de Russie.

Au sujet de l'art. II, les Plénipotentiaires Ottomans tiennent à constater qu'il demeure entendu que cet article n'a qu'un caractère déclaratoire en ce sens que les énonciations y contenues ne sauraient se prêter à aucune interprétation qui soit en désaccord avec le caractère des engagements pris dans le Traité de Berlin.

S.E. le prince Lobanow, en accueillant cette déclaration des Plénipotentiaires Ottomans, constate que, de son côté, le Gouvernement impérial de Russie n'a en vue que la stricte et fidèle exécution du Traité de Berlin, dans sa lettre comme dans son esprit.

L'art. V donne lieu de la part de M. le Plénipotentiaire de Russie aux explications suivantes:

S.E. le prince Lobanow déclare que la somme qui y est spécifiée constitue un maximum auquel la totalité des réclamations ne pourra vraisemblablement jamais atteindre; il ajoute qu'une Commission *ad hoc* sera instituée à l'Ambassade de Russie pour examiner scrupuleusement les réclamations qui lui seront présentées, et que, d'après les instructions de son Gouvernement, un délégué ottoman pourra prendre part à l'examen de ces réclamations.

Quant au terme d'une année fixé par cet article comme date à partir de laquelle les réclamations pourront être produites à la Sublime Porte, il est entendu qu'une exception y sera faite en faveur de la réclamation de l'hôpital russe, s'élevant à la somme de L.S. 11,200.

À l'égard de la dernière partie du paragraphe *c* (art. 4) du projet primitif, il est convenu, sans rien préjuger, que les Principautés de Roumanie, de Serbie et du Monténégro étant aujourd'hui indépendantes, ces stipulations du Traité de San-Stéfano ne sauraient trouver place dans le nouveau Traité, sauf aux parties intéressées à s'entendre directement.

Le paragraphe *d* de ce même projet étant supprimé, M. le Plénipotentiaire de Russie se réfère à la déclaration faite à ce sujet par le comte Schouvalow dans la séance du 2 Juillet du Congrès de Berlin (Protocole XI) et d'après laquelle aucune obligation ne pourrait résulter pour la Russie de l'interruption par le fait de la guerre de la navigation sur le Danube.

Le paragraphe *f* du projet russe est aussi éliminé; mais, afin de prévenir tout malentendu, S.E. le prince Lobanow déclare que cette élimination ne saurait en aucune façon être invoquée contre le *statu quo* administratif existant dans la Roumélie Orientale et que ce *statu quo* y sera maintenu provisoirement, jusqu'à l'introduction de la nouvelle organisation qu'élabore la Commission Européenne.

De leur côté, les Plénipotentiaires Ottomans déclarent qu'ils ont précisément demandé la suppression de ce paragraphe parce qu'ils n'entendent rien préjuger en ce qui concerne la Roumélie Orientale, dont la situation est fixée par le Traité intervenu entre les sept Puissances à Berlin et qu'ils n'ont ni qualité ni mission de discuter dans ce moment.

Le paragraphe *g* du même projet est également retranché, et l'on convient que S.E. l'Ambassadeur de Russie adressera à la Sublime Porte une note pour lui déclarer que le Gouvernement Impérial s'engage à donner, immédiatement après la ratification du Traité de ce jour, l'ordre d'évacuer les territoires occupés par les troupes russes en dehors des limites de la Bulgarie et de la Roumélie Orientale.

De plus, S.E. l'Ambassadeur de Russie prévient qu'il appellera l'attention de la Sublime Porte sur la nécessité de prendre pour le maintien de l'ordre et de la tranquillité publique certaines mesures transitoires dans les territoires évacués.

Les Plénipotentiaires ottomans, de leur côté, affirment que leur Gouvernement a toujours tenu à ménager autant qu'il dépend de lui la transition de régime dans les territoires qui sont évacués par les armées russes.

Pour ce qui est enfin de l'art. IX, il est entendu que l'amnistie dont il y est fait mention, ne saurait empêcher l'administration locale de prendre à l'égard des personnes compromises telle mesure de police qui serait exigée par les nécessités de l'ordre et de la tranquillité publique.

On procède ensuite à la signature du Traité; S.E. l'Ambassadeur de Russie fait remise de la note concernant l'évacuation et les Plénipotentiaires apposent leurs signatures au présent Protocole.

Constantinople, le 27 Janvier–8 Février 1879.

Signé: AL. CARATHÉODORY. — ALI. — LOBANOW.

(Traité définitif de paix avec la Russie.)

S.M. l'Empereur des Ottomans et S.M. l'Empereur de toutes les Russies, désirant consacrer le rétablissement de la paix entre les deux Empires et régler définitivement par un Traité les clauses du Traité préliminaire de San-Stefano qui doivent faire l'objet d'une entente directe entre les deux Etats, ont nommé pour leurs Plénipotentiaires:

S.M. l'Empereur des Ottomans, d'une part, Alexandre Carathéodory-Pacha, son Ministre des Affaires Étrangères... [titles omitted by me]

et S.M. l'Empereur de toutes les Russies, de l'autre, le Prince Alexis Lobanow Rostowsky, son Ambassadeur Extraordinaire et Plénipotentiaire près S.M.I. le Sultan... [titles omitted by me]

Lesquels, après avoir échangé leurs pleins pouvoirs, trouvés en bonne et due forme, sont tombés d'accord sur les articles suivants:

ARTICLE PREMIER. — Il y aura désormais paix et amitié entre les deux Empires.

ART. 2. — Les deux Puissances sont d'accord pour déclarer que les stipulations du Traité de Berlin intervenu entre les sept Puissances ont remplacé les articles préliminaires de paix de San-Stefano qui ont été abrogés ou modifiés par le Congrès.

ART. 3. — Les stipulations du Traité de San-Stéfano qui n'ont pas été abrogées ou modifiées par le Traité de Berlin sont réglées définitivement par les articles suivants du présent Traité.

ART. 4. — Défalcation faite de la valeur des territoires cédés par la Turquie à la Russie en conformité du Traité de Berlin, l'indemnité de guerre reste fixée à la somme de 802,500,000 francs. Le mode de paiement de cette somme et la garantie à y affecter (sauf les déclarations contenues dans le Protocole XI du Congrès de Berlin relativement à la question territoriale et aux droits des créanciers) seront réglés par une entente entre le Gouvernement de S.M. l'Empereur des Ottomans et celui de S.M. l'Empereur de toutes les Russies.

ART. 5. — Les réclamations des sujets et institutions russes en Turquie à titre d'indemnité pour les dommages subis pendant la guerre seront payées à mesure qu'elles seront examinées par l'Ambassade de Russie à Constantinople et transmises à la Sublime Porte.

La totalité de ces réclamations ne pourra, en aucun cas, dépasser le chiffre de 26,750,000 francs.

Le terme d'une année après l'échange des ratifications est fixé comme date à partir de laquelle les réclamations pourront être présentées à la Sublime Porte, et celui de deux ans comme date après laquelle les réclamations ne seront plus admises.

ART. 6. — Des Commissaires spéciaux seront nommés par la Sublime Porte et le Gouvernement Impérial de Russie afin d'établir les comptes des frais résultant de l'entretien des prisonniers de guerre ottomans.

Ces comptes seront arrêtés à la date de la signature du Traité de Berlin. On en déduira les frais effectués par le Gouvernement Ottoman pour l'entretien des prisonniers russes et la somme qui en résultera, une fois établie, sera payée par la Sublime Porte en vingt et un termes égaux, dans l'espace de sept années.

ART. 7. — Les habitants des localités cédées à la Russie qui voudraient fixer leur résidence hors de ces territoires, seront libres de se retirer en vendant leurs propriétés immobilières. Un délai de trois ans leur sera accordé à cet effet à partir de la ratification du présent acte.

Passé ce délai les habitants qui n'auraient pas quitté le pays et vendu leurs immeubles resteront sujets russes.

ART. 8. — Les deux Parties prennent mutuellement l'engagement de ne sévir ni de laisser sévir d'aucune manière contre les sujets ottomans ou russes qui auraient été compromis par leurs relations avec les armées des deux Empires pendant la guerre. Dans le cas où quelques personnes voudraient se retirer avec leurs familles à la suite des troupes russes, les Autorités Ottomanes ne s'opposeront pas à leur départ.

ART. 9. — Une amnistie pleine et entière est assurée à tous les sujets ottomans compromis dans les derniers événements des Provinces de la Turquie d'Europe, et toutes les personnes détenues de ce fait, envoyées en exil ou éloignées de leur pays rentreront immédiatement en jouissance de leur liberté.

ART. 10. — Tous les Traités, Conventions et engagements conclus entre les deux Hautes Parties Contractantes relativement au commerce, à la juridiction et à la position des sujets russes en Turquie, et qui avaient été supprimés par l'état de guerre seront remis en vigueur, et les deux Gouvernements seront replacés l'un vis-à-vis de l'autre, pour tous leurs engagements et rapports commerciaux et autres, dans la même situation où ils se trouvaient avant la déclaration de guerre, le tout sauf les clauses auxquelles il serait dérogé par le présent acte ou en vertu du Traité de Berlin.

ART. 11. — La Sublime Porte prendra des mesures efficaces pour terminer à l'amiable toutes les affaires litigieuses des sujets russes pendantes depuis plusieurs années, dédommager ces derniers, s'il y a lieu, et faire exécuter sans délai les sentences rendues.

ART. 12. — Le présent acte sera ratifié et les ratifications en seront échangées à Saint-Pétersbourg dans l'espace de deux semaines ou plus tôt, si faire se peut.

En foi de quoi les Plénipotentiaires de Turquie et de Russie y ont apposé leurs signatures et le sceau de leurs armes.

Fait à Constantinople le 27 Janvier/8 Février 1879.

(Signé): AL. CARATHÉODORY. — ALI. — LOBANOW.

(Protocole séparé)

Afin de définir la manière dont l'art. XI du Traité de ce jour devra être exécuté, les soussignés sont convenus des dispositions suivantes qui auront la même force et valeur que si elles étaient insérées mot à mot dans le texte même du Traité.

La Sublime Porte s'engage à exécuter et à faire exécuter dans le plus bref délai possible les sentences exécutoires rendues avant la guerre contre les sujets Ottomans et contre les différentes administrations Ottomanes.

L'exécution de ces sentences devra être poursuivie avec toute la diligence possible par les Autorités compétentes. Mais, afin de hâter le résultat désiré, le soin de veiller à l'exécution de ces sentences sera dévolu à une Commission composée de deux Délégués ottomans et de deux Délégués russes, lesquels auront, le cas échéant, à indiquer les mesures efficaces qui devront être prises dans ce but.

En cas de divergence, les membres de cette Commission désigneront d'un commun accord un surarbitre qui tranchera la difficulté.

Les réclamations des sujets Russes pendantes depuis plusieurs années à la charge des sujets Ottomans, seront déférées à la même Commission, qui recevrait un mandat de conciliation.

Lorsque les moyens de conciliation auront été épuisés relativement à une réclamation, si cette réclamation est à la charge de l'État et s'il y a eu avant la guerre une entente diplomatique pour la soumettre à un arbitrage, elle sera déférée à un arbitre nommé par les membres de la Commission.

Toute autre réclamation à la charge de l'État pour laquelle l'essai de conciliation aura échoué, sera déférée au Tribunal qui sera désigné par la Commission. Si la réclamation est à la charge d'un particulier, elle sera déférée au Tidjaret, et, en cas d'empêchement légal, elle sera également déférée au tribunal à désigner par la Commission.

De son côté, l'Ambassade Impériale de Russie promet de ne pas laisser en souffrance les sentences rendues en faveur de sujets Ottomans contre des sujets Russes.

Fait à Constantinople, le 8 Février (27 Janvier) 1879.

(*Signé*): AL. CARATHÉODORY. — ALI. — LOBANOW.

BIBLIOGRAPHICAL NOTES

THE following bibliographical notes cover only what I have consulted for the writing of this book. I have omitted standard reference works, various general books, and most of the references in the footnotes to Chapters I and II. Abbreviations used in the footnotes are printed in heavy type. N.B. *Addenda* on p. 697.

A. and P. : *Accounts and Papers; Parliamentary Proceedings.* The references are given by year and number of volume, by command paper number, and by number of document.

Actenstücke *aus den Correspondenzen des k. u. k. gemeinsamen Ministeriums des Äusseren über orientalische Angelegenheiten* (Vienna, 1878; 2 vols.). The Austrian Red Books, covering May 1873 to November 1878.

ADAMOV, E. A., 'Le problème bessarabien et les relations russoroumaines', in *Le Monde slave*, 1928, no. 1. Very polemical: replies to it were made by M. C. Kogălniceanu (the son of the minister for foreign affairs) and N. Iorga in no. 4.

AKSAKOV, I. S., *Slavyansky vopros* (Moscow, 1886). The first volume of his collected works: consists of his articles on Slav questions, 1860–86, and his speeches to the Moscow Slavonic Benevolent Committee.

ANUCHIN, D. G., 'Knyaz Vladimir Aleksandrovich Cherkasky kak ustroitel Bolgarii', in *Russkaya Starina*, 1888, vol. lix. Written up from his diary. A. was Cherkasky's right-hand man in the civil government of Bulgaria: a strong and careful defence, in reply to Dabizh (q.v.).

—— 'Tyrnov i Shipka v iyule i avguste, 1877 g.', in *Vestnik Evropy*, 1893, vol. v. Includes details as to the arming of the Bulgars.

—— *Kongress Berlina* (St. Petersburg, 1912). Appeared, in the same form, in *Russkaya Starina*, 1912, vols. cxlix, cl, clii. His diary: detailed and important. A. was one of the Russian military experts at the Berlin congress.

(ARDAGH, LADY), SUSAN, COUNTESS OF MALMESBURY, *The Life of Major-General Sir John Ardagh* (London, 1909). A. was an engineer officer, employed by the British war office from September 1876 in the Balkans; attended Berlin congress, and served on the Bulgarian and Greek boundary commissions (1878–81); numerous diary extracts on the work of the commissions, but the earlier portion is brief and formal.

ARGYLL, THE DUKE OF, *The Eastern Question* (London, 1879; 2 vols.). Mainly based on blue-books; trenchant attack on the Disraeli government, particularly its Afghan policy. A. was secretary of state for India 1868–74.

Aus dem Leben König Karls von Rumänien: Aufzeichnungen eines Augenzeugen (Stuttgart, 1897, 1900; vols. 3 and 4). Anonymous, but actually the diary of Jehan de Witte, King Charles's doctor and personal secretary, supplemented by many letters, &c. Indispensable.

Avantyury russkogo tsarizma v Bolgarii (Moscow, 1935). A very incriminating collection of documents from the Russian foreign office archives covering 1885–95, edited by P. Pavlovich; includes an article by A. Popov on Russian policy in the Balkans, 1860–78.

AVRIL, ADOLPHE D', *Négociations relatives au traité de Berlin et aux arrangements qui ont suivi, 1875–86* (Paris, 1886). A. was a French diplomat on the Danube international commission.

BADDELEY, J. F., *Russia in the 'eighties* (London, 1921). Then Russian correspondent of the *Standard*; a friend of Shuvalov.

—— 'The rising of 1877 in Daghestan and Tchetchnia', in *Georgica*, London, 1936, vol. i, nos. 2–3.

BAKER PASHA, LT.-GEN. VALENTINE, *War in Bulgaria: a narrative of personal experiences* (London, 1879; 2 vols.). Mainly military. B. had been in charge of the Turkish gendarmerie and during the war served on Mehemet Ali's staff.

BAMBERG, F., *Geschichte der orientalischen Angelegenheit im Zeitraume des Pariser und des Berliner Friedens* (Berlin, 1892). B. was in the German consular service in Turkey; valuable for Turkish internal affairs; very anti-Russian.

BAREILLES, B., *Le Rapport secret sur le Congrès de Berlin, adressée à la Sublime Porte par Carathéodory Pacha, premier plénipotentiaire ottoman* (Paris, 1919). The report is dated 1879. B. does not state how he came by it: is it published *in extenso*? It deals with the general situation and European Turkey, but not at all with Asiatic Turkey.

BRUNSWIK, BENOÎT, *Le Traité de Berlin annoté et commenté* (Paris, 1878). A useful analysis of the treaty of Berlin in relation to previous treaties, &c.

BISMARCK, *Reflections and Reminiscences* (London, 1898; 2 vols.).

BOBRIKOV, G. I., 'Uchastie Serbii v poslednei voine', in *Russky Vestnik*, 1889, nos. 10 and 11.

—— 'Vospominaniya o Berlinskom Kongresse', in *Russky Vestnik*, 1889, no. 12.

——, memoirs under varying titles, in *Russkaya Starina*, 1912, vols. cl–clii; 1913, vols. cliii–clv. B. was an influential staff officer with a good knowledge of the Balkans. His memoirs were written long subsequently, in part after 1905: they are valuable for his missions to Roumania (early 1877) and Serbia (Sept. 1877 to Mar. 1878) and the Berlin congress, at which he was one of the military experts. I have been unable to use his account of the second Serb-Turkish war, 1877–8, in his book *V Serbii* (St. Petersburg, 1891).

BONGHI, RUGGIERO, *Il congresso di Berlino e la crisi d'Oriente* (Milan, 1878). A useful analysis and criticism of Italian policy by a moderate supporter of Corti.

BOTKIN, S. P., *Pisma iz Bolgarii 1877 g.* (St. Petersburg, 1893). Letters to his wife of a well-known doctor, at imperial G.H.Q.: delightfully written, critical descriptions, with no pretence to inside knowledge.

BRĂTIANU, G., *Le Problème des frontières russo-roumaines pendant la guerre de 1877–8 et au congrès de Berlin* (Bucarest, 1928). Useful for the Roumanian point of view.

Bratskaya pomoch po stradavshim semeistvam Bosnii i Hertsegoviny (St. Petersburg, 1876). Published by the St. Petersburg Slavonic Benevolent Committee. A propaganda volume chiefly of literature and poetry; but includes a general historical article by Lamansky and an informing article by G. K. Gradovsky, 'Russkoe obshchestvo pered litsom bedstvii v Hertsegovine i Bosnii'.

BUGISTRE-BELLEYSAN, D., *Les Intrigues moscovites en Turquie; la vérité sur les massacres de Bulgarie* (Buda-Pest; first ed. January 1877, second ed. February 1877). Good example of Magyar anti-panslav propaganda.

BÜLOW, FÜRST BERNHARD VON, *Denkwürdigkeiten* (Berlin; vol. iv, 1931). B. entered the foreign office in 1875, was in St. Petersburg till April 1876, and was in Berlin during the congress: of very little value for these years.

BUSCH, C. A., 'Die Botschafterkonferenz in Konstantinopel und der russisch-türkische Krieg', in *Deutsche Rundschau*, 1909, vol. cxli. His diary, edited by L. Raschdau: valuable for his period at Constantinople, Jan. to Mar. 1877, and the Berlin congress, of which B. was a secretary: he had been dragoman at Constantinople and consul-general at St. Petersburg.

BUTKOVSKY, I. YA., 'Tainstvennaya ekspeditsiya v Ameriku v 1878 g.', in *Istorichesky Vestnik*, 1883, vol. xi. Russian naval preparations against England: no indication of sources used. See also below under Strakhovsky.

CARATHÉODORY PASHA; see above under Bareilles.

CHAMBERLAIN, J. P., *The Regime of the International Rivers: Danube and Rhine* (New York, 1923; Columbia University Studies in History, Economics, and Public Science, vol. cv, no. 1). An enlargement of his State Department memorandum drawn up for the American delegation to the Paris peace conference.

CHASTEL, COMTE ADOLPHE DU, *Les Événements d'Orient et le Congrès de Berlin de 1878* (Tournai, 1908). Written in 1878; covers Constantinople conference and Berlin congress; du C. was in the Belgian legations there at the time. Slight.

CHIALA, LUIGI, *Pagine di Storia contemporanea* (Turin, 1892–8; 3 vols.). Vol. i covers 1858 to 1878: contains much of interest on Italian foreign relations.

CHICHAGOV, L. M., *Dnevnik prebyvaniya Tsarya-Osvoboditelya v dunaiskoi armii v 1877 g.* (St. Petersburg; 2nd. ed. 1887). Semi-official compilation.

COQUELLE, P., *Histoire du Monténégro et de la Bosnie* (Paris, 1895). Useful for the Montenegrin campaigns 1876–8, and map.

CORTI, E. C., *Alexander von Battenberg* (Vienna, 1920). A full study, based on his private papers.

—— 'Il conte Corti al congresso di Berlino', in *Nuova Antologia*, 1925, vol. ccxl. Based on the family papers, but not of much interest.

—— 'Conte Corti alle catene', in *Historische Vierteljahrsschrift*, 1926, N.F., vol. xxiii. Substantially the same as the previous article.

—— *The Downfall of Three Dynasties* (London, 1934). Tr. from the German. Based on the letters and diary of Prince Alexander of Hesse, brother of Alexander II's wife and father of Prince Alexander of Battenberg.

ČUBRILOVIĆ, V., *Bosanski ustanak 1875–1878* (Belgrade, 1930). Uses valuable Serbian MSS. and printed sources, and to some extent the Vienna foreign office archives.

CUMMING, A. N., 'The Secret History of the Treaty of Berlin—a Talk with the late Lord Rowton', in *The Nineteenth Century*, July 1905. Journalistic record of a conversation in 1898 with Disraeli's private secretary.

DABIZH, PRINCE V. D., 'San Stefano i Konstantinopol v feb. 1878', in *Russkaya Starina*, 1888, vol. lvii. Anecdotal descriptions. Written up in 1887 from contemporary notes. Antagonistic to Cherkasky.

Disraeli: *The Life of Benjamin Disraeli*, by W. F. Monypenny and G. E. Buckle (2-vol. ed.; London, 1929). References are to vol. ii.

D.D.F.: *Documents diplomatiques français (1871–1914): Ière série (1871–1900)*. Unless otherwise stated, the references are to vol. ii.

Dokumenti za blgarskata istoriya (Sofia; vol. i, 1931; vol. ii, 1932). Official correspondence of Naiden Gerov 1857–76: indispensable for Russo-Bulgarian relations: see also below, under Gerov.

DRAGOMANOV, M. [P.], *Turki vnutrennie i vsneshnie* (Geneva, 1876). Violent attack on the panslavs and the volunteers to Serbia by a well-known Ukrainian radical in exile.

DRAGOVIĆ, M. P., 'Vospominaniya Chernogortsa iz vremen hertsegovinskago vozstaniya i chernogoretsko-turetskoi voiny, 1876–78 gg.', in *Russkaya Starina*, 1883, vol. xxxviii. Written in 1882.

DREUX, A., *Dernières Années de l'ambassade en Allemagne de M. de Gontaut-Biron 1874–1877* (Paris, 1907). Based on G.-B.'s papers and diary.

DRIAULT, E., and LHÉRITIER, M., *Histoire diplomatique de la Grèce de 1821 à nos jours* (vol. iii; Paris, 1925). This volume is by L.: based on the Athens and other archives. Important.

DRUMMOND WOLFF, SIR HENRY, *Rambling Recollections* (London, 1908; 2 vols.). British member on the Eastern Rumelian Commission 1878–9: well-known foreign affairs expert and parliamentarian. Contains the bulk of his journal notes privately printed in 1878 as *Notes taken in Paris, Vienna, Pesth, and Berlin, during the Easter Recess 1878.*

DUKMASOV, P., *Vospominaniya o russko-turetskoi voine 1877–1878 gg. i M.D. Skobeleve* (St. Petersburg, 1889). Typical of the hero-worship of Skobelev: D. was a Don Cossack adjutant of his.

DURNOVO, N. N., 'K istorii serbsko-turetskoi voiny 1876 g.', in *Istorichesky Vestnik*, 1899, vol. lxxv. Valuable account of the antecedents of Chernyaev's expedition to Serbia by an active panslav who was in close touch with the Metropolitan of Serbia.

ECKARDT, JULIUS, *Distinguished Persons in Russian Society* (London, 1873).

—— *Russia before and after the War* (London, 1880). Both published anonymously and translated from the German original; the latter with additions by E. He was a Baltic German who settled in Germany and worked on the Russian press for Bismarck: strongly anti-panslav; able, biased journalism.

EDWARDS, H. SUTHERLAND, *Sir William White* (London, 1902). Not at all full. W. was consul-general at Belgrade 1875, at Bucarest, 1878; and ambassador at Constantinople, 1885–91.

EGERTON, MRS. FRED, *Admiral of the Fleet Sir Geoffrey Phipps Hornby* (London, 1896). By his daughter. H. was in command of the Mediterranean fleet from Mar. 1877.

ELLIOT, SIR HENRY G., *Some Revolutions and other Diplomatic Experiences* (London, 1922). Edited by his daughter. Begun in 1883; privately published in 1900. E. was ambassador at Constantinople 1867–77.

EVANS, A. J., *Through Bosnia and Herzegovina on foot during the Insurrection, August and September, 1875* (2nd ed., revised and enlarged; London, 1877). First ed. 1876.

—— *Illyrian Letters* (London, 1878). A revised selection of his letters from Bosnia to the *Manchester Guardian* in 1877.

EVREINOV, B. A., 'Voina za osvobozhdenie balkanskikh slavyan (1877–8 gg.) i cheshskoe obshchestvo', in *Trudy V^go syezda russkikh akademicheskikh organizatsii za granitsei*, vol. i (Sofia, 1932). Largely based on the contemporary Czech press.

FEOKTISTOV, E. M., *Za kulisami politiki i literatury, 1848–1896* (Leningrad, 1929). The memoirs, based on diaries, letters, &c., of a well-known journalist and official of the ministry of education; an adherent of Katkov and D. A. Tolstoi; vivid, biting, and informing.

FORBES, ARCHIBALD, *Czar and Sultan* (London, 1894). F. was born and brought up in Giurgevo and knew Bulgarian, Turkish, and Russian: was *Daily News* correspondent with the Russians during the war. Based largely on his war letters and personal notes.

FOURNIER, AUGUST, *Wie wir zu Bosnien kamen* (Vienna, 1909). Based on much inside knowledge.

FRAHM, FR., 'Bismarck vor der Option zwischen Russland und Oesterreich im Herbst 1876', in *Historische Zeitschrift*, 1934, vol. cxlix.

GALLENGA, A., *Two Years of the Eastern Question* (London, 1877; 2 vols.). By *The Times* correspondent in Constantinople; covers Nov. 1875 to Apr. 1877; he had not been there before, but was well informed; a friend of Sir Philip Francis, the British consul-general, and correspondingly hostile to Elliot.

GARDINER, A. G., *The Life of Sir William Harcourt* (London, 1923; 2 vols.). Contains some evidence on his relations with Shuvalov.

GATHORNE-HARDY, A. E., *Gathorne-Hardy, first Earl of Cranbrook* (London, 1910; 2 vols.). G.-H. was secretary of state for war, 1874 to Mar. 1878, when he succeeded Salisbury at the India Office: useful on cabinet divisions.

GAULD, W. A., 'The Making of Bulgaria', in *History*, 1925, vol. x.

—— in *Cambridge Historical Journal*, 1925, vol. i, prints text of Russian *notice confidentielle* of 12 Feb. 1878.

—— 'The Dreikaiserbündnis and the Eastern Question, 1871–6', in *English Historical Review*, 1925, vol. xl.

—— 'The Dreikaiserbündnis and the Eastern Question, 1877–8', in *English Historical Review*, 1927, vol. xlii. Utilizes material from the Vienna archives.

—— 'The Anglo-Austrian Agreement of 1878', in *English Historical Review*, 1926, vol. xli. Based on the British foreign office papers.

GEORGEWITSCH (DJORDJEVIĆ), WLADAN, *Die serbische Frage* (Stuttgart, 1909). G. was, from 1873, doctor to Prince Milan, and later played an important political and diplomatic role; strongly anti-Russian.

—— (GEORGÉVITCH, VLADAN), 'La Serbie au Congrès de Berlin', in *Revue d'histoire diplomatique*, vol. vi, 1891. Based on Ristić's correspondence with Belgrade. Important. Reprinted as a brochure, Paris, 1891.

GEROV, NAIDEN, *Iz arkhivata na N. G.* (Sofia; vol. i, 1911, vol. ii, 1914). Ed. by T. Panchev. Massive collection of G.'s private correspondence 1856–78: indispensable for Russo-Bulgarian relations. See also above, *Dokumenti* . . . .

GHICA, IANCU, *Corespondenţa Generalului Iancu Ghica, 2 Aprilie 1877–8 Aprilie 1878* (Bucarest, 1930). With introduction and notes by Gen. R. Rosetti. Important collection of documents, in French.

GHIKAS, G., *Botschafter von Novikow über den Panslavismus und die Orientalische Frage* (Vienna, 1907). Panegyric of N. by a Greek-Vlach adopted by N. as a boy and taken into his private service 1867–77. A very curious booklet.

GIACOMETTI, G., *Les Responsabilités* (Constantinople, 1877): English edition, *Russia's Work in Turkey* (London, 1877), translated by E. Whitaker, the very anti-Russian editor of the *Levant Herald*. A Turkish collection of alleged Russian documents revealing panslav intrigues: see above, pp. 126, n. 1, 130, n. 4, and 244. A circumstantial account by Loftus, disp., no. 355, 15 Aug. 1876, in *F.O.* 65/939, derived from the Turkish minister in St. Petersburg and from Gorchakov, suggests that these documents may have been fabrications supplied to the Turkish legation in Vienna by a gang of Poles. Even if not genuine, most of them are in content very similar to authentic panslav communications.

GLAISE-HORSTENAU, EDMUND VON, *Franz Josephs Weggefährte: das Leben des Generalstabchefs Grafen Beck* (Vienna, 1930). Based on his private papers: he was at this time chief of the Emperor's military chancellery. Important.

GORIAINOW, S., *Le Bosphore et les Dardanelles* (Paris, 1910). First published in Russian, in St. Petersburg, in 1907 (Goryainov, *Bosfor i Dardanelly*). G. was the archivist of the Russian foreign office; of great value, but over-narrowly confined to his own archives, and to be used with caution. The French edition is fuller, particularly as regards quotations from the documents.

GREENE, F. V., *The Russian Army and its Campaigns in Turkey in 1877–1878* (London, s.d.; preface dated 1879; 1 vol. text; 1 vol. of maps and plates). G. was American military attaché to Russia; was with the army in the Balkans, Aug. 1877 to July 1878: a very useful military account.

GRIMM, E., 'K istorii russko-bolgarskikh otnoshenii', in *Novy Vostok*, Moscow, 1924, no. 5.

G.P., *Die diplomatischen Akten des Auswärtigen Amtes 1871–1914: Die Grosse Politik der europäischen Kabinette.* The references, unless otherwise stated, are to vol. ii (1922).

GRÜNING, I., *Die russische öffentliche Meinung und ihre Stellung zu den Grossmächten, 1878–1894* (Berlin, 1929). A useful study of the main organs of the Russian press since the Crimean war, and particularly from 1878.

La Guerre d'Orient en 1877–8 (Paris; vol. i, 1879). By 'un tacticien'; on the basis of Russian and Turkish official reports.

GWYNN, STEPHEN, and TUCKWELL, GERTRUDE M., *The Life of Sir Charles W. Dilke* (London, 1917; 2 vols.). Vol. i contains two interesting chapters on the eastern question.

HAJEK, ALOIS, *Bulgarien unter der Türkenherrschaft* (Berlin, 1925). Based on Bulgarian sources: mainly covers the nineteenth century, up to May 1876.

HANOTAUX, G., *Histoire de la France contemporaine* (vol. iv, Paris, 1908). Especially valuable for the use made of unpublished French diplomatic reports and the 'memoirs' of Carathéodory Pasha and Shuvalov (q.v.); very anti-Bismarck.

HARDINGE, SIR ARTHUR, *The Life of . . . Carnarvon* (London, 1925; 2 vols.). C. was secretary of state for the colonies until his resignation in Jan. 1878, in opposition to Disraeli's policy. Vol. i contains one not very informing chapter on the eastern crisis.

HARRIS, DAVID, *A Diplomatic History of the Balkan Crisis of 1875–1878: the First Year* (Stanford University, 1936). A very detailed and an important study, largely based on the London and Vienna foreign office archives; uses Russian printed material.

Hasenkampf, M. A., *Moi dnevnik 1877–78 gg.* (St. Petersburg, 1908). First published, in a less complete form, in *Vestnik Evropy*, 1905, nos. ii–v, 1906, nos. ii–iv. Letters to his wife arranged in diary form and supplemented by numerous texts of telegrams. H. was on the Grand Duke Nicholas's staff, first as press liaison officer, then in the signals section: a close friend of Skalon (q.v.). Indispensable.

HEISMAN, P., *Slavyano-turetskaya borba 1876–77–78 gg. i eya znachenie v istorii razvitiya vostochnago voprosa* (St. Petersburg; pt. 1, 1887; pt. 2, bk. 1, 1889). Covers 1876 and 1877 down to September. H. was a Russian officer and a volunteer to Serbia; gives a sober, professional account of the Serbo-Turkish war.

HELMS, ALBERT, *Bismarck und Russland* (Bonn, 1927). Dissertation. Covers mainly 1872–90; uses the MS. of Schweinitz's diary (q.v.), then unpublished.

Hertsegovinskoe vozstanie i vostochny vopros (Moscow, 1876). Panslav propaganda pamphlet on the revolt, covering 1875 only.

HOBART PASHA, AUGUSTUS CHARLES, *Sketches from my Life* (London, 1886). Breezy yarning by the English naval officer in command of the Turkish navy: of no value, except for a few points on the Cretan insurrection.

HYDE, A. M., *A Diplomatic History of Bulgaria, 1870–1886* (Urbana,

1928; Univ. of Illinois studies in social sciences, vol. xvi, no. 3). Elementary and not reliable.

IGNATYEV, N. P., in *Izvestiya ministerstva inostrannykh dyel* (St. Petersburg, 1914, bks. 1–6; 1915, bks. 1–4): text in French of memorandum of Ignatyev written in 1874 reviewing his ten years' work in Constantinople. A condensed version, down to 1870, appeared in Russian in *Russkaya Starina*, 1914, vol. clviii; 1915, vols. clxi–clxii.

—— *Zapiski* (Memoirs), in *Istorichesky Vestnik*, 1914, vols. cxxxv–cxxxvii, covering 1875–7: in *Russkaya Starina*, 1915, vol. clxi, covering January 1877; 1914, vols. clvii–clix, covering Mar.–Apr. 1877: in *Istorichesky Vestnik*, 1915, vols. cxxxix–cxli, covering Dec. 1877 to Mar. 1878, republished (Petrograd, 1916) as *San Stefano*; and 1916, vols. cxliii–cxliv, covering Apr.–May 1878, republished (Petrograd, 1917) as *Posle San Stefano*.

These memoirs were written long subsequently, at various times and with various additions. They are based mainly on his official papers and contain numerous texts of dispatches, &c., to and from St. Petersburg. The texts where I have been able to check them are correct. Very biased, but indispensable. See also below under Onou, *Slavyanski glas*, and Sumner.

IORGA, N., *Correspondance diplomatique roumaine sous le roi Charles Ier (1866–1880)* (Paris, 1923). A valuable collection of texts; in French.

—— 'La guerre de 1877–8: nouvelles informations: état d'esprit des belligérants', in *Revue d'histoire moderne*, 1928, no. 14.

ISMAIL KEMAL BEY, *The Memoirs of* (London, 1920). Ed. by S. Story. Supporter of Midhat; held various posts in the Turkish service 1865–73, and end of 1875–May 1877, when he was exiled.

I.V.: *Istorichesky Vestnik*: see under the authors of the articles.

IVANOV, I. S., 'Bolgarskoe opolchenie i ego sformirovanie v 1875–1879 gg.', in *Russkaya Starina*, 1889, vol. lxii; 1890, vol. lxvi. Dated 1888–9; partly on the basis of a diary. I. was a Bulgar, in Russian service, at Kishinev, and a panslav agent.

——, 'Iz zametok ob yuzhnoi Bolgarii 1878–9 gg.', in *Russkaya Starina*, 1892, vol. lxxv. Dated 1891.

JAPIKSE, N., *Europa und Bismarcks Friedenspolitik* (Berlin, 1927). Tr. from the Dutch. I have omitted most studies of this type in these notes, but Japikse seems to me to deal specially well with Balkan problems in relation to Bismarck's policy.

JOVANOVIĆ, SLOBODAN, 'Serbia in the early 'seventies', in *Slavonic Review*, 1925, vol. iv. Incorporated later in

—— *Vlada Milana Obrenovića* (vol. i, 1868–78; Belgrade, 1926; first ed.). The authoritative history of modern Serbia.

KAPCHEV, G. I., *Priznatelnaya Bolgariya* (St. Petersburg, 1909). An extension and revision of his earlier books on Russia and Bulgaria 1876–8: semi-official panslav propaganda, with much emphasis on the Tsar Liberator and Cyril and Methodius.

KARTSOV, YU. S., *Za kulisami diplomatii* (St. Petersburg, 1908). Originally published in *Russkaya Starina*, 1908, vols. cxxxiii, cxxxiv, and cxxxv. A lively and important account of Russian relations with Serbia, 1875–7, written in the early eighties by the nephew of A. N. Kartsov, the Russian consul-general in Belgrade, who gave him his private papers. Yu. S. Kartsov was a volunteer to Serbia and later in the Russian diplomatic service.

—— *Sem let na Blizhnem Vostoke, 1879–86* (St. Petersburg, 1906). Mainly anecdotal personalities.

KAULBARS, COL. BARON N., *Zametki o Chernogorii* (St. Petersburg, 1881). Geographical and military handbook on Montenegro, with useful map. K. was a member of the Montenegrin demarcation and delimitation commissions 1878–9.

KHVOSTOV, V., 'P. A. Shuvalov o Berlinskom Kongresse 1878 g.', in *Krasny arkhiv*, 1933, vol. lix. Gives text, in Russian translation from the French originals, of two memoranda by Shuvalov: one on the non-occupation of Constantinople by the Russians in 1878, the other, dated Aug. 1880, on the Berlin congress. These had not previously been published, though they were used by Tatishchev and, in the original French, by Hanotaux (q.v.). Referred to in my footnotes as Shuvalov's memoirs.

KLACZKO, JULIAN, *Deux Chanceliers: le prince Gortchakof et le prince Bismarck* (Paris, 1877; 3rd ed.). Not of much value: K. was a well-known Austrian publicist.

KOERLIN, KURT, *Zur Vorgeschichte des russisch-französischen Bündnisses 1879–1896* (Halle, 1926). Valuable analysis, though written before the publication of the French diplomatic series.

KOETSCHET, JOSEF, *Aus Bosniens letzter Türkenzeit* (Vienna, 1905). Largely based on his contemporary papers, written up not later than 1890. K. came of a Dutch-Swiss family; served as a doctor with the Turks during the Crimean war, and later as doctor and secretary to Omer Pasha; from 1864 he was medical officer at Sarajevo; influential with Turkish officials, and well informed.

KOGĂLNICEANU, VASILE M., *Acte şi documente din corespondenţa a lui Mihail Kogălniceanu relative la resboiul independenţei Româneiei 1877–1878* (Bucarest; vol. i, fasc. 1, 1893). The texts are almost all in French.

KOSTYRKO, M., 'Ocherk grazhdanskoi dyeyatelnosti nashi v Bolgarii v 1877–8 gg.', in *Russkaya Starina*, 1908, vol. cxxxv. Interesting, because uneventful and unassuming, account by an army officer acting as a civil administrator in the Dobrudja.

KOZHUKHAROV, K. D., *Istochniyat vpros i Blgariya 1875–1890* (Sofia, 1929). Not based on any Bulgarian sources, but gives a good view of the eastern crisis from a Bulgarian angle, particularly of the policy of the British government.

KRACHUNOV, K., 'Razlom na Sanstefanska Blgariya', in *Izvestiya na istoricheskoto druzhestvo v Sofiya*, 1930, vol. x. Covers Mar. 1878; based on non-Bulgarian printed sources.

KUROPATKIN, A. N., *Zadachi russkoi armii* (St. Petersburg, 1910; 3 vols.). Vol. 3 contains a chapter attacking Danilevsky and the panslavs. K. served through the Balkan campaign 1877–8, and wrote an important military history of it: he was later war minister and commander-in-chief against the Japanese.

LANG, ANDREW, *Life, Letters and Diaries of Sir Stafford Northcote, first Earl of Iddesleigh* (London, 1890; 2 vols.). N. was chancellor of the exchequer 1874–80: contains very little on the eastern crisis.

LANGE, OTTO, *Die Orientpolitik Oesterreich-Ungarns vom Ausgleich bis zum Berliner Kongress* (Berlin, 1926). A portion of a Berlin dissertation, dealing with the autumn of 1876.

LANGER, W. L., 'The European Powers and the French Occupation of Tunis, 1878–1881', in *American Historical Review*, 1925, vol. xxxi. This portion covers 1875–9: in part based on the Vienna archives.

—— *European Alliances and Alignments, 1871–1890* (New York, 1931). A very valuable survey, based on exceptional command of printed material, including some Russian.

LARMEROUX, JEAN, *L'Autriche-Hongrie au Congrès de Berlin, 1878* (Paris, 1915). Doctoral thesis: not of value.

—— *La politique extérieure de l'Autriche-Hongrie, 1875–1914* (Paris, 1918; 2 vols.). Perfunctory and inaccurate for the seventies.

LASCARIS, S. TH., *La politique extérieure de la Grèce avant et après le congrès de Berlin, 1875–1881* (Paris, 1924). Specially important for his use of the Greek archives.

LEE, DWIGHT E., 'The proposed Mediterranean League of 1878', in *Journal of Modern History*, 1931, vol. iii. Based on the British foreign office archives.

—— 'The Anglo-Austrian Understanding of 1877', in *Slavonic Review*, 1931, vol. x. Prints documents from the British foreign office archives.

—— *Great Britain and the Cyprus Convention policy of 1878* (Harvard, 1934). Detailed study mainly based on the Layard papers and British foreign office archives.

LEROY-BEAULIEU, A., 'Les Réformes de la Turquie: la politique russe et le panslavisme', in *Revue des deux mondes*, Dec. 1876. By a well-known expert on Russia: belittles dangers of panslavism.

LHÉRITIER, M.; see above under Driault.

LIEBOLD, RUDOLF, *Die Stellung Englands in der russisch-türkischen Krise von 1875/78* (Wilkau, 1930). Leipzig dissertation. Useful analysis of the printed sources.

LIEGNITZ, V. F. W. A., *Aus drei Kriegen, 1866–1870/71–1877/8* (Berlin, 1904). Highly placed German officer attached to Russian G.H.Q. and Gurko: based on his diary and contemporary notes: almost entirely military.

LOFTUS, LORD AUGUSTUS, *The Diplomatic Reminiscences of* (1862–79; second series; London, 1894; 2 vols.). Vol ii covers his service at St. Petersburg; of little value; see above, pp. 33–4, and below, under Sumner.

LURION, FAUST, *Campagnes de Suleiman Pascha* (Paris, 1883). By a strong adherent: contains important correspondence of S.

MACCOLL, REV. MALCOLM, *The Eastern Question: its Facts and Fallacies* (London, 1877).

—— *Three Years of the Eastern Question* (London, 1878). M. was a perfervid Gladstonian and one of the leaders of the atrocities campaign. He visited Belgrade, with Canon Liddon, in autumn, 1876. His *Memoirs and Correspondence* (London, 1914), edited by G. W. E. Russell, do not add much on 1876–80.

MACGAHAN, J. A., *The Turkish Atrocities in Bulgaria* (London, 1876). A reprint of the letters of the *Daily News* special correspondent; also gives text of Schuyler's preliminary report. M. knew Turkish, Bulgarian, and Russian.

Macmillan's Magazine, November 1877, vol. xxxvii: 'Panslavists and the Slav committees.' Initialled 'N.': he claims to know Russia well: an exaggerated tirade against panslavism.

MARVIN, CHARLES, *Our Public Offices* (London, 1879). His account, in vulgar journalese, of his employment as a copying clerk in the British foreign office and his revelation to *The Globe* of the Salisbury–Shuvalov memoranda. M. had acted as St. Petersburg correspondent of *The Globe*; he knew Russian and had been six years in Russia, up to 1875. He subsequently returned to Russia as a journalist, and wrote up Skobelev and Central Asia.

MATVEYEV, P. A., 'Bolgariya i Vostochnaya Rumeliya posle Berlinskago kongressa', in *Istorichesky Vestnik*, 1886, vols. xxiv and xxv. Contains a good many points of interest: written with inside knowledge.

MAXWELL, SIR HERBERT, *Life and Times of W. H. Smith* (London, 1893). S. was First Lord of the Admiralty from Aug. 1877.

MEDLICOTT, W. N., 'Diplomatic Relations after the Congress of Berlin', in *Slavonic Review*, 1929, vol. viii.

—— 'The Recognition of Roumanian Independence, 1878–1880', in *Slavonic Review*, 1933, vol. xi. Both based on the British foreign office archives.

MIDHAT, ALI HAYDAR, BEY, *The Life of Midhat Pasha* (London, 1903). By M.'s son and based on M.'s private papers.

MILLER, ORESTE, *Slavyanstvo i Evropa* (St. Petersburg, 1877). A leading panslav; reprint of his articles and speeches, 1865–77.

MILOBAR, FRANZ, *Der Berliner Kongress und die Bosnische Frage* (Zürich, 1902). Dissertation: mainly juridical.

Ministerul affacerilar straine: documente oficiale, 1878. Roumanian Green Book, covering Nov. 1876 to May 1877: almost all the documents are in French.

MOLLINARY, A. VON, *46 Jahre im oesterreich-ungarischen Heere 1833–1879* (Vienna, 1905; 2 vols.). M. was a Croat general; in command at Agram 1870 to Sept. 1877: the important chapter dealing with this period is mainly based on his letters to his wife.

MORLEY, JOHN, *The Life of W. E. Gladstone* (London, 1903; 3 vols.). Vol. ii includes 1875–80: much less interesting than it might be on the eastern crisis.

MOÜY, COMTE CHARLES DE, *Souvenirs et causeries d'un diplomate* (Paris, 1909). M. was secretary to both the Constantinople conference and the Berlin congress. Mostly general and anecdotal: the Constantinople portion appeared in *Revue des deux mondes*, 1 Feb. 1900.

MÜLLER, MANFRED, *Die Bedeutung des Berliner Kongresses für die deutsch-russischen Beziehungen* (Leipzig, 1927). Dissertation: valuable material from German foreign office archives on the carrying out of the Berlin treaty.

NAGLOVSKY, D. S., 'Kishinevskoe sidene', in *Russkaya Starina*, 1902, vol. cxii. Diary, Dec. 1876 to Feb. 1877, of a staff colonel at the Grand Duke Nicholas's head-quarters.

NELIDOV, A. I., 'K dvadtsatipyatilyetiyu osvobozhdeniya Bolgarii', in *Istorichesky Vestnik*, 1903, vol. xci. Covers the Adrianople armistice negotiations: dated 1902: sources not indicated; general in treatment, but accurate where he can be checked.

—— 'Souvenirs d'avant et d'après la guerre de 1877–8', in *Revue des deux mondes*, 15 May, 15 July, 15 Nov., 1915. Covers 1875 to April 1877, and San Stefano to Berlin; written in 1896; sources not indicated; not reliable.

NEMIROVICH-DANCHENKO, V. I., *God voiny (dnevnik russkago korrespondenta) 1877–8* (St. Petersburg, 2nd ed., 1879). The diary and letters of the best known of the Russian war correspondents.

—— *Posle voiny* (St. Petersburg, 1880). An outspoken eyewitness's account of the Russians in Bulgaria in 1879.

NEVEDENSKY, S., *Katkov i ego vremya* (St. Petersburg, 1888). Analyses

K.'s views as shown in his articles; frequent quotations from them.

NOLDE, BARON BORIS, *L'alliance franco-russe* (Paris, 1936). Mainly a survey of Russia's relations with the western powers 1871–93: uses Giers's private papers.

NORADOUNGHIAN, G., *Recueil d'actes internationaux de l'empire ottoman* (Paris, 1897–1903; 4 vols.). A valuable collection compiled by a legal official at the Porte.

NORMAN, C. B., *Armenia and the campaign of 1877* (London, s.d. [1878]). Republication of the war letters of *The Times* correspondent with the Turks; detailed, sober account, with good maps: became disgusted with Turkish misrule and inefficiency; poohpoohs 'the Russian menace'.

Nouvelle Revue, Paris, 1880, vol. iv: 'La Guerre russo-turque, d'après des documents inédits'. Published anonymously, though in fact by the Russian financier-journalist-agent E. Cyon, see his *Histoire de l'entente franco-russe* (Paris, 1895), p. 18. C. was on the Grand Duke Nicholas's staff: unreliable in detail, though the later part is based on his diary, supplemented from some official information from Turkish sources; should be carefully checked with Hasenkampf and Skalon (q.v.).

—— 1880, vol. vi: 'La Guerre russo-turque'. By a Russian claiming to be an eyewitness; perhaps Jomini: a reply to Cyon's article above.

O.K., *Russia and England from 1876 to 1880* (London, 1880). 'A protest and an appeal' by Olga Novikov, the panslav propagandist in England, and friend of Gladstone. Preface by Froude. Mainly based on her letters in 1877 and 1880 to Stead's *Northern Echo*: contains translations of some of Aksakov's speeches. See also below under Stead.

ONOU, ALEXANDER, 'The memoirs of Count N. Ignatyev', in *Slavonic Review*, 1932, vols. x and xi. A résumé of the memoirs; see above under Ignatyev.

—— 'Graf N. P. Ignatyev v San-Stefano', in *Slavyanski glas*, Sofia, 1932, vol. xxvi. Mainly a defence of I. against charges of violating the agreements with Austria-Hungary and of being anti-Serbian. See above, pp. 452–3, n.

—— 'Graf N. P. Ignatyev i vneshnyaya politika Rossii', in *Trudy V^{go} syezda russkikh akademicheskikh organizatsii za granitsei*, vol. i (Sofia, 1932). A general discussion of I.'s career.

—— 'Correspondance inédite de baron Alexandre de Jomini', in *Revue d'histoire moderne*, Sept.-Oct. 1935. Prints letters from Ignatyev and Onou to Jomini, Oct. to Dec. 1875.

The late M. Onou was a son of the Russian dragoman at Constantinople, and was himself consul-general in London in 1917.

Opisanie russko-turetskoi voiny 1877–78 gg. na balkanskom poluostrove (St. Petersburg; vol. i, 1901). The official history, edited by the military history section of the general staff.

OVSYANY, N. R., *Russkoe upravlenie v Bolgarii v 1877–78–79 gg.* (St. Petersburg, 1906; vol. i). General staff publication: covers Cherkasky's administration; prints important documents.

—— *Blizhny vostok i slavyanstvo* (St. Petersburg, 1913). A collection of his articles on Cherkasky, Dondukov-Korsakov, &c., and a translation of Grujić's important *Srpsko-turski rat 1876–7 g.*, originally published in 1902, Belgrade.

PARENSOV, P. D., 'Peripiska P. D. Parensova s K. B. Levitskim pered nachalam voennykh dyestvii s Turtsii', in *Russkaya Starina*, 1905, vol. cxxiv. Text of letters of P. to Levitsky, Jan.-Feb., 1877, when P. was intelligence officer at Bucarest.

—— *Iz proshlago* (St. Petersburg, 1901–8; 5 pts.). Covers 1877–81: in part previously published in *Russkaya Starina*, 1899, 1900, 1902, and 1903; specially important for his period as war minister in Bulgaria.

PEARS, SIR EDWIN, *Forty Years in Constantinople* (London, 1916).

—— *Life of Abdul Hamid* (London, 1917).

PLENER, E., *Erinnerungen* (Stuttgart, 1911–21; 3 vols.). P. was an important Austrian German political leader.

Pobedonostsev i ego korrespondenty (Moscow, 1923). The end of vol. i, pt. 2, contains letters and notes of Alexander III while Tsarevich to P.

—— *Pisma Pobedonostseva k Aleksandru III* (Moscow; vol. i, 1925). Covers 1865–82. See also below, under *Slavonic Review*.

POKROVSKY, M. N., *Russkaya istoriya s drevnyeshikh vremen* (4th ed.; Moscow, 1923). Vol. iv covers the second half of the nineteenth century: written originally about 1912.

—— *Diplomatiya i voiny tsarskoi Rossii v xix stoletii* (Moscow, 1923). A republication, with some changes and two new chapters, of his chapters in *Istoriya Rossii v xix v.* (*izd. Granata*).

POLONSKY, YA. P., in *Na chuzhoi storonye*, Prague, 1924, vol. iv: extracts from his diary, Aug. and Sept. 1876, Aug. to Oct. 1878: good example of extreme anti-government panslav views.

POLOVTSOV, A. A., 'Iz dnevnika (1877–78)', text in *Krasny arkhiv*, 1929, vol. xxxiii. Diary of a senator; mainly in St. Petersburg: in touch with Timashev and the Tsarevich.

POPOV, A., 'Ot Bosfora k Tikhomu Okeanu', in *Istorik Marksist*, 1934, vol. xxxvii. Contains interesting commercial and economic evidence on Russian expansion 1875–97.

POROKHOVSHCHIKOV, A. A., 'Zapiski starozhila', in *Istorichesky Vestnik*, 1897, vol. lxvii. Anecdotal memoirs of the panslav campaign, 1876, in which P. took a prominent part.

PRATT, E. J., 'La diplomatie française de 1875 à 1881', in *Revue historique*, 1932, vol. clxx. Mainly based on *D.D.F.*

PRIBRAM, A. F., *The Secret Treaties of Austria-Hungary, 1879–1914* (English ed. by A. C. Coolidge; Harvard, 1921; 2 vols.). See above, pp. 583–4.

PRZIBRAM, L. v., *Erinnerungen eines alten Oesterreichers* (Stuttgart, 1910–11; 2 vols.). Well informed; P. was in the Ballplatz press bureau.

PROPPER, S. M. v., *Was nicht in die Zeitung kam; Erinnerungen des Chefredakteurs der 'Birschewyja Wedemosti'* (Frankfurt, 1929). P. was an Austrian journalist working in St. Petersburg from 1875 onwards: in close relation with the Russian foreign office.

Proslava na osvoboditelnata voina 1877–8 g. (Sofia, 1929). A valuable collection of articles, in Bulgarian and Russian, in commemoration of the fiftieth anniversary of Bulgaria.

PUSHKAREVICH, K. A., 'Balkanskie slavyane i russkie "osvoboditeli"', in *Trudy instituta slavyanovedeniya Akademii Nauk S.S.S.R* (Leningrad; vol. ii, 1934). Deals mainly with 1876–7; partly based on the archives of the St. Petersburg Slavonic Benevolent Committee.

Queen Victoria, The Letters of, second series, 1862–78 (London, 1926; 2 vols.), edited by G. E. Buckle.

RADEV, SIMEON, *Stroitelite na svremenna Blgariya* (Sofia; vol. i, 2nd ed., 1911). Valuable account of the building up of the principality by a leading Bulgarian patriot.

RADOWITZ, *Aufzeichnungen und Erinnerungen aus dem Leben des Botschafters Joseph Maria von* (Berlin, 1925; 2 vols.); edited by Hajo Holborn. A favoured protégé of Bismarck. Special mission to St. Petersburg, Feb.–Mar. 1875; then at Athens; secretary-general of the Berlin congress. He wrote the chapter on the congress in 1902.

RASCHDAU, L., *Ein sinkendes Reich* (Berlin, 1934). Covers May 1877 to May 1879. R. was then a young German consular official in Constantinople; knew Turkish and was in close touch with Turkish officials: a valuable source; partly at least written in the nineties.

REUTERN, M. KH., Text of extracts from his diary, 1876–8, in *Russkaya Starina*, 1910, vol. cxliii, taken from A. N. Kulomzin and V. G. Reutern, *M. Kh. Reutern, Biografichesky ocherk* (St. Petersburg, 1910).

—— Baron Nolcken, *Die finanzielle Sanierung Russlands nach der Katastrophe des Krimkrieges 1862 bis 1878 durch den Finanzminister Michael von Reutern* (Berlin, 1914). German translation of Kulomzin. Important memoranda and diary extracts.

Revue de Paris, 15 July 1897, vol. iv: 'Les Russes devant Constantinople, 1877–1878'. Stated to be by an anonymous Russian:

very hostile to Gorchakov; gives extracts from the Grand Duke Nicholas's *Mémorial de la dernière guerre d'Orient*, drawn up by him at the end of the war; critical of the Grand Duke.

Revue d'histoire diplomatique, 1896, vol. x: 'L'Angleterre et la Russie en Orient (1876–1877)'. Dated 15 Dec. 1877; anonymous, but by a diplomatist recently (1896) dead: attributed to V. Cherbuliez. Mostly a general discussion of British policy; very anti-Elliot and anti-panslav.

—— 1934, vol. xlviii: 'Extrait des mémoires d'un diplomate russe, M. Michel de Bartholomei'. B. was counsellor in the London embassy 1871–80: anecdotal attacks on Shuvalov and Gorchakov.

RISTIĆ, JOVAN, *Diplomatska istorija Srbije za vreme srpskikh ratova za oslobodenye i nezavisnost 1875–1878* (Belgrade, 1896, 1898; 2 vols.). Very biased, but important account by the Serbian minister for foreign affairs. The last two chapters are a shortened version of Georgewitsch (Georgévitch), q.v.

—— *Pisma Jovana Ristića Filipu Hristiću od 1870 do 1873 i od 1877 do 1880* (Belgrade, 1931). Fourteen of the letters are of 1877, when Hristić was agent at Constantinople.

RIZOV, D., *The Bulgarians in their historical, ethnographical and political frontiers* (Berlin, 1917). Bulgarian propaganda atlas; includes twelve maps, from Šafarik (1842) to Cherkasky (1878), showing the different estimates available at the time of the eastern crisis.

ROSETTI, R., 'Roumania's share in the war of 1877', in *Slavonic Review*, 1930, vol. viii. Primarily military; good notes, and map.

ROSI, M., *I Cairoli* (Bologna, 1929; 2 vols.). Important for the Cairoli ministry in 1878.

RUMBOLD, SIR HORACE, *Recollections of a Diplomatist* (London, 1902; 2 vols.); *Further Recollections of a Diplomatist* (London, 1903). Anecdotal reminiscences written up in part from a diary: in St. Petersburg 1868–9; in Constantinople 1871–3; in London 1877–8.

RUPP, G. H., 'The Reichstadt agreement', in *American Historical Review*, 1925, vol. xxx. A comparison of the Russian and Austrian versions.

R.S., *Russkaya Starina*. See under the authors of articles, except where anonymous.

—— 1883, vol. xl: 'Knyaz Al. Mik. Gorchakov v ego razskazakh iz proshlago'. Anonymous; by M—sky: recounts conversations with G. in 1881–2.

—— 1905, vol. cxxiii: 'Obzor politicheskikh sobytii s 28-go dekabra 1877 g. po 15-e apryelya 1878 g'. Anonymous: no sources cited.

Russko-germanskie otnosheniya (Moscow, 1922). A reprint of documents first published in *Krasny arkhiv*, vol. i: includes texts concerning the *Dreikaiserbündnis* and the Reichstadt agreement.

Russky Arkhiv, 1897, no. 2: 'Nakanune nashei poslednei voiny'; communicated by N. I. Brailko, with a postscript by P. Bartenev. Gives text of important letter of Aksakov to his agent in Belgrade, Dec. 1876, and of two letters to him from Belgrade, Jan. and Feb. 1877: the panslavs abandon Serbia.

—— 1914, nos. 1 and 2: text of letters of Prince Milan to Chernyaev, 17 June to 25 Oct. 1876, and one of 6 Mar. 1877; printed in the original French. Important. Includes a wholly laudatory biographical sketch of Chernyaev by Antonina Chernyaeva.

SALIH MUNIR PASHA, *La Politique orientale de la Russie* (Lausanne, 1918). A recrimination of little value, by a Turkish ex-diplomatist.

Salisbury: *Life of Robert, Marquis of Salisbury*, by Lady Gwendolen Cecil. References are to vol. ii (London, 1921).

SALUSBURY, P. H. B., *Two months with Tchernaieff in Servia* (London, 1877). Breezy account by a young British infantry subaltern who volunteered to Serbia.

SALVEMINI, GAETANO, *La politica estera di Francesco Crispi* (Rome, 1919).

—— 'Alla vigilia del Congresso di Berlino', in *Nuova rivista storica*, 1925, vol. ix.

SANDWITH, HUMPHRY, see below, under Ward, T. H.

San Stefano: see above, under Ignatyev.

SARAUW, CHRISTIAN V., *Der russisch-türkische Krieg, 1877–78* (Leipzig, 1878). By a Danish officer; on the basis of Russian official reports.

SAUER, EUGEN, *Die Politik Lord Beaconsfields in der Orientalischen Krisis (1875–1878)* (Sindelfingen, 1934). Tübingen dissertation.

SAX, CARL RITTER V., *Geschichte des Machtverfalls der Türkei bis Ende des 19 Jahrhunderts und die Phasen der 'orientalischen Frage' bis auf die Gegenwart* (Vienna, 1908; with a supplement, 1913). Useful outline for Turkish internal affairs. S. was in the Austrian consular service in the Balkans.

SCHÜSSLER, W., 'Bismarcks Bündnisangebot an Russland "durch dick und dünn" im Herbst 1876', in *Historische Zeitung*, 1932, vol. cxlvii.

SCHWEINITZ, *Denkwürdigkeiten des Botschafters General v.* (Berlin, 1927; 2 vols.). See above, pp. 34–5. For 1876–7 written up from his diary: from Jan. 1878, his diary. Very important.

—— *Briefwechsel des* . . . (Berlin, 1928). Contains very little on Russia that is not in his memoirs.

SETON-WATSON, R. W., 'Russo-British relations during the Eastern Crisis', in *Slavonic Review*, 1924–8, vols. iii–vi. Texts of documents, mainly from and to Shuvalov and Gorchakov, 1875 to Jan. 1878. Indispensable.

—— 'The Role of Bosnia in International Politics (1875–1914)', in *Proceedings of the British Academy*, 1931, vol. xvii.

—— *Disraeli, Gladstone and the Eastern Question* (London, 1935). Very important, especially for his use of the unpublished papers of Shuvalov, Layard, and English liberal leaders.

SHILDER, N. K., *Graf Eduard Ivanovich Totleben; ego zhizn i dyeyatelnost* (St. Petersburg, 1885–6; 2 vols.). The 'official' life.

SHUVALOV, P. A., see above under Khvostov.

SIMPSON, J. Y., *The Saburov Memoirs* (Cambridge, 1929). A translation of Saburov's *Ma Mission à Berlin 1879–1884*, printed for private circulation in St. Petersburg early in 1914: valuable for the making of the *Dreikaiserbund*.

Skalon, D. A., *Moi vospominaniya, 1877–1878 gg.* (St. Petersburg, 1913; 2 vols.). Diary and numerous texts of telegrams: the diary was shown from time to time to the Grand Duke Nicholas. S. was one of his personal adjutants and a close friend. Should be used in conjunction with Hasenkampf (q.v.). Indispensable.

SKAZKIN, S., *Konets avstro-russko-germanskogo soyuza* (Moscow, vol. i, 1928). Very important study covering 1879–84: mainly based on the Russian foreign office archives.

S.R.: *Slavonic Review*. See under the authors of articles, except where anonymous.

—— 1928, vol. vii: 'Pobedonostsev and Alexander III' [up to 1881]. Based on their published correspondence and some unpublished correspondence of E. F. Tyutcheva. See also above, under Pobedonostsev.

Slavyanski glas, Sofia, 1932, vol. xxvi. Centenary number devoted to Ignatyev; articles by St. Danev, V. P. Nikolsky, K. Krachunov, A. Onou (q.v.), and M. Popruzhenko (on Tseretelev).

Slavyansky Sbornik: three stout volumes; produced annually (1875–7) by the St. Petersburg Slavonic Benevolent Committee: they deal mainly with the ethnography, philology, literature, and early history of the Austrian and Balkan Slavs, and not with contemporary conditions or politics. Exceptions are articles by N. A. Popov (vol. i) on the position of the *rayas* in Bosnia since 1859, by A. S. Budilovich (vol. i) on the present position of and mutual relations between the western and southern Slavs, and by A. N. Moshnin (vol. ii), consul at Rustchuk 1871–5, attacking the new *vilayet* system as applied in Bulgaria.

SOSNOSKY, T. VON, *Die Balkanpolitik Oesterreich-Ungarns seit 1866* (Stuttgart, 1913–14; 2 vols.). Highly critical of Wertheimer: important.

SPALAÏKOVITCH, M. J., *La Bosnie et l'Herzégovine* (Paris, 1897). Doctoral thesis, mainly on legal and administrative questions in regard to Austrian occupation.

Spomenica o hertsegovačkom ustanka 1875 godine (Belgrade, 1928). Patriotic collection of essays embodying reminiscences, documents, and some archive material from Cettinje and Vienna.

SPRINGER, ANTON, *Der russisch-türkische Krieg 1877–8 in Europa* (Vienna; vol. i, 1891). The main Austrian military history of the war.

STEAD, W. T., *The M.P. for Russia: Reminiscences of Madame Olga Novikoff* (London, 1909; 2 vols.). Based on her correspondence with, e.g., Gladstone, Froude, Freeman, and on Stead's paper, *Northern Echo*. She was a panslav propagandist; sister-in-law of the Russian ambassador in Vienna; was in London, autumn 1876 to Jan. 1877; her brother was the first of the Russian volunteers to Serbia to be killed. See also above under O.K.

—— *Truth about Russia* (London, 1888). Account of a two months trip to Russia, 1888; contains some friendly chapters on Ignatyev.

STILLMAN, W. J., *Herzegovina and the late uprising: the causes of the latter and the remedies* (London, 1877). S. was *The Times* correspondent at Ragusa; knew Turkey well; very anti-Turk, and biased, but well informed at first hand: see also pp. 580–2.

STOYANOFF, ZACHARY, *Pages from the Autobiography of a Bulgarian Insurgent* (London, 1913). Tr. by M. W. Potter. Unbuttoned recollections of a prominent supporter of Stambulov: describes in detail the risings of 1875 and 1876, in which Stoyanoff took part.

STRAKHOVSKY, L. I., 'Russia's Privateering Projects of 1878', in *Journal of Modern History*, 1935, vol. vii. Uses State Department and other American archives, and Russian printed sources. See also above, under Butkovsky.

STRATFORD DE REDCLIFFE, *The Eastern Question* (London, 1881). Republication of letters to *The Times* and articles 1875–8.

STURDZA, D. A., *Charles Ier, Roi de Roumanie* (Bucarest; vol. i, 1899; vol. ii, 1904). Vol. ii covers 1876 to Aug. 1877; mainly texts of documents; but also a long introduction by S.

SUMNER, B. H., 'Ignatyev at Constantinople 1864–1874', in *Slavonic Review*, 1933, vol. xi. Mainly based on I.'s 1874 memorandum and memoirs, in *Istorichesky Vestnik*, 1914, vol. cxxxv; see above, under Ignatyev.

—— 'Lord Augustus Loftus and the Eastern Crisis of 1875–1878', in *The Cambridge Historical Journal*, 1934, vol. iv. Mainly based on the British foreign office papers.

Tatishchev, S. S., *Imperator Aleksandr II, ego zhizn i tsarstvovanie* (St. Petersburg, 1903; 2 vols.). Unless otherwise stated, references are to vol. ii. The 'official' life, but based on important archive sources. T. was from 1864–77 in the diplomatic service (see above, pp. 28 and 149, note 1), was a volunteer, and from 1881–3 served in the ministry of interior. He then became a very active journalist, in close relation with Katkov, and after Katkov's death was for ten years responsible for the political section of *Russky Vestnik*, advocating panslavism and the alliance with France. He published a number of works on Russian foreign relations in the nineteenth century, of a strongly nationalist colouring.

—— *Iz proshlago russkoi diplomatii* (St. Petersburg, 1890). Includes an analysis of Russian policy towards Bulgaria 1878–87; sharp attack on Russian 'altruism'.

TCHARYKOW, N. V., *Glimpses of high politics* (London, 1931). See above, p. 583.

TEMPERLEY, H. W. V., 'British Policy towards Parliamentary Rule and Constitutionalism in Turkey (1830–1914)', in *Cambridge Historical Journal*, 1933, vol. iv. Includes Abd ul-Aziz, Midhat, and Abd ul-Hamid.

TEPLOV, V., *Materialy dlya statistika Bolgarii, Thrakii i Makedonii* (St. Petersburg, 1877). Detailed estimates, with map, of Moslem and non-Moslem population for each *kaza* in the *vilayets* of the Danube, Adrianople, Salonika, and Monastir. Over-favourable to the Bulgars, but important, and the basis for the Russian justification of the big Bulgaria of the Constantinople conference, &c. T. served in the Constantinople embassy. See above, p. 241 and n.

—— *Knyaz Aleksyei Borisovich Lobanov-Rostovsky* (St. Petersburg, 1897). Brief, semi-official life, mainly on his tenure of the foreign office.

THOMPSON, G. C., *Public opinion and Lord Beaconsfield 1875–1880* (London, 1886; 2 vols.). Almost entirely on the eastern question; very hostile to B.; useful for copious extracts from the press.

TRIVANOVITCH, VASO, 'Serbia, Russia and Austria-Hungary during the reign of Milan Obrenovich, 1868–78', in *Journal of Modern History*, 1931, vol. iii. Based on Serbian printed sources; mainly deals with internal and personal affairs.

TSERETELEV, PRINCE A. N., 'Pisma s pokhoda', in *Russky Vestnik*, 1878, vol. cxxxvii. Letters from his cavalry regiment May-Aug. 1877. See also above, under *Slavyanski glas*.

TYLER, M. W., *The European Powers and the Near East, 1875-1908* (University of Minnesota, 1925). A careful study.

VALUEV, P. A., *Dnevnik, 1877-1884* (Petrograd, 1919). A detached, cynical diary, written with an eye to posthumous publication. V. was minister of the interior 1861–8, and then of state domains: a shifty careerist; anti-panslav. See also below, p. 698.

VERESHCHAGIN, V. V., *Na voine* (Moscow, 1902). War reminiscences of the famous painter, who was with Skobelev in 1878.

Vestnik Evropy, April 1883, vol. ii: very critical anonymous obituary notice of Gorchakov.

Voenny Sbornik, 1879, vol. cxxv: 'O razvitii nashikh voennykh sil v poslednyuyu turetskuyu voinu (1876–1878 gg.)'. Anonymous article, with useful figures of number of men mobilized, etc.

VONLYARLYARSKY, V. M., *Vospominaniya ordinartsa o voine 1877–1878 g.* (St. Petersburg, 1891). Of very little interest.

WADDINGTON, F., 'La France au Congrès de Berlin', in *Revue politique et parlementaire*, 1933, vol. clvi. Makes some use of the Quai d'Orsay archives and private letters.

—— 'La Question des frontières grecques', in *Revue d'histoire diplomatique*, 1936, vol. l. A few points made from W.'s private letters.

WARD, T. H., *Humphry Sandwith: a memoir* (London, 1884). S. was an English doctor, with much experience of Turkey, who organized medical help in Serbia, Aug. 1876 to Mar. 1877; based on his autobiographical notes. There are a few of his letters from Serbia to Henry Allon, the editor of *The British Quarterly Review*, in *Letters to a Victorian Editor*, edited by A. Peel (London, 1929). See also S.'s article 'The Servian war', in the *British Quarterly Review*, Jan. 1877, vol. lxv.

WASHBURN, GEORGE, *Fifty years in Constantinople and recollections of Robert College* (Boston, 1909). W. was president of Robert College: useful on the revelation of the Bulgarian atrocities.

WELLESLEY, COL. THE HON. F. A., *With the Russians in Peace and War; Recollections of a Military Attaché* (London, 2nd ed., 1905). Of hardly any historical value; but see above, p. 34, on Wellesley.

WENTWORTH HUYSHE, *The liberation of Bulgaria; war notes in 1877* (London, 1894). War correspondent of the *New York Times* in 1877; with the Turks: not of much interest.

Wertheimer, E., *Graf Julius Andrássy, sein Leben und seine Zeiten* (Stuttgart, 1910–13; 3 vols.). Unless otherwise stated, references are to vol. ii. The authoritative life, based on Andrássy's papers, but overbiased in his favour.

—— 'Neues zur Orientpolitik des Grafen Andrássy (1876–1877)', in *Historische Blätter* (Vienna), 1921–2, vols. ii–iii. Very important material from the Vienna archives, particularly on the Austro-Russian secret conventions.

WESSELITSKY BOJIDAROVITCH, G. DE, *Dix mois de ma vie, 1875–6* (Paris, 1929). See above, pp. 157 and 160 n. Written up at the very end of his life; he died in 1930, aged 89: no indication of materials used.

WHITTAKER, E., *Russia's work in Turkey* (London, 1877). See above, under Giacometti.

WILLIAMS, CHARLES, *The Armenian Campaign: a Diary of the Campaign of 1877 in Armenia and Koordistan* (London, 1878). The able special correspondent with Mukhtar Pasha: useful Turkish general-staff map: emphasizes anti-Russian feelings among most of the Armenians.

WIRTHWEIN, W. G., *Britain and the Balkan Crisis, 1875–1878* (Columbia University Press, 1935). Detailed collection of British press views, chronologically arranged.

WITTROCK, GEORGE, *Gorčakov, Ignatiev och Šuvalov* (Stockholm, 1931). Important study, covering 1876 to 1878, based on the Vienna and Berlin archives: appendix of documents in the original German or French; for a translation of the Swedish text I am much indebted to Miss G. Fristedt.

WOODWARD, E. L., *The Congress of Berlin* (British foreign office Peace Conference handbook, 1919). A very clear outline, based on the foreign office papers.

YRIARTE, CARLO, *La Bosnia e l'Erzegovina durante l'insurrezione: note di viaggio* (Milan, 1876). Y. went to Bosnia in Sept. 1875: interesting on internal conditions.

ZANCOF, D., and BALABANOV, M. D., *Bulgaria, by her two delegates* (London, 1876). Tr. by F. H.: issued in late Oct. 1876: see above, p. 253 and n.

ZANDER, E., *Die französische Orientpolitik vom Frankfurter Frieden bis zum Berliner Kongress* (Berlin, 1936). A dissertation: slight.

ZETLAND, THE MARQUIS OF, *The Letters of Disraeli to Lady Bradford and Lady Chesterfield* (London, 1929; 2 vols.). Adds very little on the eastern crisis to the Buckle *Life*.

ADDENDA

DANAÏLLOW, M., 'Bismarck und die Befreiung Bulgariens', in *Berliner Monatshefte*, Dec. 1936. Almost solely based on the *Grosse Politik*: slight.

GOLUBEV, A., *Knyaz Aleksandr Ilarionovich Vasilchikov, 1818–81: Biografichesky ocherk* (St. Petersburg, 1882). A hastily composed memoir, but includes summary of V.'s unpublished pamphlet *Vostochny vopros* (1876) and extracts from V.'s letters on the panslavs. V., though not previously connected with the panslavs, was president of the St. Petersburg Slavonic Benevolent Committee from early 1876 until the middle of 1878: he opposed Aksakov and the volunteer movement, but was powerless.

HAINES, C. G., 'Italian irredentism during the Near Eastern crisis, 1875–78', in *Journal of Modern History*, 1937, vol. ix. Based on the Austrian and British foreign office archives and a wide range of Italian publications.

MESHCHERSKY, V. P., *Pravda o Serbii* (St. Petersburg, 1877). Written immediately after his return from Serbia at the end of 1876; see above, p. 190, n. 2.

—— *Moi vospominaniya* (St. Petersburg, 1898; vol. ii, covering 1865–81). The memoirs of the sinister, arch-reactionary proprietor of *Grazhdanin*.

ROSETTI, R., 'Din corespondenţa inedită a principelui Milan al Serbiei cu colonelul Gheorghe Catargi . . . 1877–78', in *Mémoires de l'Académie roumaine*, section historique, série iii, 1935. I have unfortunately only been able to see a very brief reference to this correspondence, which should be highly interesting.

STÄHLIN, K., 'Die Briefe Louis Schneiders an Russischen Domänenminister Waluew', in *Historische Zeitung*, 1936, vol. clv. Based on the unpublished letters of S. to Valuev, 1874–78.

INDEX